TALK ABOUT TROUBLE

Edited by Nancy J. Martin-Perdue & Charles L. Perdue Jr.

TALK ABOUT TROUBLE

A New Deal Portrait of Virginians in the Great Depression

The
University
of North
Carolina
Press

Chapel Hill

&

London

© 1996
The University of
North Carolina Press
The paper in this book meets the
guidelines for permanence and durability
of the Committee on Production
Guidelines for Book Longevity of the
Council on Library Resources.
Designed by Richard Hendel
Set in Monotype Garamond by
Tseng Information Systems, Inc.
Printed in the United States of America
by Thomson-Shore
Library of Congress
Cataloging-in-Publication Data
Talk about trouble: a new deal portrait of
Virginians in the Great Depression /
edited by Nancy J. Martin-Perdue and
Charles L. Perdue, Jr.
p.   cm.
Includes bibliographical references
(p.   ) and index.
ISBN 0-8078-2269-8 (cloth: alk. paper).—
ISBN 0-8078-4570-1 (pbk.: alk. paper)
1. Virginia—Social life and customs.
2. Depressions—1929—United States.
3. New Deal, 1933–1939—Virginia.
4. Virginia—Social conditions.
5. Virginia—Biography.
6. Interviews—Virginia.
I. Martin-Perdue, Nancy J.
II. Perdue, Charles L., 1930– .
F231.M38   1996
975.5'042—dc20   95-34700
CIP

00 99 98 97 96   5 4 3 2 1

The research for this work was
made possible in part by a grant from
the National Endowment for the
Humanities, an independent federal
agency whose mission is to award
grants to support education, scholarship,
media programming, libraries, and
museums, in order to bring the results of
cultural activities to a broad, general
public.

The publication of this volume was
aided by generous support from Arts
and Sciences and from the office of the
Vice Provost for Research, both at the
University of Virginia.

Dedicated
to the memory of
Kevin Barry Perdue
and
Gerald E. Parsons Jr.,
whose own life stories were
cut all too short,

and to all the people who
contributed their life histories to
the Virginia Writers' Project

Contents

Part II. Making a Living *From Farm to Factory,* 205

Preface

Times ain't now nothin' like they used to be,
Times ain't now nothin' like they used to be,
I'm tellin' you the truth, you can take it from me.
— Richard (Rabbit) Brown, "James Alley Blues"

"Things ain't now like they used to be nohow," a Virginia native told a state Writers' Project worker more than a decade after Rabbit Brown's "James Alley Blues," with its similar refrain, was recorded by Victor Records in New Orleans on 5 March 1927. A central theme pervading the hundreds of life histories produced by the fieldworkers of the Virginia Writers' Project between 1938 and 1941 is that of being witness to the vast socioeconomic and cultural changes ensuing from the Great Depression and the New Deal responses to it.

We, the editors, were likewise offspring of the 1930s decade and were affected by those same processes of change that were radically altering theretofore accepted ways of living and of comprehending the world. It was in the critical context of those times also that both our futures and our mutual and abiding interests in folklore, history, and people were shaped. Those interests undoubtedly guided (in sometimes serendipitous and not always easily recognizable ways) our selection of the texts included here and affected the interpretations we bring to them. Since these circumstances are of some relevance to what follows, this, then, is necessarily a very personal preamble.

To begin, we were both—as some say in these life histories—"rocked in the Democratic cradle" from early childhood. We listened earnestly to the sound of President Roosevelt's voice as he broadcast his "Fireside Chats" live on radio. And each of our families received some material benefit from various New Deal programs: for Chuck's folks, the WPA built a much appreciated, solid, new, concrete-based outdoor privy; for Nan's father, a CWA flood control project on the Los Angeles River in California provided a temporary construction job. It is of far more profound consequence, however, that both families were affected directly by the rural-to-urban transitions of the early 1930s onward, by the subsequent transformations from the pre–World War II period to the "boom" times of a postwar modern world, and more recently, to some degree, by the conditions of so-called postmodernity. The course of those changes spans several generations in each family, and those lives must also be taken into account in this process.

Nan's grandfather Martin (born in 1855) was a scout for the Texas Rangers at the age of fourteen and a small landholder and stockman in west central Texas for some part of his life. His wife bore him twelve children between 1877 and 1902, outlived him by twenty years, and died in Los Angeles at the age of almost ninety-six in 1953. On the maternal side, her grandfather Tipton (born in 1875) was first widowed in midlife and then partially paralyzed by a stroke. It was doubly difficult for him to manage three daughters and a sizable mohair goat and cattle ranch in Menard County, Texas, alone. In time, he remarried a much younger cousin of his first wife. In the next generation, this editor's parents traversed the old plank road (still in use across parts of the desert) from Texas to California and back again several times before finally moving to the "City of the Angels" in 1930. The move from rural Texas to urban Los Angeles hastened and ensured a transition, already begun among the Martin kinsmen, from farming and ranching to the mechanics and skilled craftsman trades. A first-generation Californian and native Los Angeleno, Nan nevertheless grew up primarily within an enclave of extended kin and Texas émigrés.

On the other side of this collaboration, a partial transition had been made earlier by Chuck's grandfathers Perdue and Samples—a farmer and a cotton sharecropper, both from rural Georgia—who had moved to town and become, respectively, a small store owner and a streetcar conductor. Out of necessity, Chuck's father worked and retired as a U.S. railway mail clerk, although he never really wanted to do anything but farm. And so this editor grew up in Panthersville, Georgia, took the four years of vocational agriculture offered at Southwest DeKalb High, milked dairy cows, plowed mules, and helped his father improve and farm fifty acres of red clay—nine miles from downtown Atlanta. Chuck had assumed the dream of his father and expected that farming would be his lifelong occupation, until urban sprawl and the military disrupted those plans. For him, rapid change was more keenly felt, required greater adjustments, and spurred other choices, which were themselves constrained by a limited range of experience and awareness of alternatives.

Life as an academic in a university setting was not, then, among the options either recognized as desirable or thought to be attainable. But both editors were also products of the same changing cultural values and rising expectations with regard to higher education that affected so many of the people interviewed as part of the New Deal life history projects in Virginia. And just as it is true for children and grandchildren of many of the families in the texts following, we are among the first in our respective families to obtain an education beyond the level of the secondary school. The wishes of parents for their children to have more opportunities—educationally and jobwise—than they did, to "better themselves," or to acquire "culture" with a capital *C* are also familiar to us. In other words, our understandings of class, gender, and value differences were born of personal experience or lived realities, not of later academic learning.

Elsewhere, memory events from childhood collided directly with the narrated events of a life history and unexpectedly produced other sudden recollections. Julia Keesee Carwile of Lynchburg reported that her brother Orville drowned in the Los Angeles River floods of early spring 1938. Her account prompted Nan's recall of standing with her parents and other family members watching in fear and fascination as the river washed out the Imperial Boulevard bridge in that same flood. During that disastrous season, a number of people lost their lives as they attempted to cross streets and were pulled into the city sewer system by the suction created by open drains in the curbing. Whether or not that is, in fact, what happened to Orville Keesee, his story vividly brought back the long since forgotten sensations of real terror felt as a child when confronted by swiftly moving curbside water.

Even in lighter moods and later moments, we encountered, by sheer happenstance, traces of and connections to individuals in these life histories. We did not become aware of the VWP "Tom Hand's Mule" text until the summer of 1984. But between 1969 and 1978, we lived in Rappahannock County, Virginia—little more than a mile distant from the stone remains of Hand's mill, formerly owned by Tom Hand's father, William. And while doing folklore fieldwork in that area, the county's commonwealth attorney, George Davis, told us a story about "*Cooper's* Mule." According to the story, a man named Cooper sold a mule to a local farmer, who brought it back the next day indignantly complaining that the mule was blind. When he hitched the animal to his farm wagon, it had pulled the wagon straightway into the side of the barn and wrecked it. Cooper's response was that the mule wasn't blind, it just didn't give a "damn." Since then, in neighboring Culpeper County, anyone who didn't "give a damn" was said to be "just like Cooper's mule." So, in a barroom in Manila at the close of World War II, when a soldier from Culpeper County heard a voice behind him say that someone was "just like Cooper's mule," he knew immediately that the person speaking had to be from Culpeper. He was.

A few years afterward, Culpeper native T. O. Madden Jr. (nephew of Rev. Willis J. Madden, whose life history is herein) told us a variant of the same story—except that in his version, the catchphrase was "just like Thornton's Mule," Thornton was from Rappahannock County, and the World War II soldier was in a bar in Okinawa. Much more recently, the great-granddaughter of Lycurgus Drumheller (for whom a VWP text is also included in this work) allowed in a passing conversation that her husband, a local land surveyor in the counties of Culpeper and Madison (formed out of Culpeper in 1793) also "knows" about Tom Hand's mule, again with the added element of the World War II ending.

All the names mentioned in the variant stories—Hand, Cooper, and Thornton—refer to real persons who lived at different time periods in Rappahannock County (formed in 1833 out of Culpeper County) and who were well known for their eccentricities and as local characters in the extended area. Although the names change, the existence of the variant "blind mule" stories (with their slogan in simile form) attests to the persistence of tradition, exhibited in this case in an oral expression closely identified with the region and with the reputations of local personalities. Moreover, these variants, updated to the experience of the Second World War, demonstrate the capacity of tradition to adapt to functional and historical change. In the latter form, they offer reassurance in the face of unpredictability by juxtaposing experiences of the foreign and unfamiliar (World War II and distant places) with the local and familiar (the recognized formulaic expression of identity and place, "like Cooper's mule"). Those associations in oral tradition continue as reminders of the lineal connections between the people and histories of the counties of Rappahannock, Culpeper, and Madison more than fifty years after closure of the Virginia Writers' Project, which had documented a pre–World War II version of the narrative, in passing, as part of its Tom Hand life history text.

Although common threads tie us to the lives and experiences of others in these life histories, those chance connections alone were neither necessary nor sufficient conditions for particular texts to be included here (see the "Editorial Commentary and Method" section in the introduction for discussion of the selection criteria and process). However, we do accept responsibility and sincerely apologize for any misrepresentation that may result from our interpretation of these texts.

Acknowledgments

Our lingering work on the Federal Writers' Project and other New Deal programs in Virginia has spanned twice the length of the decade under study; needless to say, our cumulative obligations over time are many. First and foremost, without the spirit and guidance of Eudora Ramsay Richardson, the diligent efforts of her Virginia Writers' Project workers, and the remarkable cooperation of the hard-pressed people they interviewed more than fifty years ago, this project would not have been possible. That is a debt that can never be fully repaid or adequately acknowledged.

We recorded interviews with or otherwise conversed or corresponded with a number of people employed by New Deal programs on various levels, among them Eudora Ramsay Richardson, Raymond H. Sloan, Laura Virginia Hale, Margaret Jeffries, Emory L. Hamilton, John S. Widdicombe, Herbert Halpert, Leonard Rapport, Richard Chase, Arthur Rothstein, Jack Delano, and Bernarda Bryson. We have been fortunate to be able to talk with these individuals, even if only briefly, for their numbers dwindle steadily.

Many institutions and individuals provided services and assistance to us in the course of this work and deserve credit here, among them Edmund Berkeley Jr., Michael F. Plunkett and the staff of the Manuscripts Department, Division of Special Collections, documents librarian Walter Newsome, and Martin Davis, all of Alderman Library, University of Virginia, Charlottesville; Robert Clay, Conley Edwards and staff (Archives Branch), Edward D. C. Campbell Jr., Publications, and Mikell Brown and Mark Scala, Picture Collections, all of the Virginia State Library, Richmond; Carol Tuckwiller, archivist, Virginiana Collection, Roanoke Public Library, Roanoke; Grace McCrowell, Reference Department, Rockbridge Regional Library; Fritz J. Malval, archivist, Collis P. Huntington Library, Hampton University; Robert Vaughan, executive director, and the staff of the Virginia Foundation for the Humanities and Public Policy; Brooks Johnson, curator of photography, and Irene Roughton, associate registrar, both of the Chrysler Museum, Norfolk, and Larry Dunn, assistant superintendent of schools, Charlotte County, Virginia.

We would also like to thank Richard Schrader, archivist, Southern History Collection, Wilson Library, University of North Carolina, Chapel Hill; Charles Ritchie and Laurie Weitzenkorn, formerly assistant curators, Index of American Design, National Gallery of Art; Richard K. Doud and staff members, Archive of American Art, Smithsonian Institution; National Archives staff members, in particular, Richard Crawford, Renee Jaussard, and Jimmie Rush; Gillian Anderson and Anne McClain (Music Library, Division of Performing Arts), Beverly Brannon and Deborah Evans (Division of Prints and Photographs), John Y. Cole (Center for the Book and Publishing Office), John F. Hackett (formerly Division of Manuscripts), Joseph C. Hickerson and the late Gerald E. Parsons Jr. (Archive of Folk Culture, American Folklife Center), Alan Jabbour (American Folklife Center), and Carl Fleischhauer and Catherine Kerst (American Memory Project), all of the Library of Congress; Joseph T. Wilson, executive director, National Council for the Traditional Arts; John Alexander Williams, Martin Sullivan, and Sally Yerkovich, who originally steered the proposal for this work through the National Endowment for the Humanities labyrinth; and

J. David Sapir, former chairman of the Department of Anthropology, University of Virginia, for "keeping the faith."

For his constancy as a dear friend and for his generosities of both mind and spirit, we give our everlasting affection and gratitude to Gerry Parsons, who could not wait with us to see this work completed. To him and to our son, Kevin Barry Perdue, we dedicate it in remembrance. Special appreciation is expressed as well to Charlie Camp and Marta Weigle, longtime friends and colleagues, for their help, encouragement, and mutual interests in the subject at hand. We owe a further debt to Marta for her cogent and constructive criticisms of this manuscript, and to Edward L. Ayers of the University of Virginia's Corcoran Department of History as well, who voluntarily read the manuscript and gave enthusiastic comments. And thanks to Anthropology Department colleagues Ellen Contini-Morava and Richard Handler, who like-wise read and commented on parts of the work and gave encouragement when it was sorely needed. Anne E. Bromley and Susan Holbrook Perdue (both of whom are working editors as well as daughters-in-law) suffered through the twice-as-long first-draft manuscript and, as hoped, made thoughtful recommendations for shrinking it. To all the above we owe much credit for the betterment of this book; the shortcomings that remain, however, are our own.

Other persons—friends and acquaintances, students, local public officials, project workers, and those they interviewed or their relatives alike—also contributed in all manner of ways, including generously sharing rare family documents or photographs for use in this volume. Appreciation for these sundry efforts and many kindnesses extend to George Kegley, Walton F. Mitchell Jr., Dorothy Jarrett, Mrs. Filmore Norfleet, T. O. Madden Jr., Clara Steele Eden, Ann Brush Miller, Dorothy Davis, Gary Grant, Joel T. Broyhill, Marvin Broyhill III, William Thomas Garrett, Mrs. Kenneth Davidson, George and Hilda Hodges, Mrs. James Hodges, Margaret Wolfe Lee, Janet P. Drumheller, and Michelle Branigan. To any we have inadvertently missed, we apologize for the oversight.

This work has also been furthered by financial and other intangible benefits extended to us jointly and separately from a number of different sources. Gail Moore and Judy Birckhead in the Word Processing Center, Office of the Dean of the Faculty, College of Arts and Sciences, University of Virginia, gave exceptional service by entering the Virginia Writers' Project life history interviews into computer files. Their good cheer and interest in the materials went well beyond what was necessary to the job and was much appreciated.

A grant from the National Endowment for the Humanities and a joint fellowship in the Center of the Virginia Foundation for the Humanities and Public Policy, in conjunction with faculty leave from an associateship awarded to Charles L. Perdue Jr. in the Center for Advanced Studies, University of Virginia, all gave material support to the early stages of research and writing on this project. More recently, the University of Virginia offices of Dean Raymond J. Nelson and Associate Dean Richard J. Sundberg, and of Vice Provost for Research Gene D. Block, in cooperation, have been more than generous in their support for publication of this work by the University of North Carolina Press. It is not too much to say that this volume would not have been possible without the aid of all these individuals and organizations. We very humbly recognize our indebtedness to all of them, but to Dean of the Faculty Raymond J. Nelson, who has given friendship and support through the years, we offer special heartfelt thanks.

Thanks, too, to David Perry, who has been kind, reassuring, and helpful through it all, despite the unforeseeable early traumas inflicted by a fire at the Press. We are grateful to him, to Pamela Upton, and to the University of North Carolina Press for their continued support of and confidence in this work.

Finally, Martin and Susan Holbrook Perdue, Marc Perdue and Anne Bromley, and Kelly and Elizabeth Steel-Perdue have all been troubled with talk about this book for far longer than should have been necessary. They have borne it with generally good humor and patience, freely given advice, encouragement, help, and love, and on occasion they provided the levity needed to put it all in proper perspective. They have also provided us with the delights and distractions of grandchildren, Emily Stoddard and Sarah Martin Perdue, Kathryn Bromley and Theresa Russell Perdue, and Benjamin Tipton and Daniel Walton Perdue. Whether they know it or not, collectively and separately, they enrich our lives and make it all worth the effort.

Abbreviations

AAA	Agricultural Adjustment Act
CCC	Civilian Conservation Corps
CWA	Civil Works Administration
FAP	Federal Art Project
FERA	Federal Emergency Relief Administration
FMP	Federal Music Project
FTP	Federal Theatre Project
FWP	Federal Writers' Project
HABS	Historic American Buildings Survey
HAMMS	Historic American Merchant Marine Survey
HIP	Historical Inventory Project
HRS	Historical Records Survey
IAD	Index of American Design
NYA	National Youth Administration
OEM	Office of Emergency Management
OWI	Office of War Information
PWA	Public Works Administration (Federal Emergency Administration of Public Works)
PWAP	Public Works of Art Project
RA/FSA	Resettlement Administration (later, Farm Security Administration)
RFC	Reconstruction Finance Corporation
TVA	Tennessee Valley Authority
VWP	Virginia Writers' Project
WPA	Works Progress Administration (1935–39); Work Projects Administration (1939–43)

TALK ABOUT TROUBLE

Introduction

There are few things more fascinating or informative than learning about the experience of other conscious beings as they make their way through the world. Accounts of their lives have a power to move us deeply, to help us imagine what it must have been like to live in different social and historical circumstances, to provide insights into the workings of lives, and perhaps, to provide a frame of reference for reassessing our own experience, own fortunes, own possibilities of existence.

—*William McKinley Runyan,* Life Histories and Psychobiography

When Virginia Writers' Project worker Anne Worrell asked a Roanoke woman about her life history, she exclaimed, "Talk about trouble!" and launched into a narration of her sons' marital woes. Her comment—the title of this volume—serves as a metaphor for the conversations, or "talk," prompted by various life history interview programs conducted in Virginia under the agency of the Works Progress Administration's Federal Writers' Project.[1] Guided by Eudora Ramsay Richardson as its full-time state director, the Virginia Writers' Project brought a number of significant books (including *Virginia: A Guide to the Old Dominion* and *The Negro in Virginia*) to publication, carried out a notable folklore and folksong collecting effort, conducted approximately three hundred ex-slave interviews, and, between October 1938 and May 1941, completed more than thirteen hundred life histories, social-ethnic studies, and youth studies.[2]

Richardson planned "to include the best of these Youth Studies and Life Histories in a book devoted to the lives of typical Virginians," but the Virginia Writers' Project ended before that goal could be accomplished. As its offices closed in June 1942, the VWP dispersed program materials to various storehouses, where, for the most part, this too-long-forgotten and endangered documentary resource has languished for more than fifty years.[3]

The remarkable circumstances of the Great Depression and of the New Deal years affected the lives and consciousness of people across the social spectrum in Virginia. Ultimately, the changes brought about by those times were reflected in many ways in the collective interview transcripts produced by the VWP and in the images made by photographers attached to state WPA offices or to the Historical Section, Information Division of the Resettlement Administration. Together, the New Deal texts and images, which form the core of this volume, offer contemporary portraits or glimpses of everyday life in Virginia in the 1930s that cannot otherwise be reproduced and consequently are at once ordinary and extraordinary.

In their range and variety, these documents illustrate the impact of historical and cultural forces on individual lives and allow us to consider the dynamics of *both* history and culture as ongoing processes and products "of interaction between the past and present."[4] Virginians of another era "talk about trouble" and also relative well-being, about the complexities of their lives and experiences, and about coping with profound economic and sociocultural change in the throes of the Great Depression.

Although the present work truly had its beginnings, in more ways than can be acknowledged here, more than half a century ago, it also represents the culmination, in part, of our more than twenty-year ongoing effort to search out, augment, and make accessible to scholars and general readers these rare Virginia documents. As the first-time publication of a selection of VWP life history texts and of many of the WPA or RA/FSA photographs produced in the state, illuminated by additional research findings, contextual information, and commentary, *Talk about Trouble* makes a substantial contribution in its own right. It also adds to the cumulative scholarship available on New Deal programs, oral history, narrative life history research and method, cultural and regional studies, and, in particular, Virginia history. Further, it will eventually serve as a companion reader to an administrative history and in-depth analysis of New Deal cultural programs in Virginia, now in preparation.

To "read" these Virginia Writers' Project texts in terms of the multiple levels on which they have meaning, one needs to know more about the historical circumstances and contexts in which they were produced, about the individual persons who were responsible for their creation, and also about the individuals who were their subjects. Since the above-mentioned administrative history will treat the background and circumstances of these programs and their products in a more comprehensive manner than is possible here, the discussion that follows gives only a brief overview of programs and political aims at the federal level. Rather, more extensive consideration is given specifically to the Virginia Writers' Project, its programs, some of its personnel, and its relationship to other, similar programs, especially William Terry Couch's FWP southern life history project and its publication, *These Are Our Lives*. Lastly, this introduction refers readers, in brief, to the general literature on the uses and interpretation of life histories, addresses some of the problematic aspects of the FWP and VWP life histories, in particular, and suggests approaches to such texts offered by other recent works that have dealt with similar written narrative forms of relating lives and experience.[5]

In Part I, "Narrating Experience," older informants in the first chapter talk primarily about the past and about how social life and ways of making a living had changed in their lifetimes. That part's remaining chapters focus on narratives illustrating how the factors of gender and race differentially affected an individual's experiences and chances with respect to work, education, social life, health and welfare, or misfortune. Part II, "Making a Living from Farm to Factory," details work experiences in specific occupations. The epilogue sums up the VWP and RA/FSA programs in Virginia and comments on some of the changes that occurred as World War II drew closer.

The missions of the Works Progress Administration and the Resettlement Administration were broadly defined and quite different. Under its "Federal One" mandate in late 1935, the WPA established federal art, music, theater, and writers' projects to provide relief jobs appropriate to the needs and skills of artists, musicians, actors, and white-collar and professional workers. The individual federal projects, in turn, fostered similar state programs, such as the Virginia Writers' Project, to carry out those same objectives at the local levels.[6]

By way of contrast, the Historical Section was organized within the federal Resettlement Administration agency in mid-1935 as a public relations unit to gather and produce files of cultural images documented by photography. These images were to be used, in part, to sway public opinion in favor of RA (later, Farm Security Administration) reform proposals affecting farmers and farm workers displaced from the land, in many cases by Agriculture Adjustment Act programs that advanced both agribusiness and mechanization.[7]

Despite critical organizational and programmatic differences and the fact that their efforts in Virginia seldom overlapped on the ground, the various VWP interview programs and the

RA/FSA and WPA photographic projects did share similar interests and subject matter. Life history and photographic projects alike focused on the problems of small farmers, tenants, and sharecroppers in rural localities. Concerns about housing, health, and educational issues, as well as about relief programs and jobs, were not limited to any single setting, and these subjects were documented by texts and photographs in both rural and urban areas.

As the depression faded into the beginning of psychological and material preparations for World War II, New Deal programs entered a new phase and dealt with different kinds of demands, subjects, and even geographic areas within the state. People were being dislocated by the establishment of new military bases or the enlargement of old ones. Defense industries were expanding, new ones were being developed, and a mass exodus from rural areas to urban centers for the defense jobs available there presented new problems. The RA/FSA turned its attention and resources away from "stranded" communities toward its projects to provide housing for defense workers and military personnel. The National Youth Administration shifted its training programs to residential centers and to skills needed for the war effort. In addition, W. E. Garnett, a rural sociologist at Virginia Polytechnic Institute, became interested in the problems of out-of-school youth and requested VWP workers to conduct narrative interview surveys among both rural white youths and urban black youths aged sixteen to twenty-four. The survey of urban black youths was carried out in various cities by the project's separate Negro Studies unit based at Hampton Institute.[8]

Calls for military readiness propaganda stimulated the photographic documentation of shipbuilding, testing of new fighting equipment, and training of military personnel, as well as the production of images projecting America's well-being and strength. By the early 1940s, both RA/FSA- and WPA-generated photographs began to be more overtly propagandistic, and talk of impending war and of patriotism began to appear in the last life histories produced by the Virginia Writers' Project.

However, the course of both the Writers' Project in Virginia and the RA/FSA's Historical Section, at their different levels of operation, was ultimately as much tied to and influenced by the lives, circumstances, and experiences of particular persons as are the collective life histories of individuals that the VWP produced. For instance, even as they hired Eudora Ramsay Richardson to be full-time director of the Virginia Writers' Project (replacing part-time incumbent Hamilton J. Eckenrode) on 9 March 1937, FWP director Henry G. Alsberg and his aide, Reed Harris, were concerned about her reputation for being "very strong willed." Richardson, a freelance writer with publications to her credit, had attended Hollins College, graduated from Richmond College (University of Richmond), and received a master's degree in English from Columbia University. She was well qualified for the position. However, her long-term commitment to women's issues and former service as a field director for the National Woman's Suffrage Association under Carrie Chapman Catt raised questions about her independent tendencies and whether that behavior could be controlled by administrators in Washington. Their worries—unacceptable now—were not unexpected or entirely without basis then.[9]

Roy Emerson Stryker, appointed as chief of the Historical Section in the Information Division of RA/FSA on 10 July 1935, was regarded by some as a testy eccentric. Certainly he was as strong minded and individualistic as Richardson, or more so. Born into a populist family in Colorado, he worked for a while in a New York City settlement house, as did other New Dealers, such as Harry Hopkins, the successive federal administrative head of FERA,

View of Stony Man Mountain, Skyline Drive. October 1935. Photo by Arthur Rothstein. [LC-USF33-02198-M4] *[This print shows the hole punched in the negative, a trademark of one means Roy Stryker used to "kill" photographs.]*

CWA, and WPA. Stryker (like Richardson) attended Columbia University, where he met and worked for his mentor, economics professor Rexford Guy Tugwell, the later assistant secretary of agriculture and head of the Resettlement Administration. In his capacity as chief of the Historical Section, Roy Stryker directed a cadre of special photographers that over time included Dorothea Lange, Marion Post-Wolcott, John Vachon, Arthur Rothstein, Ben Shahn, Jack Delano, Russell Lee, and Walker Evans.[10]

Of the estimated 140,000 to 182,000 negatives produced by RA/FSA photographers nationwide in about eight years, slightly more than 3,000 were made in Virginia.[11] The first photographer hired by Roy Stryker was Arthur Rothstein, whose first official assignment in October 1935 was to document some of the more than five hundred families being displaced by the establishment of Shenandoah National Park in the Blue Ridge Mountains of Virginia. Of the 309 photographs taken on this project, 154 were "killed" by Stryker, a fact that may reflect Rothstein's hasty work and professional immaturity at that time.[12]

As the twenty-year-old New York native Arthur Rothstein was just setting out on his photographic expedition to Virginia's Blue Ridge, the Federal Writers' Project under the direction of Henry Alsberg was also beginning its first undertaking: creation of the American Guide Series, based on the model of the earlier Baedeker guides to Europe. The guidebooks to states, regions, and territories were to highlight the distinctive values of indigenous American landscapes, culture, and heritage, while simultaneously promoting automobile travel and tourism.[13]

To produce the Virginia guidebook "mosaic" (as Eudora Ramsay Richardson perceived it to be), some amount of early folklore collecting was carried out to provide the local color cultural material demanded. But as the *Guide* was gradually "laid by," other work decreed by the FWP demanded Richardson's attention. Among the programs so specified by Alsberg in October 1938 (and for which he granted Richardson ten additional relief workers) were a full-fledged folklore project overseen by Benjamin A. Botkin in Washington, D.C.; a social-ethnic studies program directed by Morton W. Royse, also in Washington; and a southern life history documentary effort spearheaded by William T. Couch in Chapel Hill, North Carolina.[14]

All three of these FWP programs were confounded almost immediately in Virginia—either by Richardson's direct actions or under her signature. Apparently, none of the program manuals, as written by either Botkin, Royse, or Couch, were distributed to VWP fieldworkers. Instead, a two-page form letter in November 1938 announced the start of a "Social-Ethnic Studies" program, instructed workers to obtain "life histories" of persons in suggested occupational groups (those mentioned specifically in Couch's instructions), and elsewhere brought in phrases from Royse's and Botkin's manuals. A two-page interview guide accompanied the letter, and this four-page packet replaced almost forty pages of program manuals. The consequences of this action proved to be both the strength and weakness of the VWP efforts.[15]

Despite the lack of definitive directions provided by the manuals, workers on the VWP folklore project produced a sizable and important body of folklore collectanea, some examples of which are included in this work. The social-ethnic studies program, in contrast, was of little consequence in Virginia—except as an erroneous heading on some VWP inter-

Nicholson Hollow,
Shenandoah National Park, Virginia.
Mrs. Bailey Nicholson.
Photo by Arthur Rothstein.
[LC-USF33-02173-M2]

views. Perhaps this resulted, in part, from perceptions, such as those expressed by Douglas Southall Freeman in the Virginia guidebook, that most residents of the Old Dominion in 1930 were "of the same stock" and had "no deep admixture of recent foreign blood." Concerning the life history program, however, the VWP's disregard of Couch's instructions soon brought his sharp rebuke, and this was a matter of more serious consequence in Richmond. Despite long-standing, often jocular, rivalries between Virginia and its neighboring state, the allegiances of Richardson and the VWP were essentially southern and were thereby more closely aligned with North Carolina than with Washington, D.C.[16]

William Couch was a man with a purpose. He had little tolerance or time for obstacles to his plans to collect southern life histories for a multivolume series, "Life in the South." He believed such a body of oral testimony would provide "readable and faithful representations of living persons" to discredit the "merriment over psychopaths" incited by Erskine Caldwell's fictional debased southerners. In addition, the life histories of real people in diverse occupational groups ought to reflect, Couch contended, "a fair picture of the structure and working of society," by which he meant southern society.[17]

As director of the University of North Carolina Press and part-time Southeastern Regional FWP director, Couch was well placed to carry out ideas he developed while previously serving with the North Carolina Writers' Project. Even before his FWP appointment became official in August 1938, he was pushing his southern life history project forward. By February 1939 (scarcely a month after reprimanding Richardson for not sending out his instructions), Couch's edited collection of FWP southern life histories was on its way to the printer. *These Are Our Lives* was published on 26 April 1939 without including any Virginia materials. Before the year ended, Couch was no longer an FWP regional director, and no further volumes in his proposed series were published. Under Richardson's guidance, however, the VWP produced some of its best work in the period from 1939 until its life history efforts ended in mid-1941.[18]

The names and often the places given by the "real people" telling "their own stories" in *These Are Our Lives* were changed, making subjective experience anonymous and detaching it from actual contexts of community and kin. Based only on the editorial conventions admittedly used in the volume, almost half of the "real" lives presented were extensively edited; a few may have been completely fictitious. More important, the nature and scope of creative "improvements" by individual editors or of revisions to meet Couch's criterion of "literary excellence" cannot be easily determined.[19]

Without proper contextual description, "stories of ordinary people past [such as those in the FWP life histories] stand in danger of remaining just that: stories. To become something more," anthropologists John and Jean Comaroff advise, "these partial, 'hidden histories' have to be situated in the wider world of power and meaning that gave them life." Deprived of the matrix of place and circumstance that actually produced them, the stories in *These Are Our Lives* remain as disengaged, anonymous *stories,* powerful though they may be.[20]

Nevertheless, the "chorus of hosannahs" that greeted publication of that work in 1939 included the urging of one reviewer that "members of Congress should read this unbiased selection, which mediated between 'drearily impersonal' sociology and fiction." A recent comment is more pointed, cautioning that "by today's categories, the life histories [in *These Are Our Lives*] are an interesting cross between oral history and creative writing." Yet it has been this "creative writing" aspect of the hybrid that has been largely emphasized and hailed, while the contributions of these FWP life history texts as oral history or as ethnographic resource have remained inadequately considered. To the extent that this is so, the vast content of cultural and historical knowledge and information contained within these texts also remains, as oral historian Paul Thompson wisely observes in another case, "not even known to be needed." It is our job to make the need known.[21]

Contemporary awareness of the FWP life history programs and texts is still generally limited to the historic publication of *These Are Our Lives* or to recent popular anthologies (such as Ann Banks's *First-Person America*) that claim to present the aesthetically "best" or most "authentic" of these texts. Other FWP texts appear in occasional anthologies of literature as early mythic examples that presaged the canon of works by now legendary writers such as Ralph Ellison, Richard Wright, Studs Terkel, Saul Bellow, Zora Neale Hurston, or Kenneth Rexroth—all of whom were sustained by the FWP to live and write another day.[22]

One of the democratizing side effects of the Federal Writers' Project, however, was that its work relief programs gave opportunity for expression to many persons who were not normally "writers," as that term is most often understood. As a case in point, the VWP workers had varying amounts of education, and their writing styles reflected that range, with a number who wrote largely in the vernacular. Several VWP relief workers wrote poetry, and others joined or formed literary societies or later wrote for local newspapers, but none of these individuals gained any lasting fame in the world of literature after their stint on the project. Although their VWP creative contributions were sizable, such writers generally have been underrepresented and rarely treated in the literature devoted to these New Deal texts. This work seeks to bring some much needed balance to those accounts.[23]

Seven individuals, out of almost forty workers on the Virginia Writers' Project life history programs, wrote more than two-thirds of the more than thirteen hundred narrative texts. Those seven persons, Leila Blanche Bess, Gertrude Blair, Susie R. C. Byrd (the only African American among this group), John W. Garrett, Margaret Jeffries, Essie (Celestia) Wade Smith, and Mary Skeen Venable, were all native Virginians who documented themselves, their kin, and their communities in these texts.[24]

The biographies of these individuals yield some personal characteristics that may illuminate the attitudes and values expressed by them in the life histories they produced. The factor of age is significant, and in that regard the three youngest, Garrett, Jeffries, and Byrd, were about forty years old, Bess was in her fifties, and Blair, Smith, and Venable were nearing seventy as they carried forth their project work. In terms of their marital status, Venable had been married and divorced; Garrett was widowed then remarried; Smith was twice married, and possibly Byrd was as well, but the individual circumstances in their cases are unknown or not clear. The remaining three women (Bess, Blair, and Jeffries) never married but continued living at home with aged parents or extended family members.[25]

Since all of these persons occupied VWP relief jobs, we can assume that they were working out of necessity for the maintenance of both themselves and others. But this assumption masks significant class, race, and gender differences, for not only was John Garrett the single male in this group and the major provider as head of his household, but his working-class socioeconomic background was also substantially different from that of most of the women VWP workers considered here. His father (see Arthur Garrett in chapter 3) was a tenant farmer during his early life, was laid off by the Tubize silk mill in Hopewell, and was himself a WPA relief worker late in his life. After the VWP ended, John Garrett worked as a laboratory maintenance worker for seventeen years, until he retired from Hercules Powder Company in

Hopewell. And after almost fifty years' service in churches in both North Carolina and Virginia, he also retired as a Pentecostal minister about 1970.

In comparison, the five white women writers were from families that were relatively well-to-do, even privileged, at other times. Jeffries's father was a lawyer and judge in Culpeper County, and Venable's father (who was born in 1818) was a land lawyer in Alleghany County. Lycurgus Blair was a building contractor in Roanoke whose only daughter, Gertrude, had been taught early on by private governesses and then studied Renaissance and ancient art in this country and in Italy. She considered her "ability to ride horses that a man wouldn't mount" to be a special skill. Bess's father was a teacher and then a middle-class farmer and store owner, but the permanent damage to his health from a Civil War injury and to the family's financial prospects through the loss of their store and home in a fire was irreparable. By 1910, when Essie Wade Butler was married to Cabell Smith and living in her father-in-law's household in Martinsville (see Orthodox Creed Strictler [Smith] in chapter 1), she was a public school teacher. Her grandfather Henry Hobson Wade, an Episcopal minister educated at Princeton, died in Franklin County before 1860. Subsequently her infant father, Zachary Taylor Wade, was raised by his stepfather, Theodorick Webb, a Baptist minister and large slaveholder, who suffered serious property losses in the Civil War. When Essie Wade Smith died at eighty-nine, she was the honorary president of the United Daughters of the Confederacy. For the most part, these were Virginia gentlewomen, by breeding if not in economic fact, who because of their employment as VWP relief writers could retain something of their social dignity despite adversity.

Susie R. C. Byrd's situation was substantially different from that of the others, however, because of her race and the castelike separation it imposed on the conditions of her work and life. Her education and work placed her within the middle-class African American community in Petersburg, where she lived, but that status could not be translated directly into the larger social milieu in Virginia. In addition, the bounds of the Negro Studies unit at Hampton Institute limited and, to some extent, redefined her efforts within the larger structure of the Virginia Writers' Project. Following her ex-slave interviewing work, Byrd produced numerous life histories. But these were reshaped, under the influence and interests of Roscoe Lewis at Hampton, into brief descriptive case studies collectively entitled "Economic and Social Conditions among Negroes," which reported on existing racial inequality and, in almost clinical detail, the grittier aspects of life in the slums of Petersburg. These texts strike us as quite different from other narrative life history texts, and they are—another VWP by-product, thankfully, of being left to one's own devices without hard and fast procedural rules.

In the process of this work, the persons interviewed or their reputations were quite often already known to the project fieldworker, but the reverse was also true. So what was conveyed in their exchange was already affected by preexisting relationships, expectations, and experience. Inevitably, the VWP texts reflected the writers' judgments of people and of the social and moral geography of their communities. But it is within just such "moral judgments, moral prescriptions, and active comparisons," according to anthropologist Sidney Mintz, that culture and society may be illuminated by the opinions of a single informant—or a single VWP interviewer.[26]

If the responses elicited from George Strausburg by John Garrett had the self-revelatory tone of confession made during a pastoral visit, perhaps that was not accidental. Certainly, the deference exhibited by some African Americans toward "Miz Mary" Venable rightly placed her as the child of a former plantation mistress, or as granddaughter of the same in Jeffries's case. Elsewhere, Venable's reported inquiries about the subject's needs for food, bedding, or clothing suggested her visit was more in line with her role as a member of the Methodist Women's Home Mission Movement than as a VWP interviewer. Such subjective and situational factors certainly entered into the resulting VWP texts, with the consequence that they, in turn, provide commentary on multiple lives and on a variety of topics meaningful to both interviewer *and* subject. In this reflexive process, or "double frame of life history," as some have called it, "the two stories [of both interviewer and subject] commenting on each other travel alongside, simultaneously commanding our attention and creating a different world than either represents by itself."[27]

We have few clues, however, as to how the various workers actually carried out their life history work day to day. Although the VWP life histories are largely composed of "talk" transformed into written texts, which freely mix third-person and apparent first-person reportage, the writers had no modern recording equipment with which to document conversations for later transcription. A few, such as Jeffries, may have taken shorthand, but we have to assume that most just made brief notes from which they reconstructed the exchange afterward. Sketchy, penciled jottings have been found for some ex-slave interviews; none such have been located for the life history texts. What do exist in some cases are completed Youth Study forms (discarded from W. E. Garnett's initially intended questionnaire study), adapted by VWP writers after November 1939 for easy note taking with subjects of all ages, not just youths. Not unexpectedly, the narrative life histories in these cases are almost wholly shaped by the questionnaire, with the major divisions of the resulting texts closely following the format in which the questions were listed and answered on the form.[28]

The personal characteristics of the individual workers did affect how they carried out their work in one important detail: how they prepared their texts to be submitted to the Richmond office. The five white female workers all owned or had access to typewriters in their homes or in offices. They typed their own life histories in the original and sometimes kept carbon copies. Neither Garrett nor Byrd had the luxury of a typewriter, and all of their texts were handwritten in pencil on legal-size paper. But Garrett's handwritten texts suggest an important question about the processing of these works in the Richmond office: in the few instances in which there is a typed Garrett text (identified with a staff typist's name on it), no handwritten manuscript copy of that text has been found in the extant archival holdings. This would be consistent with the project's seeming practice of discarding manuscript texts after they were used, in whole or in part, in some publication in progress (observed elsewhere with regard to ex-slave interview material and *The Negro in Virginia*) or after the official copy was typed for the files.

Supplemental research also hints that life history texts were produced out of many, more varied conditions and types of interactions than the usually assumed interview situation. The fact that neither George Hodges nor Margaret Wolfe Lee remembered having been interviewed by Mary Venable or Leila Blanche Bess respectively (although he remembered Venable and Wolfe remembered Bess) may result from forgetfulness after fifty years. Or it may be that both Venable and Bess constructed some of their texts out of chance meetings and conversations, along with additions from their own common stock of local knowledge, possibly without Hodges or Lee ever knowing they were VWP youth study subjects. In other cases, it is obvious that no project interview ever took place. John W. Garrett's father-in-law,

Thomas Jefferson Broyhill, died in early 1936—several years prior to his VWP life history by Garrett (see notes for Marvin Broyhill in chapter 3). The reporting of questions and responses between a VWP worker and subject in a text is also no guarantee of a presumed interview situation's authenticity, as the complex manipulations indicated in Bessie Scales's texts with Dilcie Gum and Mollie Williams attest (in chapter 4). Although these cases appear to be exceptions to general practice, it is difficult to estimate the extent to which that is so.

The editorial acts of VWP workers and of staff members in the Richmond office alike raise other types of questions. The seven interviewers just considered were not only the most productive writers (of all those working on VWP life histories), but they also ranked among the most reliable. To varying degrees, their texts are generally trustworthy. Still, in at least a few of the texts these writers produced, they made deliberate changes to disguise the subject's identity or otherwise altered some details (see Orthodox Creed Strictler in chapter 1 and William D. Deal in chapter 7). The reasons for such modifications are not always so obvious. The types of changes made are not consistent and seem not to follow any regular pattern, even within the collective texts produced by a single interviewer.

Editors and typists in the Richmond office, through omission or by other types of manipulation, also made changes to some number of the texts they received from writers in the field (for instance, see Sam Harrison text in chapter 5). In practice, then, VWP writers and editors had various chances between them to affect the ultimate depiction of VWP life history subjects.

It is here that an application of the concept of "negotiated biography," as a kind of ethnographic text or biography produced out of interactions between persons having different cultural backgrounds or unequal social relations, might be most useful. Under compelling conditions of difference between writer and subject, negotiating a biographical text is an inherently lopsided and potentially coercive enterprise. As negotiated biography is described, "informants speak, ethnographers write," and insofar "as the final representation is concerned," the ethnographer has the last word, most often in print, and frequently without the subject's advice or consent, or possibly even (as has been suggested previously) without the subject's knowledge. In fact, all interview situations involve structured exchanges that are negotiated by the parties involved. The important issues of social or cultural difference, inequality, and control over one's narrative are implicit in each individual case and differ only in degree, not in kind.[29]

Despite the unbalanced and interrogatory nature of most structured interviews, it should never be inferred that the subject or informant is completely disadvantaged or without any agency in such a situation. The ways persons choose to narrate their lives to an interviewer are necessarily conditioned by many factors, including a certain amount of self-awareness and trust. In addition, it is the perception and interpretation of the facts (or the "truth" of the matter) that people act upon in their everyday lives—insofar as they are free or able to do so—and that shape the narratives or life stories they relate to those who ask. It is a repeatedly rediscovered truism that "no narrative can be transparent upon reality; that the constitution of the 'facts' is always a matter of interpretation," whether on the part of the writer, editor, subject, or reader.[30]

These factors existed and for the most part pertained also to the texts included in *These Are Our Lives.* Couch's editorial statements—"in the stories here printed [the "Instructions to Writers"] have been carefully followed" and "the first principle has been to let the people tell their own stories"—are insufficient disclaimers against the operation of interviewer or subject effects. Furthermore, under Couch's overview, various state editors within the southeastern region revised or otherwise added their own contributions to the texts, usually without having had any direct contact with or knowledge of the persons treated. They decontextualized and hid these stories behind the "fiction" of anonymity, while simultaneously claiming to present "authentic" experiences and "real people speaking," and without recognizing either the implicit contradiction or possible effects of their editorial changes.[31]

By chance of the programmatic differences between Richardson's vwp and Couch's southern life history project—that is, the late timing of the vwp life history efforts and, consequently, the lack of any resulting publication from them, and the lack of firm directions from the Richmond office, which set fieldworkers free to write in their own communities and among their own people pretty much as they saw fit—the Virginia Writers' Project life histories escaped some of the larger-scale emendations suffered by *These Are Our Lives* and survived more or less intact. What is even more significant, given the general conditions under which the vwp texts were produced, is how well these life histories hold up when compared with other sources of information about the subjects' lives and histories. When used cautiously, these texts can indeed be dealt with as ethnographic or historical documents.

It is evident from the analysis of vwp life history materials that no past model or single definition of what a life history "is" or "should be" can be applied equally well in all cases. However, the work of sociolinguist Charlotte Linde is suggestive and may offer a solution to the dilemma of "what is a life history?" by teasing it out of her definition and use of the term "life story." She identifies life story as a narrative linguistic form that is somewhat akin to a spoken autobiography but one that is open ended. A life story consists of the totality of the stories—their variants and associated discourse units—that persons tell, and use to convey their sense of themselves to others, throughout the course of their lifetime. The vwp life histories (and perhaps the life history in general) may best be viewed as a part of one's life story—a single frame at a particular moment in the larger production—as it is told to or written down by the other party to the story. Logic would suggest the terminology should be reversed: that life story should represent the part, and life history, the extended whole; but Linde is constrained by prior, longstanding debate about the multiple definitions and uses of the term "life history" in reference to both the object produced and to a methodology.[32]

In many respects, the Virginia Writers' Project life history texts have much more in common with the themes and conventions of oral narrative generally. It has been pointed out that Native American women characteristically emphasize the themes of everyday life, continuity between generations, landscape, and mythology and use "received traditions [adapted to] present circumstances" to shape statements of cultural identity in their autobiographies. The vwp life histories contain such themes as well, though mythology is more often replaced by other genres of expressive culture or folklore, such as the Tom Hand and the blind mule story, versions of which—updated to the World War II era—are still in oral tradition today in areas surrounding Culpeper County (see discussion in the preface and Tom Hand's text in chapter 3). If the fwp had not, in fact, rationalized dividing life history and folklore programs into separate endeavors, elements of oral tradition might have represented an even larger component of people's reported lives in the vwp texts.[33]

Nevertheless, as documents of some part of the human experience, the vwp life histories capture significant moments and relations in time, describe ways of doing things or social and economic processes at work in the past, and have the power to move and inform us.

These texts are also rare sources of testimony about tangible distinctions between people and about change. When change is measured "by paying close attention to concrete differences in people's lives," new insights may be gained that illuminate old debates. By extension, the history of everyday life in the Old Dominion during the Great Depression may appear "far newer" refracted through the lens of change provided by the Virginia Writers' Project life histories.[34]

Editorial Commentary and Method

Our underlying concern with the VWP texts as ethnographic or oral historical accounts directed the selection of particular life histories and subjects, first and foremost. In addition, we tried to select texts that (1) were produced under a variety of different conditions and programs and (2) were rich with internal details that might allow possibilities for further investigation, discovery of added contextual information, and the presentation of life history texts that are more than "just stories." Insofar as it was possible within those requirements and within the constraints of the material itself, we aimed for a general representativeness in terms of sex, race, class, age, occupation, and geographic distribution across the state.[35]

We have appended the findings from our search of census, courthouse, and other primary records, as well as secondary sources, that document a majority of the individuals in these life histories. Contextual information gleaned from our personal knowledge and experience has been included as well. Occasionally, the process of inquiry led us directly into contact with a few VWP subjects themselves or their relatives, and in those cases we were able to ask about their recollections, exchange materials and information, or obtain copies and permission to use personal family photographs and documents. In other instances, research revealed connections between people (including project workers and their subjects) that were not known and could not have been deduced otherwise.

Headnotes are used to infer or detail relationships between individuals, events, or texts; to elaborate the contexts in which a person's reported experience and its meanings were situated; or to comment on the problems of interpretation posed by specific workers' interview methods or treatment of texts.

Even with intensive efforts, however, we did not find every subject of these life histories. That fact in itself should offer a cautionary note: authenticity cannot be determined simply by an intuitive or careful reading of the text but can be revealed, if at all, only by further research and determined comparative work. In those cases of persons missing or not found in other sources, speculations or possible explanations for their absence from the record are offered in either headnotes or notes for the text.[36]

The life histories that we have included are presented in their entirety with few exceptions. Those cases, for the most part, involve the omission of unduly damaging or slanderous, personal remarks made by the VWP interviewer. All omissions have been indicated with ellipses or described in a note if more extensive deletion has been made. In addition, the page or word count (or both) as originally given on the VWP copy is included in the background data for each interview. Thus it should be possible for the reader to judge approximately how much textual material has been left out in all such cases.

Other editorial changes include the silent correction of misspellings and typographical errors; standardization of contractions, such as *did'nt* to *didn't;* consistent use of *through* for *thru* and *though* for *tho;* silent correction of punctuation where confusion seemed possible; silent capitalization of proper names and occasional elimination of unwarranted capitalization; and, where appropriate, elimination of occasional one-line paragraphs by combining them with preceding or subsequent paragraphs on the same topic. When it was obvious that interviewers used spellings such as *won't* or *want* to indicate the archaic form of *was not* in an informant's speech, we changed those various spellings to the standardized *wa'n't.*

Although the RA/FSA and WPA photographs do not correspond exactly with the life history interviews, many of the scenes in the photographs graphically reinforce or complement discussions in the interviews. Pictures add a visual dimension to a text about slum housing even if the houses depicted are not the same as those discussed. And a photograph of a field of haystacks offers a landscape that is at once a possible and an appropriate context for imagining accounts of cutting and stacking hay. We have used some photographs for such purposes. In a few cases, we put a series of photographs together to create photo-essays; in other cases, groups of pictures from the same project or lot had been designed from the outset to be presented together as a photo-essay. The latter includes those series that were intended to illustrate specific RA/FSA projects or the poor conditions they hoped to eliminate with resettlement or defense housing.

Film formats ranged from Arthur Rothstein's 35mm Leica to Walker Evans's 8 × 10–inch view camera. Letters following negative numbers indicate the size in inches of the original negative: A = 8 × 10, B = 5 × 7, C = 4 × 5, D = 3¼ × 4¼, E = 2¼ × 2¼, and M – 35mm.

Captions on the photographs are as given, with the following exceptions: when a series of photographs by a single photographer was taken within the same month and that information is cited preceding the series, it is not repeated in successive captions; and states and counties are spelled out. Any other alterations, clarifications, or additions are indicated within brackets.

Copies of exhibition-quality, gelatin silver prints of the following RA/FSA photographs were obtained from the Chrysler Museum, Norfolk, Virginia, and used with permission. The museum's accession number is given in parentheses following the page number on which the photograph appears:

Page 5 (85.1.22); p. 33 (84.78.10); p. 190 (85.1.2); p. 191 (84.78.29); p. 194 *top* (84.78.25); p. 217 *top* (84.78.110); p. 217 *bottom* (84.78.79); p. 236 *bottom* (84.78.97); p. 238 *top* (84.78.99); p. 239 *top left* (84.78.106); p. 265 *middle* (85.1.4); p. 276 (84.78.65); p. 307 (84.78.30); p. 352 *top* (84.78.17); p. 372 *top* (84.78.94).

As an important counterpart to the more widely known and celebrated RA/FSA photographers, this volume also includes a number of photographs by Virginia WPA staff photographer W. Lincoln Highton and one photograph by Robert McNeill, who was with the VWP Negro Studies Program at Hampton University.[37]

KENTUCKY

Stonega
Osaka
Roda
Esserville
Derby
Inman
Appalachia
Imboden

Dunbar
Clintwood
Wise
Tom's
Creek
Coeburn
Norton
Keokee
Big Stone Gap

Grundy
BUCHANAN
DICKENSON
RUSSELL
Lebanon
Abingdon

Jonesville
Speer's
Ferry
Gate
City
LEE
SCOTT
WASHINGTON
Bristol

Bluefield
Tazewell
TAZEWELL
Saltville
Marion
SMYTH

Pearisburg
GILES
Bland
BLAND
Wytheville
WYTHE
Foster's Falls
Austinsville
GRAYSON
Independence
Galax

Blacksburg
MONTGOMERY
Christiansburg
PULASKI
Pulaski
Bertha
CARROLL
Hillsville

ALLEGHANY
Falling Spring
Blue Spring Run
Ben's Run
White Sulphur
Springs
Jordan Mines
Sweet Springs, W.Va.
Potts Creek
Barbour's Creek
Paint Bank
New Castle
CRAIG
Callaghan
Clifton Forge
Covington
Oriska
BOT
Fincastle

ROANOKE
Salem
Roano

Radford
FRANKL
FLOYD
Floyd
Ferrum
Rocky Mo

PATRICK
Lover's Leap
Stuart
Ararat
HENRY
Martinsv

TENNESSEE

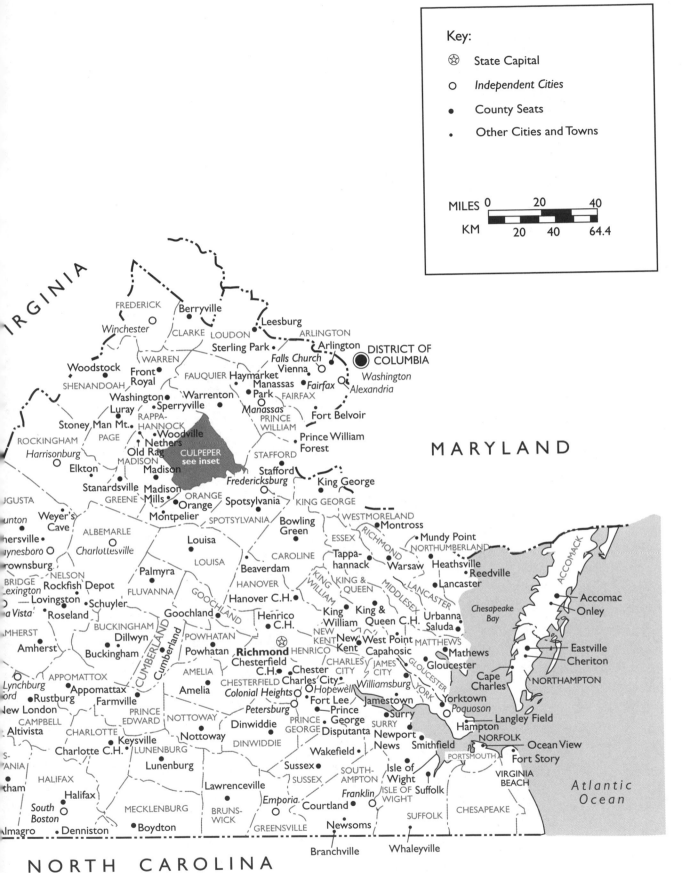

NARRATING EXPERIENCE
Virginia and Virginians in the Decade of the Great Depression

The Great Depression unleashed millions of Americans from the constraints of their previous understandings of "normalcy." Herbert Hoover's bids to ease economic problems (through creation of the Reconstruction Finance Corporation in January 1932, for instance) were widely perceived to be unrealistic and hopelessly inadequate responses to a severe domestic crisis. By 1933, when Franklin Delano Roosevelt took the oath of office as president, industrial production in the United States had fallen to half of what it had been prior to the stock market crash in 1929. And upwards of one-fourth of the American workforce was unemployed and in dire need.[1]

During his now famous "first one hundred days" in office, Roosevelt directed legislation that created a profusion of experimental federal relief programs, the so-called alphabet soup acts and agencies (among them, the Agriculture Adjustment Act, Public Works Administration, Federal Emergency Relief Act, Tennessee Valley Authority, and Emergency Conservation Work, the predecessor of the Civilian Conservation Corps). By the beginning of his second term in office, in 1937, these efforts had yielded, at best, a faltering economic recovery. National income figures had returned to the 1929 level, but about one-fifth of the workforce was still unemployed, and another downturn was under way.[2]

Still, the popular political lines between Roosevelt and his predecessor were clearly drawn, and these were exemplified in the writing of one anonymous Virginia songster:

"ROOSEVELT SONG"

> Listen, my buddies, if you want to hear,
> A story about a brave engineer,
> Franklin D. Roosevelt from Washington, D.C.
> Pulling the train they call "Prosperity."

> He received his orders that danger was ahead,
> Many were starving, many were dead.

He said to Mr. Garner, his flagman true,
"We are going to clean up a mess it's taken years to do."

So he straightened out the banks with a big holiday,
And circulated money with the P.W.A.,
And the C.C.C. and the C.W.A.,
He brought back smiles and kept hunger away.

There's a lot of people kick, say, "He did not cut his pay,"
Remember he's not fishing, he's working every day,
That's the way Hoover spent his time,
And we were always broke and didn't have a dime.[3]

Roosevelt's conception that the "first duty of government [was] to protect the economic welfare of all the people in all sections and in all groups" influenced the New Deal programs designed to stabilize and restore the economy. In time, the relief efforts born of expediency wrought physical changes upon the landscape in the form of roads, dams, public utilities, civic buildings, and schools. Those construction projects gave people work and enabled many to survive the lean depression years by feeding, clothing, and housing them. Even as Roosevelt's New Deal adaptations of federal patronage modified economic and legal structures and fostered significant technological changes, they also intervened in the socioeconomic and cultural lives of American citizens to an extent unprecedented in the nation's history.[4]

Yet even prior to the events of either the Great Depression or the New Deal, in the decade of the 1920s, another profoundly significant political and social revolution was in the making in Virginia and across the country as the result of a newly developing technology. Its instrument, the radio, was heralded by some as "the world's greatest source of knowledge, the creator of international harmony, and the invention that would stop all wars." The first commercial radio station (KDKA) was established in Pittsburgh in 1920; by the end of 1922 there were 510 broadcasting stations in the country. And radio sales, which amounted to $60 million in 1922, had risen to $850 million in 1929. By 1930 more than twelve million homes in the United States had a radio. Virginia and the world did, indeed, stand on the verge of the modern communications age.[5]

In 1923, then Secretary of Commerce Herbert Hoover was already trying to regulate the runaway growth of the broadcasting industry associated with the radio, which "captured the imagination and loyalty of the public in a way that the phonograph never had. While the phonograph was viewed as a passive instrument of entertainment and very much the machine that it was, the radio was perceived as a vibrant, living thing." The characterizations of the one invention as a passive, impersonal machine and the other as almost "another member of the family" could stand, ironically enough, as metaphors for the public perceptions of the style and personalities of the successive presidents Hoover and Roosevelt.[6]

A number of writers have observed that Hoover was admired but not loved and that he "never managed to establish rapport with working-class Americans." That message and the phonograph metaphor were explicitly linked by a woman who reported in 1981 that her father had purchased a "wind-up record player" along with a phonograph record about Herbert Hoover at a sale in the 1930s. But she said, "Wasn't any of us wanted to hear that record. . . . We just didn't like Hoover. My goodness alive, that [his term as president] was as near to starvation as I ever seen in my life."[7]

On the other hand, Franklin D. Roosevelt masterfully used the radio and his broadcast "Fireside Chats" to personalize his presidency and to communicate and win support for his political policies by making them known to the people directly. It was not unintended that FDR instilled in his listening audience the feeling that he "was talking to each one of them, personally" or unanticipated that they would respond with an unprecedented and familiar outpouring of letters to the president and his wife.[8]

By 1925, the radio was reported in Virginia as "becoming a necessity to the farmer" in order to keep track of crop prices and markets and to hear "lectures by experts [that kept the farmer] informed of the latest methods of agriculture." At that time, 3,715 farms in the state had radios. Arlington and Fairfax Counties were best equipped, with a radio for every two and four farms, respectively. Alleghany County had 54 farms per radio, and Culpeper had 37 farms to every radio. Dickenson County, on the other hand, ranked lowest in the state with regard to ownership of both radios *and* tractors. It reported only one radio for every 1,483 farms and no tractors.[9]

On 16 December 1935 the WPA educational radio project was established to use the talents of "actors, singers, directors and playwrights—in the ranks of those on relief." Shortly afterward, some Virginia Writers' Project workers were given jobs writing quasi-historical and patriotic radio plays. Others were told to ask life history subjects, such as Josephine Wright of Potts Creek and Sarah Colleen Powell of Danville, in addition to what papers and books they read and movies they had seen, if they owned a radio. Both Wright and Powell did.[10]

The radio, however, was not yet "the world's greatest source of knowledge." As Sarah Colleen Powell's mother reportedly always said, her "real education was in the school of experience. Hard to learn and not easy to forget." Powell's aphorism provides a theme linking the people who are assembled in the four chapters constituting this section on narrating experience. These chapters focus on the social and demographic attributes of age, gender, and race, which—in "the school of experience"—differentially affect an individual's life chances and expectations. The life histories, in turn, reflect the impact of those attributes in particular cases, as people relate the diverse experiences (not always pleasant to recall or easily forgotten) that shaped their lives, generated persistent symbols of identity and place, evoked memories, or served as indexes of change.[11]

The Civil War was one such experience—a defining moment in time and one of change for Virginia and for the nation. It had serious consequences for the lives and futures of those who shared that singular moment—slave and free person, slaveholder and nonslaveholder alike. The life history interviews with elderly white Virginians in the first chapter of this section offer a parallel to the interviews with ex-slaves that were previously published in *Weevils in the Wheat* and were, for the most part, conducted as a separate program by the VWP Negro Studies unit at Hampton Institute.[12]

All the speakers in chapter 1 were born before the end of the Civil War, and when they were interviewed in 1939–40, their average age was eighty-four. These individuals focused heavily on the "old days," which were generally recalled with nostalgia. Their personal circumstances at the time of the interview were described briefly, if at all, and then almost exclusively from the interviewer's observations and perspective. As a result, the extent to which the more frequent and serious side effects of advancing age (sickness, loss, loneliness, and poverty) played a part in the speakers' existence cannot be judged—except for the notable case of George Strausburg. In contrast with the histories of the other elders in this group, Strausburg's life history is too easily dismissed as relentlessly negative, even maudlin. But it should also caution us that perhaps his story is much closer to a larger truth, given the realities of his life, his class, and his time.

With a few exceptions, the individuals in the last three chapters of this section form a series of later-age cohorts, born after the Civil War on into the first decades of the twentieth century. Their commentary was foregrounded in a more recent past, and they were, to a large extent, still actively engaged in the ongoing, day-to-day problems of life and work. Yet it is the late-middle-aged persons among those in these chapters who come the closest to offering what many currently refer to as a "life review," that is to say, a fairly reflexive coverage and assessment of meaningful events, persons, and changes in their lifetimes up to that moment.[13]

The circumstances of individuals in these life histories varied widely, but Ms. Emily Palmer Stearns of "Farley" in Culpeper County and Ben James in Petersburg represent the socioeconomic extremes in this volume. Class distinctions are far more complex, however, than the simple reporting of income, real estate, or personal property alone can indicate. Cultural norms and ideas can also demean individuals or groups and contribute to their marginality. One VWP worker's judgment that a certain young woman would "naturally" be "somewhat narrow" in her attitudes because "her parents were first cousins, about the same age, same education and environment, and same name" was based on erroneous social evolutionary ideas. Another project worker similarly wondered how a particular family had "started downgrade" when its members had reportedly married "women of means and moderate education" for generations.[14]

With regard to education, the Literary Fund was established to educate poor children as early as 1810, but universal public education in Virginia did not begin officially until 1870, when the law mandated "a system of free public schools for persons between five and twenty-one years." However, that act, in response to Virginia's new constitution of 1868, basically created primary schools; publicly supported high schools were not established until after 1906. Despite legal provision for the education of all children in Virginia, in practice that development neither proceeded immediately and uniformly across the state, nor did it serve all equally, as Cleveland Buchanan, Rev. Willis Madden, and Isaiah Wallace testify. In Rappahannock County (where Wallace lived and where outmigrations by blacks had been substantial following the Civil War), there was *no* high school for black youth within the county boundaries until 1967—more than sixty years after public secondary education began in the state.[15]

Some local educational systems developing during the period withheld teachers for, or closed, rural one-room schools without being able to provide equal access to the newly built centralized schools in cities and towns and incidentally disadvantaged other social-class–based groups. One group of parents protested the closure of their rural Johnson Creek community school by the Alleghany County School Board in 1939, complaining, "Our taxes are helping to build this fine building [the new white high school in Covington], while our children can't read nor write and have no school to go to." One of the women who challenged the board's action was asked by the superintendent, "Why do you want to live up in such a place, anyhow? No electricity, no roads, no modern improvements." In response, she inquired why he had not stayed in Charlottesville from whence he had come: "It is a much better place than Covington!"[16]

Between 1920 and 1930, the number of Virginia's children (of both sexes, aged five to twenty years) attending school increased more than 3 percent. However, the increase was almost 6 percent in urban areas, with the greatest gain there being made by black males. Across all areas—urban and rural—the number of black females in school showed the greatest increase, yet the general rate of school attendance by black children remained lower relative to that of white children.[17]

The illiteracy rates for persons over ten years of age, however, reveal more about the effects of educational differences. White females in urban centers had the lowest illiteracy rate (1.4 percent) among native-born persons in 1930. In contrast, rural areas had the highest illiteracy, averaging 4.8 percent for all native whites and 19.2 percent for blacks, or a rate four times that of whites. Although the figure for blacks in Culpeper County (22.1 percent) was slightly higher than average, the illiteracy rates for both the white (15.1 percent) and black (26.5 percent) populations of Rappahannock County were more than three and five times the state's average for native whites. Only two counties, Buchanan and Greene, exceeded Rappahannock's white illiteracy rate. However, eight counties had black illiteracy rates that were above 30 percent.[18]

Among these was Charlotte County, which, despite its Central High School for black youth, had an illiteracy rate of 32.3 percent. Furthermore, the county had a higher average rate of illiteracy (including both white and black statistics) in 1930 (16.7 percent) than it did in 1920 (10.3 percent). Concerns about this rise may have been one factor in Charlotte County's decision to build a new consolidated white high school under the authority of the Public Works Administration in 1939. This Charlotte Court House school project, documented by OWI photographer Philip Bonn, also included a sequence of pictures taken at Central High. Whether intended or inadvertent, the comparison offered by this series graphically documents some of the inequalities existing under the prevailing "separate but equal" political philosophy.

Other environmental and economic factors were critically associated with questions of general health and well-being. Negro Studies Project worker Susie R. C. Byrd remarked that the backyards and gardens in the bottoms below High Street in Petersburg were breeding places "for malaria and typhoid germs." Typhoid fever had been "principally a disease of the Valley of Virginia and the adjacent mountains" during the nineteenth century. But by 1900, typhoid, smallpox, and tuberculosis were the three major diseases responsible for deaths statewide. Infections still accounted for seven out of ten deaths in 1920, but "the leading cause" by then was pulmonary tuberculosis. The decline of death rates due to typhoid fever from 27.3 per 100,000 in 1914 to 5.1 in 1929 was attributed to gradual improvements in sewage disposal and water purification systems generally.[19]

No region of the state, however, was exempt from either endemic forms of disease or epidemic. The declining incidence of typhoid fever did not soothe the anguish of Susie Young Smith, whose husband died of the fever in Portsmouth in 1928. Likewise there was little to console Charles Tucker of Alleghany County when he lost his wife and three of their nine children in less than a month through successive epidemics of diphtheria and the 1918–19 "Spanish Lady" flu. The assertion by Lillie Vaughn that tobacco steam rooms had "caused much sickness, especially TB, among [her] race" was based, in part, on her personal loss of both parents to such work-related tuberculosis in the early 1920s. But this woman's childhood experience made her acutely sensitive to the need for and grateful for "the Colored TB Sanatorium" that was finally "finished and open for patients" in 1940.[20]

Other public institutions in Virginia, such as poorhouses, asylums, and orphanages, continued to reflect the "moral treatment" and paternalistic attitudes common in practice from earlier times. Formal treatments of the insane, indigent, aged, widowed, and orphaned alike relied heavily on manual labor, religious worship, and the removal of such persons from their former associations and surroundings as means by which to establish "regular habits of self control" and to divert the "mind from morbid trains of thought." An overseer of the poor in Richmond, George Greenhow, described his relationship to those in his care in 1820 as that of a "cautious, prudent, industrious master, who has a large, and for the most part, helpless family to bring up, support and Educate."[21]

Yet these caretakers sometimes exercised more social control as masters over their charges than benevolence. In the first chapter of this work, George Strausburg, whose father had been killed in the Civil War, bitterly remembered his experience and that of other "poor critters" at the hands of a keeper of the poorhouse in Augusta County. Such abuses as existed could, and did, force painful choices on those deciding the fate of family members.

The decision either to keep a family together or to break it apart in the face of want or tragedy is a theme that runs throughout these VWP narratives. In one of the many such cases an Alleghany County woman, compelled by her husband's death from tuberculosis, had to find homes for four of her five children, including one said to have been "marked" when she "doctored a sick calf" before the child was born. The newborn baby's blind eye "looked like the calf's eye and rolled about just as the calf's eye did when it died." At the age of five, this little girl was given to an elderly couple who "wanted a child to raise" after their own children "were all gone." But the isolation and lack of educational opportunities or association with others her age further handicapped the girl with the "calf eye" and left her an economic and social cripple later when the two old people died.[22]

The life histories report more than one case of well-to-do couples offering to buy children from poor people with large families and few prospects or options. More often children were simply given to other persons to be raised as their own offspring. Sometimes they were taken in and cared for in exchange for their domestic or other service to the householder. Both of these circumstances seem to have applied to some extent in the case of the child with the calf eye. The informal alternatives to institutions such as orphanages were not necessarily more benign, especially since those solutions were often coerced by racism, poverty, or misfortune.

The collective narratives of memory in this first section provide a "school of experience" that is instructive as to how categories of age, gender, race, and also class were defined or perceived, as well as how they affected the lives of some Virginians in the 1930s. Up to that time, programs to protect workers, dependent families and children, or the elderly were few to nonexistent, but national child and wage labor laws, welfare services, and Social Security were soon to be initiated by the New Deal. Civil rights laws prohibiting racial, sexual, and other forms of discrimination were still decades away, however, and would wait until past midcentury for passage. Even though the life histories in these chapters are dated in their details, they also have a certain contemporaneity that is instructive. Despite watershed legal, and even behavioral, changes in the intervening years, the constants of age, gender, and race, remain just that—attributes that underlie abiding, and thorny, social issues.

Narrating Old Ways and Past Times
OF "INFAIRS" AND "CALLITHUMPS"

I wish to God I could go back to them days! —*Benjamin Thacker*

In describing old ways and past times, Benjamin Thacker and his contemporaries create a multidimensional tableau of social life back in "them days," often using colloquial forms of speech reminiscent of even earlier times and other places. There are numerous references to "infairs" (infares), which were feasts or receptions held "for a newly married couple usually at the home of the groom's family a day or two after the wedding," and "callithumps," which referred (in usage more often in New England) to a shivaree or rowdy disturbance of the married couple's wedding night. But it was allegedly while trying to suppress a "calathump" (in another of its meanings, as "a noisy boisterous parade") that law professor John A. G. Davis was shot and killed in front of Pavilion X at the University of Virginia on 12 November 1840.[1]

The "big callithump, or serenade," as reported by Nannie Isabel Webb Price in this chapter, served a combined function of mischief and celebration. After her wedding, she said, "The young folks wanted to dance, . . . but all our family were strict Baptist and didn't believe in dancing—thought it was the work of the Devil." In this case, the callithump was used as a deliberate strategy to sidestep the family's religious proscriptions against dancing. When the young people rushed in with their instruments and started to play music and to dance, her father gave way. Price attested to the plan's success: "So that's how they managed to dance in Pa's house." Regardless of local variations in meaning or practice, the infare and callithump represented different types of important social activities that, like quilting bees, barn raisings, wheat threshings, or corn shuckings, have aptly been called "rituals of local bonding."[2]

Dan Arritt lamented the loss of old ways. He thought people had lived better and visited more in past times and, in 1939, were in "too big a hurry." Others, such as California StClair, agreed with him: "We worked hard but we had a good time too." She continued, "In that day and time everybody would pitch in and help each other. We had *real* neighbors then." Celia McKnight Brown stated her case much more succinctly: "Those were the good days." But Benjamin Thacker expressed his feelings most strongly: "I wish to God I could go back to them days." These declarations imply more, however, than just the wishes and looking backward of a few elderly

St. Paul's Evangelical Reformed Church just north of Weyer's Cave, Rockingham County, Virginia.
Photo by John Vachon. [LC-USE6-00218-D]

persons. Collectively, these texts speak of change—economic change, social change, and changes in the way that people interacted with one another.

These changes were beginning well before the country reached a critical breaking point in the Civil War. Developing industrial and urban structures gradually overtook and then overwhelmed rural, tradition-based, agricultural patterns of organization and moved the United States on a course toward truly becoming a nation-state. Some of these changes are analogous to what happened over a longer span of time in Europe, as feudal systems collapsed in the early modern period (ca. 1500–1800). At the beginning of that era, popular or vernacular culture was everyone's culture: "a second culture for the educated, and the only culture for everyone else." But when the position of elites was no longer as clearly defined as it had been under the old regime, they began to use other means to differentiate themselves. The elite, and likewise those who aspired to such status, bought, read, and heeded books on etiquette, abandoned their native languages, and looked to the royal courts for social and cultural models both for behavior and innovation.[3]

One can see parallels in a new social and economic order, based on ideals of efficiency, progress, science, and technology, that was developing in the North before the Civil War. Those changes were further reflected in the rise of magazines such as *Harper's New Monthly Magazine* (1850) and the *Atlantic Monthly* (1857), which succeeded by "telling their middle-class audience what it wished to hear: that it was the center of the universe and the true bearer of American culture." These and other periodicals and books on etiquette and fashion increasingly advised their readers on how to act, dress, furnish their houses, and think in manners appropriate for upward mobility. Between 1820 and 1852, the *Bibliotheca Americana* listed more titles under the genre of advice books than any other—a fact that suggests their popularity.[4]

Numerous writers have attempted to bracket critical periods or aspects of change in American rural history. Walter Nugent used data on the movement, distribution, and composition of the population through time to propose a long "frontier-rural" mode, composed of certain repeated patterns of development on a succession of frontiers, that lasted from 1720 to 1870. In his discussion of Nugent's thesis, Swierenga suggests those patterns "led to a very gradual change from subsistence to commercial agriculture, but hand labor with primitive tools, powered by men and horses, remained the norm until the 1860s at least."[5]

The life histories that follow provide a window into Nugent's "frontier-rural" time frame. Although these texts give some support for his assertion that the "transformation of traditional rural communities into modern cosmopolitan societies" began in the late nineteenth century, they also confirm that where that process did occur, it did so over the course of a number of generations. Both the RA/FSA photographs and the life histories give evidence, moreover, that subsistence agriculture, as well as primitive tools and men working horses, remained the norm well into the late thirties. It is doubly ironic that those very conditions were, in fact, what some of the New Deal programs were mobilized deliberately to change.[6]

At the end of the Civil War, there was a great deal of social movement as individuals and families—especially in the South—attempted to deal with a drastically changed world. And the transition was not easy. Plantation slavery, and the southern economy based on it, came to an end. A sizable portion of an entire generation of young southern males did not come home from the war, and many of these left widows and orphans in poverty. Of the surviving veterans, many found their homes and farms destroyed or in profound disarray: animals and

Nicholson Hollow, Shenandoah National Park, Virginia. One of the Nicholson men hauling a load of cornstalks on a rude sled. Photo by Arthur Rothstein. [LC-USF33-02191-M2]

stores confiscated by forces on either side, stocks of feed and seed depleted, fields eroded or gone to waste, and little cash combined with an uncertain labor supply.

When interviewed in 1939, William West was ninety-eight years old. He had served as a drummer boy in the Civil War, and he spoke of conditions in Alleghany County when he returned at war's end.

We got twenty-five cents a bushel for corn for a long time. [But money was scarce and trade was common.] It was queer to hear the trading goin' on. Ten pounds of bacon for a chicken. One pound of sugar for a quart of seed beans. After the second year, prices came up in a hurry. Wheat came back to reason first. That was our bread crop. The millers had the business then, for they took toll and ground most of the wheat raised around here. Very little was sold away from the County till 1870. It seemed like the people were bread-hungry. Fresh meat was high. We did a lot of hunting. Deer were plentiful and opossums, quail, pheasants, and lots and lots of wild turkeys. It took a long time to get the hog-raising goin' again. Everybody had eaten their hogs and there were no breeders left. Horses to work were something great. Only the rich could buy them![7]

In some cases, individuals tried to defer the inevitable by not telling slaves that slavery had ended. James Berkley of Buckingham County gave this account about one of his neighbors:

[He] had out a big crop of corn 'en tobacco, and he didn't want the negroes to know they had been set free. So he kept them right on at their work. Along late in the summer like, a man came through the country and when he saw them negroes out in the fields at work, he went out there and said, "Look here, you negroes! Don't you know you have been set free? Why, you don't haft to work fer your masters anymore. You are free." And the very

Mr. McGahey showing P. M. Carper, Assistant County Agent for Rockingham County, sword and scabbard which were manufactured on the place for the Confederacy. Photo by John Vachon.
[LC-USE6-00253-D]

last negro dropped his hoe in the field and went out of there shouting, "We don't hafta work no more."

With unstable currencies after the war, most people were cash poor, so in lieu of wages "sharecropping and tenant systems [soon] fell into place."[8]

In parts of Virginia the old "findings," or perquisites, system, in use from colonial times, was continued with less disruption of the economy. In 1837, George Grimsley of Rappahannock County, Virginia was hired to work for John S. Green for one hundred dollars and "found," which included 450 pounds of pork, one barrel of flour, corn sufficient for bread, and a cow to milk. A century later, Fleety Dodson of Culpeper County, Virginia, interviewed by Margaret Jeffries, reported that she and her husband Charlie got twenty-two dollars a month and findings (or found): a house to live in, 350 pounds of hog meat, one barrel of flour, twenty-five bushels of corn, a garden with time off to work it, and use of a cow.[9]

After the war, some formerly affluent members of society found themselves moving down the social ladder at the same time that some members of the working class were able to move upward by utilizing newly developing opportunities in timber, tobacco, mill work, and other types of manufacture. In the late nineteenth century, northern industrialists became interested in southern timber, coal, and other mineral resources, and beginning about 1880, textile mills were being lured to the South by its large, cheap labor pool. By the early decades of the twentieth century, mills producing various types of artificial fibers, such as rayon, were also beginning to be established.

The shape and nature of communities and the economy changed dramatically as families moved to mill towns from small farms that would not support them, or as husbands went off to work in sawmills or in the coal fields — sometimes with families in tow, but sometimes leaving them back at home or with relatives for extended periods of time. In rural areas, one's neighbors were generally known, and more often than not, they were kin, who could usually be depended on in a crisis. After moving to town, parents often complained that they did not know with whom their children were associating or even where they were some of the time.

The general change from a subsistence, community-oriented society to a more impersonal, wage-labor–oriented one eventually affected even the most isolated rural areas to some extent. And in time, many traditional activities involving shared labor and communal gatherings, such as log rollings, barn raisings, hog butcherings, apple butter boilings, and corn shuckings — the previously mentioned rituals of local bonding — either shifted to wage labor, were done by machinery, or simply disappeared.

A farmer on Big Ridge in Alleghany County told project worker Mary S. Venable about the occasion, in 1927 or thereabouts, of the last log rolling in that area. He said that the "invitations were given, just like they always had been." The fellow who was hosting the log rolling had a reputation as a good "barbecuer" and for not being stingy about providing plenty to eat and drink. Yet nobody showed up on the appointed day. When he asked those who said "they *would* come, why they disappointed him," he found that they had "wanted pay for their work" but had been unwilling to say so directly. He protested that "the food and drinks had cost him about the same, [and] if they had told him he would lieve [as lief, or willingly have] given them the money." As it was, he had nothing to show for the cost of the food and drink. When one could no longer depend on customary understandings and expectations, cultural and social change followed quickly.[10]

Benjamin Christopher Thacker *by Gertrude Blair, 2 August 1939*

At the age of eighteen, Benjamin C. Thacker (born in 1860) attended the "infair" held following the marriage of his future in-laws, Thomas A. and Sarah M. Wood, in Bedford County. He "didn't think then [that] they would raise a girl for [him]." By the time he married their twenty-two-year-old daughter, Leona Pearl Wood, Benjamin was forty. They had eight surviving children when Gertrude Blair interviewed Benjamin in their home at 622 Albemarle Avenue SE, Roanoke, nearly forty years later.[11]

Benjamin Thacker's own childhood had not been an easy one. His father, Samuel, was drafted and apparently served in the Civil War, even though he was fervently opposed to it and was "a strong Union man." Then in 1868, Harriet Thacker died in childbirth, leaving Samuel a widower with six children, including her surviving infant, living at home. By the age of eight, Benjamin had lived half of his life amid the turmoil of a war that took his father away for a time; soon afterward, he lost his mother. These were doubly difficult and bitter experiences for a young child, and they clearly affected and remained with Benjamin Thacker the rest of his life.

Benjamin is the son of Samuel and Harriet Yancy Thacker, both of Albemarle County, Virginia. After their marriage they came to Bedford County to live and bought a farm not far from New London, where the subject of this sketch was born June 27th, 1860.

"I haven't very much education, for I only attended public school (and that was two miles from our home and I had to walk) three months in the year: January, February, and March. I helped my father with work on the farm through the summer and fall up to Christmas, then

Shenandoah farmers decorate their barn doors. This building, formerly used by the Mennonites and Dunkards, is on the main Valley road just north of Harrisonburg, Rockingham County. Photo by John Vachon.
[LC-USE6-00213-D]

went to school for three months—stopped every time the last of March and went back to work. I would forget what I had learned by the time I got back to school again. I remember my first teachers: Mark Traylor, Sam Dooley, Miss Sophia Rucker, Jefferson Wilkinson, and Dick Shelton. He was a tight one too, I'll tell you." Neither his father nor mother's family were slave owners. "My father was a strong Union man, was drafted for service in the Civil War; he wouldn't accept a pension, he was so ag'in it.

"My mother died when my sister Harriet was born, November 10th, 1868. She was forty-three years of age." The old man broke down and said, "I wish I could put my arms around her now, and tell her how I've missed her through all these long years since she left us. After my oldest sister died, I turned in and bought the old home place. I never was any of these tomcats to run around, never got into any trouble in my life. I am a whole lot older than my wife, I knowed when my wife's *mother* got married, I went to the infair. I didn't think then they would raise a girl for me."

"Who was your wife, Mr. Thacker?" "Leona Pearl Wood of Bedford County. She is a whole lot younger than me. She told me not to ask her mother, for she knew she would say no. So I walked out to the barn when her father was feeding his stock, and talked around. Finally I made up my mind not to fool about it any longer, and said, 'Mr. Wood, Pearl and myself have decided to get married, and I want to know what you think of it?' He threw up his hands and said 'You can't get her.' Then he said, 'She is her own woman, and if you suit her it's all right with me.' We have eight living children. My oldest son was in the World War, he was shell shocked, has a government job, and lives in Washington, D.C."

"What about the parties you had in those days?" "Well, we always danced when we got together. I always was a great hand at dancing. My brother Jim could outplay anybody on the banjo and several of the boys played fiddles, and I'll tell you we had a good time in them days. We danced the square dance. You couldn't er got a girl to dance like they dance now. Excuse me (this was an apology for his description of the dance), but I call it the *hugging* dance. In my day and time the girls wouldn't have put up with it, no indeed, Lord a mercy! I don't reckon there is money enough in Roanoke to get my wife to put on one of those bathing suits. Even the churches are different, too much style and pride in 'em now. People used to get happy and shout. If anybody shouted in a church now they'd call the police. I wish to God I could go back to them days. If a man got sick his neighbors would go and cut his wheat. When my father killed a beef he'd send all his neighbors a roast.

"We would have apple and peach peelings, at night generally. Everybody went early, for we would be invited to supper you know, then all hands would get busy and peel. The corn shuckings were great times too. One of the men would stand on top of the big pile and lead the singing. You know there was always some apple brandy on hand, but nobody got drunk. I wish I could remember some of the songs we used to sing, but my God!, its been so long. Let's see, 'Shuck away, shuck away, we'll shuck this corn, if it takes till day.' Maybe I can think of some of the old songs, if you can come to see me again sometime."[12]

"Did you go by signs in planting your crops and gardens?" "Oh yes, *sure*. We'd plant snap beans, potatoes, and corn on the sign of the twins, and lay our crossrail fences on the light of the moon, cut pine on the dark of the moon to use for fires. A black cat around the house keeps the girls from marrying. The Strongs had a black cat and somebody told Miss Cassie about that superstition. So she caught the cat, took him to the woodpile and cut his head off. And shortly after that, sure enough, she got married, t'wa'n't no time. I've always heard that any animal crossing your path with a long tail brings you good luck. We always butchered our hogs on the dark of the moon, otherwise it [would] all go to grease when t'was cooked."[13]

"There was an old Dr. Ding, he lived not so far from us at a place called Moss Town. He was er herb doctor, a lot of folks took his medicine. The colored people believed that he could cure 'em and 'conjure' 'em too. Aunt Mira, a colored woman lost her cow, so she went to talk with Dr. Ding about it. He put a needle in a ball, twirled it around several times. When it stopped she followed the way this needle pointed and went out and found her cow right away."[14]

"Did you ever hear of witchcraft down that way?" "No I can't say that I did. Miss Bettie Creasy, who lived seven or eight miles back this way from us, believed in witches and would tell stories about the mischief they did in her neighborhood. She lived to be over a hundred years old, and it was said that she put on white slippers and danced on her hundredth birthday."

Mr. Thacker told of the following superstitions which existed among the negroes in his old neighborhood in Bedford County. He said that if the negroes had been stealing anything from the "white folks," they [the whites] would get a pine root, split it open and lay it in the path leading to the house, and no darkey would pass over it. Another prevalent superstition or omen was, "If a bird sung in the middle of the night it was a sure sign of a death. Did you ever drive through the country and see a dead snake hanging on a tree? It was put there to cause rain during a drought. Old Mrs. Mullhews, whose husband was killed in the War, used to tell fortunes when I was a small boy.[15]

"The house I was raised in was log-bodied, twenty by thirty feet, four rooms, and the fireplace was eight feet wide. The chimney was built of stones picked up around on the farm. My sister could bake the finest ashcakes, I can see her now rolling them over in her hands — first one then the other — shaping them and putting them on the clean hot stones in the fireplace, mercy me! I'd like to have some right now."

Mr. Thacker and his family have been residents of Roanoke for about twenty years. He has been following the carpenter's trade since he stopped farming. He does not own the house in which he lives. It is a seven-room frame building, two stories, with a vine-covered porch extending across the entire front. He and his wife were sitting on the porch, invited me to be seated there, so I don't know how the interior looks but I judge it is very plainly furnished.

Mr. Thacker says he has been chewing tobacco for sixty odd years.[16]

[Loc.: UVA/FC, box 10, item #1546, 4 pp.]

California Elizabeth Adams StClair *by Gertrude Blair, 23 April 1940*

At the place called Cross Roads on the way to Liberty (now Bedford, the county seat), California (Callie) Elizabeth Adams was born in 1850 — after the census had been taken. As she speculated to Blair, California might have been so named because of the recent western gold rush. But the fact that her older sister was called Texanna suggests another possibility: they were both named following a popular practice in the mid- to late nineteenth century that produced many other females similarly called Oklahoma, Missouri, and Arizona, as well as America.

In 1860, Samuel Thacker and his family, with the then two-month-old Benjamin, also lived in Bedford County — only a few households away from Wilson and William A. Adams, Callie's uncle and grandfather. Despite the difference in their ages, both Callie Adams and Benjamin Thacker were taught in school by "old" Dick Shelton. Thacker did not mention the clubfoot, which distracted Adams so much that she could not remember the alphabet, but he did observe that Shelton was "a tight one," in reference to his being a strict and difficult teacher.

By the time young Benjamin Thacker attended his future in-laws' "infair," Callie Adams and James H. StClair were already married and living next to James's parents, Joseph D. and Lucinda (McGhee) StClair, in the Staunton District of Bedford County. The StClairs, like the Adamses, had been resident in the county for some time and were well established in the area as farmers, carpenters, blacksmiths, millers, and merchants. In addition, both families could depend on a network of extended kin for mutual aid in times of need or crisis.[17]

"In that day and time everybody would pitch in and help each other," Callie Adams StClair declared, but some had more resources and help available to them than others. When Callie had three infants aged one, two, and three in 1880, her eighteen-year-old cousin, Susan E. Adams (daughter of her father's brother Abram), lived with Callie's family and helped her with the child care. After his wife's death, however, Samuel Thacker faced raising his family on his own. His in-laws had moved on to Pittsylvania County, where, at age seventy-four in 1870, Jeremiah Yancy was a farm laborer.

Despite the varying experiences and circumstances of their respective families, in the end Callie Adams StClair and Benjamin Christopher Thacker both retained strong convictions about the importance of "real neighbors" and vividly recalled the rich communal life they had shared in the Bedford County of their youth.

Mrs. StClair was born November 7, 1850 on her father's farm in Bedford County, Virginia. Her father James Adams, who was a native of that county, married Elizabeth Roberts in 1846. Elizabeth grew up on a farm in Campbell, the adjoining county. Three daughters and one son were born to Mr. and Mrs. Adams, California being the second daughter. In answer as to why she was named after such a *far away* state, she said she did not know unless it was the great excitement caused in 1849 by the rush to California for gold. Naturally in her infancy, it was abbreviated to Callie, which name has followed her through the years. Her father's four hundred acre farm was on the old turnpike from Rocky Mount to Lynchburg. It was at the intersection of the road to Liberty (now Bedford) and the place was called Cross Roads. That was an important thoroughfare at that time. In the old days many a hogshead of tobacco from Franklin and Henry Counties rolled over this road drawn by an ox team on the way to the Lynchburg market.

Mrs. StClair told of her early school days. She attended a private school as there were no free schools at that time. "Old Mr. Dick Shelton was my first teacher. He was clubfooted. There was only one chair in the schoolroom. It was used by the teacher, and the children sat on slab benches with no backs. There was a big fireplace and the benches were placed around it. Do you know that Mr. Shelton kept me in at recess six or seven days straight along because I couldn't say my ABC's. I was only five-years old and Ma ought not to have let me go, but my older sister, Anna [Texanna], wanted me to go with her. We had to walk three-quarters of a mile. I could just rattle off the alphabet at home. I think it must have been his clubfoot that frightened me so terribly.

"Our next teacher was Mr. Thomas Hillsman, he was a gay young man, and all the children liked him. After the War, we had a public school and I attended that for two years. That was the end of my school days. It was not a graded school, we studied reading, writing and arithmetic.

"My father raised sheep and all the cloth for our clothes was woven right on the place. Pa bought the cotton but never had to buy any wool. Ma could weave the loveliest yarn counterpanes. We didn't have anything that we didn't make right there on the farm. We would get up Monday morning and spin and weave until Friday, then we would clean and bake for Sunday.

"We worked hard, but we had a good time too. We had parties and dances, but *no such dancing as they do now*. Pa was a fine dancer, I loved to dance with him. There was something going on all the time on the farm, quilting parties, apple cuttings, and on those occasions all the neighbors for miles around would come and spend the day. They were the main social events that the wives of the farmers had. Of course, the young folks had plenty of parties, [and] dances, especially at Christmas time, when there wasn't much work to do on the farm.

"When we went to apple cuttings we would take a paring knife and apron, and while we

Nicholson Hollow, Shenandoah National Park, Virginia. Spreading apples to dry on a roof.
Photo by Arthur Rothstein. [LC-USF34-00361-D]

peeled apples or peaches and cut them up to dry or to make apple butter, we talked about as fast as we cut. There was not an item of news concerning anybody and everybody in the community for miles and miles around that was not discussed. There was no other *news* to make conversation. It was not like today, with daily newspapers, magazines, and radios. A weekly newspaper was all we had.

"At the quilting parties, we always put on our best 'bib and tucker,' would take a good needle and our own thimble. Each one would try to outdo the other, not in the amount of work done, but in the fineness of our stitches. So Ma had a great many lovely quilts, and with her wool counterpanes our beds were the pride of the household. I don't know why it was, but housekeepers then were so much more careful about the way beds were made up than they are now. Ma never let us lay anything on the bed, not even our hats.[18]

"Ma was mighty strict with us, I'll tell you. Another thing she was strict about, when we went visiting or to parties, we had to be home by nine o'clock, even when I was a big girl. Pa wouldn't let me go out by myself with a boy. He would always go along."

Mrs. StClair told of the apple butter boilings, corn shuckings, [and] log rollings. When new ground was cleared, all the neighbors would come and help. "In that day and time everybody would pitch in and help each other. We had *real* neighbors then. Of course, everybody always prepared a big dinner or supper, with an appetizer thrown in for good measure or rather good fellowship."

"Mrs. StClair, I don't suppose you can remember anything about the Civil War, can you?"
"Oh, yes indeed, I can. I remember when General Imboden came riding up on a dapple-

gray horse. He jumped the picket fence and never before had I ever seen such a *fine* looking man, with his epaulets on his shoulders. I wondered why Pa didn't *wear a suit* like that. He was following up the Yankees. He asked Ma if she had anything to eat. She told him no, but she would fix something right quick. So she gave him and his company the best she had. She told him that she would have to give him cornbread as there was not a dust of flour in the house.

"Pa had the meat hid and the horses taken to the mountain. The Yankees passed along before General Imboden came and ate up every egg we had on the place, but they didn't do any damage. Pa was mighty willing to let them have anything we had to eat. We had an old well that had gone plumb dry. It was lined with rocks, so Pa put all the meat in there and the Yankees didn't get a single piece of it.[19]

"We used to 'put up' a lot of fruit in the summertime. There were quantities of blackberries on the place, so we canned a great many. One day we decided that we would make a blackberry pie for dinner and opened a can of the berries and found they had fermented. Several cans were opened and every one was the same, so they were thrown out where they would not be tracked into the house. Now we always raised a big gang of turkeys. In a little while after we had thrown the berries out, someone passed along and came back and told us that every turkey we had was lying sprawled out on the ground. Well, we decided we would save the feathers anyway, so all hands rushed out to pick them before they got cold and every turkey was picked clean. About the time we got our feathers put away—bless your soul!—one by one [each] of those turkeys got up and began walking around! They were the funniest looking things you ever saw."

"What on earth did you do?" "Well, I'll tell you. In those days people wore red flannel petticoats, so we took every piece of red flannel in the house, petticoats and all, and made jackets and put on them. You can imagine what funny looking things they were, walking around in the fields with those red jackets on. And do you know that we saved nearly every one of them that way?" "Were they drunk, do you suppose?" "They evidently were."[20]

"Mrs. StClair, did you ever attend camp meetings in Bedford or Campbell?" "No, we never had camp meetings. We had District Conferences. My family were Methodist, so these conferences were big occasions with us. Of course, the members of the church entertained the preachers. The presiding Elders were the 'big shots' as the boys would say today, and it was quite an honor to have them as a guest.[21]

"I must tell you a funny thing that happened one Sunday morning in our church. You know how mischievous young boys are. Well, how the boys got those yellow jackets without getting stung, I can't tell you, perhaps they did. Anyway you know how boys congregate around the church before time for the service to begin. On one Sunday morning, they put a few yellow jackets in the pulpit before the minister arrived. . . . He came and went up in the pulpit and took his seat. Then in a short time he arose and announced a hymn, which was sung. And immediately after reading a chapter in the Bible and announcing his text, he said, 'Well, friends, the word of God is in my mouth, but the Devil is in my breeches.' "[22]

"Mrs. StClair, tell me something about your wedding. How old were you when you were married?" "Oh, I was getting right old, I was twenty-five. In those days when a girl was twenty-five she was a hopeless old maid." "Was it a house wedding?" "Yes, indeed. I had a big wedding. We were married November 25, 1875 in the evening and Ma certainly gave us a big supper: turkey, chicken, old Virginia ham, and all kinds of cakes and fancy pies. I had seven or eight waiters and candle waiters. The little girls that carried the candles had on pretty party dresses. My husband had his home already. It was on a small farm over near Bunker Hill and we went right straight to housekeeping." "Was that in Campbell County?" "No, in Bedford.

"There were no contractors in that day and time, but my husband was an apprenticed carpenter and he followed that trade all his life. About 1903, I think it was, we came to Roanoke from Bedford and lived on Denniston Avenue, Virginia Heights for nineteen years. After my husband's death in 1910, I continued to live there until my married daughter who lived with us moved to Norfolk nine years ago, at which time I came to live with my son, John W. and his wife at 716 Highland Avenue, S.E."

Mrs. StClair is the mother of eleven children, eight sons and three daughters. There are only seven of the children now living. Mrs. StClair does not look like she can possibly be ninety years of age. She is very erect and alert, with shining black eyes, full of life and expression. And [she] still has a very nice suit of graying hair. She is rather tall, [and] was wearing a black and white print dress with a narrow white collar and a soft light wool shawl over her shoulders. She is slightly deaf. That is the only indication of the long span of years that she has traveled.

[Loc.: VSL/AB, box 186, 6 pp., 1,918 wds.]

George Strausburg *a tall tale, by John Garrett, no interview date given*

John Garrett obtained this "folklore" text from the same George (Strausburg) Strawsburg whose life history follows afterward. Like Strausburg, California Adams StClair told the VWP interviewer a tall tale, but she did so within the larger context of conveying her life history. In that circumstance, Gertrude Blair seems to have accepted the tale as part of StClair's natural history, and no apparent consideration was given to its nature as folklore or as living tradition.

On the other hand, the life history of George Strausburg and the text of the tall tale he told were treated as separate items, submitted to separate Federal Writers' programs, and at length deposited in separate locations — in effect, disconnecting living lore from its human agency and complex of meanings. When brought back together again, these pieces add an important dimension to our understanding of George Strausburg. It admits that another, lighter side to his life may have once existed and relieves an otherwise melancholy and self-pitying portrait of this old man.[23]

Mr. George Strausburg, an old blind man up in his seventies, tells us this story that his father [told] him:

"There was a man by the name of John Toad Willhahelm. They lived up at Rockbridge, Virginia. He said one time 'Sam' (fer that was his nickname) went to a little town like, and they were scarce of water. And they said to Sam, 'Over the mountain is a good well. If we had it over here, we could have a plenty of water.' 'Well, what will yer give me to bring the well over here?' And er, they made up the money, you know, and er, he went over the mountain and found the well and pulled it up. And he got it up on his shoulder and he carried it to the top of the mountain, and the thing busted in two pieces and like to of washed the whole town away."[24]

[Loc.: UVA/FC, box 7, item #718, 1 p.]

George (Strausburg) Strawsburg *by John W. Garrett, received 25 June 1940*

If anything, the death of his father, Ephraim, in the Civil War was even more devastating for the slightly younger George Strausburg (born in 1857) than the loss of eight-year-old Benjamin Thacker's mother had been to him. Both George's father, Ephraim (b. 1833), and his grandfather Elias (b. ca. 1806) had been blacksmiths in the town of Fishersville in Augusta County. But both these men in succession died early and intestate, leaving young children as wards of various guardians. In 1852, nineteen-year-old Ephraim bought a number of items for a total of $270.49 from the fairly sizable estate of his father, Elias Strausburg, among them a saddle, skillet, sugar box, shotgun, mason hammer and trowel, and a two-horse wagon and gear. By 1860, Ephraim's mother, Elizabeth, had contracted with Jacob Shaver to remarry, and Ephraim also had a wife, Elizabeth, and sons George, aged three, and James Watson, aged five months.[25]

Just a few years later Ephraim himself was killed in the war, and his family did not fare so well in its aftermath. Although his widow remarried, it was not a very happy union according to George, and the Strausburg children were put in other homes to be raised. Certainly it is the case that in 1870 George Strausburg (listed as age ten rather than thirteen) was indicated as a "domestic" living in the household of an aged farmer, William Carter. Whether or not Carter was the same person referred to as the "keeper of the poorhouse," who was so mean to the "poor critters" in his care and from whom George Strausburg ran away when he was sixteen, however, has not been determined.

In recounting and judging his own life, Strausburg declared, "I never had no chance fer nothing but hard work." And the hard work he eventually pursued was that of carpentry—an occupation he held in common with Benjamin Thacker, James StClair, Lycurgus Drumheller, and George Brown elsewhere in this chapter. George Strausburg worked at that trade until he became blind and could work no more. Then he had to sell his carpenter's tools in order to live.

Ephraim Strausburg and [his] wife lived in Fishersville, Virginia, Augusta County, and it was there that George was born. He had two brothers, but destiny had decreed that the young brothers were not to see much of each other. They little thought as they played around the fireside together that the ill fortune of separation was awaiting them so young. But when the Civil War came their father was called to service in the Confederate Army.

George said, "I can just remember my father, but I can see my mother now in my mind as she was crying as Father went away to fight. I was born in fifty-seven, and I was too small to remember the hardships of my home until my father was killed in battle. Then Mother, she couldn't make a living for us, and she just put us out in any home she could get us in. She didn't have no education and I don't guess Father did. You know there wa'n't no schools in them times like they are now.

"The man that got me was a keeper of the poorhouse and he was awful mean to them 'poor critters,' and to me too. I got a hard beating for nothing. I tried to please him but, why that couldn't be done. After awhile Mother married again. Did she take us back? Why, no. She couldn't git along with the old man herself and I knowed I couldn't git along with no stepfather, nobody could. I have several half brothers en' sisters, but I never knowed much of them.

"I ran away when I was about sixteen from the man that had me, en' I went to work fer meself. I picked up carpenter work along, a helper at first. And I was apt with tools and liked to work, and I soon become a pretty good workman. Of course, I couldn't read as I never had no chance to go to school. I went a part of one winter before Father died and the teacher usta beat me every day. And after that, why I never had no chance fer nothing but hard work. When I went to work fer meself, I saved all I could. I never was nobody to be wasteful.

"When I was twenty-four I was married to Martha Black. She was thirty-five. We had one girl, Bettie. I had bought us a little home and had got it paid for and after Bettie come, why Martha was allus sick. I have had a lot of 'ups and downs.' Martha, she lived on like that fer several years, but it was medicine and doctor bills all the time. But I didn't mind that if she could git any help from her suffering. But Martha kept saying, 'George, I want Bettie to git this place and I want you to deed it over to her.' Well, I wanted her to have it too after we was gone, she was our only child. But Martha couldn't rest until I had made the place over to Bettie, so I went ahead and got it all fixed up.[26]

"While Martha was living it was all right, but she died, and then it left just me en' Bettie. We got along all right. Of course, we was lonesome, but I was working and Bettie looked after the house fer me. But when she got married, why that was when the trouble started. Her husband soon got tired of me and when they didn't want this ole man, I gits out. But thar they had my house and all I had.

"Well, I had to have a place to stay. The War come up in fifteen en on, and over at Gashan [Goshen, Rockbridge County] was a lot of work going on. So I goes over there and got a job. Well, I was making me four dollars every day, worked all overtime I could git. That was the only time in me life that I ever made much money. But I didn't like boarding, so I bought me another house en' lot there in Gashan. En' paid fer it while I was working there during the War, en' I lived in it. I done my own cooking en' housekeeping. I was sixty-four and I had not got married no more, en' I thought I never would. I kept on working here en' there. After the War, of course, the work there was dull. But I farmed a little, raised chickens, and time went on until I was in [my] seventies, still living there by meself.

"One day I went over to my neighbor's house and Clara Meterspring was there. She was up in [her] twenties I thought. My neighbor's wife went on bragging on Clara, 'Why she is the nicest girl I have ever had to stay with me.' I thought nothing of it at first, but the next time I went over there after awhile I missed Clara. So I says, 'Why! Where's Clara?' 'Why,' she says, 'she's gone home to git her clothes to come stay with you, George.' Time went on and I heard that Clara was in the hospital and after awhile I heard she was at home. So I went over to see her and I thought now Clara has been sick, so I just [took] her some candy along. When I got over there, why Clara had taken blood poison in one of her feet and that's how come her in the hospital and she had to have her foot took off.

"Well, I felt so sorrow for her en' I kept going over to see her along. Clara got her a club-foot and got so she could walk again pretty good. After she got well awhile, why one day she comes over to my house and says, 'Mr. Strausburg, I have come over here to keep house fer you,' en' I says, 'Why all right, Clara.' So when spring begun to come and Clara says, 'Now Mr. Strausburg, I will stay on until March and if we are not married by then, why, I goes home.' So I thought, well now look here. Well I wus there all by meself, I couldn't live with no son-in-law. So I says, 'All right Clara, we will git married.'

"We went over to the preacher's house. I am an old fashioned hard-shell Baptist, mind you, a hard-shell Baptist. Well, we got married. And the first thing I knowed that preacher up thar was mad at me en' saying, 'Oughta give Clara a deed to my home and I wus not treating her right by not doing it.' Well, I wanted Clara to have my home when I was gone, but I had lost one home and I didn't know what Clara might do. She was twenty-nine when we wus married en' I wus seventy-five, and a 'burnt child dreads the fire,' I can tell you. So I was going to wait awhile and see how Clara done, but she had done well fer me and now I have willed my little four-room house up in Gashan to Clara.

"Well, I got old and my eyesight got bad. I couldn't work no more, and Clara, she can't work to do no good with a clubfoot. So my brother he comes up from Buckingham to git me to move down to his house. He says, 'George, I have a good six-room house, painted, don't have no screens, but I want you to come on down and live in it. If you will, I will let you have a cow to milk, you can raise your chickens and a hog, and I will help you what I can.' That cow suited Clara, she is wild for her milk. So we moved, and he done all he said and we don't pay no rent, just live here.

"But I went totally blind [three?] years ago, and can't see nothing. Clara has to do all the work and lead me around wherever I go around the house, en' I can't walk to do no good. I tell yer it's awful to be blind. People can talk about it, but they can't know how awful it is: can't see nobody, can't read, can't find yer way, can't feed yerself, can't do nothing. When people comes, can't see 'em. Talk to 'em, but can't see 'em. I have two grandchildren and some great-grandchildren, but I can't see 'em. Can't see 'em (with tears flowing from his blinded eyes as he repeats, can't see 'em), it's awful. But up yon'er I can see 'em, some day can see 'em up there.

"I sold my carpenter's tools to git money to live on. The relief gives us ten dollars a month. And sometimes Clara gits four dollars a month fer the rent of our house up in Gashon, but we can't live on that. Why if our good neighbors didn't help us, we would suffer greatly. Some people say, 'Why Mr. Strausburg, why you don't need nothing.' No, I don't need no clothes. I don't need no chair, don't need no bed, don't need nothing to eat. No, I don't need nothing, they say. Cause a ole man eighty-three years old and his wife, we don't need nothing, they say. The house don't haft to be kept up. We don't need no bed. We are thankful for all we git from the relief. But if the neighbors wasn't so kind we would suffer, but they ere allus a-bringing us something."

The old house, which seems to have been an old farm home, with its many outbuildings are all in bad need of repair. The palings around the yard are falling down, while the flowers which once grew in its yard are about all smothered by grass and weeds, except [for] a brave white peony blooming among the grass. The house is clean on the inside but scarcely furnished. The porch is in need of repair. On the porch is an old worn glider with a bed, for George Strausburg spends his days laying there or sitting as he talks to those who visit him. "The Methodist preacher comes by and sings and prays with us sometimes, and we enjoy it. It makes us feel somebody still cares something fer us."

Mr. Strausburg is white haired, tall, and feeble. His wife hops around on her clubfoot and takes care of his needs. "Clara is awful good to me, and she deserves all I could give her. There's nothing like being at home. If I want to rest, I rest. I can do as I please. Nobody says, 'You can't do that, George.' But I am glad that up there I will see — yes — see again."

[Loc.: VSL/AB, box 187, 4 pp.]

Fulton Pottery *by Leila Blanche Bess, 15 December 1936*

George N. Fulton, the "best potter in Alleghany County," was in fact born in Ohio. He noted the clay deposits in the area while serving with the Union army and returned after the war to establish a pottery kiln in the vicinity of Potts Creek. His soon-to-be helper, Daniel F. Arritt, was a mere boy of seven years when Fulton bought land from Baptist minister John B. Davis and began his pottery works there in 1867. The ware produced at the Fulton Pottery was a salt-glazed, blue-gray clay body with blue decoration—the type of pottery referred to by crafts writer Mary Nichols Rawson as "strongware, sometimes called 'scrodle ware,'" which she noted was "unbreakable on the roughest road." In 1875, Fulton supposedly removed his shop from Alleghany County to Fincastle in Botetourt County. The reasons for this move are made the more mysterious by Rawson's report in 1938 that "some sixty years ago," George Fulton "moved away with a shop full of ware set up for burning but never burnt."[27]

Leila Blanche Bess of Potts Creek, Alleghany County, who submitted the Fulton Pottery report and snapshot of the kiln site, was one of a number of workers on the Historic Inventory Project who were also employed later by the Virginia Writers' Project. The HIP was sponsored by Virginia's Conservation Commission from October 1935 to December 1938, with the purpose of surveying and documenting items and places of historic interest or significance in the state.[28]

1. *Subject:*
   Fulton Pottery.
2. *Location:*
   On Route #18, about 15 miles from Covington, Virginia, 3/4 mile from Jordan Mines. Lane 300 yards.
3. *Date:*
   Was in operation in 1875.
4. *Owners:*
   W. D. Hepler, present owner.
5. *Description:*

Fulton got clay on the Moses G. Wright place, then owned by Moses G. Wright, Mr. Arritt's step-father. Mr. Arritt says: "They dug about four feet through the soil. This, as a rule, runs from twelve to twenty feet deep, of fine, smooth clay. When through the clay, they struck rock-bed, like river or creek beds."

The clay was dug out in large blocks, loaded on a two-horse wagon, owned by M. G. Wright, being one of two in that section and hauled to Fulton's place of business. Here the clay was unloaded, put in a machine which was equipped with knives, curved something like fingers. The machine was run by a horse going round in a circle, or to be more modern, like the music, "the horse went round and round." The curved knives cut the clay up and took out the bits of grass and trash, then water was added, rendering the clay to a pulp, or something like dough. It was then turned out on a board and put on a lathe, which was operated by the foot, using a kind of petal. The clay had to be handled carefully; shaped with care and skill. Fulton had lathes of all sizes for jars, crocks, jugs, churns, vases, etc. He had all shapes too, many odd pieces were made especially for children, such as eggs, pigs, money banks, etc. After the ware was shaped it was set inside a building to dry. This required several days, probably three days. It was then put in a kiln to burn. The burning or firing process required forty eight hours of continuous burning. When the kiln and ware became very hot, a quantity of salt was poured on. This salt made the glaze. When it was seen they had a good glaze no more fuel was added to the kiln, but the ware could not be removed from the kiln until it cooled, which required about three days time. When thoroughly cooled the ware was removed and set in a building ready for marketing.

One who has never seen one of the old fashioned kilns will find it worthwhile to visit one. Fulton's kiln was built of brick, and at this time is sodded over. It is very easy to find, and interesting.

The oven or kiln is about eight or ten feet above the ground, now covered with sod and wild flowers. Some of the built-in cavities where the ware was placed are visible, although some have fallen in and the sod has almost covered a part of it. When the ware was burnt one piece was placed inside another. The largest one was put in first, a block of clay put in to prevent touching, then a second size, and so on until the smallest ones were placed. Sometimes Fulton burned as much as a thousand gallons at a time.

6.   *Historical Significance:*

George Fulton was said to be the best potter in Alleghany County and surrounding territories. He bought a small plot of land from Rev. John B. Davis, now owned by W. D. Hepler, near what is now known as Jordan Mines. He built a log dwelling house and houses for drying and keeping his stoneware. Nothing remains of the building but the kiln where the ware was fired still remains.

Mr. D. F. Arritt gave a very interesting account of the making of stoneware. Mr. Arritt is an authority on the subject, for he worked with G. N. Fulton for a long while, in every stage of the work from digging of the clay to selling the finished articles. . . .[29]

7.   *Art:*

   Photo.

8.   *Sources of Information:*

   Informant: Mr. D. F. Arritt, Jordan Mines, Virginia. Informant: Mr. T. O. Crowder, Mill Branch Road, Potts Creek, Virginia.[30]

   [Loc.: vsl/hip, reel #3, Alleghany County]

Site of Fulton Pottery kiln. Photographer unknown. vsl/hip. [49020]

Daniel F. Arritt *by Leila Blanche Bess, rec. 24 April 1939*

"Child, I'm old, what would you want with my life history?" "Uncle" Dan Arritt (born in 1860) asked Leila Blanche Bess when she came to interview him for the second time. The first occasion had been for the WPA Historic Inventory Project more than two years before. He talked with her then of his work for George Fulton's pottery, and she reported, incidentally, that Moses G. Wright was Arritt's stepfather. That bit of personal information was not contained in the subsequent life history even though almost a quarter of its text was adapted by Bess from the previous Fulton Pottery report and resubmitted—this time to the WPA Writers' Project.

Daniel Arritt's father, John L., died during the Civil War and left his wife, Phebe, with four children under age ten. Phebe Arritt, unlike George Strausburg's mother, was able to keep her family together during her widowhood before she married near-neighbor Moses G. Wright by 1864. Indeed, it was Wright, not John Arritt, who was referred to in the life history when Daniel Arritt said his "father was a farmer, and a good one too."

In April 1882, Rev. John B. Davis, who formerly sold the land for the Fulton Pottery, married Daniel F. Arritt and Mary Emma Riddlesbarger (the daughter of Martin and Mary A. Riddlesbarger) of Botetourt County. When Dan Arritt died in 1945, he was survived by eighty-seven-year-old Mary Emma and seven of their children: two sons were in Seattle, Washington, and Kalamazoo, Michigan; the others all remained in Alleghany County.

"Child, I'm old, what would you want with my life history? I had never thought of havin' a history, but I reckon we all do have somethin' in our lives that might be called by that name, stop to think of it," and the old man folded his gnarled hands across his lap in a restful pose. His face was a study. The expression changed often as if he were living over again the years he had left behind him. For a few moments he seemed oblivious of my presence.

"Life Histories," he mused, "they sorta got me to thinkin' of my young days. Things ain't now like they was then. It 'pears to me that folks had better times and lived easier in them days than they do now with all the machinery we have to work with. Not as I'm down on any improvement, not a bit. I like the newer, better way of doin' lots of things and they's been a lot of improvements in farmin' and keepin' up the land an' all since I started farmin'. But what I mean is, we live in such a hurry these days we don't see as much of each other now as we did long ago before we had cars to go in. It used to be common fer neighbors to go on Saturday evenin' and stay with another one 'til Sunday after dinner. It was easy to git some other neighbor to 'tend to the stock fer you. They was glad to do it. And maybe next Saturday they would want to go, and you would do fer them the same and no thought of charges. It would have been an insult to mention payin' fer a little neighborly act like that." Uncle Dan's pale blue eyes looked a bit hard as he looked out from under shaggy brows, and his old toil-worn hands worked together nervously.

Uncle Dan looks at least ten years younger than his age (eighty years); he is small and quick, there is nothing in his movements that would denote old age. His cheek bones are high and he has a thin Roman nose. The handlebar mustache, sandy in color, completely hides his mouth. His chin is rather sharp but has strength, too. The fortune tellers would say that his chin denoted determination. . . . [31]

It was a beautiful, bright, warm day and Uncle Dan was sitting on the porch of his home. He takes great pride in keeping his home in good repair. There are no leaky roofs or un-

Daniel Arritt's home.
Photographer unknown.
VSL/HIP. [49029]

sightly, sagging gates about his house or barn. The house he occupies is very old and carries with it an interesting bit of Alleghany County history. It was built by one of the very early settlers and was for many years used for a kind of courthouse and many trials have been held there. It was also used for a regular place of worship before there was a church in the community, and is still used for a tax-collector's stand.

"Farmin' is my occupation now, and there's nothin' better to my way o' thinkin'. I like it better'n anything else I've ever done. No, I wasn't always a farmer, part o' my life I wa'n't anything," he said sadly. "I was borned and raised on a farm and always liked it. But you know sometimes it takes a boy several years to find out what he wants to do, so I didn't start out as a farmer, but I ought to. I didn't know where I was startin' to, but I come mighty nigh goin' to the devil, before I found my way," he said gravely. He sat silent for a little while, twirling his thumbs. He leaned his chair back against the wall and sat his feet upon the rounds.

"My father was a farmer, and a good one too. I don't know how it come that he allowed me to go away to work, but I got work with a potter. He lived about two miles below here and wanted a boy to help him, so I hired to him. He had a fine business, made stoneware, and sold it by the thousands of gallons. 'Did you ever see a potter shop in operation?' he asked suddenly. "Well, it's an interestin' thing. I worked with him in all stages of the work from diggin' the clay to sellin' the ware. I'll tell you how it was done. First we had to find a good bed of clay, just any kind won't do. Then we had to dig down about four feet until we found the choice kind of clay, then we cut it out in great big blocks, loaded it on a wagon, and hauled it to the shop. There we unloaded it and it was put in a mill and ground up; the mill run something like a cane mill, round an' round. It was pulled by a horse. The mill had a lot o' little blades or knives in it an' they cut the clay up and helped to rid it of any trash. It was then mixed with just enough water to make the clay pliable, something like wheat dough. It was then turned out on a board, this was operated by the foot, using a kind of pedal. The clay had to be handled carefully and shaped with skill. We made all kinds of jars, crocks, vases, churns, and many odd pieces, such as eggs, pigs, money banks, and many others.

"When the pieces were shaped it was set inside a building to dry. After this, it was put in a kiln and 'fired' for forty eight hours. When the kiln and ware become very hot, a quantity of salt was poured on, this made the glaze. When it was seen that they had a good glaze no more fuel was added to the kiln, but the ware had to remain in the kiln until it was cooled.

This required about three days. When it was thoroughly cooled it was set in a building, ready for marketing. When we were ready with a load, I loaded up my wagon with an assortment of ware and drove all over Alleghany, Botetourt, Craig, Giles, and Montgomery Counties, sellin' ware."

Uncle Dan tells an amusing story of a competitor he met at Blacksburg who tried to "run down" his ware: "I had just driv into town with a load of ware, when an older man came swaggering up, looking at my load. After lookin' it over, he said with a sneer, 'Young man, your stuff is no good.' An' I said, 'I'll show you that it's better'n yours.' So I just picked up a stone jar an' throwed it across the road, it didn't break either. And says I, 'Can yours stand that? An' whats more,' says I, 'I bet you can't bile water in'm.' The fellow just stood an' looked, never aimed to show what his stuff was made of. So I took up a jar, poured some water in it, an' set it on the stove and 'bilt' it good an' hard. Then I told him his wares was glazed with red lead, an' was rank pison." It seems that his competitor was convinced of the superior quality of his ware, for he bought seventy-five gallons right there.[32]

"I was married when pretty young, got a mighty good woman, too. We started out with nothin'. We lived with my people for awhile. Well, it was several years before we went to housekeeping to ourselves an' really started a home. You see I wasn't settled even then. I finally decided to try to buy a home and did buy a little farm, only about forty acres of land an' no house, but then it was not so hard to build a house as it is now. I cut the logs on my own land and hauled them in. And when I got all the materials to the site, I then invited all my friends and neighbors in and we had a raisin' an' in one day I got my logs up and the rafters on. It wasn't any trouble to get your neighbors to help you then, they enjoyed it, we all did. We had raisins' an' cornshuckins' an' logrollins'. Just any time a fellow had a big job on hand, all he had to do was to let his neighbors know about it an' they was ready to help. The womenfolks cooked up a big dinner an' they had a lot o' fun too. Well, I finished my house myself as soon as I could, an' we moved in.

"I've always managed to provide fer my family. We had nine children an' we tried to raise 'em right, to be law-abidin'. An' I tried, too, to give them a better chance than I had. I could have had more 'larnin" but I jus' didn't take it. I went to pay schools an' had some as good teachers as anybody would wish to have. One I went to was an awful good teacher. He was tight though, but Lord, he had to be. It's a wonder he didn't kill us boys. There was ten of the meanest boys that ever set foot inside a schoolroom. Some days that man whopped the whole bunch, an' still we was mean as the devil. We was afraid to let him ketch us at our worst meanness. I've had my durn'd hide tanned more times than I can count," the old man grinned a little shamefacedly.

"Yes," he went on, "I've tried to raise my children better. When my two oldest ones was right smart chunks of boys, I took them to town and took them through the jail. They wanted to know why people had to [be] kept locked up behind barred windows. I explained the best I could an' tried to impress on their minds that if they didn't want to be confined like those people, they must be good boys an' abide by the law. I then took them outside an' told them how the people that done wrong used to be punished. I explained all about the old whippin' post, an' how the prisoners were brought out on the court yard an' stripped naked to the waist an' was tied hand an' foot, then they was throwed across the post an' whopped by the sheriff. They got so many licks dependin' on what they had done. The limit was forty-nine, save one. The whippin' strap was made of leather soaked in oil, an' sometimes when a nigger was

Farm land in Alleghany County, Virginia. January 1939. Photo by Arthur Rothstein. [LC-USF34-26812-D]

whopped, the strap come down so hard it left a white strip on the black flesh. I don't know what impression all this made on the little boys, but I've never had a child in jail," he said in a thankful tone.

Two small husky boys came romping in. "These are my grandsons," said Uncle Dan proudly. "Their mother is dead an' their father is married again, so we keep these boys," he explained. "They're a sight o' help, an' company too," he added.

The sunlight fell in long, slanting rays across Uncle Dan's thin face, lighting it up with a youthful expression. He looked very serene and peaceful as he looked out over the newly turned earth, rich and dark, and we breathed a prayer that he might live to enjoy the fruits of his labors.

When my visit was ended Uncle Dan rose from his chair, holding his old felt hat in his hand. "Now don't make this the last time you come to see me. Come back an' stay longer. I don't call this much of a visit," he said kindly.

Uncle Dan is one of the most outstanding farmers in his community. He engages in up-to-date farming and raises good cattle and horses. When he wants to pass a delightful day, he saddles one of his horses and rides to the top of Potts Mountain.

He sold the small farm which he described as his first buy, and bought the one on which he now resides. This is a much better farm, most of it is smooth creek bottom land. It is on this we find the old historic house. Uncle Dan has improved it. He tore down one of the chimneys which was staggering and built a flue. In this room he holds court, he is still magistrate and many local troubles have to be settled. The room serves as sitting room and office; he has a large desk and chair very much like those we see in the courthouse.

The view is good from the small-paned windows looking out over the main highway and a beautiful stream, while far away in the distance, the mountains rise high and misty.

Uncle Dan and his good wife have taken several children and given them good home and training. Some they took from the county poorhouse and reared them as if they had been their own. Uncle Dan has done remarkably well. He has paid for his farm and we don't think he owes anyone a penny. He is, in addition to being a good neighbor, a fine veterinarian and will go anywhere at any hour to doctor a sick horse. . . .

And we believe he will have many stars in his crown for the many little kindnesses he has done for his neighbors and for the relief he has afforded the dumb animals of God's creation.[33]

[Loc.: VSL/AB, box 185, 8 pp., 2,338 wds.]

George and Celia (McKnight) Brown *by Maude R. Chandler, 4 December 1939*

George Brown was thirteen when he left his native Scott County in 1875 to live for a while with a Kelly family on Looney Creek in Wise County. The section around Looney and Callahan Creeks, where the "more capitalistic mountain natives" John Kelly and Joe Kilbourne lived, "had just begun to develop" in 1876. Otherwise, according to Brown's description, the area at the time was still largely a sparsely populated backcountry.[34]

Sometime after the Civil War, the same General J. D. Imboden who rode his dapple-gray horse into Callie Elizabeth StClair's yard in Bedford County would also lead a group of Pennsylvania investors to the rich coal fields of Wise County. The alliance between northern speculators and civilian lawyer and land agent Imboden resulted in the founding of the Virginia Coal and Iron Company in 1882 and the eventual development of the Stonega mines in the vicinity of Looney and Callahan Creeks, not far from Big Stone Gap. Already in 1880, however, overly zealous boosters were predicting in the Big Stone Gap *Herald* that it would become "one of the mightiest manufacturing cities and railroad centers on the continent."[35]

Commenting on Captain John Ferdinand Dalziel Smyth's travels and remarks about land speculation on the borders of Virginia and North Carolina prior to the Revolutionary War, Alfred James Morrison gave his own view in 1922 of the requirements for future development in the area. Because there was a "continent of land to be exploited" in the beginning, he observed, "it was very difficult to corner even a small part of the market. . . . Land could not be handled as capital, until a sufficient number of settlers had come in, each contributing his accumulations to enhance the value of the common stock."[36]

By 1880, the population of Wise County still consisted of only 5,939 people, with that number increasing by a little more than a third by 1890. But in 1900 the population (19,653) had more than tripled, and by 1930 (at 51,167) it was more than eight and a half times its size in 1880. The condition of transforming the area into a settled territory, which Morrison described as necessary to its use as a resource for capital formation, was not well met or sufficient in Wise County, given its size, until the early decades of the twentieth century, even though the stirrings of such development were there by at least the 1870s.[37]

When George Brown and his wife, Celia McKnight, were married more than fifty-three years ago, they had practically nothing at the time of going to housekeeping. They had many hardships to face but, as the wife remarked, "We thought nothing of hardships at that time." They went to housekeeping in a one-room log house and they even kept two boarders in this one room. Later, when the mining camps began to build up, their boarders were the Superintendent and the Scrip Writer. Later on they built a "lean-to" and used it for their kitchen. But one day when they were away from home, their house burned up and not a thing was saved. They had two big feather beds and eight pillows to get burned up with the rest of their household goods. These things were hard to replace. But they didn't let that discourage them and as the years advanced they became more prosperous.

George Brown is a native of Scott County and was born February 10, 1862. His parents, John and Lizzie Edens Brown, were pioneers of Scott County and they lived near the station of Spears [Speers] Ferry, a point where the Southern and C.C. and O. Railroad cross the Clinch River. The gap is the place where all the old settlers came in from the East and ferried the river on their way to Kentucky and other western settlements.[38]

His parents made their living by cultivating the rough mountain farm. In this family were four children: one girl and three boys, George being the eldest. When he was only thirteen years old he left home in Scott County and came to Wise County, [where he] lived with a Kelly family whose home was on Looney Creek, which is about a mile from the present corporation limits of Appalachia. At this time this place was covered with virgin forests with small clearings, where the people eked out an existence, with only two or three mountain trails for roads: one leading toward Cumberland Gap, Tennessee; one toward Tazewell, Virginia; and another across the [Black] mountain into Kentucky.

After staying here for awhile [Brown] went over into West Virginia and stayed eighteen months, [then came] back to the same place to live. And again he left, this time going back into Kentucky where he stayed for two years, after which he came back to the same place again to live. He stayed on there for sometime then went to Inman, about two miles from Appalachia, to prospect for coal. He worked at this while the railroad was being built at Clinchport. He worked on the tipple for eight years. When prospecting from early dawn until dark, he got only one dollar and ten cents per day.

He was thrifty and saved his money. Coming to Appalachia, he bought property on what is now Main Street and paid fifteen hundred dollars for it, lived in it five years and sold it to Dr. Stallard for three thousand dollars. He then bought a big house and four lots up on the hill in 1907. He farmed these lots, worked at the carpenter trade, and made a good living. They lived in this house until about two years ago, when they moved out into a smaller house which they own. They sold the larger house.

The house they live in now has five rooms and bath. It is ceiled on the inside and painted. It is very well-arranged and is well-kept. Their furniture is not modern, but is very good and kept clean. The house is painted on the outside. They have running water in their house and electric lights, but few electric conveniences.

Mr. Brown tells some interesting stories of his boyhood days, during [which] . . . this section had just begun to develop. "There were no roads and a very few mountain trails. One of these trails led to [the] head of Callahan Creek through what is now Stonega, about six miles from Appalachia, into Kentucky. From the time they left Appalachia going to Stonega, they crossed this creek forty-two times. There were only a few families living on this trail, viz: Jim Elkins, Will Shepherd, Henry Creach, Eden Sturgill, and Joe Kilbourne. This was in the year of 1876. The section was covered with laurels, spruce pine, poplar, and oak. A few years later, a band mill was brought in and the virgin timber cut and sawed into lumber. Then families began to come in and small houses to go up." Mr. Brown tells us that these were happy times, that they all had good times, more so he believes than the young people of today.

Cecilia McKnight Brown was born in Letcher County, Kentucky, April 4, 1859. Her father Anthy [Anthony] was born in 1812, and her mother Susanna was born in 1818. Her mother lived to be ninety-two years old. She had measles at the age of ninety. In their family were eight children: five girls and three boys. Mrs. Brown has one sister now living in the state of Kansas. She also has two brothers living, who are farmers. In those days everyone in the family helped and their biggest aim was to raise enough money to pay their taxes. This money was made by farming and ginsenging.

Mrs. Brown says, "We would go sengeing [looking for ginseng], sometimes fifteen and twenty in a group, and we would camp out for a week or two at a time. We would carry our food with us and at times would kill wild game. We usually made our camp under a big cliff and fixed a furnace where we could do our cooking. We would come over into Big Black Mountain, which is between Kentucky and Virginia, [on the] line." Mrs. Brown says they would make johnnycakes by stirring together meal and salt and water, making it out in cakes and putting it on a buckeye board, and leaning it to their open fire to bake. "Those were the good days."

She also tells this very interesting story. "One time me and my brother were out senging. We noticed and heard something that kept following us all day, and the dogs kept barking. During the day we had caught a groundhog and put it on a stick, and [were] carrying it around with us, and as we came around a bench in the mountain there was a panther coming around on a log. We had our dogs with us, and we begun to hiss him, hiss him, hiss him, until the dogs ran it into the slick foot of Black Mountain. But that night about dark it came close to our camp, but [it] would keep out of our sight. I never slept any that night. I laid with my face on the ground for I was afraid I would see it. We had a good time as well as hardships. We would hunt chestnuts, and at night set around the campfire roasting them and singing. I have hunted squirrels and pheasants lots of times. Even after I was married, me and my husband would go hunting together, I always liked to hunt."

Mrs. Brown lived on the border of two counties in Kentucky. Her house was in Letcher County and her smokehouse in Harlan County. She had a sister that was married and lived here in this section of Virginia and she was over here staying with her sister when she met and married George. They were married in 1886 by Rev. Johnny Sturgill, a Primitive Baptist minister. They have had fifty-three years of married life together. She is now eighty years old and he is seventy-seven years old. They have gone through hard times together but as she said, "We thought nothing of hardships in them days."

When Mr. Brown begun prospecting for coal in the Inman hollow, they lived there in a small house. [It] and one more [were] all the houses in that section. He made $1.25 a day at this work. They later sold their house to the company for $50.00 for a right [of way]. At this time the coal land was being developed and he helped build Imboden. And [he] moved there and rented a house for five dollars a month. While working there he made $1.10 a day. He says, "The most I have ever made a day was during the World War [I], when I got eighty cents an hour doing carpenter work. I have no work now. I was cut off at the age of sixty-five."

Mrs. Brown says, "I forgot to tell you about killing six partridges at one shot. One day I had some company and we was standing out in the yard talking and a covey came down right at my house. And I told them just wait till I went in the house and got my gun, and I did and went to the front gate, and shot into [the partridges] and got six at one shot. I gave two of them away and I cooked the other four."

Mr. and Mrs. Brown are members of the Baptist church. They don't go very regular for they both are getting old. They neither went to school very much, but both have a very good education. Mr. Brown is a well-read man, keeps up with the daily news, and reads books. . . .[39] They say back in those days they just had school three months out of the year and were taught from the old Blue Back Speller, and were taught geography and arithmetic and reading. There was a little log schoolhouse, eighteen by twenty feet, on Pigeon Creek that children from near and far came to. They would have fifteen or twenty students. Our present superintendent of Wise County schools, Jack Kelly, Jr. and his sister attended school in this little log building. Mr. Brown is well acquainted with the prominent men of Wise County.

Mr. Brown likes to visit the sick and talk with them and give them encouragement. He and Mrs. Brown are both very interesting to talk with and seem so glad to have you come [visit]. They really seemed to enjoy telling of their experiences.

Mrs. Brown is a tall, slender woman and a brunette, and Mr. Brown is a tall [man], large and dark-complected. Their heads are almost gray now. They seemed to have spent their married life in happiness with each other. They have no children.[40]

[Loc.: VSL/AB, box 189, 6 pp., 1,844 wds.]

Lycurgus Drumheller *by Gertrude Blair, 13 May 1939*

Lycurgus Drumheller (born in 1848), or "Curgus," as his wife and others called him, kept meticulous records in an old leather-bound ledger, which was formerly used for his father John Drumheller's store accounts at Rockfish Depot. The one page remaining from that era is dated 14 June 1834; the other early records have been cut out. Lycurgus's first and only entry for the year 1873 was dated 2 October—the day after he married Sarah Louise Kidd; on that date, he was paid $4.00 for "4 days hauling logs" for miller M. W. Woodson.[41]

The accounts show that, in addition to general farmwork, "Curgus" Drumheller did get "plenty of [carpentry] work to do," including riving shingles and making various items such as tables, barrels, coffins, cow yokes, and cradles (both for babies and wheat). For Hawes N. Farrar in 1875, he hauled and stacked oats ($.50), repaired a plough ($.20), made a garden rake ($.15), and also made and fit a six-light sash "in school house" ($1.25). Between 1875 and 1895, Lycurgus also did many other jobs—often in exchange for meal, flour, wheat shorts, bran, or seed—for M. W. Woodson. He worked on the mill, its dam, and waterwheel, replacing cogs on gears and pecking burrs on millstones; made bolts and strip hinges; worked cornfields; and built a house, stable, shed room, cellar wall, and chimney.[42]

In 1878, Lycurgus Drumheller and his family rented a house from Mrs. Anna M. Roberts, and between February and November of that year, she paid him almost $42 cash for a variety of work done for her. In a memorandum for that year, Lycurgus noted that his family had used 5 1/2 barrels of corn and 24 pounds of sugar. He also itemized everything he had bought or paid cash for during the year, including $1.73 in taxes on his own property for 1877. Altogether, the family purchases for the year totaled $39.72.[43]

Through the years, Lycurgus tallied the debits and the credits in the old ledger without comment, with two notable exceptions. In one case, he wrote that a certain hired man "shall do no

Lycurgus Drumheller.
Photograph taken in Yorktown, Virginia, 1941;
used courtesy of Janet P. Drumheller.

more work for me," but five days later he recorded that he was making a coffin for the man's wife. And when one especially vexatious debt of $3.90 was paid in full in 1879 by way of six and a half days' labor planting and working corn and with Lycurgus having to provide his own board, he wrote following the entry: "this Cr [credit] By damnation forever," and then with a flourish, "End."

When he was interviewed in 1939, VWP worker Blair described Lycurgus Drumheller as being "about six feet, rather slim, quite erect for his age, alert physically, and especially mentally." At ninety-one years of age, he had outlived his wife and three of their eleven children and at that time resided with one of his sons at 1334 Pinkney Street SE, Roanoke, Virginia. He later returned to his native Nelson County, where he lived and died at his home in Rockfish Depot.[44]

His great-grandfather, William Drumheller, came to America from Germany and settled in Albemarle County, date unknown. He lived to be one hundred and four years of age. His firstborn, a son, was given his name. William Jr.'s firstborn, a son, was named John, and John's firstborn was named Lycurgus after the old Spartan lawgiver. William Jr. went to Nelson County and settled on land near Rockfish, where he continued to live and where his son John, the father of Lycurgus, was born. John could neither read nor write. He married Elvira Jane Dameron; she was born and raised in Fluvanna County. There were seven children in John's family. Only two survive: the oldest Lycurgus, and the youngest, a brother who lives in Ohio. Lycurgus was born in Nelson County, September 12, 1848, at Rockfish Depot, which is about halfway between Charlottesville and Lynchburg, Virginia on the Southern Railroad. He had few educational advantages, "learned all that I know at home," so he told me. He remembers when the Southern Railroad was built. He was about eleven years old at that time. His father lived on a farm in Nelson County; later he opened a general merchandise store at Rockfish Depot. He was in the Civil War for four years, and was wounded in two battles.[45]

"I enlisted when I was seventeen, but Lee surrendered before I got in the army. Soon after the close of the War, I was in Culpeper and strolled out to the cemetery. The following inscription I read on a tombstone there:

> Here lies the body of Robert Gordon,
> Teeth almighty, and mouth accordin'
> Step light stranger over this wonder,
> If he opens his mouth, you are gone by thunder.

"I decided to learn the carpenter's trade when I was about eighteen and I soon got plenty of work to do. 'Can I tell you when I was married?' Well I guess I can, that's one time I'll never forget. On October 1st, 1873, I married Sarah Louise Kidd, that was sixty-six years ago." He laughed and said, "That's a long time to live with one woman, isn't it?" "Was she a Nelson County girl?" "Oh yes, she lived on Dutch Creek. She died in February of this year, eighty-four years of age. When I went courting I rode horseback, there were no roads in those days—just bridal [bridle] paths through the woods. Grain was taken to the mill in sacks thrown across the horse's back. Some of these old mills, tucked away in mountain hollows, had great blocks of stone that ten men couldn't lift. God Almighty only knows how they ever lifted them in place."

Mr. Drumheller and his mother made a trip to Lynchburg during some celebration there, and John W. Daniel was the orator on this occasion. His speech was delivered on Daniel's Hill. Lynchburg in those early days was a big tobacco market. Mr. Drumheller had explained to me how the tobacco was hauled in hogsheads drawn, generally, by oxen, how it was packed in there with the pole going through the center, and extending out at each end far enough for the shafts to be fastened to [it]. For advertising purposes they had one of those big hogsheads, with two oxen hitched to it, with an old negro man driving the team singing:

> I'se gwine down to town,
> I'se gwine down to Lynchburg town
> To carry my 'bacco to Lynchburg town,
> Bacco's selling high, and money's gittin' *skace* [scarce]
> Do pray young man sell my 'bacco
> And let me leave this place.[46]

Mr. Drumheller sang this as he remembered the old negro singing it. He really has a remarkable voice for his ninety-one years—strong and clear. (The suggestion in the manual on Folklore [was] to "let the person interviewed ramble on": I didn't have any choice in the matter with Mr. Drumheller, he took the floor and held it.)[47]

He told me of J. W. Foster of Leesburg, Virginia coming and opening up that big soapstone quarry at Schuyler, Nelson County, about four miles from his home, and where he worked for several years. Leaving there he went to Ohio and worked on a farm not far from Columbus, and lived there for three or four years. During an election there he was the only Democrat to cast a vote at that precinct.[48]

During his residence in Ohio he formed quite a friendship for a young lady named Jennie. She took one of the children's slates, and wrote the following verse on it, and put it in his room:

When you are sitting all alone,
Reflecting on the past,
Remember that you have a friend,
Whose friendship and love will last.

Jennie

"It was seventy years ago when I read those lines." "And, you didn't marry Jennie!" "No, I came back to Nelson and married my boyhood sweetheart, bought the farm I live on now, and set up housekeeping.

"We had a good time when I was young."[49] We had a dance nearly every week: old Ned Faulkner played the fiddle, all square dances, no waltzing. We danced the old Virginia Breakdown and 'Johnny Picking Up Rocks.' I know you've played 'Killyme Kranky.'" "No, I don't remember that I ever did." "It was more like a march, it went like this:

Farewell Dick and farewell Tom,
Farewell old Aunt Franky;
Every time I think of you
I'll wind up Killyme Kranky.

If you have been where I have been,
And seen the sights that I have seen;
Four and twenty girls,
All dancing Killyme Kranky.[50]

We used to play those games and dance 'til daybreak.

"'Chickamy Crany Crow' was one of our favorites:

Chickamy Chickamy Macrany Crow,
I went to the well to wash my toe,
When I got back my chicken was gone.
What time is it old witch? 'One o'clock.'[51]

In this game there is a 'witch' and an 'old hen.' A long string of children hold hands and repeat the verse, until the witch says it is twelve o'clock. Then in a chorus they all sing 'Old hen, old hen, your house is on fire.' When the hen gets back, the witch has all the old hen's chickens and a battle ensues between the old hen and the witch. The last chicken caught will be the next 'witch.'

"Another game we played was 'London Bridge.' This is sung:

London Bridge is falling down, my fair lady
London Bridge is falling down, my fair lady
London Bridge is falling down, my fair lady.

Build it up with silver and gold, my fair lady
Build it up with silver and gold, my fair lady
Build it up with silver and gold, my fair lady.

Hold up the gates as high as the sky (all arms are raised)
And let King George's troops pass by.

Here comes the light to light you to bed,
Here comes the hatchet to chop off your head.

A boy and a girl stand holding hands as high as they can and let them fall on the heads of the couple passing under, and ask, 'Which do want to be, a peach or an apple?' When they announce their decision, they begin to form an apple line and a peach line. After all the couples pass under and have their heads chopped off, and take their stand—either on the apple or peach line—the greatest number of apples or peaches wins the game." [52]

Mr. Drumheller used to go fox hunting. "I'd rather hear the cry of a pack of fox hounds than the sweetest music." He told of many exciting fox hunts, and possum hunts at night.

"My grandmother used to call her hogs by note.

"Miss Blair, when I was a boy in school and thought of my parents, the more I would study. My old uncle wrote these lines in my copybook: 'Command you may, your mind from play, every hour in the day.'"

"How have you managed to keep your teeth?" He laughed and said, "Eating corn bread and black molasses." He is a Democrat, [a] Baptist, and an enthusiastic Odd Fellow. [53]

[Loc.: UVA/FC, box 10, item #1542, 6 pp.]

Orthodox Creed Strictler (Smith) *by Essie W. Smith, rec. 13 March 1939*

There is compelling evidence that Orthodox Creed Strictler is, in fact, Orthodox Creed Smith, the father-in-law of Celestia Wade Butler Smith, otherwise known as the VWP interviewer Essie W. Smith.

In 1742 a colony of "Presbyterian Protestant Dissenters" from Pennsylvania led by John Irvine settled in the Hat Creek area of what was then Brunswick County, but later became Campbell County. Paulett Clark, who came to the county in 1798 to teach school at Hat Creek, stayed with the family of Major John Irvine (son of the above John) and within the year married the major's daughter Mary Ann. Paulett and Mary Ann Clark's family included fraternal twins, Orthodox Creed and Catherine F. W. Clark, each of whom named sons Orthodox Creed. But Catherine married William B. Smith, and it was their son, Orthodox Creed Smith, who was the subject of this life history. It was a "proud and distinguished" patriarch of the Cabell family who disapproved of Creed Smith's courtship and later marriage to his daughter, Mary Winifred. And in 1899, their son Cabell Smith married Essie Wade Butler, the widow of Benjamin Waldo Butler of South Carolina. [54]

Essie Smith changed the surnames or first names of a number of her informants for reasons that were not always apparent. She also changed some other details of Orthodox Creed Smith's life; for example, his mother, Catherine Smith, did not die when he was born. She was still alive in the 1850 and 1860 Campbell County censuses, but his father was absent in 1860 and presumably was dead by then. There are a few other disparities as well. But at least in this case, we can assume that Essie Smith made alterations based on personal family consideration and obligations.

Mr. Strictler is a spare, lean man, of average height and austere demeanor. His intensely black hair, which is thinly sprinkled with white, curls abundantly around a bald spot on top of his head, and grows high on his forehead and back from his temples. His skin is a deep red, rather rough, and under his heavy beard, which he keeps well-trimmed, his neck is very dark and scrawny.

Like the village blacksmith, he goes on Sunday—every Sunday—to the Church. He is a Presbyterian by name and a Presbyterian by nature, as all his father's [people] were, and his given name, incredible as it sounds, is Orthodox Creed. In the churchyard where many of his family are buried, there are no fewer than seven Orthodox Creeds carved on headstones. He is generally known—by the few familiar enough with him to address him by his first name—as Creed, but the Orthodox is always present in their minds. He is considered a very just man, but he believes not only in eternal punishment but present punishment for anything which his own mind designates as sin. Once when he was asked to help rehabilitate a man who was in need as the result of too much dissipation, he said, "No, I cannot help him. I do not desire to balk Providence in His efforts to convict the man of sin."

He rises early in the morning from lifelong habit and everyone on the place, regardless of physical or mental condition, must rise also and have breakfast at seven o'clock, winter and summer. The morning papers are all placed in his room and no one can touch them until he has finished every sheet, no matter what time of the day he completes his slow perusal. He insists that no one bring in the mail except himself and it must be left in the box until he can personally distribute it. His house is very large, with huge rooms and high ceilings, and inadequately furnished. When it was built he bought extravagant mantels and woodwork, but refused to put in a furnace because he preferred an open fire.

[Strictler] was an early associate of R. J. Reynolds, who made that tobacco company famous and amassed a huge fortune, and he remained with the company until the death of Mr. Reynolds. But he could never be persuaded to invest in any of the stock, being a "conscientious objector" to buying stock of any kind. So that while all the men he recommended (and his recommendations were always accepted) grew enormously wealthy, no arguments of Mr. Reynolds could induce [Strictler] to change his mind and he was the only one of the men in that vast company who did not have an almost unlimited income. He was devoted to Mr. Reynolds and was perhaps the most sincere mourner at his large funeral. A fine autographed picture of the tobacco magnate, who left such an enormous fortune to his family, is Mr. Strictler's most valued possession.

When interviewed the old man seemed at first indisposed to talk, but once he began he became apparently interested in his own conversation and said, "I was born in Campbell County, Virginia, and barely raised by a sister much older than myself, as my mother died when I was born. We were a large family and my sister had a busy life taking the place of housekeeper and mother when she was only a girl. She was sixteen when my mother died. We lived on a farm, and I went to the schools there about five months in a year. I was always thin and delicate as I am now. I was born a scrawny baby. I never could eat like other people, and perhaps this habit was a blessing in disguise when I was in a Yankee prison.

"When the War came on my older brothers and all the men in our neighborhood went. One of my brothers was killed and his body was never recovered. I was sixteen the last year of the War, and two young cousins and myself enlisted early in 1865. We were in Coit's Battalion, but I do not remember much about the organization. I do know that I was terribly excited and frightened. We were sent to Petersburg, Virginia, the three of us going together. I did not have many clothes and I gave the few I had to a colored woman in Petersburg to wash for me, my cousins doing the same.

"There was a battle near a place called Cocke's Church. And there one of my cousins and myself were captured and taken to Hart's Island, where we remained in prison for several months. My cousin could not stand the rigors of prison life and when he took dysentery, he soon died and was buried there. I did not suffer so much. Never having been able to eat much, I could save part of my meager fare and sell it to others with better appetites, and procure a few comforts. I do not recall being so badly treated, but I tried not to give the guards any trouble. I did not arrive at home until June after the surrender. When I got there I was tired, filthy, and lousy. My sister called to me to go down to the washpot, which was in the yard, and take a bath. And she would send me some clean clothes and just burn what I had on in the fire under the pot. A negro boy brought me the clean clothes, and you can imagine my surprise when I found they were the ones I had left with the colored woman in Petersburg. The cousin who had not been captured [had] returned to Petersburg and the woman had brought him the clothes. And he had brought them home when he arrived some time ago.

"I stayed on the farm some time, but the work there was very strenuous and I was not strong. So I got a job traveling, and in a few years I met Dick Reynolds and began buying tobacco for him. I was always a good judge of tobacco, and I do not hesitate to say that I helped him get his start by buying the right kind of tobacco for his needs at a reasonable price. He did not have easy sailing in the early days of his business. At one time his entire assets were reduced to ten thousand dollars and he called me in consultation. He decided to invest this entire amount in advertising, which brought tremendous results as the world knows today.

"I had become pretty wild in those days. I had acquired the habit of drinking and, consequently, was in debt and the outlook for my future was not promising. About this time I met one of the most beautiful women I have ever seen. Her father was a very proud and distinguished man and looked with extreme disfavor when I came to pay her marked attention. He soon forbade me to come to the house. I think this helped my suit more than anything he could possibly have done, for she continued to meet me at other places and finally consented to run away with me. We went to North Carolina and were married. Our life was anything but an easy one. I still drank to excess and we had a number of children in rapid succession.

"The children were very delicate and several of them died before they were old enough to gain my deep affection. But one beautiful and loving daughter lived to be seven years old and her death from scarlet fever nearly broke my heart. I resolved from that day never to take another drink and to live as nearly as I could like my father and other members of my family who had been Presbyterians for generations. I have never taken a drink since that time. I joined the church. She [the daughter] had been a fine Christian character and attended Church regularly in spite of her youth. I have given one-tenth of my income to the church and have done all I could to make up to my family for my shortcomings during the time when I was not walking in the narrow way.

"We raised only two children of all our large family, and although both of them are married, there are no grandchildren and I am afraid the name will not survive. There will probably never be another Orthodox Creed, but the young people who have an aversion to unusual names will probably not regret the passing of this one.[55]

"I like our new minister. He is not a young man and he preaches rather long sermons which the younger members of the congregation criticize, but I do not mind. I can hear him, as he talks louder than most preachers. I am beginning to be quite deaf but I sit in the amen corner, which is usually shunned in these days, and I hear nearly all he says. He believes in the old fashioned doctrine of eternal punishment and can paint very lurid pictures of the future life of sinners. But he also tells a lot about the joys of the righteous and there is consolation in that." [56]

[Loc.: VSL/AB, box 179, 5 pp., 1,500 wds.]

Nannie Isabel Webb Price *by Gertrude Blair, 2 June 1939*

The town of New London, where Benjamin Thacker was born in Bedford County, was built on land ceded in the mid-eighteenth century by William Callaway, a forefather of Nancy Callaway Webb—Nancy (Nannie) Isabel Webb's grandmother. The Callaways were "conformists to the Anglican church" and part of that group that formed a middle stream of migration into the area in the 1750s. They "enjoyed a certain prestige" from that alliance, for, as Early noted, "at that time church moved with state; other sects were classed as dissenters and were not accorded equal privileges." Among the latter were the earlier colony of Presbyterians near Hat Creek (in an area of the county that became Campbell County in 1781) and the Quakers who established a meeting site on the south fork of the James River in the late 1750s. [57]

Nancy Callaway's husband, Theodorick F. Webb, was a Baptist minister and successful farmer. He owned "nearly a hundred slaves," according to Nannie Isabel Webb, whose childhood memory was not unexpectedly exaggerated. In fact, he owned eleven slaves in 1830, and these had increased to thirty-seven by 1860. At that time, Webb had a personal estate valued at more than twenty-nine thousand dollars, real estate worth twelve thousand, and significantly, a second wife. Nancy Callaway Webb likely died in 1856 when her daughter Nancy was born, for the next child—born two years later—bears the name of Theodorick's second wife, Julia (Patterson), the widow of Episcopal minister Henry Hobson Wade. Three of Henry and Julia Wade's minor children were living in Webb's household in 1860, including eight-year old Zachary Taylor Wade, the father of VWP interviewer Essie Wade Smith. [58]

Before the war and for sometime afterward, Theodorick Webb's eldest son (Nannie Isabel's father), Tazewell Armstead Webb, continued to farm and operate his gristmill, sawmill, and brandy still. He and his wife, Jemima Adaline (Darnall), and family were listed in the 1860 census in the household next to that of Jemima's brother, Richard F. Darnall, his wife, Susan, and their children, the youngest of whom at the time was Henry Mauze Darnall. The lives of Nannie Isabel Webb and her same-age first cousin Henry M. Darnall exhibit interesting parallels as well as contrasts.

In 1878 Nannie Webb married Edward Hairston Price. Edward's father, Owen Price, and Theodorick Webb seem to have been farmers of comparable scale. But Price died during the war or shortly thereafter and left his widow, Mildred, to tend their own children as well as several others, who were wards of the Prices. When the census was taken in 1880, Edward Price was farming and his father-in-law, Tazewell Webb, was teaching school in Franklin County.

In the meantime Nannie Price's cousin, Henry Mauze Darnall, finished school, worked as a store clerk and superintendent of a tobacco factory in the county, and so began a career in business. In 1881 Darnall married Mary L. Hairston of Martinsville and by mid-decade, they moved to Roanoke, where he worked in banking and insurance for some years. [59]

Edward and Nannie Webb Price quite likely moved to Roanoke County because they already had family members in the area and knew of job possibilities through Henry Darnall. Whatever the case, they were living in Salem, Virginia, where they owned their home free of mortgage and

Edward worked as a foreman on the railroad in 1900. Their older children, who would have been working on the farm or in the home in an earlier time, were moving into various jobs for wages to help support the family. Sons Charles and Luther, then eighteen and twelve years old, were both day laborers; daughter Hattie, fifteen, was a weaver in a textile mill. By 1910, however, fifty-three-year-old Edward was a laborer in a local tannery, where his son Luther also worked as a mechanic. In that same year, Henry Mauze Darnall was appointed commissioner of revenue for the city of Roanoke.[60]

Over the several generations sketched here, some member families made the move from rural farm to urban industry, whereas others did not and remained in Franklin County. The persons in Nannie Webb Price's family were, in many ways, much better prepared to make that transition than most: they were fairly well educated; had family members and friends with good "names" and useful contacts; and were moving from a former base of relative economic affluence. Still, the large-scale social changes set in motion by the Civil War and by later technological developments scattered remnants of families and communities abroad on the land and fostered a new process of social differentiation.[61]

Mrs. Price's father, Tazewell Armstead Webb, was the son of Theodorick Webb of Franklin County, Virginia, who was a large land and slave owner and a widely known Baptist minister. He married Nancy Callaway, whose ancestors were closely identified with old Lunenburg and Bedford Counties. It is said that they came to this section in 1740, and were the first men who cleared land and planted corn on the Otter River. Colonel William and James Callaway were among the original owners of the land on which the western frontier town of New London in Bedford was laid off. At a court held for Bedford County in 1754, William promised fifty acres of land, and fifty acres when patented, to be used for a court house and prison—the land to be situated at the forks of the road near his home.

In 1785, Franklin County was formed from Bedford and Henry Counties and quite a settlement of Callaways was made in the new county, which later on had a post office bearing their name. The name of Webb is legion in Franklin County also. Theodorick was the father of six sons and five daughters. As his sons grew to manhood, he gave each [one] a hundred acre farm cut from his big plantation. In the deed to the one hundred acres to each son, there was a clause restricting the sale of any part of it. Theodorick owned nearly a hundred slaves. According to Mrs. Price, when any of [the slaves] died the funeral was preached right in [her grandfather's] parlor, and he had them buried in his family graveyard.

Mrs. Price's father, Tazewell [Armstead Webb], married Jemima Adeline Darnall; seven children were born to this union. Nannie Isabel (Mrs. Price) was born February 3, 1858. She was the second child, the firstborn being a son whom they named Henry Tazewell.

"My father taught school for fifteen years." "Wasn't he in the War between the States?" "Yes, but he was never in a battle, he served all through the war in hospitals, nursing the sick and wounded. He was in Winchester a long time." "You were so young, you don't remember anything about the War, do you?" "Oh yes I do, while there was no fighting down our way, we children were scared to death for fear the Yankees would come over. The darkies talked so much to us about the Yankees we thought they were some kind of terrible monsters who would rob and plunder and carry little children away on their horses, and leave them in the woods to starve and die. We were mighty poor after the War and the 'niggers' all set free. But they didn't all leave us, Pa was mighty good to his negroes.

"Pa had a gristmill, sawmill, and a big copper still. He had so many apples and peaches we couldn't begin to use them all, so he would make big barrels of apple and peach brandy. He had a huge trough, made from the trunk of a big tree — you have seen the watering troughs made from big trees in the country, I know. Well, the apples and peaches were put in there and mashed to a pulp with a heavy pestle, then the pulp was put in barrels and barely covered with fresh boiling water and left to ferment. Then the juice was racked off and put in the copper still, which was always so clean you could see your face in it. A hot fire was made under it, and [the distilled extract] would run off through a pipe and flow into tubs. *That* was called, 'singling.' Then the pulp was emptied out, the still washed clean again, the juice put back, a big fire kept going, and as the boiling juice passed through the pipe the second time ["doubling"], cold water flowed on the hot pipe condensing the steam." "Wasn't sugar added to the fruit juice at any time in the process of making brandy, Mrs. Price?" "No, only what sugar the fruit contained. Pa never made brandy to sell and he never made what is called 'corn liquor.' We had big apple and peach orchards and he only made brandy for his own use every year: put it in barrels, and set it away, and let it age.

"I must tell you a little story about his brandy. Miss Bettie Price had a private school in the neighborhood. It was a pay school, of course, and I was one of Miss Bettie's favorite pupils. She boarded around with the parents of the children, but she was not boarding with us at that time, however. One morning I decided that I would take some of Pa's brandy to school and give the children a little dram before school opened. So I found a bottle, washed it out nice and clean, and slipped down in the cellar, pulled out the bung, and stood on tiptoe so I could push the bottle in. And after a few minutes when I pulled it up, there wasn't a drop in it. So I pushed my bottle further down, and I heard a gurgling sound. So in a little while I pulled it up and it was full up to the neck. I corked it and wrapped it up. And off to school I went so as to get there before Miss Price, and [I] gave each of my little friends a nip all around. I must have gotten into one of Pappy's barrels of old brandy, for when the teacher arrived the children were getting pretty happy, in fact, quite hilarious. Miss Bettie knew Pappy always made brandy every fall and her eyes were instantly glued to me. I was perfectly innocent of knowing of any wrongdoing, I never saw anybody drunk in my home and saw it passed around any time to friends. I was so small I didn't do any thinking about it one way or the other, I only wanted the children to have some. The grown people seemed to like it so well."

"Did Miss Bettie give you a 'flogging,' Mrs. Price?" "No, but she kept me in for about an hour. She sat there working on some papers, giving me ample time to reflect and repent. My brother Harry always carried my books for me. So that evening when I couldn't go home with him, he went on down the road to an old tobacco barn, climbed out on a ridge pole and kept peeping out to see if I was coming. He wanted to go the *rest* of the way with me and also find out if Miss Bettie whipped me. He said he was afraid to come down when he saw Miss Bettie coming along, but he did. She was surprised to see him there and asked why he hadn't gone home. He told her, 'I was waiting for Nannie.'"

"Well, what did your father say when Miss Bettie told him, did he whip you?" "No, as I think of it now, it must have been all he could do to keep from laughing. I can remember now how Miss Bettie looked; she wore one dress *all winter long*. It was a black worsted, trimmed in red, and she always had on an apron with a bib, and it was as white as snow. Another teacher I had was Miss Julia Turner. She wore the same dress all winter too; it was a blue flannel trimmed in black braid. I'll tell you people were poor after the War, yes sir! They

Arlington, Virginia. June 1943. Dancing the Virginia reel at a bi-weekly Saturday night "open house" dance at Idaho hall, Arlington farms, a residence for women who work for the government for the duration of the war. Photo by Esther Bubley. [LC-USW3-25737-E]

didn't dress anything like they do now. We had a little brown jug and Ma would fill that jug with fresh buttermilk and Aunt Marcia, our faithful old cook (she and her husband, Uncle Patrick, wouldn't leave us after the surrender), would bake pones of cornbread for us to take with the jug of buttermilk for our lunch at school. Yes sir, that is all we would have. Pa went to Rocky Mount and bought two tin cups—one for brother Harry and one for me—to use at school and we passed about our cups, not knowing which was which. So Pa cut a deer on Harry's with his knife and a little house on mine. We often had nothing but ashcakes and cold souse meat for supper. Those ashcakes of Aunt Marcia's with plenty of fresh butter, nothing will ever be as good again as they were.

"There were two old ladies who lived in our neighborhood, they were old maids, Susanna and Ursula Leviss. When a child, I loved to spend the night at their house, chiefly, I think, because their beds were so high. I would have to stand in a chair to get into them big old fat feather beds." "Where was your father's home in Franklin?" "It was not far from Sydnorsville, it was a log house, two stories, and a mighty happy home it was." "You haven't told me who you married, or when." "I married Edward Hairston Price, Christmas week in 1878. I would have been twenty-one come the third of February. We were married at home in the late evening and during the ceremony Pa and Ma both cried and cried. They were willing for me to marry, but they hated to see me leave home. We had a big supper. I'll tell you that night Ma 'put the big pot in the little one' for that supper. The young folks wanted to dance, of course. Everybody danced square dances then, but all our family were strict Baptist and didn't believe in dancing—thought it was the work of the Devil. So the young people arranged to give me a big callithump, or serenade; planned then to rush in later and start up the fiddle and banjo with a dance tune, and everybody start in dancing. So that's how they managed to dance in Pa's house. As soon as they began dancing Pa left and went out and sat in an old house we used for a washroom. They danced all night. I didn't, for I had to go to bed to be in style, you know. So I left them dancing, and they kept it up till break of day, yes sir'ee."

I found Mrs. Price sitting on the front porch on that pleasant June morning. She was occupying one of those old-time split-bottom rocking chairs, dressed in a dark grey print (she would have called it calico). She had a sun bonnet on her head that completely hid her face, and the proverbial gingham apron. Before leaving I asked her to remove her bonnet. Her hair is quite gray, combed straight back and coiled about midway between the crown of her head and the nape of her neck. Her eyes are gray blue, with a kindly amiable expression, nice features, with rather long, instead of round, contour of face. She doesn't approve of girls smoking or the present style of dress, but she thinks the girls are pretty fine to step out and fill so many responsible positions in the business world.[62]

[Loc.: RPL, 6 pp.]

Narrating Women's Experience
"LIVING THE LIFE OF A WOMAN"

I've done the work of a man . . . at the same time I was

living the life of a woman. —Josephine Wright

When Josephine Wright said she had "done the work of a man" and lived "the life of a woman," she was not just speaking figuratively. In her partial accounting, she had built rail fences and palings, taken a partition out of her house, rebuilt furniture and a stairway, and frequently planted corn while carrying a baby on her hip. Even her husband, John, allowed that there "never was a better worker than Josie" and that "her mother before her was a good worker" too. Such statements give rare glimpses into the dynamics of gender operating among certain people in particular times and places. In addition, the experiences Wright and other women recount in these VWP life histories lend support to the contention that "there can be no unified history of women, only a multitude of histories of women as members of specific social groupings, groupings to which men also, usually, belong."[1]

Among the workers in the VWP life history, social-ethnic, and youth studies programs, women outnumbered men almost two to one and contributed all but one of the texts in this chapter. These narratives of women's experience are, in effect, the products of particular social groupings of females. Most often female interviewer and subject were members of the same communities (if not always of the same class or race), and in many instances they shared common experiences or were, in fact, related by kinship or marriage.[2]

Sometimes, distinctions between interviewer, subject, and other persons were collapsed by intermingling these separate voices in a single life history, as in an extraordinary report of spouse abuse submitted by Mary S. Venable in 1940. An anxious neighbor told the VWP worker about the white figure that knocked loudly at the adjoining house in the middle of the night and ordered the young husband within not to beat his wife again. Venable interpreted this incident as a warning from the Ku Klux Klan, which had "ceased to operate in Alleghany *excepting for wife-beating*." And though she had not heard of any such happening in the previous two years, Venable noted that she herself had reported an abusive husband about five years earlier. She was advised to state the case in a letter, sign her name, and send it to the "Klan, address Coving-

Fairfax County, Virginia. January 1940. Three girls at a Grange meeting representing Flora, Ceres, and Pomona.
Photo by Arthur Rothstein. [LC-USF34-29279-D]

Fairfax County, Virginia. January 1940.
Master of the Grange.
Photo by Arthur Rothstein.
[LC-USF34-29287-D]

ton, Va." Within three days after the letter was sent, the "drunken husband changed his attitude"; two weeks later he and his family left the county for Roanoke."[3]

By its actions, the Klan asserted limits on inequitable relations between women and men, as well as assumptions about the nature of some women, particularly white females, who fit the ideal of a "good woman" and thus merited protection.[4] Since judgments about others vary both among individuals and within different social groups defined by various attributes of race, rank, education, or occupation, clearly "some good women are better than others." In the case cited, however, both Venable and the Klan agreed that the "child-wife," who "spent eighteen hours out of every twenty-four caring for five babies" (including triplets) and still suffered a jealous husband, displayed all the virtues of the feminine ideal.[5]

Indeed, as they described other women's lives, most project workers revealed their own subjective criteria defining the ideals of womanhood. For example, Anne Worrell talked with a woman, whose husband of forty-four years worked in the Norfolk & Western railroad shops in Roanoke. She noted the woman's pioneer Scotch-Irish Presbyterian background; the cleanliness of her house; her two hundred cans of food put up the previous summer; her well-tended garden, pigs, and chickens; and her appearance, even down to "the neat darn in her well-worn glove." In summarizing this matron's life, however, Worrell's final approving statement went awry. She wrote, "Since the days of Lot's wife, women like this have been the salt of the earth"—an unfortunate association considering the fate of Lot's wife.[6]

Directly and indirectly, the women interviewed also voiced their personal opinions on the broader issues of social life, education, marriage, divorce, and work, in terms of and relative to conventional gender ideals and roles. Changing mores and attitudes not only produced different forms of behavior but also generated potential for grievous conflict between generations. Thus the eldest daughter of an entrepreneurial family in Alleghany County thought her parents were "mossbacks because they [would] not allow her to go on weekend camp parties without a chaperone." In another example, spinners in rayon plants, female and male alike, had to pay close attention to their hands and nails because a hangnail could snag a reel of fine thread and result in a several-week layoff from work. Although seeming innocuous, such cosmetic constraints could significantly alter family social relations and behavior. So despite one mother's protest that "ironing don't make hangnails," her daughter—the spinner—used the conditions of her work to avoid general household chores, to justify costly manicures, and, less directly, to argue her need for leisurely activities and long car trips on weekends. And a number of speakers remarked further on the connections between cars, major changes in courtship practices, and the "speed age."[7]

Even though the number of females in school in Virginia was increasing in 1930, much of the commentary in these life histories about the value of educating women was still embedded in notions of the essential choice of a woman's life being that between marrying or not marrying. When asked in 1940 about education for females, Margaret Wolfe (who had graduated from high school in 1938) poignantly described the dilemma, "We can't go any further in school and most girls just marry as soon as they get out, so what's the use?" But the double standard in terms of education and gender is even more explicit elsewhere. Lizzie Gibson reported that both she and her husband wanted their son to graduate from high school, but as for their daughter Sue, it didn't "make much difference about her schooling" beyond the grade school level. They did not want Sue to work, but Lizzie guessed she would probably "marry when time [came]."[8]

Norfolk, Virginia. March 1941. The mother of a farm family from North Carolina who have come to Norfolk to get defense jobs. Photo by John Vachon. [LC-USF34-62517-D]

Marriage posed its own problems, however, and female project workers likewise noted and often reported on the affective strains in their subjects' relationships. One Richmond woman worked in a paper mill to support her family after her husband—despondent about his layoff and unemployment—began drinking and drifting from place to place, "lost his mind [and his memory] for awhile," and eventually came home to recover. She apprehensively told the VWP worker, "I guess if I *had* to choose between my husband and my children, I would take my children. I know I can trust them." Another woman described how six years of ministering to a husband stricken with "creeping paralysis" had "just about wore" her out. She candidly declared, "Try as hard as I can, I don't love him like I used to. My love has worn'd out too. . . . But I tends to him all right." Love, loyalty, and sense of duty might ordinarily have survived, but sometimes even those common bonds were victims of mistrust or misfortune aggravated by the depression and hard times.[9]

Now and then, feelings between husbands and wives and other family members were transformed more immediately by specific events, such as the wrenching conflict that followed Anna Watts's abortion and the ethical and gender issues associated with it. She had resorted to abortion twice: once by her own efforts, and once through the clinic at St. Phillip's Hospital in Richmond. Her actions were allegedly provoked by a disintegrating marriage and erratic husband, by the poverty she and her several children already endured, and by fears for her life—reinforced by the stated concerns of doctors.

Under not dissimilar economic conditions but with a strong marriage, Anna's mother-in-law had borne sixteen children, would have welcomed more, and declared, "God gave them all to me." Similar views of children as God given, along with developing sentiments that modern women were refusing to bear children simply because they did not "want to be bothered with 'em," are echoed by others elsewhere in these life histories. Indeed, the conflicts embodied in this case transcend the historical person and situation of Anna Watts in 1941; they remain central to arguments over the issue of abortion as it affects women today.[10]

With regard to another important women's issue, the dissolution of marriage, rural farm women in every region of the country have consistently exhibited a lower divorce rate through time (even into recent decades) than women in urban and nonfarm settings. Reflecting on this pattern, a perplexed Alleghany County farm widow, who lost her husband a month after their fiftieth wedding anniversary, wondered "what causes so many divorces now." But there was no confusion in the mind of a nonfarm woman in Roanoke as to the reasons for rising numbers of divorces.

> Talk about trouble, I've had my share since my children got away from my apron strings. The marriages they have made have caused half of it, too. . . . [One daughter-in-law] works in [an unnamed department] store, making sketches of the merchandise for the papers, and if they starved to death she wouldn't stoop to fix a meal. All he gets, he fixes for himself. Thank goodness, there's no children, she sees to that. I tell you, women nowadays are not fitted for marriage—just dressing and gadding. Yes, I have one son at home that is divorced, and another one up here that ought to be.[11]

This Roanoke mother's remarks clearly blame changing gender roles and attitudes for her sons' marital rifts. And a sign on the window of a South Boston, Virginia, restaurant just before Thanksgiving in 1940 further reflects the change under way—from wives as homemakers and helpmates to women as "pets" and objects of material possession and status.

South Boston, Virginia. March 1940. A sign on a restaurant window during Thanksgiving week. Photo by Marion Post Wolcott. [LC-USF33-30770-M2]

Alexandria (vicinity), Virginia. March 1941. The wife of a torpedo plant worker is talking with her neighbor at the Trailer camp on U.S. highway no. 1. Photo by Martha McMillan. [LC-USF34-14365-D]

Matters of gender and of race, however, are not simply fixed features of biology. These are also culturally defined categories that place different limits on people, especially when combined with other factors, such as occupation. As important elements of class and status distinctions, occupational roles can confound gender definitions of femininity or masculinity and can shape identity as powerfully as can race or ethnicity.

Two examples can serve here: A destitute widow in Alleghany County was appalled by the naïveté of her assumption that "any honest work was no disgrace" after she went to the welfare superintendent in 1938 and was given a job cleaning the courthouse. At first she was glad to have the work, but then she found herself "*classed with the colored people there*" and "hardly noticed or spoke to by anybody else." She was treated as "not white" and was shunned by others of the white community because she occupied a position defined as "colored people's" work.[12] In Nola Thompson's account, her mother Minnie Fowlkes, a widowed black woman with eleven children, "went to the sawmill [in Chesterfield County] to work to keep from starving." In that case, Fowlkes could be degraded or treated as unfeminine and "not woman" because of the normative definition of sawmill work as "man's work."[13]

Domestic service for white families who were perceived to be inferior was demoralizing for other African American women. Placed in such a position by the Mother's Helpers Project, a Petersburg woman stated that "lice would stand on top of the water just like fish scales [when she did the family's washing]. I couldn't complain because I needed the money." Yet she spent her own sorely needed money for sulfur to treat *their* bedding. Later this same woman "carried baskets of dirt, rock, gravel, trees, and dug honeysuckles in the field" for the WPA project at Lee Park, but she was at a loss—comparing the park work's sheer drudgery with the domestic service—as to "which was the best job."[14]

Given the general absence of work relief programs for women and seeing great hardships among them, Ella Agnew, head of the Women's Work Division under the Virginia Emergency Relief Administration, convinced officials to hire women for manual labor creating bird and wildflower sanctuaries, such as Lee Park. She also worked to establish hundreds of sewing rooms, putting the skills of both black and white women to work making clothes and bedding for other needy people, costumes for children's pageants, and at one Richmond site, replicas of Revolutionary War uniforms for National Park Service personnel at Yorktown. But some urgent measures to provide work relief for women, such as Lee Park and similar programs elsewhere, were regrettably marred in practice by discrimination.[15]

The attempts by governmental agencies and individuals such as Ella Agnew to provide work for women, however, were not the only efforts to have unintended consequences. The Virginia Art Goods Studios was an independent enterprise begun by two ladies in Lynchburg to produce hand-embroidered purses. Their business at first depended on the needlework talents of "society girls." But, according to Julia Keesee Carwile's account, it grew from a cottage industry into a sweatshop hiring "unfortunates."[16]

Textile mills in towns such as Front Royal, Harrisonburg, Lynchburg, Roanoke, Covington, and Danville over time provided new occupational opportunities for many former farm families. But moving into town for economic advantage also inevitably brought about important cultural changes in many areas, including gender relations. Migration itself loosened the holds of kin, community, and tradition and exposed young people to other behavior patterns and values. And it simultaneously provided a much larger pool of potential mates, most of whom were essentially strangers insofar as families were concerned.

These new prospects were well understood by a young textile mill spinner, who vowed never to return to the farm and hinted at her social ambitions in the rayon plant. She admitted, "The first fellow that I went with was just a forty-cent-an-hour man. I had just come in from the country, but the fellow I go with now is a room-foreman." Her comment calls to mind the wishful lyric of a textile mill song recorded by Nancy Dixon, who, at the age of eight in 1900, started working in a North Carolina textile mill for eight cents a day.

> Yonder stands that spinning room boss,
>   He looks so fair and stout,
>   I hope he'll marry a factory girl,
>   Before this year goes out.[17]

It was widely held to be true by the speakers in these life histories that a woman's proper destiny was that of matrimony and motherhood. But the elements of social mobility and of defining one's identity as a female in reference to that of a male's rank and earnings in the industrial hierarchy represent a significant transition from the ideals of an earlier class of yeomen.

Mrs. J. L. (Josephine) Wright *by Leila Blanche Bess, 2 June 1939*

At the age of twenty, Josephine Lipes married John L. Wright at Barbour's Creek in Craig County. More than forty years afterward, she recalled how she had first met the visiting Baptist preacher's son and they "got to goin' together . . . just for pastime." She admitted good-humoredly, "I didn't know what I was goin' into." The "pastime" ultimately led "into" a lifetime of hard work, ten children, and a few regrets.

One of Josephine's regrets was that she "never had any chance to do anything better at home" before her marriage. She wanted an education, but her father did not believe in the "foolishness" of studying grammar and geography or of "spending much time in going to school." Although Wright and her contemporary Emily Palmer Stearns had vastly different backgrounds, both women were keenly aware and resentful of the limits imposed on their schooling because of prevailing patriarchal attitudes. Josephine Wright tried to "do a better part by" her children but was disappointed yet again when none of them finished high school.

Josie Wright's life history provides an important counterpoint to that of her husband, John L. Wright, in the following chapter. The two texts show some obvious gender-related differences in content: she focused on her domestic economy, her home, pigs, and garden; he talked about past work experiences, failing health, and his increasing inability to fulfill his role as family provider. But there are also substantial topics of mutual concern and overlapping discussion: they both talk about past struggles, the present circumstances of other family members, and their generally pessimistic views concerning the future and the effects of change.

Josephine, or Josie as she is familiarly known, is small and very straight and rather slender. Her black hair shows no sign of grayness and the dark brown eyes are still bright and young looking. Josie is sixty-six years old, but does more work than either of her daughters. Just how she stands the daily routine of hard labor is beyond the understanding of ordinary human workers.

"I was born in Craig County on Barbour's Creek and lived there on a little farm with my parents until I was married. I was young, only twenty, I didn't know what I was goin' into," she said, laughing heartily.

"I never had any chance to do anything better at home. Papa didn't believe in spending much time in going to school. He thought if we learnt to read, write, and figure a little, that was all we needed. He would never buy me a geography or grammar. He said there was no sense in studying such foolishness. I did want to go to school and study the same books that some of the other scholars had, but he wouldn't hear to it. We had no such chance as my kids have had. There was no high schools anywhere near. I have tried to do a better part by my own youngin's, but they don't seem to care. I never got a single one of mine to finish high school. I thought sure the two youngest ones would go on and finish, but they wouldn't. Fannie quit and went to work at the rayon plant expectin' to make a lot o' money. And what did she do? Nothing, just played around awhile and spent the money as fast as she made it.

"She begged me to let her go and work and said she would send me part of the money. And I did need some help then. It was in the spring and everything was kinda' scarce. You know how 'tis in the springtime when the winter's supply is about run out and nothing has come in yet. So I let her go. Her papa didn't favor it much, but I knowed other girls to go there and make money. And I knowed Fannie could work if she would. She's not too fond of hard work, but she's fast with her fingers and she could make good at that rayon plant if she had stayed long enough. But she got homesick and come back in November. Then between Christmas and New Years she took appendicitis and had to be operated on. She was awful bad off, but got along fine. Next notion she took was to get married. That's usually the way.

"I've raised ten children, seven girls and three boys. They are all livin' but one. One of my girls died last August with T.B. Another one had it and was in the Catawba Sanatorium for a long time. I always believed it was workin' in factories that brought it on her. She worked in the silk mill in Covington when it first started up, and then she went to Richmond and worked in a cigar factory until she was married. She broke herself down so that she was never well after she was married, and after her two children come, she got down with T.B. She's well now though, and does all of her own work.

"I've sure had some time raising my family. If either of my girls had to work and get along like I've had to, they'd think they couldn't do it, but a feller don't know what all he can do, 'til he has to. When I was first married and before, I thought I could get along just like my mama and papa did. They always had plenty to go on and we never had to worry about anything. But I've had a time to make ends meet, and God knows it hain't been because I hain't worked and tried to save and manage so's we would have something. And John has worked hard, too.

"Things ain't now like they used to be nohow, it jus' naturally takes more to live on. Folks used to be content with less and was as happy or happier than they are now. We never had no finery at my home, no lace curtains or linoleum rugs. Mama had a rag carpet on the best floors, and the others had to be scrubbed every Saturday with a broom made out of hickory or white oak splits. Them brooms sure did fetch the dirt up and Mama kep' her kitchen as clean as anybody keeps their'n now with all their rugs and sinks and kitchen cabinets. It's all right to have them conveniences if you can, but I'm jus' sayin' how we used to do, and get along.

"They was eight of us—I was the only girl—but my family purty near turned the other way. I had seven girls and three boys, raised all of 'em. I used to take the baby one and go to the field to help John with the work in the spring. We both had to work hard to get things planted in time. I've carried a baby on my hip and drapped corn a many a day. But when you ketch one o' mine a'doin' anything like that, jus' let me know, will you? They wouldn't no more think of it, than I would think o' startin' to New York today, a'walkin."

She leaned against the fence for a moment in a restful pose, and I noted that she was a very attractive woman and did not look much older than one of her daughters who was visiting there. The big flowered print dress was a late pattern and was neat and clean. She had removed the bright little sunbonnet in order to better wipe the perspiration from her brow, and it was surprising to look at her bright glossy hair, so free from gray streaks or even threads of gray. Her complexion had been coarsened by the sun and wind, and of course, she had used no lotions to protect her skin which had been very clear and smooth.

"I started to tell you how I started out in married life. John and me was married with nothing in God's world to start on. His daddy had twelve children and of course, he had nothing to spare toward helping John. But nobody objected or told us we had better think twice before we married. You may wonder where or how I happened to know John. Well, his daddy was a Baptist preacher, and come once a month to Barbour's Creek to preach at the school house—we didn't have no church there. Well, everybody looked forward to goin' to preachin' and the preacher got to comin' to our house for dinner, and sometimes come to stay all night of a Saturday night. He took a likin' to me, and brought John along with him. So that's how I met him and we got to goin' together. At first, it was just for pastime, but it wasn't long 'til we was a'goin' together regular.

"We lived with my parents for awhile after we was married, then we moved to his father's place. We didn't live in with them. I couldn't stand that, there was too many. After we had three children, we had a chance to rent a farm of over a hundred acres. It had a log house on it, but the house was in a run-down fix, but it had a good fireplace, good floors and walls. There was four rooms, three downstairs, and one up. The two lower rooms was small and I decided to tear out the partition. I done it myself and I liked the room so much better. I rebuilt the stairway too, and made it not so steep. There was a lot of flowers there: old-time roses, lilies, phlox, honeysuckle and hollyhocks. The old people who lived there before we went [there] had planted them. The old man had cleared the land and lived there most of his life. When he died his wife left and went to live with her children. The old place was right purty and I liked it from the first day I saw it. That was when we moved, I had never seen it before.

"We didn't have much to move, brought it all on a one-horse sled. We had one horse and one cow, and our little household stuff, and some canned fruit. I was glad to find a table there, one of the old falling leaf tables. It was a little rickety, but I fixed it up and it served for our dining table until about six years ago. As the family increased, I tore the table up, made a new frame and laid the top crossways using some other boards for a part of it, but used all that was in the table for it was walnut and the legs was turned. So I made a long table and we all had room to eat at one time. I let one of my married sons have the table when a daughter moved away and gave me her table.

"Come in, what's the use of standing here in this hot sun if we are goin' to talk." And with the words, she left the garden work for another time and led the way into the house which was cool and inviting after the intense heat outside. There was a fragrance about the whole place coming from the old-time flowers then in full bloom. There were many box flowers growing too. But it was the old-time cinnamon roses and clove pinks which gave out the sweet fragrance, and brought to memory the gardens of our mothers and grandmothers.

"You see I hain't [got] anything to brag on yet, but I don't owe for any of this stuff." She pointed to a new Singer sewing machine. "This is the last piece I bought and I was glad when I got it paid for. A few dollars a month don't look like it would be so hard to get, but it comes due before you know it and sometimes before I can get it. We have added a few things as the years have come and gone, and I still need so many things—many I never expect to have now.

"But what we need now more than anything else is a house to live in. This one is just about gone as you see. We worked and skimped and saved until we bought this little rough farm, and I thought we would have had a new house long before now but we hain't had the money to begin. John is afraid to start without the money to finish, but if I had my way I'd start and I know I could manage to get a small house built. One thing is certain: if we don't begin we'll never have it, and I've wanted a nice house ever since I went to housekeeping. But it looks now, like I'll never have it," she said disconsolately.

The house is truly about to fall down or so it looks. The foundation has given way and the roof has gone down in the middle, giving it a swaybacked appearance. The porches are roofless and the posts are ready to fall out. The floors are rottening into holes. In one room the floor has sunken until it rests on the damp ground and it is always damp; and in rainy or damp weather it molds and smells badly. "I am glad we have a home though," she said. "And we have paid for it. It is rough and rocky, but there is some good land and as long as we can work we can live all right.

"We don't get any pension. I wouldn't want it if I have to sign away my little home. There ought to be some other way for old people to live after they are wore out with hard work anyhow. There is so much talk about the Old Age pension, Social Security, and this and that, but what does it all amount to after all. We thought the Old Age pension would be a benefit to

A rocky farm in Alleghany County, Virginia. January 1939. Photo by Arthur Rothstein. [LC-USF34-26746-D]

us, but the way it is I don't like it. I'd sooner have what little I have and know it's mine to do as I please with, than to be paid a little sum of money and have nothing of my own. I don't intend to quit work until I have to, so I reckon we will find a way. We always have.

"When the children come so many and so fast some people said, 'What in the world are you going to do? What do you want with such a family and no way to provide for them?' I always told them I was willing to try to take care of jus' as many youngin's as the good Lord saw fit to give me. I hain't no patience with this thing of not raisin' any children. The women don't want to be bothered with 'em. And such women ought to have a dozen to raise." Josie looked serene as she talked about the ten children she had brought into the world, and certainly she looked none the worse from the experience.

"The young people are different now. My girls are no more like I was at their age than if they was no akin to me. I reckon the whole world has changed and in some ways I don't think it is for the better. When I was a girl the courtin' people done then was mostly as we went and come from preachin'. If a girl had a beau she expected to meet him at the church, and he knowed that's where he'd find his sweetheart on Sundays when there was any meetin'. But now, how many girls and their beaus do you see at church? Very few and oftener, none at all. The girl either stays at home and waits till he comes and 'honks' at the gate and goes runnin', or goes to church and hurries home to be there ready when he does come. And they start away in the cars about the time young girls used to know to be at home. Their mothers lay awake at night waiting and listening for the car, imagining all kinds of things that might have happened and too often they do happen.

"I often think of a cousin of ours—one of the sweetest girls I ever saw—that went for a drive one night after preaching, when her father wanted her to stay at home but allowed himself to be persuaded. And when she was brought in a few hours later it wasn't to her home, but to the hospital with her poor back broken. He has never forgiven himself and life has been very sad for them all. The girl lived for four years and for a long time was able to go out in a wheelchair and seemed to be happy. But I know she only pretended to soothe the feelings of her people and her boy friend to whom she was engaged, and that boy was true and loyal to their love as long as she lived. He felt responsible for the accident and has something to regret all the days of his life.

"The girls are no worse than the boys. My girls have not give me as much worry and uneasiness as my three boys. My baby boy is still at home and that boy has nearly run me crazy. He has a car and drives it like nobody's business. Oh, he's so reckless and he drinks too, and when he leaves home I'm in hot water till he gets back. Sometimes he's left to be back at a certain time the same day and don't come for two or three days. I can't sleep a wink. I can almost see the old car smashed up and him a'layin' dead. It's awful to raise children that weary the life out of you when they ought to be a comfort." She sat tense and still for a moment and a tear fell over her tanned cheek. Then with a resolute movement she got to her feet quickly and said, "I'll show you my pigs, I think I got a bargain. I traded twenty-five cans of berries for the three," and she smiled brightly.

"You say you are writing life histories. Mine ain't worth tellin', but if I'd tell it all nobody would believe it for I've done the work of a man and at the same time I was living the life of a woman. I've built rail fences and put up palings and helped to build everything on the place except the barn, and all the time I was raisin' children. When my youngest girl was born there was an awful fire in the woods around here, and I had not a soul with me except my other kids. I waited on myself with the help of my oldest girl. I got along as well as if I had a doctor like everybody has now [but] I think that is as it should be. No woman has any business trying to wait on herself at a time like that.

"I have had a lot of experience as a midwife and our doctor wants me to take out [a] license, but I don't want to. I don't want to have to go at any hour in the night to wait on somebody. I have too much to do at home to try waiting on so many others. My oldest son offered to pay for the license but I refused. No wonder he would want somebody handy all the time: he has twelve living children, and one dead, and his wife is still [in] her thirties.

"My oldest girl has a big family, too. She has nine children. Her husband is a railroader and they get along purty good. None of the others have such big families. They are all married and gone, except the youngest boy. I told you about him. It's jus' me and John now—kinda like it was with us at first—but I don't feel quite so spry as I did then but I hain't no reason to complain. I'm able to work and enjoy what I do, and I'm thankful for it.

"You must step out and look at my garden before you go. It looks fine and I'm proud of it because it means so much to us. And then I'm always proud of having good luck with plants, I love to see things grow.

Her garden is something that anyone might well be proud of. It is a large plot of ground and it is completely filled up with vegetables of all kinds and everything is in a flourishing condition. It looks very prosperous. Indeed the corn crop and oats and grass all look fine, top-notch I should say, only the house shows ruin and decay. "If I only had a house," said Josie, "I would feel like taking a fresh start, but it looks hopeless enough now. But maybe John will start soon. If it was just a good new log house, I would be pleased with it," she said wistfully.

"John jined the Methodist church a long time ago and I went with him. We are neglectin' goin' to preachin' too, but on Sundays we're tired and we don't try hard enough to get ready. We used to go regular. John has been puttin' out some pulp wood—that's how we paid for the place—and he ain't so well, has an awful cough." She was silent then.

"Vote? Yes, my feller, I vote. I never miss an election. We are Republicans and stand by our party too. Everybody ought to vote. We elect the wrong one sometimes, but when we do all we know to do we've done our duty. It is sometimes hard to know who to vote for. Now this year we have several good men out for Sheriff—two have served together as deputies—and they're both good men. One is from our own neighborhood, and is the son of an old neighbor, and a fine man. In such cases it is hard to decide which one would serve best. But I've got my mind made up and will vote that way.

"As I said at first, there ought to be some means provided for all old people so they could live and not feel like paupers. They can't always work. The churches do help a lot, but they are not able to do so much. Then we never know when we might get sick, might be down helpless for a long time. What would become of us? We have spent hundreds of dollars for doctor bills. Why one time John run a thorn in his finger when he was out at work and it turned to blood poison, and just that little thing cost us a hundred dollars. But we was glad he didn't have to have his hand took off. He never would have been much account with only one hand. We've had plenty o' sickness in our family, but have been lucky to have good doctors. Two of the girls had appendicitis, and one of the boys got his foot mashed and had to lay in the hospital for months.

"We work hard most all the year. Of course the hardest work is in the spring when we have to plow and get the ground ready to plant. And then when the crop and the garden come in to be worked it is the best season for peeling pulp wood, so you see we have to keep busy. In the late fall when everything has been gathered in and put away, we have a little rest period. The men like to have a little time off to hunt then, and in the spring, they fish a little. We don't have no regular income. All we have is from the wood, and that depends on how much we can spare time from the farm work to get out and get it hauled.

"I don't study much about balanced diet. I cook what I have and put it on the table and it's always et. We generally have plenty of milk and butter. We always have our own meat—pork I mean—sometimes we kill a beef. And I never fail to have plenty of fruit either fresh or canned.

"How do we spend our evenings? We usually sit and listen to the radio. We both like it and it is a rest, as well as hearing all the news. I like the music too, all kinds. I used to dance and I still like to hear the fast music. My folks was all musical. Every one of my brothers played some kind of instrument and Papa played the fiddle," she related with pride in her voice.

[Loc.: VSL/AB, box 185, 11 pp., 3,500 wds.]

The wife of a successful rehabilitation client in Virginia. Photo by Arthur Rothstein.
[LC-USF34-00697-C]

Margaret Wolfe *by Leila Blanche Bess, 10 July 1940*

Two older brothers such as Arthur and George Wolfe *might* get overlooked among six sisters, but it is doubtful they would be forgotten altogether. So Margaret Wolfe's assertion that "there are no boys in our family and they have made boys of all the girls" recognizes, instead, the dynamic, socially constituted bases of gender roles, which her family modified according to its needs existing at that time.

Margaret's father, Frank Wolfe, was stricken with a degenerative arthritic condition, which required the use of crutches even in July 1940 and which soon after restricted him to a wheelchair. Both brothers, Arthur and George, as well as their three sisters listed in the 1920 census, were by then married or living independent of the family home. Despite the possibility of occasional outside help from them, the major responsibility for farming or of otherwise providing for the family fell upon those who remained at home and were able to do so: in 1940 that was Rose Wolfe and her three youngest girls (who were "made boys of"), including Margaret.

Each of the three older Wolfe sisters before Margaret had, in turn, "worked on the farm before they got work in the mills." In comparing work on the farm with mill work, however, Margaret Wolfe acknowledged the impact and needs of a cash economy. Farm work—whether done by male or by female—did not keep "a check coming in regularly every two weeks" or keep a family "from worrying about the taxes and things that only money can take care of." But working in a textile mill, she concluded, wasn't what it was "cracked up to be" either. Octogenarian Nannie Isabel Webb Price (in the preceding chapter) had thought it "pretty fine" for modern young girls in 1939 "to step out and fill so many responsible positions in the business world." Nonetheless, in 1941, Margaret Wolfe chose marriage and a life of farming over the world of business and mill work.[18]

"I'm so doggoned tired and sleepy I can hardly hold my eyes open. And it will be ten o'clock before I get home and I don't know how long after that until I get to bed and to sleep. Yesterday I didn't sleep over three hours. It was so hot I couldn't sleep. I got up about three in the afternoon and bummed around until time to start back to work. I work at the old silk mill over in town and I have to get there any old way I can. I ride with some of the boys who work at the paper mill. They work different shifts, but I work from eleven to seven all the time. And I'm tellin' you it ain't what it's cracked up to be."[19]

"I go to work with whoever I can and I come back in the mornings with the Potts Creek mail carrier. That's why I don't get home any earlier. If I had a way to drive in home in the mornings as soon as I come off from work, I would be at home before eight o'clock. But the way I have to sit and wait until eight-thirty to leave town, I am plum worn out before I start. I have fallen off until I hardly weigh anything any more. In fact, I'm afraid to get on the scales. I have to come here to the Post Office to meet the carrier and I'm not takin' any chances on missing him, so I always come early. And sometimes it takes them so long to get the mail made up that I almost croak before time to go. I have to sit here on the edge of the porch in the hot sun until he comes; then I go and hop in the car.[20]

"We are only getting three days out of a week now. If there was anybody else to work, I'd be takin' me a vacation right now. But I am the only one workin' at home, I mean, I am the only one workin' away from home.

"Papa isn't able to do anything on the farm. He has rheumatism, has had it for years. If it was not for Mama, we couldn't run the farm at all. She tends to all the stock and to the working of the corn. She asked me the other day if I wanted to go with her to the cornfield, and I asked her where? And she said: 'Margaret Wolfe, is it possible that you don't know which fields are in corn?' I felt real foolish, but I didn't know she had corn over there. I went along and helped her hoe some of it. There are no boys in our family and they have made boys of all the girls. We wear overalls when we work on the farm, and we have a good time riding the horses and looking after the cattle. We range some of the cattle in the mountains, and we go once a week to give them salt and to see that they are all there.

"Here of late a number of cattle have been stolen from the herds in the range. The heads and hides have been found hidden away where they have been butchered, and others disappeared. We think they were loaded on trucks alive and taken to some stock market and sold, or taken away off and butchered. Several people have lost cattle the same way. They have never been able to catch the thieves, but we all have a good idea as to who they are. Since the Government has taken over so much land and has men out watching, it will not be quite so easy for the outlaws to get by with their meanness. The men who stay in the towers can see all over the country and that will help the cattle owners some.[21]

"I have five sisters, three are married. They all worked on the farm before they got work in the mills. My two older sisters graduated from high school, and the third one ran off and got married before she finished. I graduated, but I sometimes wonder if it pays. We can't go any further in school and most girls just marry as soon as they get out, so what's the use? I did think of taking up nursing, but I can't because I never could understand Latin and I would have to know it to train for a nurse. I don't know why, but I didn't like that study and never got along. I guess if I had buckled down and tried hard as I could, I could have made it, but I didn't try very hard.

"When I got out of school I wanted to get a job, and my sister tried to get me on at the

Rayon Plant where she has been working ever since she finished school several years ago. Now talk about pull: some say that is the only way to get a job, have a pull. Well, I thought she could help me, but she couldn't. The manager told her he would like to take me on, but said he was not hiring any girls and didn't know just when he would. Clara said the very next day he sent in several for her to instruct. She was good and mad, but it did no good. You can't talk back to your boss. I told her not to ask him any more, I would get myself a job—pull or no pull. I made up my mind I'd make a pull for myself. They all told me it was wasting my time to try to get a job unless some one helped me. I went to town and to the old silk mill and put in my application. They asked me about my education, how much high school I had had, and talked to me a little while. I went back home and was called to work in two days.

"I have worked there ever since—not all the time—but I have had no other job. When we were laid off for awhile last year, we got part-pay through the Social Security. It is a very good place to work. But it is hard to have to go as I do—with Tom, Dick, and Harry—just any way to get there and then get home so late next day. I do not get the rest that I need and I am not feeling as fit as I would like."

Margaret's home is practically new, newly painted and screened. It is located near the road [and] surrounded by shade trees, many of which are Catalpas and when in bloom, they are beautiful—resembling cherry blossoms—they are so full and so white. The girls have paid for the improvements: the buildings, the fences, and paint and labor. The house is well furnished with modern furniture, radio, and telephone.

"I always have a job when I'm at home, what time I'm awake. We have the telephone switchboard, and every one of our folks will get out of 'tendin' to that thing if they can. I do despise to talk over the 'phone' anyway. Before we took it, I was in school and the switchboard was just above the school house. I had to go there every day at noon and learn how to operate the thing. I would just as soon have taken a beating as to have to go. Mr. Evans would make me do the work. He sat and told me how, and listened to all my talk.

"The thing I've always hated worse than all others, is when the Government man—the one who has charge of all the forestry work—comes in to send messages or talk to some of the men in the fire towers. He sits by and makes me do all the calling, and if he does any talking, he cusses with every word. I never in my life heard a man swear like he does. Sometimes I have a message for him from some of the tower men and once when some one spilled some paint on the floor up at the tower, I never heard such cussin' in all my born days. I tell you I just hate to talk to that man and listen to his cussin'. It's worse than workin' at the mill and getting home late.

"I don't know what I'll do, whether I'll keep on at the mill or not. I would like to get something better if I could. I hardly think I'll get to go to school any more as someone has to help out here, and Dorothy has not finished school yet. Until she gets work or something else opens up, it looks like I would have to stand by the folks at home. Papa is improving some, but has to walk with crutches and as long as he has to do that, he can't work on the farm. We could live by working on the farm, but it is not like a check coming in regularly every two weeks. If we work we are sure of that, and it keeps us from worrying about the taxes and things that only money can take care of."

Margaret is a small attractive brunette, dark complexion, dark brown eyes, and hair. She has an up-to-date permanent and wears good clothes. Her viewpoint is somewhat narrow as to education and marriage, but probably this comes naturally. Her parents were first cousins, about the same age, same education and environment, and same name. They are in comfortable circumstances and really have no need to worry about the future. Their daughters have been thoughtful and helpful. The mother was anxious to give the girls an education, and it has been by her untiring efforts that she got three to finish school. When Margaret said there were no boys in the family, she meant there were none at home. There is one son who is a first-class garage mechanic and has steady work in one of the best garages in Covington.

[Loc.: VSL/AB, box 185, 6 pp., 1,526 wds.]

Lizzie (Sallie Newman) Gibson *by Anne L. Worrell, rec. 14 April 1939*

Six-year-old Susan J. Howell, the future grandmother of Sallie Lou Newman (alias Lizzie Gibson), lived with her parents, Fountain Howell, a thriving farmer, and his wife, Nancy, in the region of Patrick County served by Ararat Post Office in 1860. In time, Susan Howell Newman named her firstborn son (Sallie's father) after her older brother, Elijah Howell. Subsequently Sallie Lou's older brother, the eldest son of Elijah G. Newman and his wife Jettie, was given the family name Howell U. (Eugene) Newman. Census records not only give evidence of residential proximity and patterns of naming that establish family relations, but they also suggest that it was necessarily Sally Newman's great-grandfather, Fountain Howell (*not* a grandfather Howe), who served in the Civil War as the text describes.[22]

When Noah Lee Gibson and Sallie Lou (Lizzie) Newman applied for a marriage license in February 1926, they lived in the same block of Penmar Avenue in southeast Roanoke, a few houses down and across the street from each other. Curiously, given the description of their courtship in the text and their residence at the time, Noah Gibson's occupation was listed on the marriage license as "farmer," not mill worker. But no records have yet been found to indicate either that Noah and Sallie N. Gibson worked otherwise than at the American Viscose plant or that they lived anywhere other than Roanoke after their marriage. In June 1973 Noah Gibson died at age seventy-one; three years later his widow Sallie sold their property at 1623 Stewart Avenue SE for ten dollars "and other good and valuable considerations." The "Dutch Colonial" house that Noah Gibson had dreamed about, built a scale model of, and hoped to actually build for his family someday does not stand at that address today. There is, however, a Dutch Colonial–style house on the corner, just a few houses away from the site of the Gibsons' former home.[23]

The lives of Sallie N. Gibson and her sisters may have been no different, as she purportedly claimed, from those of "hundreds of the other girls that was raised on the farm" and became spinners and weavers in the mills in towns such as Vinton, Roanoke, and Covington. But the lives of these young women as a group *were* markedly different from those of their mothers, as previously observed by Josephine Wright.

Sallie Gibson's mother, Jettie, spun and wove "as pretty as ever you saw," but unlike her daughters—the mill workers—she did so in a setting in Patrick County that included the beauty of flax fields in bloom. And even though flax was "lots of trouble" and Sallie was glad she could "buy [her] linen over the counter," she still "set lots of store" by items that had been woven by hand by her mother. The thread of connection between mothers and daughters, as well as of ambivalence arising out of shifts in cultural meaning and social and economic change, was thus woven into the complex patterns and fabric of individual lives.

Old Rag, in the Shenandoah National Park area, Virginia. October 1935. Mrs. Brown, wife of the former postmaster. Photo by Arthur Rothstein. [LC-USF33-02195-M4]
[The negative for this print was missing in Prints and Photographs Division, Library of Congress. This copy was made from a negative copy of a microfilm positive and has lost some resolution in the process.]

"Tell you the story of my life? Why you sound just like Jo here, beggin' me to tell him about when I was a girl and walked three miles to school in the winter, and always getting my toes and heels frostbit two or three times before the cold weather was over.

"Well, I guess my life's no different from hundreds of the other girls that was raised on the farm, come into town to work in the mills, and ended up by marrying and going to raisin' kids. I was born in Patrick County, right there in the mountains and not so far from Lovers' Leap. That's where they say the Indian sweethearts jumped to their deaths sooner than be parted. The fairy stones come from Patrick, too. But me or my folks never had so much luck there that I'd ever be sorry we all got away.[24]

"My father was a hill farmer. We lived on a piece of land he got from his Pa and it was too rough to grow more than enough to feed us all. Nine of us children and we all got out as soon as we could. The two oldest boys went to the West Virginia mines up the North Fork hollow; and one was killed there when they had the big slide. I have one brother in Illinois working on a farm, and it's a sight to hear him tell how many hogs they raise every year for the Chicago slaughter pens.

"No, Pa and Ma didn't have much education. Right after the War lots of folks didn't. And Ma never learned to read or write, but she could spin and weave as pretty as ever you saw. Even after I was a big girl—and I was the baby of the family—she used to plant her a patch of flax every year. Did you ever see a flax patch in bloom? Well I do say! You sure have missed a mighty fine sight. It grows about waist-high and when it's waving in the wind, all covered with blue flowers just the color of the sky on a hot summer's day, you'd have to go a far piece to find anything half so pretty. Lots of trouble though, flax is, and I'm glad I can buy my linen over the counter. But I set lots of store by some towels and such that Ma wove and give to me when we first set up housekeeping.[25]

"Yes, I left home the week after I was twenty-one and got steady work in the mills right from the start. Noah was already working at the viscose, and him and me got to courting right away. I wanted to wait awhile to get married, but evenings got mighty lonely and we thought I could keep right on with my job after we got hitched. You know how that was. Pretty soon my first boy was on his way and I had to quit.

"He was a pretty little fellow and lived to be three years old. When Jo here was just past his first year he [the oldest child] took pneumonia and died almost overnight, you might say. That most killed Noah, and me too. He was such a cute little tyke and crazy about his mom and pop. The next year I had a stillborn little girl, and the third little boy died with diphtheria the year Sue was born. That one was the spit image of Noah. Just seems like I loved all my babies too good and the good Lord took 'em away.

"Yes, everybody says Sue looks like me. A great big girl she is for three years, but I used to be big and strong too. I didn't need no powder or coloring for my face either. And Noah used to tease me about my blushing when he was coming to see me. I've got skinny and sallow in late years and don't feel so good anymore. Ma enjoyed her health until she was past seventy, but seems like I've got sickly and all run to skin and bones.

"You want to hear more about my folks? Well, let's see. My granddad Howe fought in the War four years. And when he got home he didn't have anything to plow his land with but one old ox, and no seeds, or nothing else much. He lived to be eighty-nine years old and used to say he was of fightin' stock. He had three boys and divided his land three ways, deeding them all a little piece to farm. I have two sisters in Roanoke, and one here in Vinton. They work in the mills, except Kate, the oldest. She is around fifty now and has two girls and a boy working. And they want she should take a rest, though she is a fast weaver yet.[26]

"Not much I can tell you about Noah's folks, except they are country folks same as mine. He was born on a farm in Bedford County, and his Pa is still living out there near Thaxton. He has a right smart bit of land, and the oldest boy stays on there and tends it. The children love to go out there in the summer and wade in the branch and pick blackberries. I like that, too, if the briars wa'n't so mean to stick a body.[27]

"Noah got more schooling than I did. I went to a two-room school and didn't get through the seventh grade. But Noah had one year of high school. He's an awful smart boy and always was. And big-hearted, so's we'll never have anything for he'll give it all away faster than he can make it—always helping some of his folks or mine one. But land sakes, it's better, I say, to be too open-handed than tight-fisted any day. And I never could abide a stingy person.

"Well, what you know! Talked all this time and never told you what kind of work my man does. He works in the engineering department at Viscose. It's mighty dirty work but he has daylight [day shift], the pay is good, and Viscose is always grand to them as works there. There's not a lazy bone in Noah's body, even if I—as shouldn't—says so. And even after his day's work is done, he is always pottering around here doin' something.

"We have a garden on our lot we own in the next square, and he already has that planted. Spaded it up his'self. And did all the planting with Jo here to drop the beans as he put in the corn. For years we have planned to get us a little home on that lot, but seems like something always comes along to get our nest egg. We rent this house, and it's convenient and all we need, I guess. We have a good old Ford, and my washing machine and refrigerator are both good as new. Christmas we got us a new Philco radio and it's a sight how we all enjoy that, even the baby.

"You're asking me something now when you ask what we plan for the kids. I do know that I want Jo to get through high school. And then I guess he will want to go with Viscose. Noah and me would both like that. As for Sue, well it don't make much difference about her schooling just so she gets through the grades. Guess she will marry when time comes and we don't aim to let her work if we can help it. Noah always says just so they grow up decent and honest is the main thing.

"Amusements, you say? Well, we go to the pictures once in a long time. And I visit some with the neighbors and keep Noah company after the children are asleep. We are still plannin' and hopin' to build us a house someday. And we used to talk about that a heap, you know: how we would set out the bushes, and have some fruit trees, and a whole lot of chickens fenced off from the garden. He used to argue me down about the color to paint—me being all for a dark color that wouldn't show smoke so quick and him all set for a pure white with dark green blinds at all the windows.

"Get off my lap, Sue, and let's show the lady the little house that your pop built. Watch the step and don't let the baby put her sticky hands on your coat. There it is. Noah calls it a Dutch Colonial house, if you know what that means. He built it right to a scale and it's a mite over four feet tall. All the little windows are puttied in like real ones, and the outside blinds and all the doors are on real little hinges. Noah built on it—off and on—for over a year, and the children played with it until they got over liking to open and shut all the dormer windows.

"How come I took it for a chicken house? Well, the old hen dragged the little chickens all over the place in the wet, so's Noah just built this little paling fence around the house and put them inside. It's nice and dry in the house, but land [abridged "land's" or "lord's sake"?] it ought to be, with the best tin roofing money could buy and the real little gutters all soldered into place. Yes, the old hen can step over the fence when she feels called to, but not one of the little ones can follow her—without Sue gets to fooling with them, lifting them in and out, or opens the little gate, and forgets to shut it again.

"I hated [it] someway, though, when Noah put the old hen in [the house]. Makes me feel like he don't feel like we'll ever get our Dutch house started. He laughs and says it's too good a house to go to waste. But just the same I'd soon he had left it empty. Already the good white paint is getting dirty and the floor inside will never be fit to be seen after them filthy things feed awhile longer. Shoo, you hateful old hen! I know she is the stubbornest old thing in the world, climbing up on Noah's nice little back porch. I always plan to plant me a wisteria vine over the back porch if we ever get the place." [28]

[Loc.: VSL/AB, box 182, 6 pp., 2,030 wds.]

"The House on the Farm Owned and Operated by a Woman": A Case Study in Pictures *by John Collier, August 1941*

The woman depicted in this series of photographs is Miss Mary McKim Crane Jr., who purchased a farm of twenty-seven and one-half acres near Haymarket, Virginia, on 23 October 1940 and immediately sold a half interest in it to Miss Marjorie Lee McLeod. Successful or not, Crane and McLeod sold the farm on 11 December 1944, so the enterprise was relatively short lived. That this "farm owned and operated by a woman" was deemed worthy of documenting suggests that such a circumstance was, at the very least, considered to be unusual, whether it was in fact or not. Moreover, out of all the Virginia RA/FSA and WPA photographs of farm scenes, the one here of a woman with a tractor is singular in its display of modern mechanization on a Virginia farm. This further suggests that both conditions were of interest because they were, in effect, atypical.[29]

Haymarket (vicinity), Virginia. August 1941. The owner and operator of a chicken farm driving a tractor. Photo by John Collier. [LC-USF34-80527-D]

Haymarket (vicinity), Virginia. August 1941. The house on the farm owned and operated by a woman. Photo by John Collier. [LC-USF34-80518-D]

Haymarket (vicinity), Virginia. August 1941. Feeding chickens on a farm. Photo by John Collier. [LC-USF34-80531-D]

Haymarket (vicinity), Virginia. August 1941. An old farm house on the property of a woman who owns and operates a chicken farm. Photo by John Collier. [LC-USF34-80513-D]

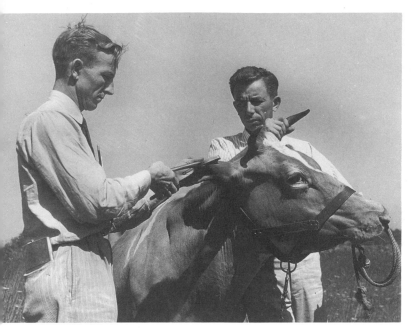

Haymarket (vicinity), Virginia. August 1941. A Department of agriculture veterinarian stapling identification tags on a cow's ears after conducting a disease test. Photo by John Collier. [LC-USF34-80539-D]

Haymarket (vicinity), Virginia. August 1941. Woman who owns and operates a chicken farm holding a calf. Photo by John Collier. [LC-USF34-80538-D]

Haymarket (vicinity), Virginia. August 1941. Creosoting the floor of a prefabricated metal hen house on a chicken farm owned and operated by a woman. Photo by John Collier. [LC-USF34-80505-D]

Haymarket (vicinity), Virginia. August 1941. The owner and operator of a chicken farm. Photo by John Collier. [LC-USF34-80512-D]

Letitia Jane Lumpkins *by Essie W. Smith, 16 May 1940*

Letitia Jane Lumpkins, or "Tishie," got her name from both her grandmother and her husband Sam's grandmother, who were one and the same person: a Letitia, born in the mid- to late 1850s, who married their grandfather, James Lumpkins. By 1900, this Letitia was a widow with six surviving children—out of the nine she had borne. Among these were Sam's father, John; his younger brother, Obie, the father of Tishie; and their sister Sallie, the aunt who took in Letitia Jane and her siblings after their mother Jennie died.[30]

When VWP worker Essie Smith spoke of a noted cook known in the area as "Aunt Viney," Letitia Jane responded that Viney was her grandmother. Viney Boothe was, in truth, the maternal grandmother of Tishie's husband, Sam, and so far as is known, Tishie's grandmother by affinity only, not blood. This distinction seems to have mattered little insofar as the stated kinship to Viney was concerned. Of far more consequence, however, Tishie's relationship with Viney (and possibly with her own maternal grandmother, Eliza Lumpkin, who, though not mentioned in the text, was herself a cook of some renown) provided other vital meanings and models. She learned, "Anybody that does something real well, I don't care what it is, gets a name for theirselves and gets remembered, too." And in spite of her former troubles, Letitia Jane aspired to have a "good name," just like her Aunt Sally and her grandmothers. [31]

A small, very black man came rushing in the back door of the physician's home, a terrible stream of blood gushing from a gaping wound in his throat. The doctor was not well and was lying on the bed when he heard the hoarse scream. His wife happened to be in the kitchen to witness the gory sight as blood flew copiously in every direction. One bound and the doctor had seized the severed jugular vein in capable, experienced hands and held it with grim zest, while his wife telephoned another physician who lived near and was fortunately at home. Together the two men who had spent years in preparation for just such emergencies worked swiftly and expertly to save the worthless life of a trifling character. The woman who witnessed the near tragedy and did her part to avert it, marvels each time she sees the man pass her home in full vigor. She cannot forget the spurts of blood, and the hoarse cries for help which she had thought would be so futile. "My wife, she got mad and cut my throat with a pocket knife," he managed to mutter.[32]

Letitia, or Tishie, as she is called, is a dark brown girl about twenty-three years old. She is slender and capable with small, quick, glancing black eyes, hair combed in a pompadour in a weak effort to straighten its naps, and a broad purplish mouth which almost cuts her face in two. She conceals her white teeth instead of exhibiting them as most of her race do with such telling effect.

She has a wide, flat nose and high cheek bones and a head which sits with splendid poise on her straight, slim shoulders. She moves with quick, brisk strides, and accomplishes a surprising amount of work in a quiet, unostentatious way. As she told her story she was industriously waxing the floor and dusting the room, and she did not pause or look up, even at the most vital parts of the recital.

"I wuz four years old when my mother died. My father was allers a cripple on account of scrofula and he never could take no care of us, so we went to live with his sister. There was three of us: my older brother, and sister, and me. She (the aunt) had a whole passel of children of her own and it was pretty hard on her to have us, too. So after a year or two we went back to live with our daddy. We stayed with him awhile, and we got awful thin and hungry cause he never was no hand for steady work, even if he had been able to stand it. Then my mother's sister saw how it was, and she come and got us. She didn't have no children of her own, but she had done raised two or three other famblys. How she raised and fed all them children, I never will know, cause her husband drank up most he made. And she had to work out for about every mouthful they all eat. I stayed there until I was fourteen and then I married my cousin. He was a slim black fellow 'bout nineteen and didn't have no more sense than I did.[33]

"He never had done no work then and he ain't never done none since. I allers would work. I never could a'bear to hold my hands. I stayed in a restaurant a long time. I liked it there and they looked like they liked me. I used to give Sam money sometimes, but he mostly spent every cent he could lay his hands on for dram. He drove the car some for the doctor, but he never did get nothing out of that but fun and whiskey. But finally he did get his life saved by that same doctor.

"No'm, I never did have no children, so I wasn't bothered none in my work. But I never did save nothing. Look like my wages went faster than I could get 'em to save my life.

"Well, we had been going long right well, just sorter living like. I rented a room and paid the rent. My pa had done married again. And now he had a stroke and he ain't got over it. The doctor and everyone said he was bound to die when he got the third stroke, but he is alive yet and getting some better. He gets five dollars a month from relief and some food stuff, and his second wife she looks after him.

"Then Sam, he took a notion to go fooling round with a frisky little gal that worked out in the same restaurant I did. She wa'n't no account and I didn't like no such doings. He finally got so bad and mean that one night I got so mad, I upped and cut him with a pocket knife I had with me. It scared me nearly to death when I saw how he was bleeding. And then he run up to the doctors that lived near and got fixed up, and they said I done most killed him. They arrested me that night and put me in jail. But the next day my boss that I worked for got me bonded out. And Sam got well and didn't make no complaint and they never did do nothing more about it. Then I lost my job at the restaurant cause they said it wa'n't safe to have me around, though goodness knows, I wa'n't go'n' ter do nothing to none of them.

"I had done gone back to live at my daddy's and he wouldn't let Sam come on the place. So we done separated, but we ain't got no divorce. I missed my work and didn't do nothing for a good while. But now I am getting on all right. I been cooking for Miss Lucy about six months and we get on fine. All the fambly is good to me. I has to work right hard, cleaning up and the like, besides cooking and things like that.

"Yes'm, I takes a dram sometimes at night. I sorter got the habit from Sam, seeing he liked it so well. And it seemed to help him so much. I goes to the colored dances sometimes, but when they begins to get rowdy I allers tries to get away. I ain't been to the moving pictures in a long time. I likes them all right, specially the love pictures. But I don't want to get the habit of going, it costs too much money. I likes to smoke cigarettes, too. But they costs and I don't have many, except them that is give to me.

"Yessum, Aunt Viney you talking about was my grandmother. She had 'leven children, and was a powerful smart colored woman, and cooked for lots of the quality folks around here. She sure was a good cook and some of her children was good cooks, too. I just hope I can be as good some of these days and have folks talk about me like they does about her.

Anybody that does something real well, I don't care what it is, gets a name for theirselves and gets remembered, too, even after they is dead. My Aunt Sally that raised all them children, she has got a good name, too. And ev'rybody says how fine it was of her to take them all in and feed them. I know I never could have done that. I never was much of a hand for children nohow. And maybe the Lord knowed that [and that's] the reason he never give me none."

[Loc.: VSL/AB, box 179, 4 pp.]

Mrs. Susie Young Smith *by Sarah W. Moore, no interview date given*

Susie Young Smith did not know for sure whether her parents were English or Irish, only that they had "come from some'ers over there." But in 1910 the Portsmouth census indicated that her father, Robert H. Young, a fifty-two-year-old machinist in the railroad shop, and her mother, Mary J. Young, aged forty-five, were both natives of London, England. The couple's two older sons, Robert and Richard, were listed in 1900 as naturalized citizens, born in England; however, in 1910 they were both indicated as having been born in New Jersey. Like their father, the brothers also worked for the railroad, as a boilermaker and machinist, respectively. Sixteen-year-old, Virginia-born Susan Young was a machine worker in 1910 — presumably at Parker's Hosiery Mill. These persons and four other children at home composed the Young household at the time.

The VWP text gave no information regarding either the name of Susie Young Smith's husband or the date of their marriage, but it did mention the date of his death as 6 June 1928. An article in the *Portsmouth Star* for Sunday, 10 June 1928, offered the headline "Death Takes Victim of Typhoid" and reported that "Theodore A. Smith, . . . died Friday night [8 June] at a local hospital at 7:30 o'clock after an illness of a week. . . . The five children in the family also have typhoid and are thought to be seriously affected with the disease." An obituary from the day before added that Smith was a "native of Portsmouth" and had been "employed at the Navy Yard as a machinist." He was survived by his father, Theodore J. Smith; his widow, Mrs. Susan Smith; five children; and four brothers and two sisters. He was a member of St. Paul's Catholic Church and St. Paul's Council, Knights of Columbus.[34]

Mrs. Smith is forty-five years old, has a very pleasant face, large blue eyes, light brown hair and would be a very attractive woman if she were not so fat. [She] weighs at least 200 or 225 pounds and is as neat in appearance as one of such dimensions could be.

She was born in Newport News, Virginia but has lived in Portsmouth for forty-one years, her parents having come here to live when she was four years old. She is not sure whether her parents were English or Irish, but thinks they were English. "I know that I've heard my mother say that they come from some'ers over there, but I ain't sure which.

"My mother was Catholic and raised up her children in the Catholic faith. My father was non-Catholic and they used to have some awful arguments over that, but Papa turned to the Catholic faith before he died. He didn't join no church but I know he believed Catholic, so I had him buried accordin' to my faith. He lived here with me a few years after my mother died. And he was the most particularist person I ever saw, so clean and all.

"I never went no higher than the fourth grade in school. I stopped school when I was fourteen years old and went to work at Parker's Hosiery Mill. I had to work and get my own clothes and help Mama out. Papa, he was a drinking man, and I had to work. I was a'working

Portsmouth, Virginia. March 1941. The mother and child of a destitute family of five who are living in one room at the Helping hand mission. Photo by John Vachon. [LC-USF34-62614-D]

there when I was just twelve years old—in vacation time—had to stand on a crate to reach the work. You see, there wa'n't no child labor law then. I earned $4 to $5 per week.

"Then after I was married, we had to struggle to get along. But my husband was one good man, and he *did* love his children. They could do just anything in this world to him. We were just as *pore* as anybody could be almost, before he died. But, woman, if I haven't been through something these ten years since he died—or is it eleven? Yes, I think it's eleven. It was the summer of 1928.

"My boy was almost sixteen years old. He was working for Mis' Sykes around there on Sixth Avenue. You know Mis' Sykes that run the little store? Well, the child got so he didn't want nothing to eat and he'd have crying spells. I took him to a doctor, but he said he didn't

Portsmouth, Virginia. March 1941. Singing hymns at the evening service of the Helping hand mission. Photo by John Vachon.
[LC-USF34-62515-D]

think nothing much ailed him. So it run like that till May. And he took a fever and then the four girls, they took a fever. And at first the doctor thought maybe they were a'getting scarlet fever. But after a few days he said to me, he said, 'Mis' Smith, I believe these children has got typhoid fever.' So he give them a blood test and they did have typhoid fever, all five of 'um, mind you. Melvin was sixteen, then there was Elsie a'most fourteen, and Mildred twelve. Harriet here was nine and Mary Catherine, the baby child, was a'most six.

"I had been sick all of the year myself, had kidney trouble, and a specialist in Norfolk treating me all of the time. But I nursed them day and night until my husband took sick. When his family heard that he had went down with it, they put together and hired Mis' Miller, a nurse, to take care of them at night and so that I could rest. And then I nursed them in daytime. There my husband had been a'going to the Navy Yard to work everyday when he was sick enough to be in bed.

"Well, he didn't last long. One morning he asked the nurse to call me and when I got upstairs he says, 'Mama,' he says, 'I'm so sick. Oh! My stomach hurts so bad and I hurt all over. Oh! I'm so sick.' We called the Dr. and when he come he says, 'I think we'd better take him to the hospital.' That was the pitifulest sight, five children and my husband, all so sick in two rooms.

"They carried him to the hospital that morning and he died that night. I didn't know he was so sick, and the Dr. didn't tell me that he was dying when they took him to the hospital. But he said he did it to keep the children from seeing him die. I've got a little piece I cut out of the paper about him. It says 'Father gives life to save children.'

"They were too sick to be told of his death. He had been dead almost three months before the Dr. thought they should be told. My boy would say to me, he says, 'Mama, have you been to see Papa today?' And I had to pretend that I was going at night after the nurse come. And when they asked how he was, I'd say he's not much better. I don't know how I ever went through that summer. My boy's birthday was June 23rd. (And my husband had promised him a bicycle for his birthday, but he died June 6th.) But the day before his birthday—after he thought I had been to the hospital to see his daddy—he says, 'Mama, did Papa say anything about my bicycle?' I says, 'No, son, your daddy's too sick now to think about that.' And he would say sometimes, 'Mama, how will we ever pay all that hospital bill?' And I had to smile, for it would never do to let him know that we didn't have *no* way to pay anything.

"They all pulled through. And when they begun to get stronger we knew they would have to be told about it. But how was I ever to tell them? Finally, I sent for my priest and asked him if he would tell them for me. And he agreed to do it, but didn't like the job."

There was some insurance and Mrs. Smith very wisely paid off the indebtedness on the home, which they were buying when Mr. Smith died. "If I hadn't, we wouldn't have a roof over our heads today." They have had a hard time of it and seem to be having it hard yet. The children are all grown but unable to get work.

When the boy was strong enough to work he got in [the] Navy Yard as messenger, salary $13.00 per week, and has been promoted to junior clerk, $22.00 per week. And Elsie, the oldest girl, worked for awhile in a ten-cent store [for] $8.00 per week. But [she] married about five years ago and is back home now with her three children and no support. The other girls get a few day's work occasionally, but don't seem to be able to get anything permanent.

Mrs. Smith tried selling soup and doughnuts but realized very little from that. She also worked for awhile at the Hosiery Mill but "I am so heavy on my feet and suffer so much with my kidneys I just couldn't hold out at that." Her brother-in-law helps her out some, and people give the girls clothes and that helps a lot.

Elsie and Harriet are very attractive girls. The other one, Mildred, is not as attractive or intelligent looking as the other two. They were all neatly dressed: Elsie and Mildred in sweaters and skirts; Harriet, in becoming black and white checked gingham dress.

The little grandchildren are all pretty, especially the oldest, a girl of five years. She has beautiful light curly hair, very sad hazel eyes, and although she was dressed in a dark blue coverall playsuit, she was a perfect picture. Sandra, the next, is three years old, and Dickie, fifteen months. The home is in a very nice section but sadly in need of repairs. It had been painted, no doubt, when first built, but very little of that is visible now. Some window lights are out and walls have naked places where paint has cracked off. Mrs. Smith says they have a bathtub but that it is out of order.

The living room is a large square room with a hot blast coal heater (but very little heat), a daybed over which was a faded cretonne cover, Singer sewing [machine] above which hung an oval-shaped mirror, one rocking chair, and several dining chairs (all oak finish), an oak buffet, and baby's playpen. One or two inexpensive pictures hung on the walls, and [the] floor was covered with blue and white linoleum, all very much worn.

Mrs. Smith says, "Some folks tells me they don't see how I've ever been able to smile after so much trouble but I says, Heck, you don't get a dern thing for crying."[35]

[Loc.: VSL/AB, box 183, 5 pp.]

Mrs. Nola (Geneva Fowlkes) Thompson *by Susie R. C. Byrd, rec. 24 July 1939*

Nola Thompson was, in fact, born Mary Geneva Fowlkes, about 1904, in Chester, Virginia. The key in this case to a pseudonymous given name and the lack of a maiden name was provided by a Hopewell City marriage record for 12 May 1930, which linked Mack Thompson, a native of Asheville, North Carolina, to Geneva Fowlkes and named her parents, Thomas and Minnie Lee Fowlkes (also variously Folkes, Foulkes, Fulkse, or Fultz). The search for Thomas and Minnie Fowlkes and their family in census records and city directories slowly built a case but also brought a sudden realization: Geneva's mother was the same Minnie Folkes whose ex-slave interview (also by Susie R. C. Byrd) was referenced in *The Negro in Virginia* and included in *Weevils in the Wheat.*[36]

These accounts, taken together, give witness to the adaptive strengths of female kin networks both for mutual support and for maintaining families in the face of poverty, misfortune, and unrelenting work. In addition, they trace fragments of the struggles of three generations of women from plantation slavery to urban tobacco factory.

As a child, Geneva Fowlkes Thompson worked with tobacco in the fields; as an adult, she was employed in the factories of the British American Tobacco Company in Philadelphia and in Petersburg. In the latter city, there were 927 African American women working in cigar and tobacco factories in 1930, and Thompson was one of that number. Nine years later, she was no longer able to work because of her health; still, Geneva Thompson vowed to Susie Byrd that she "liked to work in the factory and fool with tobacco better than eating."[37]

The 1937 city directory for Petersburg listed the then widowed Geneva Thompson, tobacco worker, at 12 East Byrne Street (where she lived also when Byrd talked with her in 1939), but that is the last trace of her found in such documents. On the other hand, her mother Minnie Foulkes was indicated as occupying the rear of the house at 12 East Byrne in 1941, but Geneva Thompson had been replaced up front by a David Moore—relationship unknown.[38]

"There were eleven of us children raised in Chesterfield County. Lou, Rose, Sarah, Jim, and John are my older sisters and brothers; then come me, Henry, Hattie, Skinny, Retta, and the baby boy, Sammy. Mother lost four of her children in infancy; glad to say that the rest of us are still living, all scattered in different cities.[39]

"I went to school in Chesterfield County for only six months. I walked five miles to school with my tin pail with my lunch in it, holding [it] in one hand and my books in the other. Some of my brothers and sisters didn't go to school as long as I did, so you see none of us had much learning. We might have gotten more if our father lived. I always said if I had children when I grew up, I would try to let them go to school for this reason: by knowing things and how to do things makes it easier for you to get a job and live a good life in the world.

"After our father died, Mother went to the sawmill to work to keep us from starving. We had nothing: lived in a two-room house, all sleeping in one bed that could, while the other children slept on the floor. Our clothing was scant, and you know that we must have been

Newport News, Virginia. November 1937. A negro woman carrying groceries on her head. Photo by John Vachon.
[LC-USF33-01011-M2]

hungry most of the time. We only had to live on the small salary that Mother earned at the sawmill.[40]

"When I was seven years old, Mother sent me to stay with my oldest married sister, Lou. After being with her two months, I went out working in the tobacco field. Sister gave me one meal a day and a place to stay. She taught me how to sow the tobacco seed, plant slips and how to cure tobacco. We would go in the field at five o'clock in the morning, and would work until it was so dark that you couldn't see your hand before you.

"All this was done when I was seven years old. I stayed with sister until the year was out and the tobacco sold. She gave me a load of prunings after the tobacco was cured for my pay. I sat up keeping fire curing this tobacco night and day; when sold, it brought $800.

"Sister and my brother-in-law decided to move from Chesterfield and go to Disputanta, Virginia [Prince George County], because Nat got a job firing at a sawmill making a salary of $10.00 per week, supporting five in the family. When living in Disputanta, my sister would [not] send me to school but hired me out to work in a peanut field for $.50 per day. After work, I had to come home, cook supper, and house clean.

"After staying here awhile, we moved to Wakefield [Sussex County] following the sawmill man who employed Nat. Here we were given, free-of-rent, a four-room house. Nat sends to his sister and gets his son, Melba, by his first wife. Our family now has six children: Pearl, Becca, Buba, Ella Mae, Mel, and me. Mel is hired out for waterboy on a farm for $1.00 per week. While here I kept the family clean.

"In the meantime, [I] worked at the white folk's house minding Mrs. Allington's baby. Mrs. Allington paid me $1.00 per week when I first went to work, but soon started paying me $5.00 per week. I worked here a long time, saved what I could, and as soon as I met Charles Hardy, courted a piece. And I ran away from home, got married when I was sixteen years old. We had one child, Rosalia, and lived with Katy Green, renting one room for one year. Charles died, and I butted around here and there with my child, working [and] supporting the two of us.

"[In] 1930 I married Mac Thompson. He worked in Hopewell, Virginia [Prince George County] at the gas conduction plant as a janitor. We rented a four-room house—438 Sycamore Street, in Newtown, Hopewell—paying $3.00 per week. I had a little living room suit of furniture that I bought secondhand, paid $49.00 for it on installment plan. Payments were $1.00 per week because I was buying a dining room set too.

"When Mac was working in Hopewell, I worked in Petersburg for British American tobacco factory making $15 and $16 per week. A number of us, who worked together at the same table, paid John King $1.50 per week to take us to and from work. We left home every morning around six o'clock. If the factory gate closed on you at seven o'clock you would lose a day's work. We all knew this and would be standing on the corner waiting for John to pick us up. During the whole three years, rain or shine, we were late only once. The 'fliver' had engine trouble.

"The factory closed down the third year that I worked. I went to Philadelphia to work. I was fortunate in securing work with a branch of the British American tobacco factory. I sent money home to my mother to care for my baby. While working in Philadelphia in the factory I took sick. Mother and Mac persuaded me to come home; I did. All the few pennies that I had been saving to help Mac buy a home went for medicine and the doctor's bill.

"After I got well from under the doctor, I persuaded Mac to move to Petersburg from Hopewell. This he did. I grew restless and wanted to go back to work. I was reemployed the very first day that I went to the factory asking for a job. Mac lost his job while I was sick. He made enough cleaning yards to pay house rent.

"The first three-room house we rented when we decided to live in Petersburg was down in Smoky Hollow. This settlement is east of Wythe Street down in a bottom. Upon the hill surrounding, we find several factories (peanut, tobacco, cleaners and dye plant), dairy plants, with other industrial plants. The wind carries the smoke from the chimneys of these plants into the settlement. So I imagine that's why the place is called Smoky Hollow. It's an all-Negro settlement.

"This house needed repairs and was in a bad condition. We took it because we couldn't do no better. The location was a long distance from my work. The rent was only $1.00 per week. The house furnishings were just enough to make out with: a double bed, several chairs, a cooking stove, and a cot for the child.

"The second week that I got my pay, Mac got on in the factory too. The following week we were fortunate enough to move from Smoky Hollow to 12 East Byrne Street, near my mother and closer to work.

"This house is one side of a double tenement. I don't care for double tenement houses for several reasons. One is you can lay in your bed and hear clearly a conversation in your neighbor's house. Secondly, often very undesirable and careless neighbors will move next to you. Sometimes you will plant flowers beautifying your home, [but] the other fellow will neglect [his part].

"We have been living here for six years. Mac died the third year after moving here. I continued my job in the factory. I liked to work in the factory and fool with tobacco better than eating. I was considered a swift worker. Anything you like, you will do well and get a kick out of it.

"The saying is true, 'Sometimes up and sometimes down, Sometimes almost level with the ground.' It seems that all my life has been that. For the last year I haven't been able to work.

Rosalia had to stop school in sixth grade and go to the factory to support herself and me. I always wanted her to have an education. She is a good worker, makes $15 and $16 per week. She pays her insurance and my insurance. For less expense, I had the man to cut our lights off. The furniture payments were back, so the man came and carried part of it away last week. We have no cooking stove only a wood tin heater. I had almost finished payments too.

"The Bible says, 'Put your trust in God and you'll overcome obstacles.' That I've done and that's why I believe it's as well with me as it is. All of my people are Baptist denomination. I used to go to Sunday school and to church, taking Rosalia by the hand. She goes now, but I can't go since I've been suffering with this kidney trouble. The clinic has been giving me treatments."

Mrs. Thompson, although sick, is cheerful. She wears a pleasant smile on her dark-complexion face. She has big, bright black eyes. Her hair is of good texture; she wears it plaited in two braids pinned around her head. Whenever seen, Mrs. Thompson is neatly groomed in one of her housedresses or a green uniform that she wore when working in the factory. She weighs, I guess, around 135 pounds. Though sick and having endured many hardships, she has not stopped her habits of casting the benefits of her pleasing personality on those that she has contact with.

[Loc.: HU/REL, box 5, 13 pp., handwritten ms.]

Julia Keesee (Carwile) *by Mack T. Eads, rec. 22 December 1938*

In her recollections, Julia Elva Keesee grew up in a happy home, in a large family of eleven children—only ten of whom were living (of fifteen that had been born to Willie Kate Keesee)—at the time of the 1910 census in Campbell County. Despite her pleasant memories, the life of a dark-tobacco farmer—especially one with eleven children—was not easy. Even her parent's "congenial" marriage and working partnership on the farm could not protect them from the successive effects of war, the Great Depression, change, and loss.[41]

The First World War was admittedly a factor when Julia Keesee secretly married Watson M. Carwile on 15 June 1918 in Bedford County. Both gave their ages as twenty-one, though by her own admission she was only nineteen at the time. Shortly, Julia went to live in her in-laws' home, and within months, Watson was serving a brief stint in France—along with his wife's older brothers, Clarence and Orville—just before the armistice.

By 1925, a combination of health reasons and wanting to "do better" finally caused Watson to leave his family's farm for a series of jobs with grocery store chains, including the A&P Tea Company, Bibees, and Penders. His work with these companies took the family to various locations in West Virginia and Virginia, and eventually they came to Lynchburg. There, VWP worker Mack Eads noted, Watson and Julia Carwile lived in the lower apartment of a house rented jointly with "her" sister-in-law. But the "sister-in-law" who shared the house on Federal Street was actually Mattie H. Keesee Carwile, Julia's sister who married Watson's first cousin, Paul E. Carwile. The assumption by Eades was apparently based on the two women's shared surname.

In the spring of 1938, Julia and Mattie's brother, Orville Keesee, drowned in California in what were at the time the worst floods in the recorded history of Los Angeles. Their mother Kate, grieving about her lost son, who had left home, died without ever learning his fate. Julia missed her mother most of all, admitting that she was "jealous of people who have mothers" still living. Before the end of 1939, however, Julia Carwile also lost her father, Charles V. Keesee, who outlived his longtime companion by only a few years.

"I was born in Campbell County near Rustburg. My father, Charles V. Keesee, was of Scotch-Irish descent. My mother's maiden name was Willie Kate Boley and she was of English descent. Papa, as I always called him, was what you might call a prosperous farmer. Dark tobacco was his main crop. My mother was a very capable person, she did all the sewing for our family, and there were eleven children to sew for. She also did her own housekeeping.[42]

"I was reared in a very pleasant home. Papa use to come in from the work on the farm and we would be back in the house laughing, talking, and playing and I've often heard him say, 'Who is here?' and mother would say, 'Nobody, why?' and he would answer, 'I thought you had a house full of company, you were having such a good time.' I am glad and thankful I was reared in that kind of a home; when I see the conditions a lot of children are raised under today, I feel sorry that they couldn't have had such a home as mine. When father bought anything new for the farm he always would come to the house and get mother to go out and look at it and get her opinion. My father and mother were so congenial they worked and planned together.

"Olive and I were about the same age and always went together. One day we were visiting grandma and she was entertaining a guest in the parlor and was telling her what good grandchildren she had, never heard a cross word from any of them. Olive and I laugh today about that because we were back in the next room having the biggest spat but we were so quiet about it, grandma did [not] know it.

"There use to be an old colored man that went through the neighborhood called 'Old Pete Bradley.' He always carried a bag on his back and we were scared of him and we would ask him what he had in that bag and he always said 'none of your business.' One day Olive and I went to the watermelon patch and we saw old Pete coming towards the patch to steal melons, I suppose. We were just little tots around six or seven. We were so scared of him we ran into the cornfield, and we kept running and got lost and separated from each other. I thought old Pete had Olive and she thought he had me, and we ran out of the field screaming and crying until we reached home. We were not satisfied until Mama went over to see if old Pete was gone.

"One night Olive and I heard rats in the attic and we thought someone was sawing the door down and we were scared and Mama again satisfied our little minds by going up in the attic and searching every corner for us.

"I think I will tell you what our home looked like before I go any further. It was a seven-room red brick house. Our old home originally belonged to the Franklins and is now over one hundred and fifty years old. It was built on a rock foundation. There is a large basement, also an attic. In the basement, the huge old rafters can be seen that support the house. The basement walls are constructed of rock. In the attic, the flooring is original and the planks are unusually wide and very smooth. Two of the upstairs rooms have original flooring also. The dining room and the living room have deep panelled-wainscoting. Fifty years ago, the house was condemned by the neighbors, so Papa had an iron brace put between the two floors, and it is just as sound as ever now. When I was a child the old kitchen used by the Franklins, was partly torn down and made into a smokehouse and we always called it the new house. And until a few years [ago] it always went by that name. The new house is gone now also. The windows had small panes of glass and very deep sills. The doors were unusually wide, the old locks are gone.

"In the living room was a built-in bookcase to the right of the fireplace. This cabinet came down even with the wainscoting. Underneath this cabinet was a secret closet, which could be reached by just sliding up one of the panels in the wainscoting. This made an opening. Mother used to keep her wood in there out of sight. As children we used to wonder if the Franklins didn't hide there during the War between the States. There is a burying ground near the house which is not enclosed. Two old markers remain. The one over old Mr. Henry Franklin, who is said to be the original owner of the house, bears the date 1841. Mr. Franklin was very wealthy and owned many slaves, also owned the old Hayden place near our home. It is said many slaves are buried there too. Miss Jane Campbell was buried there in my lifetime. She was a very old lady and said to have been very wealthy. My mother is buried at Bethany Church near Rustburg.[43]

"We used to hear that some of the younger Franklins were infidels. One of them was named Miss Joanne Franklin. She died in that old home. Late one evening when we were quite small Mrs. Wheeler, one of our neighbors, came to call on us. She began to talk about the Franklins and telling us about the death of Joanne Franklin and, as I've just said, she was an infidel. She died as everyone thought: they shrouded her, and she suddenly raised up in bed and began to shriek that she was in hell and wouldn't some one try to save her. After shrieking for a few minutes, she stretched out and was dead. My mother said she knew when Mrs. Wheeler was telling that story that she would have company in her bed that night as Papa was away from home. Sure enough eight of us slept in her bed that night—too scared to move.[44]

"Mrs. Wheeler told us about another one of the Franklin women. She walked in her sleep and one night she fell out of one of the upstairs windows, got up, and walked into the house unhurt. Some of the Franklins were very fine and good people and the others very wicked.

"In our front yard were several old locusts, whether they were of original growth I cannot say. But they were there when I was a little girl, also some dwarf boxwood of considerable size.

"I started to school when I was seven years old—to a little one-room school about a mile from home. I walked whether the weather was good or bad. My first lesson was written on a chart placed on an easel. Then they gave me a primer. I skipped the first grade and continued on at this school until I reached the seventh grade. Olive and I were sent [then] to Concord to school. We stayed at Grandma's and went to school. I finished there at the age of seventeen. My last winter at school I boarded at Mrs. Dickey's, as Grandma had moved. They didn't have any children and they let me do as I pleased, but were very particular about who I played with. The Dickeys were such nice people, so devoted to each other.[45]

"Old Mr. Dickey had just sold a colt for one hundred dollars. Mrs. Dickey was looking for new hired help the next day, so she was up early preparing breakfast. When she heard a knock on the door and thinking it was her new help, she opened it quickly and there stood a masked man holding a gun in his hand. He said, 'Hand me over that hundred dollars.' She didn't understand what he said and asked him again what he wanted. Old Mr. Dickey was over eighty years old. He jumped out of bed, grabbed a sabre off the wall, and rushed at the door. The masked man took to his feet and left. Mr. Dickey shot at him twice and missed him.

"I met Watson, my husband, when I was twelve years old. My cousin brought him to our house to see my sister who was five years older than Watson. She was just as much too old for him as I was too young. When I was seventeen years old we started to going with each other. We were married when I was nineteen. The War was going on and we decided we would get married and keep it a secret. We were young but went on to Rustburg and got our license asking for secrecy in the matter. Down the road to the parsonage we went. The preacher came out and we told him we wanted to get married and wanted it to be kept a secret, so he promised. We thought we would do something different, so we asked him to marry us sitting in the little old Ford car. He asked us to stand and we said we could clasp hands sitting, so he said all right. Watson took me on to my home and he went to his own. We decided we wouldn't live together until after the War, but some one told our parents and after two weeks I went to his home to live.

"Yes, Watson went to France but don't make me think of that day. I already had one brother, Clarence Keesee, in service. My brother Orville left for service the same day Watson left. I went to the station. They landed in France the 9th of November, the Armistice was signed the 11th. Watson came home March 26, 1919. We started to housekeeping the 4th of April on his father's farm. We farmed for about six years. My first and only child, Morelle, was born a year after we went to housekeeping. After six years on the farm we left because we thought we could do better elsewhere. Watson suffered with hayfever and every time he worked in tobacco it made him sick. My husband started to work for the A & P Tea Company. We boarded with one of his brothers. He worked for them three years and was transferred to Princeton, West Virginia. We stayed there one year. Some of my best friends live in Princeton.

"He was transferred then to a little place called Davey. He asked permission to bring me back to Lynchburg as I was sick. While here he got a job with Penders as manager. We moved to Altavista and stayed two years. Then was transferred to Penders in Bedford. Watson's father died and he came back to Lynchburg, Virginia.

"There is an incident I'd like to tell before I go any farther. My brother Orville left home when my boy was just a baby. He told us he was going and told my mother goodbye. He wrote to her, but each time from a different state leaving no address and promising to send it at the next place. Finally the letters stopped coming entirely. Mother grieved a lot over it. She searched the papers for some clue. She studied pictures. Just before she died, I saw her studying a group picture so intensely and she looked up and saw me and said, 'I thought maybe I'd see Orelle [*sic*] in that picture.' We appealed to the American Legion to make a search for him. After mother died, we received a letter from him.

"One day I was in the store talking to my husband and looked up and noticed someone standing there and at first I didn't know him. I was so shocked and surprised, I began to laugh and cry at the same time—it was Orville. He stayed at home several months and left. Last spring we got a letter from his wife in California. Orville had been drowned during the flood there. It took ten weeks to find his body. It was dug out from under some buildings.[46]

"Watson stayed with Penders for a year and was transferred to Chatham, Virginia. I was sick and couldn't go there. I was ill for eleven weeks, and he came home and is now working for Bibee's Home Owned Chain Grocery Stores. He has been there for five years. The hours at the Atlantic and Pacific, also Penders were long and hard. He never got home until two or three a.m. on Sunday mornings (after a hard day's work on Saturday). He goes to work now at seven a.m. The store closes at six-thirty p.m. He always gets home later. Bibee's hours are long and hard. Managers get paid fairly well. Clerks who have been there for years only get

$13.00 a week. I believe in eight hours for women and I certainly wish that my husband could be at home with his family a little more than he is.

"I went to work at the Virginia Art Goods Studios Inc. about six years ago during a rush season in the spring, and it was a rush season. It is a non-union shop run by two Lynchburg women. How they started their business on a little novelty bag is very well-known, so I won't go into detail about that. They started business—as you might say—as just 'one of the girls,' now she (Miss Rohr) tries to be too hard-boiled for the size plant she is running. That first season I made sixteen and two-thirds cents per hour. Often we worked until nine and ten-thirty p.m. She did pay us for overtime, but when closing time came we had already worked so fast and so hard we were not able to work any longer. But we did and didn't dare to even show a frown. They called the shop a studio. They put on market lovely hand-embroidered bags done by people here in Lynchburg. At first she gave the work to society girls around town who didn't need the money. The business was small. Later the work was given to unfortunates who had to take what they could get for their work. Eyelets and all embroidery were done for the concern at little cost; they have the work done in Madeira now, and have eyelet machines. We worked so hard all day and so fast, and just about closing time the big orders poured upstairs with [demands] to get the work out that night or else the orders would be canceled. Everybody would grab bags and rush, and then the next morning there would be all the bags unshipped.[47]

"Some girls received as little as $5.00 a week. There was a little lunchroom close by, too small to accommodate the crowd, so we sat around on the curbing outside. We used to get forty-five minutes for lunch, now we get thirty minutes. When the N.R.A. went in effect things began to run smoother, hours were shorter, outside work was done, but done in the name of someone else.[48]

"I went to work at Craddock and Terry Shoe Company, I think it was the next fall. That is a union organization. I believe in unions to a certain extent. I think places like Virginia Arts needs something to make life easier for the employees. Still I don't think it's good for the country to have any one organization that is too powerful. It seems the government is the one to set rules and regulations for industries. When the government intervenes it seems things are done in a more orderly way. I notice there is a lot of disorder at times throughout the country caused by union strikes.[49]

"You can never depend on work at Virginia Arts. They will employ a person one season who will work themselves to death for them and the next season they take on someone else in their place. The pressers worked so hard last spring, just as hard as they could press, perspiration just rolling off them. Most of them are old women and they never get up to even get a drink of water. Near the close of the season, Miss Rohr came upstairs and said they were not pressing fast enough. Usually in the middle of the season Miss Rohr makes a very dramatic appeal to her employees. Calls them all together, usually says that if they work harder and faster perhaps the concern will run the whole year and won't cut off anyone. In a week or so she cuts off five or six a night until the season closes.

"One Easter we had worked so hard and everyone was planning for Easter, and Miss Rohr sent word around that she couldn't pay off but if anyone needed $5.00 she could let them have it. Last season we were supposed to get paid off every two weeks. We got it when she gave it to us just before Easter. She said she couldn't pay off, but had received a little money for an order and she would pay off as long as it lasted. Nearly every employee went through the office. Mrs. Thornhill said, 'Why it looks like a bread line. Why I didn't know I had so many poor people working for me.' She didn't consider that those girls worked hard and had obligations to meet.

"I'd rather live in the country if Watson could still work in the town. I believe I could live cheaper. I like to see things growing, the air is purer and the water tastes better. I have no car at the present time. I wouldn't like to live in the country unless I could have city conveniences. I have been keeping house for six years. We usually have a garden. Sometimes a garden pays, if the season is good.

"My boy will graduate next June from the E. C. Glass High School. He is interested in photography. He wants to go to college. I hope I'll be able to send him. He wants to study art."

When I called Mrs. C. for an interview she was nice to give me an appointment the next day at two p.m. When I called, she met me at the door neatly attired in a dark dress smiling cordially, and invited me into her living room. I have known Julia for several years. She has recently moved from the outskirts of town to College Hill nearer the business section. She and her sister-in-law rented a very nice house together. Julia took the lower apartment, which consists of four rooms; her apartment is comfortably furnished. Recently Julia bought a new bedroom suit. Like her father and mother, she and Watson work together for each other's interests. She takes extra work when she can get it. She asked me not to call her name as she expressed herself freely about Virginia Arts. She will probably work there next spring.

Julia is forty years old [and] still has a youthful appearance. She is the type of person everyone loves. She is never too tired to do a favor for anyone. She speaks a good word for everyone. She loves to do for people, enjoys life. I heard her say once, "I am jealous of people who have mothers. I want my mother so much." She said, "I guess it's wrong to say such a thing." I was a little surprised because I had never heard her say a thing like that. Julia usually has a roomer or a boarder. I noticed her new place has a large garden space. She is a good manager too. Julia can enjoy a good joke and bring a smile into other's lives, but still at the proper time, she can be so gentle, kind, and serious.[50]

[Loc.: VSL/AB, box 190, 10 pp., 3,333 wds.]

Emily Palmer Stearns *by Margaret Jeffries, 26 March 1940*

Ms. Emily Palmer Stearns inherited the estate "Farley" in Culpeper County from her father, Franklin Stearns Jr. The land had originally been granted to William Champe Carter, sixth son of Edward of Blenheim, who married Maria Byrd Farley—the source of the property's name. Emily Stearns's parents, who were newlyweds in June 1870, reported $9,000 worth of personal property and $100,000 in real estate in the census for Culpeper County that year. Her grandfather Franklin Stearns Sr. was listed in 1860 Henrico County census records, however, as having $155,000 in real estate and $200,000 worth of personal property in association with his occupations in "finance" and as a "distiller."[51]

Ms. Emily Stearns spent a part of her early life in Washington, D.C., as an independent working woman and as a suffragette with Alice Paul. Later, she returned to Farley, where she lived, espoused socialism and vegetarianism, turned the estate into an orphanage of sorts for a multitude of stray cats and dogs, and was eventually referred to by some as the "Culpeper Cat Lady." In the latter years of Stearns's life and the decades since her death, the historic old house fell into a state of dilapidated ruin—in large part owing to her use of it as a feline sanctuary. The house has recently been refurbished by new owners, and the recent spate of activity in and around the property has yielded a number of sightings of the ghost of Miss Emily. Stories currently in circulation report that she has "been seen a few times in front of the house sitting in a rocking chair." And one of the workmen in the house is said to have "met Miss Emily in the upstairs hallway and had a conversation with her."[52]

Certainly, Emily Stearns's background and experiences place her in a class apart from that of most persons interviewed by the Federal Writers' Project programs. Thus her life history, both in its aspects of wealth and privilege and its unconventionality, serves as a small but important corrective to the imperfect public record.

"Thou Shalt Not Kill" is the motto at the head of Miss Emily Stearns's writing paper. The same motto is the one which she has adopted for her life. And she is not content with the negative expression of her belief, but goes to work in a positive way to preserve life in every way she can. She believes every animal has a right to as long a life as nature has decreed for it and does not think that man has any right to cut it short by even as much as one hour.

"Show mercy that you may have mercy shown to you," she was heard to say on one occasion, as she rebuked a colored man (who was working for her) when he tried to find something with which to kill a snake. And she herself got a stick and, running it under the belly of the snake, carried the quiescent reptile off, down into the woods where she gently lowered him to the ground. And the wonderful part of the whole incident to the writer was the fact that the snake did not once try to wiggle off the stick. It may have been because he was just out of the ground, but it seemed because Miss Emily—through her love of animals—had imbued the snake with confidence in her intention not to hurt him.

Miss Emily loves all animal life but she is especially fond of cats. And she has concentrated her not inconsiderable efforts on saving homeless cats and dogs. Any old kind of dog or cat is welcome at FARLEY, her old home in the country, ten miles to the northeast of Culpeper Courthouse. In fact she prefers the strays because they have no one to love them and care for them. "The world has not begun to realize yet what we owe to the animal," she says earnestly. And working on that theory, she is striving to do all that she can to make life more pleasant for stray cats and dogs to counteract, in a degree, the harsh treatment they receive at so many careless hands. "Of course, I know that my work is just a drop in the bucket," she often remarks. "But then, it is the beginning, and I am happier in doing it than I would be in not trying to relieve the situation at all."

Miss Emily is often interviewed and so she was not bothered the least bit in the world by another inquisitive person asking her questions. In fact, she is so interested in her work that she is anxious for the chance to explain to people how she feels about it. She realizes that she is probably looked upon as pretty much of a crank. But then, all people who are different from the general run are so labeled. She does not mind that because she knows that she is right, and she would not be happy any other way. She is intimate with that attitude because members of her own family often express their wonder at the things she does. "Even my family does not understand how I feel," is her way of putting it.

Miss Emily's immediate family is rather a large one as families go these days. And her lineage is one of which to be proud. Her mother, formerly Miss Emily Somers Palmer of Boston, was educated in New York and moved in the best society circles of both cities. Her father, Franklin Stearns II, [was] educated in Paris [and] made his home—after the death of his own father—in Richmond, Virginia, where he and his wife took their place in the best circles of the southern capital. Franklin Stearns I was in real estate and owned countless farms throughout Virginia. The care of these he left to his son, Franklin II, and the caring was considerable. So that although he was said to be in real estate, he was not a real estate agent, but devoted his time to caring for his own property and making it pay. Mr. Stearns met Miss Palmer at a reception given at the Governor's mansion in Richmond. They were both rather young when they were married, she being eighteen and he, twenty-one. They came to FARLEY as soon as they were married, as Mr. Stearns, Senior made that his wedding present to them.

FARLEY was an immense place and immensely old, too. Situated in the midst of over eleven hundred acres of land, the great old house had then stood there for more than a century. It is, architecturally speaking, a good example of the period in which it was built. Back about a quarter of a mile from the river (then used for transportation), it was, architects say, placed in exactly the right spot. Of course, the grounds around it are not so spacious now, nor are they so well-kept as formerly, but one can see the extent to which they reached in the old days. Measuring about one hundred twenty-five feet in length, the house itself is built upon beautifully simple lines. Just the width of one immense room and a hall, it is five rooms in length. The plan is not unique. Beautiful entrances on each side, back and front, have above them exquisite old fanlights of colonial design. The pillars inside and out, the type windows used, the high ceilings and large rooms, the spacious halls, the old six-panel doors, and chair rails, all denote a plane of living above the ordinary, even in the days of Champ Carter, its original owner.

Franklin Stearns (the first) bought the property in 1862 and ever since that time it has been in the family. When his son Franklin II was married, he presented it to him and he, in turn, left it to his children. There were nine of these children. Franklin III was the oldest of the lot and he is the only one who is not living today. The rest of the family are Mrs. Charles Rixey, who makes her home part of the time at FARLEY; Mrs. R. F. McClannahan of Washington, D.C.; Miss Alice Stearns, who is still single like Miss Emily; Charles Palmer Stearns of Washington D.C.; Mrs. Pressley Rixey, whose husband was a nephew of Surgeon General Rixey, for so long White House physician; Mrs. George A. Gray of Washington, D.C.; and Palmer Newcomb Stearns of Arlington, Virginia.

All the children were born and most of them started to school at FARLEY. But when, in 1888, Franklin Stearns, Senior, died, it became necessary for his son to move to Richmond, the better to look after the business his father had left him. "But Father promised us that we could come back for the summers," Miss Emily smilingly said. "He thought we would be less brokenhearted if we could come back in the summer. You see, this was our world then and we hated to give it up. So after that we had a summer home and a winter one." Miss Emily, like the rest of them, was born at FARLEY. "But one thing I won't tell is my age," she said laughingly.

And she commenced her schooling here too. In the yard still stands a small schoolhouse where all the little people who have lived at this old place have been taught their three R's. "Father had a governess for the older children and of course, for the little time I went to school before we moved to Richmond, I went to the same governess," she explained.

One would not think the place such a bad one in which to go to school, this little building, standing aloof from the main house, with the fanlight over the door an exact replica on a smaller scale of that one over the big front door. The tall old windows, one on each side,

Farley, home of Emily Palmer Stearns. Photo by W. Lincoln Highton. VSL/PC. [A9-7340]

must [have] let in more than a'plenty light for little eyes and the huge old fireplace must have been cheerful and warm for little toes coming in cold from play.

"When we went to Richmond in the winter, we went to Miss Mary Johnson's School," Miss Emily continued. "One of Father's friends told him that it was a good school for us to attend and there is where I finished my education." But she had never been able to talk her father into letting her go to college. "That was one of the great crosses of my life," she admitted. "Father did not think it the proper thing for a young lady to do. He told me that if I wanted to take up special classes in Richmond with Miss Johnson, I could take all of them I pleased. But he just wouldn't let me go to college." And so the young Emily had taken extra classes in French and Philosophy, and such cultural subjects. But they had not filled her mind entirely as was to be seen later in her life.

"I dabbled in several things when I went to Washington," she replied when asked about her work. "I never did any work until I went there to live. I guess I just wasted those other years." And she told of how she had "dabbled" in Woman's Suffrage. She always did her own thinking, did this young girl. And her thoughts became directed toward Woman's Suffrage, along with those of many other women of that day. She joined the movement under Miss Alice Paul, and was right away made National Membership Chairman of the National Women's Party. For two years she worked hard with these women—receiving no salary, but content—because she was helping a cause in which she believed thoroughly. She was one of the women chosen by Miss Paul to picket the White House and Congress.

"My brothers and sisters and mother thought it was terrible for me to do it. But they did not understand how I felt about the injustice of not being allowed to vote when [women] really had the right under the Constitution. Oh, we weren't violent. We weren't outwardly militant. But we were morally militant." Her voice showed even yet how great had been her interest in the movement of that past day. "The membership grew from ten thousand to thirty thousand while I was chairman too," she added.

Farley, home of Emily Palmer Stearns. Photo by W. Lincoln Highton. VSL/PC. [188145]

Her interest turned to the real estate business after the women received the vote. And for the next two years she worked hard, in and around Washington, trying to sell property. "I did try hard at it. But I wasn't much good at that, I'm afraid," she dismissed that phase of her life.

She then started telling of her war work. And interesting work it must have been, too. For she was one of twenty-two young women who were chosen to investigate and inspect the homes, which were thrown open to the young ladies hired to carry on the work of the government during the World War. "You see, these young ladies were coming here from every part of the United States to get government jobs," she explained. "And they had to be housed. You know the government called for the homes of Washington people to be thrown open to them. Many people — some of them people who needed the extra money that the rooms brought in, but many of them rich and not needing the money they received — offered their rooms for use. Well, they had to be inspected and investigated before the workers could be sent to them."

It required a person of tact and diplomacy as well as one thoroughly capable of judging homes and people. And it required a person of untiring zeal. Such a person Miss Emily was. She told how she liked the work so well that she worked at it overtime. She even went on Sundays, knowing that the need was pressing. That she was good at the job was shown later when the twenty-two workers were cut to fifteen, and cut again, until finally there was only one needed and the one chosen was Miss Emily Stearns. The young ladies were finally all housed and her job with the Registration Division of the Housing Corporation was ended. For this work she had been paid three dollars a day and her car fare up to a certain amount.

Just as in the case of her suffrage work, she had thrown herself wholeheartedly into it. And that is the same way she went to work at welfare work which she took up after this. "But I never did do any organized welfare work," she assured the writer. "I just helped some of my friends who were doing it."

It was in 1926 that she got to thinking seriously of the sad plight of poor stray cats in the cities. All the time she was employed at other things, she had been befriending homeless fe-lines she saw on the streets. "I would take them to the apartment my sister and I had," she said. "But my sister didn't like that. She was not so fond of animals as I am, and of course, there was so little room there for the poor things."

But it was from her deep compassion for homeless things that she one day conceived the idea of opening up the old house down in Virginia and making it into a home for cats. Upon the death of her father and the division of the property he left, she had fallen heir to FARLEY and a considerable acreage about it. The house was just standing there. The family sometimes used it for summers. She would just take all the cats, and go there and take care of them. "It is not an ideal situation for the work," Miss Emily explained. "It is too far from the city. But it is the best I could do just now."

And so she went to the S.P.C.A. and asked them for the cats, which they had collected and were going to put to death. She explained her idea and was much disappointed that they would not let her have the animals. Her purpose was too idealistic, they said, and they could not turn over their cats to her. Their policy was to kill all those not wanted by people as pets.

"And so I just loaded all the cats I could gather together into a big truck and brought them along to Virginia," she exclaimed. "My ambition is to have a place nearer to the city where I can gather in more of the poor things. Here I am limited in my work. I mean one day to have a hospital and clinic with an ambulance. Then I feel that I can really do the work that amounts to something. I have money enough to purchase the land but it will take quite a bit for the other things. Every time people send me money I put all of it I can into the bank for my hospital. And someday I shall have one."

Miss Stearns has had quite a bit of publicity about her work. "The reporters say that it is the fact that I am using an old Virginia home for my cats and dogs that puts the kick into the stories they write about me," she said laughing. Reporters have visited her from New Jersey, New York, Richmond, and many other places. Pathe News interviewed her and took pictures of the place, and of her with her cats all about her. Fox made pictures, too and altogether, she has been well publicized. And all of it has helped.

Quite frequently some animal lover sends her a check. And one lady sent her twenty-five cases of large cans of Red Heart dog food, with the promise of twenty-five more every five months. Two ladies send her fifteen dollars each a month regularly, and this she uses to run on. Other checks she usually puts into the fund for her hospital. One lady who was interested in the work gave a card party and raised sixty dollars, which she sent to Miss Stearns with the suggestion that she buy a cow so that the cats might always have milk. "And I never use a bit of that milk for myself or for the dogs either," she assured the writer. Every now and then some animal magazine will write something about her and she will hear from its readers who are in sympathy with her work.

"I didn't mean to take dogs too," she explained. "But I had one little dog given to me and I just couldn't turn her away. So I decided I would keep her and now I have nine altogether. I just can't see them suffer. Animals are so loyal and true. I just couldn't be any other way to them." It was in 1927 that she started taking dogs. Now, besides the nine dogs, she has about fifty cats. They walk around everywhere. Two friendly dogs always greet the visitor, jumping up to be petted and showing their friendliness with every wag of the tail.

"The whole place belongs to them," Miss Emily will explain, as she hands her guest a little switch to fend them off with. "I don't mind their jumping on me, but you'd better show them this little switch to keep them off your clothes. You see, I dress for my work in these old clothes and it doesn't matter if they do jump up on me." And indeed she does dress in a practical way to take care of her animals. An old coat—heavy and warm, but sturdy enough to bear the scratchings of dog and cat claws—is her usual outer garment. A cap pulled down over her ears keeps the cool wind out, and stout old shoes on her feet finish off a practical outfit suited to the exigencies of her task.

Miss Emily is an attractive woman when she is fixed up. She is a few inches over five feet tall, and slender as many a younger woman would love to be. Her hair is very gray now, but this rather adds to her youthful appearance than detracts from it. Her cheeks are plump and although they are not so smooth as those of a woman who lives an indoor life, they give little evidence of the passing of the years. Her blue eyes are interested and young looking. Her manner is vivacious and friendly.

Besides running the Farley Refuge for Friendless Cats, Miss Emily is much interested in politics. "I know when I tell you that I am a socialist you will disown me," she said laughing. But really, Miss Stearns is not the least bit ashamed of being a socialist. She is proud of it. She is sincere in believing that it is the only party for Americans. "When I became old enough to vote," she explained, "I looked into all the platforms of all the parties. And after a lot of examining and looking into [it], I came to the conclusion that the Socialist Party is the only one that is right for Americans. Now, I am not a Socialist as the Germans are, or as the Russians are. Not at all. I do not believe in the equal distribution of wealth. I think that each individual should have his reward for his own initiative. But I do think that we should have equal opportunity. And we don't have that here in America. I am a socialist because I believe that true socialism is the truest democracy and the most clear-cut expression of the Constitution of the United States. Both of the old parties are worn out. Why should we stick to them when they do not meet our needs?"

Miss Stearns is a very convincing speaker. When she expresses her views on a subject, the listener immediately begins to believe in the same views. It is no wonder that she has made a success of almost everything she has attempted to do. She is so thoroughly a part of her work and believes in things so strongly.

"My people have always been Episcopalians," she said when asked concerning her religion. "I joined the Episcopal Church in Richmond, and then when I went to Washington I just attended first one church and then another. I never allied myself with any special Episcopal church there. My mother did, but I didn't. And I go to Christ's Church here at Brandy whenever I can. That is not often, as I have no way to get there."

Miss Emily feels very strongly on the subject of war. "If people felt more compassion for each other and for the animals about us, they would not have war," she said. "Our love for animals makes us different. I tell you that that is the beginning of it all." She has quite evidently been asked why she did not direct her talent and energy toward helping human suffering, for she expressed herself quite freely on the subject. "There are thousands of people helping the orphans," she said, somewhat defiantly. "There are thousands of people helping human derelicts. But there is hardly anybody helping the poor homeless animals."

Her policy, she said, was to use the same methods towards her animals that were used toward humans. "When a human gets sick, do we kill him?" she asked, and went on to answer her own question. "Of course not. We put him in a hospital and do all we can for him. And that is the same policy I am trying to carry out with animals. I want to build my hospital and take care of the sick ones there. My sisters will ask me why I don't kill a dog that is sick. I ask them would they kill a person that way, and of course, they say no."

She got up abruptly and went into the house coming back presently with a sheet of stationery and an envelope. The letterhead read:

THOU SHALT NOT KILL
Farley Refuge for Friendless Cats
Emily Palmer Stearns, Founder
Brandy, Virginia

And the envelope bore the same inscription. Pointing to the top line, she remarked that it did not say "unless."

"People ask me if I eat meat," she continued. "I tell them I do not. I am not rabid about the matter. My sisters stay here with me, and they have their meat. But I do not need it. I eat my vegetables and get along on them. My system doesn't call for meat. I say that people have to settle that question for themselves. I make no criticism of other people for eating meat and not feeling about things as I do. But as for myself, I do not eat meat and I would not be happy if I did other than I do."

And that simple fact is her creed. Her soul is filled with compassion for the less fortunate of the world, be they dumb animal or human. As an example she told of an incident that happened while she was still living in Washington. She happened to be passing through a department store one day and glimpsed the face of a boy wrapping packages. "It was so sad, so pathetic," she said, "that I could not help stopping and looking at him."

She went to the store management and obtained his address from them. She then forthwith went to see his people, and after talking to the boy's mother invited the lad to come and visit her for the summer at FARLEY. "My mother asked me why in the world I had done such a thing. I told her I didn't know why I had done it, but I thought that Christ must have felt that same way many times. They were much opposed to my bringing him here, saying that I knew nothing about him. I told them that, of course, I knew nothing about him, except that he was a human in need and that was all that I needed to know. Well, he came and spent the summer with me. He still comes to see me sometimes. He is a grown man now, and he often says no one knows what that summer meant to him."

In her reading Miss Emily sticks to her subject. She devotes most of her reading time to animal magazines. "I take the *National Humane Review* and *Anti-Vivisection Magazine*," she said. And she does not content herself with merely reading the magazines, but often contributes to them—writing articles. "Mostly about animals and against war," she said humorously.

For her religious reading she prefers *Unity,* but reads other magazines of like nature. For her political reading she takes *Labor Power* and *The Call.* She also subscribes to two Washington papers, *The Evening Star* and *The Times Herald;* and one local weekly, *The Virginia Star.* "I don't have any time for anything else," she admitted.

"Sometimes I would like to go to the city and have a good time for awhile. But I just can't desert my animals. I couldn't leave them with anyone. No one feels about them as I do, and no one would treat them right." And so she lives on in this bleak old house, working over her sick animals, rubbing salve on their wounds, tending to their feeding, fighting with mange and fleas. It is not an easy life, but the compassion in her heart for unwanted homeless creatures drives her on. She loves every one of the dogs and cats and knows them by name. She knows where every one has come from and the disposition of each. To her they are the sub-human race and must be treated as human beings are treated. And in order to carry out this ideal she has adopted the sixth commandment for her own and has set up before her the flaming words:

THOU SHALT NOT KILL.

[Loc.: VSL/AB, box 184, 15 pp., 5,200 wds.]

3 Narrating Men's Experience

"WE MEET WITH SO MANY CHANGES"

When I got so I could do as much work as a man,

I got fifty cents a day. I felt like a man then. —Charles Tucker

Some writers have argued that "universal" histories of change in politics and economics, society and culture, are, in general, representations of the past as experienced, deduced, or claimed, primarily by men. Certainly, it is true that the lives and perspectives of women have for the most part been missing from the chronicles of earlier times; but all men have not been created equal in those works either. The lives of the majority of men have been almost as neglected by the histories of elites, important events, and ideas as those of women. The omission of men from the historical record, however, has usually been determined by issues of class and status rather than of gender, which is more often the case for women.[1]

Some recent scholars analyzing narrative texts suggest that gender is "an unmarked category" for men and that the "dynamics of gender emerge more clearly in the personal narratives of women than in those of men." In the life history texts produced by the Virginia Writers' Project, the conditions of men's work and leisure were at the core of most of their accounts. From these, it is proposed that personal narratives about negotiating the world of work and social change *are,* in fact, a marked gender category for men. The epigraph cited for this chapter is certainly so marked: it reveals Charles Tucker's awareness of the point in time when he became a full participant in the gender domain of men's work, both in terms of its social definition in a particular time and place and for someone in his particular socioeconomic position.[2]

Despite the developing depression, almost three-quarters of all males above the age of ten in Virginia were gainfully employed in 1930. Ninety to 97 percent of all men in every age group from twenty through sixty-four years were working; and 46 percent of all men aged seventy-five or over were still employed. As these figures evidence, a man's work (carried out in primarily male-dominated social groups and contexts at that time) occupied the major part of his efforts through most of his lifetime. A man's occupational life—which also established his identity in the role of "good provider" for himself and his family—was, perhaps, his most significant gender-defining experience. Indeed, we may *not* read statements about work as gen-

Newport News, Virginia. Newport News shipbuilding and drydock company. October 1941. These are the men whose skill is devoted to the building of the finest, most powerful fleet of naval vessels the world has ever seen. They are leaving the gates of the yard, after their regular shift. Photo by Alfred Palmer. [LC-USE6-01688-D]

der marked because the subject matter itself is so confounded with ideals of male identity and masculinity as to become indistinguishable and essentially invisible.[3]

There are occasional narratives in the life histories about the common experience of men as members of specific male groups; these accounts often reveal how the gender ideal of masculinity was defined and expressed in that shared set of relations. For instance, John Lee Wright vividly recounted how he and a group of men making railroad ties on Iron Mountain in December 1890 almost lost their lives in an unexpected and severe snowstorm. In remembering the event, he said, "It looked like starvation an' freezin' was goin' to be our doom."[4]

Wright himself took leadership credit for suggesting that the stranded group cook the last of their food, bundle up all their clothing and bedding, and try to find their way down the mountain before the storm worsened. They spent all day struggling through deep snow and fortunately found a farmhouse just as it was turning dark. After being taken in, fed, and put up for the night by the farm family, they walked the rest of the way home the next day. Wright added a coda to his story reporting that his family was worried about him and had their own "trouble a'plenty" in the storm, "but it wasn't nothin' to compare with bein' lost in the mountains."[5]

Through their cooperative efforts, the group of men survived what otherwise could have been a tragedy. All the men faced similar distress; those who did not display their fears or become dependent upon their companions were, by implication in Wright's testimony, more manly. One man's breakdown (though he "was too big to cry") was, nonetheless, excused on the basis of his acute exhaustion. But in Wright's recall of the event fifty-years previous, it is clear that he thought of himself as the best man of all in the measure of masculinity forged in that encounter with Mother Nature.[6]

There are other forms of tacit information about male gender roles and identity in particular historical and occupational contexts in these texts as well. They suggest that adaptation to drastic change was most difficult for those bound to a particular occupation or lifestyle or constrained by other factors such as age, race, class, or health. And beyond those considerations, there was individual variation with respect to motivation, ability, and experience.

In the face of technological change and developments that altered or eliminated whole categories of customary work, some texts reflect individuals' symbolic efforts to understand and accept those changes. Early in his life, one man had begun work as a teamster, which "was a good business then, before the trucks took the place of horses," and he lamented: "If I could have done what I liked best, I would still be drivin' an' workin' with horses. They's nothin' else like it in the world to me. When I work with horses, I feel like I'm dealin' with friends. They seem to understand me an' I understand them. We get along." His sense of loss concerning the passing of that enterprise, in which he had invested so much personal identity and sentiment, is evident.[7]

At the time he was interviewed, however, this same man was working at "railroadin'." The transportation categories, whether by horse, truck, or railroad, at base all involved moving people and goods from place to place, but the work activities of a railroad section gang bore little resemblance to the individualistic behavior of a teamster working with horses. And this man's statement "We meet with so many changes, we hardly know where we're at" points up the ambivalence he felt about those developments and that still remained some decades and many other experiences later.[8]

Other men underwent numerous changes over the course of their working life but to

Planting corn in the fertile farmland of the Shenandoah valley, Virginia. Photo by Marion Post Wolcott.
[LC-USF34-57511-D]

some extent were still able to remain in their chosen occupation. A seventy-year-old North Carolina native told project worker Maude Chandler that "he had spent most of his life in mining. . . . *mining was the only work he ever wanted to do.*" He had worked in ore mines in Foster's Falls and Bertha and zinc mines in Austinsville, Virginia; copper mines in Ducktown, Georgia; the soda ash department of the Matheison Alkali Plant in Saltville, Virginia; coal mines around Welch, West Virginia; for the Virginia Iron and Coal Company in Keokee and Esserville; and finally, for the Stonega Coke and Coal Company in Dunbar, Virginia. That he had worked in so many different places and kinds of mining operations may not have been a matter of personal choice but more likely corresponded to instability or changes in that sector of the industrial economy through time. Nevertheless, this man *had* spent his working life as a miner—doing what he said he most wanted to do.⁹

Sometimes these documents shed light on how individuals make the sundry decisions that

Sam Bens and Noah Booher, drivers for Associated transport company having dinner with a textile mill truck driver at a highway stop along US highway route no. 11 near Wytheville, Virginia. March 1943. Photo by John Vachon.
[LC-USW3-20370-D]

"give shape to each life story" and cumulatively affect the "direction and scale of major social change." For instance, while cutting extract wood one morning an Alleghany County man, who had "heard of the fabulous sums of money to be made" in an Akron, Ohio, rubber factory, suddenly decided to go there. He "left his axe sticking in a log, went home and told his parents about his decision," and gave the extract wood he had cut to his father. With little preparation otherwise, he left his rural home to make his fortune in Akron.[10]

The motif of "leaving the axe in the log" and of following an impulse to seek one's fortune elsewhere is apocryphal—the very stuff of legends. As to his success, this man eventually returned home to the farm at the age of forty, after working twenty years in the rubber factory and then being laid off for over a year because of a union dispute. "True, I've made easy money," he reported, "but it was easy to spend it and I have very little to show for my years of work there." He added that factory work was "hard on a man's health. One hour out in the country is worth a month in the city."[11]

The "seizing of economic chances" is represented in another form in the case of Marvin Broyhill: work with his father in the lumber business in North Carolina gave him valuable experience in preparation for his later real estate and construction businesses in Hopewell, Front Royal, and Arlington, Virginia. Only Marvin Broyhill's life history is included in this volume. But VWP texts with multiple members of the Broyhill family suggest the links in the migration chain that brought him, his parents, and several of his brothers to Hopewell and then assisted them in making use of the opportunities they found there.[12]

Reliance on the shared resources and mutual help of family-based networks, which are especially adaptive for dealing with conditions of poverty, crisis, or even migration, is a theme that appears in many of the life histories of both men and women. Yet some of the differences in the way these networks functioned, in terms of the sexes, reflect traditional gender roles. Generally, males used their own contacts or reputations as workers in a particular context or locality to help find work for their kinsmen (such as John Ernest Bess, Isaiah Wallace,

Luray (vicinity), Virginia. November 1940. Hog killing on a farm. Photo by Marion Post Wolcott. [LC-USF34-56412-D]

and others), who were strangers in places where they were newly arrived or were distant from their homes or whose job qualifications were otherwise not known. Reciprocal arrangements and helping between females were of a different order and more often involved the exchange of domestic resources and duties, especially child care, which then allowed other mothers to work and support their families. But women, as a rule, did not have the same possibilities in the occupational sphere (or "pull," as Margaret Wolfe termed it) for directly helping their female kin obtain jobs or advancement. The work-oriented, politically institutionalized "good old boy" network, which explicitly admits its gender base, did not then—and largely does not now—work the same in most arenas for women as for men.

Some male groupings did form, however, for the sole purpose of communal work on a specific task, such as "log rollings" (a cooperative effort to get logs cut and brought to a neighbor's proposed house or barn site), house or barn raisings, corn shuckings, and butchering of animals. For instance, an Augusta County native recounted the "spontaneous cooperation" and "neighborhood sociability" that accompanied hog butchering in that area. In his narration, this man invoked traditional beliefs concerning the proper phase of the moon for such practices as planting, harvesting, or, in this case, butchering. He also detailed both a process of food production and a social context for the exchange of gender-related items of traditional expressive culture such as hunting stories and brags:

> Some farmer would say at the corner store or on the road, where a neighbor on his work horses waited at the "draw-bars" for the friend-neighbor to unhook and join him, jogging

Luray (vicinity), Virginia. November 1940. Hog killing on a farm. Photo by Marion Post Wolcott. [LC-USF33-31162-M1]

Luray (vicinity), Virginia. November 1940. Rail fence and farm home. Photo by Marion Post Wolcott.
[LC-USF33-31165-M2]

Newport News, Virginia. March 1941. Men eating at the Salvation army. Photo by John Vachon. [LC-USF34-62719-D]

Christianburg (vicinity), Virginia. June 1936. Cradling wheat. Photo by Dorothea Lange. [LC-USF34-09197-E]

Rustburg, Virginia. March 1941. A day in court. The eye of God surrounded by a glory on the wall behind the judge's seat.
Photo by John Vachon. [LC-USF34-62758-D]

along as the sun set: "If the weather stays this cold, I'm going to kill my hogs next Tuesday. The moon is right for the meat to dry up and not turn soft and slimy. I'll get the wood in on Monday, unless it turns warm." That was all said. There was no offer to exchange my help for your help later. The announcement was heard in silence but when the "right-moon-Tuesday" dawned, out of the fog, would come those whom the farmer had wanted, and whom he would help, when *their* butchering was scheduled.

[After the hog was dispatched, and the scalding and scraping of the carcass was begun], the party would hear the conclusion of the tales of what fine shots the men were. Of course there was nothing to marksmanship in killing a hog in a pen. But it was nonetheless true, that he who had the best championship record always did the shooting. Therefore, to dispel any doubt in the minds of the assembled party that each speaker was not the equal of the man who was merely "so lucky" as to have been seen make extraordinary shots "last year on the deer hunt," each promoted his own stock in sportsmanship. And if time got short and two talked at once, *there were no women around to know it. . . .*

After several hogs were hung on the long propped log, if the first had cooled, we would see who could cut one up and have the best shape to the hams, shoulders, the lard pieces cut off, and do it the quickest. . . . That would be about four or five o'clock P.M. and we would have had our dinner of chicken and dumplings, mince pie, and milk in a pitcher not in a bottle. If the day was freezing cold, coffee would come around once or twice and it was not percolated. It would make New Orleans drip coffee, in comparison, baby food to this "man-coffee." Every visitor brought his razor-sharp knife to a butchering. Every man's knife was the "best sheffield steel" that "would take an edge."[13]

Like John Lee Wright's recall of being the best of the lot of males in the Iron Mountain incident, this man proclaimed himself the same. "As they are gone and I am here, [he laughed], *I* am *the one,* who *always* cut the best shaped hams and got through the whole hog, five minutes before the next best could get his cut into shape." Despite his recollections that no women were present at such occasions, the chicken and dumplings, pie, and "man-coffee" were presumably prepared by the womenfolk. Yet it is very clear that in this man's memory hog butchering was strictly a male domain—a place for socializing and bragging without interference or insistence on truthfulness by those of the female gender.[14]

Other accounts document the demise of such cooperative endeavor as a result of social changes. The intrusion of a cash economy was directly implicated in the account of the last known log rolling in Alleghany County, related in the introductory text in the first chapter in this section. Regardless of such change, however, it is still evident from these accounts that each man, like each woman, "is not simply a member of one definite social category" but is necessarily a member "of a multitude of coexisting and competing social groups and relationships."[15]

Warrenton, Virginia. May 1941.
Bookies taking bets at the horse races.
Photo by Marion Post Wolcott.
[LC-USF34-57426-E]

John Lee Wright *by Leila Blanche Bess, 22 April 1940*

John Lee Wright was interviewed by Leila Blanche Bess at least twice, not to mention the several occasions on which she also interviewed his wife, Josie, and several of their children and grand-children. But her initial interview with John Lee—submitted to the Richmond vwp office more than a year prior to the text following—did not mention him by name and was simply titled "A Visit to Rocky Point Farm." Her reasons for not identifying him are clear in this case: on that occasion, she was less than generous in her judgments of his character and behavior.

Although he had acquired a farm and "paid for the place" by selling pulpwood, Bess condemned him for having done nothing "in the way of improvement" and for having "no pride or ambition." She concluded further, "Beauty? He doesn't seem to know the meaning of the word, all he thinks of when he sees a tree is: How many sticks of pulp wood will that tree make, and how many dollars will it bring? . . . Where there [once] was magnificent trees and great natural beauty, there is [now] only ugliness and desolation." The appearance of an aged and infirm Wright a year later seems to have prompted sympathy and, perhaps, to have softened Bess's previously harsh view of his past actions and of him as an insensitive, opportunistic exploiter of the land.[16]

John Lee Wright was born seventy one years ago on a small farm in the southwestern end of Alleghany County. The farm was owned by his father, John Nickson Wright, who was then a young man and a Baptist preacher. John Lee was the second child of a family of twelve children. They were very poor, often not having enough to eat, and as to clothing, they went half naked and had no shoes until they were half grown.

The father and mother eloped when very young. They stole away in the darkness of midnight riding horseback. John N. took his bride-to-be on behind him on the bony old nag and rode to Lewisburg, West Virginia, a distance of about forty miles, where they roused a sleepy old preacher and were married. Mounting the tired old horse they rode back to the home of John's father, George. They lived there for a short time, but soon began making a home for themselves on a portion of the home tract.

The farm was practically level and [was] fertile at that time. They knew nothing about soil conservation and the land has been run down and does not produce much now. The place was all in an open farm then, but has been cut up and divided until it is well dotted with small clapboard houses with rusty stove pipes sticking from the roofs. The fences are broken and some have been patched up with pieces of barbed wire.

The family increased so rapidly that John Nick and Barbara could not provide food for the hungry children. The story has been often told that John Nick went out hunting one day, hoping to kill enough game to provide fresh meat for the children. Luck seemed to be against him and he only got one squirrel. When Barbara made a fire to start supper, John N. said: "Cook the whole squirrel Barbara and make a lot o' gravy, we'll live while we do live."

The children just "grew." They were not reared or trained or educated. They learned someway, to read and write and to keep time. If they worked for a neighbor they kept strict tab on the number of hours and knew to a penny the amount [that] would be due them. John Lee went to school for a few months and learned more than some of his brothers and sisters. He has good common sense and practical ideas. As he was the oldest boy and the family was in distressingly poor circumstances, he was hired out as soon as anyone would employ him.

"Well, it seems like a long time since I got my first job. I was just a chunk of a boy when I first begun lookin' out fer myself. I helped pa an' ma an' the other children some too, as long as I stayed at home. I was about twelve years old when I got my first work. Mr. Lynch lived about two miles of us and he had a good farm. But he was a stage driver and every summer when the season opened at the old Sweet Springs, he was called to drive a stage from the Sweet to Alleghany Station and haul the guests as they come and went. They had big crowds there in them days.

"Mr. Lynch always farmed, but he had to hire the work done after he left. So he come over one day and asked me to come the next day to hoe corn for him. He had Bob Matheny to plow. So I went. I was glad to go, fer we was purty scarce of things at home. It was just the season of the year when the winter's supply had run out and nothin' had come on from the garden, that is, they wasn't enough fer our big family. I got fifty cents a day and my meals. And my feller, what meals they was!

"Mrs. Lynch was the kindest old lady I ever seen an' the best cook. I got three good meals every day an' plenty o' sweet milk and sweet cakes in between meals. She had a great big jar that she kep' full o' sweet cakes all the time. I don't know when she ever got time to bake 'em, fer all the kids in the neighborhood run there to git sweet cakes. I've et a many a cake in my time, but I've never tasted any others like the ones I et at Mrs. Lynch's. When I went to the house fer a drink o' water she would say, 'Come an' git you a cake John, I know you're about starved.' And believe me I didn't miss goin' fer that sweet cake jar.

"In between corn hoein', I went with pa ''sangin'' [looking for ginseng]. Pa went often as he could. That's the way I learnt how to tell 'sang. We would go an' stay fer days at a time, camp out, an' eat what we could find, except sich times as we drapped in at somebody's house around mealtime. They always asked us to eat, fer pa he knowed most everybody. He preached at different places, but he was regular goin' to Barbour's Creek. After I knowed 'sang well, I went by myself. I stayed in the woods an' dug 'sang every year. But when I was sixteen, I got work on the section up above Callaghan. I was there fer a right smart while.

"Then I got me a job makin' ties up on Iron Mountain. There was about twenty-five o' us fellers went up there. We all camped an' done our own cookin', but we wasn't all in one camp. We was gittin' along fine. It was in December, I think if I recollect right, it was the sixteenth, 1890. We set by our fire that night makin' plans about what we was a'goin' to do fer Christmas. Boys, we had big plans an' little did we think what we'd go through with before another day passed. When we got up the next mornin' early so's we could git ready fer work an' opened the door of the shanty, the snow was piled more'n halfway up the door, an' all outside everything was kivvered up. There wasn't a sign of a road, branch er anything, jus' a white wilderness. We was dumbfounded. We looked at the snow an' we looked at each other, every feller a'wonderin' what was goin' to become of us. We hadn't much in the camp to eat; it was our day to go fer supplies an' our eatin's was low. It looked like starvation an' freezin' was goin' to be our doom. We didn't say much, but started breakfast. We couldn't eat much either, jus' set a'thinkin' what to do.

"Allen Bush was the first feller to mouth a word. He said, 'Boys, I hain't but one dollar in my pocket.' He got up an' started walkin' the floor. It was awhile before anybody said a word. Then I says, 'I've got ten dollars.' An' Edd Simmons, he was about twenty year old, he sez, 'I've got a dollar, but what in God's name air ye a'goin' to do with money. What difference does it make how much or how little we have, it ain't a'goin to help us none now. Can't you see that we air a'goin to freeze an' starve right here? We can't git out an' nobody can git to us.

That snow is more'n four feet deep an' you fellers a'talking about money, what do we need money fer? A grave up here ain't a'goin to cost a cent.'

"Edd's talk made us all feel creepy an' fer a long while not a word was spoke. Then I sez, 'Let's cook up every bite we got here, an' take our blankets an' see if we can get down off this mountain. Maybe we can take it by turns an' break a road.' I thought it might not be so deep anywheres else. Sez I, 'Maybe we can git somewhere to git us somethin' to eat.' 'It looks like a poor chance,' sez Allen Bush, 'but what's a'goin to become o' my family if I don't git home.' 'An' mine,' sez another feller, [I] fergit his name now. We packed our little grub an' our beddin' an' started.

"I took the first turn at breakin' the road. I didn't go fer till Allen Bush offered to take my place, an' I was glad to give it up. Then Edd he tried it, an' first one an' then t'other, but it looked like we wasn't gittin' anywhere. Every direction we looked in was jus' like a white kivver, except the trees a'stickin' up here an' yonder. We couldn't figger no way out; we couldn't tell which direction to take. We would start one way an' somethin' would turn us, an' we didn't know which way we was headed. But we had to keep a'movin fer we knowed we'd freeze if we stopped long. Edd was in the lead when we struck deeper snow. In places it had drifted 'till it was ten foot. 'There ain't no road nowhere,' Edd complained. One of the fellers fell in a hole where the snow was a good ten foot. We had hard work to pull him out. Lord, what a time we had. We lost our way so often an' we all was a'gittin' weaker every minute.

"'Long in the evenin', when we was still in sight o' nothin' jus' snow, Edd he jus' busted out a'cryin' an' said, 'We're a'goin' to freeze to death right here tonight, I know we air. I can't go a step further.' Edd was too big to cry, but he was plum wore out, an' cold, an' wet. Allen, he give out, an' we had to put down some o' the beddin' an' let him rest awhile before we could go on. An' toward sundown we had him to carry a'piece. We didn't know where we was, but we was a'goin' down a holler. It was about dark then, when all of a sudden we saw a light.

"We let into hollerin' but nobody answered. We hollered a'gin, but still no answer. We was puzzled. But we saw a feller come from the house with a lantern and go to the chimney and then back in the house. Our spirits took another drap then. But in a few minutes we saw him a'comin' carryin' a big pine torch. We had been carryin' Allen an' had laid him down while we rested an' watched. The man come right on up to where we was a'standin' an' said, 'Hello fellers. You are about froze, ain't you?' We told him we was, fer a fact. Then he said, 'Mr. Fudge sent me up here to tell you to come on to the house. We heard you holler an' knowed that somebody was in distress. Come on. I'll lead the way.' We guthered Allen up an' carried him in, but we could hardly make it. When we got to the house to a good fire, we was ready to drap off our feet. We was cold, wet, and hungry, and plum give out. We jus' fell down before that good fire.

"Mrs. Fudge was an awful kind woman an' jus' like a mother. She fixed supper fer us an' we shore put away a lot o' grub that night. After we got warm and dry, they showed us to a warm room an' good beds. We was too tired to talk an' drapped off to sleep as soon as we hit them good old feather beds. Next morning, Mrs. Fudge packed plenty o' lunch fer all of us an' we started home. After we broke the road fer a'piece, we struck the trail where the other fellers had broke. We knowed then that the others had gone in too. It was not bad after we got on their road, an' we made purty good time considerin' how tired an' sore we was. We all got home that day.

"That was the awfullest time I ever had an' home never looked so good to me. They [his family] didn't know what had become o' us, fer they was no way o' findin' out. They was wearyin' [worrying] about me. They was havin' trouble a'plenty there, too, gittin' wood an' makin' roads. But it wasn't nothin' to compare with bein' lost in the mountains.

"I kep' on workin' on public works anywhere I could git a job. I worked sometimes by the side of a nigger. I didn't like it but I never bothered them, an' I had no trouble. I've worked in the iron ore mines prospectin' fer the Virginia Coal & Coke Co.; we used a lot o' dynamite an' then dug out the ore. I made good money on that job. That was about the last public work I done.

"When I was married, I started to save a little money an' go to housekeepin'. But we went to live with Pa an' Ma fer awhile an' we couldn't save anything. An' it wasn't satisfactory, there was too many there. So we moved to Barbour's Creek, that is, we moved ourselves, we had nothin' else. We lived with Josie's people fer awhile, but that was no more satisfactory than it had been with Pa an' Ma. So I come back to Potts Creek an' rented the old Hubbard place. The land had been worked to death an' the house wasn't hardly fit to live in. But it was better'n livin' in with another family, even if they are your own kin. So we got a few pieces of furniture together, picked it up here and there, an' went to work in earnest fer ourselves. I don't think anybody could call me lazy, an' they never was a better worker than Josie. An' she knows how to work, too, her mother before her was a good worker. We 'lowed to show people that we could make a livin' an' we did. It was tough sleddin' fer a time but we made it.

"We lived at the Hubbard place fer several years. We had three children when we moved from there to this place. Virgie was the baby an' she was eighteen months old. Poor child, she's in the asylum now, don't know anybody. The man she married was so mean an' abused her so was what put her crazy (the old man was quiet and in deep thought for awhile, looking very sad). I've had ups an' downs a'plenty, more downs than ups. But it did look fer awhile like I would be able to make it, an' I would if my boys had not turned out so bad. I had hopes of havin' plenty o' help on the farm an' in the pulp wood, but they shore have disappinted me.

"We had ten children: seven girls an' three boys. But my girls have done a sight more fer us than our boys. I tried to raise 'em to do right, but they got past me long ago. I've warned 'em about this whiskey business, but they won't mind an' some of 'em will land in the penitentiary, I'm afraid.

"Trouble an' overwork is what brung on this heart trouble an' this awful cough, it's a'killin' me. I kep' a'goin as long as I could—keepin' up the fires an' carryin' in the wood an' doin' the feedin'—but I can't do it any longer. I split a little pine this evenin' but it took all my strength to do it. I hate to see Josie doin' all the work. These boys have plenty o' time to keep wood in but they don't do it. Josie has even had to hitch up the horse an' drag in wood. Me an' Josie has done more work than all our ten children will ever do.

"Youngsters these days don't want to do nothin'. [They] think somebody ought to hand 'em everything they want, an' they hain't no respect fer their parents ner nobody else. Some o' mine hain't, I do know. Some o' the girls are good to us. There's Effie, she lives in Richmond. She married a Swede. I objected to it because I had never had no use fer foreigners, but she married him anyway, an' he is a fine man an' they are doin' well. Effie has been sendin' money along, an' Roxie too. She lives in Ohio an' her man works on the railroad. Bessie lives in Roanoke. She has been sick a lot an' hasn't had so much to send, but she does what she can.

"We've got good beds, an' wood fer fires if anybody will git it. An' we got plenty to eat now, but I don't know what will be here this time next year. I don't expect to be here long, an' some of the others will have to take more interest in things here if they expect to make a livin'. I know I'll never be able to make a livin' fer 'em any more. I was a'tellin' a feller just the other day how we used to visit the old neighbors, an' if anyone got sick we went to see how they were. An' if they needed wood, we cut it an' made fires, done the feedin', milkin', or anything that was to be done. An' when they was poorly, we set up night after night an' waited on 'em, an' was glad to do it. But now, a feller can get sick an' die, an' nobody comes. Sometimes I feel awful blue a'settin' here with no company.

"What has become of the new preacher" he asked suddenly. "I couldn't blame the man if he never come back here. I don't know what made me git it in my head that he was one [of] the Holy Rollers. An' I said some things I am sorry fer now since I've heard that he was the new Methodist preacher that had been sent to this circuit. I never did hate anything so bad, an' I 'spect I said some things I oughtn't to. But after he left I sez to Josie, 'How could a man have sich a good countenance an' be one o' them rollers?' I've been distressed about it ever since an' I sent him word that I had an apology to make. I want to have a chance to tell him about my mistake. I'm a Methodist, but Pa was a Baptist.[17]

"I thought I was goin' to get this place fixed up an' I did git that little porch built. But I never got the house fixed up like I wanted, ner like Josie wanted. This room was cold all this winter. We kep' a good fire in the heater all the time but it was still cold. The floor is so open an' the cold comes in around the windows too. The wind lifted this old rug a'way up from the floor and we got awful cold sometimes. But it will soon be warm an' we will get out in the sunshine, or I hope to anyway. It will soon be time to plant corn, an' I don't have a furrow plowed.

"I'll tell you, when I was doin' the farmin' here I always had my land ready at the right season an' I planted at the right time. I don't know whether these fellers here, Grady an' Allen, [his sons] will git anything planted or not. I used to work my own land an' rent from ten to twenty five [acres] from the neighbors, an' I raised plenty o' stuff. But I don't expect to crop any more. I would like to see the ground in good shape an' see the boys takin' an interest in farmin' fer its the surest way of havin' an independent livin' that I know of. I've tried public works of different kinds, an' I've peeled cords an' cords o' pulp wood, but farmin' is my choice every time. A man may make more money, but he don't live as easy. An' if he does make more, he has to spend more an' he's always under a boss on the other works. So give me the farm life every time."

John Lee is very thin. His brown eyes are very bright, but appear sunken and, at times, look a little wild. A short, stubby beard covered his chin and his hair, which is white, was long. He was in need of a shave and haircut, but hardly looked able to sit for so much primping. He was comfortably clad in brown flannel shirt, blue trousers, sweater, and coat. He wore heavy shoes and wool socks. He sat in an arm chair, with long, bony legs crossed but did not seem to be resting. One arm is noticeably shorter than the other and he can barely reach his face with that hand. He said his arm had been broken but did not explain how it was done.

The house is dilapidated. The roof is patched with various colors of paper roofing and the logs are partially decayed. The front porch has no roof, but the small one running in front of the kitchen has been newly built and has a roof made of hand-split oak boards. The interior of the house is more inviting than the exterior. The walls are painted white, the windows are clean, and green shades and white curtains lend a dainty appearance to the room. There is a comfortable iron bed, nicely made with heavy flowered spread and pretty embroidered pillow cases. A good looking Singer sewing machine stands in one corner. [There is] a dresser and a table with several potted plants; some were in bloom. A large heater, a day bed, and a few chairs complete the furnishings in the living room.

There is a radio too. John Lee enjoys the radio a great deal, sometimes sitting up until midnight or after listening. He also enjoys the daily news and reads the papers regularly. He is a constant reader of the Bible and enjoys talking about it, sometimes getting into quite a heated argument over some question. In his younger days he was quite a fighter. He did not always keep to fistfighting, but often used rocks or some other weapon to defend himself. However, he was not mean about picking a fight, but would scrap when [an] occasion called for it.

John Lee is a prompt taxpayer and a loyal Republican. As long as he was able to walk the distance of two miles to church, he was faithful to attend, and enjoyed every service. He owns the little rough farm where he lives and has made good for a family of ten.

[Loc.: vsl/ab, box 184, 12 pp., 3,844 wds.]

John Ernest Bess Sr. *by Leila Blanche Bess, 15 August 1940*

In 1860, John Ernest Bess's grandfather Hamilton Bess and his family lived next to Daniel F. Arritt and his parents in the Boiling Spring District of Alleghany County. John Ernest's father, twenty-three-year-old John L. Bess, was a teacher in a "commercial" school at the time and was just beginning to accumulate some property. But within two years, he and several of his Arritt neighbors were driven by the Civil War to enlist in a Confederate army unit—Company G, Twenty-second Regiment—called the "Rocky Point Grays." Shortly afterward, John L. Bess was wounded at Lewisburg, West Virginia, and he carried the minié ball, which lodged in his shoulder too close to an artery to be removed, "to his grave." [18]

For the rest of his life, though, the injured arm, which was "never strong again," caused John L. Bess considerable trouble: for one, he could not farm with it and had to hire others to do that work for him. The injury was also a factor in John Ernest's later judgment that his father "had never been a strong man." But the strength and resources of the elder Bess were taxed further by the loss of his store and home by fire in 1896 and the loss of his son Walter to Bright's disease between 1900 and 1910. Those events left wounds as enervating and irreparable as that caused by the minié ball and that just as surely troubled Bess for the rest of his days.

In the trying time after the fire, the Bess family's recovery depended largely on the efforts of the sons and on the connections and assistance of kinsmen. In response to a written request for help, an uncle in Pocahontas County, West Virginia, was able to find a job for John Ernest, who then also found work for his older brother. Presumably, the uncle and his family provided lodging and board for both young men until spring, when they returned to help on the farm in Alleghany County with enough money saved to replace their team of horses.

From the distance of time and living in town, it might have been just wistful thinking when John Ernest Bess insisted that farming was the "happiest and most independent life one can live." But he had decided much earlier to stay home on the farm to help his parents and he continued to live there, along with his widowed mother and unmarried sister, following his father's death. In 1917, John Ernest Bess married Nannie Reid, and she, too, joined the other women living at

(Opposite) Roanoke County, Virginia. March 1941. A farmer plowing. Photo by John Vachon. [LC-USF34-62751-D]

the Mill Run home place. By 1927, however, John Ernest's mother had died, and a "dissatisfied" Nannie Bess insisted on moving into town. Thirteen years later, he was still thinking that the next year would find his little family living happily back on the farm, but that apparently was not to be. When John Ernest Bess died just before Christmas in 1955, his widow, son, and married daughter were all still living in South Covington.[19]

"Yes, I'm mail carrier from Covington to Paint Bank, a distance of nearly seventy miles a day. I go up Potts Creek to Paint Bank, returning by way of Mill Branch, Wrighttown, Ben's Run, and Blue Spring Run. From the Blue Spring Run post office back to Covington, I travel over the same road that I do as I go to Paint Bank. I handle a lot of mail and around Christmas, well for about three weeks before until after the New Year, the mail is awfully heavy. I sometimes have to take two cars to haul it all. I've been on this job now for over three years—three years this past July. My time will expire next July. I don't know whether I'll bid on the route again or not. I won't unless I get more money. I bid it in too cheap. It's a hard job, every day except Sundays, and I do not get any holidays as this is a star route instead of a rural. The rural carriers get all holidays with pay, but I don't get any.

"I have, in a way, enjoyed carrying this mail and building up friendships and confidences along the trail. I think I have the confidence of the people for they send by me for everything from a spool of silk thread of a peculiar color to their money orders. Some times I carry quite a lot of money for people. I do not have to take the money or buy stamps for them and put them on at the post office, but I do it for an accommodation for a lot of the people live a long distance from the post office and it is almost impossible to keep stamps all the time. I am not allowed to carry stamps and sell them, nor can I carry money orders like the rural carriers, but I am allowed to bring money to the post office for money orders and also for stamps. My people send by me to do all kinds of shopping from machine needles to mill feed and hay. I haul passengers, too. I am always pretty well loaded and sometimes, overloaded.

"Yes, I travel through some pretty wild looking territory and where there are known thieves and outlaws of different kinds, but I have never had any trouble. The only time I've felt like anyone might be going to hold me up was one day when I came from Paint Bank. I had to pass a bunch of Gypsies going and coming. As I came back, some of them tried to wave me down and stood pretty well in my path, but I didn't slow up a bit and they stepped aside. They didn't have mail to go out, at least they didn't show any, and I kept moving.

"It takes a car a year to carry the mail in [a car lasts a year carrying the mail]. It is awfully hard on cars. A car soon gets dirty and scarred up, and a part of the road I have to go over would shake a road wagon to pieces.

"What did I do before I took this job? Well, I am a farmer and like it better than any other work. But I had not been farming for ten years and had no job. I have done a lot of little things to help along with our living, but farming is what I like best of all. I live in the new part of Covington, called South Covington, near the Rayon Plant. I moved there with my family when the plant was being built. I hoped to get work there but never did, and later we took boarders, and then the post office. My wife is postmistress there, but I have always helped her with all the work until I got this job. The mail I carry does not go through the South Covington office. I get the mail out of the Covington Post Office and go directly to the Blue Spring office. Before we moved to Covington, I lived on a mountain farm and a very good one. It is run down and the buildings need fixing up, but it would be a fine place to graze sheep and cattle and a man can make some money there.

"Before my parents died we were fairly prosperous. That was when we were all at home and before any of us were married. We got burnt out in 1896 and from that time on, things didn't go so well. Father had never been a strong man but was a good manager. He did not attempt to do the farm work himself for he was not able. He taught school and ran a store. He had a good business for a number of years. When the house and all in it was burned, it was a big loss. We had no insurance. We had to begin from the bottom and build up. And I want to say, it was an uphill business. Father would not go in debt. And as he didn't have enough money to build with, the house was never finished and his mercantile business ran down, too. I didn't understand then, but I think now, he was so broken up that he lost confidence in himself and did not venture far enough to help himself as much as he might have done.

"We had always had plenty, not that we were rich at all, but we had never known want until after we were burnt out. Nowadays when people get burnt out people pitch in and help them to get on their feet again, but it was not so at that time. Father had a good deal of money out, he did a credit business, you know. And when he needed money so badly, only one man came forward and paid up his bill. That was why the business went to the bad, so many people owed big store accounts and did not pay. Some didn't have the money, but others could have paid and wouldn't. There were no industrial plants in the county then where we boys could get work. And the only work we could get was on the farms around home and the pay was short.

"I worked for the most prosperous farmer in our section and worked from daylight until it was too dark to see to plow or hoe corn, then go in, put up the horses, feed and curry, then have supper. Sometimes we had to go in and cut stove wood to do the next day's cooking. It was a hard way of living. They give fine board, and a good bed to sleep in, and were kind and good. But he only paid fifty cents a day and if he could, he paid off in bacon and flour. I took some of my wages up that way that first year, for we had nothing to eat. Our house was burnt in the fall and with it, our meat, and all canned fruit, and an abundance of dried fruit and beans. We lost everything. I remember walking home, after I finished a days' work, carrying a big hunk of bacon and fifteen pounds of flour. It was three miles, and seemed longer when I was tired [than] when I started, but I wanted to go. And when I got home, mother would fry some bacon and eggs and bake biscuits. I thought nothing ever tasted better than those meals. I was hungry, but mother was a fine cook. I've never tasted better cooking.

"It looks sometimes like one bad thing is followed by another. After the fire, we lost two horses. Both got choked and we couldn't get them unchoked. So we were left with only one horse, and it's a poor go on a farm with only one horse. Well, we boys worked around and got another one and did what farming we could. By the second year we were beginning to get on our feet, when we lost another horse. Our only hope then was to borrow and all we could get was an old mule. I never did like mules, but I had to work one that spring with our old sorrel horse. He was a grand horse and lived to be twenty-seven years old and gave no one any trouble. He ate his supper one night and—it was a practice of mine to go to the stable each night before I retired to see that everything was alright—I went over as usual. And old Chub, that was his name, had dropped dead off his feet after he had eaten his supper. We had owned him for so long it was sad to bury him. He had been with us in our days of prosperity and of near-famine. My youngest brother had to plow corn with Chub for a few days one summer without having corn to feed, just pasture, and it was almost more than he could stand. He said he would rather not eat than to hitch up old Chub without feeding him. But that's what it means to be too poor.

"My oldest brother finally got a job in West Virginia soon after I went there. We had to do something for we couldn't make a living for us all on the farm at that time. So I wrote to my uncle who lived in Pocahontas County and he was lucky enough to land a job for me in a store there. After I had been there awhile I got a job for my oldest brother. We made it pretty well there. And the next spring we bought a team of good horses and I came on home to help farm. You see, father was not able, and my youngest brother was hardly old enough to depend on, and the other brother was never stout. He always did the milking but we never depended upon him to do any heavy work.

"After we got started that year things went better. But again it seemed that we were doomed to be broken up just when we felt like we were going to pull through. I had a job with the civil engineer at Thurmond, West Virginia, was making good money, and my older brother had a good job with a lumber company. We were making enough then that we decided we could manage for me and my next older brother—the one who was not strong—to go to school that year. We started in after Christmas and were doing fine, when Walter seemed to take a deep cold. However, we did not think it serious, but after a few days called the doctor. He didn't seem to be alarmed but told him to keep quiet for a few days. Walter did not seem to improve and said he thought he would go home for a few days. I thought he was homesick. He went home and they had the family doctor to come. He said he had Bright's disease and in less than twenty four hours after he told them, [Walter] was dead.

"His death was such a shock that none of us knew what to do. We were lost for awhile. Father and Mother were almost prostrated with grief, and the youngest brother took sick. I couldn't see anything for me to do, only to quit school and go home and do what I could to help out. So I did just that and I never got to go back again. It seemed that they depended on me after that and I stayed by. Father died next, six years later. Mother lived for several years longer, but was never the same.

"I married in 1917 and we lived on the farm until we moved to Covington. I would like to be there now and hope to go back and build it up and have a lot of sheep and cattle. I know a dairy and poultry will pay well, and also sheep. I would never have left, but my wife become dissatisfied and wanted to go. She says she likes farm life and I don't know why she wouldn't, for she was raised on a farm. I think the next year will see us on the farm. My boy likes the farm and the girl [does] too, but she has a little job in town and just now feels that it is important. But when dad and mom go back, she will come too.

"I think farm life is the happiest and most independent life one can live. There is nothing I like better than to get out with a good team of horses in the early spring and begin turning the earth for the spring crops. I love the harvest, too. This year I got off one day and went up to the farm and helped the tenant stack wheat. I had not stacked any for over ten years. I sure got hot and tired, but I never slept better and believe it or not, that day's work never even made me sore. I enjoyed every minute of it and wish I could spend more time there showing that fellow what and how to do the work. He's a right good fellow and doesn't mind being told what to do and how.[20]

"So you see I've had a pull at several different jobs but if I could have my choice today, I would take the farm and stick to it. I came from a long line of farmers and ministers. Not

Sperryville (vicinity), Virginia. June 1936. Wheat stacks in the field. Photo by Dorothea Lange. [LC-USF34-09544-C]

that I ever expect to preach, but I do enjoy listening to good preaching and would like to hear more old-fashioned talk, more real Bible preaching.

"My hobbies? Well, I hardly know. I like good horses and dogs. I go squirrel hunting occasionally but do not care much for fishing. I spend my leisure time in reading. I enjoy any kind of good story, but like Westerns a lot. I love a good, clean garden and flowers and a comfortable home—not too nice to sit down in and have a comfortable chair with my feet on another—but reasonably nice. I like good cooking, milk fresh from the cool dairy house with good corn bread."

This man has a host of friends who depend upon him to do any odd shopping they don't want to take time out to go to town for. He is a member of the Methodist Church, Southern Branch, and a loyal Democrat as were his ancestors for several generations. He holds the office of steward in his church and serves well and with success. He has been greatly missed in his home section and his old friends hope he will return to the farm at an early date. He probably missed a great deal of enjoyment and a better job by leaving school, but he has the pleasure of knowing he made glad the hearts of his parents when they so sorely needed him.[21]

[Loc.: VSL/AB, box 185, 8 pp., 2,500 wds.]

Arthur Garrett *by John W. Garrett, rec. 3 February 1940*

Arthur Watson Garrett clearly had an itchy foot: he "could never be satisfied to live in one place." And according to his wife Emma's summoning up of the traditional wisdom that "three moves are equal to a burnout," they had suffered the equivalent of almost seven fires during their married life. At least one of the Garretts' many troubles actually did involve fire. The only son of their son John (the VWP worker) and his first wife, Susie, tragically "burned to death" in an accident in Arthur and Emma Garrett's home.[22]

In 1930, Arthur and Emma's daughter Hester married Albert L. (Allie) Crocker, and afterward the young couple lived with the Garrett family for a year. Later, as Hester was staying in her parents' household temporarily to await the birth of a second child, her husband was killed at his father's house in North Carolina. Relative to other young widows facing such conditions during those hard times, Hester fortunately had her mother Emma 'to take care of the babies,' so she could soon afterward find a room and take back her former job at Standard Drug in Richmond.[23]

From 1940 through 1943, Arthur and Emma Garrett were listed in Richmond city directories, together with Hester Crocker at the same address. However, it was Hester who then rented (out of her twenty-five-dollar-a-week salary) the "nice five-room cottage, with modern improvements, . . . [and] a nice yard where the children could play in the sunshine" on Cowardin Avenue. After her parents came to live with her in Richmond, Hester was able to use the money she formerly paid for room and board to "help support" them. In turn, her mother did "most of the housework," mended the girls' clothes, and helped them all get off to work and to school. Hester declared, "We all work together to keep our little family together."[24]

Her father, Arthur, was not so charitable, however, in judging the contributions of the distaff side of his family and complained that the women's economy—in the domestic sphere of home and children—was extravagant or, worse still, frivolous. On the other hand, he recalled with some pleasure the years spent truck farming on the Eastern Shore—the last time father and sons spent together as a socially bounded and distinctly male working unit.

When Arthur Garrett married Emma Carter, he was twenty-four and Emma was two months his senior. That was forty-four years ago. As a young man Arthur liked dancing and had often carried Emma [to dances]. She sometimes played a banjo for the old Virginia Reel. The square dance was the fashion in those days. Arthur had high ideals and never drank or went to immoral places.

Though his parents were poor and had to rent their farm and often plowed oxens in his young days, they were highly respected. Arthur says, "I've plowed a yoke of oxens when I was a boy and Emma usta tease me about hearing me call my oxen across the field. [I'd] call 'Whoa Buck' and 'Come here Jerry,' but I had a good pair, [and] lots of people worked oxens in them days."

Arthur, as a young man, had clean habits—standing straight and tall with clear blue eyes and a fair complexion. "Wearing a mustache was the style then and I never shaved it off until now. I wouldn't look natural," [he] says. As Arthur stands or walks he either has his hands in his pockets or crossed behind him. In his old age, he is given to worry over his financial problems.

When he was married, he and Emma went to live with his parents. He had one sister; he was the only boy. After his father's death, his mother wanted to live with her daughter who

Plowing in the Piedmont. Photo by W. Lincoln Highton. VSL/PC. [43650]

was married. So that left him and Emma on the farm alone. This farm he continued to rent for a few years, but Arthur could not be satisfied to live at any one place for long. So he moved over to Nelson County, renting a farm on the James River [and] leaving Buckingham County where he had been born and reared. Distant pastures seemed to be the greenest, and Emma and Arthur were often moving from one good farm to another. Emma said, "We have moved at least twenty times since we have been married. And three moves are equal to a burnout, they say. But Arthur could never be satisfied to live in one place. But then, we have got to see things, and people, and learned a lot we'd never know, if we'd stayed up on James River in the mountains."

[In response, Arthur explained how they came to move to the Eastern Shore.] "In nineteen and twenty, [one] of my kinfolks, Sam Davison, had gone over to Eastern Shore Virginia, and had made good money at truck farming. And he got at me to bring my family and move over there and rent a truck farm. My boys had got about grown and was a lot of help to me, but the girls never worked in the field. Jimmie, my oldest son, was working in Newport News on a streetcar as conductor, and Charlie and John was wild to go. So in December we moved over there, rented a good truck farm, got ready and planted ninety-six barrels of Irish potatoes, besides corn and sweet potatoes.

"We made good money that year. And in the fall the whole family wanted me to buy a car, so I bought a T Model Ford. The boys went wild over it and they were allus on the go.

Roseland [Nelson County], Virginia. April 1938. A boy sitting on the porch of the general store.
Photo by John Vachon. [LC-USF34-08381-C]

And run her until all the gas was out before they'd come home. The next night they [would] beg me for money to buy more gas. John, he was the worse one, allus out to some dance or nother. I just got so I'd buy him five gallons of gas a week. That went pretty hard with them, but I didn't see no use of them being gone all the time.

"We made so good that year, I rented more land. And [we] planted two hundred and eighty-one barrels of potatoes and ten acres of cabbage, and sold thirty-five hundred crates of cabbage and I don't know how many potatoes. The third year the depression come on potatoes—and we had planted a lot of potatoes—and couldn't sell 'em for expenses. And we lost everything we'd made. Jimmie en' John had got married, and Charlie was the only boy I had left.

"The girls had gone to Hopewell and gone to work in the silk mill there. So we concluded to quit the farm and move to Hopewell. And I got a job there in the silk mill—denitrating silk. I worked there for ten years and made good money, and the girls did too, and Emma kept boarders. I saved some money but the girls spent theirs, dressing and buying furniture. And we was getting along good until a big cut come in the plant, and I was sorta old and they cut me off. I couldn't get any work nowhere and we had to live on my savings, en' it went fast.

"Hester, my married daughter, and her husband were living here with us and they had two little girls. The baby was just seven days old when Allie, her husband, was killed and we had to help her. Hester soon went to work but Emma had to take care of the babies. Viola got married and went to live in Florida. She helped us a lot. She often sent us money and things, but she was killed in a automobile wreck last year. Viola was a good girl and a great help to us.[25]

"Charlie is married. He works in a dairy. He has a large family—a fine boy—but he has all he can say grace over. I had to go on relief until the WPA come on. I went to work on it, and I still am. They have been awfully nice to me and give me easy jobs. I was a guard over at the city playground for one summer. Then they put me on as night watchman down here at the schoolhouse while it was being built, and now I am waterboy.[26]

"Emma en' Hester have moved [to] Stop ten on the Richmond Pike and I go home when I am off from work. I have been trying to save money to get me a suit. But the family is so extravagant, they want the best house and everything. It takes about all I make. If they think I've got any money they are after me.

"I get along tolerable well," says Arthur. "I like to attend church and Sunday school. I've been a member of the Odd Fellows for years, but I got so I don't like 'em so much. They do tolerable well when your dues are all paid up—alright, I guess for a young man.

"I hear the pension will begin this year. I don't know if they will let me have it or not. So long as I can work on the WPA I guess I'll keep trying to knock along. It takes so much to keep the family up and I am getting so I can't do like I usta. Times look mighty hard to me. Even the young men can't get no work. And rent is so high and it seems like everything except wages are allus going up. We have paid enough rent to buy a dozen homes, but it looked like I could never save enough to buy a house.

"We have had a heap of trouble, lost two girls with sickness. And Viola was killed, that like to of killed Emma. I don't think she will ever get over it. Viola was awfully good to us and her husband was too. And he is still good to us, but we will always miss Viola—to think she had to go like she did. Automobile drivers are so reckless. It's getting to be a man's never safe on the highway. But I tell Emma, we'll make out some way," says Arthur, as he stands with his hands clasped behind his back.

While Arthur never had a chance to get an education and had to leave school when he was a boy of thirteen years to help his father on the farm, he likes to read books and keeps up with the daily news. Though he is showing age and worry, he is liked by his neighbors. He is very firm in his manner of speech and can't tolerate evil speech and low living. His ideals are now—as they were as a young man—that of wholesome living.

[Loc.: VSL/AB, box 188, 7 pp., 1,353 wds., handwritten ms.]

Mr. and Mrs. Charles Crawley   *by Susie R. C. Byrd, rec. 22 January 1939*

When asked who had resided longest in the bottoms of the old section of Petersburg below High Street, several persons interviewed by Susie R. C. Byrd gave Charles Crawley's name. Certainly, Sarah Crawley had arrived from Lunenburg County (where she had formerly been a slave of "Colonel" Robert Allen), along with her son Charles and daughter Sarah, before the Petersburg census for 1870 was taken. Charles's father, Armistead Crawley, either died beforehand or for some other cause did not come to Petersburg with the family.[27]

Armistead Crawley would be unknown except for his appearing as "father" of the groom on the marriage record for Charles Crawley to Martha Tylor on 7 July 1880. In the census for that same year, Charles was enumerated in his mother's house at 207 Plum Street, along with a stepfather, William Goode. Twenty years later, Charles was absent from his mother's household (possibly working in Hopewell), when James Givens was listed as its head in the place of William Goode. At the end of the next decade, Sarah Givens was a widow, and her son Charles Crawley was again living at home. Only after forty years of marriage and of working far from home did Mattie (Martha) Crawley finally appear in the 1920 census, together with her husband Charles and her mother-in-law in the Petersburg household.[28]

The Crawleys survived better, perhaps, than did many ex-slaves in the postbellum years. At her death in 1923, Sarah Crawley Givens left a house and lot at 515 Plum Street to her son and daughter-in-law, money and personal property to her daughter Sarah, and a lot each to a granddaughter and great-grandson. Still the transition from being considered as property herself to being a property holder was not made by Givens and her family without considerable effort and sacrifice. The living arrangement of the Crawley family—that is, of one member working in a distant location for great lengths of time while others stayed behind at home—was and is common among many peoples, including African Americans following the Civil War. Although such a pattern was hard on family life, it was an adaptive strategy that enabled many black families to survive, or possibly move up the socioeconomic scale, until such time as those arrangements were no longer necessary.[29]

Mattie works for Covington's in Chesterfield County. She comes home once a week and is off one Sunday in each month. They pay her $6.00 per week. "It's hard to get any wages around Petersburg."

Before working for Mr. Covington, she was hired by the Misses Layton. When they left Petersburg for Quaker Hill, New Jersey, she went with them. Last year the last one of that family died and she came home. She worked in that family more than thirty years.

"I haven't worked in twenty years. While working in Hopewell with Dupont Company, I was injured.

"All of my life, I have lived in this neighborhood. My mother bought this home soon after the War. She bought it from a Mrs. Jackson, a colored lady. Mrs. Jackson, at that time, owned a number of houses all through this section. When we first bought the house it was a cottage, [but] Mother rebuilt [it as] a two-story frame house. And it has four rooms, two rooms upstairs and two down. We have a front porch, but no back porch. A platform leads to the kitchen outside.[30]

"This street is in a bottom, drainage comes off High Street. The dampness rotted the porch boards. I had it cemented when I was working years ago. The cement is still in good

Historic American Buildings Survey. Pig Alley Block Study (VA-930), *Hurt St., Plum St., and Grove Ave., near Appomattox River. Mid 19th Century village complex of cottages, built for laborers in nearby flour and cotton mills. (1968) [This particular photograph shows row houses at 705–713 Plum St. Built ca. 1835.]* LCP & P. [HABS VA27-PET 23E-I].

shape. It hasn't cracked yet. The fences need repairs and the house needs paint. We are not able to have repairs done. It takes what little Mattie is making for us to live on. The front yard is very small. We have no driveway, but a walkway on the side.

"This house needs general repair inside, too. All the floors are in bad shape. The walls are good in the rooms upstairs; downstairs they need fixing badly. Some of the plastering has fallen. All the window panes are in and we have screens for all of them. Mosquitoes and flies are terrible around here. Yes, all the floors are covered with linoleum and rugs. They are passable. Shades and curtains are in fair shape.

"We have just odd pieces of furniture in all the rooms. Mattie worked away and we never bothered about getting expensive furniture. We have electric lights. Toilet is outside and it needs repairs. All of our rooms are small. Our bedroom, in the winter, is used for everything. In it, we cook, sleep, eat, and receive our company."

This room was very congested, having a double bed, bureau, trunk, table for preparing meals, and wood and coal packed behind the stove, on the side, and under the table. A large oak wardrobe [took] all the space on the side of the room by the chimney. At the foot of the bed was a rocker, and in the center of the floor, there [was] a big arm chair. A small bookcase was also seen in the corner by the bureau. This case was filled with books, papers, and magazines. [The] floor [was] covered with linoleum and [there was] a rag rug beside the bed, and [one] in front of the stove. White curtains and green shades were at the windows.

"All the pleasure I have is a good smoke. My pipe is my comforter. My worries are hard times and my wife having to take care of me these 20 long years. Yes, if I had a sum of money given me, I would stop my wife from work, repair this house, pay our back bills, and live on the other.

"In a way the poor man is worse off now than he was in slavery time. Reason is, he has to hustle now, or die. When [a man] had a good master, he would look out for him. Race problem can be solved when idleness is stopped—give people work. When [the] poor man works it helps the rich, because he exchanges his money with him. Yes, I belong to Church. And I didn't vote this last election because I had no money to pay my taxes."

[Loc.: HU/REL, box 5, 5 pp., handwritten ms.]

Marvin Broyhill *by John W. Garrett, rec. 18 March 1940*

Although Marvin Broyhill was born near Moravian Falls in Wilkes County, North Carolina, his family came full circle back to Virginia, for the Broyhill (or Broughall) family traces its history in this country to William Broyhill of Caroline County, Virginia, in 1732 and through his grandson James to Wilkes County by 1806. James Broyhill's great-grandson Thomas Jefferson Broyhill (Marvin's father) was a farmer, carpenter, and millwright who brought the first steam engine into western North Carolina. With it he set up the first of a number of sawmills that became part of a small-scale lumber and building business and the initial training ground for Marvin Broyhill and his brothers.[31]

In 1912 the E. I. DuPont de Nemours Company bought a large tract of the Eppes family's Hopewell Farm in Prince George County with the intent of building a dynamite plant. With the advent of World War I, the plant was expanded in 1914 to become "the largest guncotton plant in the world," and "Hopewell" persisted as the name of the city that rapidly surrounded it.[32]

Ruel Vandenberg Broyhill seems to have been the first of the Broyhill brothers to go to Hopewell in response to DuPont ads. Another brother, Gibson, joined him there in the summer of 1915. By the end of that year, their parents, Thomas Jefferson and Sallie Gilreath Broyhill; Ruel's family; and brothers Felix, "Pete" (Lincoln), and also Marvin Talmadge had all migrated to Hopewell, either to work in the plant or to join in the related land speculation and building rush. It was surely a time of optimism and abundance for Marvin T. Broyhill when he married Nellie Magdalene Brewer (also a Wilkes County, North Carolina native) on 8 April 1917—notwithstanding Congress's declaration of war two days before.[33]

A disastrous slump followed the end of the war, when the powder plant, as some suggest, "shut down abruptly" and was boarded up by the DuPont Company very shortly after the armistice in 1918. Although the building business went down much more quickly, the actual closing of the plant may have been somewhat more gradual than stated, since the census shows both Marvin T. and his brother Gibson working for the DuPont Company, as a clerk and a mechanic, respectively, in 1920. Nevertheless, as Hopewell continued to rise and fall repeatedly with successive waves of new industries, such as the Tubize Artificial Silk Company and Hercules Powder, so too did the fortunes of Marvin and Ruel's business Broyhill Realty Company, until at last it was shut down by the depression. In January 1937, Marvin T. Broyhill and his family moved to northern Virginia, where he began again, along with several of his brothers.[34]

When Marvin Talmadge Broyhill died in Arlington at the age of seventy-eight on 23 November 1966, the founder of M. T. Broyhill and Sons Corporation, which combined "development, construction, insurance and realty," was credited with a number of accomplishments. In the early days in Hopewell, he "concentrated on building for the low middle income brackets" and on a project "to build better housing for Negro workers living in Hopewell." In northern Virginia his company "built and sold more than 15,000 houses and apartments," many of these in response to the housing shortages following World II and the demand of returning servicemen. His last major project was the planned community of Sterling Park, which joined government financing, U.S. Steel, and his own Sterling Park Development Corporation in one grand venture.[35]

"When I was a boy on the farm, where I was born in eighteen hundred and eighty-eight (my father had bought the tract of timber—as he was a lumber manufacturer, and contractor and builder—and after he had sawed the timber on the place and [built] a home on it), the Cleveland administration came and with it the panic. And during these years my father had the place cleared and brought into cultivation, more to help the poor people than anything else. As I have heard him say many times, he didn't intend to make that place his home, but it was a good farm and he liked the community and so we lived there for around twenty-five years.[36]

"My oldest brother had finished the seventh grade some two years before I did, and had gone to Lynchburg, Virginia to do some special studies and had returned home. And when I had finished the grades—that was as far as the county schools could take one—I told my father I wanted to leave home and take up some business course when the fall came. And he consented to send me. So I answered some advertisements of various schools and decided I wanted to go to Omaha, Nebraska. I remember one day as I was hauling up corn from off the farm, I had been teasing my little five-year old brother—telling him I was going away and he would be sorry to see me go. Pete was the pet of all of us and he said, 'Yes, I want you to go and I want you to go right now.' But when I left, little Pete was crying along with the rest of us. Leaving home wasn't so easy. But I had made up my mind to go, and I wanted to make good and secure more of an education.

"When I arrived in Omaha, the government was calling for wireless telegraphy operators, and [I] investigated the positions they had to offer and thought I would like the work. So I entered the school to study wireless telegraphy. It didn't take me but a few months to graduate. But to get a position, I had to join the United States Signal Corps and I was only eighteen. So I would have to secure my parents signature to my enlistment papers. I wrote home and asked them if they would sign for me to enlist for four years. My parents were willing, but wanted me to come home on a visit first. So I went home for two weeks and returned with the papers all signed. After I was all signed up and passed the examinations and gone through the sham battles as operator, one day the Captain came in our camp and was selecting a number of boys to go to Alaska for the government. And to my surprise, I was among the number chosen. 'Now boys, we don't compel you to go up there, but it's a good opportunity if you want to go. Alaska is a country with opportunity and hardships, you will get double time on your retirement record while you are up there.' Well, I was full of adventure and anxious to go.

"We sailed from Seattle, Washington in nineteen and six, and arrived at Nome, Alaska in about three weeks later. We saw lots of icebergs, which made sailing both slow and dangerous. Alaska was an interesting country: a lot of Americans came up to hunt for gold, some of them got rich, and many went home broke. I was furnished with a dog team of six fine dogs and sleigh, on which I traveled during the winter when I went from one road house to another where our stations were located. The summer day is called six months long and

the winter night is also six months, and we longed for the first of the sun in the spring. We had snow all winter, and when spring come and the sun came up, it was beautiful. And the Northern lights are wonderful, worth a trip to Alaska just to see them. But I wasn't conscious of the sun's glare on the snow and the first thing I knew I was snow blinded. That's why I have [had] to wear glasses ever since.

"I wrote home to my parents every week, [even] though the mails were irregular. And often I would have to wait a month for a letter from home and friends on the 'outside,' as we called it, only to receive a nice pile all at once. And how glad we were when it come. I stayed up there until nineteen and twelve—around six years—and the longer I stayed the more I wanted to go home. So I come out to the States, and bought myself out of the Signal Corps, and home I went.

"My father was still in the lumber manufacturing business and was operating a number of mills and I wanted to work with him. And so I bought a mill from my father and stayed with him until the depression come in nineteen and fourteen and the lumber business went down, and we had to quit or go broke. We had a lot of contracts, but the people said we can't pay you for sawing as we can't sell a foot. So I still had my trade, and I secured a position with the Southern Railway Company as telegraph operator. My father moved to town, sold our farm, and I was again at home.

"Then the war come on and my oldest brother had gone to Hopewell, Virginia to work with the DuPont Nemours Powder Company. And he found it easy to sell real estate and was soon a leading real estate agent. He wrote home telling us all about the prosperity of Hopewell, Virginia, so my father and mother went out there with the family. I was left alone in Wilkesboro, North Carolina, and it wasn't long until I resigned my position and went to Hopewell. And my parents, my brother, and I were in the real estate business and making money fast. We had a lot of options on lands. My mother often warned us, 'Boys, you would better be careful, a crash is coming.'

"And in the meantime, I had left in North Wilkesboro the sweetest little girl I had ever seen and in the spring of nineteen and fifteen, Nellie Brewer and myself were married at her home in Huntington, West Virginia. After our honeymoon we come back to Hopewell to make it our home, where I was in business.[37]

"In a few months after that, one day the DuPont Company made a statement that their plant might be temporary and next morning, why I couldn't give a tract of land away. We had all our money invested, and we found ourselves broke. We got a job with the DuPont Company and went to work until we could get on our feet again. The war come to a close and with it the plant closed down and Hopewell was a dead city, people left by the thousands. I told Nell we might as well stay on and see what would come, as I felt sure the city would come back.

"And soon the Tubize Silk Company came and then other plants, and I again opened my office dealing in real estate. We had three boys then: Marvin Jr., the oldest; and Joe [Joel T.]; and Hurbert. We wanted a girl but we had all boys. The town began to build up, and I began a building project of a restricted district in Crescent Hills and built and sold around a hundred houses. Then the depression of twenty-nine came. We had a lovely home in Crescent Hills and with it our two girls, Joy, and Nellrose, and we were happy and enjoying prosperity. I thought I could sell my farm and save my other property, but I couldn't collect and I couldn't survive for long. A house here lost and then another, and finally we sold our home, and moved to Arlington, Virginia.[38]

"My family lives there and I keep my office in Front Royal. And after my week's work is done, I go home [to] Arlington to spend the weekend with Nell and the children. Junior has finished high school and is working in Washington, D.C. Joe had to have five more units, so last year I sent him to Fork Union Military school and that cost me around a thousand dollars. But he is through school and is selling real estate with his mother. She is a good business woman.[39]

"I am getting a bit gray now, but I am still young. A bit heavier than I used to be, around one seventy-five pounds. [I] enjoy a good joke and a game with the boys when I go home, or a game of bridge with the family. We enjoy the Sabbath day, when we attend church together and often take a drive through the country in the summer when it is warm. Joy and Nellrose are getting to be grown girls, and they enjoy music and dancing. Mother is a good cook and housekeeper (though we always have a maid); she sees to the work, and she is a great lover of flowers. That's her hobby, but she grows some prize-winning roses, chrysanthemums, and other [choice?] ones. But I would like to have her to give up her work at Arlington and live at Front Royal, so I could be home more of the time. I enjoy the home life with the family and it's a treat for the week to pass, when I can run home for a weekend and be with Nell and the children."

[Loc.: VSL/AB, box 188, 8 pp., 1,658 wds., handwritten ms.]

Charles Tucker *by Leila Blanche Bess, 6 May 1940*

Charles Tucker allowed that the only thing that could take his mind off his troubles was to get his "gun and [his] dogs and go coon hunting." And he had enough troubles in his life to give him cause to "spend many a night on the mountain" alone, just he and his dogs, seeking its solace. In the space of a month in 1918, Tucker lost two children to diphtheria, his wife and another child to the flu, and he was suddenly left a widower with six other children, including a four-month-old baby.

The so-called Spanish Lady flu epidemic of 1918–19, which killed an estimated 550,000 Americans, including Jane Wolfe Tucker and her child, appears to have broken out first in Camp Funston, Kansas. From there it was carried by World War I troops to Spain and around the world before it came back to Alleghany County in the mutated and much deadlier form that caused highest mortality among the normally hardiest age group—persons twenty to forty years old. In the known history of pandemic influenza, the 1918 flu epidemic is unique in this age pattern. But that was no comfort to Charles Tucker.[40]

Tucker's youngest son, who was orphaned at four months, claimed his mother's red hair when he was later interviewed by vwp worker Leila Bess. "I reckon my daddy had a purty tough time of it after mother died," he told Bess. "[But] we never broke up, Dad kept us all together, two girls and four boys. He done the best he could by us, but Lord, no man can do much of a job keepin' house an' raisin' kids an' farmin' an' blacksmithin' for a livin'." He guessed that was why his father had married a widow and "mighty fine woman" three years later. In the end, however, his stepmother's sense of obligation to her own grandchildren separated and kept her and Charles apart and left him to seek consolation in solitary pursuits.[41]

When Charles Tucker was born in Alleghany County, fifty-nine years ago, at the home of his grandparents, James and Elizabeth Tucker, there was the usual stir and excitement that attends a birth but to this was added much gossip, for his mother, Josephine, was not married. She was young and attractive and very intelligent in a natural way. Her education and religious training had been sadly neglected. Her parents were poor and there was a large family. They were honest and worked hard, but could not provide the necessary food, clothing and books for the family, so several of the girls as they grew up were "hired" out to work in more prosperous homes. . . . [42]

[Charles's] mother was fond of him, but could not give him any assistance in an educational way, even if she had been so-minded. She had to work out to get food and a few clothes for herself and Charles. Their raiment was often very scanty. Charles was often clothed in a pair of old trousers, given to him by someone who had outgrown them and expected them to last until Charles could grow into them. One suspender usually kept the old trousers from falling off, and a much patched shirt about three sizes too large completed his outfit. He went barefooted most of the time until he got large enough to work for himself.

Charles began picking up little jobs around among the neighbors when he was very small. He did his work very well and soon people began to comment on his good work. . . . He lived on with his grandparents on a little farm, close to Potts Creek, in the Arritt section. There was a post office near called Arritts. He was fond of his grandparents and worked steadily to help them all he could, but finally decided that he could be of more service if he had a job outside of the farm, where he could make more money. . . . [43]

"When I first got work away from home, it was on a farm, I didn't know how to work anywhere else then. I hoed corn and was taught how to bind wheat, then I was taught how to cradle the wheat. I loved to swing a cradle in a good wheat field.

"I was only paid twenty-five cents a week, whenever I first started to work. I worked at that price for a good while. Then they raised my wages to fifty cents a week. I worked at that for a spell, but when I got so I could do as much work as a man, I got fifty cents a day. I felt like a man then. Fifty cents a day was the usual wage for a man, except in wheat and hay harvest, then he got $1.00. As I said before, I always liked farming better than any other kind of work and I still like it best. I worked and saved all I could of my wages. I always give my mother and granddaddy part of my money, for they had took care of me when I couldn't take care of myself, and I felt like I wanted to do something in return.

"I heard of a job over in Craig County, where I could make better money if I had a horse. They wanted a man to haul timber for the mines. They used heavy stuff to brace up the mines to keep the dirt from caving in. I took out one day and went over there to see for myself what [there] was to do and how much I could make. I looked the job over and saw it was a dangerous job, but it paid more money than I had ever expected to make. I come back, got out my little savings and counted it over. I had found out where I could get an old horse. He was big and strong and in good shape, but he was old. I got him and went to Craig County and began work. My first job on public works.

"I didn't cut the timbers, they was cut and ready to haul. I had to haul them right up to the mouth of the mine—or the 'man hole'—where the little cars was loaded. I dumped the timbers off right over the mine. There was some danger of going a step too far and the horse might fall into the open shaft. I made money there. When I quit I had money enough to buy me a good team. I got a job of hauling from off Potts Mountain then. I hauled ties and tan bark. I was awful proud of my team and my work. I got along all right.

"When I was around twenty-two years old, I married a girl I had knowed all my life. Her name was Jane Wolf. We went to housekeepin' on the mountain and lived there for several years. We had nine children and was doin' fine when the children took diphtheria. We was far from a doctor and it was in the dead of winter. I seen they was gettin' worse and I got on my horse and rode off that mountain one awful cold night for Doctor Carter. He come and give medicine, and told us it was diphtheria and how awful it was. We done everything he told us to do, but nothin' done any good, and one night two of the children died. We was alone there on that cold mountain, no way of lettin' anybody know until daylight. Everybody was afraid to come, when they did hear it, and we had an awful time. I tell you nobody knows what trouble is, till they have to set by, helpless to do a thing to help, and see their children die. We couldn't do a thing only watch and wait. We had an awful time to get a coffin and to get the little bodies down off that mountain to the graveyard. The other children was all sick, too. They got better of the diphtheria and then we all took the flu.

"It was the winter of that first awful time that the flu come around. My wife had it and all the children was sick. I was sick too, but kept goin' about. One of our neighbors was awful bad off and sent for me. Our folks seemed to be better and I got ready to go. One of the little boys wanted to go with me. I didn't want him to go, but he begged so hard that I consented, and he went with me. He had got over diphtheria, but seemed weak-like. After we went over there, he took flu and died. Then his mother died next. I had four deaths in my family in less than a month. I was stunned, broke up. I didn't know which way to turn, and there was the six motherless children. Oh, nobody knows what death is till it comes like that and almost wipes out the whole family with a single stroke. Their mother had always taken care of the children and then I had nobody to look to. But I determined to keep the kids together and I did. It was hard goin' with a four-months old baby to look out for. I had to get milk for him just anywhere I could. My cows was dry at that time. I stayed with the children as much as I could for three years.

"My oldest girl got married and then I got married. I married a widow with two children, a boy and a girl. She was a good woman and I've never seen a better cook or housekeeper than Maggie was. We got along fine and I had plenty of everything. I had a fine team of horses, several good cows, hogs and chickens and a good crop. I was livin' on Doctor Carter's farm then. We left the mountain some time before. We had a good show for bein' more prosperous, when her daughter's husband was caught with bootleg whiskey and sent up for two years. Maggie felt like she had to go to her daughter and help to take care of her children and to save them from goin' to the devil like their daddy. I tried to persuade her not to go, and told her it would be a waste of her time for them youngins' would do just as they pleased anyhow. I couldn't do nothing to keep her from goin'. She washed up every single piece on the place and ironed them and put 'em in the dresser drawer. My shirts and everything.

"Little did I think that she would be gone all these years. I told her I would take the small children, her grandchildren, and take care of them if she would stay. But she couldn't bear to turn any of them away. And I couldn't take the whole family, for it was already public that some of the boys was into the same trouble and I wouldn't have it. So she went away and it has turned out just as I thought it would. The oldest boys are as mean as their Dad, and Maggie has no influence over them. And her daughter's husband has left since he got out of the pen and is livin' with another woman. And Mag is left with the bag to hold. She still has two of the children and all she has to depend upon is six dollars a month she gets — old age pension. One of the boys was in CCC Camp but got tired and left. He said he was tired of giving his money away and just walked out. Now he has nothing to do, and his grandma has him to feed what time he ain't loafin' around somewhere.

Chopawamsic [now Prince William Forest Park], a U.S. Resettlement Administration recreational project in Virginia. April 1936. Making "shakes" (hand-made shingles). Photo by Arthur Rothstein. [LC-USF34-01562-E]

"After Maggie left me, I sold everything I had on the place. My team and cows and chickens and most of my furniture. I went to livin' around with my children. It ain't satisfactory, but its the best I can do. I never got no divorce. I've always hoped that Maggie would come back and we could make another start. I go to see her sometimes, and I send her groceries and anything I know she needs. I have never quit work. I rent land every year and raise a good crop. I only have one horse now. I just double-team with others that have one horse. I am not happy and I'm restless. I would like for my wife to come back and we could spend our last days together. I'm not old, only fifty nine. I can make a livin' for her and would if she would come back."

"The only thing that takes my mind off my troubles is to get my gun and my dogs and go coon hunting. I've killed a many a big fat coon on the mountain. I killed twenty, one fall, from one dog. I have spent a many a night on the mountain by myself, just me and my dogs. I was out one night, right on top of the mountain, when the dogs began to bark like they saw something. I looked, the moon was shining a little, and I could see something walking. It looked like a bear walking on his hind legs. Next, two come in sight, then four. The dogs were raging, and I raised my gun and took aim right in the breast. I didn't fire, but raised my gun again, and the third time something stayed my hand. Just then someone called: 'Don't shoot, for God's sake, don't shoot.' I let my gun fall to my side. I felt weak. I had come mighty near shootin' some of my neighbors, takin' 'em to be bears. They never did explain how they happened to be there at that time o' night. They wasn't huntin'.

"But the closest shave I ever had when out huntin' up there was when my dogs fell in a big hole in the side of the mountain. I thought they was after a groundhog and followed in after 'em. I soon found that the place was deep and slippery, and I didn't know where the bottom was, and the dogs was fightin' something in there. So I scrambled out and set fire to the leaves, but before I got out of the way the smoke was about to smother me. I barely escaped that time with my life. The dogs got out and we left that place, and I've never been back there any more. I never found out what the dogs had back in there.

"I'm farmin' some this year, but not as much as I usually do. I'm tryin' to help my boys along too. They kinder depend on me to tell 'em when and how to do things. I done the best I could by my children, but I know it was not what it would have been if their mother had lived, or even if their stepmother had stayed with us. Most of my kids liked their stepmother, especially the youngest ones. She was good to them, and took a great interest in keepin' them clean and give them plenty to eat of well-cooked food. She taught the girls how to cook and how to keep the house nice and clean. She was very particular about the housekeepin' and wouldn't stand for any dirt around. She worked all the time and no wonder we missed her.

"She has had some hard times, too, and is about up against it right now. She lives in an out-of-the-way place in a little old shack. She told me she almost froze there last winter. There are holes in the walls big enough to stick your arm through. The last time I ask her to come back, I told her I would rent a farm and buy all the furniture we needed, and the stock, too. I had one cow then, and would let her bring the two grandchildren with her. And I could take care of them all and be glad to do it. But she said: 'No, Charley, I can't go back now. I ought never to have left your home. You was good to me and have been good since I left, but I can't go back now and take these children. They would be a worry to you, as they have been to me. You was right. I have failed to make of them what I hoped. The two I have are good children yet, but when they get older they may do like the others have done. But I'll have to stay on. When they all leave me, I don't know what I'll do then.'

"It all looks so foolish for us two old people to be living apart this way, when we could be so much happier together."[44]

[Loc.: VSL/AB, box 185, 11 pp., 3,122 wds.]

Isaiah Wallace *by Margaret Jeffries, 11 March 1940*

On the road up Red Oak Mountain in Rappahannock County in 1900, the census enumerator located Charles and Annie Wallace, their eleven children, and his widowed mother, Martha Wallace, who was born in 1824. One of Charles and Annie's sons, Isaiah (or Isaac, in the listing), at about age fourteen, ran away to an uncle's house in Pittsburgh and afterward worked for a number of years in Pennsylvania, Ohio, and West Virginia. But Isaiah was at home for a brief interval in 1900—between going to work in Rhode Island and returning to marry Malinda Payton in 1901. Some natives of Rappahannock County, who remember Isaiah Wallace or stories of his youthful ramblings, still refer to him as "Hobo Ike."[45]

Isaiah Wallace's lifelong interest in education may have begun under the influence of his first employer and mentor, the "beloved Mrs. Belle Mason, who taught him so much." But his second marriage (as a widower) to teacher Lila Dangerfield and his subsequent diverse efforts to organize a "league of colored people" to obtain Rosenwald funding for schools in Rappahannock and Culpeper Counties went beyond the seed "to know" implanted earlier.

Jeffries was not ready, however, to address the possibility that Wallace had the capacity on his own to chafe against inequality, either in education or in voting. From her vantage point, Margaret Jeffries could only conclude that Isaiah recognized and accepted the "limitations of his people and their dependence upon the white race" and understood that it was solely "through education . . . that the Negro [could] hope to take his place in the world among other races."

A good old Bible name has Isaiah Wallace. And his last name is that of a good old Virginia family. All of which is reasonable enough because Isaiah's father and mother were brought up to read the Bible and they were trained by good old Virginia families. For Isaiah's father and mother were slaves.

"My grandfather belonged to the Wallace family," Isaiah said. "Folks called him Strother Wallace, after Colonel Strother Wallace. My father was Charles Wallace and he was servant to Dr. James Kemper during the war. I went down to Lynchburg not long ago and went to the old hospital where he used to work. He died sixteen years ago last December."

Where they got the spelling of the name Wallace is hard to say since the family to whom they belonged and whose name they took after the War between the States, spelled their name Wallis. After the emancipation of the slaves the family was more or less scattered. "Didn't but one of 'em go off with the Yankees though," Isaiah remarked.

Isaiah's grandfather went to live in Rappahannock County and seems to have stayed there until his death. And there is where his son, Charles, the father of Isaiah, lived the rest of his life too.

"My mother belonged to Miss Matilda Brown up here near Eggbornsville," he continued. "Miss Matilda and her sister—they was both of 'em old maids—taught her how to knit and sew, and she used to knit socks and gloves and take them over to the Confederate soldiers many a time. She's eighty-eight years old now. She fell some time ago, and someway or other she has never been able to walk since. She lives up here at Woodville, in the house my father bought and lived in. One of my brothers and one of my sisters live with her. My sister's not just normal but she does pretty well for somebody like her."[46]

There were thirteen children in all in Isaiah's family. Only ten of them are living now: five boys and five girls. And all, except the sister who is not normal, are married. "No'm, they don't own their own homes," he answered a question. "Seems like they never been able to buy homes." All of the family with the exception of Clarence, who is a blacksmith, and Isaiah, who was a stone mason and plasterer, work out by the day at any kind of work they can get.

"Times were pretty hard right after the war," Isaiah said. "Many's the time when Mama couldn't give us nothin' to eat except a little potlikker made from cress salet or some kind of other greens and ash cake. But it tasted mighty good, I'll tell you. It sure tasted mighty good."

He then went on to tell how hard it was to get hold of anything with which to make clothes. "The way we got the wool for our stockings was, Mama would send us all out in the fields. And you know, the white folks would wait a long time to clip their sheep, and the wool would get long and pull off on the briars. Then we would go along and pick it off the briars and take it home to Mama, and she would wash it and card it and make it into stockings for us. She made all of us—boys and girls—learn how to weave and knit and sew and cook too. And the first pair of shoes I ever had she made for me out of the top of an old pair of boots. She used the leather legs of the boots for the soles and made the tops of cloth, that woolen cloth that was made up here at the Swartz Woolen Mills." His mother did not go out to work as many colored women did. But she did take in a little ironing from people who wanted things done especially well.

"To get money to buy us clothes, we used to pick shumate [sumac] and dry it," Isaiah reminisced. "And when they were ripe, we picked blackberries and sold 'em. We picked cherries for folks too. And we sold chestnuts for two cents a pound to get shoes and shucked corn for ten cents a barrel."

His face broke into a grin when he thought of a story of his youth and he could not keep from telling it. He said that one time he remembered some of the brethren of the church were at his home having a lengthy conference on some point of church work. His father generally did the butchering for the neighborhood and quite frequently was given the tripe and the livers. "You know the white folks wouldn't eat tripe or liver or chittlings," he said smilingly. "So my father generally got all that when he butchered a beef."

On this occasion—all during the conference—the pot was boiling on the stove, cooking up the tripe and chitterlings from a beef just killed that day. The aroma from the pot became better and better to the dusky brethren. Finally, it was time for the company to depart. But that tripe smelled so good cooking! In bidding her guests goodbye, the woman assured them that if she had some bread baked she would invite them to have some of the contents of the pot. "They all said right away that it wouldn't take long to stir up a little hoe cake," Isaiah was laughing right out now. "So Mama made some hoe cake and put it on the griddle to bake in front of the fire and sure enough it didn't take long. And did those folks eat? They kep' on eatin' and eatin' until all the tripe was gone. Then I sidled over to Mama and said: "Please Mama, don't let 'em eat all the chittlin's too.""

Isaiah said that his mother was half Indian. Her name was Annie Perry, although her father called himself Fields.[47]

Isaiah's school career started when he was nine years old. He was still at home then. It did not last long, eighteen months being the sum total of all of it. At first he attended school in a little log school building which measured, he said, fourteen feet by twenty. And this room, small as it was, housed eighty-eight pupils when they were all there. "They just stood all 'round the walls," he answered the query concerning the method used to get that many children into one room so small. "The benches were made out of slabs and didn't have backs to 'em. There were four grown people there, but they had to pay a dollar a month to go. I learned most from Mrs. Belle Mason."

He then explained how he was working for Mrs. Mason for eighteen dollars a year and board, and was sent to school for three months during each year. "She made me study my lessons every day with her children," he said. It was this same plan that was used during the most of his school life. He was working at the same time he was going to school. He stayed at the home of Mrs. Mason for three years.

He then went to work for Mr. John Butler for fifty dollars a year and had three more months of schooling. "Miss Lucy Butler helped me with my books then," he added. "The second school I went to was a little bit bigger than the first one. It was taught by a one-legged white man. The little school was taught by a colored man, John T. Williams."

The subjects he studied were reading, writing, arithmetic and geography. The schools were not graded at that time and a child was promoted by readers. Isaiah was in the third reader by the time he went to work for Mr. Billy Mason, brother-in-law to his beloved Mrs. Belle Mason, who taught him so much. He was still working here and had finished the third reader when he ran away.

"It was the eighteenth of January," Isaiah related with a sheepish grin on his face. "The snow was deep in Pittsburgh and I didn't have a sign of an overcoat. I didn't have but a quarter in my pocket either. If I had had nine dollars and a quarter more I would have come right along back home. But I didn't have it. I had borrowed nine dollars and fifty cents from the postmaster at home, and it took the rest to pay my fare."

Luckily for the young colored boy, he had relatives in the city. His uncle, he said, was very well thought of in Pittsburgh and helped him to find a job shoveling coal in a factory. Here he worked for three years saving, during that time, forty dollars. And then hard times struck again. Along came a depression, "the one during Cleveland's administration," Isaiah said.

"You know they had to have soup lines and such things. Well, I never had been used to gettin' my food that-a-way, and I had a right hearty appetite too. I had just forty dollars I had saved and I knew—what with havin' to pay out three dollars a week for board—that wouldn't last long. So I said to myself I had better try hard to get some work, and I finally did. I went to a employment agency and they asked me what kind of job I wanted. I told 'em I'd take anything I could get. So then they told me about a place in the country near the city. It was in Idlewood, Pennsylvania, and I stayed there workin' on the farm for some German people for two years. They were real nice people too."

He did not say why he quit this job on the farm, but started telling of his next job which was in Liverpool, Ohio, working in a livery stable. He did not like the work there very much and quit after nine months time. In Charlestown, West Virginia, he secured his next job working on the C. & O. Railroad loading freight. He had worked at this for four months when the freight he was on stopped over in Culpeper to load on some flour.

"Well, me and a redheaded man that worked with me went up the street," Isaiah took up the tale. "It was our day off. And I met my aunt and she told me about my sister that was sick. I didn't know she was sick. And she pleaded with me until I went home. Didn't any of 'em know me but the sister that was sick."

After this he worked for different farmers in the neighborhood. Two years he spent as a hand for Mr. Will Yancey and then he went north again. This time he found employment in Newport, Rhode Island where he worked for two seasons—or eight months—farming. This brought him up to the time of his first marriage.

"It was in 1901," he continued. "Malinda Payton met me in Washington, D.C. and we was married there by a justice of the peace. She had been cookin' for Mr. Will Yancey and that's where I come to know her." This marriage lasted for twenty-two years, at the end of which time Malinda died.

During that time Isaiah began his trade of stone and concrete work. At first he worked for other people, contractors. He began working for John Johnson and then later did some work for another contractor, Mr. Charlie Hawkins. At this he worked off and on for four years. All this time he was learning his trade and finally got so he could contract for small jobs himself. He proudly exhibited a list of houses he had plastered between 1917 and 1923. After running a crooked finger down the long list of names, some of which had the figure one beside them, and some two, or even four, according to the number of houses he had plastered for that man. "Forty-nine houses in Culpeper County," he stated and started counting again. "Thirty-five in other places with two in Rappahannock County, and one apartment house with a hundred and fifty bedrooms in it."

He then announced that he had built seventy-one flues and chimneys during that time. Continuing his story of his work experience, he told of three years when he had worked in the lime kilns of West Virginia, baking lime. For the rest of the time, he worked for other people around his home in Rappahannock. Finally, he started buying a little place of his own near Rixeyville, in Culpeper County, and devoted his time to that.

"I was doin' fine, keeping up the payments on my place, until I got hurt," he explained. And [he] went on to tell that in 1931 he was in an automobile wreck from which he came out with a fractured skull, a broken jaw bone, his teeth all knocked out, and an injured arm. "And somethin' happened to my neck," he stated. "It hurts me when I turn my head round. And there is somethin' feels like corn flakes inside of here," he said, putting his finger on the spot on the side of his neck. "I didn't go to the hospital though," he ended triumphantly.

Since the wreck he has never been able to work as before. He did fairly well for a year or so by hiring two men to work his place for him, and getting himself a job collecting for the Southern Aid Insurance Company among the colored policy holders. For this he received eighty-five dollars a month all told, counting his expense money and the commission paid him by the company on the receipts. He paid the men for working his farm twenty dollars a month, and in that way had enough to keep up the payments on the debt. But unfortunately another depression cut short his career again. Policy holders became scarcer and scarcer until there were not enough to make it worth his while, since he had the pay of his hired men to take out of what little he received. He threw up the job and rented out the farm. "But I'm afraid I'm goin' to lose it yet," he said sadly.

Isaiah married again in 1923. His wife, Lila Dangerfield, generally known as Mary Dangerfield, was a school teacher already in her forties. Lila's father was a well doing colored man who owned his own land and made a decent living for his many children, even managing to send Lila off to normal school at Petersburg to fit her for her profession. And she had been teaching ever since. Isaiah, although he could not go to school very much himself, was very much interested in seeing that other people of his race got a chance to get an education. He had, even before his marriage, been active in school work.

Just after the World War, when the soldiers had come back from France, he got to thinking that something should be done about them not having had any education. "I had kept an account," he said smilingly, "of the number of dollars that I calculated the school board owed us in schools. You see a certain amount was appropriated for colored schools in Rappahannock County and for several years we didn't have any schools at all. Well, after the war I went to work on it." He then told how he had organized a league of colored people and got them interested in getting schools for their children.

"Some of the white people thought I was trying to start trouble between the whites and the blacks," he said deprecatingly. "But I wasn't. I was just tryin' to get schools for my people. Well, Mr. Will Yancey came to me one day and asked me about it. He told me what some ignorant colored folks were sayin' about me, and then I just explained how it was. And he said right away that he would do all he could to help us."

Finally, when the matter came to the attention of the school board, the members were inclined to do nothing and he thought he was defeated but one of the board, Mr. Will Cannon, was interested enough to get to the bottom of the affair. "He asked me how much money us colored folks could put up," Isaiah continued the story. "And I told him a thousand and that we already had six hundred and sixty-two in cash. Then he told the rest of the board that somethin' had to be done about that school. So they did agree to give the rest of the money."

This controversy had begun in 1919, and by 1922 the schoolhouse was completed, the first model school in Rappahannock County for colored people. "Lots of white people helped us," Isaiah said. "You know the Misses Lewis up here at Rixeyville? Well, they gave us right much money. And others gave us some too."

And now, after his second marriage, he went to work to organize a league at Eldorado where Lila had secured a school. The building in which she was teaching was too small for her pupils and a very crude building besides. Through the efforts of these two working together, the school board was brought to realize the needs of the community and the people were aroused to the extent that they raised the amount of twelve hundred dollars. Application was made for the Rosenwald Fund and six hundred fifty dollars secured.[48] This, with the amount the people had raised and the amount the school board was willing to give, put up the first model school for colored people in Culpeper County. And a very nice little schoolhouse it is too.

By this time the Wallaces were living at Eldorado in a rented house. They moved partly because they would be nearer to Lila's school, and partly because they thought that by renting the farm to someone who had more strength than Isaiah had, they might be able to make the payments.

"I tried to start leagues at Jeffersonton, Rixeyville, Alanthus, Buena, Norman and Brandy," Isaiah explained. "But the people would not work together."

The actual work that Isaiah can do now is very little. He drives the school teacher who boards with them to and from her school each day. He works his garden and jobs about the small place they rent but he is always mighty glad of a chance to make a dollar or two.

The house in which the Wallaces live is not a very large one, being comprised of only four rooms. A nondescript fence surrounds the small yard which shows little care and few flowers. A small front porch gives entrance to the front hall. And inside, this hall runs straight back to the kitchen. To the left is the room in which the Wallaces live and have their company. Here, the double bed, very neatly arranged, occupies the corner back of the door. A mantel on the opposite wall from the door, bears on it an ornate clock and a few pictures among which is one of the Madonna. Against the wall to the left, a table stands, cluttered with papers and books and a very old model typewriter, as if here most of the work of the teacher is done. The corners of the room are occupied by a bookcase holding a mass of old books and papers, a bureau quite modern in style, and a wash stand with pitcher and bowl. Chairs are arranged comfortably about the small wood heater through whose pipe dancing flames may easily be seen at times. The windows, one over the table and the other across the room from it are neatly, though inconspicuously, curtained. Around the walls, portraits—apparently those of the family—hang in their wide wooden frames, and on the back of the door and behind the bed, wall pieces—appliqued and embroidered—attest the skill of Lila's fingers.

The room is not complete without a picture of Isaiah himself. There he sits, his round mulatto face creased in a ready smile, his nose saddled with glasses, his hair cut close and nearly white. He is a man of sixty four, having been born in Rappahannock County on September 29, 1876. Ill health has stamped his shoulders with a stoop. He is a man of about average height, not stout and not thin. He dresses very neatly in a gray suit and an overcoat ornate with worn fur collar.

"I used to be interested in the elections," he said, switching to a new subject. "But now I just vote for the man I think is the best man." Whereupon he entered into a story of how he had started out as a Republican. He had worked with the Republican Party in Culpeper until one time when—the chairman of the party being absent—a Negro was elected as a delegate to a convention in Chicago. "When Mr. Elkins came back, he was mad because we had sent a Negro to the convention. He said he was for a 'lily white' party. Well, I just gave him my hand. I told him I didn't have any hard feelings, but I just couldn't agree with him in that. And ever since then I haven't worked with any party. Some of my people don't think I should vote for a Democrat. They think we all got to be Republicans. But I tell them, we get our living from the Democrats, all the country round us is Democrat and the Democrats give us work, so we can live. Then we ought not to feel like we just got to be Republicans."

He then launched forth into another story of his Northern experiences. He said that one time when he was working in Pittsburgh for a large company, a meeting was called before the election of McKinley and one of the men in charge of the company told all the workers that they must vote for McKinley. He said if they did not vote the right way and he found it out, they would be fired. "He made some remark about the way the Southern people had treated the slaves before the war," Isaiah went on. "And said that we had all come up there to get a chance to be free. And so when he said everybody caught not voting for McKinley would be fired, I couldn't help speaking right up. I told him I thought they were trying to do the same thing to us that he was condemning the Southern people for doing. And I got layed off for ten days too. It was right then that I made up my mind I was not going to work for people like that."

Isaiah is of the Baptist faith, though he is not very regular in his attendance at any church just now. "I go up and talk with my mother most every Sunday now, though I used to go to church every third Sunday when we had preaching," he said. He belongs to Shiloh Baptist Church in Woodville, not very far from where his mother lives. He has belonged to this church ever since he was a boy of fifteen. When asked why he joined the church when he was young, he said that his parents were religious and always saw that he went to Sunday School, and he had just joined. They had taught him about the Bible when he was young too. "When I joined, the church was just a planked up and down building with strips nailed over the cracks," he explained. "But in 1905 we built a new church. I was made chairman of the building committee and we finally got together enough money. The white folks helped us."

"Yes'm, I like to read," he made answer to another query. "I just been readin' a little ancient history in regards to General Washington and—who was that other man? Yes'm, lived 'bout the same time. Yes'm I guess it must a been Thomas Jefferson. I been readin' about the time France had that insurrection in San Domingo [Santo Domingo, Dominican Republic] too." He hesitated and went on to tell the story of how General Washington had made his servant, Primus Long, sleep under the same blankets with him. He seemed much impressed with the incident and chuckled appreciatively to himself over it. He says he likes history best of all the things he reads. But he likes the Bible too, and books about the law.

When he was asked where he had obtained all these books he said that he got some of them from Mr. Albert Johnson. The man who settled up Mr. Johnson's estate had told him to burn a pile of books. "Long time before that Mr. Johnson had tried me out of one of those books," Isaiah explained. "He was a justice, you know. And when I saw that same book on his desk one day, I took my finger and dipped it in the ink bottle and made a mark like this," and here he drew his finger down across a paper lying before him, "on the book. I wanted to be sure I'd know that book later if I ever got a chance to look in it. And when the man told me to burn the books, there it was on top of the pile. So I saved that one and a few others. If I had known as much as I know now I would not have burned any of 'em. But I was young."

He went on to tell how he had procured some of the law books he had read from a library in Washington, having a friend in the city to vouch for him. He had also fallen heir to a lot of the books given his father by Dr. Kemper after the War between the States. "I've got some books that must be two or three hundred years old," he said proudly. "They got those funny letters in them, 'f's' instead of 's's,' you know."

In speaking of other leisure time pursuits, Isaiah said that he used to like to hunt and fish, but he did not go anymore. His leg gives him so much trouble since his accident that he is afraid he will fall when going over rough ground. "Two or three times I fell down and the gun went off, and I was afraid I'd hurt myself or somebody else, so I just quit. But I used to bring birds to Dr. Chelf and Mr. Waite both, here in town real often," he said.

Isaiah is very proud of his mother and the things she accomplished. He states with pride that her mind is just as clear as ever. "Mama sent for me the other day," he started again. "She had heard about a little accident I had had," here Isaiah stopped, hesitatingly and then went on. "Oh, it wasn't anything much. I just bumped into a fellow's car. Didn't hurt it much but he had me up in court. I told Judge Reams I would pay for it if somebody would tell me how much it was. But you know a certain class of people start hollering right away when anything happens. Nice people don't do that way, but a certain class —," he smiled ruefully and let the sentence drop.

Isaiah and Lila have lived in the little rented house for ten years now. Three years ago Isaiah had a slight stroke, which makes his strength even more uncertain than it was before.

"I didn't go to school much myself but I've taught myself a lot since," he stated simply. "I've learned a lot from Lila since we've been married. And I've got some of it for myself from reading. But if I had had a better education, say even just what I could get in the grades, I would have had a chance to get a better job in Pittsburgh when I went there as a boy. My uncle could have got me a place on the police force or carrying the mail. Then you didn't have to have so much schooling as you do now. But I just didn't have the education and I had to just take any kind of job I could get and keep on doing that."

Learning seems to be something that Isaiah never tires of and of which he is very proud. He likes to keep records of everything that happens, bringing them out at times to show to people. He is intensely interested in schools and proud of the work he has done for his people, getting schools for them. A satisfied look spreads over his brown cheeks when his wife gives him the praise for getting a better school at Eldorado where she was teaching. And he is bewildered when some of his race do not seem to appreciate his efforts to help them.

Isaiah is proud of his family too. He likes to recount the happenings of the period just after the War between the States and to tell of how gloriously his mother came through those hard times. He is also proud of the fact that his father belonged to a good old Virginia family. A thorough mixture of the old time Negro and the present day Negro, is Isaiah. Intelligent beyond most of his race, he evidently realizes the limitations of his people and their dependence upon the white race. And he firmly believes that it is through education, and education only, that the Negro can hope to take his place in the world among other races. For that reason he is doing all he can to bring about the wider education of the Negro.[49]

[Loc.: VSL/AB, box 190, 17 pp., 5,700 wds.]

Tom Hand *by Margaret Jeffries, no interview date given*

Down the Hawlin Road a little distance from the village of Woodville, the stone foundation of a mill that belonged to William Hand, a Civil War veteran and father of Tom Hand, still stands. Born the same year as Isaiah Wallace (1876), Tom Hand was actually a little older than Margaret Jeffries described in her not very complimentary account. There is, however, a much more significant contrast between her portrayals of Hand and his contemporary: Jeffries presents Wallace as "intelligent beyond most of his race," that is, a deserving Negro; but she is at a loss to explain Tom Hand's garrulousness, apparent disdain for social amenities, and erratic working career, for he was white and came from a good family.

Indeed, by her measure, Tom Hand was related to some of the best families in Rappahannock County, or even Virginia. On one family line, he descended from William and Frances (Byrd) Eastham. Their granddaughter Nancy Eastham married William Hand (Hand's great-grandfather), and the couple lived on the farm adjoining Captain William Walden's "Glen Farm" on the Hazel River at Slate Mills. The 1860 census lists their son, Thomas Hand, Sen., with his three sons, William, Eastham, and Robert; three daughters (none of whom married); and personal property worth $13,098. Although the eldest son, William (Tom Hand's father), was indicated as a "farm hand," he owned real estate valued at $4,000. (It was likely one or the other of the adjoining farms above, which Tom Hand and his cousins later held in partnership.) The Tom Hand of the VWP life history, as depicted by Jeffries, was something of a rude roustabout or a trickster figure. But Hand's family lineage and social status was apparently of quite a different order; those assets, it seems, are what Jeffries felt had been squandered by downward social mobility, and for that she had little sympathy toward Tom Hand.[50]

"Just like Tom Hand's mule" is a favorite saying about the town of Culpeper. And there is no other citizen just like Tom Hand himself. The way the story started is this:

Tom Hand is a horse trader of quite a bit of renown in these parts, known for sharp dealing and not always too careful as to the truthfulness of the merits he ascribes to the beasts he sells or trades. One day he was trying to sell a mule, in which—according to him—all mule virtues existed. There was absolutely no fault to be found with the animal. The customer went around the mule and noticed a funny bluish appearance about one eye. He asked Mr. Hand if the beast were blind and got a very indignant denial of any such state of affairs. The man decided to test it out for himself and whacked [the mule] on the rump to make him go past the tree under which he was standing. With that the animal walked squarely into the tree. "If that mule ain't blind what made him walk into that tree?" the man demanded angrily. And Tom Hand, not to [be] outdone, replied as quickly as he could, "Why that mule just don't give a damn." Ever since that day that saying has been a by-word in Culpeper County and town.[51]

Tom may be seen any time of the day, standing in front of stores, talking to whomever will listen to him, or loafing inside of some office, talking about the cattle market. In his greenish brown coat with sagging pockets, a dilapidated felt hat on his head and a stout walking cane in his hand, he is a well known figure about town. "Take a fool's advice and sell," you might hear him say, as you pass him where he has cornered some man to talk to him. Or you might hear him telling someone about a deal in cattle which he has just made.

Born in Rappahannock County, Virginia—about fifty-five years ago—on the farm of his father, Tom Hand made his first trip away from that farm when he was seventeen, at which time he got his first look at a train. "I went to work for myself when I was twenty-sree," he told me, "And that was in nineteen and sree." (He has an impediment in his speech which does not permit him to pronounce the combination "thr" properly.) He told me that he went to work at first in a furniture store for eight dollars a month, room and board, rooming over the store. Part of the time he repaired furniture and when there was no furniture to repair, he worked on the farm belonging to the owner of the store.

After one year here, he went to work for the owner of a hardware store driving an oil wagon. This was hard work, as he had to drive mules hooked to a heavy oil wagon over very rough and frequently muddy roads, in all kinds of weather, for miles about the county. For this, he received twelve dollars a month, room and board. At the end of four years he went back to work in the same furniture store he had started working in—the store, meanwhile, having been sold to another man. Here he stayed for several years, starting in at twenty dollars a month and ending at sixty.

His next job was in Washington, D.C. as a baggage man in the Union Depot; here he received one hundred ten dollars a month. He was working here when he was married. He was still working here when he contracted typhoid fever and was taken back to Culpeper to recover. For weeks he lay flat of his back in the Waverly Hotel, but finally was well enough to go to work again. Not being very strong, he first accepted a job as a bill collector. However, he was soon back in railroad work having secured a position as baggage man for the Southern Railroad at the Culpeper station.

After having held this place for several years, he quit to go to farming. He, together with some of his first cousins, had inherited a large farm at Slate Mills from his uncle. The cousins went into partnership and appointed Tom as manager of the farm. After some years the partnership was dissolved, and Tom retired from active labor.

He took up horse trading, cattle buying, buying up old horses for the glue factories, plowing people's gardens, and other odd jobs. And now he may be seen at any time of the day standing or sitting about the offices and stores, or limping on to another corner to stand and talk over the cattle market with anyone who will stop long enough to listen.

As I walked past the huge pile of sawdust and approached the wagon gate which led into Tom Hand's place, I wondered if I would find him at home. I was approaching a small, new, stuccoed house of one story. I walked past a high pile of long wood, up a slightly rutted road, and over a new path to the front steps. On the small front porch I knocked at the new looking door before me. It was immediately opened by a little girl whose small, pointed and none-too-clean face had a pleasant smile as she bade me enter in a prim little way. Trying to keep out the small dog which had followed me up on the porch and utterly failing, I gathered as much dignity as I could to greet my hostess. She was a short, pudgy little woman, peering at me through huge horn-rimmed glasses. Behind her stood a tall brown-eyed girl with her brown hair caught in a bun at the nape of her neck. Across the cluttered floor, in a pen made for the purpose, an eighteen-months old boy yelled to be taken. While I was being seated by Mrs. Hand, the younger woman, Tom's daughter, went to the boy and took him from the pen. Such a wide grin greeted this concession that I found myself talking to the youngster just to make it appear again. Hopping about on one foot, the little girl watched proceedings.

Seated in a small rocker, I divested myself of my coat, for, although I could see no stove, I felt the heat of it. I looked about me, as my hostess pulled up another chair and removed clothing from it so that she could sit down. The room was a pleasant one, opening into another, which I gathered was a dining room though I could see no dining room furniture. To my right, the young mother seated herself on a cot, dressed up as a couch. Across from me I could look into a bedroom, where all I could see was a wide mirror. To my left a high backed chair stood up under a shaggy, rug-like affair thrown across its back, its bright colors catching the eye. And by the side of the bedroom door stood a large what-not, its shelves literally full of dogs, cats, dolls, and many other small objects.

After answering several questions about my own family I asked a few questions myself, learning that the two children were Tom's grandchildren and the offspring of the young girl, Bessie, whose husband sent a little—a very little—money to help support them. She was forced to live with her father and mother, and was trying to find employment. "Bessie has nothing except what her father gives her" was the mother's summing up. And I found that she had gotten a few day's work now and then clerking in some store, that she had managed to get a little sewing to do, and was registered with every employment bureau available.

"Little Tom can't give her anything, now that he is married," Mrs. Hand added, referring to her other child, named for his father and known as Little Tom Hand to differentiate him from his father. Little Tom, I knew, was driving an ice truck and had recently married, though rather young for it. And thinking of Little Tom reminded me how some years ago, Tom had spent several days in jail because he refused to pay the fine imposed for his failure to send his boy to school. The officers had finally concluded that it did no good to have Tom sitting up there in jail, as he showed no inclination to pay the fine or to send the boy to school, and released him.

And thinking of the jail experience brought to mind another difficulty Tom had just been through. He, together with one of the well-known lawyers of the town and two younger men, had been arrested for fox hunting without a license. And I remembered Tom telling me that he had merely been sitting in a car listening to the dogs baying. He had got out of that without a fine or jail sentence either.[52]

"I know my Granddaddy is going to bring me something whenever he comes home from town," the little girl was hopping around on one foot again. Her statement was drowned out by a wail from the little boy and a resounding thump, which sounded as if it might be accompanied by the crash of glass. We held our breaths as Bessie extracted the little fellow unhurt from the crevice between a book case, I had hitherto not noticed, and the high backed rocking chair. Over his crying, she explained to me how her father spoiled the children by bringing them nuts every night. "Just a handful, so they won't eat too many of them," she finished.

"I know he'll bring me something," the little girl chanted, hopping about and nearly tripping over a spool left on the rugless floor. And then she rushed off only to come back with a wagon, into which she carefully lifted the little boy, pushing him about the room with a great clatter.

I rose to go, agreeing to see whomever I could about trying to get Bessie work, as I fastened my coat. "Come back to see us again," the little girl urged primly, her bright smile flashing from her dirty face, as I went through the door. I turned to wave from the path and saw the little dog that had followed me in being forcibly ejected after me.[53]

[Loc.: VSL/AB, box 190, 6 pp.]

Narrating the African American Experience
"DEMOCRACY PAID FOR"

The race problem could be solved by working on an equality base. —Bernice Reid

Although African Americans were excluded from many social groups by processes rooted in the historical fact of slavery, by the end of the eighteenth century in Virginia blacks and whites already "shared family, clan, and even folk histories that could not be separated one from the other." In this chapter on narratives of the African American experience, the vwp text with Rev. Willis J. Madden offers a specific case in point. In Culpeper County, Madden's white, indentured ancestor and her free black progeny are known and documented through family papers dating from the eighteenth century. Still, project worker Margaret Jeffries in 1940 found Madden's "mixture of satisfaction in the accomplishments of his race and pride in the white blood that flow[ed] through his veins" worthy of comment.[1]

Even though they shared much in common, progressive demands in the nineteenth century to differentiate freedmen from slaves, and slaves from masters, had led to a hardening of attitudes and social boundaries and required increasingly restrictive laws to govern behavior between the races. Such views were explicit in an 1823 letter that warned Rev. Willis J. Madden's ancestors that they "should be careful in their conduct with slaves 'otherwise they would and ought to forfeit the good opinion which the [white] people [were] disposed to entertain of them.'" These circumstances were not resolved by the Civil War; rather, the bitterness in its aftermath, the divisiveness of Reconstruction, and, later, the "Jim Crow" laws generally intensified separation along racial lines.[2]

Dilcie Gum pointedly referred to Jim Crow practices when she replied to Bessie Scales's question about white people attending her church "to hear the singing." She told Scales, "When they do come to our branch of God's House we doesn't Jim Crow 'em, but ask's them right up to the front." But not everyone felt so inclined to forgive the affront of Jim Crow—even in church—and sometimes the positions were reversed. After the Dillwyn Baptist Church, five miles away, stopped sending its bus out to pick up worshipers, one of its members commented that he sometimes went to a nearby "colored church." He thought it was "better to go over there than nowhere,

Newport News, Virginia. March 1941. The Shipyard at 4:00 p.m. Photo by John Vachon. [LC-USF34-62645-D]

and the colored folks [had] some pretty good preaching. They [gave] the white folks a seat in the back by hisself." [3]

However, it was generally a harsh and hostile world that African Americans confronted in Virginia and elsewhere in the years following the war and on into the twentieth century. These conditions were reflected in the life history interviews as well. One white informant from Fauquier County was working as foreman of a bridge gang when "the Southern Railroad was double-tracking its main line" (about 1900) "at or near the Rapidan River." He reported almost offhandedly that he "saw them kill two negroes and push them down the fill and cover them up in it. Nothing was done about it because nobody told about it." [4]

In the description of another case, violence against African Americans was seen as justified because of their open defiance of the white-imposed Jim Crow laws. Jimmie Garrett reported that after he left Hopewell during World War I, he went to Newport News and got a job as a streetcar conductor.

This was a dangerous job in those days. The Negroes had been a problem and had wounded several conductors, and they had to carry a gun. One night two big Negro men were setting up in the front seat of the car. [I] went up to them, "You'll hafta move back." "No, we won't move back neither, we are as good as any damn white man." "Yes, you will move back, too," taking [my] gun out of [my] pocket. A soldier boy [was] standing by. "Let me have that gun," said he, "and I'll shoot the d. Negroes." Taking the gun he shot between them, skinning the side of one of their heads. One of the Negroes jumped off the car while it was running, the other ran to his place in the back. [Laughing], "No, I never had any more trouble with Negroes after that."[5]

Almost always when black Americans stepped out of the roles or definitions assigned to them by whites, dared to defy Jim Crow laws, or just define their lives in their own terms, they were—at the very least—deemed to be "uppity." A Hampton Institute graduate, whose father was a janitor, recognized this reality in 1940. He told the VWP interviewer that he might not return to Danville to practice law after his planned study at Harvard because, as he said, "people might think I had gotten above myself, that I should do my father's kind of work."[6]

Many of the VWP life histories *by* and *from* African Americans—as opposed to those *by* whites *about or with* African Americans—reiterated essentially the same message offered by Bernice Reid when she said, "The race problem could be solved by working on an equality base." Reid, who had been a former schoolmate of Susie R. C. Byrd's at Virginia State College, ruefully recalled their classroom discussions of the social problems in the very same Petersburg neighborhood to which she and her family were confined as a result of her husband's layoffs, first from the tobacco factory and then the WPA Colonial Heights' project.[7]

It was there also that Byrd found "a settlement of approximately forty ex-slaves" about two blocks from her own home. Some of these she interviewed, and some were recorded for the VWP Negro Studies project headed by Roscoe E. Lewis at Hampton Institute. A number of these persons likewise emphasized the many problems—the lack of jobs, inadequate pay, hunger, high incidence of disease, and terrible housing-that existed in the slum areas near Virginia State College.[8]

The RA/FSA photographs of the Aberdeen Gardens Homesteads in Newport News (discussed more fully below) documented efforts toward such an "equality base," as suggested by Reid, through the provision of decent housing for African Americans. Those photographic images contrast with other pictures of black housing and with the interview descriptions of living conditions in Petersburg and elsewhere. Like some other Resettlement Administration housing projects, the Newport News effort suffered from assumptions, based both on race and class, about the nature of the persons it would serve. Accordingly, the project was altered somewhat in the planning stages and greeted by ridicule in the white press on completion; nonetheless, it was a substantive success. Initiated by African Americans at Hampton Institute, Aberdeen Gardens was the first, and only, suburban resettlement project built for blacks in the United States.[9]

Aberdeen Gardens was, in addition, the site for an NYA "Civilian Defense" project, which used eight of the houses in the settlement as residences for forty-two African American girls. Under the supervision of NYA employees and "instructors furnished by the State Board of

(Opposite) Chopawamsic recreational project, Virginia [now Prince William Forest Park]. April 1936. A laborer. Photo by Arthur Rothstein. [LC-USF33-02325-M2]

Education and Hampton Institute," these girls got work experience in "all phases of foods, sewing, laundry work, and child care." In addition, they received "daily instruction and training in all phases of domestic service," using textbooks on "foods, maidcraft, and home-making" furnished by the local school board and Hampton Institute.[10]

Even though working conditions had been precarious for African Americans from at least the end of the Civil War, their relative position worsened even more with the depression and the extension of severe unemployment to broader segments and massive numbers of the population. Some jobs were provided to both blacks and whites by early Resettlement Administration projects to develop park and recreational areas such as the 1936 Chopawamsic project, which was later renamed Prince William Forest Park and transferred to the National Park Service. Still, the benefit from such efforts was hardly noticeable given the widespread general need. Increased migration to take advantage of opportunities perceived to be better elsewhere and a pervasive competition for scarce jobs and resources intensified strains between racial, ethnic, and class groups, as well as between regions.[11]

One elderly female tobacco worker's account of a heated exchange between herself and another woman worker—a North Carolinian—reveals sectional differences and antagonisms that are often only insinuated elsewhere. She told how in her haste, when she was late to work

Rustburg, Virginia. March 1941. Judge of the local court on the right. Photo by John Vachon. [LC-USF34-62755-D]

one morning at the tobacco factory in Petersburg, she had accidentally run into a woman who told her to get out of the way, calling her an " 'old sore back.' " "I called her 'old tar heel.' We had it for a time. I told her, 'You all come to Virginia from North Carolina and we can't get you away. If you steal a $.05 hat in North Carolina the law gives you 5 years, and if you steal [the] same amount in Virginia our law gives you 'bout 15 days and turns you loose.' Virginia to my mind is the best place on the map and I am glad that I was bo'n in Virginia. You can't fool Negroes from Virginia to live in North Carolina, but them tar heels will come here and try to take us." [12]

Harrison Blair, who "waited in the employees' dining room at the White Sulphur Springs for awhile," complained about foreigners and also unions. "They have only fureigners in the main dining room. I dunno why! They is everywhere in the cities! Just a few hotels use the colored waiters! They is unionized, them fureigners. And you can't crack in, not if you is American, white or black! Looks like they has everything their way, even if we is American-bo'n." [13] And though he had a job in the shipyard in April 1941, James Cooke regretted that the Newport News shipyard did "not permit Negroes to attend the trade school which they conduct[ed] exclusively for white boys" and which was "one of the finest of its kind in the country." [14]

The series of photographs of the Charlotte Court House schools also managed incidentally to show the separate, but not exactly equal, base between the black high school and its newly consolidated, PWA-built white counterpart. The picture of the black high school auditorium being used by elementary school students to practice for a pageant suggests the multiple ways that space served the black community. It accentuates as well the deeply felt disappointment expressed by Cleveland Buchanan about the newly built black high school in Alleghany County having no auditorium and thus no adequate place for public assembly by the black community. Although it was a "democracy paid for" by years of service, for African Americans it was not yet a democracy gained. [15]

Aunt Mattie Perndon *by Margaret Jeffries, 15 May 1940*

Mattie Perndon (born about 1848) shares much in common with Charles Crawley's mother, Sarah Givens, in the previous chapter. Both women were born in slavery, both had several husbands, both worked hard, and in time both managed to buy houses of their own. But Sarah Givens was sufficiently older than Perndon to have married during slavery, and her first husband, Armistead Crawley, like Perndon's father Edmund Stewart, may have been sold away. After the war, Givens left the plantation, against the wishes of her previous owners, and went with her children to the city of Petersburg. What is more surprising, in contrast, is that Fannie Stewart, Mattie's mother, against the persuadings of Yankee soldiers, chose to stay with "ole Miss" Hill Brown, who had beforehand so callously sold Fannie's son Frank to "nigger traders" while the family was out picking blackberries.

By 1870, however, Fannie Stewart, with a nine-year-old boy of the same surname, was living with her daughter Mattie (Martha) and son-in-law Joseph Ficklin, a farm laborer, in the Jefferson-ton District of Culpeper County. Mattie reported moving with her husband Joe "to the various farms on which he lived as a year hand," but she added ambiguously that "she finally saved up enough money to buy a little place for herself." Whatever the case, her marriage to Joe Ficklin seems to have been of short duration: a Martha Stewart appears alone, working as a servant and cook for store clerk James Burdett, in the town of Culpeper in 1880. Moreover, only two decades later, Henderson and Mattie Perndon reported having been married for twenty-three years. Before two more decades passed, Mattie Perndon was a widow.[16]

Unlike Sarah Givens, who was able to live until she died in the house she had labored for, Mattie Perndon's "little place for herself" burned down. Since she had no children from either marriage (in contrast also with Givens), Mattie was fortunate to be able to move into her niece's house and be cared for in her old age and blindness by a nephew and great-nephew. And finally, Perndon's niece, Josie Stewart Bradley, who sent money to support the Culpeper household out of her salary as chambermaid to Mrs. Staunton in Stockbridge, Massachusetts, was, in effect, the counterpart to Sarah Given's daughter-in-law, Mattie Crawley.

Aunt Mattie is a plump old Negro woman even if she is bedridden. She has been in bed for nine or ten years she thinks, but the passing of time is a thing that Aunt Mattie cannot keep up with. For in addition to being bedridden, she is also blind in both eyes. "I jes' kin see whar dat dere window is," she explained when asked if she could see anything at all.

But Aunt Mattie does not look old except for her kinky white hair, which she wears in tight little braids and which is very, very white indeed. Her face is large-featured, with a broad forehead, wide flat nose, and spreading mouth. Her eyes appear normal until close inspection reveals little blue spots covering the pupils. Her shoulders, covered with a soiled outing night gown, are broad and plump. Her hands, long and capable-looking even now, give no sign of the numbness which she says makes them practically useless. The nails have been allowed to grow so long that they are clawlike and caked with dirt underneath.

On the day the writer visited her, the bed upon which the old woman lay was a tumble of bed clothes. The sheets pulled every sort of way were not of the cleanest, though of good material. The brown quilt was lumped midway of her body, leaving her toes sticking out from under. It was an iron bed, which had been painted a light shade of green with pink trimmings, and appeared to have a very good mattress on it.

The room was a fairly large one, though one with a low ceiling. It was square and held a bed in each of the corners to the north. The other bed was seemingly a cot, having neither headboard nor footboard. It was made up meticulously with a striped pink and white cotton spread, probably of homemade construction since there was a wide stripe of pink goods alternating with a wide stripe of white throughout. At the foot of this, and across the space occupied by the window, was a small cabinet which served as a washstand. On this, there was an assortment of articles including an old candlestick of the saucer type, a small tin bucket, two enamel-ware cups and a box of matches, all of which were kept from scratching the surface of the cabinet by the presence of a scarf, half-blue and half-white. On the opposite side of the room from this and in the southeast corner, an old fashioned bureau with little side shelves, tall narrow mirror, and marble top held an oil lamp, a bottle of Yager's Liniment, two empty bottles with prescription labels across their sides, and a glass in which a spoon stood. On the wall, between the bureau and the door by which entrance to the room was gained, hung three calendars advertising some kind of patent medicine. Only one of these showed the correct day and month, and over one was suspended an almanac. A high-backed rocking chair stood in the floor in front of the bureau, and two other chairs of the straight-backed type, made up the seating arrangements of the room. Between the two beds, the wood heater—now heatless — stood on a tin mat which had been nailed down to the floor. In the middle of the floor, which had been stained brown and was in need of mopping, a patch of varicolored linoleum protected the boards. The window was curtained with some thin material.

Aunt Mattie does not know how old she is. "All I knows is one time when I was sick, the doctor-man he come to see me. An' I heared him ask my ole Mistis when he was a'feelin' my pulse, 'How ole dis little nigger?' An' my ole Miss she say, 'Oh, I guess she 'bout thirteen year ole.' An' dat was de firs' year er de War," the old woman will say when questioned concerning her age.

She was born on the place belonging to her master, Mr. Hill Brown, about seven or eight miles south of Culpeper Courthouse. And there she lived until after the War between the States came to an end. "De Yankees tried to 'suade my mother to go 'way an' leave ole Miss," Aunt Mattie reminisced. "But Laws a'mercy! My ole Miss she wuz so pitiful. My mother jes' couldn't leave her, no ma'am."

The old negress did not know much about her father. "His name wuz Edmun' Stewart," she said. "But he wuz sold 'way 'way from us when I wuz jes' a little nigger. I never seed him no mo'." Her mother's name, she said, was Fannie Stewart and there were twelve children in the family, she being next to the youngest. Five of these children were girls and seven were boys.

"I 'members when my brother Frank wuz sold ter de nigger traders," she went on. "We wuz all out walkin' 'round pickin' a few blackberries an' we wuz a'stragglin' out kinder, not noticin' each other much. An' when we got home, Frank he wuz'n with us. We went back an' looked an' looked for him, an' then my mother she went to ole Miss an' tole her Frank mus' be los'. An' ole Miss she say, 'no, she done sole him ter de nigger traders.' None us never seen him no mo'."

None of Aunt Mattie's sisters lived to be grown except one. And she too is dead now, leaving Aunt Mattie the sole survivor of all of her family.

Aunt Mattie can tell some interesting tales of the war times. Her home was located not many miles from the country over which the Battle of Cedar Mountain was fought.

"My Mistis' house wuz a horspital," she said. "Laws a'mercy! De wounded soldiers wuz brought in dere an' laid down all over de yard an' dey wuz lef' dere all day an' all night an' us niggers had ter step over de soldiers ter go ter de spring ter bring 'em water. It sure wuz pitiful ter hear dem soldiers, po' things, a'hollerin' water, water, all de time. An' de balls wuz a'whistlin' through de yard an' through de trees, Laws a'mercy!"

She said that she had two young masters who were in the War, "Marse William Dan'l' and Marse Hill." Marse Hill was her master after the slaves were divided. "Marse Will'am Dan'l, he would call all his servants up eve'y mornin' an' whip 'em whether dey needed it er not," she continued. "When his wife ast him what fo' he done dat, he say it wuz one his rules. But Marse Hill, he didn't do his servants dat away. Yas ma'am, when ole Miss would tell Marse Hill ter whip some de servants he would make like he wuz a'whippin' 'em somepin' awful an' dey would holler an' yell an' he ain't done laid de whip on 'em 'tall."

Aunt Mattie has been married twice. Her first husband was Joe Ficklin and she was married to him about four or five years after the War between the States. Her second husband was Henderson Perndon. He too has been dead for many years now. She never had any children by either marriage. "I never wished fer no children," she explained. "I liked children but I never wished fer none er my own."

And now since her husband is dead and since she has no children of her own to care for her, she lives with her niece. "Yes ma'am, I would a'had ter go ter de po'house, if my niece hadn't took me in. Yes ma'am, Josey's mighty good ter me. My house wuz right 'cross de road up dere, an' when it burned down I jes' didn't have nowhar ter go." Josey is the daughter of Aunt Mattie's brother and she holds a position as chambermaid for Mrs. Staunton in Stockbridge, Massachusetts.

"Dere ain't no woman in de house 'cept me," the old woman explained. "I gets a woman from cross de road ter come in an' do fer me, straighten up de room an' bed, an' turn me over eve'y mornin'." The household then consists of three persons, Aunt Mattie, her nephew, Arthur, who she explained was "not bright," and Roland Stewart, who is her great nephew. Josey sends money there to keep things going. Roland works whenever he can get work to do. Just now he is working with a house mover and has had a day or two at it. Arthur seems incapable of work, though he seems anxious to please his aunt and do whatever he can for her.

Aunt Mattie herself gets ten dollars a month from the old age pension and with this she pays for the few things she needs. "I pays de woman ter look after me three dollars a month, an' you see dat don't leave me but seven," she explained. She went on to explain about the various things she had to buy for herself. Among those was the stove in her room for which she said she had paid six dollars.

This old woman has worked hard all of her life until now. After the slaves were freed she went to work at anything she could get to do, working in the field, taking in washing, working as chambermaid, or anything else at all. After she was married she moved around with her husband to the various farms on which he lived as a year hand. She finally saved up enough money to buy a little place for herself and then she went out to work by the day, washing and ironing at night after she got back to her little house. It has been twenty years, she said, since she came to live with her niece.

"No ma'am, I never did go ter school none," she answered another question. "Dar wa'n't no schools fer colored folks 'fore de War an' after de War I had to work hard. My mother tried ter get me ter go but I wouldn't do it." And so Aunt Mattie cannot read or write, even if she could see how to do so. "I wished many a time I had a'gone though," she added as an afterthought.

Aunt Mattie has belonged to Antioch Church, a Baptist church for the colored folks in Culpeper, for forty years. "Rev'ren' Madden, you know he preaches dere," she said. "He ain't been here fer a long time. Seems like he don' like black ones like me. He likes 'em light colored like he is," and the old woman shook with her chuckles. "Yes ma'am, his father wuz a thoroughbred white man, he wuz. Laws a'mercy! I 'members when Rev'ren' Madden wa'n't nothin' but a little shaver." [17]

And she stopped, panting for breath. "No'm, I ain't never voted," she answered yet another question when she had recovered her breath. "I ain't never bothered with sech things."

Aunt Mattie said she reckoned it had been about fifty years since she and Henderson Perndon moved into the neighborhood. He has been dead, she said, for fifteen years, but since she had said already that she had lived with her niece for twenty years, it is evident that she is vague concerning the lapse of time. "Sometimes I jes' don' know nothin'," she explained. "But I 'members things that happened long time ago."

She then started telling of a hanging she had witnessed one time. "The man killed his own dear uncle," she said. "An' when he wuz a'standin' dere on de platform wid de rope 'round his neck, he prayed an' sang a song, an' den he said he jes' hoped he'd be a lookin' glass fer de worl'. Yes ma'am, he done killed his own dear uncle fer his money an' den he didn't have ary quarter ter his name. I jes' don' see how folks could do sech things. I 'clare I don' know what dis worl' comin' ter dese days, way folks a'killin' an' a'robbin'. Seems like dey jes' steal fer pastime."

The house in which Aunt Mattie lies helpless, as before stated, belongs to Josey Stewart Bradley. It is a very nice-appearing house as it is approached from the road, fenced-in with a plank fence and with its setting of flowers and shrubs. The grass in the yard is uncut, but the rose on the end of the long front porch gives the place a homey air. It is a six-room frame house with two stories and is painted a rather bright shade of yellow. It is equipped with electricity too, a recent innovation acquired since the coming of an R.E.A. line through the neighborhood. In the hall through which one must pass to Aunt Mattie's room, a new, white refrigerator is the first thing to catch the eye, though Aunt Mattie says that it is not run by electricity. The hall is narrow and has barely room for the narrow stairs which go up to the left. On the wall, opposite the stairs, hang three rather large pictures all of Biblical characters and scenes.

"We keeps de screen do' fas'ened all de time," Aunt Mattie assured the visitor. "You never know dese days who's a'comin' in yo' house."

The shrill cheep of little chickens could be heard to the side of the house and Aunt Mattie said that they had chickens and a garden too, though the latter had not yet been plowed for this year.

"I b'lieve yo' visit done me good," the old woman said when her visitor was leaving. "When you firs' come, looked like I jes' couldn't git my breaf but I feels lots better now." And so the writer went away leaving the old woman helpless on her bed, her breath, though quieter, coming still in gasps at times. And Arthur, the nephew who is "not bright," sitting in the room with a vacant grin on his bearded face.

[Loc.: VSL/AB, box 187, 9 pp., 2,800 wds.]

Willis J. Madden *by Margaret Jeffries, 11 January 1940*

The common knowledge, according to Mattie Perndon, a member of Madden's Antioch Church who had known him since he was a "little shaver," was that Rev. Willis J. Madden's father "wuz a thoroughbred white man." The Willis Madden who was told to others to be his father was, rather, his grandfather and namesake. That earlier Willis Madden (clearly not "direct from Africa") was born in 1799 of a free black indentured servant named Sarah—herself the illegitimate daughter of an Irish woman, Mary Madden, of Spotsylvania County. It is *that* Willis who in his will, probated in April 1880, left his home—the old Madden Tavern—to his daughter, Maria Fields (the mother of Reverend Willis), and a granddaughter, Margurite Taylor.

The nephew of Rev. Willis Madden, nonagenarian Thomas Obed Madden Jr., currently owns and lives in the family's old homeplace—the former tavern. While repairing the roof in 1949, he discovered in the attic an old leatherbound trunk containing business records and receipts from the Madden Tavern; family papers including bastardy and indenture papers for Sarah Madden; the free papers for both Willis Madden and his wife, Kitty Clark Madden; and other documents. T. O. Madden Jr. also reports a family tradition that links the Maddens to George Washington's coachman, and this life history with Rev. Willis Madden suggests the family's connection to the household of Thomas Jefferson. There is documentary evidence, however, that proves Sarah Madden's original indenture in Spotsylvania County was, in fact, transferred to James Madison Sr. of Montpelier, Orange County, and was later deeded by him to his son, Francis Madison of Madison Mills, Madison County.[18]

Professor Madden, as he is known to most of Culpeper, is a Negro. He was for many years teacher of the school for the colored in Culpeper but is retired now. However, he has not retired from his position as preacher at Antioch, one of the Negro Baptist Churches. He looks the part too. He is truly preacher-like, with his long, graying beard which covers the lower part of his face, and his almost white hair. He dresses the part too. He generally wears black, his hat being wide of brim and his coat long of tail. He is not a tall man but full of the dignity of his position.

The house in which the Maddens live is a commodious one. It is situated well back from a much used road, the Sperryville Pike, about a mile west of the courthouse. The ground slopes gently up to the house which stands in a grove of trees. There is no fence about the yard and no flowers soften the contours of the place. The house itself is an eight-room structure painted white, having a long porch across the front of it. Inside, the rooms are not overly large but are adequate. The walls are white coated, having picture molding about a foot from the ceiling. The house is equipped with electricity, the fixtures being of an ordinary, old-fashioned variety often seen in houses of people of moderate means.

There are four rooms on the first floor, a room used as a living and entrance hall, having in it a small wood heater, a bookcase with a two-volume dictionary atop of it, a table littered with various papers and a heap of books stacked on the floor. To the left of this room is the parlor which is tastefully furnished with a modest three-piece suite, a bookcase, an organ and a tiny wood heater. And back of the entrance hall is the kitchen, the same size as the other two rooms, but well-filled with two tables and the big wood range, on top of which a huge black pot was boiling on the morning of the interview letting out a most tantalizing odor of cooking beans. Here a worn linoleum covered the floor and red dotted curtains adorned the windows. Dishes were piled ready for washing in the dishpan and many articles of kitchen ware filled the tables. A straight backed, split-bottomed chair was drawn forth for the visitor.

"My wife says it is a disgrace not to have a fire in the front room," the Reverend Madden expostulated as he ushered the writer into this room.

"Here, let me take your coat," the wife put in her word hospitably. And seated at last by the side of that huge range, the writer could look around.

Willis J. Madden, retired teacher, was born near Maddensville, a small place in the vicinity of Lignum, in Culpeper County. Maddensville, in fact, has been named for his people. There is there an old, old tavern, now used as a house, which being located on the old Fredericksburg Road, was the stopping place of the wagon drivers in the days when shipping was done by wagons.

"I wasn't born right there, though," the old man assured the writer. "I was born just a little ways away from there at a place owned by my mother. You see, I always tell people that my father was Willis Madden, but that is not the case really. My father was a member of Congress and a member of the House of Delegates later too," this last was said with a curious little smile, half of pride and half of shame. "But it's best not to mention that, I think," he continued in his gentle way. "My mother was Maria, daughter of Willis Madden and my father

fixed her up with her own little home and some land. But someway, I don't know just how, it got away from her. Whether it was paid for in Confederate money or just what was the reason, I don't know. But she lost it."

He then explained how Maria was the daughter of a white maid in the home of Thomas Jefferson and a black man, afterwards called Willis Madden, who was direct from Africa. Therefore, although she was colored herself, she was free, because her mother was white.[19]

He had been born to Maria in August of 1862 and had never known slavery. As a boy he had attended the little school for the colored that was near Lignum, Virginia. And he received his first chance to teach in this same neighborhood.[20]

"But I want to tell you, I had some oxen and I hauled the lumber to build that schoolhouse where I first taught," he ruminated. "I had help with the building but I made every one of the seats with my own hands. I used to be very good at that kind of work." This he was willing to do in order to get the school, a little one-room affair between Lignum and Richardsville. And although he had not been off to college anywhere then, he continued to do the best he could for the colored people who came to sit before him for four years. And then, for three years, he taught the school at Maddensville.

But the young colored school teacher was not satisfied with his education. He felt the urge to preach and with that end in view, sought entry in Howard University in Washington. He attended this institution for three years. "But I always managed to get a school in vacations," he said. "One year I taught in West Virginia, one year in Culpeper, and one year in Loudoun County." While he was at Howard University he covered such subjects as moral and mental philosophy, international law and science of government, history, which he assured the writer took the church from the time of its beginning up to the nineteenth century, evidences of Christianity and natural theology.

And then he went to preaching. At first he had a very small church near Harper's Ferry. He next preached at a small church in Madison County, Virginia. [He] came to Culpeper to take charge of the Antioch Baptist Church in 1896, and he has preached here ever since.

He first came to teach in Culpeper in 1889, holding school in the old building where white children had received instruction at the hands of Mr. Stone, a retired missionary and teacher of note. This building was located in a part of the town of Culpeper known as Jeffriestown. "There were just two rooms," Madden continued. "And you could put your hand against the wall and push and the whole building would rock." [21]

Altogether he taught in Culpeper for forty-seven years. And for many of these years he gave instruction in two years of high school work. "And thirteen of my pupils went to teaching without going off anywhere to college," the old man boasted gently. "Several of them entered colleges at different places. One of the best known of them to go on and finish his education was Dr. Roberts, of Roanoke."

But when the new Culpeper Training School was started in town Professor Madden was considered too old to hold the children down. However, he should have a lot of the credit for the colored people of Culpeper having a modern up-to-date school building, well located and well cared for, in which they may receive full instruction in all high school subjects. The present commodious building is in great contrast to the small, drafty, brick building, badly located on a lot much too small for a school, where Willis Madden taught them.

To Madden also there should go a great deal of credit for the way in which he has reared and inspired all of his children. "I was married when I was thirty-eight," he stated hesitantly. "Well, I was married before that but you can't really say—well," he hesitated. And then he continued, "I was married before but it was an unfortunate marriage. You see, the woman was very young and you see, well, the baby came a bit too soon. She died. A very unfortunate circumstance."

And it was from an old neighbor that the whole story was learned. He had married a very young girl of a respectable colored family and was very happy for a while. But as is the case with so many young mothers, her baby came too soon, sooner than her husband thought compatible with a virtuous life. Suspicion entered the little home and lived there, an unwelcome guest, until the early death of the wife and child. And that is why Willis Madden, himself the offspring of a union unsanctioned by society, will not speak of that early marriage of his and will always tell the inquirer that he has had only ten children.

He was married again when he was thirty-eight years old and his second wife, a rather pretty, mulatto woman with an intelligent face and carefully polite manners, was the mother of his ten children. In this large family, the members are equally divided as to sex; and too, they are equally divided as to marriages—there being one boy and one girl married.

"The oldest boy," Madden ruminated, "is not so well able to take care of himself. You know what I mean, he just can't seem to get along like the others. Dr. Kelly told me that he thought he had something pressing on his brain, possibly. He does very well for a while and then again he will not get along so well. He likes to read things: history, and all about the stars—I mean those out in Hollywood. But he never did go to college like the rest of them."

He then told of his second son who is living in Philadelphia and is what is called a cement worker. "He calls himself a stone setter, I believe, though," he added. And he went on to tell how talented the boy was at erecting stone arches and particular bits of work where an extra dexterity of the hands and especial precision was needed.

"The next boy is Samuel and he is Supervisor of Adult Education and travels all around. He is at present at Hampton, Virginia," he stated proudly. And he entered into a dissertation on the accomplishments of Samuel who, he said, had laid out a course of study that was being followed not only by the colored people but by some white people as well. And then he took the visitor into the parlor where he showed with pride, several oil paintings done by the boy. And very well done they were too. There was also a framed wood cut which the old man said the boy had used for his Christmas cards, having designed it himself. It too, showed unmistakable signs of good workmanship.

"Samuel wanted to go to the University of Virginia and study law," the old man stated precisely. "But I insisted upon his not trying that. I told him it would just cause a lot of trouble and I did not want that kind of trouble."

The next boy, according to the old man, was teaching in a high school in Richmond, Virginia and the other boy is in college at Petersburg, Virginia.

Of the girls, he is just as proud. One of them is married and living in New Jersey. She had gone to college for several years and after finishing had taught for four years before marrying a very well-to-do undertaker. The second girl finished college, and is teaching home economics in Rustburg High School in Campbell County.

"We think she is quite talented in dress making," he said, the note of pride creeping in again. "She made a suit of clothes for the head of the school and for several of the others too. And she made some clothes for Mrs. Hendricks when she was home last summer." Mrs. Hendricks, be it noted, is the wife of the Superintendent of Schools under whom Madden taught for many years.

"We want her to get a better position somewhere where she can advance more," he continued. "And she was offered a place in Richmond, but for some reason she stayed on where she was. The school there is kind of an experiment out in the woods, like your Fredericksburg School was at first. That was in the woods wasn't it?" The old man peered questioningly over his glasses and then went on. "The conditions there are rather rough."

Two of the other girls are still in college at Petersburg and the youngest one, just fourteen years old, is still in high school here in Culpeper.

"We couldn't keep all of them in college and high school ourselves," the wife and mother put in her oar. "The others help with them. We just couldn't do it ourselves. Why, we both even need shoes right now and have no money to buy them with." And she stuck out a foot badly clad in an old broken shoe. There was no complaint in this statement, just mere fact.

Madden has in the lot on which his house stands, nineteen and a fraction acres, not enough to do any farming on but enough to support the one cow he keeps. "I don't have a horse any more," he said. "So all I need is room for a garden and for the cow to pasture." And he himself is unable to work the garden very much. "You see, I am very lazy," he said with a quizzical smile at his wife, who immediately protested his unfitness for such work. "You know you can't bend over any more," she reproved him.

And indeed this old man, although he is not at all feeble, at nearly seventy-eight years of age, finds himself unable to do the things that he could once do. He feeds his cow and milks her and does a few odd jobs about the place and then devotes the most of his time to his preaching.

"I don't know just how many members we have now," he considered thoughtfully. "Can't say exactly. But I can say that I expect I have buried more people in the last year than any other man in the county." And with that he hesitated, deciding something in his mind before saying that there were exactly thirty-eight funerals among his people during the past year. "And that takes out a lot of the members of our church," he said sadly.

And turning to his wife, in a quiet voice he asked her, "Will you bring me one of those little papers in my satchel?" And then while she was gone to do his bidding, he continued, "I don't expect there are many more than two hundred in all of our association. And of course, so few come to church any more. I was thinking of getting a preacher from New York here to preach for awhile, but he asks ten dollars to be collected before he will agree to come and then there must be another ten dollars collected for the people," he said. "That would make it too expensive, I am afraid, ten dollars a day for him and ten dollars for the people."

When his wife came back he took from the brief case she held a bright pink covered pamphlet and passed it to the writer. On the cover it said in bold black letters:

ADDRESS
of
Moderator W. J. Madden
at
FIFTIETH ANNUAL SESSION
of the
WAYLAND BLUE RIDGE BAPTIST
ASSOCIATION
held with the Bethel Baptist Church
of Mitchells, Va.
Rev. W. F. Smith, Pastor
AUGUST 16,17,18, 1939

Inside there were a list of all the meetings of the association since its organization in 1888 and the address itself which commenced with the salutation, "Dear Brethren." The address went on for considerable length and then ended up with the words of the old hymn, "LOOK AND LIVE."

The old fellow pointed to the words and asked if his visitor were familiar with the song. When some doubt was evidenced he stood and—looking over the writer's shoulder—sang in a quavering old voice the first verse of the hymn. So old and uncertain was the voice that the melody came out somewhat vague. "I want to revive that tune," he said when he had finished. "I think it is a shame for it to have been forgotten. But I can't find the music anywhere. Maybe some day I shall get my daughter to pick out the music on the organ, and put it down for me as I sing it. She might be able to do it for me."[22]

Madden was very vague in answering the question concerning his spare time. He agreed that it took most of his time preparing his sermons and doing the little visiting he was able to do. "I can't do much visiting these days," he said. "But I do what I can."

He admitted reluctantly that there were no young people's organizations in his church and that there was no missionary society either. But he said that there was a flourishing Sunday School. "Though the people do not come like they should," he said sadly.

He admitted also that he did some reading but did not enlighten the questioner as to just what he read. A copy of *The Woman's Home Companion* was on the couch in the parlor and a few odd papers were scattered about the table in the entrance hall, but aside from that there was not much evidence of just what the family read.

"I think so many bad things come over the radio," he remarked when asked about his listening to that. "Of course, some of it is good." And so he goes on day after day, this aged man, reading a little, listening a little to the radio, jobbing about outside when he is able, and preaching to the few people who come to his church to hear him.

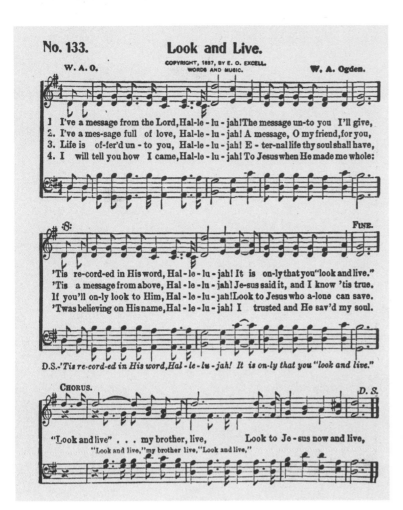

Text and Music for "Look and Live,"
from Wonderful Jesus and Other Songs
(1927) #133. UVA-KBP.

He has done much for his family, seeing that each member received as much education as he could and encouraging them all he could to fight for position in a world greatly biased against his race. More white than colored himself, he is yet careful not to offend the white people of his acquaintance. Of irregular origin himself, he could not help having suspicions of his young wife so that he does not think of her dead child as his.[23]

Supposedly broad-minded far in advance of his people, he still holds to that view of an older generation. Working hard for the advancement of his people, he still harbors a shade of ill feeling that they should have thought him too old to manage the new training school in his home town. Too old to exert himself to hold his congregation together and acquire new members for his church, he is yet resentful of the fact that so many of them stay away from his sermons on Sunday morning. He is a mixture of satisfaction in the accomplishments of his race and pride in the white blood that flows through his veins.

He feels deeply the inequality of privileges between the races, having told the writer of how he had paid out as much for the education of his daughter as a white gentleman of his acquaintance had paid for his, and yet his daughter had received a position that paid not half as much as the position given to the white girl. But he is not one to push against impassable barriers. He is not one to antagonize the white people by trying to gain for his children privileges not accorded them freely. He is courteous to all, intelligent in his thinking and mild and gentle in his manner. And he has done much for the advancement of his people.[24]

[Loc.: VSL/AB, box 187, also box 184, 12 pp., 4,050 wds.]

Lillie R. Vaughn *by Bessie A. Scales, 26 August 1940*

Lillie Vaughn was born in Almagro, a portion of Pittsylvania County later annexed into Danville City. Written across the top of a page in the county's census for 1920 is the identification "Almagro Village," followed immediately by "Means All Negros." And, indeed, what followed was a settlement—then unincorporated—composed of 265 Negro families, among whom a large number of persons were originally from North Carolina and 62 percent of the families were property owners.

Both Weldin Yancey, a teamster and later a plasterer, and his wife, Henrietta, were North Carolina natives. But their nine children (including fraternal twins, son Jollie and daughter Knowledge) were all born in Virginia—most of them in the city of Danville at 142 Rison Street, where the Yanceys rented a house for more than twenty years before moving to Almagro. In that community, the Yanceys were listed as living on the corner of Branch and Winslow in 1935.[25]

At some point, Henrietta Yancey met and became a close friend of Lillie Vaughn's mother, and she "adopted" the child after both of Lillie's parents died in the early 1920s. Insofar as Lillie Vaughn could recall, "Mama Henrietta" was the only mother she had ever known. Interviewer Bessie Scales added her own testimony as well about Henrietta Yancey and her fine reputation. It is of some further relevance here, however, to know that Henrietta's daughter Ada Lee Yancey was the person who contacted Bettie Stevens and Lessie Johnson of Almagro and arranged for Scales to interview them about folklore. It was also likely Ada Lee Yancey, acting as go-between, who earlier led Scales to conduct a life history with Lillie R. Vaughn.[26]

In talking of the experience she had gotten in her work for the NYA—on the playground and in the library of the "colored" school—Lillie commented, "I guess they have improved and so have I." She liked the work better "than any [she had] ever done" and hoped to stay on with the program until she was "past the age limit" of twenty-five. But the NYA, which was established within the WPA by Executive Order No. 7034 on 6 May 1935, was closed down by the end of 1943—before Lillie reached her age limit. In the period between 1935 and 1943, however, seven thousand black youths had been put to work on NYA projects. This number included not only Lillie Vaughn but also an unidentified group of "negro boys" in Charlotte County who "built an addition to [the] white Home Economic Building"—depicted in the photographic essay on Charlotte Court House schools later in this chapter.[27]

"I have heard so many complimentary things about you from the N.Y.A. Director, Lillie, that I've come to ask you to tell me about your busy life." "Certainly ma'am, I will be glad to tell you anything you want to know. I was born in Almagro, Virginia (which is part of Danville now), in 1919, so I've been told. My own mother and father died when I was real young, and I was adopted by a friend of my mother's named Henrietta Yancy. My parents were both factory hands. And the steam room in which they worked caused their death, I've been told, as they both died with TB. Whenever I think about my parents and the many other colored people who have died with TB, I am so thankful the colored TB Sanatorium is at last finished and open for patients. Working in a tobacco steam room has caused much sickness, especially TB among my race.

"I don't remember either of my parents and Mama Henrietta has been the only mother I've ever known. She sure was a good one though and she learned me about everything I know. She was always saying, 'Lillie, politeness don't cost you nothing and it will always serve you as a friend.' Ma Henrietta was mighty religious, too. She believed in keeping the Sabbath and she made me believe in keeping it too. She was always mighty strict but mighty good to me, and I knows I lost my best friend when she died. She made me 'tend school regular and learned me to wash and iron, an' cook and sew, and do about everything. She couldn't read or write herself but, don't you know, every night she would sit by the table and sew while I was studying, and made me study everything out loud.

"We lived in a two-room house, and as her other children were grown — some of them married and moved away, and some living out in service — I was the only one at home with her. She worked hard, took in washing, to educate me, and I always had good clothes and shoes. She always said I was the only one of the children who was refined enough to want to go to school and study and be somebody. The night I graduated she said, 'Child you sho' has made Ma Henrietta proud,' and she just sat and cried because she was so happy."

"I knew your Ma Henrietta, Lillie, and she was a splendid woman and had many friends among the white people. And I'm not surprised that you are making a success in life having been trained by her. How old were you when you started to school?" "I begun school when seven years of age and attended regularly till I graduated at the age of eighteen years. I liked school and as I had decided to be a school teacher I tried hard to make each grade. I did not repeat a grade nor skip one. I liked all my studies and got along with all my teachers. The subjects I studied and liked most were History, English, and Domestic Science.

"During my summer vacation I would always help Ma with the house work and washing and [with] my being at home to help, we could take in more washings and make more money. Some weeks we would make nine and ten dollars together. In the evenings we would sit out on the porch and I'd read aloud to Ma. I got books from the Library. We always liked the love stories best and Ma and I would talk about the people in the books, just like we knew them and they were really living folks. Ma always said she was going to buy me an organ and let me take music lessons, but we never could save up enough for that. I wish they would teach music lessons in every school. But they did teach singing and I liked that.

"After I graduated I wanted mightily to teach but I didn't have the money to go off to school, so I got a job dressing hair." "What do you mean by dressing hair?" "I ordered a dozen bottles of hair tonic and was appointed an agent, and I had an outfit that I carried around from house to house. And everywhere I went, I demonstrated and sold a bottle of the tonic that would take all the kinks out of the hair and make it straight and glossy. I made good money for a while when I was the only demonstrator. But pretty soon, so many were selling tonic and dressing hair that nobody could make a living.

"I worked out in Danville some, but times got so hard I couldn't find regular work. And the laundry is begin doing family wash, which nearly put all the washerwomen out of business. During one winter I worked in a laundry. But the over-heated work rooms kept me with a cold all the time and I had to give up that work.

"I applied at the office of the N.Y.A. and was given a job at one of the recreation centers. I've been working on N.Y.A. for about two years. This summer I've had charge of the children's playground at the colored school and I also have charge of the Library. I like the work better than any I've ever done, 'specially the library part. On fair days, I teach games, sewing, handcraft [and] modeling out-of-doors and when the weather is bad, we move in the Library. I've taught the children how to take care of the books they borrow to read and to return them when they are due to be returned. I also read aloud right much. When I started, only a few children were getting books and just to look at the pictures, mostly. But now, about every child wants a book and most of them read. Over [the] week, we have a few boys and girls to tell us about the books they have read. We all enjoy hearing each other tell a story they have read.

"The N.Y.A. Director [called] on us at one of their meetings and she said it was wonderful how the little children could tell about a story they read or [had] read to them. It certainly is teaching the children to read. And I require them to take care of the books, too. If they abuse a book they have to mend it. I've seen such a big improvement in the care they take of books, also. And the children have even learned to wash their hands before they handle the books.

"Last winter, I worked in the school cafeteria. I helped with the cooking, made up menus, and waited on tables. I liked this work and hope to get on again this coming school term. I work seven hours and my pay is $19.40. I also get my dinner free when working in the cafeteria.

"After Ma Henrietta died, I went to live with her oldest daughter who is married. She owns a nice home in Almagro. Her house has five rooms, is painted, has plastered walls, electric lights, and running water. Her husband has a good job with the city, and her two girls are in school. I pay her two dollars a week for my room and board, but she pays me back fifty cents a week to hair dress her two girls hair—also her hair once a month. She has a radio and her husband has an auto. I stay in the room with the girls. We have nice furniture in all the rooms. I help with the cooking, housecleaning and laundry. We all are good to each other and don't live like no trash.

"I save a dollar a week in a Xmas savings and I have nearly two hundred dollars in a bank on interest. I also carry sick benefit insurance, and if I should get sick I would be protected and could go to the hospital. I don't spend much for clothes. I work in a uniform, which is easy to keep clean by laundering it about twice a week. I learned sewing at school and make most of my clothes. My ready-made cost me around fifty cents a week if I'm paying on a coat or nice dress. We all read the Danville Bee, a daily newspaper, and I read many books aloud but most of them are children's books. I go to movies about once a month. We have a nice sitting room which is furnished just like a parlor, but we entertain most of our friends in the kitchen. We cook on a wood stove and it is always warmer in the kitchen. We have a nice big coal stove in our parlor and always make a fire in there on Sunday when we have so much company.

"Yes ma'am, we are all church-going people. We go to High Street Baptist Church. I am a member and I go about every Sunday afternoon. And Sunday night we go to the Holiness Church. I don't go to Sunday school and don't hold any kind of office. My cousin's husband is a deacon. And for that reason we don't have no card playing or dancing, and I never have been to a dance but go to parties every Xmas. Of course, I have to manage the children and maybe I do enjoy doing so. Some of them are mighty bad, but I guess I get on with them as well as anybody else. No ma'am I have never paid any poll tax or voted. I don't care to mix up with politics."

"What plans have you for the future Lillie?" "I don't suppose I have any. I hope I can keep on working for the N.Y.A. till I'm past the age limit. I'm keeping company with a nice young man. We might get married sometime, but he is too poor now and I don't want to marry anybody that can't make as good living as I can. I'm just proud that way." "Maybe you want to be an old maid?" "I don't know, Ma Henrietta used to say 'single blessedness was better than doubled cussedness,' and I guess she knew."

"Do you have any trouble keeping order at your play center? I heard some of the Directors have a time with so many children. How do you manage them?" "When they get to fighting and doing bad and won't mind me, I just form them in line and make them march all around. And they try to behave, because they don't like to march, and they do like to play. I don't have any trouble now. I did at first, but they do real well now. I guess they have improved, and so have I."

[Loc.: VSL/AB, box 178, 7 pp., legal-size, handwritten ms., 1,843 wds.]

Cleveland Buchanan *by Mary S. Venable, rec. 31 July 1939*

Undertaker Cleveland Buchanan had done some traveling in his life; his wagon had not spent much time in the shed. Given his pronouncement that "the wagon, put up in the shed, did not wear out"—relating decreased African American mortality rates with the forced inactivity brought about by the depression—perhaps he should have been concerned about his own wearing out as a result of much activity and many adventures.

That was not yet an issue for the twenty-two-year-old Grover C. Buchanan in 1910, when he was working as a gardener on the farm of Hunter J. Breckenridge in the Amsterdam District of Botetourt County, Virginia. Since he ran in track in that same year and graduated from Tuskegee Institute the following year, Buchanan presumably was working his way through college between semesters or in the summer, when he was fortuitously picked up in the Botetourt census. It is not known, however, if the Breckenridge farm was related in any way to the Catawba Stock Farm, where Buchanan later worked for a time—after World War I and before going to Covington in 1927.

Archival references to the film *Democracy Paid For* confirm the information reported in the VWP interview about it and its United States premiere. But it has not been determined whether any copy of the film is still in existence at this time.[28]

"I was named for two Democratic Presidents, Cleveland Buchanan, I'd HAVE to be a Democrat, wouldn't I?," says the bearer of that honorable combination.

"My father, down in Shelbyville, Tennessee where I was born, was what you might call a diplomat. When he talked with a Democrat, he was a Democrat. If it was a Republican he was talking to, he was a Republican. Isn't that a diplomat?, his son wants to know. It is a great mistake to think that the colored folks belong only to the Republican Party. They do *not* in Virginia and we vote to the issue, in both national and local elections. But I have always chosen the candidates of the Democratic Party on my ballot, so I'm a Democrat.

"I came to this town twelve years ago, that was 1927, and opened up an undertaker's business. I chose this town rather than many other places I might live—France, New York, Tennessee, Alabama, North Carolina, California and Washington, D.C.—because I liked it best and because I saw the demand. I bury about ninety-eight percent of the colored around here and go into West Virginia, White Sulphur [Springs], and over into Greenbrier County, when I get calls. The latest town directory gives this town a shopping population of fifty thousand people. That is rather high figures, but with from twenty to twenty-five percent population in the county, 'my people,' it gives me a wide territory and practically no competition.

"I have never regretted living here. I would not leave. The mountains hem us in and many of the families have never been beyond the ridges, but somehow, I like them better than any other folks. We have some educated negroes: doctors, teachers, and many of the well-to-do have educated their children, till we have a pleasant and progressive group. My wife and I find it a nice place to live. She belongs to all the clubs and does a lot of civic and church work. The Recreational Center, she has found, reaches closer to the homelife than some of the other progressive projects. We were disappointed about getting an auditorium for our new High School building. And Manual Arts left out of it!! Major Beirne stood by us and re-signed from the school board when he could not do anything toward getting the auditorium. We will remember him."

Merging from a somber note to brighter, he continued: "But I started to tell you about business conditions here in my work. Here is a most surprising thing, for which I have the figures to prove. You see I'm educated and keep my statistics. I was educated at Tuskegee, B.S., majored in Agriculture, 1911 class. The DEATH RATE of negro mortality DECREASED WITH UNEMPLOYMENT of 1932–33–34–35. Here is the way I have figured it out, and by the way, a representative of the Institute of Public Affairs got my figures and wrote me concerning this matter. They found it very interesting. When the depression hit Virginia, in this county, where there are not so many but those comparatively few had not gotten into regular work since the iron business dropped them, the negro population suffered more than any race. They were harder hit: no labor; no money to carouse on; no pork chops; no ham; and my books will show that the death RATE DROPPED 42 per cent. He had nothing to do but sit and take what welfare would give him. That caused him to live longer. The wagon, put up in the shed, did not wear out.

"Since times are better, these last three years: money better; livin' better; dying is better, too. In 1934 I buried eight paupers for the county. In the past five years, I have had one each year, five, in all. Compare that with one bad year."

Cleveland thinks the "sanitary instruction by state and county nurses has greatly reduced TB among our people. There was a time when our county rated low on the state list of that disease, but we have come up. Pneumonia is the worst disease, I find. Dropsy and heart disease comes next, from what I have listed.

"I have not put extra capital into my business. The profits are carrying it. The profits are sufficient to give us about—well—I pay my debts and bought this eight-room brick house in 1938. You can see we have plenty of room, bath, good lot, no garage, but I keep my hearse and car near my office. Profits have not increased in the past three years. We got a raise from the county for pauper funerals, but private patrons would not stand for a raise and so it has stayed where it was before the advance in manufacturer's prices. The average I get is two hundred dollars for a burying.[29]

On the wall is a framed group of four pictures, accounting for the highlights of Cleveland's life: 1910, in track suit, when he ran in the track meet for Tuskegee (he does not mention the winning); 1915, on horseback, he was farm manager at an agricultural college in Montgomery, Alabama; 1923, Fleet Steward, Merchant Marine, U.S. Shipping Board; 1929, in his handsome hearse, Covington, Virginia. In the center is a World War souvenir, seal and ribbon. On another wall are his honorable discharge, recommendations, references signed by notables of the period on official letter-head paper. The District Attorney of Los Angeles County, California recommends Cleveland to be a "reliable, sober, industrious and efficient employee, May 1917." His U.S. Army service discharge gives his number 1765997 of 349th Field Artillery; during the World War he enlisted in California.

He says he was discharged at Fort Bourguen, France, [as] a regimental sergeant, and became secretary to the Negro Y.M.C.A. in Paris. "Later I became the business secretary of the Y.M.C.A. and handled from forty to fifty thousand dollars a month. Over there, they speak of Colonial French. They are all one people. I was thrown with the high-ranking officers of our army in my Y.M.C.A. work. And the French army officers are used to their Negro citizens and make no difference. It was a great experience, living in Paris! The Y.M.C.A. work, established for our soldiers, closed out with the embarking of our troops for home. But in the meantime, having high rank in the army I had the unusual opportunity to film our troops or to get pictures of certain occasions, which could not have been gotten excepting by permission of authorities. [This] gave me a chance to work up a movie which I had written. I called it 'Democracy Paid For.' It was produced in Paris by the Eclair Societie Industrille Cinematographique, Paris. Here is the press account of its presentation."

The name of the paper is not on the clipping, but it states the author's name mentioning that it is a three hundred-thousand francs production; the first ever seen of camp life of Colonials; shown September 2, 1919 at the Manhattan Casino; made for the Buchanan and Franklyn Cinema Corporation by the Eclair company. The notice mentions "one of the clearest pictures ever made of the Argonne Forest." Cleveland has two of the photos and says he has had trouble keeping these; his friends want them for souvenirs. One is of a color bearer with the stars and stripes, troop in middle foreground. The other is of a line of soldiers in French uniform. "They are the French Colonials."

Asked how he got a "backer" for the production of his play, Cleveland becomes animated in his glowing description of his warm friend in Paris, whom he loved as soon as he met him. "He was a millionaire. As we would walk down the street together, he was recognized by notables of the army or by men of civic importance in a way, one felt, was due his prestige. He was born in Paris and had made his money in a wine and liquor shop. Why, President Roosevelt, walking down our streets, would not be more highly saluted or honored than Franklyn! They called him the 'black Frenchman.' He had a palatial home at 12 Roune a Que. One of the most popular citizens of Paris! The Manager of the American Express Company introduced me to him and he was in for producing the play as soon as he heard about it. The people over there thought a lot of it. And then I wanted to bring it to America, of course.

"Oscar Hammerstein, a personal friend of mine, and Bert Williams tried to get the New York Board of Censors to let the picture be produced here just as it was given in Paris. But there was some objection, so it was cut. But what was taken out did not ruin the plot and I really did not care. It was complimented in New York." The author had no press account of the play as given in America, but the Parisian notice was very complimentary. "Why don't you write another play? Something of the history of this place you have chosen for your home?" we asked Cleveland. "I think I will, but you know how it is when everyday there is plenty of business. The time never seems right to get at it." (He takes cinema writing for a hobby.)

Although he has had an eventful life and made the most of the period, so plentiful in opportunities, there is no braggadocio in Cleveland's manner—rather a gladness and continued enjoyment through memory of the praise from others, whose names are well-known.

Continuing his story of varied employment with eager zest and, at the end of each new phase, bringing out some letter, press clipping, or picture, as though he had prepared for

Missouri doubters: "I was the personal friend of Harry S. New. He had the same place in the government as Mr. Farley has now. He had influence in government circles and got me a place in the Merchant Marine through the U.S. Shipping Board."

He shows a copy of official appointment, February —— 1923, Fleet Steward numbers 1 & 2, Steward's Department. "I had seventy-two boats—got to be Chief Steward—passengers and freighters under my charge! On the Antigone, I had as passengers Mrs. Harry Payne Whitney and Mr. James J. Hines. We don't speak so much of him since the trial. But anyhow, they both said that I had one of the cleanest ships they had ever sailed on and they told Mr. New that. The Antigone was a grand yacht that had been the private yacht of the Kaiser's wife. It had been taken over by the United States. The furnishings were very handsome, every convenience!

"In 1924, I married Dorothy Dudley of Clarkesville, Tennessee. She had graduated at the Agricultural and Mechanical College, Huntsville, Alabama. She takes charge of my office when I have a burial on hand or when I am collecting. I have to count twenty-five percent loss per year on my accounts, even though I do the collecting, or try to, myself. We belong [to] and attend the First Baptist Church on Lexington Street—the brick church! No, I am not an officer in the church."

In reply to an inquiry of how he happened to find the little village he prefers, Cleveland explains that "after the World War commotion had ceased," he learned through Emmet Stock, secretary of the late Booker T. Washington, that the Catawba Stock Farm of B—— County wanted a farm manager, and he had been recommended. "The owner was a millionaire or, that is, he had a rich wife. The farm was equipped for stock, fine horses! We had everything that would tend to put good racers on the track. But things got to going bad: domestic troubles, and there was a divorce. I would not boast about how I managed the farm, but it must have suited Mr. ——. For he sent a check to Tuskegee for ten thousand dollars, because he said he knew from my training it was doing good work as an institution. While I was there I found that this town had no undertaker for Negroes nor had the . . ." [part of the text missing here].

No children came to this couple, so they adopted one. He is being given the best of care and one hears that he is mentally above the average. The foster mother is musical and she encourages choral work in church and clubs. She thinks the women's clubs have resulted in much good and broadening of interests among her people. The branch of the Progressive League, of which she is a member, has planted shrubs and flowers on unsightly vacant lots, helped in alley sanitation, and cooperated with town authorities in waste disposals, which was a problem for those on the outskirts of the corporation.

Cleveland replies, when asked for a constructive criticism regarding employment: "We are running top-heavy in employment. I would like to see the white public open avenues for those of my race having had high school and college education [who are] prepared for professional service."

Asked to explain "top-heavy" his reply is enigmatical, since it repeats adding to the top. He adds that women should have courses in home economics and takes up a local condition in which he has had the backing of the best citizens:

"Our newly finished high school is back against a hill away from the center of negro population. There is no space provided for manual arts. No vocational training room! We asked for an auditorium, since we have only the church auditoriums in this town. What we got was two rooms that can be thrown together, seating less than one tenth of the parents. The old school building, which has done duty for more than thirty years, at least was well located. I hear that it will be sold. It was good enough for us last year. A little repair would provide space for the first four grades and keep from crowding the high school, which is too small for the school population. If the small children could be kept off the dangerous crossings where the cars whiz by, it would save lives. But we will not be allowed to use that old building. It will be sold. Can you guess to whom? I will tell you, though there has been no mention as yet of its sale (he names two; both from Northern descent, Ohio and N.J.). Maj. Beirne went down before the gang. He resigned [from the school board] because he could not beat the majority against him. (Maj. Richard Beirne, owner of the paper, Covington, Virginian [actually, the *Evening Virginian*]) The best white people stood with him, but they were outnumbered. There's NOTHING we can do about it. We have tried and failed." (NOTE: His criticism is correct. Sadly true! M.S.V.).

[Loc.: VSL/AB, box 181, 6 pp.]

"Working on an Equality Base" I: Charlotte County Schools in Black and White *photographs by Philip Bonn, June 1943*

Philip Bonn was a photographer with OWI in the period just before Roy Stryker left it for Standard Oil Co. of New Jersey. Bonn's photographs are no better or worse than many taken by other, much better known RA/FSA photographers, but his life and career seem to have received little, if any, serious consideration. As a result, the extent of Stryker's influence and of Bonn's place with regard to the RA/FSA "canon" is not known.

In Virginia, Bonn had only one assignment: to photograph in June 1943 the state's first consolidated white high school—Randolph Henry in Charlotte Court House (Charlotte County)—erected with funds from the Public Works Administration and a private donation of five hundred thousand dollars from statesman and county native David Bruce.[30] One hundred and three photographs of the white high school, along with three photographs of the town of Keysville, survive. In all, Bonn took 209 photographs in Charlotte county; 76 of them were killed.

For reasons unknown, Bonn also took pictures of Central High, the county's black high school in Charlotte Court House. Whatever his intent was, Bonn's twenty-seven surviving Central High School photographs graphically illustrate the instructional programs available to black and white students and offer a paradoxical twist on the pervasive separate-but-unequal theme. The picture *not* taken by Bonn— a full front view of Central High School itself—would have shown a solid, but aging, brick structure that had been built in 1921, had undergone some renovation in 1941, and was, relatively speaking, a better building than those sundry frame structures, documented by Bonn, that spread across the county and that previously served the secondary school needs of the white population. Nevertheless, in 1943 the older educational facility for black youths was, in comparison, no match for the splendid and modern new Randolph Henry High School. The more glaring and important visible differences existing then, however, were not between structural facades but between the separate educational programs and unequal curriculum content that trained one group to repair farm equipment or identify leaf forms and prepared the other for advanced studies with courses in chemistry, math, and language skills.[31]

Randolph Henry High School continued to serve white students from the eighth through twelfth grades until 1969, when the county integrated its schools. At that time, Central High School, which had been renovated further in 1963, became the county's consolidated junior high school, serving eighth- and ninth-grade students—both black and white. Central Junior High became Central Middle School in 1985 and finally closed its doors altogether in 1994. Since then, the Charlotte County School Board has been considering plans for rehabilitating the old building for new uses. These include possibly using some space for county offices, turning the still usable gymnasium over to the Recreation Department, or even using part of the central portion as a museum dedicated to African American schooling.

Keysville, Virginia.
[LC-USW3-33304-E]

Central high school [black].
June 1995.
Photo by Charles L. Perdue Jr.

Randolph Henry high school
[white]. Students entering main
building. [LC-USW3-33447-E]

Central high school. Lunch room. Students usually bring lunch from home and buy one or two things in cafeteria. [LC-USW3-33492-E]

Randolph Henry high school. Students eating lunch in the school's cafeteria. [From the caption on another view of the cafeteria] Students don't have much money so they bring produce from farms for which they receive tickets. Lunches cost about 15 cts. Typical lunch for 15 cts: candied yams, macaroni and cheese, fruit salad, devilled eggs, dessert, and milk. Milk is free and children can have as much as they want. [LC-USW3-33861-E]

Randolph Henry high school. Home economics cottage. Girls learn to plan, cook and serve meals. They usually have a guest. [LC-USW3-33410-E]

Central high school. Girls in the kitchen of home economics cottage. [LC-USW3-33347-E]

Randolph Henry high school. Interior of vocational shop where boys learn to repair farm machinery, carpentering, and welding. Machine shop is 3-year course. [LC-USW3-33459-E]

Randolph Henry high school. Exterior of vocational shop. June 1995. Photo by Charles L. Perdue Jr.

Central high school. Shop where boys learn to repair farm machinery. [LC-USW3-33338-E]

Central high school. Exterior of vocational shop. June 1995.
Photo by Charles L. Perdue Jr.

Randolph Henry high school. Girls' gym class. [LC-USW3-33308-E]

Central high school.
A combination gym and auditorium
where the seats are movable.
The elementary school has no auditorium
so the children have come over to practice
an operetta.
[LC-USW3-33428-E]

Randolph Henry high school.
School band which played for
graduation.
[LC-USW3-33482-E]

Central high school band every month
or so marches up Main street to give
drills and a concert. Players must buy
their own instruments and costumes and
pay for their own lessons. Lessons are
given during school hours.
[LC-USW3-33394-E]

Dilcie Gum *by Bessie A. Scales, 23 July 1940*

Letitia Jane Lumpkin commented previously on her grandmother Viney's reputation as a good cook, saying that "anybody that does something real well . . . gets a name for theirselves and gets remembered, too." One of the few venues open to African American women in which to make a "good name"—both in the antebellum years and for a long while afterward—was as a cook.[32]

Dilcie Gum was allegedly one of those cooks. She was the "one-and-only cook in this town," according to Scales, and had contributed "nearly every other recipe" in the cookbook called *The Key to the Pantry.* But an 1898 copy of that cookbook, which had belonged to John Staige Davis of the University of Virginia, contains not a single reference to or recipe from "Dilcie of the Country Club." There are fifteen recipes (in this collection from the Ladies of the Church of the Epiphany in Danville), however, that were contributed by Miss Augusta Yates—most surely the "Miss Gusta" who it is said paid Dilcie ten dollars for her "resceits." [33]

Dilcie Gum was allegedly one of the numerous home owners living in Almagro Village, yet no one by that name has been found in courthouse and other records for the city and county or in the censuses for that section between 1900 and 1920. The search did find one woman with a similar name, Dilcie Ingram, who—though she was a laundress, did not own her home, and would have been over ninety in 1940—*was* in Almagro Village records throughout that time period. But that information merely muddles the identity of Dilcie Gum further.[34]

Considerably more relevant to this case is the fact that Bessie Scales interviewed another subject, Mollie Williams, and submitted a folklore text and personal history forms for her that bear significant similarities to the Dilcie Gum life history. According to the information given for her, Mollie Williams owned her home in Almagro and had lived in Danville for more than fifty years, "cooked in one home [for] thirty-five years," was a lodge member, and attended the Holiness Pentecostal Church. Other details clearly disagree with those asserted for the life of Dilcie Gum, but in any case, Williams, too, cannot be positively identified in the records.[35]

It is altogether possible and probable that Dilcie Gum is a pseudonym for Mollie Williams. But what is far more likely the case is that the person identified as Dilcie Gum is, in fact, a composite of the histories, experiences, and lore of several unidentified or otherwise obscured women interviewed under the heading of several different VWP programs. And that would be all the more a shame, for in so doing Bessie Scales deprived more than just one African American woman of her "good name" and of being remembered.

Up a slippery path [on] the top of a hill sits a dilapidated, unpainted three-room house, built so high up from the ground on stilt-like underpinnings, that it seems even a slight gust of wind would cause it to tumble head-long down the hill, and into the branch-like creek at the bottom. This house is entered by a flight of five broken-down swaying steps that lead to a porch, almost entirely enclosed by hop-vines running on strings. Several old tin cans filled with flowers growing profusely were by the edge of porch. A short walk was outlined on both sides with ends of glass bottles stuck in the ground. A Mimosa tree in full bloom wafted a delicate fragrance and shaded the front yard. Several lilac bushes, hollyhocks in full bloom, with old-fashioned spice-pinks [were] growing in clumps everywhere. Sitting in a rocking chair that had seen better days was Dilcie Gum. Dilcie was dressed in a clean, freshly starched, gingham dress that made her look like she weighed three hundred pounds, instead of just two hundred.

"You certainly look comfortable and contented sitting up here where you can view the town, but what in the world are you knitting?" "Honey, I'se knitting myself some socks for winter wear." "I know they will be warm because they certainly are the largest, longest ones I ever saw, but who taught you to knit?" "My Mammy did, she were pow-ful perttickler to learn all we chilluns how to do everything.

"Come in and say howdy to me ma'am. Sit right here on this chair. Won't fall down." "I don't suppose you remember me but I've seen you many times when you were the cook at the country club." "But that's been a long time ago." "Not long [enough] for me to forget that you were always considered the one-and-only cook in this town. And even now I have a copy of that cookbook called, *The Key to the Pantry,* and you know nearly every other recipe in it is signed *Dilcie of the Country Club.*" "Yes'm I does 'members that book, and you know Miss Gusta—she's the lady what got up the book—gave me ten dollars and said my resceits [receipts or recipes] were the mos'n and best she got.

"I'se glad you spoke of that book, I can't seem to make up my remembrance about things like I used to. I ain't so vigorous in my mind seems. Who is you anyway, honey? Seems as I ain't never seed yo' face befo' as I knows."

"What is that you've got your head tied up with?" "I'se got headache, and these here tansy leaves he'p's me right smart. I keeps them on till the headache is gone, but I'se feeling tol'able."

"I was wondering how old you are?" "Honey, I'se nigh eighty." "Well, you certainly don't look it. Tell me all about yourself. Were you born in Danville?" "Yes'm I were and I'se lived in this house might nigh all my life. This place used to be in the country, but now we is annex' with the town, and we have City running water, but we don't have no 'lectric lights like some of them does here in Almagro. I still uses a kerosene lamp and cooks on a wood stove like I'se always been used to. I went to school some, and I kin read and write. My son and his wife lives with me, and both of them kin read ennything. We gets the *Danville Bee* every day and we all sho' do enjoy that paper, but we don't read no books. This is all my house, bought and paid for and I have a little money I put away in the bank. I saved up this money during the twenty-two years I was in service at the club. My house is right nice. I got all my walls plastered, and I aims to have it painted some day."

"Have many children have you?" "Just one son now and his wife which is just like my daughter. My son he drive a warehouse truck. He do sho' know tobacco and he got a good job. His wife, she work out in service. I can't do much washing for the white folks now, case I'se too heavy to be on my feet much and I always liked to do my work unaided."

"Is your husband living?" "No'm he isn't and for many years I's been better off to git shut of him. He was just no 'count, leaving me with all the burdens to be a'staggering under. While he jest set and brag and big-talk about 'my house this,' and 'my house that,' and t'wasn't his a'tall, and he jest tetchus about ev'ry thing. And some folks is tried to persuade me to for-git my spite and marry agin, but no honey, not me, I's drank at the branch. So when he taken sick and died I jest knowed 'twas proper to miss pestications but tain't good sense to mourn their loss. But when my boy he died it might nigh kilt me."

"Was he sick long?" "Yes'm, he took sick at Christmas and lived till summer." "I know you did all you could and all were good to him." "Yes'm, we were, but 'tis sho powerful grieve-some to see somebody you love laid out with miseries, but nobody can't lucidate my troubles like the Lawd. Tis just like the Rev-und ——— said, to not be studyin' by no kind of trouble, that it is all out of my understanding, and he'd jest sit by me and smoke his pipe, and it would jest ease down my mind. The Rev-und ——— and I is kinnery, and he jest goes around giving religgus advices, but you can't always fault folks when they is griefed." "O cheer up Miss Dilcie." "Yes'm honey, I will, but somehow his kind of talk gave me trouble in my mind when he came to converse me about that."

"I imagine you are a mighty good church member and that you attend regularly. What church are you a member of, and do you attend Sunday School also?" "Sho' I's a church member. We call our church, The Christian Holiness Church, and I used 'tind regular but I don't get there much now. But the church members all knows I have nouf miseries in my limbs to be a po' saint, and they also knows po' saints ain't expected to rise from they beds of woe when they can't even walk to church. And none of us 'tends Sunday School. My son he sing in the church choir, but my daughter she ain't made up her mind yet. So she ain't suppos'n sing in the choir, an I does sho' pray hard she will come through."

"I'm sure the singing at your church is lovely. Do many white people attend?" "Yes'm, sometime they bring they visitors to our Tabernacle jest to hear the singing and when they do come to our branch of God's House we doesn't Jim Crow 'em, but ask's them right up to the front."

"I wonder if you remember much about the war?" "O yes'm, my son he attended the war. He blowed on the bugle, and he went all the way over to France, but praise be de Lawd, he returned and didn't get kilt nor nothing." "Well, do you remember much about the other war— the War between the States—when the North came down and outnumbered the South?" "No'm, I don't member nuthin' much about that war, but I members hearing my folks tell about them Ku Kluxes, how they was ridin' 'bout in the night-time all civered up in sheets. They mighty nigh scared folks to death and when we chillens was bad my Mammy would always tell us the Ku Kluxes was comin' and git us." [36]

[Scales allegedly leaves at this point but returns for another visit later on a very hot day. She continues the second interview on the same page without any break, but she comments on the bad road to Dilcie's house and her trouble getting there.]

"Well now honey, isn't we house owners done everything we could to have a few loads of cinders put in them holes. We is 'gwine petition the Mayor for a street, but I's feared I be cemetery dead before anything is did." [37]

"You haven't your head tied up today and didn't I hear you singing?" "You sho did. I never was one to dwell on troubles. "But I don't believe you have many troubles. You look too happy and well, and while you say you are most eighty years old, you don't look it. Just what do you do to keep yourself so spry?" "Now go on honey, ain't you white folks just a sight." "Do you work hard?" "Yes'm I sho do, and when I works, I works hard and when I sets, I sets loose." "But you don't worry?" "Yes'm I do, but when I worries I most always jest goes to sleep." "Well that certainly is a fine recipe, the best one you have ever given out. And I'm sure if everybody would adopt it and pay you for it, you would make a fortune." "Yes'm." [38]

"Why do you hang a towel over the face of your clock and over your mirrors?" "Don't you know, honey, you does that when there is a death in your family and it stays civered up 'till the mourning period is over." [39]

"Have you ever been to a movie?" "No'm. I'se heared all about them, but they ain't for the likes of me. I jest stays at home and tends the house, I don't never go nowhere but to funerals, you know I's a lodge sister."

"How many sisters and brother have you?" "There were twelve in [my] family. I jest don't know what become of all of them. My five brothers worked around here. Two of them live with their families in town, and the others just scattered. Yonder over there is where one of my sisters live. One died and two of them been living in the North a long time. I's the oldest and they don't come see me often."

"Do any of you have an automobile or have a radio?" "No'm us don't, but I'd sho' like a radio. How financial do you have to be to buy one?" "When you have electric lights put in your house you can get one real cheap." "My son and daughter all the time wishing we had a radio. Some of these times I'll make inquiries about one. You think I like to have it?" "I'm sure you would. You could just sit and listen and be entertained." "But honey, I reckon I go to sleep likes I always does, but if I buyed all the things they is always pestering me to buy it would be like my mammy used to say, 'I have to charge my debts to the dust and let the rain a'settle them.'"

"Well, if I don't leave now the rain will settle me, and maybe in that branch. It looks like it is going to pour." "Now honey you come sometime again when I's making pickle and try some of my pepper-hash. You knows the kind I make, tis in that cook book." "Thank you I will and I'm going to put you in a book." "I sho be proud, but I ain't got no picture."

[Loc.: VSL/AB, box 178, 8 pp., 1,997 wds., handwritten ms.]

Mollie Williams *by Bessie A. Scales, 9–13 September 1940*

On the "Form A—Circumstances of Interview" for Mollie Williams, her parents Royal and Eva (Jones) Williams were indicated as ex-slaves. Scales noted, too, that Williams had three sons and four daughters. Two of the daughters lived with their mother and cared for her in the home in Almagro, Danville, where Molly Williams was interviewed on the subject of "Folklore." It is useful to compare Scales's entry for item #8, description of room, house, surroundings, and so on with the text for Dilcie Gum. She wrote:

> This home which is owned by Mollie Williams is located on top of a hill. A path leads up to the front steps from a foot-bridge over a branch. This house is built on a foundation of brick columns, which are so far apart as to leave the impression that a hard gust of wind might blow it over backwards. There are three rooms, all plastered and furnished with odds and ends of massive golden-oak, veneered mahogany, and crude home-made furniture. A swaying porch extends across the front of the house which is reached by picking your way up five rickety steps and holding on to a hand rail. Hop vines running on strings make a dense shade over the porch, excluding the morning sun entirely. On both ends of each step is a worn tin pan, can or bucket filled with petunias blooming profusely—a riot of color. A path leads around to the back door which is only one step from the ground, making an easier, safer entrance, than the front door. A large old oak tree grows at the front of the house, its branches spreading in all directions overhead, or its roots growing along the top of the bare ground. There are such conveniences as electric lights and running water in the house. Both the house and surroundings are clean and everything in fairly good repair. Mollie had owned and lived in this house twenty-five years.

This is essentially the same description given in Scales's life history of Dilcie Gum. And she continued:

After many years in active service as a cook, [Mollie] is now unable to get about much on account of rheumatism, but keeps busy making patch-work quilts from scraps of cotton cloth. She does all the sewing and quilting by hand. These quilts are made in the old-fashioned log-cabin and Peacock patterns, are colorful and attractive and so well-made she cannot make as many as she can find sale for. This work brings in a tidy income, quite enough to meet her simple needs.   [Loc.: UVA/FC, box 12]

"Yes ma'am, chile, I'se glad to see you and I'll sho' be glad to talk to you. Set yo'self right here in this chere and rest yo'self. I'se always 'sociated with high-class quality folks, and I'se proud that you is come to make inquirement. Yes ma'am, it sho' is nice and pleasant this A.M. but you can't trust the Sun when he come up warm so soon. I don't reckon I'se got much to tell you, case I allus belive I must a'got started in this world wrong-end foremost. For I'se never see's nothing 'till I'se gits past it. But who is you, ma'am, chile, I ain't never seed yo favor befo'. I can't seem to make up my remembrance about you.

"Yes'm, most of my folks is cemetery dead. It jest looked like at one time that soon as I took the kiveren of'n the mirrors & started up the clock somebody done up and died agin. Sho' you allus stops the clock and kivers up the mirrors when somebody dies. Ef'n you don't they sho' will come back here and hant you.

"My son-in-law name Mac was so mean he was counted a two-head man case he was mean as Hell. He took and got mad with me and tole me he was a'gwyin to fix me. And mighty nigh right away I'se begin to have pains in my jints, so I'se knewed right off he done put the conjure on me. So I searched and looked everywhere and when I looked the second time under this here back step, I saw a little bundle way back and when I'se pulled it out and opened it thar was nigger har [hair]. Mac had put it thar to conjure me with. So I'se took that har and burnt it up—but in the yard—case if I had gone up that step and stepped over that har I sho' would a'been conjured and sho' been killed too. But it did set me back some, case the very next day I'se was a'walking down the Street and I met one of my friends and she say, 'Did you know Ada is dead?' I'se answered quick like, 'you a liar.' Then she said, 'you come see.' So I'se walked right in and bless Gawd, thar she lay in corpse. For a long time jest to hear talk of Ada give me trouble in my mind and I'se didn't get complete rid of that conjure or vigerous in my mind ag'in 'till the Rev'nd come see me and tole me, 'Sister Mollie, can't you know and b'lieve nobody can't lucidate your troubles like de Lawd?' And right there I ease down on my mind and persuade myself to forgit my spite and that conjure left me. I've hearen tell that if you keep a rabbit foot tied 'round your waister it would keep off the conjure. But a plain rabbit foot won't do, it must be the left hind foot of a graveyard rabbit killed on a moonlight night by a red-headed nigger, and that kind is sho' hard to find.

"No ma'am, chile, I don't know nothing about no ghost stories. I don't rest no oneasiness no mo' 'bout hants, but I'se do know talking about the old booger man will sho' skere up his imps. [Sho'], Ma'am I'se is a Church member.[40]

"I'se gives biggus 'vices [advice] ef enny one comes to converse me 'bout it. Don't you never turn back unless you make a cross mark and spit in it, if you don't want to have bad luck. And if you ever put your left shoe and stocking on befo' you put your right shoe & stocking, you sho' is goin' be an old maid. Always 'member, sass is wurth a'heap mor'n sense.

"When I'se sets and sews I'se sing's, sho! I'se allus sings. I muss tell de good Lawd all of my trials. I can't bear dese her' burden 'lone."
    [Loc.: UVA/FC, box 2, folder 3, #305]

Rev. J. H. Coleman *by James Taylor Adams, 1 October 1940*

This brief interview with John Coleman gives a slightly different slant on the African American practice of and belief in conjuring from those expressed either in the preceding text by Molly Williams or by Benjamin Thacker in chapter 1. The following statement by James Taylor Adams prefaced the text from Coleman in the document originally submitted to the vwp folklore project.

The Reverend Coleman was standing on the cokeyard of the Norton Coal Company, at the east end of the battery as he leaned on a coke fork and told me how to become a conjure man and how the art was practiced. He said:

"I was born in slavery . . . two years in slavery . . . in old Pittsylvania County . . . a one-room log cabin. I've heard my father tell how one become a conjurer, and how it was practiced. All old colored people believed in it. Of course I didn't believe in it. No educated person does. But the old people all did. My father said to become a conjurer one had to kill a black cat and cook it whole. Then take the pot to a stream of running water and pour it all in the water. The conjure bone would float upstream."[41]

"I've heard them tell how they practiced curing sickness by conjuring. It was nothing but a graft, as we'd call it today. Several persons would get together and agree on what and how to do. People that were sick in the neighborhood would be selected to work on. One person of the group would go at night and bury a bottle at the door of the sick person. The bottle would be filled with spider legs. The next day, maybe, another one of the group who had some reputation as a conjure man, would show up at the house of the sick person, ask them some strange questions and announce that they had a 'spell on 'em.' Somebody had cast a spell on 'em. And that there was a bottle of spiders buried at their door. And to show the sick person that he knew what he was talking about he would go and dig right where the other fellow had told him he had buried the bottle, and sure enough there was a bottle full of spider legs."[42]

"Did the sick person believe in him?" "Of course they did. And nine times out of ten they got well or better at once. You see they just believed it so strong that they did get better. People are that way, if they believe anything enough it will just about be that way.

"Father said that to keep conjure men and witches from casting spells on you, you had to sleep with a knife under your pillow."[43]

[Loc.: uva/fc, box 2, item #273, 1 p.]

"Working on an Equality Base" II:
Aberdeen Gardens Homesteads Project Photographs

by Paul Carter, Arthur Rothstein, and John Vachon

Inadequate housing for low-income black families was a long-recognized problem in the South, and when the New Deal programs began, several individuals at Hampton Institute began working to establish a subsistence homesteads project in the Newport News area. The Division of Subsistence Homesteads was organized within the Department of the Interior in the late summer of 1933. By January 1934 division officials were in contact with Dr. Arthur Howe, president of Hampton Institute, and William M. Cooper, secretary of the Hampton Subsistence Homesteads Corporation. Cooper was also director of the Extension Service at Hampton.[44]

"Aberdeen Gardens," the name eventually applied to the project, changed in concept, cost, and function over time. Initially, there was a goal of 10 homes, which was increased to 25, then 50, then 100; upon completion there were 159 units. In January 1935, two hundred acres were purchased at the intersection of Mercury Boulevard and Aberdeen Road, three and one-half miles from Newport News. The *Newport News Daily Press* on 27 February 1935 announced, "Government approves $280,000 project for 100 colored families." A news release dated 13 March 1935 stated that the aim of the project was to give the homesteaders "an opportunity to utilize their spare time in the production of the food they require[d], and to lift them to a higher social and health level." Accordingly, there were to be 24 houses on one-acre lots; 20 houses on two-acre lots; and 14 houses on three-acre lots. The cost per unit was expected to be $2,000 to $2,600. Twelve homesteaders would have mules to work their own and neighbors' gardens, and twelve would have cows. Each homesteader would have chickens, a garden, and orchard, and there would be poultry houses, pig pens, and stables.[45]

The Aberdeen Gardens project was barely on the drawing boards when, on 15 May 1935, the Division of Subsistence Homesteads was transferred by executive order to the newly created Resettlement Administration.[46] The project was then completely replanned and became a Suburban Resettlement project rather than Subsistence Homesteads. Eventually it became a "small Negro housing development surrounded by a greenbelt of farms and gardens." In the initial planning, Aberdeen Gardens was the first Subsistence Homesteads project for African Americans and, as it turned out, the *only* African American Suburban Resettlement project.[47]

Newport News, Virginia. September 1936. View of life in the negro section. Photo by Paul Carter. [LC-USF33-10161-M1]

There were many complaints and criticisms of the RA housing projects, and Aberdeen was no exception. A *Newport News Daily Press* report of 14 August 1936 was merely snide in its comments: "They are attractive houses, as houses of their kind go [to be sold to] Negroes of this community on a long time payment plan—providing buyers can be found. . . . There were 376 Negroes at work yesterday, to say nothing of the one who strutted a badge bearing the label 'Special Officer.' "[48]

On 9 March 1937 the Board of Directors of the Virginia Peninsula Association of Commerce protested that the eventual boundary of the project, as called for in the plans, was too close to white farmers. The controversial project increasingly became a political liability for Governor Price. And when the formal opening was finally scheduled for 8 May 1938 (with forty-one families already living in the project), Price indicated by letter that he could not make the opening and, in fact, was so busy that he would not be able to schedule any time for the opening, no matter when it might be held. Instead, he sent Sidney Hall, supervisor of public instruction to take his place.[49]

The final cost of the Aberdeen Gardens Project was $1,353,896.29, rather than the $280,000 anticipated, and the unit cost for the 159 homes built was $8,515.00—about three and one-half times the original estimate. Still, from many perspectives, the project was a notable success.[50]

The RA/FSA photographs in this essay illustrate various stages in the housing project's development and set it in the context of a crowded and rapidly expanding metropolitan area. Today, the houses of Aberdeen Gardens remain and are still occupied largely by African Americans in Newport News.

Newport News, Virginia. September 1936. A market in the negro section. Photo by Paul Carter. [LC-USF33-10164-M4]

*Newport News, Virginia.
September 1936. A high class
Negro mansion in the negro
section. Photo by Paul Carter.*
[LC-USF33-10164-M1]

*Newport News (vicinity),
Virginia. September 1936.
Newport News homesteads,
a U.S. Resettlement
administration housing
project. The negro office staff.
Photo by Paul Carter.*
[LC-USF341-11293-B]

Newport News (vicinity), Virginia. September 1936. Newport News homesteads, a U.S. Resettlement administration housing project. A street lined with partially completed homes. Photo by Paul Carter. [LC-USF341-11294-B]

Newport News (vicinity), Virginia. September 1936. Newport News homesteads, a U.S. Resettlement administration housing project. Negro workers on the project. Photo by Paul Carter. [LC-USF33-10159-M3]

Newport News (vicinity), Virginia. September 1936. Newport News homesteads, a U.S. Resettlement administration housing project. Front view of type A and B houses. Photo by Paul Carter. [LC-USF341-11295-B]

Newport News (vicinity), Virginia. September 1936. Newport News homesteads, a U.S. Resettlement administration housing project. Lunch hour. Photo by Paul Carter. [LC-USF33-10157-M4]

Newport News (vicinity), Virginia. November 1937. Newport News homesteads, a U.S. Resettlement administration housing project. The house formerly occupied by one of the tenants. Photo by Arthur Rothstein. [LC-USF34-25990-D]

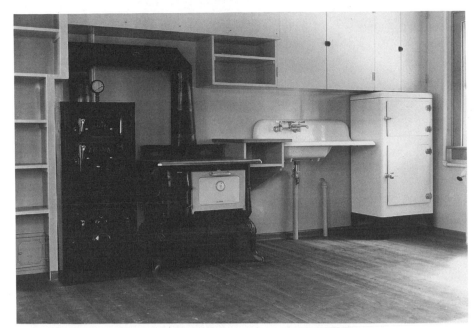

Newport News (vicinity),
Virginia. September 1936.
Newport News homesteads,
a U.S. Resettlement
administration housing
project. The interior of a
kitchen showing the
arrangement of facilities.
Photo by Paul Carter.
[LC-USF341-11298-B]

Newport News (vicinity), Virginia. November 1937. Newport News homesteads, a U.S. Resettlement administration
housing project. A young couple moving into one of the new homes. Photo by John Vachon. [LC-USF33-01001-M3]

Bernice Reid *by Susie R. C. Byrd, rec. 3 January 1939*

Bernice Inez Dyson and her future husband, Odell Reid, were both born in Petersburg—he near the beginning and she near the end of World War I. In the census for 1920, however, four-year-old Odell was neither with his parents, Walter and Lelia Reid, nor in Petersburg; he was living, rather, with his grandfather Turner Chatman (a farm laborer) and step-grandmother Mary in Zion Magisterial District, Greensville County. How long Reid stayed with his grandparents or when he returned to Petersburg is not known, but it is certain that he was living there at 435 Doans Alley in early 1936.[51]

In 1935, Bernice Dyson was a student at Virginia State University, along with Susie R. C. Byrd. On 20 April 1936, the eighteen-year-old daughter of Eddie and Mamie Dandridge Dyson married Odell Reid. By the time Bernice was interviewed in 1939 by her former schoolmate, she and Odell had two small children, Arthur McDaniel and Rose Dicie, he had been laid off by the WPA, and they lived at 317 Low Street, Petersburg—in what she referred to as a "bum neighborhood." Bernice was more than a little distressed to have Byrd and her other schoolmates know where she lived and spoke of wanting most of all to get away from "that section of the City."[52]

By 1941, it seemed as though things were looking up. At least by then the Reids were listed in the city directory at another address: 517 S. Dunlop Street. And Odell Reid apparently was trying to further his education, for he was listed as a student. In September 1941, however, Bernice Inez Reid, aged about twenty-three, died, leaving her husband, a four-year-old son, and three-year-old daughter.[53]

As a postscript to Bernice Reid's brief life, Odell Reid, still of the same address, was inducted into the navy at Richmond in 1944. And six years after her death, on 13 September 1947, he married for the second time to Eula Mae Williams, a North Carolina native.

"Odell hasn't a job now. I do wish that he could get work. He was layed-off WPA; formerly he worked on the Colonial Heights Project. His wages were, when on the job, $36.40 monthly. Every two weeks he got his check.

"Once Odell worked at the Brown and Williams tobacco factory. When he was working they had no unions, but now Brown & Williams have a union. Yes, I think unions are good because all stick together and get some things you want, decent stopping-work hours, fair-wage pay, and [you] stand a chance of steady employment. Yes, workers should strike for justice and equal consideration where there is efficiency.

"We pay $1.50 per week house rent when we have it. Sorry to say our rent is right many weeks back."

Neighborhood:

"This is a bum neighborhood and I hate for you or my friends to know where I live. But since I married Odell and have the baby four months old and Arthur three years old, with no work in view—Odell still unemployed—I just swallow it all. I made my bed hard. It's an awful lay, Miss B[yrd]. I certainly regret that I did not finish Virginia State College. Remember in 1935, we were in several classes [together].

"My companions led me off. I didn't know what a plight that I was in until it was too late. Just think, I was the honor graduate in my class at Peabody, won a scholarship to State, and acted such a fool. The saying is, 'You shouldn't grieve over spilt milk,' but I can't help grieving over my lost opportunities.

"Going back to this neighborhood, you know how we discussed slum areas in Petersburg—especially this vicinity. Little did I ever think that I would be living down here. Everything under the sun is done in this vicinity. Nobody is married on this street but me and the lady across from me. In the fall, a woman stabbed a man next door from me. Plenty whiskey joints and big time houses are down this way.

"Mostly this neighborhood is residential but we are on a back inland street; nothing to be seen but backyards, stables, garages, [and] vacant lots. All drainage from High Street comes to this street.

"On this side of the street, it's much lower than on [the] other. We have Grove Avenue at the back of us. A branch divides us from the whites. The City cleans this branch now and then. Other streets near us are Bank, Sycamore, and Market.

"Yes, we have a small garden space. We had a few vegetables and flowers last summer. Wire fencing is all around this home except the division from the neighbor's backyard: for side fence, two pair of bed springs serves as fence. Yes, we have a walk and driveway. The City takes care of garbage and trash. Yes, I couldn't do without screens, the mosquitoes and flies are plentiful. So much standing water around."

[Byrd's description of the Reid's house, following, appears not so much as narrative, but rather as hastily jotted field notes.]

Exterior:

This house is a two-story, double-tenement, pretty fair looking, much neater and cleaner than the other houses. Paint in fair shape.

Interior:

Floors, wood, are in good condition. Floor coverings: rugs and linoleum in bedroom and front room. Kitchen floor: no covering.

The walls in the bedroom and living room were papered very nicely. Kitchen wall was all wood ceiling, top to bottom. No pictures on walls.

The living room was very neatly furnished with a cheap overstuffed suit of furniture. No furniture in kitchen, but a table, stove and a bench, two baby chairs, and a carriage.

The bedroom very neatly furnished with a suit of furniture and two baby cribs, which makes it rather congested.

A railing was built around the stairs because there were no balusters. Just a hole and a few steps to get up stairs was seen with this large opening. Window panes all were in. Shades and curtains hung very neatly at the windows. Lamps were filled with oil, nice and clean on the mantle.

Luxuries or Conveniences:

"Our water is outside by the kitchen door, also toilet outside. It's in a bad shape, boards all off, also door. No seat, just bowl to sit on. You know how cold it is to sit on iron and porcelain these cold days.

"No, we haven't any musical instruments. I wish so much for a radio. The first time you see a house, please let me know, I want to get away from this section of the City. Please help me. Mother has 10 children. I'm the oldest, and I can't go home to live."

Quite a bit of reading matter was seen on the table, in the bedroom, [and] on the kitchen table. There was a *True Story* magazine and a novel that Mrs. Reid had been reading.

"Well, I have no pleasures now, but to stay in this dungeon. Worries? I told you already my worries. Yes, I go to church when I can leave children with someone.

"I think the poor man is worse off now than in former years, due to oppressions by the white race. The race problem could be solved by working on an equality base.

"No, I should vote and will. I see the need of it, nowadays, more than ever. The thing for the Negro to do is to make himself efficient [competent or competitive] for jobs, and fight and demand his rights, and he will get them."

Mrs. Reid is a tall brown-skin girl, 20-years old, weight 125 pounds. There was no hesitation in giving me her story.

[Loc.: HU/REL, box 5, 7 pp., handwritten ms.]

Mr. and Mrs. Ben James *by Susie R. C. Byrd, rec. 6 March 1939*

Ben James is an "invisible man" on many levels. A search of the index for the 1920 Virginia census yielded a person of the right age to possibly be the twenty-one-year-old Ben James who, in 1939, lived with his wife, Elsie, and three children at 533 Squaw Alley in Petersburg. But this turned out to be a false lead.

What is left, then, of the traces of Ben James's life are fragmentary bits and pieces of records assumed to relate to the same person who appears in the VWP interview done by Susie R. C. Byrd. One Benj. James, a laborer, living on East Franklin Street appeared in the Richmond city directory for 1938; he was not listed in that city again until 1942. But in 1939, the Ben James of the VWP life history resided at 533 Squaw Alley in Petersburg (where he could easily have remained for the several years in between), only twenty miles from Richmond. When he reappeared in the Richmond city directories from 1942 through 1944, Benj. James lived at 609 N. 9th Street—in a house later bequeathed by barber John S. Powell to his brother Frank and since replaced by a parking lot behind the John Marshall Courthouse for the city of Richmond. James's occupation was again listed as laborer, *except* in 1944, when no occupation was given. Instead, his employer at that time was indicated as "U.S.A." Nothing further on Ben James was found.[54]

"I've been out of work since December 1937 when Mr. T. Richie Jones said that he didn't need me anymore. Since that time, I've only been able to get pickup jobs, never making more than $.50 or $.75 per week. This is all that I can get to support my wife and three children.

"Elsie manages to get a day's work at Mrs. Brown's, Colonial Heights. She pays her $.50 a day and two meals. She cooks, does the washing and ironing, and cleaning. Time she makes is never but one and one-half days to the week.

"The clothes the children have were given to us. We all are hungry. Some days I go and sit on the riverbank all day trying to catch fish to feed us a meal. I get all our wood from the riverbanks.

"We rent this shack and I haven't been able to pay any rent since July. We live near Virginia State College. Appomattox River and the Norfolk and Western railroad tracks are back of us. Grove Avenue is in front of us; front scenery [is] backyards. We have no fences around the house, front or back; no driveway or garden. The backyard is small. There is no wood house.

"No, I've never voted but if ever I get a job I want to vote, move from this place, and pray to God for help."

[The interview is discontinued on this page, but then begins again on the next page as follows:]

"The rent is $1.00 per week. We want a better house and to live better, if I could only get a job. This house is not fit for people to live in. It's just a hull. A hard wind will blow it down.

"[In] the two rooms upstairs all the plastering is down from [the] sides and ceiling [and the] laths are falling from the ceiling and sides. The windows on the front and sides have no sash, but are covered and nailed up with rusty sheets of tin. It rains through the top like outdoors. All the weatherboarding is so dry that they are falling off. Birds are making nests all under the boards.

"Downstairs in the kitchen, we have gotten pasteboard packing boxes nailed all around the side walls to keep from looking through the cracks and to keep some of the wind and cold out. This, however, doesn't keep rain from pouring in. We use only two rooms downstairs.

"In the kitchen, we have just a table that I made . . . out of boxes . . . to eat on, two stools for children to sit on, one chair, and stove. The floor is [of] rough, wide boards. We have no covering on [the] floor.

"In our bedroom, Elsie and I begged old newspapers, and papered it trying to keep cold and wind out. Nothing is under the papers but laths and it rains in the room so badly that we move the bed in[to the] center of [the] floor. And when the wind blows I start praying to God, 'Please don't let the shack blow down and kill us.' We have only one bed in the house. All of us sleep in it: my wife; Bertha Lee, six years; Robert, five years; Ruby, two years; and me. We have to lay all kinds of ways. Our bed covering is scarce and although we sleep piled up, we get cold.

"The floor is covered with scrap pieces of old linoleum. The stove is tin. It has no bottom. I have it filled half full of ashes, setting in another piece of tin made like a trough. This stove and trough sets on four bricks, raising it from the floor.

"We have no toilet, but asks permission to use the one next door. This one is about to fall down."

[Loc.: HU/REL, box 5, 4 pp., handwritten ms.]

Mrs. Catherine Johnson *by Susie R. C. Byrd, rec. 20 February 1939*

Catherine Johnson, with fewer persons to feed than Ben James, made more money in a month on relief than he and his wife Elsie combined made by working. But that relative fact is also not very meaningful, since an income of only six dollars a month guaranteed to both families a similar level of meager existence, want, and misery. If possible, Johnson is, for reasons of gender, more invisible in the records than Ben James. The search for Catherine Johnson is thwarted by the lack of both her maiden name and her husband's given name, as well as by a profusion of Johnsons in the Petersburg area.[55]

When Susie Byrd interviewed her in 1939, Mrs. Johnson and her two children lived at 639 Plum Street, a fact confirmed also in that year's city directory, which listed "Kath Johnson, (c) domestic" at the same address. If "Kath" or "Cath" was used consistently to indicate Catherine Johnson, then she was listed as a laborer, living at 6 Goodrich Row in 1937. And in 1946 and 1948, she was a stemmer for Beech Tobacco Company and living at 327 Low Street—in the old "bum neighborhood" just a few houses from where Bernice Reid had lived earlier. From these bits of evidence it appears that Catherine Johnson did survive the scanty years of the depression, but survival in itself is not the full measure of a life.[56]

"I have two children: Louis, eight years old and Benjamin, eleven years old. I used to work at Lee's Park [for the] W.P.A., salary: $18.20 per every two weeks. This park is supposed to be a flower preservation and bird sanctuary.

"But we had to carry large trees, two workers to a tree; carry gravel in a bushel basket. Some workers actually rolled gravel in wheelbarrows. We [were] sent in the field to find wild flowers, dig them, and replant [them].

"I had to dig, and dig shrubbery, and go up very steep hills. This made my breath short. My weight is 200 lbs., I just had to stop to rest between digs. It was for this reason the Supervisor cut me off. She put on my slip 'Careless Worker.'

"The day before I was cut off, I sawed wood all day with a crosscut saw: Martha Jane Buford at one end and I at the other end. After sawing wood, we had to stack it to be burned when it was cold. It was very cold that day. The white workers sat by the fire all day, picking pine tags for making baskets and hats. We were not allowed to stop to warm until lunchtime. This is the truth! No one knows but the one who goes through with it. We poor folks had to work this way or get nothing to do. We wanted to tell someone but didn't know where to go, because all the supervisors were white.

"A big rope was tied around my waist and to a tree. I had to go down a very, very steep hill to the edge of the lake to pick leaves from the edge of the water. I want work and will work but, I couldn't stand going to the park doing what I did last fall.

"I pay $1.50 per week house rent. Six dollars per month—since I've been out of work—is given me by the relief. This is every penny I have for two children and myself to live on. I eat one meal a day to give the children two meals, as near as I can. I buy beans, peas, herring, [and] white meat, trying to stretch. The children have no nourishing [food] as they should. My sides and back is sore from carrying wood from the riverbank. Daily I walk the city streets trying to get work."

[They] live in a three-room house. The floors and walls need repairs. The water is inside the house. There is no garden. Fences are in fair shape; no driveway. The toilet outside and the woodhouse are in fair shape.

The only furniture in the front room is a [iron] double-bed, one chair, stove. The floor is without covering. All window panes were in; worn shades hung at windows. The half-room upstairs [was] unfurnished and seldom used.

In the kitchen, we find only a table [and] cooking stove—small and broken door held together with wire (coals of fire may fall from stove causing the house to be burned). On one side of the room was a woodpile; no covering on floor; [and] one bottomless piece of chair. [That] is all that's in [the] kitchen.

[Loc.: HU/REL, box 5, 3 pp., handwritten ms.]

Anna Watts *by Louise B. Gow, 14 May 1941*

The interviewer Louise Gow included her own sympathetic assessment of Anna's circumstances: "Anna married very young—too young indeed. I cannot blame her for not wanting a large family, but she doesn't know of effectual birth-control and is entirely too timid and too dependent to ask." A little further on Gow declared, "With her great marital trouble, few clothes, no money, very little food, no education, little courage, I cannot get Anna's case out of my mind and am hoping that in some small way I may be able to help this girl. And I do hope for her a better future . . . than the past has been."

Anna was born 4 July 1916 in Florence, South Carolina. A former investigator had commented that she was "another North Carolina victim!" Anna told me her story as follows very reluctantly and timidly.[57]

"I can scarcely remember my father, because he died in Florence while I was very young. My father and mother, Mr. and Mrs. Hampton Timmons, were farmers. There were six of us Mama had to look after. Mama sure had a tough time running the farm, which was very large. Some man helped her and seemingly he cheated her, because we never had enough of anything. I went to school until I was nine years, and then Mama said I had to work on the farm in the cotton and tobacco fields. Oh yes, I had time to play a little and I loved it. Mother never did come to Richmond though. Just before I married, Mama died. And South Carolina is kinda like a slavery place, so my husband Arnold Watts and I decided that it was better living here at Richmond. So we've been here for eight years.

"My husband was very good to me at first. My mother and father-in-law have been most kind to me whenever I was sick or needed help with the children. But Arnold started to drinking and several times he fought me and took out a knife. I guess I woulda been kilt if I had not run over to 'Cousin Mary' (her mother-in-law).

"Three times he left me," continued Anna, "once for eight months at a time. I suffered, the children also. We were left without food and clothing, while he worked to support other girls. The last time, he lived with Elizabeth Payne who now lives at 907 Hickory Street. I could not stand it any longer. And since he was working as a WPA laborer, I reported him. He was given one year on the road and I was promised his salary of $40.00 a month. I haven't received anything yet. It is only recently that he's gone away for the third time. He is now at Beaver Dam, Virginia. He will behave for a while on his release, but most likely he will leave me again. He writes the children such lovely letters, but when he is here he neglects them. I am *not* willing to ever live with him again. Not ever. I want to be rid of him, because our love for each other is ended.

"I did not desire to have too many children, because I am small and the Doctor told me that I'd die if I had more children. I have three living and two miscarriages and I just don't want any more."

"Anna has no plans for the future. She is merely existing in a miserable manner," said Mrs. Mary Watts of Anna, her daughter-in-law.

[Gow interjects] However, I'd like to say that I found the old Mr. and Mrs. Watts a very picturesque and quaint couple. They were sitting side by side in a poorly furnished room. No heat in the rusty looking stove, and since they were both sick some heat was needed as the room was quite chilly.

Mrs. M. Watts is a mulatto and Mr. Watts a very dark man. She had a towel tied around her head and greeted me with a charming smile. A friendly sort of person who smiles as if she'd known you long.

"Come right in and sit down," she said. "This is my husban', Mr. Watts. He's known me since I was thirteen years old and he raised me. We married when I was thirteen and we have had sixteen children and 'leven of them is living'. God gave them all to me and I'd be one happy soul, if someone would give me a baby now. We ain't never proven ourselves unfriendly to nobody, ain't never been to no law, nor arrested. And wherever we's lived, we can always go back and receive a friendly welcome. As long as Mr. Watts and I have lived together for forty-three years, we ain't never been apart one day. God don' never put no more on you than you can bear, and we believes if we git it rough here on earth we'll be blessed in Heaven. My husban' Mr. Watts, is a sick man: he's had a crushed shoulder, broken leg, broken hip-bone, and has had two operations on his stomach. Sometimes his hip bone jumps up and I have to sit on him to get it in place. He screams because it is so painful. Because he's been so sick, I had to go out and do day's work while he minded the children. They've been blessed to have their father at home.

"Yes, I knows Anna since she was a baby. I he'ped to nuss her. I knew she and my Arnold would marry someday. And before he married her, I went to Emporia, Virginia to live. My husban' and I farmed for a while.

"Arnold, Anna's husban', was mighty good to her at first. I cot every one of her babies and I was a mother to her. When I die, I don't want anyone to say anything bad about me. So I've been kind to all my in-laws.[58]

"Well, in February 1939, Anna found herself pregnant again. She used to jump over the ditches and I would warn her, but she would say 'I'm so happy today but I gonna quit jumpin' ditches.' That day I had done her washing for her and had left the big tub of water. I said to her, 'Now don't you lift that tub, but wait until your husban' comes in.' She promised that she would wait. However soon afterwards, the child ran over to say that Anna lifted the tub and was screaming away. Well, I scolded her, but called the Clinic doctors and three of them came down. The baby was born premature, seven months, but was alive and kicking. I wrapped it up nicely and laid it aside. In the meantime, there was a strong smell of turpentine on the baby. The doctor and I questioned her about this, and Anna said she rubbed turpentine on the outside and it must have gone in. However, we knew that she drank turpentine and lifted the tub in order to lose the baby. The doctor then asked her what should he do with the child. And in the presence of her husban' and Mr. Watts, Sr. she screamed 'Take it away, do anything with it, burn it up, I don't want it.'

"I knew this was the beginning of the end of her married life. Arnold went into the backyard and the Doctors carried the baby away and I haven't seen it from that day to this. Her husban' began to change from that day. But he was mortally wounded when she went to the hospital and had an abortion without his knowledge. She did it this way.

"One day Anna came over to me and asked me to go with her to the [St. Phillip's] Hospital to get her medicine. I said, 'Anna, I've taken you so many times to the clinic, you should know the way by now.' She said 'I might get lost.' Well I consulted Mr. Watts and he wasn't pleased at my going, because I'd been havin' faintin' or falling out spells and this was a very hot day in August.

"When we reached the Hospital, Anna told me to sit in the Clinic and she took the elevator. Well I sot and I sot between high noon and low dusk. I was gettin' madder all the time, because I knew Mr. Watts would be worried about me.

"Finally Anna came down and asked me to go upstairs with her. I was angry, but I went, and then I heard the doctor ask her if she wanted to be operated on. I was shocked when Anna told me she had found another baby and it was two months old in her womb. I begged her not to have an operation without her husband's consent. She defied me and laughed at me, as did the sister or nurse in charge. The nurse said to me, 'How many children have you? What a fool you are to have had sixteen? What did it get you?' Then I answered her and said 'God gave each one to me and I would not want Anna to lose another baby.' But the doctors persuaded her and asked me if I'd go up with her. I said 'No' and came home.

"My husban' and Anna's husban' were sad when I told them what had happened and I knew this was the end of Anna's marriage. Her husban' Arnold never forgave her for killing his child without his knowing. I, too, have only this against Anna, but she brought her trouble on herself. She told me that she would grow fat and healthy, but Anna is going back every day. I am still a mother to her, and would beg my son to take her his wages. But he would say, 'O.K. Mama, I'll take Anna some rations, oil, etc.' and that would be the end. Anna would not see him, nor wages, nor rations. I, as his mother, would rather that he be on the road, because he must learn how to take care of his wife and chilluns. Maybe when he comes out, he'll do better."

Mr. Watts, Sr. said, "I am not worried about the boy, because non-support is not an unpardonable sin in the sight of God. I am worried about Anna, and I am wondering if she has committed murder and whether it is unpardonable."

[Loc.: VSL/AB, box 186, 10 pp., handwritten ms.]

MAKING A LIVING
From Farm to Factory

With the "exception of the over-worked tidewater region," so one commentator proclaimed, the state of Virginia was an "agrarian paradise" in 1933. "In a state so perfectly designed to serve as a background for mellowed charm and quiet grace," he continued, it is "sacrilege to speak of commercial progress. . . . Virginia really should be endowed. Nobody should have to make a living there."[1] Despite the writer's pronouncements, most Virginians—even those outside the Tidewater area—did have to make a living, and much of the content of the life histories focuses on that singular experience.

In reality, the agrarian paradise that Virginia was alleged to be was already experiencing the effects of change toward a more urban, commercial, and industrialized economy. The social and political tendencies to Bourbonism, noted satirically (some say piously) by the author above, did contribute, however, to the state's reluctance to initiate adequate and timely relief measures in response to change, to the depression, and to the actual needs of its citizens. When New Deal programs were begun at length, they reflected the new realities and their associated concerns. It was not coincidence that the Virginia Writers' Project received state sponsorship for youth studies directed toward "Rural White Youth" and "Urban Black Youth," aged sixteen to twenty-four. These two particular groups were perceived to be especially vulnerable to changes in the occupational structure and to high unemployment, and thus they posed potential social problems.[2]

Between 1910 and 1930, the population in Virginia increased (15 percent) from just over two million (2,061,612) to almost two and a half million (2,421,851) persons. White Virginians made up 73 percent of the inhabitants (an increase of almost 22 percent), whereas those persons listed as "Negro" had lost slightly more than 3 percent of their number since 1910 and constituted 27 percent of the total in 1930. During the same period, the population of urban areas increased 39 percent, whereas rural areas gained only 3 percent. Although the absolute number of rural residents showed a small increase, the percentage of the rural population relative to that of the urban population was declining steadily. In 1890, 83 percent of the Virginia population was rural and 17 percent was urban; by 1930 the ratio was 68 percent rural to 32 percent urban. That shift in later decades would tilt the balance toward urban areas.[3]

In addition, increasingly, people who lived in rural areas were not necessarily engaged in agriculture; this gave indication of an even more basic and profound change for many Virginia localities. Between 1920 and 1930 the number of rural residents who were farming declined 11 percent, whereas those engaged in nonfarm activities increased 20 percent overall. The counties of Alleghany and Culpeper, which were the settings for numerous life histories in this volume, were both designated by the census as rural counties, and yet as distinct cases, they provide a useful contrast.

In 1920, Alleghany County (including the independent city of Clifton Forge) had a total population of 11,787 urban and 9,709 rural inhabitants. By 1930 the 13,377 residents of Covington and Clifton Forge made up the county's urban population, and its rural population of 13,650 persons consisted of 3,329 farm and 10,321 nonfarm residents. Fewer than 10 percent of the county's white workers and not quite 2 percent of its black workers were gainfully employed in agriculture. Females constituted slightly more than one-fifth of the county's white labor force and almost one-third of its black labor force. Within those numbers, 76 percent of the black women were in domestic or personal service; only 19 percent of the white women were so employed. Rural white youth (aged fifteen to twenty-four in the census categories) accounted for 22 percent of the population, and black youth added another 2 percent to that age group.[4]

The distribution of occupations in the county census for 1930 indicates the impact of commerce: of iron mines and furnaces, the railroad, silk mill, rayon plant, and the Westvaco pulp and paper mill with its associated chemical by-product plants. These workplaces employed more than half the labor force in Alleghany County, and these industries were not depression-proof. Rather, they were highly sensitive to the vagaries of the market economy, as witnessed by Joseph Hippert's 1938 account of the closing of the Low Moor iron furnaces and mines. Other factories managed to keep operating through the depression, but their workers often suffered the loss of wages or pensions by way of layoffs and reduced working hours or were subjected to hazardous working conditions about which they dared not complain for fear of losing the scarce jobs they had. The 1930 census indicates the extent to which the inhabitants of Alleghany County were then dependent on industrial employment; the personal experiences reported in Virginia Writers' Project life histories later in the decade show the joint results of that dependence and of the depression.[5]

In contrast, Culpeper County listed no urban residents in 1930, and its rural population of 13,306 persons included only 5,905 nonfarm residents. Slightly more than half of the county's gainfully employed whites and more than 55 percent of its black workforce were engaged in agriculture. Likewise, a greater percentage of its female labor force (in comparison with Alleghany County) was employed in domestic or personal service: 81 percent of black females and 42 percent of white females worked in such jobs. A little more than 19 percent of Culpeper's population was aged fifteen to twenty-four years; 13 percent were rural white youths.[6]

Of the area's county seat prior to World War II, project worker Margaret Jeffries wrote, "Culpeper just misses being a city . . . in point of size. [But] the spirit of the place is far from being that of a city." She went on to describe a typical Saturday when the people from the countryside came to town and took up every parking space all day long while they shopped, sold their produce and goods, watched and visited with passersby, and perhaps ended the day in one of the town's two movie houses—one of which showed only westerns.[7]

Jeffries also enumerated the businesses in the town that was first called Fairfax (before it became Culpeper) and observed that "all of them directly or indirectly cater[ed] to the farmer." These included some number of produce stores, which bought, sold, and shipped the farm commodities, and two feed stores—one with an associated hatchery and another that also sold "coal and farm machinery." Three other stores sold only fertilizer and seed, three hardware stores sold farm machinery in addition to building supplies, and two other businesses supplied only the latter. The farm community also supported two blacksmith shops; one harness shop; three creameries, one of which made butter for local sale out of the cream not shipped elsewhere; and an ice cream manufacturer, which also used local dairy products and supplied ice cream to lunch counters in two of the town's three drug stores. Culpeper also had a silk mill with about a hundred looms, a community-owned garment factory, a chair factory, broom factory, and a Coca-Cola bottling plant.[8]

In addition, the town had eleven restaurants (apart from the four that catered to "the colored trade") that were supported by an abundance of tourists from the "Skyline Drive traffic." The state and federal government's development of Shenandoah National Park and Skyline Drive—though outside the boundaries of Culpeper County—not only created new demands for businesses within the county but also unintentionally produced some new forms of discrimination. A waitress who worked at both the High Hat and Ritz restaurants in Culpeper explained the social boundaries that pertained to each one. These adjoining restaurants had the same owner, but they served different clientele. The Ritz welcomed working people, just as they were, coming in directly from their jobs. "But the people who go into the High Hat are mostly tourists and those who do not want to eat with folks in their working clothes." This young woman observed that the food was "served differently" in each establishment as well.[9]

Although the sexes approached equal distribution in some of the one hundred rural counties in Virginia, the number of males exceeded that of females in all but three of those counties. Conversely, in urban areas females dominated the populations in eleven of the fourteen Virginia cities having ten thousand or more residents in 1930. Norfolk and Portsmouth with their navy yards and shipbuilding industry had more males than females overall, as did Hopewell. But virtually all of the fourteen cities had larger populations of black females relative to the numbers of black males.[10]

Between 1920 and 1930, Newport News, Petersburg, and Portsmouth went counter to the trend of urban growth, losing 3, 8, and 16 percent of their respective populations, whereas most of the other cities grew in number from 3 to 30 percent. The exception, Hopewell, reported an increase of 9,930 persons—a phenomenal growth of more than 710 percent during the decade. This fact confirms one stage in the series of Hopewell "boom and bust" cycles referred to by Marvin Broyhill in chapter 3. Some have described Hopewell in its early DuPont de Nemours Powder Company "boom" days as similar to an early "Wild West" mining camp: a rowdy place of tents, shacks, and saloons, with a brothel coexisting next door to the police station on its main street. Be that as it may, legitimate occupational opportunities were expanding in Hopewell, and African American and white women achieved relative equality in their labor force participation, with each constituting 25 percent of the respective black and white workforce.[11]

The occupational structure in cities was obviously broader and offered a greater range of jobs and opportunities for many persons, but male employment, with less concentration of workers in any single job category, best exhibits this diversity. Among white males in Portsmouth, only four categories employed more than 10 percent of the number of workers: iron and steel industries (16 percent); public service (15 percent); steam and street railroads (15 percent); and wholesale and retail trade (12 percent). The next largest number of white workers (5 percent) were employed in the building industry. Among the ranks of black male workers, only railroads, iron and steel, and other transportation and communication industries employed slightly more than 10 percent each of that workforce.[12]

The comparable levels of employment for white males in Norfolk were in wholesale and retail trade (16 percent); public service (15 percent); and other transportation/communication (13 percent). Twenty-one percent of black males were also in the last category, and 13 percent of them were in wholesale/retail trade. However, domestic service (at 6 percent) ranked as the third largest employer of black male workers in Norfolk. The remainder of the male labor force—white and black—in both Portsmouth and Norfolk was employed across the spectrum of jobs in relatively small numbers. The rankings of job categories in the adjoining cities of Portsmouth and Norfolk suggest the close complementary links between the two cities and the relative importance to both of the United States Navy, the shipbuilding and shipping industries, and the railroads, which brought raw materials from Appalachia and the interior to be transported to Europe and elsewhere.[13]

Ironically, the depression, which brought about high unemployment rates for men in general, pushed many women into the labor force for the first time. The female workforce in Virginia in 1930, however, remained largely concentrated in the jobs already deemed to be gender related: professional service, such as nursing and teaching (15 percent); some manufactures (20 percent); trade (11 percent); and domestic service (38 percent).[14]

Although most working women statewide were engaged in domestic service, the numbers of black and white women so employed showed considerable variation from the average above depending on their residence in rural areas—such as the counties examined here—or in cities. In Norfolk, for instance, 6,766 (40 percent) white women and 6,335 (66 percent) black women worked as domestics. The figures for Portsmouth were comparable (43 percent versus 66 percent) despite a smaller population base. In Richmond, 8,011 (28 percent) white and 7,253 (64 percent) black women were "in service."[15]

Tobacco factories, which employed 4 percent of the female workforce throughout the state, were second only to textile mills of all types as the largest industrial employer of women. In Richmond, cigar and tobacco factories employed 4,068 white and 1,560 black women (or 14 percent each of their respective workforce), as well as 3,159 (6 percent) white males and 1,641 (11 percent) black males. Norfolk employed 419 white and 418 black women in tobacco factories, but these persons amounted to only 2 percent and 4 percent, respectively, of that city's female labor force. In nearby Portsmouth, a total of only 19 persons were employed in cigar or tobacco factories.[16]

Tobacco was doubly important, however, in other regions of the state. In Pittsylvania County, most of its agricultural population—nearly 60 percent of both the white and black labor force—was engaged in growing tobacco. Processing it in factories occupied another 2 percent of the county's white workers and 7 percent of its black workers. In the city of Danville (located in the county), however, 8 percent of the city's white labor force and 22 percent of its black workers were employed in tobacco factories. By its associations with the tremendous financial success of R. J. Reynolds, the tobacco industry also held other important local and personal meanings, as Danville tobacco appraiser Orthodox Creed Strictler (Smith) recounts in chapter 1.[17]

The lack or loss of a job had immediately felt consequences for family living conditions and social life. In the extreme case, loss of livelihood could, and did, literally mean the loss of one's life. The widow of a marine engineer in Norfolk told project worker Edith Skinner in 1938 that her forty-one-year-old son—depressed about his lack of work—had committed suicide. The only employment he could get was with the WPA, using a scythe to cut weeds on vacant city property one day a week. Other men just reported feeling ashamed of their WPA work, much of which they perceived to be aimless, beneath their capabilities, not suitable men's work, or a combination of these and other reasons.[18]

For the slightly more than 1 percent of Virginia females employed in public service in 1930, education and class offered important advantages, but more so for white than for black women. Later in the decade, the daughters of a college president, general, and judge, as well as those of a policeman, boatbuilder and oysterman, and former planter, were among those employed by the state Writers' Project. The jobs provided by this and other WPA cultural programs, which were perceived by some men to be degrading, offered welcome relief and opportunity for some women.[19]

The characteristics of people and of context clearly varied from one place to another, but summary statistics for the state as a whole reveal little about such variations until those reportings are broken down into their smaller, constituent parts of county and town, black and white, and male and female. In the Virginia Writers' Project life histories, the consequences and meanings of those differences for individuals in diverse social or occupational groups are more directly evident.

Making a Living from the Land
PAID IN "CHIPS AND WHETSTONES"

Farmin' ain't what it used to be. These is hard times. — Sam Harrison (Buzzell Peebles)

The 1930s *were* "hard times," especially for farming, and if anything, Peebles (known as Sam Harrison in the VWP life history) understated the case. As Mr. Newsome, for whom he worked, reportedly said: "The day of the small farmer is past. You got to farm by machine to show a profit, an' . . . there ain't no use farmin' no more lessen you got a thousand acres or more." But in some areas, many would-be farmers could not easily buy land to farm even if they had money for the purchase.[1]

By the early twentieth century, much land in the southern Appalachians was held by lease or owned outright by timber and coal interests, and millions of acres of "marginal" farmland were being removed from production and incorporated into national or state parks, forests, and recreation areas. Other governmental agencies and New Deal programs also sought to retire poor land and to modernize farming and in the process deliberately altered both traditional agricultural practices and attendant social relations. In Norton—as in many Virginia localities—such interventions were not necessarily greeted with either enthusiasm or favor. In the *Crawford's Weekly* of 3 January 1934, headlines declared, "Govt to Destroy 50,000,000 Acres of Smaller Farms." The accompanying article reported that this new farm plan would pay $350 million to "owners of the land . . . and then forbid all cultivation on it." This practice, it asserted, would do what the crop reduction program of the AAA was already causing to happen in Texas, that is, it would drive more tenant farmers and small farmers off the land and intensify "the control of agriculture into the hands of rich farmers and banks."[2]

People as well as land could be "marginal," and based on his rural life studies at Virginia Polytechnic Institute, rural sociologist W. E. Garnett offered his own rationale in support of such public policy. In 1934 he observed, "Poor land generally produces poor folks as well as poor crops." He warned further, "[As] standards of living for many are being lowered, approaches to peasantry become more and more evident." For the most capable of the 41 percent of all Virginia farm families who— according to his criteria—fell into the "rural marginal farm" category, Garnett recommended a cooperative program of assistance and service between local schools,

Nottoway County, Virginia. October 1937. Gullied area caused by running crop rows down hill. U.S. Department of Agriculture. Soil conservation service photo by Cousins. [VA-10304]

churches, extension and home demonstration agents, and federal programs, such as the AAA and RA. These agencies, he hoped, would inspire and motivate the more promising farm families to make greater effort toward increasing their living standards and capital investments in farming or else ease their transition into other kinds of life work.[3]

Garnett also saw social deficiencies as contributing to some undetermined part of the excess marginal rural population in Virginia. Many of the persons in this category resulted, he believed, from early "degenerate family strains" that had "spawned a numerous brood of ne'er-do-wells and folk of low mentality." For those persons, Garnett recommended expanding the scope of the state's already active eugenics program, including use of its involuntary sterilization law and of other birth control measures.[4]

Toward the end of the depression, however, other forces were removing land from circulation and pushing more people toward expanding industrial sectors of work—not on the basis of alleged social or genetic deficiencies but on the requirement of need and national interest. A Farm Security Administration news release, dated 9 April 1941, noted: "In all parts of the country, but particularly in the Southeast and the Middle West, military and industrial defense projects are taking over land which last year was farmed by American families. By March 1, 1941, more than a million acres had actually been acquired by the Army, and the acquisition of nearly 4 million more acres was under way, with funds already authorized by Congress."[5]

The major transition from farm to factory and the shifting of populations in the United States from rural to urban living—accomplished, roughly, in the second quarter of the twentieth century—was given momentum by a combination of forces including economic and environmental factors, governmental and social policies, and at length, by world war. But the changes in agriculture, forcible and otherwise, in that period did not affect farm families evenhandedly or occur uniformly across the landscape. By 1925, only 3.4 percent of the population in Massachusetts still lived on farms, whereas Virginia had 40.2 percent of its population on farms and the comparable figure for Mississippi was 63.0 percent. Even within states such as Virginia, there was obvious variation depending on the degree of urbanization in a given area: in Pittsylvania County, 64.0 percent of the population lived on farms, but only 7.1 percent so resided in Arlington County. It is more significant, however, that the number of farms and the average size of farms in Virginia were steadily decreasing between 1920 and 1930. And in comparison to an average farm size in 1850 of 339.6 acres, by 1925 the average Virginia farm had dwindled to only 88.8 acres.[6]

At the same time, crop-lien systems, which advanced yearly provisions against future crops (mortgaged at high interest rates), contributed to increasing landlessness through default, as well as to sharecropping or farm tenancy. A commission established by President Roosevelt to look at farm tenancy in the South found that "there was a sixty-nine percent increase in the number of white croppers between 1920 and 1930." That commission also determined that these tenant farmers moved often hoping to find "a better farm and a better deal with the new landlord." Ironically, a farm labor system that largely developed to replace slavery in the South led to the progressive and widespread dispossession of many small-scale farmers and landowners among the numbers of whites and former slaves and free blacks alike.[7]

The extent of farm tenancy, however, varied considerably from state to state, so that 25.2 percent of Virginia farmers were tenants in 1925, whereas 68.3 percent of Mississippi farmers were so categorized. But these figures are also state averages. Within Virginia, farm tenancy ranged between the high of 62.6 percent in Southampton County and the low 3.9 percent in Mathews County. Culpeper County, in comparison, had only 10.3 percent of its farms operated by tenants.[8]

The terms of wage labor under farm tenancy were generally established by custom; however, certain rights—as John E. Bess Sr. discovered in his misadventures with a crafty tenant—could be enforced by law. With regard to the amount and form in which wages were paid to hired workers, there was considerable discretion allowed in practice. In Alleghany County, Reginald Shires complained to the VWP interviewer about the wages paid by some local farmers to their hired farm labor: "They want him to take [his pay], as Ma says, in 'chips an' whetstones.' She means a little meat, flour, or 'taters, something people have an' don't want theirselves." Emma Lou Lee made a similar complaint about the white people she cooked for in Franklin County: "They wants you to work every minute without stopping, and they most generally don't want to pay nothing or have you take it out in 'chips and whetstones.'"[9]

Farming has always been a demanding and risky business; thus the landowner or farmer often felt as much put upon as the cropper or hired hand. With good luck, good weather, good markets, and a lot of hard work, a farmer could get by on his own land—maybe even get ahead. As Minnie T. Kilbourne of Lee County optimistically maintained, "You can say what you want to about farm life, but we old southern Virginia farmers do have good things to eat." However, misfortune, death, or simply the normal process of aging could very quickly wipe out the work of a lifetime. And increasingly, farmers—especially younger ones—were agreeing with the sentiments expressed by another Lee County native: "We are growing tired of so much hard work and have about decided we would like to make an easier living if we

A farm covered by the rising waters of the Shenandoah river. March 1936. Photo by Arthur Rothstein. [LC-USF34-01863-E]

can. Farm life promises you only one real thing and that is a good table but it's hard to live by eating only. One likes a few of the amusements of the world and it takes a little ready cash for this." Speaking of these things may have made the decision for this young farmer, because shortly afterward he left his Lee County farm and went to Cincinatti—presumably in search of some amusements and ready cash.[10]

Certainly, life on the farm looked better for many people when they were working at something else. Minnie T. Kilbourne, who had formerly been a teacher and was a court stenographer for Lee County in 1938, spoke about farming from the vantage of not having to depend entirely upon it for a living. Likewise, as Margaret Wolfe pointed out, jobs in the silk mill could cover taxes and other necessities if crops should fail. The wish for more of the world's material goods or for just a little more security against the risks of farming was sufficient to push many families off the farm or into the wage labor force, with or without the added prod of government programs or social policies.

The life histories in this and subsequent chapters document people *making a living* in various occupational contexts from farm to factory, but they also document the *move* from farm to factory. In some cases, added findings from other sources or research make possible an intergenerational approach that can trace various steps in that movement. For instance, in the span of three generations, the course of social mobility took some members of Nannie Isabel Webb Price's family from an affluence based on agriculture and slavery in Franklin County to wage work in Roanoke. Comparing inventories for the estates of Julia Keesee Carwile's grandfather and father in Campbell County gives evidence of other kinds of agrarian change. Among his personal property in 1878, Richard Keesee left a team of oxen and an ox yoke, as well as a horse and a mule. His son, Charles V. Keesee, described by Julia as a "prosperous" dark-tobacco farmer, left two mules and a two-horse wagon when he died in 1939, but *he* had no oxen.

The nature and scale of farming were changing, but few people in the life histories were aware of the more encompassing shift: agriculture was gradually being shaped by a presumed rational business mold—toward a model of farm *as* factory. In its modern-day form, even though a southern farm may repeat cycles of activity and processes not unfamiliar to the operation of a "self-contained antebellum plantation," as Pete Daniel observes, "in other respects it more nearly [resembles] a factory. Instead of managing slaves," present-day farms are concerned largely with "the management of land, chemicals, implements, and ledger books."[11]

Raising Tobacco Is a Thirteen-Month Job:
Images of Tobacco Culture from Farm to Market

When Captain Samuel Argall arrived in 1617 to become governor of Virginia, he found that the "building of the community [of Jamestown] was deemed second in importance to . . . the cultivation of tobacco." And the settlers "were devoting practically all of their time and labor" to that end. During the colonial period and at other times when currency was in short supply, tobacco was the coin of the realm—goods of all description, including land and labor, were bought and paid for in pounds of the golden leaf.[12]

Although it has long been a major Virginia crop, tobacco is also a labor-intensive crop—hard on the soil and hard on the people that work it. Still, the cash made on even a small harvest of good leaf has often meant the difference between being able to pay the taxes on one's farm or being forced out of farming and into public work. Whether tobacco is viewed as "golden leaf" or "evil weed," it is not surprising that the subject of tobacco provokes intense and ambivalent feelings, reflected in many ways in the traditional verse reported by one former tobacco factory worker in Danville:

> Tobacco is an Indian weed
> From the devil it doth proceed,
> It picks your pockets, burns your clothes,
> And makes a chimney of your nose.[13]

Danville (vicinity), Virginia. May 1940.
A tenant farmer in a rain washed tobacco field. He has lived on this place
twenty-seven years. Photo by Jack Delano. [LC-USF34-40631-D]

*Chatham (vicinity), Virginia. September 1939. Tobacco barns and strip houses on the Ward farm.
Photo by Marion Post Wolcott.* [LC-USF34-52077-D]

Caroline County, Virginia.
June 1941. A field of tobacco
in the area being taken over
by the Army. Photo by Jack
Delano.
[LC-USF34-44875-D]

South Boston, Halifax County, Virginia. November 1939. A truckload of tobacco being taken to a warehouse.
There are eleven warehouses in this small town. Photo by Marion Post Wolcott. [LC-USF34-52900-D]

Danville, Virginia. October 1940. Farmers placing their tobacco in baskets from the trailer the night before the tobacco auction. Photo by Marion Post Wolcott. [LC-USF34-56247-D]

Danville, Virginia. October 1940.
Farmers waiting to sell their tobacco at auction in the warehouse.
Their tobacco is piled in baskets ready for the sale.
Photo by Marion Post Wolcott. [LC-USF34-55966-D]

Danville, Virginia. October 1940. A tobacco auction in a tobacco warehouse where many Caswell County [North Carolina] farmers sell their tobacco. Photo by Marion Post Wolcott. [LC-USF34-56117-D]

Sam Harrison (Buzzell Peebles) *by Roscoe Lewis, no interview date given*

There are multiple texts, or versions of texts, of the life history of Sam Harrison, alias Archie Davidson, alias Archie Jackson, located in various depositories. However, a small bit of quoted material in *The Negro in Virginia* offers credible evidence that Sam Harrison is also an alias—in this case, for Buzzell Peebles of Southampton County. Peebles, a native of that county, was living there in Branchville (not Whaleyville) when he married Virgie Worrell of Newsoms on 18 December 1920. The Peebles family lived in Boykins District, close to the state line, and there seems to have been considerable movement across the border to Northampton County, North Carolina, and between Southampton and neighboring Greensville County, as well as shared kin ties with others of the same surname in those various areas.[14]

There is nothing in the records, however, to suggest the connections to Chatham and Danville in Pittsylvania County purported by the life history. It may be that the textual details about tobacco culture and growing up in Pittsylvania County were simply adapted from Peebles's real life and experiences in Southampton County. But there is also some chance that those portions referring to Pittsylvania County were borrowed, in whole or in part, from some other source that has not yet been identified.[15]

Neither the original Peebles text, from which the fragment appearing in *The Negro in Virginia* was taken, nor the manuscript containing the tobacco-planting description has turned up in searches of archival sources. But that is not surprising. There is some evidence from earlier research indicating that after vwp editors cut and pasted the bits of interviews they wanted for copy in the above manuscript, they often discarded the rest of the interview text. If the original texts were thus destroyed, then what remained untouched in the files were the interim attempts by various vwp editors in the Richmond office to rework the original material for other purposes.

One of those editors, Thomas C. Leonard, produced just such a reworking of the already revised Sam Harrison life history. In it, he changed the Archie Davidson designation to "Archie Jackson" and titled the interview "A Black Mr. Peanut." In addition, he reduced the text to four pages and recast it in a caricatured African American dialect—for instance, replacing "Is that you, Sam?" with the phrase "Am thata you, Archie?"

Another version of the Sam Harrison text was sent with six other Virginia life histories to southeastern regional director William Terry Couch for the fwp publication *These Are Our Lives*. None of the Virginia texts were included in that work, but they were deposited in time, along with other project materials from the region, in the Southern Historical Collection at the University of North Carolina, Chapel Hill. From there, a copy of the Sam Harrison text was transformed even further and published in 1981 as an interview with "Will Clennon" of "Jetersville, Virginia," under the title "These Is Hard Times." Through all these changes, Buzzell Peebles would hardly recognize himself.[16]

The house, a hundred yards off the county road, was an amazing collection of wings and additions. The central portion, a single-story, two room shack, was of substantial construction. On each side and on the back, rooms had been added with a mind to utility rather than to uniformity. Pieced together planks, rough-hewn slabs, and packing box boards had effectively, if unsystematically, sealed the four separate additions from the elements. A single huge chimney of slab and clay separated the solid portion of the dwelling from its fragile, two-room right wing. On looking through the door of the annex, I verified what I had suspected: there was no space for a door between the house proper and its wing on that side.

The sound of creaky bed springs told me that the room was occupied. I stood in the open doorway, trying to adjust my eyes to the gloom of the windowless interior after the brilliant sunlight.

"Is that you, Sam?" inquired a weary voice from the darkness. It was a woman's voice.

I explained that I sought Mr. Sam Harrison, her husband, I assumed.

"He's down to the creek," she answered in a forced voice, as though in pain.

"Are you sick?" I inquired. "Is there anything I can do?"

"No. Nothing. Just a slight spell I git now an' then. I'll be all right."

She told me to go to the kitchen and tell Lucy to call her father. I found Lucy, a tired-looking girl of sixteen, peeling bird-egg size potatoes. She pointed out the path to the creek.

I found Sam Harrison at the water's edge repairing a shaky hand bridge, which crossed the muddy stream. He was about fifty, I decided, and he had the deliberate and almost fumbling manner of a man twenty years older. Life had not been easy, his appearance suggested. Prematurely gray, with furrows seaming his hollow cheeks and his forehead, he gave the impression of having been mentally, as well as physically, worn. His eyes, dull and weary, scanned me without expression; his voice, low and unhurried, greeted me without enthusiasm.

I apologized for disturbing him at the time and offered to wait until he had finished. He laid his tools aside, wiped his brow with a ragged sleeve, and murmured that he would do no more that day. When I explained that I wished to talk with him about farming and his experience as a farmer, he straightened up, swept the desolate-looking wasteland with his gaze, and began speaking.

"This here ain't my land. Sometimes I'm sorry and sometimes I'm glad. Farmin' ain't what it used to be. These is hard times. They say it's better over in the tobacco country. I was brung up near Danville, and I'm really a tobacco farmer. Ever been in de t'bacca country? No? Well, you've missed half your life. You know, my grandaddy used to say: 'Ev'y person who smokes oughta be made to work a t'bacca field, dey'd never smoke no more.' I was brought up with t'bacca. Don't reckon there's anything I know so much about. I think sometimes how funny it is that here I am a t'bacca farmer growin' peanuts. Why, I never knowed that peanuts growed in de ground till I come to this section.

"I started wormin' t'bacca 'fore I went to school an' for nigh onto thirty years of my life I worked t'bacca. Funny, but I never smoked it but oncet [once]. Tried it oncet when I was 'bout nine years ole jus' to be smart like de big boys. I went up in de big oak tree by de well an' lit up a corn cob [pipe] of my granpaps filled with good ripe weed. Made me so sick I like to died, sittin' up there wid de ground a'swimmin' an' a'holdin' on for dear life. I heerd 'em hollerin' me to supper but I couldn't answer an' I couldn't git up or down. Pretty soon my Pap spied me up de tree an' he brung a ladder an' histed me down. Didn't whip me an' he didn't tell it at de house. He figgered that I done learnt my lesson an' he sure was right.

"Want me to tell you 'bout t'bacca growin'? I reckon I knows as much 'bout it as any man livin'. You see, you sow de seed 'long 'bout March first over Danville way. Plant it in little beds of rich manure soil, good an' moist, an' sometimes you cover it with burlap sacks to keep a frost from killin' de tender plants. Takes about a month fo' de plants to grow good an' strong. Then about April first when de plants git about four inches tall they're ready to transplant.

First you go through de bed an' cull. That means you pluck out of de bed de shoots an' leave de runners. Now here is somethin' that don't many people know. You don't pull de strong shoots that has grown taller than de res' in de bed. You pull up de weak ones—de shortes', cause these is de ones that's gonna grow to leaves 'stead of to stalks. You lay de small shoots in a cool place till you is ready to transplant. Course you got to have your field ready, all plowed an' hilled.

"Here's how we used to set the plants out. One would stake an' de other would plant. You got to work together on dat cause ef de staker don't make de holes de right distance apart, it causes de planter a powerful lot of trouble. De planter walks de row an' lays out de plants, pickin' up de young shoots, stickin' it in a hole, clampin' de dirt rounst it, all wid one stride. Now you see, ef de holes is too far apart you gonna waste time takin' two strides, an' ef they is too close together you gonna git runt plants. Plantin' is mighty hard work. You gotta be bent over all de time, 'cause it's waste motion to straighten up 'tweenst holes. You plant by hundreds—go long steady fo' one hundred hills, den you stop a second an' drop a grain of corn in yo' pocket fo' each hundred hills so you know how many you done planted. I reckon I used to hold de record fo' plantin' in Pittsylvania County. Best I ever did was 12,000 plants a day. I ain't never seen nobody else equal it.[17]

"Once de plant gits in de ground de fun begins. Got to tender de plants along, replantin' those that dies. Four weeks after plantin' you got to top de leaves to keep the sap in de leaves. Den de suckers commence. You got to pull de suckers oncet a week or oftener ef its dry weather. All kinds of bugs is aimin' to eat de leaves. De worst is de cut worm—brown, like a grub worm—dat cuts off de stalk close to de roots. It's funny, but he won't eat up high where you can see him. Cuts down close to de ground so's you got to crawl along on yo' hands an' knees in order to see him. Then there's de wild worm that's black an' has got sections to his body jus' like a string of beads. He bores straight up through de center of de stalk an' de bes' way of tellin' when he's eatin' up de plant is by de ends of the leaves turnin' brown too soon. Plenty of time in de ground is de bes' thing to kill him.

"Then there's de bone worm that gits his name 'cause of his backbone stickin' out of his tail. He's dark green, jus' de color of de leaves, an' he's got enough sense to stay on de bottom of de leaf where you ain't likely to see him. He eats a leaf a day ef you don't get him off, but dat ain't his only fault. He lays eggs, thousands of 'em, an' pretty soon you got thousands of t'bacca moths crawlin' round. In 'bout a week dese [is] hatched into more worms, an' ef you ain't ready fo' 'em wid a spray or somethin', dat whole patch is a gonner.

"Course, all de time you got to be pullin' de suckers from de base of de leaf an' prunin' off de scaffolds. You see, de bottom leaves gits beat down in de soil by de rains, which makes 'em spotted an' torn. Some farmers save dese leaves fo' shag lug—dat's what dey make nicotine out of fo' some kind of medicine—but I never bothered wid any but de best grades of leaf. De top leaves never gits very large, so de best thing to do is to prune 'em off, ef you want de best grade of t'bacca. Only de middle leaves is worth savin'.

"You see, there's five grades of t'bacca leaf: shag lug, good lug, short leaf, long leaf, and premium. Cain't no farmer grow all one grade, but de care you take wid de plant decides how much of each grade you gonna git. I ain't boastin', but my Pap an' I used to git as much premium grade as de next an' a heap sight mo' long grade dan most farmers. I recollect in 1915 we sol' 600 pounds of premium at 98 cents a pound an' about 900 pounds of long leaf at 84 cents. That was de year my mother took sick.[18]

"I guess you might like to hear 'bout my mother, 'cause it was due to her death that I quit t'bacca farmin'. Pa and' Ma was more companions than man an' wife. It hit him powerful hard, Ma's death. It was settin' out time, an' Pa jus' let de young plants go to seed. Didn't seem to care 'bout nothin' no more. After de funeral we did what we could but Pa didn't pay no 'tention to de crops. Never did see such a sudden change in a man. Seem like he los' all his ambition. Wouldn't eat or sleep, would git up an' go out in the woods nights an' stay way fo' two an' three days at a time.

"I was de oldes', an' Rebecca was fifteen, an' little Joey was eleven. 'Course I got a fam'ly of my own now an' I can appreciate what it means when a man's wife passes on, leavin' de children motherless. But I wonder sometime what kind of sign is put on a man dat make him fo'git all 'bout his dear wife's children. It been puzzlin' me an' it always will. Fo' 'bout two years Pa was jus' like a stranger to us. He would come an' stumble to the bed an' lie there fo' hours like as if he was in a trance. Wasn't drunk, either. I would fix him up somethin' hot an' have Becky take it in to him, 'cause then maybe he'd drink it. Becky was de spittin' image of our mother.

"Pa never did do no mo' farmin'. I growed what crops I could but seem like I had lost interest in farm life too. Finally Pa went into Danville an' pretty soon I heard from a neighbor that he was workin' in a factory. 'Bout a year afterward he sent fo' us to come into town an' live wid him 'cause he done sold de farm.

"When de man come to take possession, I packed up all de things we could carry in de wagon an' drove into Danville wid Becky an' Joey. I didn't grieve none 'bout leavin' de farm. Henry Carter, who had bought de farm, was a good steady-goin' man, an' he promised me that he would keep de grass out an' put flowers reg'lar on Ma's grave. In Danville I found dat Pa had a decent place fixed up fo' de chillun an' had his sister livin' there wid him. She say dat she was gonna look after de children an' see dat Joey was put in school. I knew dat my duty was finished. I stayed round Danville a couple of days, but when I met a fellar who was drivin' a truck to Suffolk, I come east wid him. Sometime I wonder if I did right, but I got my home here now an' a wife an' children of my own an' it don't look like I'm gonna go back.

"This here section is home to 'Tildy, my wife, an' while we ain't got nothin' much, we ain't got no cause to complain. We got six children of our own—all girls—an' they's all good children. It's sorta hard keepin' 'em in school, but neither of us ever had much schoolin' an' we want 'em to have de advantages we never had. 'Course, I cain't help wishin' sometime dat one of de children was a boy, 'cause it's mighty hard fo' a man not to have a son to work 'long wid him. But de girls helps out all dey can. If I had my own place, I reckon they would give me more help dan dey do, but Mr. Johnson don't like to see girls in his field, lessen peanuts is ripenin' durin' a good market. Then he don't mind if de whole fam'ly goes to diggin'.

"Mr. Johnson owns all this land. I've been sharin' fo' him nearly six years now. He's de best man in dese parts to share crop for. But times is been gettin' worse ever since I started in here. First year I come I cropped nearly four hundred dollars as my share. Ain't been no season like that since. Last year the whole crop wasn't worth no more'n five hundred, Mr. Johnson said. My share was two hundred an' six dollars, an' outa that I owed Mr. Johnson forty-seven dollars. Haven't been outa debt to him now for four years. He don't mind carryin' me, though. All I got to do is go to his store in town an' sign for whatever I need. He keeps most everything in his store, even tonics an' medicines. I try not to run up a bill during de winter, but you know how it is with a man who's got a ailin' wife an' six growin' girls to look after. Last winter my Lucy—she's next to de oldest girl—she got pneumonia an' I had to git de doctor from town. His bill was $14. an' the medicine was $4.75. The public health nurse come out an' looked after Lucy reg'lar, an' when Lucy got well, the nurse wouldn't let her go out till she had new shoes. Mr. Johnson gave her a pair an' wouldn't let me sign for 'em.

"This public health service that the government runs is a great thing for the farmer. I don't know jus' what we'd of done if it hadn't of been for Nurse Roberts. She been comin' out here now every week or two for three years an' she say that she ain't supposed to have no money for it. It worries me sometime, 'cause I like to pay for what I get even though it ain't much I can pay. 'Tildy got chronic rheumatism, and soon as the cold weather comes, it knocks her right out. She always try not to show it when a spell comes on, drags herself 'round the house gittin' de girls ready for school an' fixin' breakfast, but the nurse always seems to know. 'Tildy was took down bad yestiddy an' even though it ain't cold yet, I'm figgerin' dat Nurse Roberts gonna know an' come out here in a day or two.

" 'Tildy don't need no doctor, 'cause the nurse always knows what treatment she needs. The nurse told me private one day that it was the climate got in 'Tildy's joints, and as long as she stays here she gonna ache in damp weather. Seem like it always damp. I cain't do nothin' 'bout the weather, an' it looks like I cain't do nothin' 'bout movin' 'long as I stays in debt to Mr. Johnson. It ain't his fault, though, 'cause he does everything he can to help me out. Last winter whilst Lucy was sick, he let me help out in his store an' paid me $2.00 a week. That was a big help, I tell you. I'm hopin' he's gonna use me again this winter 'cause crops been so poor, but I hope it ain't sickness that makes me need to work for cash. I kinda hate to see this winter come along. Something tells me it's gonna be cold and damp.

"Mr. Johnson says that the store is all that keeps him goin'. He says that the day of the small farmer is past. You got to farm by machine to show a profit, an' he says that there ain't no use farmin' no more lessen you got a thousand acres or more.

"I reckon you might like to hear 'bout the farm I was buyin', 'bout eight years ago. Seventeen and a quarter acres it was, 'cross the railroad, with good top soil an' timber. It belonged to a white man named Simpson, who dropped dead in the field one day, whilst he was hoein' sweet potatoes. I was new here an' had 'bout a hundred dollars, so his widder sold me the farm for $20 a acre — $345 — with $75 paid cash down. Her son, Henry Simpson, the undertaker, fixed up a note at the bank for me for $310 payable in three years; the 'greement was that I got all the land 'ceptin' a single acre that the house stood on. You see, the old lady still lived there. Well, the first season I made out pretty good an' paid up $110 on the note, $10 more than I was s'posed to pay. Things was lookin' mighty good. I done fixed up the barn for a house an' I was hirin' a mule from a neighbor.

"The next spring I planted five acres in peanuts, two more'n the year before. Durin' the summer it looked like I was gonna have a better crop than the first one. But in August the rains come. Don't know whether you was in these parts in '33 or not, but if you was, you musta read 'bout the big flood. Rained for three days straight, an' the water backed up in all the streams 'cross the banks onto the lowlands. You see, all this land round here is below sea level, an' it's all right 'long as don't no flood come. But when the creek overflows, the water runs down in the lowlands an' lays there till it dries up. Durin' that time most all of my peanuts lied under a foot of water. When the water dried up there wasn't more'n half the crop that wasn't rotted an' washed out. Wasn't $20 worth of peanuts in de field.

"I went to Mr. Henry an' explained the situation an' asked him to postpone the note. First he said he would do it, but later on he came an' told me there was nothin' he could do, 'cause the bank had the note. I went to the bank, but they told me there was nothin' they could do, an' that I still had thirty days grace on the note. Every other farmer I knew was 'bout as bad off as I was that season, an' there wasn't no way I could raise the money.

"One day Mr. Henry come to me an' tell me that he didn't want the sheriff to put me off, so he would buy the place back an' give me back $25 of the money I had paid for it. Said, too, that I could stay on in the barn for a year an' work shares for him. Well, it seemed like at the time there was nothin' else to do. I signed over the farm to him an' went ahead workin' on shares 'stead of for myself. 'Fore the next crop was in, Mr. Henry come an' told me I'd have to move 'cause the county done bought the place from him an' was gonna run a new road through, right where the barn was. I moved over here on Mr. Johnson's place an' here I been ever since. After I started in over here, Mr. Johnson told me that Mr. Henry knew 'bout the road all the time an' that's why he made the bank take up my note. He said that Mr. Henry sold a strip of that farm to the county for a thousand dollars.

"But I ain't no one to cry over spilt milk. I'm gettin' old now, an' I don't reckon I'm ever gonna have a place of my own. Couldn't do much with it if I had one, I don't reckon. I guess I ain't as bad off as I might make it seem. All the farmers in these parts is havin' hard times, those that share crop an' those that got they own places. Seems like whenever the crops is good, the prices is down, and whenever the crops is poorly, the prices go up. Fertilizer eats up most of the profits from a farm these days. Used to be a time when a load of good rich manure was all that a farm needed, but now you got to feed it chemicals before you can grow a crop that you can sell. One of the government agents who came through here told Mr. Johnson that this soil wasn't nothin' but dirt, not even fitten to grow alfalfa.

"I ain't got no complaint 'bout the way Mr. Johnson treats me, though. Now an' then he sends down clothes an' shoes that his children has outgrown. My wife picks up odd jobs cookin' an' sewin' an' cannin' now an' then, whenever she is able. Mable my oldest, had a job last spring after school mindin' the baby for a white lady in town. She made a dollar a week. She's hopin' that Mrs. Nelson will want her again this winter.

"Even if I ain't got no home of my own for my girls, we all gets along tol'able well. They're good girls, without none of these city ways that young folks take style in nowdays. We all go to church. I'm a deacon in the Methodist Church, an' all the girls go to Sunday School. Sometime I wish I was able to visit out Danville way an' see Pa an' the children. I reckon they is all grown now wid fam'lies of they own. I heard from Becky a few years ago an' I writ her but she never answered. She said she was thinkin' of gittin' married. I been fixin' to write her again, but I ain't got round to it. Mebbe they'll all come visit us here some day.

"Sometimes I wish that I could get a job in the city so's I could do better by my wife an' girls. Last month I heard they was takin' on men in the lumber yard in Suffolk. I went right over there, but the man said that they had all the men they was needin'. Someone told me that the government paid relief to people who wasn't able to find steady work, but I don't reckon I need government charity yet awhile. All I want to do is to hang on here till my girls is full grown an' gits homes an' fam'lies of their own. The only thing is, I hope don't none of them marry farmers. There sure ain't no future in farmin'. But soon as they get fixed, I'm gonna quit the farm for good. 'Tildy an' me can get along somehow."

[Loc.: VSL/AB, box 186, 7 pp. (6 1/2 of these are typed single spaced)]

Herman Hooker *by Mary S. Venable, rec. 13 November 1939*

In the 1910 Alleghany County census, two young men bearing the Hooker surname—Henry, twenty-one, and George, eighteen—were boarding in the household of farmer Austin A. Robinson and working as farm laborers. No further record was found for Henry Hooker, but the younger of the two men, George Washington Hooker, married Lillie Margaret Landrum in December 1914, and they are likely Herman Hooker's parents. Certainly, the G. W. Hooker family was living in 1920 near S. (Samuel) Brown Surber, the county agricultural agent and farmer for whom Hooker worked for a while as a tenant farmer.[19]

"The sharecropper, or half-hand," as Donald Holley states, "was the most disadvantaged and least secure tenant. He had no livestock or farm equipment; all he had was his own labor and that of his wife and children" to exchange for half of whatever crop they were able to produce on someone else's land. Even though he worked on shares for "the best man in the world" (as Herman Hooker's father termed his absentee landlord in Richmond), one who lived up to his agreement and did not cheat his tenant out of his share of AAA payments for reduction of the wheat crop, this half-hand could not make a fair wage for the four male laborers in his family.[20]

The Hookers—father and sons—had all "started farming as soon as they were large enough to 'hold a hoe,'" and their farming practices were skillful enough to produce an overall income from the Sills farm that was above the average for Virginia farm operations. Yet the Hooker family's six-hundred-dollar share of that income placed them among an estimated 875,000 Virginians considered by rural sociologist W. E. Garnett in 1934 to be a "marginal" rural population.[21]

On January tenth, 1922, the stork dropped Herman Hooker into a family of four boys and one girl. Since then the old bird has come again, twice, and the youngest of the Hooker family is two years of age. Inclusive of the parents, there are ten in all. Herman is a tall lad, about five [feet] eight [inches] and weighing no more than one hundred and thirty pounds of lean muscle. Not an ounce of fat!

The neighbors will tell you that Herman's father is the best farmer "anywhere around this part of the country and the Hooker boys are good workers." Herman shows that he has grown in the environ of cheerful activity. His genial grin would go far toward assisting him to find a place in the commercial world, but he has no plan to do aught but farm. Herman has learned from hearing his father defend the occupation that there is dignity and independence in farming. He takes his profession seriously and throws his 'whole soul' into his work.

The farm which the Hookers crop on the shares, belongs to Mr. N. D. Sills of Richmond, Virginia. "The best man in the world to work for. Lives up to his agreement in dividing the wheat and corn fifty-fifty, and he even divided the pay from the government when we cut down our wheat crop." There is only one trouble that [Herman] Hooker's folks' mention: the farm is a grazing farm, with too little acreage tilled to employ four men. The sales proceeds from cattle belong to the owner, which "is but fair when he put up all the money to invest in the stock." However, it cuts the farm cropping area to less than a living wage, so the family sees it, and Herman follows this argument with intelligent and comprehending expression. There is no muddled thinking in the Hooker forum. Their father is liberal, acquainted with national and state current events, though he says they have no time to read when they "rise before day and go to bed with the chickens."[22]

"I'll show my books to anybody, and see if a better man can find the cash to come out of my farming to get the start the Federal government is offering in its loans to dirt farmers. [The government program] is a dandy thing, but it just don't click where the people who planned it meant it to. If I could show a little cash I could put it in stock and get a start. I see the government's side: if you are any account you'll work and put aside money from year to year. They have to have some way of knowing if a man is worth lending to. But here, pinned down on wheat, I have to grow my flour. We raised eighty bushels last year, forty for me [and] that won't *bread* us. If I had put in more and had some to sell this Fall, the market price wouldn't have been enough to pay out on the seedin' [and] fertilizer. You can't come out even on ninety cents a barrel for corn neither. In spite of your eye teeth, it will cost you more, if you count in the time."

All told, Mr. Hooker and his three boys got off the farm produce, so they state, six hundred dollars for the year 1938. [Herman] says "He can't feed us off *that*." The eldest boy gets work on neighboring farms at one dollar per day, and the daughter is in private employment at three dollars per week. "If it wasn't for their cash, I don't know how we could keep from goin' naked. The boys have to keep their feet dry and we don't have what anybody would call *good* clothes. The most we can manage is overalls, and work clothes.

"Now, I've figgered it out. Six hundred dollars for four men's time—say fifty dollars a month—that is one dollar twenty per day for all and thirty cents per laborer. It is true that the farmer does not work three hundred and sixty days, but on a grazing farm the cattle are hungry three hundred and sixty-five days. It takes the whole time of one man in the winter to feed and bed the seventy head of beef cattle and breeding cattle on this place. There is one hand that gets thirty cents a day for eight hours. For by the time he gets around with the morning feed, it is time to start to clean the stables or bed 'um clean, and then the evening feedin' comes on before early dark."

Herman can tell you about the load of "finest cattle you ever saw, we took to Staunton in a truck. The market down there was no better than up here and we took what we could get for Mr. Sill's thirteen cattle, of best quality beef. The man what bought 'um took 'um on to Jersey City and sold 'um to, I don't know who, but he said that he made more than fifteen hundred dollars off the truck load. Just like Dad says, it is the 'middle-man' who robs the farmer of profits." "AND," says Dad, "it will never be any different till the *Federal* Government takes it in hand. They've got to have *time* to set up their workin' plan of market."

[Herman's] indifference to voting is the same as that of his elder brother, who is over twenty-one but has never registered. Thereby hangs the tale of the misfortune of having once voted by mail. It was Mr. Hooker, himself, who was to be gone on a business trip on Election Day, so he voted by mail.

"I've been hearing about that vote for the past five years. I thought, of course, that the mail vote was on the secret ballot plan and I'm not beholden to any politician, so I voted to suit myself. It was a local election. Seems like *everybody* got a chance to read the ballots sent by mail. I didn't vote to suit the courthouse-county ring, and so they had a lot to say about why didn't I vote for them?

"Not long ago a man got after me again about it, and that was five years ago I done the votin'." They laugh in this family conclave about the defeat of independent voting. But Mrs. Hooker says, "It is a pity to fall out with those who have a *say* in a *lot* of things that *tell* on the farmer." She is very serious but [Herman], shoulder to shoulder with the independent member of the household, appears to back up the decision that voting is a waste of time.

"Tell 'bout that man th' other day," he urges. Mr. Hooker is not loath. "One of the candidates for next month's election come handin' me a card. I says to him, 'You keep it. You fellows promise the farmers a lot and you never do a thing for 'um after the election. I'm through votin'. I'll never vote again as long as I live.' He says, 'Why?' I says, 'Cause if I' have to vote to suit somebody in the ring, it ain't my honest vote. And if I don't, they get my mail ballot and come tell me, and hold it ag'in me if they get a chanct.' "

The Agricultural Bulletin comes to this farm, but they take no other magazine and have no books from any source. They were, in the past, regular attendants of the nearby church, which is Presbyterian. But during the past year they have not attended. Mr. Hooker claims that there is snobbishness on the part of the church leaders, and prejudice, dating from the time when his vote did not suit a prominent member. [Herman] is not a member of any club. They did not attend the farmer's picnic last year nor this year.

Both father and sons started farming as soon as they were large enough to "hold a hoe" and none have known any but a farmer's existence. In the past ten years they have been on the same farm. Before that Mr. Hooker was tenant for the county agricultural agent, Mr. S. Brown Surber, on his farm close to the 296 acres farm of Mr. Sills. Aside from entering into the Soil Conservation group, they have received no help from county, church, or Federal Government.[23]

The up-to-date mechanical appliances extend not only in the barn and farm, but set the Maytag washing machine going with gasoline motor. Its putt-putt advertises to passers-by on the famous Hot Springs route running by the home, that here is an intelligent mechanic. Electricity is several miles distant. None of the near neighbors use it.

No sickness of serious nature has visited the family, but they would have the best of medical care, so they say, in case they needed it. During the last year, Herman has not seen a movie. His leisure time activities are fishing and hunting. His ambition is to be the best farmer in the county. He expects to farm and "do just that" the rest of his life. He thinks a trip to Blacksburg would be fine. Such a great holiday is apparently beyond the fondest hopes of father or sons. "If we keep out of debt and keep well, that is about all we can do."

[Loc.: VSL/AB, box 180, 4 pp., 1,178 wds.]

John E. Bess *by Leila Blanche Bess, rec. 7 August 1939*

The sharecropper portrayed by John Bess in this manuscript, titled "A Land Owner Speaks His Mind on Share Croppers," bears little resemblance to the persons of tenant farmers Sam Harrison and Herman Hooker preceding. Not only is Bess's antagonist the embodiment of a rogue, but he could stand as a metaphor for the villainous sharecropper anywhere.

This text, however, can be distinguished from most of the VWP life histories by one significant feature: it is a deliberately polemical piece. The VWP worker, Leila Blanche Bess, used the interview to give her brother, John E. Bess, a forum from which to express his political views in a tirade against various classes of sharecroppers and government relief programs, including the WPA. At the same time, this use of the life history allowed Bess to present and comment vicariously on elements of her own biography that were mutually shared with her brother. Thus the multiple meanings hidden in the story of the sharecropper drowning the big "yellow cat" in the well become clear when one knows that the cat, in fact, belonged to Leila Blanche Bess.[24]

"The greatest problem confronting the land owner today is to secure honest, competent labor." Mr. Bess' blue eyes were direct and keen and his hair, which is almost white and very thin on the top of his head, blew in the spring breeze as he looked out over a four-hundred acre farm, which had run down [with] brush allowed to grow where formerly good crops had been raised. He is rather short and quite stout. And he says he is fifty-eight years old, although he does not look it — except [for] his thin white hair.

"I was born and raised right here and followed farming all my life until about ten years ago. My wife was teaching and we left the farm and moved to South Covington when the Rayon Plant was built. There was not much in farming then and we thought we could do better there; we had two children to educate and it takes money to do it. I like the farm better than any other work, have always liked it. I love the livestock and there is nothing I like better than to prepare the ground for planting. I like to do the work thoroughly and was taught how to farm by one of the best farmers in this section. I reckon that's one reason I get so impatient with these fellows who won't do anything right. When I give a man a good chance to make a good living for himself and keep the place up, and he won't do it or won't live up to his contract, it makes me want to pitch him out in the road." He spoke with some heat, and then explained.

"I've had so much trouble with sharecroppers. I hate to hear them mentioned. There are all classes: I've tried hiring men and have not found one who was capable and willing to work on the farm. If they stay more than a month, when they draw their first paycheck they begin telling the owner what to do and how. They are not willing to be told what is expected of them; they call it taking orders and they won't do it. But when a man pays to have his work done, he wants it done right and according to his way. And it is exasperating to tell a man what you want done and go out and find that he has not followed your instructions. And he has the nerve to tell you that he thought his way was best and he had set up a system of his own. I begin to see his finish right there. I can't help but get hot around the collar and want to pay him off right then, but a fellow can't always do it. For these things usually happen when you need help the very worst, maybe right in wheat harvest or time to cut corn. The good-for-nothing devils know it, too. That's why they are so worthless.

"If you fire him, you have to get out and try to find somebody else to take his place. And this is no easy job even when there are plenty of idle men, loafing around the country stores, lamenting the fact that they can't get a job anywhere. Relief has ruined more men than any one thing I know of. I know men who were good, honest laborers, who never knew anything but to do an honest day's work when they were hired. And they were on the lookout for work all the time and got it, too, and since they went on relief, they aren't worth a darn. If you succeed in hiring one of these fellows, they consider it an insult if their employer or boss tells them what to do. No, they think they should tell the owner how to farm and manage his affairs. They would rather have a little food doled out to them than to work at a fair wage and be independent. Yes sir, relief has had that effect on more people than you would think. Not all, mind you, there are others who would almost starve before they would ask for food or anything else. And that class will still do an honest day's work and seek to better their way of living.

"But to get back to the land owner's problem, let me say it is real. When I worked this land, the place did not look like it does now. I did most of my own work, too. Occasionally,

I hired a boy to help me in the busiest times, and I always had to hire some help in wheat and hay harvest. But I did all my own plowing. I liked to do it and it has always been hard to get men who knew how to plow. That sounds funny, but it's true. Not one man in ten knows how to plow a piece of land right or to judge land. Some soils require deeper plowing than others. I always tried to get my plowing done as early as possible so it would freeze, that loosens up the soil wonderfully.

"I liked good fences and clean fence rows. I had a good string of rail fences then, but look now, they are made of most everything: some rails, some poles, and some wire. It's not very pleasing to the eye, nor satisfactory, but the tenants have burnt the rails until they are nearly all gone. When they wanted good, quick, stove-wood, they just hooked a fence rail and chopped it up. They slipped one off here and one yonder, so that it would not be noticed at once, and then they slip out. But such work has ruined my fences, and they have been patched up to save the crops from outside stock. They are an eyesore to me, but I can't afford to spend much the way I've been stung by renters the last few years.

"There is the cash renter, though there are fewer of them. And often if they do rent for cash, they gather everything they can get, and just before the year is up they slip out and you get no cash. Sometimes, they are so sorry, you are glad for them to go even without paying, just so they leave. I've had several like that, but by George, the worst I've ever run up against yet is some of the sharecroppers. There are several classes of them, too. Some are all right. Then there is a middle class. They are honest in a way, that is, they wouldn't steal anything. But they are lazy and have no ambition. Don't care for anything.

"Then there is another class. They usually come wanting a two or five year lease or contract. They have the fairest kind of promises. They relate their experiences and tell what all they can do. One told me about the wonderful crops of corn, wheat, oats, potatoes, and barley he had raised over in the adjoining county [and] the dairy herd he had tended. He knew all about rotation of crops, soil conservation, legumes, etc. In fact his knowledge covered every point that a scientific farmer should know. He was well-informed as to all the latest methods in agricultural work and was a first rate veterinarian, and this is a valuable piece of knowledge on a farm where stock is raised. He had also handled successfully large flocks of poultry, and knew how to keep down diseases and to keep the egg basket filled. He knew sheep care from A to Z. He referred me to the best people in the county, and I thought how lucky I was to find such a man loose. So I lost no time in writing a contract, I didn't want any of my neighbors nabbing onto this treasure.

"I furnished him a good house, a large garden, ground for all the potatoes and roasting ears, sweet potatoes and beans that he wanted, free, and furnished one third of the fertilizer for the corn crop. He was to do the work and I was to have one third of the crop. He was to prepare the ground, do the planting, cultivate the crop at the proper time, and harvest and haul in the grain. I also told him I would give him all the work I had to hire done, and pay him one dollar and a half a day. The work was to be done when he was not busy in the crop. I considered myself lucky, for this big Irishman said he could do any kind of carpenter work, and I needed quite a lot of building done and repairing of other buildings.

"Two days after the contract was signed, he with his wife and three little boys moved in. I was delighted when I went up to the farm in a few days and saw how much work he had done. When I rounded a turn just above the house, I saw the newly plowed ground, so much of it that had not been turned for several years that the place looked strange even to me. He had done a good job of plowing and was still at it. He worked with a vengeance and proved what he said. He did know how to farm. I went back and forth right often for a few weeks and watched his progress, and thought how lucky I was to grab this fellow before some of my neighbors got him with a better offer than I could make. I was there after the corn come up and it looked good. I began measuring the grain that would be raised there barring a drought or something over which we have no control. The planting had been well-done, in well-prepared soil and everything looked fine and promising. I was so sure of this man's ability, honesty and his willingness to work that I felt perfectly safe in turning the farm over to him. I went back to my work in town well-satisfied.

"A few weeks after this, he came to me and asked me if I wanted some certain trees cut, as they were shading the crop too much and offered very kindly to cut them. And said he would peel them, so I could sell them for pulp wood and there would be no waste about the cutting. I thought he was very thoughtful and told him to cut them, but specified which trees were to be cut, and told him definitely not to cut any maples or sugar trees. He said he would cut and peel the timber for a dollar and a half a cord. I agreed to pay him that price, and he went on back to the farm.

"I was very busy just then and could not get up to the farm as often as I had been going. But finally, there came a day when I did break loose and got in my car and drove up, picturing as I drove along how nice the crops must look by this time, especially the corn. I knew it must be great big, for it was almost time for corn to be laid by. It was a glorious day to be out of doors and to work even though the sun was hot. I enjoyed every minute outside. When I drove up, to my amazement, I saw no one about. The sharecropper was nowhere to be seen, but I thought he was busy in the field. I looked at the corn near the road and was terribly disappointed. It didn't look a bit good and I soon saw the reason—it had not been worked since I was there before.

"I went around to the kitchen and Mrs. Sampson, looking ashamed, told me Ed had taken his gun and gone out, she didn't know where. She is a good, honest, hard-working woman, and I'm sure it hurt her the way her husband did, but she couldn't help it for he was Lord over all his family and they feared him. I was puzzled and made my way to the big field where the best corn grows and where it looked so good when I had seen it before. There had been no plowing done nor a hoe stuck in that field. I was amazed, and just stood and looked. It was evident that there would be no corn crop, nothing worthwhile.

"I looked about me and saw that the star-farmer had done no farming, but he had been busy butchering up the trees. He had cut the timber and left ugly piles of limbs scattered about here and there. The very trees I had told him not to cut were the ones he had cut. He had even cut some sugar trees and just left them, not even peeled, just plain destruction. I got mad then, I was not only mad, but it hurt to be treated in such a devilish way. My heart felt like it was too big for my insides and I wanted to get my hands on that big deceitful devil, and throw him off the place. Then I remembered that I had a contract with this fellow, and I begun wondering if there was a way to get rid of him now, instead of having to wait until his time is up, and I felt like I couldn't stand him that long.

"When I returned to the house, sorely disappointed, I was surprised again, to see the Irishman's old ugly mules turned out in the yard, grazing peacefully as if they were in the pasture where they belonged. My sister had worked so hard and had taken such pride in making and keeping that lawn pretty; the roses and other flowers that she had planted had been destroyed.

And to cap it all off, there lay a great big calf on the porch along with its filth, which had not been cleaned up that day. I'm not blaming Mrs. Sampson, for she had everything to do: all the feeding and milking, the gardening and the wood chopping, her washing and ironing, and her children to look after, and that vagabond of a husband to wait on. He needed a good kicking out, and if I could have done what I felt like, I'd have done it, too. But when I cooled off a little, I knew it would do no good to raise a row with the old scalawag, so I decided to go to town and consult the Commonwealth [attorney] about it and see what could be done. I didn't get to see my tenant for some time, but when I did I asked him why he had not worked the corn. He said it got too dry and he waited for it to rain, so he could plow. A fine excuse for a scientific farmer to make, wasn't it?

"When hunting season came on, my son—a boy of seventeen—went up to the farm to hunt. The old Irishman refused to allow him to hunt or to occupy a room there which was reserved when the contract [was made], with the understanding that any of my family had the privilege of going or coming at any time. (This was written in the contract.) Well, the old man got so mad when my boy went to hunt, out alone, [that] he took his gun and followed him. He failed to overtake him or lost his trail, and went to a neighbor's house and inquired which way the boy went and said if I didn't take that boy away, he would put him out of the way. He said, 'I am carrying my high-powered gun this morning, and I can kill anything away up on that ther knob.' (The knob was about three miles distant.) I was so mad when my old neighbor told me about this, and said: 'You had better take John home, I'm afraid that man will kill him.'"

At first I refused to take John home. He didn't want to go and had planned that little vacation up on the farm for so long, I thought it would be a shame to allow that old devil to spoil it all. So I left him up there and went to town. When his mother and her sister, who happened to be there at the time, heard about it, they took on so that I had to go back and bring John home and let him go somewhere else to hunt. I managed it so that old Sampson never knew we took him away on his account. He thought John's vacation was over. It looked as if he followed John with the intention of killing him, but I have always believed he was more than half bluff. . . . [25]

"Well, you would think after all this and his making threats, that [Sampson] could have been put out. But the Commonwealth's Attorney said he could stay until his year was up and advised me to get by with as little trouble as possible, as the man was pretty well-known and was mean, and it would be better to lose something than to have more trouble.

"Sampson refused to gather the corn. He went in the field and hauled out his share and left mine in the field. He also refused to allow any one else to go in for my part, so it stood out all winter and all he put in for me was a little fodder for the cow. In the spring, not long before he moved, he went to the field and gathered my share of the corn and put it in the garage. When he moved he took it all with him. Still I had to live up to my part of the contract, while he had broken every letter of his. I have never been able to understand it. I could do nothing but wait until his year was up. By golly, it seemed a long time, but just a few days before his time would have been up, he moved out and was I glad. While he was there the old farm looked like a junk yard. He had the most old stuff around: old parts of wagons, old cars, pieces of plows, old steel barrels, wheels off wagons, trucks, rakes and mowers, riding plows and every old thing you could think of, and he had them scattered everywhere.

"When I went back to the farm after he got out, I saw that it would take at least two years to repair the damage he had done. He had strung up barbed wire right through the middle of some of the fields; of course, that had to be removed. The fences were down, the gates off the hinges, and the lawn was positively filthy. The house was in a terrible condition; it took several days to clean it and remove the odor. The old cuss had kept apples and potatoes in the living room and allowed them to rot on the floor. He had cured his tobacco in the dining room, and that left an awful smell. It was the old-time strong kind. He smoked an old pipe, strong as I don't know what and that perfumed the whole house. The entire place was in a deplorable condition. It was a happy day for every one and all the animals when the Irishman departed. The cows, horses, the dog, and even the chickens were glad and came to meet me, rubbing around my legs to show their gladness. The hens cackled and the old rooster [crowed] more loudly than was his want, in celebration. I was glad to be alone once more on the farm, and thought I was forever through with this sharecropper and wondered how I could have been so fooled in a fellow man.

"As I said, I thought I was through with this man, but I was not. One day, several months after he left my place, I received a summons to appear at the office of the Commonwealth's Attorney to settle with Ed. I went and Ed also came, but our attorney failed to show up—he was out of town. So we agreed to meet on the following Monday. I went back and Mr. Collins told me that Ed had been there and gone out, saying he would be back soon. I waited as long as I could and he had not come back, so I asked Mr. Collins what claims Ed had brought up against me. He laughed and said he wanted pay for fertilizer, and for hauling a lot of pulp wood from the woods, and five dollars damage to his corn field made, he claimed, by having a hole dug prospecting for Barytes [barite], and a few other charges. There were so many I have forgotten some of 'em." Mr. Bess's blue eyes twinkled a little behind the horn-rimmed glasses as he finished telling about the many charges Ed had against him. [After all was told,] "he never did come back for a settlement.[26]

"I'll say again, I thought I was done with him, but when we opened our well to clean it this spring, what should we find but my sister's yellow cat she prized so much and which had disappeared when Sampson was here. She had been so distressed about the cat and had asked about him, but could find no trace of him. He was a beautiful yellow with a little white on his breast, and was perfectly harmless and such a good mouser. There were no mice or rats around when he was here. He often sat on Sampson's lap, and he [Sampson] pretended to think so much of him.

"The reason we feel sure he did this mean low-down thing is because [Sampson] met a boy who lives there now and asked him if he used the well water? I think that is about the lowest down thing I ever knew a man to do, to put a cat in the well, not knowing what trouble it might cause or to whom. It was providential, I suppose, that no one had used the well water since Ed Sampson left the farm. There is a stream of good mountain water running by the house and that had been used instead of the well. We had the water tested in Richmond and they said there was no germs in it, but who could use it? Just the thought of that poor old cat lying in the well would keep a fellow from ever enjoying the water again. And it is a fine well, too; the water is almost as cold as ice-water. It would never do for me to know that Ed Sampson did put my sister's cat in that well, he'd pay well for it. I bet he'd run from the next cat he saw. My sister grieved so about it and said she imagined that he put the poor old fellow in alive and let him drown. Darn his ornery hide," he said with bitterness.

He took off the horn-rimmed glasses and took from his pocket a clean, white handkerchief and polished the lens carefully. I noted his strong square hands, somewhat gnarled, truly the hands of a farmer. Just as carefully, he adjusted the glasses and remarked: "I never finished college and never went to an agricultural school, but I think I know pretty well the main principles of good and successful farming, and I repeat it that it is a problem. Now this year, I've hired all my work done and I don't know whether it is going to pay or not. I furnished one horse and her feed, and boarded a man and furnished hay for his horse—he had his own corn—and paid him two and a half dollars a day for plowing. It cost me twenty five dollars to get about nine acres ready to lay off for corn—I did the laying off myself. But I've had to hire a man to plow it and a boy to hoe it and it has not had as much cultivation as it should have had, I know what it takes to raise good crops. Unless they are worked well and at the proper time, they will not be worth much.

"I couldn't get off from carrying the mail to [take care of] my oats and couldn't get a man anywhere to cut them at the right time. So when they were cut, I lost nearly half the crop because they stood too long and so many fell down and went to waste. Now it is almost time to sow wheat. And I want to get the land in grass again and some kind of pasture, and I am right now worried as to how I'm going to get it done. I could rent, yes, but I don't want to get stuck again with another Sampson, so I'll have to go slow this time. If I can get the old farm in grass again, I'm not going to try to raise much corn next year. I'll graze cattle and let someone else do the corn raising—some fellow who has some help of his own." He mopped the perspiration from his brow as he talked.

"Now, don't get me wrong about relief work. The W.P.A. has been a great help to a lot of people, and some people have made good use of it and tried to keep independent. But I can't say that for everyone who has had a chance. So many think it is all right to play around and do nothing, and seem to think it is all right for the Government to pay whether they do anything or not. But there are others who try to do their best, whether they understand the work assigned to them or not. The W.P.A. workers have done some very fine and necessary work, too, and deserve credit for it. I am not condemning the relief work as it is set up or its intention, but it has, in some instances, been abused. I think it could be improved upon."

[Loc.: VSL/AB, box 185, 16 pp., 5,534 wds.]

Following the Crops:
Images from the Lives of Migrant Laborers

The first official assignment given to RA/FSA photographer Jack Delano was to document the lives of migrant laborers who followed the crops along the Atlantic seaboard. There were far fewer migratory workers in Virginia than farther south and in the West, but they were still generally overworked and poorly housed—sometimes in compounds that looked more like prison yards than housing for free laborers. Delano himself reported in an interview several years ago that "field hands worked from 'ten to fifteen hours a day' and were paid 'ten cents an hour,' [while] workers grading cabbages were paid 'twenty cents an hour.'"[27]

In this series of photographs, which Delano took in July 1940, migrant laborers from Florida are shown leaving potato fields in Belcross, North Carolina, and being transported to their next job and temporary, new homes in Onley, Cheriton, or other nearby farm towns on the Eastern Shore of Virginia.

Belcross, North Carolina. Florida migrant agricultural workers getting aboard the truck which is taking them to another job at Onley, Virginia. [LC-USF33-20617-M4]

Belcross, North Carolina. Sam Cooper, a Negro leader of a crew of agricultural workers from Florida, driving the truck which is carrying them to Onley, Virginia, where he has gotten them another job. They have been picking potatoes.
[LC-USF33-20618-M3]

Norfolk-Cape Charles ferry, Virginia. The dock at Little Creek, Virginia.
[LC-USF33-20576-M4]

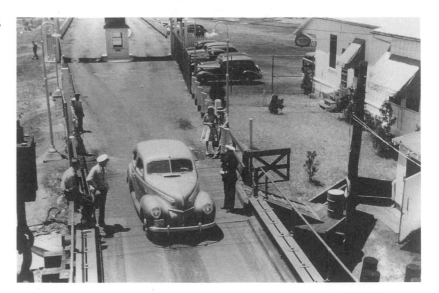

(Above)
Norfolk-Cape Charles ferry,
Virginia. A migratory
agricultural worker on the ferry,
writing a postal card to his
parents. [LC-USF34-40871-D]

(Left)
Onley (vicinity), Virginia.
Sleeping quarters for a group of
Florida migratory workers.
[LC-USF34-40913-D]

Onley, Virginia. Cooking facilities for a group of thirty-five migrant workers. [LC-USF34-40922-D]

Accomac (vicinity), Virginia. Migratory workers in an onion field. [LC-USF34-40945]

Cheriton, Virginia. Barbed wire surrounded barracks for Florida negro migrants working at the Webster canning company.
[LC-USF33-20589-M3]

Cheriton, Virginia. Barracks for negro migratory agricultural workers at the Webster Canning company.
[LC-USF33-20584-M5]

John Gregory *by Essie W. Smith, rec. 20 June 1939*

John Gregory supposedly owned and worked his own one hundred and more acres of land, had a year of agricultural training at Virginia Polytechnic Institute, practiced modern farm methods with diversified crops, and, given his scale of operation, would appear to have been a progressive farmer of the time. Despite all efforts, however, the farm income made by John Gregory and his family was no more than six hundred dollars "even [in] the best years," and at that amount, it was no more than was made by the Hooker family, who were sharecroppers.

This circumstance presented Virginia Writers' Project worker Essie W. Smith with an unforeseen dilemma. To rebut claims in an earlier report that most Franklin countians were moonshiners, Smith had chosen John Gregory's life to "illustrate the average" of that 64 percent of small farmers who Virginia Polytechnic Institute's William E. Garnett had said were typical of the Franklin County area. However, by the measure of gross income alone, the Gregorys would have fallen into the category of "rural marginal population" proposed by Garnett elsewhere. By posing John Gregory as representative of the typical Franklin County small farmer, Smith inadvertently placed most of the county's farmers in that same category.

This raises the question, then, "How typical was John Gregory?" Almost a year after submitting this life history with Gregory, Smith sent in another with a young unmarried woman identified as Elva Lee Beheler, whose father was indicated as James Beheler. But the circumstances described pertaining to Elva Lee were almost identical to those of John Gregory's eldest daughter, and they are very likely the same person. Both the Gregory and Beheler surnames can be identified with old Franklin County families. Yet courthouse and census research and communications with members of both families have failed to identify either a John Gregory or James Beheler who would fit the person detailed in this life history. So the further question is not only how typical but, "Who is John Gregory?"[28]

The Wickersham Report of a few years ago stated that ninety-nine percent of the inhabitants of Franklin County were engaged, either directly or indirectly, in the liquor business. Of course this was a gross and malicious exaggeration.[29]

Mr. W. E. Garnett of Virginia Polytechnic Institute says in one of his reports that sixty-four percent of the population of Franklin are small farmers who own from seventy-five to one hundred acres of land, which they live on and cultivate. He also gives other interesting statistics, which prove that this class of men and this occupation is the only strictly typical one of this section.

Mr. Gregory, whom we have selected from the large group to illustrate the average life of these men, is forty years old. He lives on a dirt road three miles from the highway. He cannot get his Ford car to this highway in bad weather as the road is deep with red, sticky mud, through which the vehicle cannot plough. His house has six rooms and a hall which they can use for a dining room in summer. In winter they eat in the kitchen.

His wife is a pretty, brown-eyed woman with a nice figure and much animation. She taught school before her marriage, at a time when you needed only a certificate, and not a degree, to teach in a country school. She is chef, dairy woman, scrub woman, laundress, dressmaker, market gardener, trained nurse, welfare worker, and many other professions combined. She is also advisor-in-chief to her husband, who is industrious and sober—two characteristics not the invariable possession of neighbors.

He is a slim, likeable man with brown hair, remarkably large and intensely blue eyes, and a pleasant smile. He was amusedly tolerant of the interview, and answered all questions in a painstaking manner. One could recognize instantly why he had the name of good neighbor and public-spirited citizen.

"I have been living on this place nine years. My father had a family of twelve, too large I think, especially for these times. It might have been all right in pioneer days when increase of population was in demand, but now, well, two or three children are all any working man can say grace over. My wife's father had only two children and [he] could manage to educate them properly. She went to high school and had two years at a state normal school. Then she taught four years before I could get her to marry me. Her brother studied for the Methodist ministry. He is now a missionary in China, and I expect he is wishing he was at home.

"Our folks were the first settlers in this section. They took up adjoining land and have always been friendly. I inherited a small part of my father's land, about fifty acres, and we lived in a small house on that until I managed, with what my wife had saved, to make a down payment on about sixty acres more with this house on it. The house and land were both terribly run down, but I had learned something about bringing land back while I was at V.P.I. I had been there at school a year when my father died, and I had to quit and go to work at home. So I gradually improved the land and now I have as good a small farm as any man in the county. I had learned something about carpentering from an uncle who lived in a nearby town and worked at this trade. So I could patch up the house, and by hard licks, I have it in good shape. I have paid for it all, and bought a Ford car which is nearly paid for, and put a little by for a rainy day.

"We are hoping to send our daughter, who is sixteen and will finish at high school this year, to a state normal. She says she would like to teach. I am thinking of V.P.I. for the boys, as they seem to want to farm, and that is the best outlook for them. But lately Jim has been talking a lot about electricity. If he wants to make a specialty of that, his mother thinks it would be best to let him try. The oldest boy goes to high school with his sister about three and one-half miles from here. When the roads are good I take them in the car, but if it is bad they ride the horse. Often they walk home. The other boy goes to the one-room school, which is only half a mile down the road.

"I would like to make some improvements on the farm, get some up-to-date machinery, and have water and lights in the house, but with the children needing so much the chances do not seem any too good at present. We had to get a car. Seems like you just can't make out these times without one. It takes too long to get anyplace by any of the old means of transportation. Everybody is in a hurry, and you feel as if you must not let everyone get ahead of you.

"I make a considerably larger crop now than I used to. I have more land and I have improved it a lot, and the boys are large enough to be right smart help. We make all our own bread and meat and vegetables, and plenty of stuff for the stock. My wife cans and preserves and pickles, so we have nothing in that line to buy. But there is always coffee, tea, sugar, soap, starch, and things like that, besides the store foods which the children have learned to like. We have plenty of chickens and generally, ducks and geese. The cows furnish plenty of milk and butter, and often we have some left over to sell. Our groceries cost about fifty dollars a year all told, but we exchange products for some of that amount. Clothes, and taxes, and running the car cost most of the ready money.

"I have always thought farmers with homes that they occupied themselves and worked should be exempt from paying taxes. They should be encouraged that much, for what with rains and droughts and beetles and all the other vexations, they need something to keep them reconciled to their disappointments. With all my managing and all my wife and children's help, I cannot make more than six hundred dollars on my farm even the best years. Besides other necessary expenses, fertilizer bills have to come out of this and fertilizer costs a lot, but you naturally have to have it. If I could make as much as a thousand [dollars] a year, I think I could get along all right and save a little. If I worked in town I could make more, but there would be house rent and living would cost a lot more, and I would not be my own boss, which means plenty to a man. As it is, I can get off a day or two most any time, except in the very busy season, and not be docked for it.

"I make it a rule to vote the Democratic ticket straight. My wife does the same unless she happens to know and like the other candidate. She is not hidebound as I am. There was a time when the white men of the South had to vote solidly Democratic. My father had to do it. He was a Confederate soldier, as all his neighbors were. I inherited my politics from him. I know times change, but there are some things better not changed although not many young folks agree with me.

"We are Methodists. We go to church once a month, when they have preaching at the church about two miles from here. They have Sunday School, too, and the children go to that. There is a Dunkard church nearer, where they have a big foot washing every fall. This is a part of their religion. They have this instead of Communion as in other churches, although they always serve bread and meat to every member before the rite of foot washing begins. Every Dunkard takes off one shoe, and other members go through the audience washing their foot. It sounds queer, but it is impressive to witness. We always go. These Dunkards make good thrifty citizens, although they are conscientious objectors to war.

"They had a terrible tragedy in the road out in front of this church a year or so ago. The sheriff was coming by in his automobile with a negro who had been arrested on a minor charge, when his car was fired on. The windshield was plum shot to pieces. [When] the Sheriff and the negro jumped out and started to run, both were shot in the back many times. A man, coming by a short time afterwards, found both bodies dead in the road and the motor still running in the car. There was a great hue and cry, and they tried and tried to find who did the deed. A post on a fence near the church was discovered to be half-burned where a candle had been placed that night. The shooting occurred around nine o'clock at night and it was powerful dark, too.

"Lots of folks were arrested, but the whole thing remained a mystery until sometime last year when they brought two young men here for trial. They had ballistics examine bullets from guns shot by these men, and they were found to be the same as those taken from the bodies of the two murdered men. There seemed to be nothing left to do but send the men to the penitentiary for a lifetime. It seemed awful, for they were pleasant, presentable young fellows and might have been useful homemakers. There are some people who yet do not believe they were the right ones, but those people did not hear all the testimony. And we can only hope [the two men] are not innocent sufferers. It was an awful cold-blooded deed and somebody should be punished, but I am glad I was not on that jury.

"My wife had to go to the hospital once for an operation, but apart from that and the removal of the children's tonsils, the neighborhood doctor has been able to manage all our ills. We keep a stock of simple home remedies on hand, and my wife does most of the physicking that is done. She learned something about a balanced diet at school, but she says she had to forget most of it on account of being obliged to use what she had on hand to cook. But none of us have ever been more than normally hungry. We try to get some new furnishings for the house every year, even if only one piece of furniture. Last year we got a Victrola and the children keep that going most of the time.

"I do most of my plowing in the fall and sow about twelve or fifteen acres in wheat. In good seasons this brings about ten or fifteen bushels to the acre. I plant ten or twelve acres in corn, and this is plenty for us and the stock. I make from five to seven houses of tobacco. An acre of good tobacco makes a little over one house. When prices are right this does right well. I plant some rye and try to make enough oats and hay to do me. I often improve the land by planting peas. Sometimes I turn them under, and sometimes cut them for hay. I generally plant a right large field in tomatoes and sell some of them to the cannery, but they never pay much.

"We have a garden, and nearly live on the vegetables in summer. I generally have a fine watermelon patch which we enjoy. And sometimes I sell a few of these, but the market is generally glutted when they come in. We have cantaloupes, too, in great abundance when the season is right. I have an old apple orchard, but it never amounts to more than enough for our needs. I have planted a number of young trees of nearly all the fruits that grow in this section, just to have enough for our own use. My land is not especially adapted to fruit growing on a large scale. I try to keep my barns and fences in good order, and get this done and my winter wood sawed, when the work in the fields is not pressing.

"Sometimes we get in the car and go to town to see the moving pictures, if anything comes along that my wife especially wants to see or the children hear about at school. We saw 'Jesse James' last week, because we had heard about him all our lives and wanted to see what he looked like. He was handsome if he was anything like the man who took the part. We all thought it a fine picture. It pays to get out sometimes and see what other people are doing and seeing." [30]

Jesse Jeames and Frank they robbed a many bank,
And they flagged down the eastbound train,
They would fall upon their knees and deliver up the keys,
To Frank and his brother, Jesse Jeames.

Jesse Jeames, Jesse Jeames—
To Frank and his brother, Jesse Jeames,
They would fall upon their knees and deliver up the keys,
To Frank and his brother, Jesse Jeames.

Jesse Jeames had a wife, she was a mourner all her life,
But the children all grew brave,
As they stood on the spot where they saw their father shot,
And they laid poor Jesse in his grave.
    Repeat last two lines

When the people in the west heard of Jesse's death,
They wondered how come him to die,
He was shot on the sly by a coward, Robert Ford,
And they laid poor Jesse down to die.
    Repeat last two lines

The children cried aloud when they saw their father's shroud,
Saying, "Mother we are left alone,"
But she trembling replied as she stood by his side,
"God will prepare us a home."
    Repeat last two lines

[Loc.: UVA/FC, item #697E]

"We try to keep up with the times. I take a daily paper, though I don't always get time to read it. And my wife takes some magazines and fashion books. The children bring home books from the high school library. I generally look over them and if [one] happens to suit my taste I read it. My wife reads most of them, too. Sometimes we do not think much of the things they put in the hands of young folks to read, but since they already know so much more than their elders it may be all right.

"I haven't told you much about our baby. I was afraid I might say too much. She is eight years younger than the boy next to her and came as a great surprise to us. She is two years old and, if I do say it myself, about the likeliest child you ever saw. We spoil her something awful, all of us. She is certainly the boss around here. By the time she grows up, we want to have things in good shape for her, but nobody can tell what will happen by that time. With all this talk of war, and dictators, and mixing up in foreign doings, it may be no fit place for her to live in anyhow. But we have to do the best we can, here and now, and let the future take care of our children, if we cannot."

[Loc.: VSL/AB, box 180, 8 pp., 2,200 wds.]

Marietta Holley *by Essie W. Smith, rec. 25 March 1940*

Although she had not yet convinced her mother to leave her "bothering" over the farm and move to town, Marietta admitted, "I keep on harping on it and maybe I can get her to listen some of these days." One specific benefit attributed by state director Dr. Walter S. Newman to the National Youth Administration's residential projects was that they got young people into "a different environment, . . . the first step in getting them into employment" as well as away from marginal farms such as the one described discontentedly by Holley. Other localized nonresidential NYA programs, such as the one in Franklin County that Marietta Holley participated in, were concerned specifically with the tasks of supplying training and jobs or of helping young people to stay in school while also providing some amount of needed support. Holley's assessment of her NYA experience was that it was "a lot more profitable than sitting at home moping." [31]

Marietta, or Etta, as she is called, is a tall, angular girl, with stiff unruly red hair, pale blue eyes covered with great disfiguring glasses, and coarse, rough skin. She is awkward in movement and inclined to stoop, but she is clever with her needle and can accomplish more in a day than most women who have had far more experience. She wore a dark red dress of some smooth woolen material, and it was well-fitted and neatly made. She had tried to curl her hair, but the effect was not pleasing. Her finger nails were darkly crimson and made striking rays of color as they flew in and out the hemstitching she was so carefully, yet rapidly, doing.

She is the youngest of a large family, all of whom are married except herself. One married sister lives at home with her husband and three children, and Etta's mother. Her father has been dead five years. . . . [32]

There are two renters on the farm where Etta lives. But they have lived sparingly since her father's death. . . . [M]ost of the farm work is done by the renters, Etta, her sister, and her mother. The farm is too far from town for the products to be marketed without a truck, and the land is poor, needing intelligent cultivation to bring adequate crops.

Etta was glad to join the N.Y.A. classes, both for the subjects taught and the small stipend which she sadly needed. She had stopped school in the first year of high school to assist at home. She would not necessarily have been compelled to do this, but she did not like her teacher and was not interested in school work. . . .

"I am glad to work here. I get powerful lonesome at home with nobody but old folks and babies. Our house is so far from the highway and the road is so muddy in winter that nobody can come to see you. There is not much you can do and the days get long, even when you know they are short.

"We go to preaching once a month on Sundays. The church is about a mile from our house. The preacher is a young man, and all the girls are crazy about him, but I think he has a sure enough girl way off somewhere. My mother has been a church member ever since I can remember, but I haven't joined. I aim to, some day.

"We try to raise most everything to eat on the farm, but looks like we don't have much success. Our tobacco never brings in much more than enough to pay fertilizer bills. Fertilizer sure costs a lot, and don't do much good as I can see, but they say you can't raise anything without it. I beg them to try just one year, but they won't listen to me.

"Our corn never is as good as that growing in the fields right next to it, and looks like crows skip all the other crops to get to ours. Bugs are worse on our potatoes, and weevils is worse on our beans. Hawks always find our young chickens before they do anybody else's, and when our sow has pigs there are always more runts than any other litters. Our wheat makes less bushels to the acre, an' we never do make enough oats or rough food to do us.

"Our fences rot down quicker, and our cows go dry quicker than any you ever saw. I been begging my mother to move to town and sell the place, but she has got used to the country and thinks she couldn't do without her cows and pigs. I sure could, for I never did like to milk, or churn, or tote slop to hogs, and that's what you always got to be doing in the country. Folks say it is cooler in the country in summer, but I know it never could get any hotter than it is at our place sometimes. They say wood is easier to get but it does not seem that way to me, for we never do have enough to keep properly warm and have to go out in the worst weather to get that. They say you ought to fix for winter in the summertime, but we are always so busy in the summertime fooling with the crops there never is time for anything else.

"We got some powerful good bottom land on the place, that is, a small stretch of it. But every time we plant it the floods get it, and when we plant on the upper land it gets too dry. There is always something to bother about, and I think a heap of the bothering is the kind there is no use of having. Mother is used to it though, and maybe she couldn't live without being worried about something. But I can't help thinking we would be better off in town, and I keep on harping on it and maybe I can get her to listen some of these days. Until I do, I hope I can keep on coming to these [NYA] classes, for it is a lot more profitable than sitting at home moping."

[Loc.: VSL/AB, box 178, 4 pp.]

Portraits of Peasantry or Pastures of Plenty?: Pastoral Scenes of Virginia

The few photographs taken early on in Virginia by RA/FSA photographers (or by other agencies and borrowed for the RA/FSA files) were largely project related and intended to illustrate conditions the Resettlement Administration or other New Deal programs were working to mitigate or change, such as flooding, eroded land, and tumble-down farms. But by the late 1930s to early 1940s, when the bulk of the documentary efforts in Virginia were carried out by RA/FSA and WPA photographers, the need was, in part, for depictions that emphasized stability and the country's abundant resources in the face of the coming war.

Ironically, in these pastoral and rather picturesque scenes of Virginia farms and farmers, the images are predominantly of individuals who plow fields with oxen or horses, load rye by hand on wagons, cradle and shock their wheat, and kill hogs for meat. These are not the pictures one might expect of a mechanized and rationalized large-scale agriculture geared up and ready to feed millions for the war's duration. Rather, these are depictions of the very kinds of traditional (and self-limiting, in terms of scale) farm practices that some believed were associated with an impending peasantry in this country. Yet on the brink of war, fields of shocked wheat and rail fences and yeoman farmers, with all that those familiar symbols implicitly conveyed about tradition and cultural conservation in the face of change, were reassuring, even comforting.

Roanoke County, Virginia.
Negro plowing with mountains
in background.
Photo by W. Lincoln Highton.
VSL/PC. [43550]

(Above)
Mending a plow which was
purchased through funds
advanced by the U.S. Resettlement
administration in Virginia.
November 1935.
Photo by Arthur Rothstein.
[LC-USF34-00691-C]

(Left)
Marion (vicinity), Virginia.
October 1940. Rolling farmland
showing shocked corn and
several types of fences.
Photo by Marion Post Wolcott.
[LC-USF34-56105-D]

(Top) Denniston (vicinity), Halifax County, Virginia. November 1939. Hog killing on Milton Puryeur's place. Puryeur is a negro owner of five acres of land who used to grow tobacco and cotton but is making only a subsistence living now. He burns old shoes and pieces of leather near the heads of the hogs to keep the flies away. These hogs belong to a neighbor land owner. Photo by Marion Post Wolcott. [LC-USF34-52880-D]. *(Bottom) Vienna (vicinity), Virginia. May 1941. Farmers harvesting rye. Photo by Marion Post Wolcott.* [LC-USF34-57533-D]. *(Opposite) Smithfield, Virginia. Spinach picking, April [?], route 10. Photo by W. Lincoln Highton.* VSL/PC. [42902]

Gloucester County, Virginia. The spring harvest of daffodils for the market.
Photo by W. Lincoln Highton. VSL/PC. [42931]

6 Making a Living on the Water

"TAKES A MAN WITH A GOOD BACK AN' STRONG ARMS"

Ain't a thing around here worth a crawdad hole no more. —Amos Harris

Land is a primal resource, but so, too, is water. Many Virginians had made their living for generations from the commonwealth's waters, particularly the Chesapeake Bay with its rich complex of varied marine life. But through time its productivity decreased in response to degradation of its physical well-being by natural processes as well as those imposed by humans and to repeated cycles during which particular species were heedlessly overharvested in response to large-scale market demands. Not all classes of fish and shellfish were affected in the same way by these workings and generally as one resource became scarce, the fishing industry shifted its dependence to another variety. Over the long term the famous Chesapeake Bay oysters and, more recently, its blue crabs were, or are becoming, seriously depleted. Like brothers Amos and George Harris, a number of the individuals whose life histories follow in this chapter were outspoken about the changes in the Virginia fisheries witnessed during their lives and offered a warning to the future about the nature of the bay's decreasing yields and viability.[1]

In the first quarter of the twentieth century, the increasing concentration of urban populations and of developing industrial sites along various freshwater tributaries or tidal waters all spawned their own form of contaminants. Thus sewage dumped into the James River at Richmond, as well as chemicals from the pulp and paper mill at West Point on the York River, added to the progressive and cumulative pollution of the bay. But as much, or maybe more, of the effluent came seeping from farms and industrial operations along the drains of the Susquehanna River in Pennsylvania and New York far to the north, for the bay does not exist independent of its sources, however far removed they may seem to be. Despite political and jurisdictional distinctions, those sources all contributed their share, in varying degree, to the decline of the Virginia fisheries and oyster industry specifically and the livelihoods of the independent Chesapeake Bay watermen generally.[2]

Heavy commercial exploitation of the bay's resources greatly increased after the Civil War. "Almost immediately after Lee's surrender at Appomattox," one writer states, "fishing concerns in New York and New England began fishing Virginia's

West Point, Virginia. March 1941. Paper Mill. Photo by John Vachon. [LC-USF34-62678-D]

Chesapeake waters." The oyster beds in Long Island Sound and off Cape Cod had already been exhausted by dredging, and Chesapeake Bay oysters were being imported northward in great quantities. At the same time, former oystermen from New York were exported, so to speak, to the Chesapeake Bay.[3]

In at least one instance (reported in the vwp life histories), several former neighbors on the Great South Bay in Patchogue, Long Island, New York, all decided to move to Capahosic, Gloucester County, on the York River in Virginia. Among this group was vwp worker Lucille Jayne's father, George Jayne, a native of Long Island, a boatbuilder, and an oysterman. Jayne's family first moved to Crisfield, Maryland, in 1884, when she was seven years old. Three years later, when one of her brothers fell ill, the family went back to New York for medical treatment. But in 1889, they returned to the Chesapeake Bay, staying in Crisfield for a year with another brother while their house was completed in Capahosic before moving across the bay. Jayne's account of their move recalls a time when it was still possible to sail inland from New York to the Chesapeake Bay, by way of the locks of the Raritan and Delaware and the Delaware and Chesapeake canals.

Several of our neighbors had already moved to Capahosic, down the York River to go into the oyster business. Father then made up his mind that he too, would move to Capahosic and . . . we did move the first week of October. Both times, we moved from our old home on father's sloop but he chartered a schooner for our furniture.

I can remember but very little of our first trip to Maryland, for I was just seven, a week or two before. One thing I can remember is, I thought it such a lark to sleep in the little berths in the cabin. Mother and we three girls had the cabin, while father and the boys had beds in the hold of the boat. Then I thought it such fun to watch the cooking over the little boat stove, for I had never seen anything like it before. . . . It was kind of like Gypsying on water instead of land. . . .

Our second trip down to Maryland, I can remember quite distinctly, for I was just twelve years old at that time. . . . The weather was good, with just enough breeze for good sailing, and we crossed the Great South Bay, then out Jones Inlet to the ocean. And I'll never forget when we reached the ocean. Though there was only a light breeze, there had been a heavy wind the day before which left the ocean very rough, and I had my first and last experience in sea sickness. But it was only a short distance that we had to go on the ocean, for which we were all thankful. Then we put in to Princess Bay [at the tip of Staten Island, New York] and sailed till after sunset. Then father made for harbor for the night.

The next day we crossed the bay. The next body of water we sailed on was the Rairdain River [Raritan River across New Jersey], and I will never forget our experiences there. First was trouble with one of my cats. . . . A few days later when we were in the canal and a large barge was anchored right up to us and Tom was then tied out on deck where he could be watched, he thought he would visit aboard the barge. . . . He didn't meet with any disaster, for his chain was just long enough for him to land safely on the deck of the barge but no farther. . . .

Our trip was very pleasant and interesting all the way down till we reached the Chesapeake Bay, and that we didn't care so much for, for quite often it was rather rough sailing. We enjoyed the sail down the Raritan and Delaware Rivers for we were often close inshore. And whenever we made harbor for the night we would go ashore for a little exercise and if near a store, we would go in and buy any little thing that we needed on the boat. And of course we children always wanted candy. One time when we were at anchor close to shore we saw, as we supposed, several cows out in pasture, and we all thought we would like some fresh milk as we had nothing but [canned] milk. So we went ashore for milk, but soon found out that our cows were not cows but oxen, and of course we got no milk. In sailing by [the] Philadelphia yards we were all very much interested in watching a big ship that was about [to be] launched.

We children, and mother too, enjoyed the canals. The first one we went through was the [Raritan] and Delaware and the last one the Delaware and Chesapeake. We loved to watch the mule teams as they towed us through. We liked too, to see the people passing by near the tow paths, for we had been on the boat so long that we found most anything we saw going on onshore interesting to us. But there was one thing mother and we girls didn't like so much in going through the canals—that was going in the locks. Father would always send us down in the cabin when we came to a lock, for the locks were dangerous and he was afraid that we might get hurt. . . .

We were about two weeks on our trip for father would not sail nights or Sundays, or when the breeze was a little too strong. But fortunately, the weather was good all the way till we nearly reached our destination. We then knew that a heavy September gale was coming, but luck seemed to be with us for we managed to reach a very good harbor before the gale struck. We dropped anchor close inshore at Popular Island just ahead of the storm. . . . The storm did not last but a day or two, so we were soon on our way again and reached our destination safely without any mishap in a short time. We never had any trouble the entire way down, . . . our whole trip was indeed very pleasant.

Our married brother . . . was very much worried about us during the severe storm. He was afraid that we had not made harbor before it struck. He was very much relieved when his wife sighted the sloop sailing up East Creek, for that [was] where we anchored and my brother lived close to the creek. His wife recognized the boat at once, for my brother had drawn the sails for her on the hard sand not far from their yard, so she would know it when she saw it coming. . . .

[After spending a year with her brother's family in Crisfield, they set out again for Capahosic.] We left the creek in a small boat about five thirty Monday afternoon, October 6, 1890. We sailed down the creek and boarded the schooner, which was at anchor in the sound (Tangier Sound). The sails were soon unfurled and we were on our way just about dusk. There was a good breeze all the way to the Chesapeake, fully as much as we needed by the time we entered the Bay.

We had quite an experience along in the night when we were well out in the Bay. The boy that was helping on the schooner had failed to fill the colored lights when he was told to before dark. Consequently they were hung up not knowing that they had not been filled. The result, of course, was that they went out in the night, just at the time we sighted a large tramp steamer bearing down on us and the wind was blowing a good breeze. But I know that the lights were never filled so quickly before as they were then. The captain did not take time to hang them up for the steamer was creeping up closer and closer on us. So they relighted them and held them at the place they should have been hung. Well the steamer cleared us, but not leaving much of a margin. We all began to feel a bit shaky to put it mildly. . . . But providence must have been with us, for we came safely through our experience that had come so near being a serious disaster. And we sailed up the beautiful York River the next morning and dropped anchor at Capahosic, ten o'clock October 7, 1890. It was what you would call a perfect day.[4]

The Jayne family arrived on the York River a little late for the "hey-day of the oyster fishery in the 1880s when over 18 million bushels were caught." Still, for more than two decades the Chesapeake produced 40 percent of the world's oysters.[5] And George Jayne lived to see once again a decline of the oyster fishery on the bay similar to that he had previously witnessed in Long Island.

In addition to the fishing of individual watermen, there were 2,567 drudge boats licensed to operate on the Chesapeake Bay in the 1880s. Their use of dredges was much more efficient but also more destructive of the oyster beds than the tongs used by small operators. Owned by large fishing combines, the drudge boats and their practices, which included shanghaiing crews and poaching, were a major factor in the "oyster wars" that developed in the late 1870s and continued off and on into the twentieth century. In addition to increasing competition over a steadily diminishing resource of oysters, these "wars" were abetted by long-term conflicts between Virginia and Maryland over their state boundaries in the Chesapeake.[6]

There was considerable dispute over just which areas should be designated as part of the "public rock" and open to general use and which should be withheld and restricted to private leasing, from which the state could derive more income. The Baylor Survey of 1892, which first established the boundaries of the public and private oyster grounds in Virginia, was faulty at the outset and was made even less accurate by the passage of almost four decades of fishing and other physical changes.[7]

Nevertheless, the U.S. Bureau of Fisheries recommended that the "only remedy for rehabilitation" of the Virginia oyster industry was to lease all the area *within* that survey's bounds "to private interests for oyster farming." Although the leasing of public oyster rock within the survey was strictly prohibited by the Virginia constitution, the limits *could* be legally redefined so as to increase the amount of leasable area outside the survey's boundary. It appears that is what the engineers with the Virginia Commission of Fisheries were undertaking to do in 1933.[8]

The conservation issue was complicated in Virginia by its "sharp competition with states on the Atlantic seaboard to the north," whose oyster industries had large bases of capital and other resources with which to make inroads into the state's trade. In the end, the description of efforts to regulate the Maryland oyster fishery might apply just as appropriately to Virginia. "Nominally justified in terms of conservation," most of its regulations "in effect [protected] special interests and [increased] the cost of taking oysters without protecting either the capacity of the resource to reproduce itself or the return to individual oystermen."[9]

The total value of all products of the Virginia fisheries in 1930 was $7,487,303. But in terms of their individual rank order of value on the market, oysters were at the top, followed at some distance by shad and menhaden, then closely thereafter by crabs (hard and soft shell combined). The first factory for processing oil from menhaden fish opened in 1868. The menhaden catch in 1930 was only about one-third its 1912 volume, but menhaden still constituted, by weight, about 63 percent of Virginia's fin fish catch for that year. And in 1931, despite their declining numbers, eight factories—most of them in Reedville—processed 156 million menhaden into dry scrap, meal, and oil, representing nearly half the value of all the country's menhaden products. Before many more years passed, though, concentration of the menhaden fishing industry would shift to the Gulf of Mexico and other sites. And as mechanized power blocks to hoist the nets, heavy with fish, came progressively into use, the sounds of men, who formerly pulled in their nets with bare hands and the accompaniment of work songs, fell silent on the bay.[10]

In 1930 the Virginia crab fishery yielded 32 million pounds of crabmeat valued at $738,000 and employed 2,622 crabbers, in addition to processors and packers. And Hampton, which was the "center of the hardshell crabbing industry," in 1938 shipped "100,000 barrels of crabs, 50,000 gallons of oysters, and 30,000 bushels of unshucked oysters."[11]

Today, discussion continues to raise the specter of the destruction of a bay resource; new surveys are being conducted, and Virginia and Maryland are discussing limits on the catch—this time of the crab. Currently, about 2,600 persons hold Virginia commercial crab pot licenses, and the catch in recent years has varied from 53 million to nearly 100 million pounds (considerably more than the catch in 1930). The higher levels of efficiency and production combined with an ever increasing demand suggest that concerns about harvesting beyond the crab population's capacity for regeneration may not be unwarranted.

Amos Harris's statement "Ain't a thing around here worth a crawdad hole no more" plainly conveyed the message that making a living on the water in the late 1930s was as much in decline for many people as making a living on the land was for others. And Harris's brother, George, no doubt would have agreed with the contemporary advice of one ship captain who declared, "If I was a young man looking for a way to earn my living, I'd run as far away from the water as I could." [12] After all, George Harris, though not so well spoken, had given pretty much the same advice to his own son.

John H. Flemming Jr. *by Sarah W. Moore, no interview date given*

Comparing crabs to "rich folks . . . that go to Florida or some place warm every winter," John Flemming Jr. talked about various facets of the crabmeat-packing business he operated in Portsmouth. Flemming (born about 1880) hung around his father's crab and oyster plant as "a kid" and joined his father in the business shortly before the turn of the century. At the time he was interviewed, Flemming had been engaged in the seafood industry "close onto forty years." Reportedly, the first commercial crab cannery in Virginia was that of James McMenamin in Norfolk in 1878. John Flemming Sr.'s operation in Portsmouth, established not long after that date, was certainly among such early commercial ventures in Virginia. [13]

Two developments in the decade between 1930 and 1940 eventually had important consequences for the Chesapeake Bay crabmeat industry: by 1940 the prices for crabmeat were triple what they were in 1920; and a Virginia fisherman, Benjamin Lewis, obtained a patent in 1938 for a wire crab pot that would in time be widely adopted by crabbers. John Flemming Jr. (in this interview, which probably dates from 1939) described his workers as using dip nets and "tow" or trotlines, but did not mention the use of such crab pots. Although they could increase work efficiency, the transition to crab pots required some initial costs, as well as changes in cultural practice; these factors may have inhibited the crab fishing industry from adopting such an innovation for a time. [14]

On the banks of Scott's Creek, on the northern boundary of one of Portsmouth's better residential sections, stands an oblong structure covered with corrugated iron sheets with a wooden, somewhat rotted wharf going down into the water on the northern side. There is a bulkhead stretching for about 200 yards with sufficient depth to take care of incoming tides. Nearby, along the waterfront, are several similar buildings, but all but one are vacant at the present and in poor repair.

Mr. Flemming, the owner, has an office to one side of the large room where workers prepare crabs to be shipped to points north. When I entered the office, Mr. Flemming was standing by an old-fashioned, small, iron stove in one corner. It was then about eight in the morning and the stove didn't seem to be warming the room very well.

"Just pull up a chair here and warm yourself," he said amiably, indicating one of the three unpainted pine chairs in the room. I took the one from before his old desk by the window, sliding it near the stove. It *was* cold in the office.

"I hope I won't take too much of your time, Mr. Flemming," I said, edging my feet closer to the side of the stove.

He was a large cheerful man with a red, weathered face and startling bright blue eyes, so bright they seemed improbable. He spread huge gnarled hands before him in an expansive gesture.

"Nicest thing about this business is that it runs itself. Don't make any money here, but I could die and it would be a year before they'd realize it here." He yawned luxuriously, then beamed at me to show the hypocrisy of his last words. We immediately had a secret between us, that of his subtle importance to his business. I explained my mission. It appeared to amuse him very much, but he was quite gracious about helping me.

"You know, my father ran an oyster and crab business before me, and I used to hang around the place a lot when I was a kid. Time I got to be nineteen years old I guessed I knew about as much about the business as my old man so I quit school and went in with him. It suited me and I've stuck with it right along. I've done right well in past years. I've got a nice little home over on Yancey Street, and I'm putting three kids through school. My oldest boy, Jimmy, wants to go up to the University of Richmond next fall and I'm going to try to put him through. That boy's got ambition. Wants to be a doctor.

"I've always been able to keep the wife in right nice clothes, and we get a new car every couple of years. I don't guess I've got a right to complain. Things have been getting tight in the last few years down here in Portsmouth, but I'm managing to keep going somehow and break even too. A lot of houses have gone busted in the past few years."

"Would you tell me something about crabbing?" I asked. "Be glad to. You know, a crab is just like some of the rich folks you hear about that go to Florida or some place warm every winter. When winter is coming on and the water in the shallows gets too cold for him a crab picks himself up and moves on out into deep water. Then he hikes for the capes and stays there until spring. I've been in this business for close onto forty years and I've noticed that when we have a particularly bad winter, it affects the supply of crabs for two to three years afterward. It takes that long for the baby crabs to get over their growing pains. But if the crabs aren't killed out by the cold by the middle or last of May, our local waters are pretty thick with them."

"How do they catch them"? "Simple enough. Our crabbers go out in small motorboats and let down tow lines baited with raw meat. They put tomato cans or something like that on the ends of the lines for buoys and put the pieces of meat in little loops in the lines about eighteen inches apart. The lines are usually about two hundred feet long, so by the time a crabber has his line all settled down he can turn his boat around and return to the opposite buoy and start tolling it up again. The crabs hang on to the bait until they're pulled out of the water and then the man has a hand net under him to catch them when they let loose. The crabbers set these lines and take them up again until they figure they've got a fair catch or they're just plumb tired. Then they bring them in to the packers. They get anywhere from two to four dollars a barrel for them, depending on supply and demand of course."

"But, Mr. Flemming," I asked. "If the crabs leave the local waters in winter what happens to the supply? Do you only pack them during the warmer seasons?"

"Oh, the crabbers go out to the Chesapeake Bay waters in winter and use dredges towed by their boats. That is, after the first of December. There's a state law against using dredges before the first. My workers are on pay all year, but right now they only work five days a week. Some days they don't put in a full day's work. They get paid for piece work or at five cents a pound. Some make more than others, depending on how fast they work. I've got one girl here that always gets at least ten dollars a week. She's really a hairpin, that girl! The others average about eight to six dollars a week and there are a couple in there that don't usually make more than four. Some of them don't come in every day; that accounts for it.[15]

"Would you be interested in having a look around inside?" Mr. Flemming had become immersed in his subject, obviously, and was enjoying himself immensely. He probably hadn't talked shop with a stranger in a long time and his sense of authority seemed to please him. He even grew a little wistful. "It might interest you," he said shyly.

Near a door at the north end of the white-washed, beaver-boarded room stood a huge wire basket filled with live, seemingly angry crabs which had just been brought in from the wharf. As we watched, two ragged men raised the basket and placed it within a large iron pot situated over a fire.

"You see, they steam them in the pot maybe forty minutes. Then the crabs are put in the trough over here," Mr. Flemming said. I looked where he pointed. It was a long, round trough with an iron handle at one end. An old Negro was turning the crank at the moment.

"They put them in that trough (there's a batch in it now, I reckon) and he turns the crank until the crabs get thoroughly washed. Then they're ready for the pickers." Here, Mr. Flemming indicated some colored women working at long narrow tables stretching the length of the room on one side. The pickers were seated on stools on either side of the board tables with piles of the freshly steamed crabs between them. Most of them were colored women. They wore white aprons similar to those affected by butchers and grocers, and worked rapidly with bare hands, separating the meat from the shells.

"Hell, it's warmer in here than it is in my office," Mr. Flemming said wryly.

I looked about and discovered a large iron stove in the corner by the cleansing trough. It was literally white hot. "They burn old tire casings," explained Mr. Flemming. "They give off better heat than anything else."

We wandered about the room, watching the workers. They spoke to Mr. Flemming without the deference usual in the relations between employer and employees. I soon realized that their casual attitude came from a lack of caste feeling.

Once back in the office after our tour, I asked about Mr. Flemming's markets.

"Well, very little crabmeat is consumed locally. We ship mostly to New York and the large northern cities, and some of it goes out West."

"What about the oyster business in Portsmouth?"

"*What* oyster business?" he said, laughing. "Portsmouth hasn't got any oyster business anymore.

"Up until 1900 we had the finest oysters on the Atlantic Seaboard out here in Farmer's Creek and the western and eastern branches of the Elizabeth River. Why, in 1900 there were four big oyster plants in Portsmouth and they employed about 5,000 people, including the shuckers, tongers, and the rest. Now there is one little plant operated by a Norfolk packer. It's open only during November and December.

"Why, I can remember when the oyster was one of the principal foods. The best grade could be bought for two bits a quart then. When Portsmouth had a population of 15,000 folks, there were two restaurants on High Street that alone used twenty-five gallons of oysters per week. Now we've got a population of about 50,000 and don't use fifty gallons per week.

"You can't really say just one thing caused this. There are a lot of things to blame. But the main trouble, as anybody can tell you, is that the production has been cut off in Virginia because the packers and folks aren't made to put the oyster shells back in the natural beds.

"There is a natural abundance of seed oysters, but unless they have something to catch onto they're carried on to some other section where they can find something. If the packers were forced by law to put at least a part of their shells back into the beds there would be a lot better supply of oysters around here. Of course, with small production, prices have to be higher and that places them out of the reach of the average consumer.

"I understand that over in England they require every oyster shell taken from a natural rock to be put back after the oysters are opened. That's like it ought to be. The State of Maryland requires one-tenth of all the shells to be put back. But Virginia allows the supply of oysters to be taken away and unless something is done soon there won't be anymore oysters in Virginia.

"Then too, the dredger is kind of hard on the natural supply. Oysters tonged by a right-minded oysterman are *culled,* that is the oysters hanging to the shells are chipped off and allowed to settle back on the rocks where they can mature but the ones raked in by the dredger are wasted.

"Now, an oyster to be ready for the market must measure, in the shell, three and one-half to four inches. Many of the shells brought in have from one to three baby oysters clinging to them. They're just entirely destroyed.

"Another thing that hurts the oyster business in this section is pollution of the waters. That comes from sewer dumpings from the cities nearby and from oil from boats in the harbors and chemicals from industrial plants on the water. The oysters have gotten infected and in order to use them they have to be taken up and replanted in clean water until clarified. This makes production cost more and of course jumps the price to the consumer.

"A man with small capital can't afford to grow these oysters and many folks who have never known any other way of making a living are unemployed. Some of them are on relief and some of them are in jail. They seem to figure that if they get in jail they'll at least get fed and have a roof over their heads. I'm not fooling you there, either. A good many of these oystermen are living in hell right here on earth because of being hungry and cold.

"Most of the people employed in this oyster work are native Americans and pretty decent folks. About two-thirds of them are niggers. As a general rule they are people next to useless in any other kind of industrial plant. They're unskilled, uneducated, and ignorant about any other kind of work.[16]

"I reckon in 1900 there were 15,000 people earning their living in the oyster and crab business in Virginia. Right now there aren't over 2,500 employed in this business."

"That does seem depressing, Mr. Flemming. Surely something can be done about it soon. How long does the oyster season last?"

"About nine months."

"But how did these people earn a living during the other three months?"

"They had work from September to the last of April in oysters. A good many of them were employed in the crab houses in summer, and the others worked in truck fields, digging potatoes, picking beans and so on.

"I tell you, those politicians up at Richmond better get busy if they mean to help their state. There's a lot could be done to help us."

Mr. Flemming's large, red face was set in lines of serious concentration. He plainly showed that he thought of himself as one of the fishermen.

Presently he aroused himself from his absorption with the problem of Virginia's seafood industry and smiled at me. "You shouldn't have got me started. I'm kind of a bug on the subject, I guess." I protested warmly and prepared to leave. "But just the same," he said at the door, frowning slightly, "something ought to be done about it."

[Loc.: VSL/AB, box 183, 9 pp.]

Elsie Wright *by Edith C. Skinner, 10 February 1939*

When the Virginia *Guide* was published in 1940, it noted that the Tanner's Creek estuary (by then the Lafayette River) was "lined with the mansions of the commercial and professional aristocracy." But in the 1870 census the Tanner's Creek section of Norfolk County was the site for a mixed economy of farmers and fishermen, including three generations of Lamberts: the great-grandfather, grandfather, and father of Elsie Wright.[17]

Wright's grandfather Hillory Lambert and his brother William F. Lambert were indicated as oystermen in 1870. Another younger brother, J. S. Lambert, was a farmer who owned no land but nevertheless headed the household, which included William F., his wife, and child; the elder Lamberts, seventy-year old James and fifty-nine-year-old Ann; and their youngest son, Charles. This extended kin group apparently occupied the family homeplace.

Henry J. Lambert, a farmer with nearly two thousand dollars' worth of real estate, lived one household away from the family group above and next to Hillory Lambert. It is likely that Henry (as the oldest son) received the land belonging to his father, James, in keeping with the custom of primogeniture. Since fishing—like farming—also had its seasons, it is probable, too, that the several brothers helped one another on the family farm when they were not working as oystermen.

By 1921, however, when Ellie E. (Elsie) Lambert worked as a clerk for her father in the Lambert Fisheries at Ocean View, the men were no longer oystermen. Their business instead relied primarily on finfish, including shad and spot—among the most valuable and important of the thirty-seven species of fish represented in the state's fishing industry.[18]

Elsie Wright was a fisherman's daughter, a fisherman's granddaughter, and is now a fisherman's wife. She is the daughter of James E. and Mary L. (Carter) Lambert, and the wife of Joseph T. Wright. Joseph was born at Leesburg, Virginia and the son of a civil engineer who traveled to various parts of the United States, finally settling in Mississippi. The son, Joseph, was also educated as a civil engineer and was engaged for several years in the building of roads, bridges and other engineering enterprises. Fourteen years ago, Joseph and Elsie were married after a year's courtship. They have two children: a boy thirteen years of age who attends Blair Junior High School, and a girl twelve who is in the seventh grade of the grammar school. The parents plan to, at least, send the son to college after graduation from high school. Elsie's father did not believe in sending girls to college, so she and her three sisters completed their education at Maury High School.

Ten years ago Joseph changed his business of a civil engineer and went into the fish business with his wife's people. He enjoys the life on the seashore and this business has been a very successful one. A short while ago he took over the management of this fishery, renting the plant from the present owners.

Teddy Lambert, a brother of Mrs. Wright, had owned the fisheries until recently when it went into other hands by foreclosure of a mortgage on the property. This debt had happened because of the fact that the owner had developed cataracts on both eyes, requiring an operation and hospitalization. When going away to the hospital, he had temporarily turned the fisheries over to the wife expecting them to be turned back at his recovery. When he tried to get them back, his wife tried to prove that he was not mentally right; not succeeding, she took the two children, left home, and went to some unknown destination, and he lost the property. Teddy Lambert—whose real name is Edward—had received title to the property in 1936 when his two brothers, James R. and Hiliary E. Lambert, had each assigned his third share to him, for their father had given the fisheries to his three sons in 1922 (probably then retiring from business). He died six years ago. All three of these sons had received college educations, so the brothers had preferred other lines of occupation. Teddy is employed now in an official capacity by his brother-in-law.

The Lambert Fisheries have been very successful, because of the famous Ocean View spot caught here. Mrs. Wright says that the fish feeding on these fishing grounds must find an unusual kind of food for they are better flavored than any other spot and [have] a golden yellow hue, while those of nearby waters are white. James Lambert, the father, made $10,000 in one year from his spot. He was one of the first to establish fishing on a large scale at Ocean View.

[James Lambert's] father was also the owner of a fishery, but his location was at Lambert's Point. His method of fishing was somewhat different from that of the present day. He caught his fish in pounds, which were made by driving stakes or long poles into the water and fastening large nets to them to hold the fish until they could be visited by the fisherman. These nets were knit by his wife and were much better in construction than the ones that are made by machinery at the present day. The present company also uses some nets that are knitted by a woman in Newport News. The other men of the Lambert family did not follow the fish business, but became truckers sending early vegetables to markets in the North and getting good prices for them. This was a lucrative business then, for the large truck with earlier vegetables from farther south had not [yet] cut in on their profits.

At the present day, the methods of catching fish has been changed. While some of the fish, such as shad, [are] still caught in pounds, most of the fish are caught in seines. The season for the former catches is in the early spring and only five Negro men are needed to bring them in. But the seine is hauled from the first of July through November, and about twenty Negroes are employed for the work. The seines are very long nets that are fastened to stakes a long distance from shore, [and] which are drawn onto the beach twice a day at a time set by the tides. The ends of the seines have long ropes attached that are wound on something like a turnstile as the huge net is gradually drawn to shore. The process is aided by men in boats, while the seine is a long way from the shore, and by men standing in the water as the big hauls are brought closer to the beach. Years ago the ropes were wound on [the] turnstile by a number of Negroes pushing the four arms around; at a later period, mules were used to turn the stile; now electricity is employed.

The net is emptied when far enough on the beach to prevent the escape of the fish. Sometimes the catch is enormous, covering a large area on the sand. In former times, the fish [were] placed in small fishcarts with very large wheels, especially designed for navigating in the wet sand. Now a roadway has been made (which can be removed in times of storm) to the water's edge and immense trucks drive right down to the place where the fish are loaded in ice-filled boxes, and drive away to deliver them to the shipper without any transfer. A great many of these fish are sent by Ballard Fish and Oyster Company to all parts of the United States; while others are delivered to wholesale companies in Norfolk, such as the Pender Company, which operates about half of the grocery stores in eastern Virginia and North Carolina. A regular supply is also delivered to the retail fish markets of Norfolk and Portsmouth.[19]

The Wright family live almost directly opposite the fisheries. Their home, a recent purchase, was built about sixty years ago for a clubhouse. It is a bungalow with a wide front porch across the front. There is a storm door, as well as the main door into the house, used during the winter; and these are in the center of the front and open into the living room, which is a very wide and long room. Two bedrooms on either side open into the living room, while the entrance to the dining room is at the back of the room. A baby grand piano stands on one side of the front door and several pieces of overstuffed furniture are placed in the front half of the room, which is divided in two sections by the placing of the davenport across it.

Although Mrs. Wright had been interrupted in the self-assigned task of painting some woodwork—having paint splotches on her arms and clothes—she was very cordial and gave the information written in this article. She also said that her maternal grandfather, named Carter, was born on a plantation on James River and was a direct descendant of "King" Carter, so well known in colonial history and from whom some famous persons are descended, including General Robert E. Lee. Her paternal grandmother was a milliner in Norfolk before marriage and went on a trip to New York on the first steamship sailing there, taking seven days for the trip. All of her family and friends [bid] her farewell as if they never expected to see her again.

[Loc.: VSL/AB, box 178, 4 pp., 1,326 wds.]

(Opposite) Northumberland County, Virginia. The day's catch, Mundy Point, near Kinsale.
Photo by W. Lincoln Highton. VSL/PC. [A9-10679]

Making a Living on the Water: Photographs of "Boats up the River"

Boat's up the river,
And it won't come down,
Believe to my soul, babe,
I'm water bound.[20]

Middlesex County, Virginia.
Fishermen with warehousemen
from the Railway Express
Agency on the dock at
Urbanna.
Photo by W. Lincoln Highton.
VSL/PC. [43437]

Essex County, Virginia.
Loading lumber at
Tappahannock.
Photo by W. Lincoln Highton.
VSL/PC. [8650]

Loading lumber for Baltimore
from the Northern Neck.
Photo by W. Lincoln Highton.
VSL/PC. [43563]

Express boat for Baltimore
loading freight.
Photo by W. Lincoln Highton.
VSL/PC. [43441]

Newport News, Virginia.
September 1936.
Fishing boats in the harbor.
Photo by Paul Carter.
[LC-USF33-10162-M]

Newport News, Virginia.
September 1936.
Fishing boats in the harbor.
Photo by Paul Carter.
[LC-USF33-10163-M4]

Charlie Johnson *by Edith C. Skinner, 24 February 1939*

Charlie Johnson fished from a rowboat in the Elizabeth River near the Campostella Bridge, but he declared he caught all the different kinds of fish—though not so many—that the Lambert Fishery got at its Ocean View site. Unlike the Lamberts, however, who sold to large distributors that marketed fish nationwide, such as Ballard Fish and Oyster Company, or to the Pender Company grocery store chain, Johnson sold his fish to poor folks in his own neighborhood for whatever price they were able or willing to pay.

Charlie Johnson is a short, slender Negro with a shuffling walk, caused by the fact that his eyesight is very bad and makes him move along cautiously. His clothes were very much worn and one of his sleeves was ripped half way out of his coat. As he talked, he nervously picked at a small streak of dirt on his sleeve, evidently thinking it was a strand of thread.

Charlie was born in Plymouth, North Carolina fifty-six years ago, and was one of twelve children. The parents lost nine of their babies in infancy and only raised this man, a younger brother, and sister. Charlie received very little schooling, for when he was nine years old, his father died and a part of the support of the family shifted to his young shoulders. He went to work then and earned twenty-five cents a day. The mother of the family did not stay a widow long, for she made two matrimonial ventures after the death of her first husband, but she outlived both of these men. There were no other children. Now she is ninety-one years old and lives in the country in North Carolina with a cousin.

Charlie married about thirty years ago to Mary Williams, one year his junior. Five children were born to this couple, but none of them survived babyhood. The father remarked: "I'se glad dat none of dem chillun lived, I is, on 'count of de way youn' folks does des days. Most en all goes astray. Den, how yer goin' a raise yer chillen properly and make 'em behave, lessen yer sometimes chastise dem. Den, what happens? Yer has de law agin yer. Yes, ma'am, I'se glad dey is all gone. 'Nother thin', how cud I take car' o' dem, de way things is nowadays, cullid folks has a hard row to trabel, I tells yer."[21]

"How do you make a living?" I inquired.

"Oh, I fishes, I do. I takes a rowboat and goes out in der big ribber near de Campostella Bridge an' I fish with hook and line. I done catch all de diffent kinds of fish dat dey ketches at Ocean View, even if tain't so many. I ketches diffent kinds of fish at diffent times o' de year. Lets see, I's ketched: croakers, white perch, eels."

"What do you do with eels?" I interrupted.

"Why, lots of folks like eels, they skin an' eat 'em. Den I ketches trout, an' bluenose perch, an' brown perch, an' catfish, an' rock, an' even drum. Lots o' toadfish gits on my line, but I jest chunk dem back into de wadder again, for nobody wants toads. Dere's something else I sometimes ketches, dat's crabs. But I don't like foolin' wid dem fellers. Yer has to be quick to git ahaid of crabs, an' dey don't care who dey bites. Dey jest as soon bite through yer shoe as not an' rather. It's on a'count o' my bad eyes dat I don't fool 'long wid dem much."

"Do you ever use a pole for fishing?" I put in.

"Oh, yes, lots of times. When de wedder is not so good, an' I'se 'fraid maybe dere'll be a squall, I don't go in no boat, causin' I cain't see good enuf to make much haidway in rowin'

Norfolk, Virginia. March 1941. Backwater. Photo by John Vachon. [LC-USF34-62549-D]

fast and gittin' to shore in a hurry. So when I think dere's goin' to be fallin' wedder, I fishes from de bridge, for I don't want no duckin'. I has to use a long pole on de bridge to reach de wadder."

"When does your fishing season begin?" I questioned.

"Wal, I thinks I ken start fishin' next week, if de wedder stays fine like dis. Den I keeps on fishin' 'til 'mos' Chris'mus."

"How do you make a living the rest of the year?" I queried.

"Wal, I knows how to put pumps for wadder in de groun', so some folks in de country has me do dat. Den I finds odder odd jobs to do. I ain't always bin no fisherman. When I furst come to town, I was a helper to a plasterer. Den when wurk got slack, I went to wurk in a lime kiln. 'Nother time, I wurked at a place where dey makes fertilizers for farm land. I jest bin at dis fishin' business fibe, six years, after my eyes gits worse. Thirty-two years 'go, I got hit plumb on de side ov my haid and I cain't see nohow. By en by det gits better, but de doctor says, I'd lose my vision in a year. But I kin still see some. One doctor gimme some thick glasses, and I got 'long fine 'til I broke 'em, den I looks everywhere for some more, but I cain't fin' no more like dem. But de doctors won't gimme no more glasses, dey says tain't no use."

"Do you get good prices for your fish?" I asked, wishing to complete that subject.

"Wal, I sells dem in de neighborhood. Sometimes de prices is gud, sometimes pore, but I jest lets de people set deir own prices, cause dey knows what dey is willing to pay, and I don't. Dey's mos'ly fair. Mos' folks 'round here don't have much money, yer know."

"I guess you are getting along all right then," I ventured to say.

"Wal, my wife and me'd have a tough pull, if it wa'n't for her brother. We all lives together. He's an oysterman. My wife bin keeping house for him an' lookin' after his chillen for seben years, eber since his wife ran off and left him. She was crazy about goin' to dances, an' would set out jest when he was comin' home an' den danced all night. When her husband remonstrated wid her, she ups an' leabes, takin' free o' de chillen wid her, an' leabes four chillen here, two boys and two girls. De younges' is nine. Dey didn't git no di-vorce, causen he ain't neber wanted to marry agin an' I don' reckon she has, anyway she's up north somewhar."

The family lives in a house, built with one wall joined to another house, and constructed of clapboard, which is now practically bare of paint. There should have been three steps to the front porch, but the bottom one is completely gone, the other two are broken in places. The only water to the house runs to the sink in the kitchen, the toilet is in the back yard. The only heat is in the range in the kitchen, using wood or coal, and light is obtained from old-fashioned kerosene lamps. The rent is two dollars a week. I did not go inside of the house, but I glanced in the front window, seeing a bureau in the corner. It was neatly arranged with a white scarf, a toilet set of brush, comb and mirror, also a few trinkets, such as two small china dogs and a china basket containing two tiny kittens.

Charlie seems to be very religious and attends church services on Sunday and midweek. He says the happenings of the present day are a fulfillment of prophecy in the Bible: "Yer know de Good Book says at de en' o' time, dere'll be earthquakes, an' famines, an' pestilence, an' wars, an' al'll be confusion."

[Loc.: VSL/AB, box 178, 4 pp., 1,261 wds.]

Louisa Chase *by Edith C. Skinner, 17 February 1939*

In contrast to Charlie Johnson's experiences, Louisa Chase's husband, John, apparently spent most of his life working in marine-related occupations in Baltimore and New York, as well as in Norfolk. And though Chase also used a rowboat for fishing, he did so in the waters of the Chesapeake Bay out from Willoughby Spit—a narrow peninsula of sand claimed in 1680 by Madam Thomas Willoughby.[22]

To get to his fishing grounds, John Chase had to travel back and forth to the beach six days a week by streetcar. Considering the racial tension on Newport News streetcars alleged in the incident related by Jimmie Garrett (see introductory remarks for chapter 4), the late-night trip may not have been entirely without hazard. Once at the spit, Chase then had to rely on the good will of a white resident to provide a place for him to sleep and to keep his boat when it was not in use. Among his activities as an "independent fisherman," Chase shucked oysters and dug clams during periods when he could not fish. He also depended on selling his catch in his own neighborhood but evidently could not always collect from his debtors. Thus Louisa reported in the interview that he was at the time owed the amount of almost ten days' earnings for clams sold on trust.

Louisa Chase's testimony hints at some of the complex connections between white society and the conditions of African Americans' labor and social interactions. It further suggests the underlying patterns of movement operating within the maritime industry, whether one was working the docks or following the fish.[23]

Louisa Chase was born forty-two years ago in King and Queen County, Virginia, where her father worked on a farm. Then they moved to Baltimore. The mother died when her daughter was scarcely more than a baby; the father when she was ten years old. A cousin took the orphan for a while, but she was soon given into custody of a white family who "raised" her, "treating her like a member of the family." However, she received very little schooling. She said, "I helped myself learn to read." Since she was young when she left her family, she knows very little about them.

Louisa was married when sixteen years of age to John Chase, a widower who was thirteen years her senior. The husband spent a great part of his life in Norfolk, but when he met his wife he was living in Baltimore and working as a longshoreman, because he received better wages than he did as an independent fisherman. He also tried living in New York, but he could live cheaper and was better satisfied in Norfolk, so he moved his family here ten years ago. There was only one child, a daughter, born to them. She is nearly twenty-four years old and was married six years ago, making her home in New York City. The girl did not receive much education although she did learn to read and write.

John Chase makes his living from the middle of April to the last of November by fishing. At other parts of the year, he shucks oysters for an oyster company or digs clams which he sells to colored people in his own neighborhood. He sells a great many of them to the Long-shoreman's Club, located about three blocks from his home. Sometimes he has a hard time collecting the money due on clams he has trusted his customers with. Right now over twenty dollars is past due.

When John fishes, he goes out in a boat at Willoughby Beach. His custom is to leave downtown where he lives, catch the eleven o'clock streetcar, which is the last at night to go to Willoughby and go to the home of a white resident of this beach who has granted him permission to sleep in his basement and keep his boat on his premises. At four o'clock in the morning, he gets up, launches his boat and rows to the best fishing grounds where he fishes until ten in the morning. His wife prepares a hearty meal for him before he sets out and also gives him a lunch. When he has his catch, he goes back to his home, eats his breakfast, then sells the fish through the streets of his neighborhood. He averages between two or three dollars a day and works six days a week, unless the weather is too bad for safety. Since he owns his boat, the only expenses are the lines and, sometimes, the bait. But he uses the real sportsman's kind of fishing, with hook and line. He generally uses "swimp" as the wife calls the bait, but more correctly "shrimp," which is a small water animal having a crustlike shell. He can also use hard or soft-shelled crabs, which he may catch a little closer to shore than the fishing grounds. Sometimes he buys his bait the night before in order to get at his self-appointed job early in the morning.

The family home is located on a short narrow street, less than a block in length, and they have lived here eight years. It is a six-room residence, built of clapboard and painted white, renting for fifteen dollars a month. A porch runs the width of the house. The front door leads into a narrow hallway with the living room on one side and a narrow, straight flight of stairs to the second floor on the other. A door at the back of the hall probably opens into the dining room. The living room door was partly opened showing a narrow library table, covered with a runner, setting in a slanting position across the center of the room. It contains a radio and probably the usual living room furniture. Since there was no heat in the living room, the visitor was conducted to the front bedroom on the second floor where there was heat from a small wood stove. The hot embers of the very low fire showed through small holes burned in the sides of the stove, causing one to wonder if with a few more burnt places the heater would not fall to pieces and set the house on fire. A set of bedroom furniture was in this room. A nice looking spread covered the double bed in one corner, while a bureau set on one side of the chimney, the dressing table with its caned seat before it was on the other side. There were also several chairs and a table. The mantel was draped with a somewhat soiled white lambrequin and was used more for convenience than decoration, since it contained only a water glass, a bottle of medicine and a few other small objects, irregularly placed upon it. The bedroom opened on an upper back porch, which ran past two other rooms to the end of the house. One of these rooms is rented out to a lodger, in order to cut down the cost of rent.

Until about six years ago, Louisa worked as a domestic in the home of a white family. Then her health broke down. But from the appearance of this woman, she would seem to be strong, for she is a large, hefty person with a full round face. The face is covered with dark spots, giving the impression that she has had smallpox. However, the bad health is caused by nervousness. She has had an acute attack since Christmas, requiring a two-weeks' stay at a local hospital. There was a little girl of five years of age, who kept running back and forth from the room to the porch. Louisa said that this was an adopted child and had attended kindergarten until she was taken sick recently. The child is the offspring of an unwed mother who was very glad to be relieved of the child at birth, but who now refuses to sign papers of adoption. The foster mother fears that after she has given the child opportunities to amount to something, the real mother will take her away from her. This causes her to worry a great deal.[24]

[Loc.: VSL/AB, box 178, 4 pp., 1,088 wds.]

George and Amos Harris *by Sarah W. Moore, no interview date given*

With their jointly occupied, old houseboat tied up at Scott's Creek, George and Amos Harris—former oystermen turned eel catchers—were among those folks whose plight troubled crabmeat packer John Flemming Jr. in 1939. Although the brothers Harris claimed to be sons of a fisherman themselves and to have fished all their lives, George Harris admonished his son that "he warn't to be no fisherman" because "there ain't no chance now for a white man to make his living a'fishing."

The Harrises and Flemming all agreed, however, on the need for a resurvey of the state's "natural oyster rocks," the existence of which determined whether a site could be leased to private oyster planters or fished as common ground by independent watermen. Certain that such a survey would bring an indictment against big planters for wrongfully claiming public rock forbidden to them, it was the only prayer the Harrises had left.

George and Amos Harris, gnarled veterans of strong winds and restless waters, were sons of a fisherman and found no quarrel with their early environment, each becoming a fisherman at an age so early in his memory that the date is uncertain. However, both seem certain they attended school, though for how long is beyond their ability to state.

One, Mr. George, was married and had a family. His two children, he will tell you with pride, finished high school. The lanky old man with gray hair and horizon-seeking blue eyes snarls somewhat when he says, "That boy of mine had it drilled inter him that he warn't to be no fisherman. I said, 'Son, you just go to work and larn yerself a trade cause there ain't no chance now for a white man to make his living a'fishing.' He knowed I meant it too, 'cause now he's a'workin in the Navy Yard and doing fine." [25]

He looks you in the eye when he talks to you, does Mr. George, and you sense a deep well of strength in the old fellow, despite his years. "The hell of the thing is, Miss, if you don't mind an old futz cussin," Mr. Amos broke in plaintively, no smile on his thin, drawn face, "they just ain't no way for us to make a thing. Ain't a thing around here worth a crawdad hole no more." Mr. George looked carefully at Mr. Amos and Mr. Amos picked up a stick from the ground and began breaking it in his hands. Mr. George cleared his throat. It was clear he dominated his younger brother, perhaps by virtue of his having been married. Mr. Amos was a bachelor.

"You see, Miss, it's this a'way. We used to make a right fair living once. We tonged oysters when the time was right and when it warn't, why we took it kinder easy and caught crabs. We did right well that a-way. But now the pollution has ruined our oysters and the big packers is forced the little man off'n the public rocks. And they just ain't no way for us to make anything."

Mr. George looked down at the sand, scuffling his feet. Mr. Amos looked up at me and nodded in solemn agreement to his brother's words, then bent over to pick up another twig to break up. I suddenly noticed that each of the old brothers had patched his boots with pieces of tire-tube and wire. Their overalls were patched too with curious types of materials, such as sailcloth and oilcloth. Altogether they were charming, with their blend of aged gray hairs and resilient strength.

"But aren't you getting any oysters this season?" I asked. "No mam," Mr. George replied, "The only thing we can do now is to catch a few eels. You see that trap in the water by the boat?" I turned toward the boat near where we were standing. I didn't see anything at first but he pointed a twisted brown finger and I finally saw the trap. It was a curious box-shaped object made of wire. I could just see a huddle of dark, attenuated things inside the trap. The eels looked very much like plump glistening snakes.

"What on earth do you do with them?" I asked, hardly able to restrain a shudder. The brothers looked at me quickly, then exchanged amused glances. "Why, Miss," Mr. Amos said, "Eels is just like chicken!" "Yes mam," Mr. George said, "We go out most every night and set our eel pots and put the catch in that there trap until we get enough to ship. Then we ship 'em to New York. I hear them Eyetalians up there likes 'em fine." He reached into a bulging hip pocket and produced a shapeless hunk of black chewing tobacco and a knife. He cut off two pieces, gave Mr. Amos one, and pointed carelessly at me with the evil-looking fishing knife.

"Tell you, Miss, what we oystermen need is a resurvey of the public rocks. These cussed big packers have bought up all them oyster beds they could get and they leased so much of the public rocks that they got control of the whole works. A man like myself and Amos here don't even have a prayer no more."

"That's the truth," Mr. Amos said, nodding sagely. After a moment of chewing and concentration Mr. George continued. "I figure that if there was a resurvey made they'd find these here packers have got too much territory staked off that they ain't payin' no taxes on."

Mr. Amos turned around politely and spat in the other direction. He wiped his mouth furtively. "I figure that way too," he said.

The two old men stood and silently reflected for a few minutes with something of mute commiseration for each other in their attitudes. I took the opportunity to examine their boat tied up along side the western bank of Scott's Creek. The ancient and dilapidated houseboat rested low in the gray water, perhaps twenty feet off the bank. The dirty white paint was flaked on her ragged deck structures, but the hull had evidently received a fresh coat of paint not long before for it glistened a dull red in the pale sunlight. The small, newer motorboat tied to the stern also looked recently painted.

Mr. George noticed me staring at his boat. "Miss, we've been a'living on that old floating shanty for twenty year now, me and Amos here. You know, it's right comfortable. Amos, he rigged us up a bathtub a couple year ago with a pumping arrangement leading over the side, so you might say it's as good as most land houses and a heap better than a lot of them. And there ain't no rent and no taxes to pay. Course we have to carry our drinking water in a barrel now and then but it ain't much trouble and I figure it's worth it all in all."

Mr. Amos pawed the sand with his boot and snickered. "Smells awful fishy out there sometimes when we've had a haul aboard for a day or two. That old barge seen many a fish come aboard in her day."

Mr. George gave his brother a sardonic glance. "You always was a sissified cuss!" At this, both old men broke into an embarrassed, shrill laughter. Mr. Amos prodded Mr. George in the ribs gently. They subsided.

"How do you feel about labor unions and such organizations? You must have some experience of them here in Portsmouth."

Mr. George, as usual, took the answer upon himself. "Why, Miss, I can't say as I've had much to do with such carryings on. But I figure this a'way: I figure unions ain't never helped working folks and I can't see as how they would help us oystermen neither. There's a few of them union organizers come diddling around Portsmouth now and then but most of us folks don't pay them no mind. I figure the little fisherman won't never be no better off until the State of Virginia does something for us. They got to make the big companies be fair to the little man, but I ain't seen no union do it for the fishing folks yet and I ain't thinking they're a'going to pay no serious mind to them red fellows." [26]

Mr. Amos lifted a timid glance from beneath heavy, gray eyebrows. "But some of them factory unions seems to be doing some good. They seems to work right well now and then."

"I don't put no trust in anything but the govemint," fiercely countered Mr. George. "I don't have no dealings with them red fellers." He spat contemptuously.

"Ain't necessarily reds, now George."

"I hear they is."

That decided it. Mr. Amos retired to a bewildered silence. Mr. George eyed me suspiciously. "You ain't no red, Miss?"

I assured him that I wasn't a "red." It seemed to relieve him. He laughed amiably.

"I wasn't thinking you was. No harm done. I was reading in the paper t'other day where a lot of these college girls is joining the reds these days. Seems like a pity, don't it? Well, I reckon me and Amos better be getting along. Getting nigh on lunch time, I reckon."

They ambled along the sand toward a rotted pier where they no doubt had a row boat waiting. Their movements were neither ambitiously rapid nor snail-like. Mr. George and Mr. Amos stepped certainly toward their common destination.

[Loc.: VSL/AB, box 191, 6 pp.]

7 Making a Living in the Trades and Business
"A HIGH STANDARD OF OUTPUT"

I always had a good trade, my trade being the cream of the crop. —*John S. Powell*

"The tempo of American business has speeded up to an almost hysterical pitch," wrote a state adviser on National Youth Administration residential projects in Virginia. And the challenge he saw for the NYA in 1938 was to "fit young men and women for working under such conditions without losing their sense of balance." Individuals in other settings also spoke of hurrying to keep up with the speed of machines, and increasing numbers of automobiles added possibilities for geographic as well as social mobility in the workplace.[1]

Accepted patterns that had earlier guided one's choice or training in a trade or contributed to success in business were altered in the 1930s. In an age of new technologies, the training of new skills would be necessary and expected. But no indication of that was given on 26 June 1935 when the NYA was established. Rather, President Roosevelt's announcement emphasized doing "something for the Nation's unemployed": "We can ill afford to lose the skill and energy of these young men and women. They must have their chance in school, their turn as apprentices, and their opportunity for jobs—a chance to earn for themselves."[2]

At its outset, the NYA programs were conducted locally and trained young people as domestics, carpenters, and brickmasons—occupational skills and knowledge that many could gain from family or other community members by already existing informal arrangements. It was by just such traditional forms of apprenticeship that most of the individuals in this chapter learned their trades.

The purpose of helping young people keep their "sense of balance in business," claimed later by Bernard Fagelson for the NYA "Civil Defense" residential projects, was, in fact, directed toward creating and conditioning a mobile and skilled body of urban, defense, and industrial workers, not necessarily toward developing the entrepreneurial skills of managers or independent businessmen and -women. In replacing local self-help and educational programs with required residence at some remove from one's home environment and with formalized instruction to fit the needs of industry, however, the NYA (and other New Deal programs) may have inadvertently provided the model for vocational training by experts and professionals in modern-day corporate America.[3]

Many of the merchants and business leaders of the New South in the late nineteenth century fit the general profile described by historian Edward Ayers. That is, they were the children of an earlier "broad range of Southern landowners," and the course of their rise in business was not usually direct. They often began work in local stores near their homes before setting out in "their teens and early twenties" to look for better prospects in nearby counties and cities. There they worked long enough in a business "to learn its ways and accumulate some capital. Then they either became partners in that business or opened another in the same line. Eventually they broadened their investments into real estate, banks or other businesses." In addition, these men quite often emphasized affiliations with various secular organizations and booster groups over church membership.[4]

The example of Henry Mauze Darnall, a first cousin of Nannie Isabel Webb Price (in chapter 1), fits the pattern of the New South business leader well. Born in 1857 in Franklin County, Darnall attended local schools and clerked in a country store there. Later he became superintendent of a tobacco factory and then traveled for a wholesale shoe firm in Lynchburg. After moving to Roanoke in 1885, he worked in banking and insurance and in 1893 organized the State Bankers' Association. He was secretary and treasurer of the Roanoke Land and Improvement Company and for some years served in the same positions for the Roanoke Gas and Water Company. Before becoming the commissioner of revenue in 1910, he had also served on the city council and the city school board and was author of the city's "present Magisterial system" (in 1912). Darnall was the state secretary of the Grand Lodge Knights of Pythias, a member of the Red Men and the Odd Fellows, and a Presbyterian.[5]

Henry Darnall moved to the "Magic City" of Roanoke at a time when it was growing rapidly as a transportation and marketing center, and the prospects for his success as a business leader were greatly enhanced by that fact. By 1933, Roanoke would be one of the ten wholesale trade centers serving the state of Virginia and would include within its territory Alleghany County. With more than eight million dollars in retail sales, Alleghany County ranked second only to Roanoke itself in its territory, in terms of sales, wages paid, and the value of its products in 1929—even though that year was not a harbinger of good business news to come.[6]

Certainly, location, timing, and supply and demand—as well as knowing one's competitors—were all critical factors affecting one's commercial success. Cleveland Buchanan (in chapter 4) was well aware of these things when he judged the market in Alleghany County for his services as an African American undertaker and deliberately made the decision to move to Covington. Having the experience and knowing his business at the critical time when an opportunity presented itself helped Thomas McCaleb along on his career path toward business owner. Prior to that he had lived and worked in Covington, first as a hardware store salesman and then as a clerk and a manager in both independently owned groceries and chain stores. Sometimes the timing just was not right: in the depression years people could do without photographs before they went without groceries. Thus when his father died at a relatively young age, George Hodges took over as photographer in the family's photography studio, but within a few years he had to quit and go to work in the paper mill. He returned to his career in photography after World War II, however, and worked in his own studio in Portsmouth until he retired.

Richmond, Virginia. Sixth Street Market. Photo by W. Lincoln Highton. VSL/PC [43486]

Norfolk, Virginia. March 1941. An iceman.
Photo by John Vachon.
[LC-USF34-62489-D]

Almost all of the persons in this chapter were small tradesmen. Although most had some prior knowledge or apprenticeship in their trade or experience in some family business beforehand, not all of them started out in the trades at which they were working when they were interviewed by VWP workers. Roxy Dodson became an operator of a boardinghouse after her union activities at the local cotton mill caused her to lose her job in the factory. At previous times in her life, however, she had worked in her father's cleaning establishment in Danville.

On the other hand, William D. Deal (this chapter) and F. W. Lilly (in the next chapter) were both forced out of their jobs in different sectors of public work by the ruse of a physical examination required when they reached the age of forty-five. Both had worked for several decades on their jobs—Lilly at the Westvaco pulp and paper mill in Covington, Virginia, and Deal in the coal mines of Fayette County, West Virginia—before their forced retirement. They shared with many other men the negative effects of impersonal bureaucratic regulation imposed by the industrialized sector on different occupational groups.

The responses of the two men to the situation reflect on other aspects of their personality and culture. Both men were angry and bitter about the accumulated years of experience, skills, and loyalty that were laid waste by an economic decision that devalued and was unmindful of those qualities. In addition, both shared a deep distrust of politics, a belief in the futility of voting, and a strong resentment of taxes. The interviews indicate that Deal and Lilly were both opinionated and outspoken men as well, and perhaps this speaks to strong personalities that were determined to overcome such obstacles.

In both cases, these men fell back on the occupations of their fathers, which they too had learned in their youth. Lilly's father had been a blacksmith, and after his death, the son had been apprenticed to another well-known blacksmith in the area. When Mary S. Venable interviewed him, Lilly had been working as a blacksmith since the time he had been declared "too old" by the pulp mill's examination. William Deal's father had been a shoemaker, so W. D. Deal subsequently opened his shoe repair shop and continued working at that occupation. Certainly, VWP texts show that other men in the same circumstances as Lilly and Deal did not fare so well; some worked at odd jobs for a while and began to fail, and others never worked again.[7]

All in all, a life in the trades or business could offer some amount of personal satisfaction, dignity, and pride and a measure of control over one's time and labor that was not so possible for most wage workers subject to the sound of the factory whistle. And in some cases, such as that of Marvin Broyhill (in chapter 3) in the building trades, one might achieve a sufficient degree of respect and success to be referred to as "a captain of industry" or, in barber John Powell's case, as "a knight of the razor."[8]

Mr. John S. Powell *by Susie R. C. Byrd, no interview date given*

African Americans have long occupied and even dominated some trades, such as that of barber. In 1734, a South Carolina planter advertised the services of a slave who had "serv'd his time to a Barber" and was available for hire. Although John Powell allowed that he knew "the barber trade inside out," he also chided Susie Byrd for expecting him at his age—he was born about 1867—to know about the trade "'fore the war." Despite his protest, he went on to give a good accounting of older Richmond barbers he knew, in person or by reputation, some of whom had been slaves.[9]

By some accounts, Powell began working as a porter in the shop of barber William B. Lyons in 1879 and was an apprentice to Lyons two years later. When Powell bought the business from Lyons in 1900, the collection of gilded personal shaving mugs and some of the customers they belonged to—both of which had been accumulating from the late 1850s—came with it. One of these customers, Samuel P. Waddill, the clerk of the Henrico Court, was considered "one of the assets" of the shop when Powell bought it. In 1934, Waddill's patronage, which began in 1864, had been continuous for some seventy years even though the shop had changed location several times in that period.[10]

"So you want to know about the starting of the barber trade, how old do you think I am anyway? Won't guess will you, well, I'll tell you, I am sixty-eight, so how you 'speck me to know what went on 'fore the war? But I know. I know the barber trade inside out, why I been in a shop since I was nine years old. Well, let's get started. What you want to know first? I ain't a educated man, though I rekon I talk like one. Education ain't all book learning anyway. What you mean? Do you want me to tell you first how I got my start, or how the barbers way back got started? Well I am going to tell you how Negroes come to go into business.

"In slavery times, certain Negroes, or I rekon I should of said slaves, was subject to shaving their masters. The slaves that the masters would pick to do it was usually part white—many times being their own sons—and wanting to give them some easy task, they let them shave them. As time went on, they practice on themselves and other slaves, they would [then] go to [barbering for] their masters. So the first men to go into the barber trade learned from the common practice of waiting on their masters. Some of these men got paid for doing this; several saved their money, bought their freedom, and set up a little business of their own. One or two were helped by their white fathers.

"Yes, I know their names and I will tell you later. John Graves was one of these, so was Dick Baker. But the one I know best was my old boss, the man I learned the trade under, Mr. William B. Lyons. He used to be his father's barber. He got paid well for his work, soon was able to buy his freedom. And his father set him up in business. As I said, he was the son of Mr. Lyons, one of the wealthiest men in the city. They lived where the Westmoreland Chief was located until last year.

"William B. Lyons and Hill went into business together, around 1855. They had their shop on Broad Street, between Elizabeth and Ninth Streets. A few years later they moved their barber shop to Fifteenth and Main Streets, under the St. Charles Hotel. Lyons dissolved partners in 1865. At that time he was the most prominent colored man of his day. He served on all juries, was thought well of by all, both white and colored, and supposed to be wealthy. He ran his barber shop until 1900, then he sold it out to me. Before I go into that, I'll tell you the names of the most prominent barbers at that time and before.

"Lomax Smith ran a barber shop in the old Exchange Hotel. I believe he got started in about the same way as Lyons. He left his work and went as a soldier in the Confederate Army. They say he was a bugler. I don't know what company he was with, but I know it caused a lot of talk at the time. Then there was William Ferguson, William Mundin, and Richard Baker in old Manchester [a former independent post office in Richmond]. Oh, yes, John Graves. I think that takes in as far as I know before the Civil War.[11]

"Oh, bye-the-bye, I forgot to mention two very prominent barbers. They were R. S. Hopson and John Scott. Old man Hopson was a man that bought his freedom. He was able to get on well in business, buy property and he used some of his property to help slaves get away.[12]

"Now since the war the most prominent barbers were: William I. White, most excellent Christian gentleman that ever lived in Richmond. Oliver and Robinson, Ben Harris, Powerton Johnson, James Sampson and Buddy Chappell. These had shops on Broad Street. Now to Main Street, we have Peyton and Long. Peyton got to be a very wealthy man in the city. R. M. Clark came here in '67, worked for Lyons and opened his shop on Main Street. William Tennant made quite a little fortune out of it. I guess you might mention Miles Debress', he made a fortune out of the business they say, but I think it was also speculation.

"Now you want me to tell you about my start. I went to work for W. B. Lyons in 1879 as a porter boy. I worked for him until 1885 as porter boy. This was how I learned the trade, I did anything that needed to be done. I was a bootblack, later I made lather, then I started shaving my friends. Then Mr. Lyons gave me lessons, and then he started me off on his free customers. I didn't tell you about that man did I? Well Mr. Lyons always had a free customer so we could practice on. (He [also] had two other porter boys.) This man [the free customer] that he had so long was Buck Fisher from Manchester, who sold old bony horses [for] from one dollar up to three. We would have drunks to work on too. He couldn't teach us on our friends because the shop was all white, and you know what would happen if a colored boy came in an' sat down for a shave or haircut. Also people had more time then and they wouldn't mind the porter boy working on him, if he could take a nap in the chair.

"All of these people taught us what I needed, and in 1900 I bought the shop from Mr. Lyon.

I paid him a good price for it too. I got the money to buy it from saving my money that I made in wages and in tips. I was a hard worker, and wouldn't let anything pass me. I carried the business on up until 1936 when I retired. I had from three to six barbers and two or three porter boys. Lord, yes, I have taught at least fifty the trade, many of them going out and making good.

"Now my trade was of the better class of white people. Many of my people were the richest in the city. I went to some of my customer's houses because they didn't want to come to the shop. Many of the richest old men I have given their last earthly shave to. W. S. Fogs was the richest man in town, and I always went to his house to shave him and cut his hair and I was well paid for it too. My mugs were the largest collection of any in America. I had the names in gold of my best customers. I have had several pictures taken of them and me, and [a] long write up too. When I retired, the *Times Dispatch* had a two hundred dollar write up of me with pictures of the most famous mugs, and I got letters from all over the world—some from the men, others from their relatives.[13]

"I'll tell you, barber business has certainly changed from when I started out. Of course, the instruments are about the same. Well, they are razors, shears and clippers. When I started they didn't have anything but the hand clippers, now they have the electric clippers. I didn't explain the shears. There are two types: the German type with no finger brace and the French type with a brace for the small fingers. The other implements are horns [hones] (I like the water horn best. It is a soft clay colored stone used to get a very fine edge on a razor), straps (leather and canvas), combs (hard leather and bone), brushes (three types: hair, hair dusters, and leather brush), and mugs. I have already told you about my mugs. Today the chairs are so much easier to handle. When I started out, the chairs reclined but now they do everything.

"You know that barber bill has been defeated every time in Virginia. I think it is because there is so much sympathy for the colored barbers, because the whites have taken it away from them. You don't find many young men taken to barbering as a life work. One thing that stops them is the child labor law that won't let children learn the trade young, and after they reach sixteen, they feel like they know it all. When I started out we didn't have to pay any tax or license but now it is high. Now you have to pay twenty dollars on the first three chairs, and ten dollars extra on each other chair.

"You know in those days a barber was a doctor, as well as a barber. Do you know how the pole came into being in front of the barber shop? If you want me to tell you, I will. You see, in the beginning, the pole was red and white and at the top it had a gore on it. The red stood for blood and blood letting. The white for bandages and the gore was used to catch the blood in.

"Ever since I have been in the barbering business I have sold leeches. But I don't sell or use the local ones, they are no good. I always got mine from Sweden. Doctors say that it is not good to use these, but I think that way of letting blood is better than the way they have today. Do you know about cupping? Well you take a rubber bulb and after you put the leech on the place that you wanted the blood drawn from, and the leech has dropped off, you cover the place with the bulb or cup and draw as much blood as you wanted. If you didn't use the cup, then you would use the gore. After the leech had dropped off, you would take a piece of paper and put it in a glass and light it, then put it where you wanted the blood drawn from and as much as you wanted would come in the gore. I still think that is the best way to draw blood. Then we would bandage the place, sometimes it didn't stop bleeding right away, then I would use other methods. Nowadays the poles in front of the barber shops are red, white

Harrisonburg, Virginia. January 1941. A barber. Photo by John Vachon. [LC-USE6-00206-D]

and blue, and most of them have light bulbs on top of them. Some shops used to pull teeth too. I don't know much about that.

"Oh yes, let me see, I'll tell you about the powder business. You know people buy powder in these fancy boxes, the smaller the box the more they pay. But don't you know they are getting fooled. I made all the powder we used at my shop. Do you know that all powder is made out of either rice or corn starch? I used rice, had it grinded very fine and used a rose perfume to give it that sweet smell. I used to put it up in boxes and sell it very high. People would come and get it; I also used it on my customers. These things were part of the special services I had to offer, and I always had a good trade, my trade being the cream of the crop."

[Loc.: VSL/AB, box 191, 5 pp.]

Mrs. Nana Cipriani   *by Everett Anderson, 10 February 1939*

The stem of the tobacco plant—which was necessarily purchased with "the leaf from the farmer"—could represent as much as one-third of the leaf's cost, required further expense to remove by hand or by machine, and was largely "pure waste for the manufacturer." Tobacco companies such as R. J. Reynolds sold some stems from their bright-leaf tobacco to the Virginia-Carolina Chemical Company to be processed into smoking tobacco, which was sold by the nickel bag. The bags, made by Millhiser Bag Company (formerly at 1413 East Franklin Street, Richmond), were distributed by the Virginia-Carolina Company to contract workers such as Nana Cipriani to job out for finishing with strings and tags.[14]

Italian American Nana Cipriani related that she began stringing tobacco bags as a child about 1879 and continued to do so until 1919. Then she began working on contract, supervising others paid by the lot for stringing bags in their own homes. Under such an arrangement a fast worker—one who claimed to be able to string twenty-five bags in seven minutes—had to work almost five hours to string a thousand bags and earn her pay of fifty cents.[15]

The work arrangements of Cipriani, and of those who worked out of the number of storefront stations described, represent an aspect of the tobacco industry seldom mentioned. In addition, the materials these jobbers worked with served a secondary function in women's domestic economy. Tobacco bags were recycled in small articles of clothing, handkerchiefs, or quilts, such as those documented by several Virginia Index of American Design watercolor plates.[16]

"I have been stringing tobacco bags since I was twelve. And they were doing it before then. And you can see for yourself how old I am." She is seventy-two. Her dark grey hair is fastened at the top of her head with tortoise shell combs, her pale eyes under the round forehead do not focus easily, and she is heavy. But there is unusual animation in her compressed lips and no wrinkles in her thin smooth skin. Her voice is vigorous.

"When I started, mostly kids were doing it. They made pin money that way. But now it's the older folks, those who don't go out very much that do it. The young ones, they won't have anything to do with stringing. They'd rather work in a store or drive a truck, but string bags? They won't think of it." She shifts her weight and gives her head a strong shake.

"No, I stopped stringing bags about twenty years ago, when I got a supervising contract with the company." "It must be much easier getting others to do it than to do it yourself." "You're telling me." She presses her lips together, folds her hands, and rocks a little.

"Yes-s-s, some people do depend on stringing bags for a living, that's true. But there are still people who do it to make extra money. There are lots of people who come to me before holidays—like Christmas and Easter and Thanksgiving—who string bags to make fifty cents or a dollar for a picnic or a show. Unless I have a big rush order at those times, however, I don't give them anything. I give the work to my old hands, who work all the year round. They are the ones that deserve it. They do it because it helps them out, not for some pin money. They're my best workers too.

"You know who my slowest workers are? Relief people. That's because their food and coal is given them on a silver platter. So they don't string many bags. Who wants to work when they get their stuff free? . . .[17]

"I've got from 200 to 250 people under me. They've come to me through the years, not all at once. When anyone is given the bags and strings and tags, the amount of each is put

*"*PATCHWORK QUILT, CALICO.*" Index of American Design plate by artist, Mrs. Elgin Moncure Styll. Quilt made by Mrs. Helen East of Richmond, Virginia, ca. 1874. "Fine cambric; white with narrow black stripes, ¼" apart; red with black stripes ¼" apart; border green, of tobacco bag cloth [emphasis added]; white dots and stars; large squares and diagonal pieces. Some other IAD plates of Virginia quilts also indicate the use of "Tobacco bag cloth." Courtesy IAD, National Gallery of Art, Washington, D.C. NG/IAD #9C5 [VA-TE-15].*

down and [when] he comes back, his account is checked. Every stringer has a number, and he writes it on a tag that he ties to each bundle of 100 strung bags.

"The company delivers the order and the materials for filling it to me or to the station, see? My home is just like a station. I do the same kind of work here. You see this big canvas bag? Five thousand bags came in that—the tobacco bags. You remember that little tag a sailor used to let hang out of his breast pocket? That's the kind, it has the name of the brand and of the tobacco company on it. Well, they're not weighed out like they used to be. It's more accurate to fill a Maxwell House Coffee can to that corrugated line just below the top, that's about a thousand tags. The yellow string comes in bunches of 1000 strings—or enough for 500 bags—all cut ready for use.

"A station is a store rented by the bag company. The materials are distributed and collected there just like I do here, only the company has the store rent and the salary of the girl who works there to pay. I don't know how much she gets, maybe $15 a week. A station opens at eight and closes at four every day, except Saturday and Sunday. And if a stringer is late or comes during lunch hour, he has to come back because he won't be waited on. There are three or four stations in Richmond, and one in Petersburg, I think. One of them is over on R Street between 20th and 21st Streets."

"Are there many people stringing bags?" "I should say so. Let's see, I've got around 250. Then there's the stations . . ." "About 2000 persons?" "Yes. At least 2000. They're all in the east side, you know, Church Hill and Fulton. They make fifty cents a thousand now. It used to be sixty a long time ago. [Then] it was forty-five, but they raised it to fifty last summer.

"If a person works hard all day long, he might do a thousand. You see there are two strings now, instead of one like they used to have, and they have to be knotted on both ends and tagged. So it takes about twice as much time now as it once did. And then some [of] the people doing this, don't start until after breakfast and the house is straight in the morning."

"Didn't you say that there [are] persons working for you who depended on this for a living?" "Yes, there are some." "Do they string a thousand bags a day?" "Well, some of them are weak, you know, . . ." The door bell rings. She answers it. I hear a woman's voice, "Have you got any bags?" "No, not a one. I've given them all out." "When do think you'll have some?" "Well, I can't say. You might drop around next week and see." She reenters the room that is made warm by a large wood stove in its center.

"This isn't steady work, is it?" "Oh no. It all depends on the tobacco manufacturers' orders. For instance, we haven't made any 'Stud' brand bags for over a year. Of course, when there isn't much doing, I give what work there is to my steady workers.

"The Millhiser Bag Company has the machines that sew the unbleached cotton into a bag about the size of a cigarette pack. These machines, after the strip of cloth has been doubled and hemmed at its 'top,' sew the side of a continuous row of bags without breaking the thread, so that the bags come to us in a ladder-like row. The stringer breaks them apart, turns them inside out, and uses any kind of needle he wants to, to put the string through each half of the hem at the top. Then the ends of the two strings are knotted and the tag slipped on. The bag is then ready for the tobacco. Until one gets the knack of it, it seems hard. The first five hundred seem never to end." She laughs.

"A hundred bags are counted into piles of twenty-five each, and then stacked alternately, the tagged ends at one end and then the other. A strip of cotton is used to wrap tightly the four sides of a stack of 100. When the stacks are brought to me, I look at both ends, judging the correctness of the count, and noticing the quality of the work.

"I think the Millhiser Bag Company turned the distribution of the strung bags to the service department of the Virginia-Carolina Company last fall, at least it [is] this service company that pays me and also pays the girl at the station. Then some of the trucks that bring tobacco up from North Carolina—Durham, for instance—go by the Millhiser Bag Company or the service department on 1413 East Franklin Street, and take bags back with them to the factories in North Carolina to be filled."

THE STATION

The station on R Street between 20th and 21st Streets is in a former store. Its door is set back in the center of its front, between the grimy panes of its two display windows. I step up from a dirt walk.

It is a long room, twenty feet wide, with shelves on either side, a wood stove about thirty feet back, and beyond it a tall wooden partition. To the right of two straight-backed chairs beside the stove is a haphazard group of white canvas bags, on whose sides are printed in large black letters "BUFFALO." The counter is around twelve feet from the entrance: on the paling gate at its right end is a sign: "Do Not Enter This Gate." On the other end, beside a shelf decorated with a large calendar and a bottle of Carter's Ink, is a box-like desk, slightly sloped and high enough to prevent anyone in front of it from reading what might be on it. On top of it is a long narrow box, three-quarters filled with square white cards: this is the file of stringers. There appear to be 200 cards. The cash drawer is in this desk.

Tacked to the edge of one of the shelves in front of the counter, on the right, are three short pieces of typewritten paper. One, brown with age, contains certain regulations. I lean toward it over a line of grey bags arranged along the floor there. There is time only for the transaction of business, it says, and warns against loitering and indulging in conversation that is not strictly business. Loss or damage to tags and bags will be charged against the account of the stringer. If some bags are received damaged, they should be set aside and record kept of their number. All materials taken out must be returned.

The hours and days on which the station operates are given. A penciled paper attached to the door reads "Open eight to four." [18]

FIVE CENT BAGS OF SMOKING TOBACCO

Measurements of strip of unbleached cotton that makes the bag: 3 1/2" × 5 3/8"
Approximate number of bags that can be made from a square yard of unbleached cotton: 81
Cost of unbleached cotton per yard: .04
2 strings to bag, each approx. 5 1/2" long, colored yellow.
Tag; may or may not be colored.
Label; two little packs of rice cigarette paper.
Tobacco: wider cut than in regular cigarette tobacco, therefore: looser pack; burns twice
    as fast. Quality of tobacco is inferior to that of the ordinary cigarette. Strong odor.
2 dozen bags of smoking tobacco, wholesale: .89
Government tax on 1 1/8 ounce bag of tobacco: .01265625

[Loc.: VSL/AB, box 191, 11 pp.]

Mr. and Mrs. Thomas McCaleb *by Mary S. Venable, 17 July 1939*

Challenging the accepted wisdom that the modern chain stores caused the demise of small independent grocery stores everywhere, Esta Tyree McCaleb placed local blame on two grocers whose personal rivalry and price-gouging exchanges, aimed to rip each other, were also catching others in their crossfire. Despite her protests that they "would sell out" for what they had invested in their store, Thomas and Esta McCaleb—the owners of the "M and M" grocery on Main Street in Covington—worked together in their store and were obviously proud of the quality of their service. One suspects they were far more tenacious in holding on to what they had built up than her remarks—for effect and the benefit of the VWP worker, it is suspected—would convey.

"There are no profits in groceries and we would sell out for what we have put into our store," says Mrs. McCaleb with impressive emphasis.

"Chain stores have the advantage of you in buying in quantity?" inquires a listener. "Not at all. The chain stores are not our competitors, [the ones] that are cutting under. It is these independent grocers who are in a cut-throat war, selling below cost though it is absolutely against regulations." Later on, rocking on her porch with a glorious moon rising behind a cut-leaf maple tree with sweeping branches, she says, "I could never understand the jealousy in tradesmen. There are two men in the grocery business here, so jealous and envious of each other, they would rather go in the red [and] give their time and work to *do* the other fellow, hoping to put him out of business. All the town grocers have to take the rap with the rival. For instance, there is a government regulation which counts a reasonable turnover to be six per cent profit, and grocers are told not to undersell or put on prices which do not bring that 'living wage,' as it might be called. Special bargain prices must come within this figure, and the grocer's books must show, on inspection, [that] the buying price of [the] article he sells at 'bargain' is not below what it costs him. It is a good law and prevents failures when the merchant is too ignorant to think for himself. But these two, of whom I spoke, are in the game of shutting out the other fellow for some personal spite. I do not know, in this case, what it might be, I merely see the results.

"Not long ago the inspector was in getting our reports. And he told me that one of these men (who [has] the store that has been offering butter at a very low price on Saturdays), had two tickets for his cost price of butter, one which was genuine and the other which was for a much lower figure—an incorrect figure—which the merchant wished accepted, but which the inspector told him he would not let pass. Consequently the low-priced butter specials were discontinued. We lost sales by it, for we could not match his selling price and not lose money, as he did.

"That is merely one instance of what the independent store owners will do. It seems idiotic that people will want to work hard—for grocery selling is *continual* service—and get no profit out of their labor. We are not interested in their cut-throat games and will sell out our store to the first good offer."

"Tom" McCaleb grew up in a country village, went through the grades and into high school, but did not finish for he went to work in a grocery store as helper. As a youth he left home to work in [Covington] for the leading grocer of the small town. Here he stayed for years. He became worthy of responsibility and when the health of his employer began to fail, he ran the store with a junior clerk. After an illness of several months duration, when his employer returned able to work, Tom accepted a place in a chain store. He clerked in this first chain store of the town, until his former employer became ill again and offered him a better wage. This he took, and on the strength of this increase, he married the sweetheart of his youthful school days. He says, she was "pretty." He is, today, a good judge of beauty—"feminine, fourteen to forty"—and there is every reason to believe he was then.

His wife is dark with a dreamy air, rather exotic in type. One thinks of her dark brown eyes, naturally wavy black hair, small mouth, perfect teeth, slender neck, and lightness of step, as needing a Mexican shawl for true setting, while the orchestra played "by request" the Indian Love Song. But for castinets, she plays a pencil on the charge accounts, taps off the incoming stock against the orders, and receives graciously not plaudits but complaints about tardy deliveries of her groceries. "Tom leaves the disagreeables for me to deal with," she says. And he acknowledges with great satisfaction, "She can do it better than I." "It is a great mistake for a woman to go into business with her husband," she tells him in the moonlight. "He puts all the responsibility on her.

"If it hadn't been for buying Tom a Christmas gift, I would never have worked outside of my home. It happened that I wanted to give Tom a watch. In the place we lived then on Second Street, our house was entered and robbed one night while I was down [the] street with the children and Tom was then at Mr. Payne's store. It was a Saturday night, so the thief rifled the house and among other things took Tom's watch. It was a good timepiece which I had given him the Christmas before. He was lost without his watch—just couldn't get along without it—and we talked of getting him another. But sixty-five dollars was out of reason on what he was making, and there was no use to buy a cheap watch. He wanted a good one or none.

"Along about the holiday rush, Mother came to live with us and I could then get out. So I got a place to sell in a retail woman's clothing store, just for the holidays, till I could save enough for Tom's watch. He did not know what I was up to till he found his watch on Christmas morning. Mother took better care of the children, or as good as I did, consequently, after Christmas when I got an offer to work in the chain grocery, I took it.

"As time went on Mr. Payne, where Tom worked, got so feeble he wanted Tom to take the responsibility of his store, and he turned it over to Tom. He had been such a fine man to work for that Tom would not quit when he got an offer from the chain store to be the manager, PROVIDED I would work there too. Tom told Mr. Payne, 'I'll take the management of your store on one condition. You have a partner. He has the right to check me up, as well as you. Therefore if I'm manager of your store, you will have to put on tickets all the groceries that you or any member of your family get, all the cash you take from the drawer, and all the cash you ask me to pay out to others, workmen, and so forth.' You see, he had a very expensive family and it is doubtful if he knew how much he and they used, all figured up, in groceries and living. I doubt but if he had had the figures, he, himself, would have been surprised, at least that is what Tom thought. So Mr. Payne said that was perfectly reasonable for Tom to require and matters were in process of turning over, when the chain store offered a much better figure for salary. Tom would not desert a sick man. He had a real affection for Mr. Payne. But [the older man] noticed that something made Tom absent-minded and asked him what was worrying him, so Tom told him about this better offer as manager for the chain store.

"'You must take that offer. It is a permanent thing, whilst I will soon be gone and then I doubt if my partner will continue this business,' Mr. Payne told me. The way he thought of me," says Tom, "ahead of his own good, just like he was my father! The tears still come in my eyes when I think of it. He and I both cried at the time.[19]

"We then managed Kroger's chain store for seven years, till we bought out the one we now have. The way we came to get it at a reasonable figure—because it is one of the best locations on Main Street—was that the manager committed suicide there at his desk in the back room. Domestic trouble, not financial, caused him to take his life. His books showed good returns. He was so popular and his customers thought so much of him that it took awhile for them to come back. They seemed horrified to enter the door for a long time. Mr. G—— was a fine man!" referring to the deceased grocer.

Tom adds a postscript to the story of his employer above: "After Mr. Payne got out of that store, he took a new lease on life and lived for years. I would have kinder felt badly if he had died soon after I left him."

"Mother, there's Sadie H—— and Alex, in the car, they want me to go out driving. May I go?" asks the attractive daughter [about fourteen years old] of this couple.

"If you will be back by ten o'clock. Don't go anywhere, that you can't get in by that time," says Mrs. McCaleb, in a tone that brooks no doubt that she is accustomed to obedience. This daughter is an accomplished musician having begun instruction as soon as she was tall enough to sit on the piano bench and reach the keys. All the soloists or choral clubs wish her for accompanist and Gypsy Smith thought her a "charming and talented child," when she played for his revival services.[20]

Tom is a member of the vested choir in the church of his choice. He thinks she inherited her gift of musical talent "from her father."

Leon, the only son, is fulfilling the ambition of his parents. He is attending a military and scientific school of the state and ranks among the highest in his class. "He is over at The Chamberlayne, I reckon, tonight at a dance. The boys in camp have an invitation to those dances. He writes that he is having the time of his life" his proud mother states. She does not see how people do justice to large families. Two are all, she thinks, their circumstances can fit as she would have them in these days.

Bob Daugherty and Butch Ryan, truck drivers for Associated transport company, having dinner at Mary's Place, 10 miles south of Charlottesville, Virginia, on U.S. highway, route no. 29. March 1943. Photo by John Vachon. [LC-USW3-20283-D]

This couple have no car. They rent their house from a bachelor, [the] owner of the comfortable home. He lives with them. Mrs. McCaleb's mother is happy to provide for the home all the things that delighted her own children. She believes that children and adults should be taught to work and take pride in excellence of doing homely tasks as well as they do pleasant tasks. She thinks life in the country preferable for children, but very complicated if they are to have advantages of music lessons and so forth. She and her daughter find themselves too tired to recreate after the usual day's routine. Mrs. McCaleb has intelligently protected the health of her family through adequate medical care. But [she] has found the cost in hospitalization far in excess of [how] she "guesses" the relative capital invested in physical paraphernalia plus cost of professional training, compares with general business along other lines, professional or otherwise. However, she thinks the imperative demand in emergencies will continue the high figures of hospitalization for those who can afford medical care, and the poor get along as best they can without it.

Mr. and Mrs. McCaleb are greatly interested [in local elections]. It touches their welfare and the condition of their neighbors. Their opinions are established on what they hear over the counter, [and] investigated later to learn whether reliable. No one hears them say much concerning national elections. They are not warm partisans. But the state and Federal regulations for the grocery business they think corrective of many unfair practices. And they are in full accord with hygienic inspection, because it brings other competitors to the standard of sanitation which they have and think necessary to protect the public. They have always been careful of refrigerating conditions. "Our trade calls for the best grades of food, in perfect

Haymarket, Virginia. August 1941. A drugstore. Photo by John Collier. [LC-USF34-80523-D]

condition. If anything goes out from the store in less than *perfect* condition, we replace it when complaint is made by our regular customers. We live up to our advertisements and want the inspector to make other grocers live up to their advertisements. If your bargain specials call for fresh COUNTRY eggs. They should not come out of cold storage. The inspector protects us against false ads and I know it helps. The public has not realized the progress in this line of food sanitation. The general run of folks know nothing about it."

[Loc.: VSL/AB, box 181, 5 pp.]

Mrs. Roxy Prescott Dodson *by Bessie A. Scales, 30 July 1940*

The namesake of her father's mother, Roxy Prescott was listed in the Danville city directory with her husband S. Guy Dodson in 1929. Their marriage was apparently over by the time the four thousand workers (herself included) left their jobs on 29 September 1930 to protest a 10 percent wage cut at the Dan River Textile Mill. Although Governor John Garland Pollard quickly offered to mediate the strike, his efforts were rebuffed by mill president H. R. Fitzgerald. When riots finally broke out on 26 November after forty mill workers had been jailed for unlawful assembly, the governor had to respond to requests from authorities in Pittsylvania County to send in the National Guard to end the turmoil. The strike, which some say "was one of the most serious in Virginia's history," ended on 29 January 1931 without the union either recovering wages or gaining collective bargaining for the workers. The strikers had been assailed by strikebreakers, evicted, and starved out, as Roxie Prescott Dodson stated it, all for "nothing, just nothing." [21]

The officials of Dan River Mills refused to rehire the leaders of the strike, including Roxie Dodson. She persevered by operating an independent boardinghouse for mill workers. For that reason her interview is included in this chapter on trades, despite the fact that VWP worker Bessie Scales was clearly far more curious about Dodson's role in the Danville strike.

Mrs. Roxy Prescott Dodson is a plumpish—bordering on the fat—matron with piercing voice, curly, bobbed, flaxen hair, flashing blue eyes, and about fifty years of age. Her round, fat face is quite pretty. She is intelligent, friendly, talkative, pleasant manners, but seems to be suspicious of all strangers and asks many personal questions in such a fast way it is impossible to get in a single question edgeways till she has satisfied herself as to who you are and "Why did you want to come and talk with me." Her clothes are flossy, gay, and varied with many colors, having a tendency to make her look shorter, broader, and fatter than she really is.

"Mrs. Dodson do you own this home?" "No indeed. I pay thirty-five dollars a month for it. I've lived in this house for ten years, and have paid so much rent and done so much repair work at my own expense it should belong to me. You see I conduct a first class boardinghouse. My boarders are all workers in the cotton mills and you couldn't find a nicer lot than they are."

"I believe you have always been kind of a leader, head of some of the movements undertaken by the mill people and the real leader and organizer during the strike some years ago, were you not?" "Yes. I've always tried my best to help the mill workers. I began work myself in the mills when I was thirteen years of age, and I know from experience what working in the mills is like. I began in the finishing room which was supposed to be the easiest department of the mills.

"I know I would not have lasted a week in one of the dark rooms where harder work was done. Goodness knows the work I was learning to do was hard enough, and it makes me boiling mad now when I remember how some of the folks—mostly stockholders—in this town used to say how the mill people were being spoiled by giving them a five-day week. I tell you one thing, mill folks work hard. And all the time I was working as an apprentice in the finishing room, I only drew seven [dollars and] fifty [cents] a week, but at that time I was sure glad to get anything. My job was tracing shirts, but you bet I didn't stay at that job long. I just tried to learn everything, and it wasn't long before I was as good a weaver as anybody and drawing eighteen dollars a week wages. But we all were working too hard, and too long hours, and too little pay, and when we all did finally see the handwriting on the wall, we woke up.

"That is why we had the strike, but right now let me tell you I wish I hadn't never heard tell of a strike. And there are lots of them wishes just like I do. You see we were promised so much, and I was just plain dumb and believed it all. I held meetings and made speeches, worked the best I knew for the cause, but it all turned out it wa'n't no cause. I suppose we were all just fooled by the ones that called themselves the big leaders, but we worked hard trying to stand up for our rights and we suffered endless struggles. We thought one of the big leaders had an amazing amount of understanding about conditions we worked under, but to our sorrow, we found out when it was too late that he hadn't been born and worked in mills as we had."

"What decided you to take such an active part in the strike, Mrs. Dodson?" "Well it was the other workers and neighbors, you know. When they demand you get up and serve them, you've got to be willing to make a few sacrifices of one kind or another and I guess I thought I could do something out of the ordinary. I never had done anything to attract attention to myself, except take part in all the meetings and I did always make a speech. I guess I just was carried away and talked about things I didn't know much about. You know when a person is around attending their own business nobody pays any attention to them, they get taken for granted and that was me. I was taken for granted, made to believe I could meet desperate ills with desperate remedies.

"We strikers lived weeks and weeks without wages. At the beginning we all felt capable of committing all kinds of outrages providing they were in a good cause, and our pride and stubbornness made us all hard to get along with. Why we all thought we were endowed with a spirit daring enough for anything. The Mill folks were clamoring for a leader—a woman leader, somebody extra special—and I let myself be fooled into thinking I filled the bill. And it seemed that no matter how hard we all tried, there was always a worse trouble insisting on coming out to break down and pull to pieces the grand things we thought we were building up for ourselves."

"But when it was all ended what did you all think you had won for yourselves, Mrs. Dodson?" "Nothing, just nothing, and I tell you it took a thick skin and a meek tongue, a great need of a little money and a smile, to hide our wicked thoughts of each other. When our only recourse was to sit and to pine, you just can't imagine the endless schemes thought of till finally we all became burdened with a kind of bitterness which almost caused a panic. And at last we argued among ourselves. Why take a second helping of commissary beans, when even a small pay was better than no pay at all. That broke up the strike. But you know, to this day, none of us leaders have never been able to get employment in the mills again. We realize we had been the goats in the strike, and none of us don't want anything more to do with unions.

"Sponging on relatives was a habit I did not like, so I began to consider a variety of schemes to make a living and I hit upon the idea of a boarding house. At first it was hard going. Don't you know I couldn't even rent a house in the mill village, but I had no intention of admitting I had been defeated. So I found this house which is, you see, close to the mills. So I moved in and hung out my sign reading, 'Room and Board for Mill Workers.' I couldn't give much at first and they couldn't pay much, but I guess I've made a success. I keep my house full, and I keep law and order too. I also rent the house next door to take care of my overflow. I keep two servants and work hard myself. These houses I rent were newly painted last spring, and I have such conveniences as electric lights, gas stove, screens, telephone, radio, and hot air furnace in both houses.

"Last year I saved about two hundred dollars. I have a niece living with me and going to high school. I give her board and clothes. She costs me about fifty dollars a year, but she is the only near relative I care much about doing anything for. The people in my house are all good people. They work and they gossip together and they eat—how they eat. But my house has the reputation of feeding mighty well. Yes, that is why I don't have any trouble keeping it filled, folks like to eat you know. There have been many changes at the mills since the strike and I'm real friendly with them again. And I know I could work there again but I hope and pray I won't ever have to work in the mills again.

"I was born in Danville, Virginia in December 1890, and I have spent my entire life here. I started to the public school when seven years of age, and finished the ninth grade. My reason for leaving school was that I got married, but I was married about three years when I got a divorce. I begun work in the mills when I was nineteen. When at school I made good averages. The subjects I liked and studied most were English, French and math; I did not skip a grade, neither did I repeat one. I've always been sorry that I did not continue my school work, and always wanted to take a business course and be a stenographer. I would like to see a commercial course in all the schools.

"My father and mother are both living on Pine St. My father is owner of a pressing and cleaning establishment. He was born in Pittsylvania County, Virginia, but moved to Danville, Virginia to live when a young man. He was educated in the country school and is now about seventy-six years of age. He and my mother have a nice home and their interests are gardening. They are both members of the Methodist Church. My mother was born in Caswell County, North Carolina. She had no occupation before marriage and has had none outside of the home since marriage. There are three boys and two girls living including myself. One married sister and her family of two live in my father's home, and two unmarried sons live with him and help in the management of his business.[22]

"I am completely self-supporting and am satisfied with my present situation. I do not contribute to my parental family. I believe my school work did help prepare me for my present job, as I keep accurate accounts of all my housekeeping affairs. The home duties I had while growing up helped prepare me for my present job. I partly help in the preparation of meals and care of my house. I have never received aid from any organization.

"There are two baths in one of the houses I rent and one bath in the other, with running water, also an electric refrigerator, and iron. There are eight rooms in one house and seven in the other." "Your house is certainly very clean and nicely furnished, Mrs. Dodson." "It sure should be. I work hard enough to keep it clean and I reckon I'll be paying for furniture when I die. If I should be sick I would go to the hospital as I carry insurance." "Are you fond of movies? And how often do you go?" "Yes, I go to movies very often—at least twice—sometimes oftener, every week. I don't get time to sew and read much and I haven't read a book for years. I read the daily newspaper, *The Danville Bee,* and very often I read a *True Story Magazine.* I am a member of the Methodist Church and attend quite often in the winter time, but I don't go anywhere much in hot weather as I can't stand the heat. I suppose I attended church at least twenty-five times during last year. I am not a member of the Sunday School and am not a member of any organization. No, I don't bother about voting and I am not registered, have never paid a poll tax or voted. I guess I do enjoy managing other property as I like for the people in the house to do my way. I enjoy having company as I have a nice place to entertain and friends drop in to visit nearly every night when I'm at home. I haven't any special future plans. I'm trying to get on and hope I can always make as good living as I am doing now." "I certainly thank you for this interview Mrs. Dodson, I've come here three times and you are such a gad-about I've found you out on the other two occasions." "Well, maybe I was, I like to talk so much I'm always visiting with my neighbors." "I hope you won't get mixed up with any strikes ever again." "Don't you worry. I've learned my lesson well. And the people are getting so little work now they are thankful for a chance to work and I'd feel sorry for any organizer who would even try to show his face here again. I know Roxy Dodson would sure turn a cold shoulder to anybody, even Mr. Gorman."[23]

[LOC.: VSL/AB, box 178, 8 pp., 2,115 wds., handwritten ms.]

George G. Hodges *by Mary S. Venable, 9 August 1940*

As George Hodges put it, "photography sought me." Photography also sought his father and his eldest son. Surely it seems that some individuals were intended to pursue specific callings, even if their path was not always direct. George Hodges left his late father's photography studio, shortly after the VWP interview, for a job as a papermaker in the West Virginia Pulp and Paper Mill in Covington. While working there in 1941, he married Hilda Frances Lockridge, and in time he went into the service in World War II. The army sent him to special schools at Duke University, then to Paramount Studios in New York, and put his photographic experience to use learning how to make army training films. He later transferred into the Fifth Cavalry and was in Japan at the surrender. After coming home, George and his family left Covington in 1946 and moved to Portsmouth, where his older brother already lived. There he went to work for another family business, O'Neal's Photography Studio, which he and a partner bought in 1960. Following his partner's death in 1979, George continued to run the studio until he sold it in 1982.[24]

"In one way, photography sought me, rather than I sought it for a lifework. It was this way. My father had an established studio and at his death, a few years ago, I seemed to be the one to take over the business, that is, to help my mother salvage the years he had given to the profession. I am not the eldest son, but my two older brothers were already at work in the mill. The principal reason, however, was that I like it. One might say I have a talent for it."

George is modest. From his appearance one might guess his artistic talent. His eyes are keenly observant, rapid in survey, deep blue in shade, wide open and well shaped. He has the forehead of a thinker, from which blonde hair waves in such regularity any girl would envy. His mouth is broad, teeth large and flinty in appearance. The spread of the bony structure of his face below his temples indicates that he has unlimited confidence in George.

Probably he is not alone in his estimation, for he is the type of handsome lad the girls would be crazy about, though he would never, never mention that. He is cut out for a leader, we think, with balance of reason that keeps him on even keel and none of the visionary optimism of most artistic geniuses. The firm books would have to show George a living or he would turn to something less to his fancy. He exemplifies the "show-me" type of youth, willing to work for his standard of living.

Born in Covington, November 6, 1917, when the World War was in progress, he is a realist, fortunate enough to have found a ready-made business suited to his talent. Just in the last year, the firm, which belongs to his father's estate, has eliminated the man employed to take charge of the studio (after the death of George's father) till the son was trained in the profession. This man has gone in business for himself in the same small town. Thus the patronage is divided, George having the benefit of location to which the public had found a path. George cannot say if the Hodges Studio gets fifty percent of their former trade. He would not like to make a guess until he had examined the books for the six months before the separation of studios.

"My mother does the bookkeeping and stays in the outside office for interviews with clients or subjects, to give them prices and to deliver the finished orders. We have a lot of Kodak film printing. I work in the lab when she is here, otherwise I have to be at the counter.

"When I decided to learn photography after Father's death, I came to work here under a Mr. Miller, who had been with Father awhile and who was then running the studio. He worked with different agreements, I couldn't say just what, whether commission or partner-

George Gooden Hodges, 1940.
Photographer unknown.
Courtesy of George G. and Hilda L. Hodges.

ship. I was in high school at the time my father died and mother made the best agreement she could to keep the studio going. She had looked forward to one of us following Father and after I graduated, with my other brothers already placed in employment, I was the logical one to start in."

George smiles with satisfaction. "I like photography. I always did! When I had gotten about all [the] instruction [that] Mr. Miller could teach me, I went to Richmond to work for Foster's Studio for a six month's course. He is one of the leading photographers [with] one of the oldest firms in our capital [and] with the sort of patronage, which calls for the up-to-date pictures. I learned about [the] newest materials, retouching with lead pencil on the negative base, lighting to minimize defects in faces and to emphasize the good points or features. The city patronage was very different in price to our town and I enjoyed the portraiture work, which was expensive. But I have no complaint of the prices here, and I think I brought back the quality of work that gives my customers the benefit of the difference in overhead costs between city and town rentals, and so on."

The Hodges Studio is on Main Street over a five-and-ten store. The steps are easy and facing the door at the top is a large showcase of beauties, near-beauties, and no-beauties; men, very good-looking, youthful and homely; and those whom we are curious to know why they had wanted filmed, what they must have seen reflected in their mirrors. Here in the hall, patrons can select the size, [and] talk without restraint over the tints and poses.

Toward the front, through a hallway, is the office: a front room facing the street, it is about ten by eleven feet. A counter intercepts entrance to the room, beyond which is the printing-room, file rooms, and has a desk for bookkeeping. In the front office is a wall cabinet filling the space of one end. It is also filled with photographs. The baby studies are especially worthy of notice. Girl pictures rank next, and some of businessmen are very good. Kodak pictures are scattered among the shelves. Some of the photographs are framed. The Hodges studio deals in frames. There is a table by the window, convenient for signing for an eight-cent film print to unlimited amounts.

A potted plant is on the table and above it is a framed picture of the Falling Spring of our county before commercialism had laid waste to the beauty-spot, which Thomas Jefferson— it is said—travelled through the unbroken forest to see. "That is the only picture of *The* Falls which has copyright. My father took it thirty years ago. You see it on postcards still on sale, though the stream has been diverted," explains George. "We get a royalty on the sales. I have made a lot of scenic pictures, but Father had covered the field pretty well. We have in those deep drawers over there, a lot of commercial stuff: interiors and exteriors, machine shops and things that are gone, like the iron furnace. The Chamber of Commerce gives us orders for much of that sort of photography. I guess we have the only complete files of the town for the past thirty years that can be found. Then I do a lot of wedding groups, family reunions, clubs, high school groups, athletic teams, local conventions and class pictures. I have made photos of roads, and lots disputed in court, or alleys where car wrecks occurred, but I have never had to be a witness, yet."

George's sense of humor is out of order when asked what type of subject he prefers working with. He has a contemplative air of serious professionalism, not a smile, when he mentions: "I like to make pictures of GIRLS. They more willingly cooperate and take time for the poses. See? I can try out new poses, better effects and various lighting. They are less [self-]conscious. I like to make baby pictures, too. There is no trick to that! Just get the baby happy. There is no artificiality about a baby. They are natural. You don't have to worry with them. They are good subjects. Here is a good study!" He brings an adorably lifelike study of a tiny baby, the daughter of a high school student, who was married before her graduation without the consent of her parents. But she finished her session with excellent marks. This baby was born the following year. We know it to be as bright as the photograph portrays. An irrefutable argument for early marriages, but playing heck with college degrees!

"All the lights in our studio are diffusion discs, they give a soft glow," continues George. "I use different backgrounds, selecting them according to color. I give the blondes a very light, almost white background, or if I get a well-molded face or profile that will stand severe contrast, I put a dark background behind her. Generally speaking though, the brunettes have a medium grayish and the blondes, white. Occasionally I give a picture a flat lighting using a gray background.

"No," George laughs, "I've sent no photographs to Hollywood." He leans back in the window, against the sill and with deep satisfaction talks of his work. "The materials in this work are very expensive. The public would be surprised to know that for the better class work, like my customers demand, at least one-third of gross income is paid out for materials. The chemicals are costly, the rough and smooth paper and mountings are all expensive. Now I like the fine grain surface for portrait work. Some prefer the rough for ordinary sized pictures, that is merely a matter of taste! But the portrait comes out better on the smooth."

George plans to go seriously in the profession and arrive at the top. He now belongs to the Virginia Professional Photographers Association and Board of Photographic Examiners. "That Board," he explains, "is a protection and makes photography a profession. It has nothing to do with state licenses, but more like establishing or requiring a high standard of output. The fee for a studio is five dollars and for a single operator is three dollars per annum. I plan to get better and better in this profession. I like it. Any talent I have tends toward art— and photography is that!"

Speaking of preparation for his work in the high school lab, George shakes his head and says, "photographic chemistry is so different, you might say it was of little or no help. My education gave me a general knowledge, a foundation to grasp what I am doing now. I can't say that it gave me any delight in cultural things for the sake of culture—the satisfaction a person might enjoy without turning it to utility. But the high school was about the same five years ago as it is now, and there I got my foundation."

He says he does no reading. His eyes are tired and he realizes that he must be careful of them if he is to continue in photography. He likes a few magazines: *Saturday Evening Post* and *Life,* but is reading along no one topic. He reads for relaxation and enjoyment and very little of that. He likes to dance [and] goes to private and club dances, and roadhouse dances. He loves to swim. It is his chief pleasure of all athletics.

He is the great exception, in our county: "No, I never played ball—no basketball, no football. I have a cousin who is great in football, I'm not *that* Hodges. Just a sandlot batter and stopped that when I got to swimming." George claims nothing except work for the six months in Richmond. He did not go to operas, such as can be heard in his town [only] over the radio. He roomed near the State Library in the Capitol, but did no serious reading.

A customer comes in. Down go George's feet, with a light bound he is over at the counter, a step to the pigeon-hole for films and he brings back the envelope containing the prints, amount due marked on the back. The man counts the printed pictures, nods at the price, and pays the cost. And now we believe we know that George is so light of tread that he must be an excellent dancer. No wonder he does not read much, this good looking young American!

What about romance? Has it had any place, "22 years, you are?" we ask. He parried the intimate question with a frank, "One BIG romance, at eighteen." A pause, more pause, and further the deponent sayeth not. He looks off toward the horizon without the least trace of despondency. When later, two younger boys are loafing in the office and an amateur palmist/customer tells one of them that he will have a love affair next year which will end in great dejection for him, George advises, "There is more than one girl in the world, if you only think so."

George comes from a well-to-do family, living comfortably in the best section of the town. He has four brothers and two sisters. The youngest is eleven years. His mother appears to be a courageous person, with amiable mien. She is about forty-seven years of age, a blonde, weighing about one hundred and fifty pounds. Up to the death of her husband, she was a "homebody," coming out with fair success into the business world, to gather and hold what was left by her husband. The family attends the Baptist church and are prominent in the Young Peoples Union. George has held most of the offices in it, but at present, he does not hold office.

George is indifferent to leading. Like most men of artistic talent, he is bent upon his individual plans but one notices his fellow classmates migrate in his direction. He is outstanding among them for owning his business, therefore ordering his own hours or so they think. Most of them, in his place, would cut the morning hours, but he is as regular as though employed by another. Perhaps his mother has something to do with this. The drugstore cowboys who flock around George have various opinions on military conscription. One who wants to join the army approves the conscription. He wants the others to go along, which they will fail to do unless conscripted. He pulls the old flag-argument and hopes he will not have to remain in this little, quiet town much longer. He might soldier here for the benefit of younger members of his family, but it would never occur to him that George is doing his march and drilling with camera in lieu of latest make of army rifle. Meeting the family grocery bill is not his friend's idea of "protecting children." The band does not play!

"This size costs four for five dollars, Ma'm. You will probably like it better than a dozen of this size for six dollars. Here is one finished on rough surface and here is one on smooth paper. Deposit? Yes, I'll give you a receipt. Come this way. I'll show you the dressing room." George and the customer vanish.

The children of George's family were: Winfred, thirty-four years; Ruby, thirty-two; Juanita, thirty; L. B. Hodges Jr., twenty-seven; William E., twenty-four; George, twenty-two; Jack, twenty; James, eighteen; and Joseph, ten and one-half. When his father came to this town in 1918, his brother, T. C. Hodges aided him with a loan taking lien on his outfit: "two portrait cameras and outfit, all scenery, backgrounds, five in all, one double head ground and two screens, three posing chairs, one roll top desk and chair, one flashlight machine, one mirror and stand, one small studio camera and outfit, one view camera and tripod, telescope, drying trays, printing rack, large table and retouching stand, one drugget, paper cutters, showcases large and small and any other equipment, not mentioned contained in the gallery now occupied by L. B. Hodges, and in the gallery now occupied by W. C. Parker, July 16, 1918." In 1919 Mr. Hodges bought a residence lot #1 on Prospect Street. In 1925, he built a frame house of eight rooms and gave a lien for materials for five thousand dollars. This he reduced to $3,500 by December 1927. By December 1930, this lien was released.[25]

George seems so alert about the financial end of his work, that it was a surprise when he said he had no idea of the gross income from the studio, nor what he was reasonably allowed for his services. No doubt the liens on equipment and other notes possibly, which he does not keep in his memory, account for his lack of information. There, too, is the estate interests. There seems to have been no settlement and his mother Cora B. Hodges is administrator; her husband died intestate. On the other hand, he may be reticent about the estate business, because it is others who are interested. The older girls and boys have married and left the parental home, but there remains Jack, James and Joseph. The latter is not yet eleven years of age.

[Loc.: VSL/AB, box 182, 7 pp., 2,950 wds.]

William D. Deal *by Mary S. Venable, rec. 3 June 1939*

Despite her best efforts, Mary Venable admitted with some obvious disappointment that she had learned little about the private life of Walter Daniel Deal. Perhaps that is why she chose to use the thinly disguised pseudonym William D. Deal, which could not keep his identity hidden for long. At any rate, records in the Alleghany County courthouse show that Walter Daniel Deal did have a brother living nearby: L. H. Deal, whose estate he administered in January 1943. Almost ten years later, on 5 August 1952, Walter Deal's own estate and his heirs were recorded: these included a surviving brother and two sisters living in West Virginia; nineteen nieces and nephews; and a great nephew. Among this number were the children and heirs of another of Deal's brothers, Milton W. Deal, who was listed with his family in the 1910 Fayette County, West Virginia, census.[26]

No doubt the curious Miss Venable herself would have been delighted if she had discovered that W. D. Deal had, in fact, been married. The 1920 Fayette County, West Virginia, census indicates not only that he was still a coal miner at age forty-four but also that he had a younger wife, Sadie; an adopted seven-year-old son; and his seventy-five-year-old father, Thaddeus H. Deal, living in his household at that time. But the solitary figure described by Venable suggests that

Walter Daniel Deal lost more than his chosen work as a coal miner before coming to Alleghany County from West Virginia.[27]

In the lower half of a frame store building of the nineties on "Upper Main" Street of the village, a passer-by may hear Mr. William D. Deal giving points on shoe mending. The doors are open to admit the spring breezes and in the side yard, an apple tree full of blossoms adds fragrance as well as beauty to the scene. The eaves of the building sag in the center, a few planks sag on the sides, but the vermillion-colored door and lintels add a freshened touch to the building's rather dilapidated appearance.

"Those shoe-butchers down street, cut a sole in half in the instep, when you get them to mend them. I call them *butchers* because they are *not* doing a good job," explains Mr. Deal. "Here now, I'll show you on this shoe. I leave the sole extending down into the toe, so as to have support for the instep of the one I sew on. If I cut it here," pointing to the sole close to the heel, "when your weight comes down on it, step after step, the joint gives way where the two pieces are beveled together, whereas if I leave it to the ball of the foot, the old sole protects and strengthens the new." "I see," says one customer making way for another, there being standing room for one only in the entrance. A worktable with wire grating around an overhanging shelf is just inside the door. To the right of it, in front of the storeroom's side window are chairs for those who "wait" for repairs. Straightening heels costs twenty-five cents. The best grade of leather is the only medium used by Mr. Deal, who produces a sample.

He is quite six feet in height and muscular in proportion. His eyes are keen and his mouth is hidden by a walrus mustache of jet black, within one-tenth of an inch of his lip, where it is snow white. His voice is brave and one would not imagine his mustache had turned white in a single night "as men's have done from sudden fright."

Fraternizing with his patron in sock-feet, Mr. Deal mentions the excellence of his late machinery. "This auto-sole sewing-machine or wire riveting machine leaves no tack tops to hurt floors. You know how the women hate to have their floors cut. Now see here," around the table he brings his work to prove the point, "these heels are held on with wire, which lasts as long as the leather and wears down even as it wears off. Competition, competition! A fellow has to keep up to the latest in his business these days. I have sixteen hundred dollar's worth of JUST machinery in here."

"Including your supplies?" "Not on your life! Just machinery. I get the best leather that is made and it comes high. I get Oakland brand from the ———— Tannery. It is real leather. The stuff C—— uses is nothing but some new stuff they make nowadays. What it really is, is PAPER." Then one is told the reason for the other man's now going out of the shoe mending business and the permanence of Mr. Deal's trade. "I allus say, it comes back to them. Whatever you do! A man dumped five pairs of shoes here, the other day. C—— had mended them and they were broke down in the instep. I couldn't do nothin' for him, 'cause there wa'n't nothin' left to sew a sole on to. He said they screeched as soon as they had been mended and they come apart right where the old soles had been cut off. Why not? There wa'n't nothin' to hold the new soles on, nothin' 'cept the uppers."

"Have you always been in the shoe business, Mr. Deal?" inquires the waiting customer. He comes from behind his "banker's cage," striking the heel of the mended shoe against his left palm, advances perilously near the sitting patron and repeats vehemently: "Have I always *mended* shoes? Why do you reckon I'm MENDING SHOES?" There is a world of scorn in the place of his hitherto proud tones and his voice is pitched in a high key. "Why am I *here?*" he roars, striking the shoe continuously on his palm and advancing as though seeking another place to beat the heel upon. "I don't know! Thought maybe you'd tell me. That's why I asked."

"FOR THIRTY YEARS I MINED COAL IN FAYETTE COUNTY, WEST VIRGINIA," he makes it impressive. "You made good money THERE. I put my youth and strength in it and when I got to be around forty-five, what did they do? Threw me out with those *radical* physical examinations. *They* ain't nothin' but for to throw men out what knows coal-mining, and put boys in. Not young MEN but BOYS, what ain't got no judgment about takin' keer of themselves or the fellows they work alongside of. It wa'n't the pensions, either, unless they were afraid the government was goin' to make 'um pension their old men. The gov'ment never thought of makin' the coal owners do THAT. It was just because the younguns was ignunt and they could run the count over 'um, where they couldn't over an old hand."

Mr. Deal leaned against the back of his worktable and his faraway expression was apparently kaleidoscoping unpleasant scenes. "They want ignunt folks from the mountains! They turn off the experienced men and put those ———— in their places." "Are you talking about unions and scabs? You talk like you were a union man," injects the listener.

"Would YOU be, if you found your working conditions were bettered where a lot of workers hung together, or would you rather have poor conditions? Take the ignunt ones fur instance. They don't join. They ain't got 'nuf education to count the weight, and what happens: they dig two thousand, two hundred and forty pounds of coal—a long ton. The operators pay by short tons. There's two-hundred and forty pounds mined and the miner not paid for it before the days of unions. The difference between the long and short ton cost the owner not one drop of sweat, not one penny. A lot of two-hundred and forties will make a ton, all to the good of everybody BUT the man who dug it out. NARY a cent for him! If it hadn't been for the union in the coal mines, there would never have been any safety. Lives weren't worth nothin' at all. Throw 'um in the scrap heap! Plenty more to come work for us!

" 'Blood-suckers' I call 'um, what comes in to work for the mine companies when the union is tryin' to make agreements with the [operators]. Blood-suckers, because they are taking the wages from families of men what has give their lives to coal-minin' industry. The blood-suckers don't know enough to be safe to work beside. The comp'ny complains that the drillers and 'stick-men' don't do but just one thing. Well, it takes years and years to learn to drill and to blast so as to keep from shootin' the pillars and endangerin' lives. Paid for what they know! What took experience to learn, same as men higher up! There is so much about any kind of work that outsiders never know, ways to take short cuts. You wouldn't know 'less you worked in a mine.

"When the company threw me out of Fayette mines, I looked for work goin' from one mine to another for more 'n a year. And to every mine I went, they didn't need no more workers. And right along behind me would come a boy and be took on then and there. I got tired lookin' for work an' I seen the coal comp'nies weren't goin' to take on no men forty-five years old. So I says to myself, I'll go in a business of my own.

"My daddy was a shoemaker an' I knowed somethin' 'bout it from the time I was a boy, so I started mendin'. The first shop I opened was at White Sulphur Springs. Trade was good in the summer season, ridin' boots an' all that. But the winter season wa'n't nothin', three months out of a year that was all! So I come over here where there were a lot of mills and factories and enough people to give me work the year 'round. You've got to have 'um come in steady for this business. Then my brother come over and opened his shop downtown."

Mr. Deal returns to the auto-machine, as he calls it, to sew the other heel. In the rear of the room is a large stove; near it sits a young woman reading some of the many papers thrown in confusion on the otherwise empty shelves. She is not as neat in dress as is the proprietor. His blue workshirt is fresh and clean, his rough trousers are also clean. He wears a sort of train conductor's cap, with a stiff bill. It suits his mustache, in Marx brother's fashion. On a long table across an aisle from his work table, the finished packages, tagged, await call. He does not examine the tag, when a customer comes. He knows him well and picks up the right pair of shoes at a glance.

Two thin little girls come rushing up to him and speak in confidential tones, to which he replies, "All you want. Over there in the pasteboard box on the floor." "I knew *you'd* give 'um to us," says one with a cheery smile. "Ain't no good to anybuddy!" he offers apology. "They want the old rubber heels I take off. They play hop-scotch with 'um. They're my pals!" he explains as they leave.

"Their ma's dead and he's got what he calls a housekeeper. She don't pay no 'tention to the chillun to make their clothes fit 'um. They're real purty, when they're clean. Smart 'uns, too, at school or they would be if they got 'nuff to eat. Their Pa gets good money at the mill, but he puts it some'ers else than on his chillun. He can't think he is goin' to Heaven with it," laughing sardonically, "not HIM. Little Nancy and Virginia come around here a lot of the time." Adding, after a pause, "Ef you're not happy when you're young, you'll never be."

"Have you a family?" the man waiting for his shoes asks. A boy comes in to get his half-soled pair and changes there in the seat beside the door. "Were you ever married?" queries the man waiting. There comes no answer.

In slow, loafing manner a politician's heeler enters and asks Mr. Deal if he has a vote in the coming town election. "I'll never vote again as long as I live, for town, county or for President! I'll leave that to the crooks to run. A vote never gets counted anyway. Look at this town!" He speaks fiercely to the ward-heeler, who withdraws the offered card. "*You* know what this town is!" With consenting silence the solicitor leaves without discussing the state of town affairs.

"Look at the taxes!" Mr. Deal continues as though to the man who left. "I pay over ten dollars for a license to patch shoes. On every mouth'ull of meat, bread, sugar, I pay tax. The President has TRIED but he's got things in an awful mess! Who's goin' ter pay?"

"Do you use much sugar? Put up much fruit?" "I put up two gallon of strawberries last week," proudly the shoemaker says, then with a glance of subtle defense, he shuts up. "You do your own cooking?" Useless all attempts to penetrate the private life of Mr. Deal. His dignity would grace a duke or laird. "Here, your heels. They'll keep straight as long as the uppers'll wear. Twenty-five cents. And that's the best leather tap that can be got, ANYWHERES."

The shoemaker's recreation is amusing children. In the late twilight, they come to sit on his step and block the walk with a marble game. They linger with him as long as he will let them. In the winter, his reading of daily papers is done close to the stove in the rear of the shop. If and when he is seen on the street, he walks briskly and can be seen with market produce. His neighbors say he never leaves the shop, excepting to go for food or to see his brother who lives two squares to the West.

[Loc.: VSL/AB, box 180, 5 pp.]

Nethers, Shenandoah National Park, Virginia. October 1935. Interior of the mill.
Photo by Arthur Rothstein. [LC-USF34-00377-D]

Arlington, Virginia. May 1942. Car refinishing plant. Photo by John Collier. [LC-USF34-82549-C]

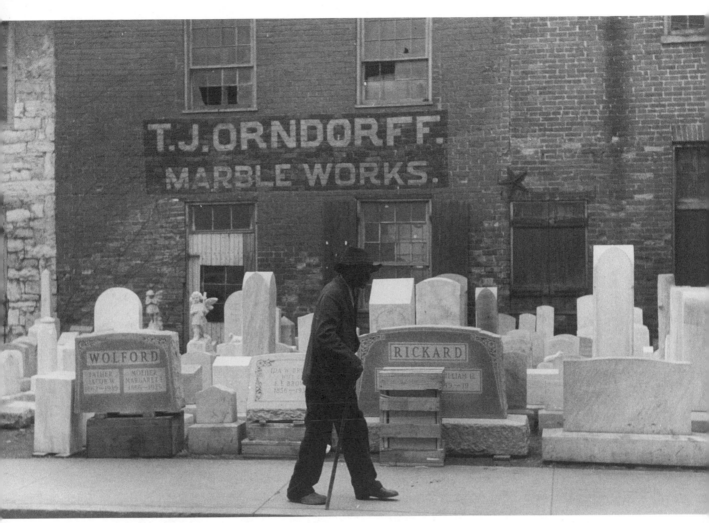

Winchester, Virginia. February 1940. A marble works. Photo by Arthur Rothstein. [LC-USF33-03463-M3]

Making a Living in Iron, Steel, and Coal
"OF EVERY ARTIFICER IN BRASS AND IRON"

If you come to think of it, all we get is out of the earth. —F. W. (Howard N.) Lilly

Iron was important in Virginia from the early beginnings of its Anglo-European history. By April 1714 a small band of German Protestants arriving in Virginia from Westphalia would be the first settlement established at Germanna Colony to work Governor Alexander Spotswood's iron mines and foundry. Before the eighteenth century was out and the nineteenth well begun, iron mines and forges dotted the counties up and down the Shenandoah Valley west of the Blue Ridge. Tench Coxe, writing in that later period, commented on the situation at Richmond, "where nature lavishly joined coal, iron, and waterfalls," conditions that were "peculiarly qualified for the iron branch of manufactures."[1]

In her interview with Joseph Hippert in this chapter, vwp worker Mary S. Venable interjected her own accounting of the history of the Jordan Furnaces in the Clifton Forge area of Alleghany County. The county's census for 1860 does, in fact, list an Edwin Jordan, fifty-seven, and an Isa F. Jordan, fifty, both still ironmasters, with real estate valued at $18,000 and personal property at $14,200 for Edwin and $10,000 and $18,300, respectively, for Isa. In the first quarter of the twentieth century, however, the Virginia iron industry was steadily losing ground in competition with the development of vast midwestern iron deposits, as reported on by Hippert. Between 1904 and 1929 the number of workers employed in Virginia in the manufacture of iron and steel products, not including machinery, was reduced by more than half.[2]

The art and craft of being a good farmer required many skills, and most farmers were, by necessity, jacks-of-all-trades: competent as carpenters, masons, mechanics, and blacksmiths. Many of them occasionally worked at other such jobs, in addition to farming, to bring in scarce cash. Thus, when a farmer decided (or had decided for him) to make the move into wage labor—either temporarily or full-time—it was relatively easy to move into a job with the railroads, in the mines, or at the foundry.

A problem inherent in the move from farm to public work, however, was that workers in these industries rarely had an economic safety net in case of mishaps or cutbacks in the labor force for various reasons, as attested to in the cases of F. W. Lilly and Oscar William Gross, or that of W. D. Deal (in chapter 7), who had spent thirty years in the coal mines. When hard times came, many former farmers had no farm to return to where they might, at least, raise enough food to subsist.

A number of men in the generation born before the Civil War (chapter 1) had moved early on from farming in areas such as Bedford, Campbell, and Franklin Counties into jobs as carpenters and blacksmiths in the rapidly growing "Magic City" of Roanoke, whose prosperity was closely tied to that of the Norfolk and Western Railroad, a post–Civil War incarnation of the old Virginia and Tennessee Railroad, which was begun in 1850 and completed in 1857. The Norfolk and Western "established its reputation and fortune primarily as a coal carrier."[3]

Since the turn of the century, railroad repair shops had been increasing in importance in Virginia, representing 4.67 percent of the relative value of its manufactures by 1929. The various railroad construction and repair shops were employing 7,345 men in 1904 and 12,427 in 1929. By the time of these interviews, Norfolk and Western with its associated shops had more than 7,000 employees in the Roanoke area alone.[4]

Coal had been mined in Virginia since colonial times, but production was relatively small until the early 1890s, when the Clinch Valley Branch of the Norfolk and Western Railroad opened up Wise County. The coal fields in Wise County were "dominated by a few large operations, including the Virginia Iron, Coal, and Coke Company, the Virginia Coal and Iron Company, the Stonega Coal and Coke Company, and George L. Carter's Carter Coal Company." By 1920, half the miners employed in Virginia were working in Wise County.[5]

Several men whose life histories are included in this work (George Brown, William Deal, and John Davidson) had spent some of their working life in the coal fields, and others had relatives who had worked in the mines. The coal industry, however, had its own depression starting shortly after the end of World War I, and most of these men had since moved on to other jobs. John B. Davidson was relatively more fortunate than many former miners. He worked in the coal mines for most of his working career but was gradually assigned to less demanding jobs above ground and retained his privileges of rent-free housing for long-term service with the Stonega Coke and Coal Company. Despite living through the worst mine disaster on the Stonega works and thinking he was "through with mining," Davidson went back. When he saw the other men going to work with their dinner buckets, he could not stay out. The "mine work culture," usefully described by historian Crandall Shifflett, would not allow him to do otherwise.[6]

F. W. Lilly *by Mary S. Venable, rec. 3 June 1939*

Lilly and shoe repairman W. D. Deal (in the previous chapter) shared a number of features in common, including the fact that Venable altered both their names in the texts of their life histories. F. W. Lilly seems, in fact, to be Howard N. Lilly, the son of Martin Miller Lilly (born in Augusta County) and his second wife, Lee Anna (Dudley), who were married in 1876. Rockbridge County birth and marriage records indicate that Miller and Lee Anna had five children: Howard, Carrie Lee, Georgeana, Nannie, and James H. By 1900 the widow Lee Lilly, with Howard and Carrie, was living in the household of widower and blacksmith Matthew Cash (also from Augusta County) and working as his housekeeper. Howard was at that time a day laborer.

In 1910, however, Howard Lilly was a blacksmith living with his wife Belle (Dunaway) and two children near Brownsburg—not far from Matthew Cash. By 1920, Lilly and his family had moved to Bath County, where he then was working as a blacksmith for a lumber company. And in 1931 he was given a homestead exemption for money owed him in Covington, Virginia (see Appendix B). The circumstances of Howard N. Lilly's life fit closely with those mentioned in the following life history; he is most certainly the person referred to as "F. W."

It was not the blacksmith in our alley of whom Goldsmith wrote, "a mighty man is he," for this one is tall, sparely built and frail in appearance. By irony of nomenclature his name is that of the white flower, the emblem of purity. In spite of his years he swings his hammer with ease and hearty action. And says to his patrons who come to this shop in preference to the one other the town affords, "You can get it this evening," referring to the job brought in.

He comes from the Scotch settlement near Lexington, Virginia; "out in the country near Brownsburg," he was born. His father died when he was ten years of age, [and left] five children and a widow. Leaving the fifth grade to go to work on the neighboring farms at twenty-five cents per day, Mr. Lilly "got no more schooling." At that time a man got fifty cents on a farm (excepting for wheat harvesting, then he got one dollar) but twenty-five cents was the regular wages for a boy. Pork was eight cents per pound and they had a good garden and cows, pigs, and chickens, so the family "made it alright."

His father had been a blacksmith. So as soon as the son reached maturity he went to Brownsburg and learned the trade from M. B. Cash, working in his shop in that large farming district. "You know what that is," he says, and to refresh one's memory he mentions the tragedy of Henry Walker. "They moved away from there after that. Had a big farm. The McClung brothers bought it after he got killed." BANG, BANG, goes the anvil as he talks and with such regularity that one cannot stop him to ask who it was that moved. The din is so great and he takes for granted that this local episode will ever live in the memory of man. "It is a good farm, one of the best around Brownsburg.[7]

"If you come to think of it, all we get is out of the earth," philosophizes the smith. "Human beings live off its vegetables, grain, meat. It was put here for us to get our food from, but nobody wants to pay the farmer what his work is worth. And so BANG, the young — BANG — farmer won't work — BANG, BANG, he just scratches around with some of these new-fangled machines." BANG, Szzzzzz goes the heated piece into the tub of water; Szzzzzz, another picked out of the dust where it has been cooling, Szzzzzz, Szzzzzz, another and another. He is tempering and sharpening his set of cold chisels, ten or more, for the day's work. "You can't find a farmer who wants to do good ploughing and work for a whole day like used to be. When you come to think of how he sees other folks gettin' rich quick, I dunno as you can blame him.

"Not long ago I was in a butcher's shop here and a farmer — Mc—— from up at Barbers — come in and asks the butcher, says he, 'I've got a young beef dressed out here. What will you give me for it?' The butcher says, 'Seven cents on foot is the best we can pay out.' 'I can't take that. Its cost me more than that,' says the farmer. After he left I says to the butcher where I had come to buy my meat, 'I want a cheap piece — say brisket, or maybe a soup bone — a bone with some meat on it, I mean. What's your *cheapest* meat wuth?' 'FOURTEEN cents,' says he. I says, 'That's your *cheapest,* double what you offered that farmer for his best meat and all? What would you make off the best, three or four times that. And here you send to Chicago and pay freight on meat what's been dead two years or mebbe more, nobody knows how long. And this here good meat, raised in this county, you won't give the farmer a decent price for [it]. That's what's the matter. You butchers want the Chicago stock yards and the railroads to eat us up with their profits. And you COULD furnish us good, healthy meat to eat, if you would.'

"He said he had to buy where he could get it regular, that the farmers 'round here would sell in the Spring and Fall, and there wouldn't be any to buy between their seasons. I told him that could be managed if the farmers were sure they could sell. There could be a slaughter house set up and regular killin' done, like used to be. There's Slaughter Pen Hollow, got its name from the slaughter house what was there. But the small man is not trying to help the small man. He wants to buy from the rich fellow in Chicago. Maybe buy back the beef sold from *here,* payin' freight both ways."

A young fellow brings a long steel rod in the door and slams it down on top of a lot of debris. It is a half-inch rod to be cut: "Four eye-bolts six inches long, and five, four inches long, a two-inch hook on the end of the four-inch. When can I get it?" "Alleghany Mill?" "Umph-hum." "This evening, about fo'."

Picking up conversation together with his small hammer, Mr. Lilly bends over the anvil, while his helper seems to be an automatic part of the cooperative plan, losing no fraction of a second when comes the instant to strike or to lift with pinchers the glowing metal from the bed of coals. Mr. Lilly decries the get-rich-quick idea of business today. "It used to be [if] a merchant was making twenty percent profit he was satisfied, and if he made a lot of money he did it by years of putting by a reasonable profit on his goods. Same way with a miller. D' ever hear of a rich miller in the old times? Well, now they got to get three prices for grindin' and get rich in a year or so. They don't leave nothin' for the other man, the customer or the farmer raisin' his wheat. They don't divide like they used to do."

"So the farmer gets to catchin' on and he wants to go up in prices. I don't blame him, for he's held the short end a hundred years. But this is what I want to know, 'WHO'S GOIN' TO FEED THE NATION?' We gotter eat. Look at these po' people all around here, out on these mountains. They got what they raise, but some ain't got no land to raise wheat on. They got to BUY flour. And there's sugar and coffee and store stuff. They ain't got enough clothes to go to school, let alone Sunday School!

"AND THE WOMEN'S CLUBS PLANTIN' TREES and makin' gardens, with naked and hungry chillun scattered all around 'um. Trees cost from two and a half dollars to fifteen, and when did those same women pay out that much for clothes for po' chillun? The young boys and girls are no 'count. Those off a farm won't handle a spade. And if they stay on the farm they won't raise enough to feed theirselves. They want six or eight dollars a day and they don't know eight-cents-worth a day.

"My wife hired a scrub woman, a young one, the other day. She knew she come to work, but when my wife told her to mop the floor, d'yer think she'd do it? No sir, said she couldn't spile *her* han's. There was red nail polish on 'um! And she *didn't* mop the floor. The girls can't sew, can't cook, *don't* do no washin', and all they kin do is to buy dresses—what ain't got no cloth in 'um—at the store, and pay six times what they are worth. They can't make a biscuit fitten to eat and they don't want to learn how. I feel sorry for the boys that get 'um for wives!"

While the iconoclast is taking in more work and memorizing the dimensions for same, it is unusual to hear nothing said of pay, costs, or any mention of money. The patrons say, "You cut one for me last year about this time." Thus they return. Perhaps the smith "leaves some for the other fellow," in naming his prices.

This shop was an old stable. The door is on the alley which parallels the river. A century ago these lots were in deeds mentioned as "ice-house-lots," when ice was cut off the river and brought up by pulleys. But since the mill polluted the river no ice has been cut off it. The square below the shop is a "court," in which modern cottages face the river and the rear of the houses across the alley have beautiful gardens to look upon. But this sole remaining stable is unsightly. Its windows lost their sashes about a quarter-century ago and the cracks in the side walls (of broad planks) permit the smoke to escape. Not all of it, as the faces of the two men show.

The helper is from Botetourt County. He is a huge man with arms like barrels. His neck and shoulders bring to mind the marvelous perfection of the created body when "Tubal-cain was a whetter [an instructor] of every artificer in brass and iron" (Genesis 4–22). From a heart in-size-proportioned, he speaks of the flu epidemic during the World War era.

"I was using my truck for an ambulance to bring the sick from the country round about. Up at Barber [Barbour] found five, a woman and four children. They didn't have no sleepin' clothes and they were lyin' on straw with no ticks. Just straw! We brought 'um to the school-house here what was turned into a hospital then. I helped all through that flu epidemic, and worked with the sick carryin' them in and out, and I never took the flu. A lot of folks did, what nursed them."

The hearth or forge is in the center of the shop. It is high off the floor on legs, a heavy molded iron square about forty inches, each dimension. The hand bellows is at one corner and a pipe runs underneath the hearth admitting the draft in the center. On one side of the room is a rack of horseshoes of various sizes. Across, on the opposite side, is a rack of tools: nippers, buck saws, rip saws, wrenches, braces, and some scraps of discarded parts. Near the anvil is a bench of files, pliers, and hammers, black with the dust of the morning. In the back of the room is a long table running its breadth. The vise is "handy" and several tins of oil are on the shelf underneath. An old water cooler lies on its side, top yawning, spigot bent. The anvil weighs three hundred and fifty pounds, the helper states, and it was bought at the auction of the old furnace when it was dismantled. The chime of the anvil is as melodious as, presumably, it was when its furnace works paid to the workers of the county eighty thousand dollars per month. "Those were great days," this man smiles at the recollection.[8]

Mr. Lilly says he has had no work on the old handmade iron since coming to this county, but that in Rockbridge in his early days, "there were a lot of *kittles* and so on," brought to him to work on. "And them pots made cookin' taste good. The cabbage cooked in 'um was yel-low, not sickly-lookin' white like that today cooked in granite or aluminum. This aluminum gives no flavor to anything. Dunno why 'tis, but them old iron pots my mother used to cook in for us chillun made everythin' taste good."

On Memorial Day he would liked to have gone to Rockbridge to the graves of two infants of his sleeping there, he mentions with depth of feeling and low pitched voice. His other children are grown and married. Only he and his wife left to provide for and he says he makes a "good living," has nothing to complain of and, with a grin, "I have a fine boss. I like him." His helper seems to be of the same opinion.

Between the clank, clank of the anvil, under the rolling clouds of smoke, with rivulet to-bacco amber from the corner of his mouth, an added smudge on his nose, he returns to his regrets of Memorial Day. "I have a truck. We could have gone if we had had the *tins* to put

Newport News, Virginia. September 1936. A blacksmith shop in the negro section, the only one in the city.
Photo by Paul Carter. [LC-USF341-11320-B]

on it (licenses). A fellow has to cover up his car with tins before he dares run it these days. Dunno when I'll be able to get mine. I need the truck too.

"I could borrow a horse but the trip would take two days and horse feed. I couldn't lose the time." He claims there "are a lot of horses around this part of the country. A lot of men owe me for shoein' 'um. I could have got some of their horses but I didn't." He says he goes out to the country twice a year to shoe horses, goes to the farms. The owners prefer that to bringing the horses to him in town. He has a scheduled route "when fryers get grown" or late in the fall "when cider is runnin' from the presses." In the one county, he states, he has the names of one hundred and twenty farmers whose horses he keeps shod.

When Mr. Lilly worked at the paper mill as mechanic, he got eighty cents per hour. He counted a ten-hour day and was pleased with his boss and his pay. He is still very indignant over losing out because of his age. "What's left for men forty-five years old? Knock 'um in the head and get rid of 'um. No place in the work that took them years and years to get experience in. Experience that benefits the company. 'Bout the time a man has got some judgement from experience in his line, out he goes! They threw me out at forty-five. I was hale and hearty. You see me now, well, that was twenty-five years gone! They had a physical examination and you put your age down. Out I went! The boy who took my place didn't know NOTHIN'. He didn't know 'nuff to be safe to the fellows he was workin' beside. But he was YOUNG and it'd be a long time before he got to be sixty, the pension age. Well, an old man can't DIE. You got to eat." Perspiration streams from his brow as he adds another smudge to his nose, and hits a knothole in the plank of the walk across the back door with a well-directed stream of tobacco juice. The log chain is finished. Cut to required lengths without any pencil note of dimensions or name in ledger.

Mr. Lilly says he is too tired to go anywhere when he leaves the shop. He never walks down to the city playground and does not read. He lives over Grime's Market. His wife missed her flowers and he would like some grass to "loaf on after the sun goes down," but "what are you goin' to do when rents are what they are?" He is not at all interested in the election for Town Council or Mayor because his vote "would not be counted." All that he wants to vote on is the reduction of taxes. "Taxes is eatin' the country up," he thinks.

The times have passed, the blacksmith of today says, when a man can make a lot of money as they did when wheel tires wore out on the rocky roads and had to be replaced every year. Good ones were of tempered metal and sold for six dollars or more. If a man failed to pay the blacksmith's bill, his wheels would probably fall down before the next year. So collections were better than today, [when] a man can get in his car and extend his limit of credit geographically to a wide radius. "But I cut the bad ones off my list. If they don't pay, they needn't come back," Mr. Lilly states decisively.

He is proud of his work. Just close to where his forge is today, what was practically "the same stand, for its been a smith's shop next to the bridge for one-hundred and forty years, Aaron Clarke shod the cavalry for General Jackson. Here is the bill." He takes from his folder a grimy sheet which is a receipt from the Provost Marshall in 1863 for mending muskets and bayonets and shoeing horses for Capt. (Stonewall) Jackson's Cavalry. "They must have stopped on their way to the skirmish at McDowell, either on their way there or on the way back. I must look up the date of that skirmish and find out," Mr. Lilly remarks as he carefully folds the scrap of yellow paper and replaces it in a worn folder.

A listener questions if that shop where the cavalry stopped was not on the east side of Bridge Street, Mr. Lilly's is on the west. He says, "it was hereabouts anyway. And my shop is the only one around now."[9]

[Loc.: VSL/AB, box 180, 7 pp.]

Joe Hippert *by Mary S. Venable, rec. 19 December 1938*

Joseph A. Hippert was the "traffic manager" and Edward Hippert was "cashier" for the Low Moor Iron furnace in Alleghany County, and one suspects that they were related. Both men claimed that they were born in Michigan and their parents were born in England, but there is nothing else to indicate how, or if, they were indeed kin. In addition, there were others of the same surname in Alleghany and Augusta Counties who were "slag engineers" or "in iron mines" and who also claimed connections to Michigan and to England. The common thread between all these persons, however, seems to lead from the iron ranges of Michigan and Virginia to common origins among ironmasters or miners in England.

The Low Moor Iron Company of Virginia, for which both Joseph and Edward Hippert worked, received its charter from the Commonwealth of Virginia on 5 July 1873 and resulted from a consortium of "New South" industrialists and northern capitalists established by merchant and shipping magnate Abiel Abbot Low of New York. In 1884, one writer reports, "eight-year-old lads" worked for "75 cents per ten hour day" and "local people, former slaves, and immigrants comprised the 'efficient, tractable laborers' acquired by Low Moor's vigorous policy of recruitment."[10]

In the twentieth century, the company's treasurer, Frank Lyman—a member of the Low family—hoped to transform its operations on large tracts in the Potts Creek section of Alleghany County and on more than four thousand acres of land around Low Moor into the "Pittsburgh of Virginia." By 1926, however, the Low Moor furnaces were shut down and a notice in the *Charleston Daily Mail* in 1927 advertised "a huge sale of its inventory," from which F. W. (Howard N.) Lilly undoubtedly bought the anvil used in his blacksmith shop. The company's offspring Kaymoor mines along the sides of the New River Gorge in West Virginia survived, but its parent Low Moor "finally closed its books in 1930."[11]

The once thriving town of Low Moor, Virginia is devoid of occupation by reason of the dissolution of the Low Moor Iron Co. of Virginia, razing of its furnace, and closing of its mines. A backward glance will disclose the causes. From 1794, Alleghany minerals were in demand. A nephew of Lord Fairfax purchased a thriving business, the Rumsey Furnace, which he operated up to the time of his death. James Swann advertised the mineral wealth of this section, whilst he was in the French prison incarcerated for America's non-payment of salaries due the French Revolutionary [War] troops. Royalty of Bavaria and Canada were stockholders in companies of capitalists; to one of these companies is deeded over one million acres of mineral properties in Alleghany and Bath counties.

From 1828–40, Col. John Jordan and [his] seven sons from Lexington, Virginia bought up or married property or held liens on tracts in various sections, thus cornering the iron industry of this locality. They were the Carnegies of their century. Their furnaces were at first charcoal furnaces, but with improved facilities they fired with coal and rebuilt the small furnaces into larger and larger ones. They gave liberally to their state during the War between the States. A resident traitor directed Hunter and his raiding soldiers to the largest Jordan furnace, where the horses were taken, the granary burned, [and] all possible damage done to the furnace. It was repaired and the whole group of Jordan furnaces commandeered for Confederate service. At the close of the war, slave furnace-labor was gone, the furnaces ruined, in fact, tumbling down through abuse by the military men sent as operating furnace-men with no experience in making iron.

The Jordans were bankrupt and penniless. They had, however, grouped in corporation ownership most of the iron deposits of the county. These scattered "openings," after passing through several "wildcat promoters" claws, became the property of A. A. Low of New York and his partner, ———— Moore of Cincinnati. Their names [became] the firm [name of] "Low Moor" (omitting the "e" in Moore). The words "of Virginia" were added by court decree after the loss of a suit by another, older Low Moor firm, far distant.

In the village of Low Moor, four miles West of Clifton Forge, on Jackson River and Karnes Creek, the central offices were situated; also a large commissary; one "mansion," which entertained the board of directors annually; twin furnaces, rebuilt to the latest model as time went on; coke ovens; twenty houses for the "office force," doctor, intelligentsia; about fifty, four- or five-room houses for white laborers; and about eighty, negro cabins of three rooms or more. Mining towns were built at each of the eight mines, consisting of thirty or more frame houses; commissaries at each town; washers; large stables and granaries for the mine mules; and churches and school buildings.

Here Mr. Joe Hippert, the Low Moor traffic manager takes up the story: "The average payroll of Low Moor Iron company, at its best days was eighty-six thousand dollars per month. There may have been a few months of seasonable occupation when the pay roll reached one hundred thousand per month, but for a long time it stood around eighty-six. That is counting all the miners in various towns, the office force, Superintendent and rentals paid out. That is the total, for its twenty-five thousand men here in Alleghany, and including Oriskany in Botetourt county, and Kaymoor in West Virginia. We paid in cash from the strong box, carried from mine to mine. And that reminds me of a funny occurrence."[12]

"There had been an epidemic of Paymaster holdups out West and North, and our Paymaster was no burly man. His trips to the lonely mining towns on our branch roads were good opportunities for rascally employees who knew the paydays and could have some idea of the payoffs. The Paymaster asked the company to furnish guards for him on these trips with the big strong box which took two laborers to lift out of the cars. The company furnished him two *big* men who carried guns, ready to touch off. The addition of two more, with the Paymaster and his two helpers who rode in the express car on the C & O Railroad and our various branch lines, made a small procession. People got to calling it the army and teasing the Paymaster about his militia, till he got so sensitive he called them off, rather be shot than hear about 'the parade.' Nothing dangerous ever happened here.[13]

"The Low Moor Iron Company of Virginia went out of business for two reasons: first, Lake [Great Lakes] ore competition; secondly, high freight rates. Our mines yielded ore twenty-nine to thirty percent metallic, expensive to smelt, requiring fifty to fifty-one percent coke. But we were close to the coal fields and if we could have had a fair rate of hauling, we could have burned the coke O.K. When we burned the coke instead of buying it, that made a great reduction in the costs. The Lake ores are richer, but for certain products our output was in demand. In fact the demand continued after we went out of business, and our patrons even wanted to know where they could get old, *used* Low Moor iron.

"The Lake ore producers fought us in the market, but we held our own. Then, through railway rates increase, they cut our territory from Ohio, the Lakes, New York and New England, our best customers! We were strangled and our Senators and Congressmen had allowed it by ignorance, negligence or worse. The Pennsylvania and Ohio statesmen had protected their territory, ours had not. Virginia has been a long time waking up.

"George L. Carter's I.C.C. fought us through the N. & W. Railroad and Virginian; the B. & O. fought us, their stockholders or their friends, also in the iron business; the C. & O. Railroad fought us, and their failure to reduce war-time rate contract finally shut us down. They killed their golden goose. Over at that little box of a station, the C. & O. R.R. was paid each month sixty-thousand dollars for YEARS, for all the Low Moor freight not delivered at this point out to all our towns.[14]

"The Low Moor Iron company was owned by a wealthy family connection. Had they held railway stock, even in the face of Virginia statesmen favoring the Pennsylvania field, there would be iron running here today. There were other stockholders in minority in Low Moor Iron Co. They, too, were rich men; this was a small bit of their business. The Means Family of Ohio and Kentucky loved this work. They were citizens who for three generations had, one might say, CARED for their laborers. I am certain that with a low profit, they would have allowed this furnace and mines to continue for they deeply regretted the fact that this town would be left to starve. But with a continual fight on their hands and a suicidal contract with the C. & O. Railroad, which the railway would not release for existence-rates for Low Moor, there was nothing [left] but dissolution of the firm and disposing of its holdings.[15]

"As you see us now, sixty percent of the heads of families [are] on relief. If it had not been for the Federal government, we would have starved. For a few of the young men, there is work at the rayon and paper mills, but very few! Our other small villages—out in the county—built by Low Moor company are in the same fix. There was no work in this locality for thousands of laborers catapulted into a meager, semi-agricultural region.

"The houses here were bought up and the people pay rent, when they can. I was traffic manager for the Low Moor Iron Company keeping track of thousands of our cars, scattered from Kay Moor, West Virginia and our Virginia mines to all our customers, both seaboards, Canada, and in all the states.

"When the break came, several of the office force stayed on here: our homes were most comfortable, and it took time to land a job. Gradually the others moved out, but here I am. My confidence in my capacities might have been shaken had I not known that the well-discharged requirements of a traffic man, for a company like Low Moor Iron Company, are not found in every applicant for lesser positions. Those acknowledged to be my inferiors in experience and activity and training, I see getting positions for which I have applied and been refused.

"For two years I held a position working several hundred men on the payroll, which I made up myself after driving an average of one hundred miles per day, inspecting and check-ing work and individuals. I did my work conscientiously and was loyal to my employer. I have always been loyal to those who gave me work. The man, who followed me on the work I speak of, had a stenographer, had a helper for his payroll. He had been on a higher salary than I at that time (but I do not know what he got at this place) but he lasted only ninety days. The office was closed and moved.

"For one year I have been out of work. I had a letter telling me to go to the County Clerk and he would explain some work in that office which was to be done. He told me that he knew nothing of it but that he would write and find out, adding, 'Why, Joe, you know you can do anything in this office. There's nothing you can't do here.' He dictated a letter in my presence but the letter never reached my correspondent, so he wrote me. I cannot go much longer this way. I have a family."

Mrs. Hippert interrupts. "If I were in Mr. Hippert's place, I would go to the clerk's office and camp till Mr. Payne, the clerk, gave me some sort of letter to mail myself—either rec-ommendation or condemnation. His kind words do not meet grocery bills. If Mr. Hippert were not capable, it would be different. He can audit a set of books. He has made payrolls for fifteen hundred men. His experience in the traffic managing for Low Moor showed that he was able to arbitrate or handle men when there is disagreement. But men inferior to him gets jobs right along."

"There was no complaint of my work, when I was put out a year ago. But perhaps my not being a native has something to do with it. But we have lived here thirty years. I wish I knew to whom to write. I would get out of here if there was any place to go for work. As I said before, but for the Federal government, people would have starved all around us. There are some pitiful cases, now, where want is great."[16]

"We're among them," adds Mrs. Hippert.

The atmosphere of the Hippert home is that of intelligence, efficiency, and industry. The family living room, across from the parlor, is well furnished: block-tiled-pattern linoleum rug; overstuffed divan; books and magazines on the tables in perfect order; canary in a high cage; Boston ferns in huge receptacles; deep, comfortable chairs with convenient electric lighting; steam heat; a desk, also in order; and, on the mantel, a clock that would inspire a "junk hunter" to theft. It is about two feet four inches in height, face has [a] few scroll design decorations but no flowers. The door has a queer painted and gilt patch-pattern. One patch is a conventionalized leaf in gilt, the next a colored hunting scene, not over an inch and a half in size; the next patch, [with] gilt leaf between, a study (with no connection whatever to the others) [of] a highly colored peach; and so on, spaced five inches by four. At a guess, the frame is brown mahogany. The top is similar to [the] Heppelwhite era of grandfather clocks. The center vase in the design has either been broken or was lacking at first. It is missing now.

How can one examine a clock in the face of two parents anxious for food for their child and grandchild? Intelligent and industrious! Efficiency, with idleness forced upon it! Even antique hunters have a heart and a yearning to examine clocks.

[Loc.: VSL/AB, box 182, 6 pp., 2,002 wds.]

A. A. Archer *by Mary S. Venable, rec. 26 October 1938*

The Covington Machine Shop, established in 1892, employed as many as 250 men, mostly from the local area. William Sanger, a Scotsman naturalized in 1899, was superintendent of the shop in 1910. But by the end of World War I or shortly thereafter, he left to go to work for the Du Val Cream Separator Company in Canada. Sanger was replaced, according to another life history, by a Mr. Alfather *not* Archer. The name Alfather does appear in Alleghany County records, whereas no evidence has been found for Archer. This appears to be another pseudonym used by Venable. Some report that the shop closed in 1931, but other evidence suggests it closed not long after Alfather took over as superintendent.[17]

"I do not know what the industrial outlook is at the present as I am not on public works any longer, but I can tell you what the union did for the Covington Machine Shops when I was there—it shut the shop down. We had always had open shop and we had never had any complaint. We had given training to hundreds of boys in this community and those were the main employees, from right around here.

"When I was made superintendent, the first thing I did was to go in and make a survey of our buyers. To give you some idea of the sum of business we had done, there was three-quarter of a million dollars [in] orders from General Electric and other large firms in ratio.

"I wrote letters to all big buyers and I said, in the past you have seen fit to trade with the Covington Machine Shops, which we appreciate and now that we are expanding, we hope for additional orders. From General Electric we got a big order, turbines for Russian trade. It was an order which, spread, would have kept us running for years. I was tickled and that morning I was in a great hurry to call the men together and tell them of this good news, when a strange man came into the office and began inquiring about whether we were open shop. I told him we were and always would be. He said he thought differently, mentioned the big order I had just gotten and what he could do if the union was not formed.

"To end a heated argument, I put him out of the office. He went around and talked to the men outside for weeks. We had several conferences, the employees and I. Finally the day came when I had to know, so I showed them the contract. And I said, 'Do you want to work? Or do you not want the work?' To make the long story short, the shops closed down. We were paying seventy-four cents to the molders. But it was the molder's union that made the trouble, and the prevailing wage for the union was seventy-two cents per hour. We were working nine hours, which was OK then. So all we clashed on was open shop.

"Had our men ever complained against anything we did, it would have been different. But up to the time when the union sent their men from a distance, we had employed native help and met their every reasonable demand. Our business, as testified by the output and the books, was good and it was on a basis to continue. The union broke it up.

"The present industrial situation, so far as I can see, will not be affected one way or another by the wage-hour law and minimum wage, because all of our mills are already over the minimum and the hours are forty, not forty-four. It may affect some small businesses."

Mr. Archer has lived in Covington since the Covington Machine Shop was closed. He opened a small foundry or repair shop. His son aids in running it, or perhaps now owns it. Mr. Archer is not on the "fire-eaters" order, but he is thoroughly convinced in the correctness of his viewpoint.

[Loc.: vsl/ab, box 181, 2 pp.]

Machine Shops of the Shenandoah Valley in Pictures and Text

The writer of the textual material following is not credited in the background data for this project, but the photographs were taken in January 1942 by RA/FSA photographer John Vachon. It is possible that Vachon also wrote the text. But it is as likely, or more so, that the writing was done by the local civic booster and businessman Luther E. Long.

Almost half of this document consists of a general and not altogether accurate description of the history, settlement, and development of the Shenandoah Valley region; that part of the text has been omitted. The remainder given here makes an overt pitch for local economic development and participation in the defense industry; the message is augmented and persuasively reinforced by the images produced by Vachon and his camera. At the very least, this sample of another type of textual material yielded by New Deal programs—in this case, the outgrowth of a documentary photography project rather than a Writers' Project interview program—is informative.

In three counties of western Virginia 320 machine tools stand idle ninety percent of the time, only a very few ever work on war production. Another fifty-five are idle over fifty

(Above)
View of the Chesapeake & Western
Car Shop, Elkton.
[LC-USE6-00227-D]

(Left)
Chesapeake & Western Railroad
runs through the Valley, 17 miles in length.
[LC-USE6-00228-D]

percent of the time. . . . These are machines that can help win the war. If a manufacturer needed similar machines to fill a war contract, he would have to wait as long as six months for one of them even though he might have the highest of priority ratings. Six months delay in the vital year 1942, when only a few hour's drive from the Nation's Capital are 375 machines—occasionally working on farm equipment or some minor industrial repairs—usually gathering dust!

It is the energetic Mr. [Luther E.] Long who is responsible for the Shenandoah Defense Cooperative and our exact knowledge of what tools are available in the Shenandoah Valley. In late 1940 he saw that this country would be playing a leading part in the fight for world freedom, and he looked about him to see what he and his neighbors could do. He saw plenty.

He saw thirty small machine shops scattered throughout Augusta, Shenandoah and Rockingham Counties. In these shops were seventy-eight engine lathes, four turret lathes, fifteen milling machines, fourteen shapers, sixteen planers, seventy-nine drill presses, thirty-nine grinders, nineteen power hacksaws, eleven power presses, fifty welding outfits, both electric and acetylene, and a host of other machine tools in smaller quantities. He spoke to the owners of these machines—to a man all were anxious to put them to work. All submitted complete descriptions of their facilities [and] convinced Long [that] they sincerely desired to do their part. These were men who "made a living" from the various odd jobs they picked up in the valley—automobile repair, repair of farm implements and frequent jobs from the half dozen large manufacturers with plants in the valley. Some had one tool; some had a dozen. The survey included even the shop facilities of the schools in the valley.

These men operated their own machines, made their own tools, hired machinists in the valley when they needed them. The men they hired were not unemployed when not working in these shops; they worked small farms, or got along doing odd jobs. Labor, competent labor, was always available to these shop-owners if an especially big job came in. The shop-owners did not set their prices high. They wanted to keep their machines busy, and they were anxious to do whatever they could to supply the armies of democracy. Realizing that they could not do high-precision work, they were anxious to free better-equipped plants to do the highly specialized work that could not be done in the valley. They discovered that there was enough of their type work to keep them busy seven days a week.

Three of the best-equipped shops were organized into the Shenandoah Valley Defense Cooperative. As these three shops were seen to be busy on work for army and navy prime contractors, Long figured, the other [smaller shops] would be more than anxious to cooperate when work came for them. An attractive brochure was prepared, describing in detail the tool facilities of the valley shops, explaining that these tools were idle ninety percent of the time and that there were enough skilled machinists available in the valley to operate them sixteen hours daily, [and] that if the orders came in enough additional men could be trained to keep the machines operating on a twenty-four-hour schedule.

In the fifteen months since the brochure appeared and since the Shenandoah Valley Defense Cooperative—with the aid of excellent nationwide publicity—began seriously to look for contracts, the three member shops have divided about $20,000 worth of work. These three shops, which include some fifty-five of the 375 tools listed, could by themselves turn out work worth at least $60,000 annually, in addition to their normal jobs. The writer has inspected each of them at length. Long estimates that if the cooperative were expanded to its full potential

Luther Long, Chairman of the Electric Cooperative, heads the Shenandoah Valley Committee.
[LC-USE6-00254-D]

size, it could turn out work worth a quarter of a million dollars per year. This reliable estimate, seen in the light of a nation full of idle machine shops, is a painful thing to hear.

The business that has come in has, of course, been a boon to the three shops that have shared it. "In February of 1941," says Raymond Van Fossen of the Braden Van Fossen Works in Staunton (largest of the three member shops), "I had to borrow money to keep me going. I've had to do that most every year during the slack season. I got through all right this year though."

Each of the three shops had added to or improved some of its machinery in anticipation of war orders. John Beery of Harrisonburg bought a milling machine; Carl Wilbarger, also of Harrisonburg, bought a turret attachment for a lathe, enabling [it] to do six operations with one setting. In Staunton, Van Fossen has acquired a heavy bending press. These tools were all bought secondhand—few completely new tools ever come into these valley shops—but the work from them is remarkably good. The men who buy them and refit them are experts.

What of these three shops? First there is J. A. Wilbarger, in Harrisonburg. Carl Wilbarger, whose late father established the shop in 1919, has three men working there now besides himself. For the largest of the war orders that have come to him he employed nine men; he could use twenty-five men were he working on a twenty-four-hour basis. He could get these twenty-five men—few of the workers in these shops are young men, most are skilled machinists fifty-five and sixty years old.

Carl Wilbarger switched on a lathe for the writer and in less than ninety seconds produced a threaded stop of the type ordered by a machine tool company for war work. "It took three or four days to make this chuck," he said, indicating a special attachment to the lathe, "but it was worth it. Without it, it takes ten minutes to make a single one of these stops."

He pointed next to another of his three large engine lathes—there are seventeen assorted machine tools in the shop—and explained how "three or four days work" had increased the capacity of the machine by two-thirds. While he was awaiting his first war job he decided that breakdowns on that lathe must be avoided. He dismantled the overhead belt and pulley power arrangement, installed a small electric motor and ripped the gear shift and transmission from an old junked Ford car. The new power setup means far greater speed for the lathe and there hasn't yet been a breakdown. In February, he followed the same procedure on his milling machine.

Claude Spitzer at the 24-inch lathe [in Wilbarger's shop]. "I have been in and out of the shop for 15 years—I am more of a blacksmith than I am a machinist." [LC-USE6-00285-D]

A few months ago Wilbarger needed some Acme thread taps, specialized small lathe attachments, required for a particular war order he was filling for the cooperative. He wrote a New York tool-house and was told he would have to wait at least sixty days for delivery. The whole job was due in ten days. He wired a Pennsylvania toolmaker and was told he could have the needed attachments in ten days. He went down the block to his friend John Raymond Beery, whose eleven-tool shop is the smallest of the three in the co-op. Beery made the taps for him in twelve hours. The cost was higher than the catalogue price—it was a custom job—but the time saved was to both men the important thing.

Beery is younger than Wilbarger and Van Fossen, a slight man of about thirty, with an alert, sensitive face. He's proud of his new milling machine, and wishes he had more work for it. He's especially happy when he can turn out jigs to speed the work of his fellow-members of the cooperative. "It doesn't pay, though, to make special jigs unless you're going to work on at least 1500 pieces," he says. Beery has one man working for him now; he could use fifteen, on a twenty-four hour schedule, if he had the work.

Early in 1942, Beery with William Dove and George Liskey, two other residents of Harrisonburg, bought an old abandoned machine shop in the city. They have put in long loving hours cleaning the eleven machine tools in this old shop, and now they have it in A-1 condition, ready and waiting for war work.

(Opposite) The terms of a small contract for walnut-picking machinery (necessary for gas mask production) given the shop of Beery & Sons, Harrisonburg, Virginia, required the turning out of four units per hour. A special jig was made for this punch press by workers at the shop, and the production stepped up to 50 units per hour. [LC-USE6-02961-D]

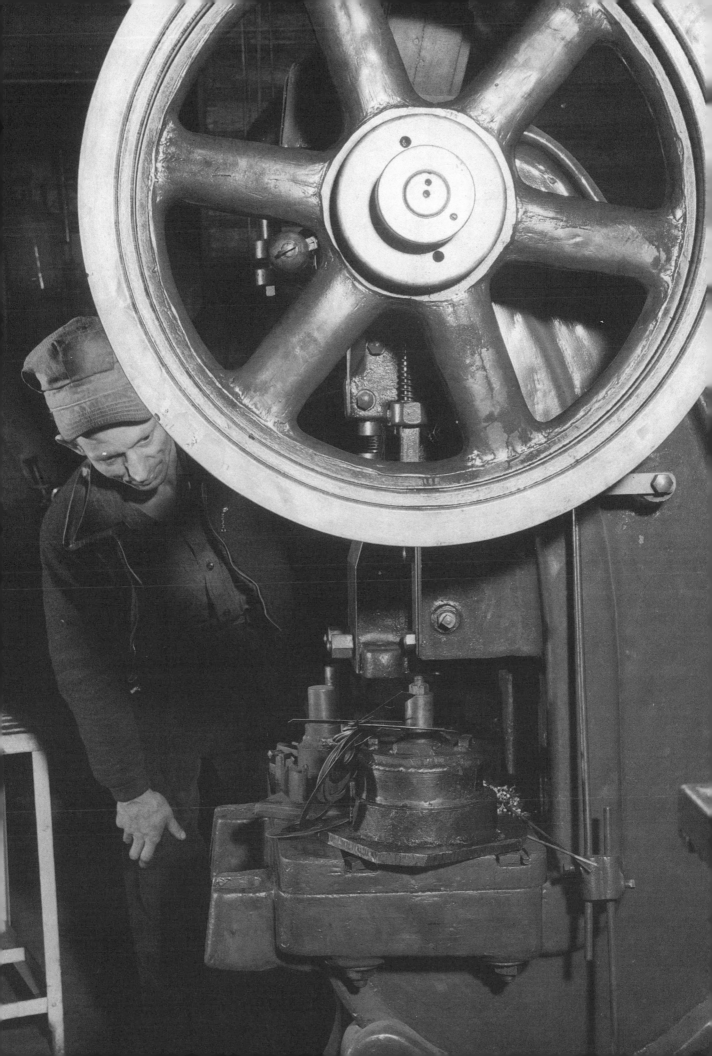

Plant conversion means machine conversion. This lathe at the Beery & Sons shop, in Harrisonburg, Virginia, is being fitted for production of a small part needed by a war contractor. [A sentence deleted here.] [LC-USE6-02964-D]

A block away from the Wilbarger shop is the large well-equipped shop of David W. Batterman, which could keep three shifts of ten to twelve men busy on war work. Batterman, a Mennonite, would not allow his tools to be used on gun parts or torpedo parts or anything destined to kill, but he would be willing to work on ship parts, parts for machine tools, etc. He hasn't yet had a single order.

Twenty-five miles down the valley, in Staunton, birthplace of Woodrow Wilson, is the Braden Van Fossen Works. A large barn with a dirt floor encloses just about as much machinery as there is in the shops of the two Harrisonburg members. Raymond M. Van Fossen is the business manager, while his partner, Dan Braden, works in the shop as a toolmaker. . . . The skill of Dan Braden is something of which Van Fossen is especially proud. "We make all our own tools," he boasts, "no shopping around for us. When we get a job we make up special tools for it. On one order we got a little time back, we were allowed ten days for delivery. Our boys got busy and made some special tools and jigs in a day and a half. Half a day later, we delivered the whole order to the Navy. That's the way we like to work."

Raymond Van Fossen has his own ideas on why the co-op has had so little work. "We feel like if the boys want it done all they have to do is let us know. But the simple jobs we know exist and are ideal for us, we just haven't been offered. It looks to me like the big boys have an idea we should be able to do anything. They send us a drawing of a gun bridge that takes close grinding and high precision work. They know we can't do that sort of thing. It looks to me like they just want an excuse to forget about us."[18]

[Loc.: LCP&P, RA/FSA Textual Records, microfilm reel 20, lot no. 2116]

Braden & Van Fossen Works, a flourishing shop outside of Staunton which does such heavy work as machining different rock crusher shafts. [LC-USE6-00223-D]

A large 60-inch lathe at the Braden & Van Fossen Works is employed to smooth down pedestals for ships' dining tables. The lathe was recently acquired and refitted to do extra large jobs. Also at the Van Fossen Works, holes are drilled in the pedestal bases for fastening the pedestals to the floor or deck. [LC-USE6-02959-D]

Oscar William Gross *by Mary S. Venable, 19 April 1940*

Oscar Gross was a "rivet-sticker" for the Virginia Iron and Bridge Works and thought it "the *best* company to work for," except during the depression, when not many bridges were being sold. In order to subsist while waiting for business to pick up and for his expected call back to steelwork, Gross worked as a cook in CCC camps, did odd jobs and gardening for well-to-do ladies, and when he could get it, did road work for the WPA.

Gross observed, however, that it was "the difference of two systems" (between federal and state WPA practice) that caused delay and problems on roadwork projects. People who needed the work, such as himself, were caught in the crossfire of their differences. On yet another level, Oscar Gross was caught in a much older system of social and economic difference that exchanged favors of varying degree and value for political patronage. Even though he referred most often to the kindness of "the lady-what-owns-the-house," it was her husband, Mr. Olin J. Payne, the clerk of the county court, to whom Oscar Gross owed his allegiance and his vote. It was Olin Payne, too, who did not respond to Joseph Hippert's repeated requests for work.

On the tenth of January, nineteen hundred and forty, Milton Joseph Gross came to live with his mother and father in the office of the old bus barn in the alley back of Riverside Avenue at the corner of Maple Avenue. To the west is Jackson's River. To the northwest is the new bridge on Route 60, its balustraded sides and bright lights taking the place of the old ford . . . near the birthplace of Milton Joseph.[19]

That ford was gone, [and] the buses were gone. They had represented the era of the building of the Rayon Plant two miles away and had carried its enterprising owners deep into the red. With a wreck from a sleeping driver and a few bumps from other careless drivers, [and] with every Rayon worker buying a car on credit, the bus company failed. And the buses filled the barn, filled the yard around it. And the horse-weeds covered their sides, fronts and tops, as though to keep from view the sight that reminded the owner of his costly venture and his thousands "gone but not forgotten."

The office of the bus barn consisted of two rooms and a small sleeping space for the man, who had to be awakened when the one o' clock bus came in or the three a.m. bus went out. It was made of stucco and had a flue between the rooms. It was never cold in the winter. Water had played on the buses in washing them, then run down in front of the office door till a pool was there. The weeds had found this spot and grew unmolested, till Oscar William Gross set up housekeeping and told the owner that he would "fix things up around here."

It was the crop of 1938 weeds that had to be cut with an extra heavy corn blade, designed by Oscar for these "trees," he called them. After the giant horse-weeds fell, Oscar had to cut again, near the ground. Then he dug the roots out, cultivated the ground, planted grass seed, put bricks along the edge of a walk to the front door and around the corner to the kitchen entrance. The space between, he filled with fine cinders. In 1939 he had a garden, which saved him cash and afforded "lots of fun" to work it.

Some of the buses were sold at about ten percent of cost, Oscar guessed from stray bits of conversation, which he could not help hearing while inspections of them were being made. Some of the worst used vehicles were junked. And Oscar gradually cleared the yard: put some inside the barn, and pushed the one remaining close against the rear of the coal-house of the "Lady-what-owns-the-place," who happened to be the one who took in the rent. When Oscar put the old bus in a shady nook, he was not planning for Milton Joseph Gross to enjoy it for a playhouse. But other boys found it before Milton's one-and-a-half-pound self came to play on the cold January morning.

Neither the neighbors, nor the grocer, nor the boss, who had seen Mildred Gross two nights before when she and Oscar took his time to the boss and stayed to talk a bit, would believe Oscar when he said there was a playmate at his home. Even Oscar's father who had seen Mildred that week said, "Yes, you're kiddin' again," for once before Oscar had "kidded" on that subject but he had never been able to offer proof. "Come down and see if you are not a Granddad" [said Oscar]. "Well I'm be darned! I'll write your mother this day and say, You went out to our girl Nell's to get a grandbaby, but I got one and didn't have to leave town to get it. She'll be *that* 'sprised!" Oscar and Mildred were 'sprised by two months, no savings, no clothes for the seven-month's doll! No "bought clothes" would fit it, so the sister of Mildred bought a doll gown and dress. The baby, by April, has grown to the size of most babies at birth. So the tiny doll dress is even now a souvenir, which one can scarcely believe once fit the still-tiny baby.

Mildred was the youngest of eight children in her family. She says the reason she knew how to care for this "incubator baby" (without any incubator) was that by the time she was able to carry a baby, her two older sisters had married. They lived not very far away, and

Mildred cared for her nieces and nephews from the time she can remember till she was married. "There was always a new baby in one home or the other!" she recalls.

"See how he notices us when we talk to him?" says Oscar, leaning over the pink-blanket-bundle in Mildred's arms. Then he speaks to "Son," who gives him a calculating glance tinged with inquiry. His mother then speaks. And to the delighted amazement of the pair, the baby turns to look at her with that wisdom of infants which seems to say, "So, this must be All Fool's Day!" "See how smart he is?" the parents ask.

In the dresser drawer are the sacque Mildred's brother bought for the baby, [and] the wrapper and two dresses "the church folks sent. They are so nice. Look at that embroidery," Mildred says. "And here is one *his* mother made, it has tatting on it. He got a lot of things, but he has just grown to them. I'll have enough to last him through the summer. He was not any bigger than this when he come" (measuring about seven inches between her outstretched hands) "and his head was not bigger than a tea cup. I wish you could have seen him."

Oscar, for [the] thirty-two years which he claims, has the glee of youth. He is never still, though he seldom reaches for the baby. But he likes to come into the event of that fateful night, "When I went for the doctor, he says to me, 'You are just scared. Tell [Mildred] to go to bed and be still. It isn't time for the baby to be here.' But, I says to him, 'Doctor, the baby is on the way this very minute!'

"He come and found out I was right. And when he looked the baby over—its fingers and toes—and saw that it was perfect all but its size, he says, 'Is it an eight-months baby?' And we said, 'No, it is a seven-months.' 'Good,' says he, 'because an eight-months never lives, but a seven-months has a chance if you know what to do for him.' And Mildred says, 'I KNOW.' Well, he [the doctor] comes real often. We ain't never had a cent to pay him. But sure as I live I aim to pay for this baby."

"Here is the bastinet [bassinet] that the-woman-what-owns-this-house brought for him. It is so pretty! She is an awful good woman. We got behind with the rent and she lets Oscar put in some time with her flowers and garden. She has not said we have to move. Oscar is out of work now," Mildred says ruefully.

The Grosses eat twice a day. It is after Mildred does the baby's daily washing and puts the bedroom in order that she gets the first meal. It was fried apples and bread on one bright April morning. The table had upon it a plaid cloth, red and white. The china was varied, but adequate to hold the meal. The coal range shone with recent polishing and the floors had no sign of mud on the linoleum, though the previous day had been stormy and the alley was muddy. The baby bastinet was near the cooking stove, and the baby was taking water from an erstwhile vanilla bottle and its very clean-looking nipple. "He knows when he wants water and will not take milk instead," mentions Oscar.

"There were eight in my family. I was the oldest boy. We lived in Craig County. I was born there on a farm. When my mother's father died, we moved to Bedford County on the farm that belonged to her mother. Sort of rented this way: my father and his boys were to do the farming, and what was raised went to feed the stock and on the table for all of us. And we were to haul and chop the wood. That left nothing for clothes, so my father had to do hauling to get in cash. That left the farming to me and my next brother. He was not strong and I, being the oldest, naturally had the most to do.

"The Blue Ridge Stone Quarry was not far from where we lived. Father hauled for the Boxleys, they owned the quarry. When it closed down, he hauled for Grubb Mines. He left at daylight and came home at dark. I got only three month's schooling a year. When you couldn't do any farming along in January and the like, I went to school. Why, the boys I started out in the class with had learned to read and were in the seventh grade the last session I went. And there I was, a big chump, still spelling out my words. So I stopped.

"My folks could have done no diff'unt! I'm satisfied with the little I got CAUSE it HAD to be that-er-way! There wa'n't nobody to do the plowin' but me. And the plowin' had to be done when the time come to do it, else the crops would have been no- good. There wa'n't no other way 'round! Ef I had er got what I wanted, it would have been machinery. But it wa'n't no drawback. Because when I went to work at the Virginia Bridge and Iron Company in Roanoke (that was several years after I was on the farm), I got along as quick at catchin' on to electric weldin' and rivet stickin' and all the shop work—just as quick—as any of them. Schoolin' don't make so much diff'unce if you got mod'rate sense.

"But I'm getting ahead of my story. I needed money that the farm did not bring in. So at first, I went to work on the section force of the Norfolk and Western Railroad for a few days in dull season on the farm. Later on, I took a steady job with the section boss. By that time, my younger brother had come on stronger as he grew up and then he was able to take my place.

"Goin' into Roanoke, I met with fellows at the Virginia Bridge and Iron [Company]. They paid good. They wanted strong fellows. I'm not so fleshy as I were then, but I was right off the farm for livin' and the road gang for work. I was taken in the shop. I went from one place to another, liked it all. The bridges that are sold from there are put together in the shop, as far as can be. We did the riveting of the long pieces, then that takes the field gang less time to get the bridge up. All that can be done is put in at the shop before they are loaded on the cars. Of course, when they are set up, there are more rivets to be put in as the pieces go together.

"I was a shop man. I never was sent out to what they called the field. I went there in '34 or 35, I don't remember which. I worked there till they stopped getting orders when the Depression came; wa'n't no bridges sold for erwhile. They laid off men they had had for years. If an order came in, a few would be called back. But I saw that my dollar-and-a-quarter-an-hour had come to an end," Oscar states the fact cheerfully.

"My father had moved to Covington. He and my mother are still living. They are on Alleghany Avenue. Both of them are sixty-six years old. He is two months older than she is. I followed them over here. I came when things were sort of low. It was no worse here than in Roanoke.

"I got a few days work by the day. All that summer I was just pickin' up a few dollars here and there. I went to the mills. If I was to tell anybody how much shoe leather I wore off going to the watch-box every morning—'spectin', no hopin', to get called—after I had put in my applications at the three mills, they wouldn't believe what I told 'um.

"I seen there was not goin' to be nothin' for me at any public works, so I went on state road work, that is, state and county. They was puttin' in a road up to Rumsey mines when I first begun. But they called me in and when the bridge at Idlewilde was put up, I got to do the rivet-stickin'."

Oscar's recollection of resuming his chosen work is filled with pleasant memories and his countenance beams, as he plants a foot on the porch and plays with a bit of copper wire that he has picked up off the ground. "It were a second-hand bridge that was put in there when the old wooden bridge gave 'way. It had been made by the Roanoke firm that I had worked for. Why, it was my old shop boss that was sent to put it up, he knew me right off. Yes, I had worked under him. He told the state foreman, 'There's a trained steel man. He used to work for the Virginia Steel [Bridge] and Iron Company. I can use HIM.'

"The reason he was so keerful 'bout pickin' his men, some of the fellows was so hard up for work they would say they had worked in steel when they had not. It is dangerous work. A fellow up on the top with me asked me what the rivet tongs WAS. He had never been on a steel job, but he had told 'um he had. Bein' a rivet-man comes from years of handlin' y'rself. This fellow took a step backwards, a rivet-sticker never does. He knows he is in the air. He fell off and broke both legs," says Oscar mixing his antecedent pronouns in a glowing pride of recital. His present garb [contrasts] so pitifully with his tale of past wages, but *his* drop has left intact his limbs and *almost* shoeless feet. And in fancy, he is, for the while, cock-of-the-topmost girders.

"When we were working on the bridge across Jackson River down at Parkling Heights, we were still gettin' thirty-five cents an hour. It was state and county work, NOT WPA. We were stickin' the rivets and we looked down at the labor-gang workin', down where it was safe, and drawing just the same as us men in the dangerous place. So we told our boss, who was a steel man, of course (he was gettin' the bridge up), we says: 'We think we ought to be gettin' half as much as we would, or as we did, when we worked for the Virginia Steel [Bridge] and Iron Company—private work. We will make it half to the state, but we think we ought to get more than those fellows down on the ground.' He says, 'Don't you leave. You can set up there, but don't you go. I'm going after one of the county supervisors and bring him down here.'

"And that is what he did. They drove down and got out and walked around. We could hear our boss talkin' to him and then they got in to go. He called the foreman over and he says to him, 'Tell the fellows to go on workin'. I haven't got it fixed, but I'm pretty sure I will and they can start up.' So we did and got our half-wages for that bridge, sixty-five cents an hour. When that was over we put up a bridge over Dunlap Creek. It was a new bridge, I believe. It has been so long I don't remember.

"'Bout that time I got married. (Oscar is unaware, but his wife smiles at his memory alibi). We lived with my folks awhile and with her folks awhile. And work got scarce. I went on WPA road work. With having to pay board and having to help with the work because we was in the families, [it] was too much. We come off here to ourselves. If I could have kept on gettin' WPA road work the same, I could have got on alright, but . . ."

His shabby overalls are clean; his blue sweater is the only whole garment on him. That is a good, warm one. His shoes are stiff, the sole-sides grinning with broken threads, spaces between. The toes are curled up. He is gardening and the ground is soft, even if there are no soles! His yellow hair curls over the edge of a ragged collegiate cap. There is a tin pin on his breast, something on the order of Hi-Lo-Silver-pin, though not exactly that. His face is unlike most rivet-stickers that we have trod the girders with: he sheds an optimistic cheerfulness and has no scar tissue in either spirit or his flesh.

"I worked for years for the Virginia Bridge [and] Iron Company," he resumes, "and never got a scratch. When I told my father that I was going to work for them, he said I would not be working there three days till I got killed. And it was true that a lot of men did get hurt; the ambulance would back up to the door nearly every day. Most workers get hurt by their own smart-aleck ways, doing something the foreman has told them not to do. The Company does not want their men hurt. But after a man works there awhile, he gets to taking chances—his own chance—at doing what the boss has told him not to do. There never was but one boss there that gave orders that turned out dangerous, and he got killed himself.

"There was a big girder 377 feet long held up by two cranes, [and] the chains were none too strong. Well, there was a bolt left in one end that ought to have been taken out before the girder was lifted by the cranes. He saw it and told me to climb up and get it loose. I told him I was not goin' up under it. He said he would, [that] there was no danger! The girders had been fresh painted and were slick. No quicker than he went up under there to take loose the bolt, them chains broke. It mashed him. He never knowed what hit him. He was from Salem. I forget his last name; Tom was his first name. He was Head-leader in fitting up. I was a helper.

"I saw a man's legs cut off. That was his own hard-headedness. [He] disobeyed orders. We had to patch gondolas. In the shop, the doors to the gondola bottoms were taken off, fixed, painted, and stacked to be put back on. They were stacked over a hole outside. To hold them up were two iron rails; the rails were small, not railroad rails. The doors were stacked about fourteen feet high in pairs; the center happened to be stacked over the hole in the ground. The rail gave away, the doors fell together, [and] the man standing on top got caught in the center, where the doors buckled together, and both legs were cut off. He had been warned about piling them so high. He did not die. They gave him a regular job in the shop. He had been a fine ball player.

"That is the *best* company to work for that I know of. They have my name and address. And when work picks up one of these days, I will get a telegram from them and money for transportation. I'll get right off and come back for Mildred and the baby on the weekend. All the men ahead of me will have to be placed by seniority and I know that business will pick up some day. Then I'm gone."

After Oscar was laid off of the steel work, he was cook at a CCC Camp near Lynchburg. He has forgotten the name. From there he got the same work in Dolly Ann CCC Camp in Alleghany. His parents had moved to Covington and he was glad to be near them. His skull cap sits at the angle of a cook's cap and one would judge from his rapid movements that he would not be awkward in a cook's place. He has an air of "Let's-enjoy-this-moment," whether it be in planting an onion, explaining that he can "wear *any* size of shoe," or planning the flower beds for the summer. He glides swiftly into relating his experiences on county road work, ere one is aware of why he quit the camp. His reputation of being a "good worker" is known, and he is in demand for all the extras that come up. The deputy surveyor for the county finds him able to keep up with the iron-muscled countrymen in climbing ridges and cliffs. The women who garden ask for him to make appointments for the days when they plant.

He has been on the WPA road force but has gotten very little time during the winter. The regulations forbid a truck carrying more than sixteen men to work. He lives at the end of a long stretch; "miles of workers" are picked up and he cannot get on the truck. The work is ten miles away from his home. How he has subsisted through the winter is a wonder. Just now the road force is laid off in entirety due to a disagreement between the district road engineer and the WPA Supervisor in Roanoke: a divergence of Federal and State ideas as to whether the drivers on the hired trucks shall take a hand in loading or merely do the driving of the individually-owned truck.

Oscar discusses the pros and cons of Federal and State roadworking policies in an intelligent manner, "It is the difference of two systems. The Federal Road Supervisor comes where we are working, and seeing the driver off his truck with a shovel helping to load, he says, 'Take that man off and put him where he was hired. He has no employment insurance under our contract. Suppose he would get hurt!'

"Then he goes away and the foreman does what he was told. Here comes Mr. I——, the State District Road Engineer. He says, 'Why is that man standing around doing nothing? The quicker the load gets on, the quicker this truck goes out.' It puts the road foreman on the spot. He does not know where he is. I heard a man who has done a lot of road work (I mean that he knows about the reports and things), he said he wouldn't give three cents for Mr. I——'s job today. One man got hurt when he got out of his driver's seat and was using a shovel. The foreman had the men too close together—the ones who were pitching dirt—and the truck driver got cut in the mouth with the other man's shovelling at too close range. So it looks like the Federal man knows what he is talking about.

"Whatever way they decide it, I hope it comes soon, for thirty of us want to eat. Ross Howell said we might know in a day or two. But the next project is a sewerage line, and there is a hang-up on the county supervisors letting lose the appropriation till the contract suits them.

"I'm behind in my doctor's bill, my rent, and our furniture payments. The doctor has not said a word and comes by real often to see how the baby is getting on. The lady what owns the house is good. She knows how little work I have had this winter and that I am willing to work for her. I paid the furniture man a dollar last month; we got $80 worth of stuff when we went to housekeeping. I kept up the payments while I was on regular WPA road work.

"We made the Rumsey Road: turn off at Dunlap Beach, and go up over the mountain. It has a sixty-foot right of way, that's a good road. There're a lot of farmers up there, and you can take it as a shortcut to Castile Run. We have about four miles yet to go. I hope when the weather opens up that I can get on the truck. It is loaded long before it gets to me. I got only two days last half. But they will manage somehow I know. Yet I'm about the only road man in this old part of town. The truck starts picking up Longdale workers and all along the way.

"I'm a Democrat, or whatever Mr. Olin Payne is. I always vote for him. He is in for his third term. I told him, no matter what I do without I always pay my head tax (he calls it poll-tax), so I can vote for you. I've helped him into office for these three last times and I hope he runs again. I don't know much about the Presidential elections, not much about the state elections, but I talk to some of the men like Mr. Payne and take their judgment. If he is a Democrat, then I am![20]

"Look yonder at that old bus, don't I know my pound-and-a-half boy will have a good time playing in that old bus? I'll have to see that the bees don't make nests in it before he gets to walking." Oscar gaily turns from trouble to the realities of blessings. "He is as big now as other children when they are born, and growing EVERY day! It won't be long before he is out here pullin' up the onions and flowers."

Mrs. Gross "reads all the time" when not caring for the house or baby. She prefers *True Stories* and *Liberty,* but we see a pile of *Colliers* and *Home and Garden* that are well worn. Oscar does not care to read. He "always has something he is puttering with at night." During the long summer evenings he works the garden. When he [had] regular WPA road work, they let something else go and took in one movie for each paycheck. "But the baby makes a difference [and] I've no paycheck coming this half, so I don't have to worry about THAT," he says.

[Loc.: VSL/AB, box 181, 11 pp., 2,162 wds.]

John B. Davidson *by Maude R. Chandler, 9 August 1940*

Just as surely as the trail from Wise County into Kentucky crossed Callahan Creek, the lives of John B. Davidson and George Brown (see chapter 1) intersect repeatedly. Both men and their families were living in the town of Appalachia in Wise County in 1910: Davidson was a store clerk for his father-in-law, Milton B. Fleenor, and George Brown was tipple boss in the coal mine. In 1886, or thereabouts, Brown had begun coal prospecting a few miles from Appalachia in Inman Hollow, a settlement consisting of only the small house he and his wife, Celia, lived in "and one more." More than twenty years later, John B. Davidson would also work for the Virginia Iron and Coal Company at Inman, which "was just being built up. Even then, "there were only a few houses, no automobiles," and transportation, he reported, was still by horse and buggy or by train.

Soon after the 1910 census, George Brown quit working in the mines and began to build on a series of lots he bought and sold in Appalachia. He continued to make his living as a house carpenter until he was "cut off" at age sixty-five. In contrast, Davidson began farming and working in the family business before he came "to the mining camps" of Tom's Creek, Inman, Imboden (which Brown helped to build earlier), Stonega, and Osaka. By 1940 Davidson was working "outside" as a timber yard foreman for Stonega, but he spent most of his decades of experience in coal mines underground as a general mine foreman.[21]

During that time he had survived "the greatest tragedy that ever happened on the Stonega Company works." Safety was, of necessity, a major concern in the dangerous occupations of both John B. Davidson and Oscar Gross (in the preceding life history). Whether one was warned not to step backward on a girder when building bridges or to set a prop under an unsafe overhanging rock in a coal mine, the possibilities for serious injury or accidental death were ever present, and both men recounted such cases involving steelworkers and coal miners as exempla. Gross observed that most workers got hurt "by their own smart-aleck ways." Davidson put it stronger, "We don't need men in the mines that are careless and go against orders." Ultimately, the obedience Davidson demanded of his men would prove to be critical when he, another foreman, and his superintendent led eighty men to safety through a water-filled room after an explosion in Stonega's Derby mine in 1934.

John B. Davidson is a tall slender man with dark eyes and grey hair. He has a good personality and he enjoys talking with people. He takes a great interest in the church work. He is a steward in the Methodist Church and is superintendent of the Sunday school.

He was born in Claiborne County, Tennessee September 24, 1876, but lived there only until he was three years old. His parents were reared in Tennessee, but they came to Lee County and bought a large farm. Land was cheap then and this was a good farm. Mr. Davidson said, "We boys worked hard and made a good living. We also raised farm products and stock to sell, and soon had the farm paid for."

He had two brothers and four sisters. They all had a common school education. Two of the girls taught school. Back then it was not necessary for one to have a college education before they could teach. His parents just had a common school education also. After coming to Lee County, they continued to live there for the remainder of their life. [Davidson's] father has been dead four years and his mother has been dead seven years. He had one brother who never married until just recently. He stayed at home and took care of his parents until their death. He is living at the home place. And his brothers and sisters were all willing for him to have the farm as his own, as he had stayed there and worked it while the others were out making a good living for themselves in other occupations.

Mr. Davidson quit school at the age of eighteen and got married. His wife, Carrie Fleenor Davidson, was only sixteen years old. They both quit school in December and were married. His wife's people, the Fleenors, were originally from Washington County, Virginia, but had also come to Jonesville, Lee County, Virginia to make their home.

Mrs. Davidson is a large woman. She has blue eyes and her hair is beginning to turn grey. She is nice looking in her clothes and she dresses well. She is [a] nice housekeeper and a fine cook. She and Mr. Davidson live a very congenial life.

They have four living children. Three boys and one girl. They are all married and living out to themselves. They have eight grandchildren. Two of [their children] live in Dunbar, one in Appalachia and one in Detroit. Several months ago one of the grandchildren was killed by a car. This child had a twin sister. It was a tragedy for them.

When Mr. Davidson and his wife were first married they lived in Lee County on the farm. He said, "I made a good living and I raised all kinds of farm products. But after farming the first year, I worked in the store for two years for my father-in-law. I could have continued to work in the store, as I was managing it. But my brother-in-law wanted to meddle in the business, so he and I didn't get along so well. So I told my wife that we would just get out. We then came to the mining camps and have lived in them ever since.

"I first went to Tom's Creek in Wise County about the year 1900, and I worked there for six years loading coal. The coke ovens were just being built, and there were only about a third of the houses there then as there are now. I left there and came to Inman and worked for the Virginia Iron and Coal Company for a year. It was just being built up. There were only a few houses, no automobiles. You had to travel by train, or buggies and wagons. I have seen livery stables with a hundred, good horses in them for hire. Of course, there were other livery stables that had only a few horses and equipment for hire. For some couldn't afford so many.

"From Inman, I then went to Imboden. These mines were individually owned by a man named Parring; they now belong to the Stonega Coal and Coke Company. I worked there for two years, and after that I began working for the Stonega Coke and Coal Company and have been working for the Company ever since. I went to Stonega, then to Osaka. I worked in Osaka for a year and was made section mine foreman. Later [I became] general mine foreman [and] served in that capacity until about three years ago, when I asked to be transferred to outside work on account of my health. The years I worked as general mine foreman I made two hundred and fifty dollars a month, and was able to save some.

"Now I make only sixty dollars, but my health has been better since I have been working on the outside than it has been for fifteen or twenty years. Now I don't have all that responsibility of all those men under my care. Some nights I wouldn't sleep over two hours for studying about my work. Now I am much freer. I am now timber-yard foreman."

Mr. Davidson said when he was hiring men to go into the mines he would instruct them in safety and the ways to take care of themselves before he would turn them over to the section foreman. He said, "After I would tell a man about his work and how to fix his place for safety, then I would go in and find him careless about it and going against orders. I would say to him, 'Now you can do as I say or get out, for we don't need men in the mines that are careless and

Coal cutter in a Southwest Virginia mine. Photo by Robert McNeill. VSL/PC. [43998]

go against orders.' He would usually say, 'If you will give me another chance I will make you a good man.' And he most always did. I found boys that had not been trained in their homes to be obedient were usually the ones that were the hardest to get to obey the rules of mining.

"I had a young man in Roda working for me that had a wife and two small children. One day I went into his place of work and I noticed a big rock in the roof that was dangerous. It was right near the place where he was working. I said to him, 'You can finish loading your car in four or five minutes, but this rock isn't safe, so you set a prop under it first before you finish loading your car.' He said, 'Do you think it is as dangerous as that?' And I said, 'Yes, Brady, I do and it is best to take the time and do it. You have a wife and two small children at home that are expecting you back each night. I don't want to have to go to them and tell them that you have been killed, for that is the hardest thing I ever had to do was to go and tell a wife that her husband [had] been killed.' He said, 'Well, if you think that it is as dangerous as that, you help me measure the timber for the prop and you needn't stay to see that it is done or worry anything more about it for I will set it.' I said, 'Well I am to meet some of the men at a certain time in another section of the mine and if you will set it, I will go on to meet this appointment.'

"In a short while, some of the other men came in to work and they saw a speck of light but didn't see or hear anyone, so they began to investigate the light and found a miner's cap

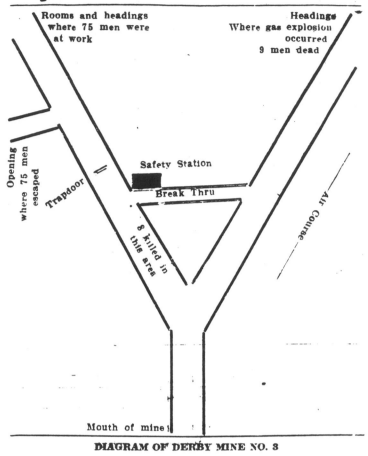

How 75 Coal Miners Escaped
Explosion Which Killed 17

Rooms and headings
where 75 men were
at work

Headings
Where gas explosion
occurred
9 men dead

Opening
where 75 men
escaped

Trapdoor

Safety Station

Break Thru

8 killed in
this area

Air Course

Mouth of mine

DIAGRAM OF DERBY MINE NO. 3

with his light still burning. And there close by, they found Brady with his head lying on one side of the log and his body on the other side. His head had been cut entirely off by the fall of the rock. He had carried the timber to the rock and decided, I suppose, to finish filling his car before he set the prop. For when he was found dead, he still had his shovel in his hands. This would not have happened had he obeyed instructions. Things like this is what we always tried to guard against in the mines."

Mr. Davidson had the experience of being in a mine explosion when he was working at Derby. He related the story of that incident: "On August 6, 1934 at 7:30 a.m., there were about one hundred men in the mines when this explosion occurred. Seventeen of the men were killed. The others were gotten out safely. Me and another foreman and the Superintendent rescued eighty men. One of the hardest things was to keep the men together and to keep them from starting out toward the entrance that they had come in through. But we knew if they went that way, they would run into damp dust and that there wouldn't be any of them gotten out alive. We stationed men [to] guard that opening [and] turn any man back that started that way. We were waiting to get in communication with the superintendent, who was on the outside, and held the men together until we could get instructions from [him].

"Victims of the Derby Blast," from
Crawford's Weekly, *10 August 1934.*

VICTIMS OF THE DERBY BLAST

CLLARENCE REED, union member, veteran, motorman, of Derby, married and father of three children— one born the day of his burial.

JESSIE DOYLE, Derby, motorman, union member, wife and three children surviving.

CLYDE WARD, brakeman, union member, single.

LAFAYETTE BLONDELL, union coal loader, Appalachia, single.

LESTER DAY, union coal loader, Derby, wife and four children.

WILLIAM BURNS, Big Stone Gap, union machine man, five children.

WILLIAM SMITH, Andover, union machine man, married.

WALTER MOORE, Derby, union member, single.

ROSCOE SMART, Derby, jack hammer helper, union, married, no children.

KYLE FIELDS, Derby, union coal loader, wife and two children.

CHARLIE REECE, Stonega, pumper, wife, 9 children.

ALEX PAYNE, Derby, married, three children.

CHARLIE MILAM, Derby, wife, one child.

RALPH BURCHILL, Derby, general mine foreman, married, one child.

RANSOM SLEMP, Derby, single.

TED JOHNSON, Derby, loading-point man, married, no children.

DAN JENKINS, Derby, assistant foreman, single.

"The Superintendent got to a phone and told us that the only escape was through a water-filled room that he had just waded through. The water [that] was in [this room] had been pumped from other parts of the mine and it had never been pumped out of it, because it was thought that the room would never be needed for an entrance, either in or out. When the Superintendent came to us, we all started out with the men. And we had to wade through water that was so deep that we had to keep our heads turned to one side to keep the water out of our mouths and noses. We were guided out by our mining lamps shining against the roof. The majority of the men were so excited that they left their coats and buckets in the mine. This was a miraculous escape.

"My wife hadn't heard the explosion, and when she saw me coming home she said to our daughter, 'There comes your Daddy. Wonder why he is coming home at this time of day?' It was then that daughter told her that there had been a mine explosion. She had been busy inside with her work and she hadn't noticed the women running back and forth to the mines.

"When I came in, I told my wife I was through with mining, that I wasn't going back inside anymore. But when the mine got ready and was declared to be safe for the men to go back to work, and I saw them go by with their dinner buckets, I told my wife to fix my bucket, that if those men were going back into work that I was too. That was the greatest tragedy that ever happened on the Stonega Company works.

"A general mine foreman has a great burden and responsibility. The Company is looking to him for the safety of the men, for a good production of coal, and the low cost of production. My forty years' experience in mining has made a lasting impression upon me, and dealing with men for years has brought me closer to them."

Mr. Davidson's wife takes great pride in housekeeping. They have a five-room house, which is nicely furnished throughout. They have just recently exchanged their old furniture for new. The house is electrically equipped. They get their rent free, because of Mr. Davidson's long service with the company.

Mr. Davidson's son that lives in Detroit is a mounted policeman and makes two hundred and twenty dollars a month. He heard of the Derby explosion in two hours after it happened and called up on long distance and said, "I heard you had an explosion there this morning." The man that answered him said, "Yes, but your father is all right." He said he couldn't ask about his father, he felt so sure he had been killed.

Another son works in Appalachia for the Southern Railroad Company. The youngest son and his son-in-law are miners.

Mr. Davidson is making very little now compared with what he used to make, but he is very well satisfied with it because his health is much better. He felt like after being under the ground as long as he had that he needed the sunshine. He would be making more if the mines ran regular. He said, "I have enjoyed reasonably good health and at the age of sixty-four years, I am able to do my regular routine of work. My health has been much better since I have been working on the outside."

[Loc.: VSL/AB, box 189, 13 pp., 2,176 wds., handwritten ms.]

The Explosion at Derby *by James Taylor Adams, rec. 1 June 1940*

The explosion at Derby mines of the Stonega Coke and Coal Company occurred on Monday, August the 6th, 1934, about seven o'clock in the morning, which accounted for the small number of lives lost. Had it occurred an hour later, the loss of life would probably [have] mounted to over a hundred. This is the first explosion of major proportions that has occurred in the Wise County field since the two explosions which wrecked the Greno Mine near Coeburn about forty years ago, and has done more to advance safety methods than any accident or happening in the history of mining in this field. While there were but seventeen lives lost in this explosion, it brought home to both miner and operator the need for improved safety methods. And today you might visit any mine in the county and you will find all miners using safety battery lamps and all other safety methods known to modern coal mining.

The ballad "The Explosion at Derby" was composed and sung soon after the disaster, but the name of the author has already been lost. While the words have not been set to music, it states on the broadside by which it was first distributed that it was to be sung to the tune of "The Picture on the Wall." Odd as it may seem, this song, while only six years from the tragedy which it celebrates, has already become a [true] folk song. For I have heard it in different forms, and Miss Pauline Carico of the Sandy Ridge section of Wise County, from whom I got this copy, tells me that the two last stanzas have been added to the original song by some poet whose name is also unknown.

Come all of you people, and listen while I tell,
Of the explosion at Derby the town you all know well.
It was on a Monday morning about seven o'clock,
When the people at Derby received an awful shock.

Cho:
In the mines, in the mines,
Seventeen dear old miners lost their lives;
Lost their lives, lost their lives,
Seventeen dear old miners lost their lives.

As I walked up through Derby a sad sight I did see,
The women were all crying, "God, bring them back to me!"
But alas! for some this never could be
For seventeen dear old miners went out to eternity.

Let us pray for the children and help the poor wives,
Of these seventeen miners who in the mines lost their lives;
For I'll tell you my friends, it is terribly sad,
To lose your loving husband and also your dad.

Soon after the explosion, there was an awful sight,
So many precious miners were brought into the light;
Mothers and children were crying, oh, how very sad,
They are gone forever, the best friends we've ever had.

Do let us all take warning, from the Derby people's fate,
And get ready for the Judgement before it is too late;
Then if the mines in your town should happen to explode
You'll be ready for the Judgement when you are called to go.[22]

Making a Living in Factory and Mill

"HURRYING TO KEEP TIME WITH MACHINES"

I feel like a machine, but it's a good-paying job. —*Nancy Carter*

The 1810 census of manufactures reports "more homespun cotton manufactures in Virginia, South Carolina, and Georgia than in the thirteen other states and territories combined [and] more flax spun in Virginia than in any other state." Cotton manufacturing continued in the South, but it was primarily domestic and small-scale manufacture. By the late nineteenth century there began a concerted effort to establish in the South industrial cotton mills with automated machinery, like those that had been built earlier in the Northeast in such towns as Lewiston, Maine, and Lowell, Massachusetts. This effort was another product of the massive socioeconomic changes taking place soon after the end of the Civil War. The movement got under way in the late 1870s through the efforts of local entrepreneurs, and the number of workers (or operatives) in southern cotton mills rose from 16,741 in 1880 to 97,559 just twenty years later.[1]

Movement is an appropriate term here. Many entrepreneurs and boosters talked more like missionaries than businessmen.

> Southern industry is a moral venture. It is an adventure in the realm of human possibility. It is the venture of seeing the potential worth of men. The pioneers of Southern industry were pioneers of God. They were prophets of God doing what God wanted done. Southern industry is a divine institution. When the first whistles blew people flocked to the light from barren places. These cotton mills were established that people might find themselves and be found. It is a spiritual movement.[2]

The mills drew their operatives, initially, from the large pool of nearby tenant farmers who were having difficulty making a living on the farm; later, mill labor began to be drawn from subsistence farmers in the southern Appalachians. "It is probable that never before or since in economic history has an agricultural population been so suddenly drawn into industry." The employment of entire families in the mills, down to children aged nine or even younger, was a common practice. The employment of children in the early days of the mill movement was seen as philanthropy or generosity, not as exploitation. And one would have to ask: Did mill work at an early age constitute exploitation any more than twelve-hour days on the farm? Some individuals, at ten years of age, simply stopped picking cotton and started spinning it, giving up a measure of independence for a steadier income.[3]

Southern workers were accustomed to long hours of hard work and to a low level of subsistence, and they came from an authoritarian culture with an emphasis on family and religion. As one writer put it: "To a child, religion, stoic discipline, fatherly authority, and the mill hierarchy seemed to be cut from the same cloth." Lois MacDonald, in her study of three mill villages in 1928, quoted workers who reinforced such judgments with their comments: "The boss is the best friend a man has" and "This is a good mill—just like a big family." But these were not the only views of mill life expressed, and many mill workers did not want their children following in their footsteps—though they often did.[4]

The labor shortages caused by World War I, as well as union activities, brought about better conditions and higher wages for mill operatives during the period. But union attempts to increase hard-won concessions after the war resulted in numerous strikes in the face of drastically changed conditions of supply and demand. During the war, there was significant overexpansion—both here and abroad—in the numbers of mills, and that ensured an ongoing, increased competition between them. At the same time, returning servicemen contributed to a larger available labor pool, and changing clothing styles required less fabric. The mills dealt with this situation by bringing in ever faster machinery requiring ever fewer numbers of workers to operate it and by attempting to break strikes whenever they occurred. In the process, some locally owned southern mills went under and were bought out by northern capital and corporate interests.[5]

The speed required to keep up with machinery eventually permeated the lives of workers, and this is occasionally commented on in the life histories. Perhaps Kate Beale's daughter, Sadie, said it best: "When you get keyed up with hurrying to keep time with machines, it sort of keeps running inside after you come off from work." Sadie kept running on weekends—to dances, swimming parties, and the movies, and she went abroad on driving trips—because by keeping up the fast pace, she said, it was easier to get back into the speed of the mill on Mondays.

Perhaps the increased speed is also reflected in music. A certain type of country music in the 1920s and 1930s utilized ever faster tempos until it culminated in 1945 in the breakneck speed of bluegrass—a music that folklorist Alan Lomax refers to as "folk music with overdrive."[6]

Mill work was always hazardous, but it became increasingly so with the speedup of machine work and with developments in synthetic fiber production. The four commercial processes for manufacturing rayon, introduced in the early twentieth century, all required the use of deadly chemicals and gases. Three of these types of rayon production were used in Virginia: the viscose, acetate, and nitrocellulose processes. For much of the industry's history prior to unionization, the Wagner Act, and various other labor laws, workers were considered to be expendable or replaceable and were not adequately protected from injury or adequately compensated when injuries did occur.[7]

Although this discussion has focused primarily on textile mills, much of it applies to other types of mills and factories as well. Henry Cowles, who left his native Alleghany County and spent twenty years working in a tire factory in Akron, Ohio, commented: "I worked in that factory so long that I was just like a machine myself. I knew the work so well that I didn't have

(Above left)
Spotsylvania County,
Virginia. Trucking pine
logs to the local mill.
Photo by W. Lincoln Highton.
VSL/PC. [43480]

(Above right)
Spotsylvania County, Virginia.
Pine logs for use as excelsior.
Photo by W. Lincoln Highton.
VSL/PC. [43481]

(Right)
Tappahannock, Virginia.
March 1941. Lumber mill.
Photo by John Vachon.
[LC-USF34-62666-D]

to use my eyes or my mind, I knew exactly when to move." [8] But Cowles's work, as well as that of Carter in a cigarette factory, was subject to the same kinds of constraints as work in a textile mill. Factory workers were, as a general rule, subject to shift work; reduced hours without warning; and layoffs as a result of loss of orders, seasonal factors, or union disputes. And regardless of the setting, many of these industrial workers remark on "feeling like machines."

G. G. Brinkley *by Mary S. Venable, 19 October 1938*

The first items sent to Richmond in response to the vwp life history or social-ethnic studies pro-grams were Mary Venable's texts with A. A. Archer (Alfather) and G. G. Brinkley on union and labor issues. In 1899, the West Virginia Pulp and Paper Company (later known as Westvaco) estab-lished its Covington, Virginia, mill, which became "one of the nation's first successful" producers of kraft paper. By the 1930s, ongoing grievances with the corporation, owned by the Luke family; depressed wages; and the hope that New Deal acts would stimulate industrial recovery finally combined to spur Covington workers into forming a union. On 4 August 1933, the International Brotherhood of Pulp, Sulphite and Paper Mill Workers of the American Federation of Labor (AFL), with headquarters in Fort Edward, New York, granted a charter to Local 152.[9]

Attached to the Brinkley text (written by Venable in a newspaper article format) was a notice from the *Covington Virginian* about a "Special meeting in Union Hall" called by G. G. Brinkley, president of Local 152, I.B.[P].S. & P.M.W., on 28 September 1938. It stated that the meeting was "Very IMPORTANT" and urged, "Come and protect your interest." But reading the text that follows, one might suspect—as did Covington plant president George Miller with regard to the seeming "sweet reasonableness" of John Burke, the national president of the union—that Brinkley "was on the side of the management rather than on the side of the union."[10]

"One thing about the industries here now and twenty-five years ago, there is no com-parison of conditions: the improvements are more efficient ways of making their product and the safety guards of the employee.

"Fatal accidents are rare now, there have been only about five men killed in five years at the Westvaco mill in Covington: Eubank and Cole, electrocuted; Cox, suffocated in the black ash, he was rodding it out when it caved in on him; two, Agner and ———— (I have forgotten the other man's name), he was from near Craigsville. He was cleaning sediment from the bot-tom of one tank. Two tanks had one exhaust, and when the one filled up it came over in the one he was cleaning. That has been fixed now, each tank has its exhaust vent.

SAFETY COMMITTEE

"There is a safety committee. And when accidents occur they chase it down and eliminate the cause, so no one else will be caught in the same trap. A safety campaign is on between every department in our mill, [and] between this mill and all others owned by the same company. In their six plants and within each plant! The Covington plant stands first for having the least accidents. The record is kept by counting 'man-hours.' As this is the largest mill, any other way would be unfair.

"In each department, they have a banner framed for perfect accident record. Our electric department got it in '36 and '37, and hope to get it in '38. The man who was electrocuted the past year was a painter not an electrician, and he was painting on the high power tower and let his feet touch the wire. He was not an electrician working in our department.

"COMPENSATION IN CASE OF DEATH
is fixed by the State Board, Workmen's Compensation. They give the widows the sum of damages, a little at a time, so the children will not be wanting food. It is a good way.

"WAGNER ACT IMPROVED RELATIONS

between the employers and the employees; it settled what they had been at for years. There is no question that it was a great thing. The employers know that the decision stands. Heretofore, the employee had no way if he was wronged to get redress and have the situation corrected. But through the Wagner Act, he gets the right, and he certainly cannot be discriminated against [by employers] and [they cannot] get away with it. Since the Wagner Act went in, there have been several cases up before the Labor Relations Board.

"GEORGE L. MILLER, PRES. OF COVINGTON PLANT

is a mighty good man to deal with. I have found him willing to listen to his employees. We have been getting along fine. Of course, we have our ups and downs like all mills. As time rolls around, the employers will see the benefit of the Wagner Act as well as the employee. People get to working together better, when each knows what to expect."

CUT IN WAGES NEXT MONTH, TEN PER CENT OF PRESENT PAY

"This company is about the only paper company that has tried to stick to NRA forty-hours-a-week code, and they say they will continue. This wage-hour law of forty-four hours maximum does not spread the wages to all who need it like the forty hours will. I'll explain about the cut: all through the summer, since October 1937, it seems that everything dropped off. Some paper factories cut the prices of paper, but this mill did not [do so] then. They are the last to cut the price of paper, but if they are to stay in the market they will have to cut too. And if they cut, labor will have to take less. The first company cut [was] in Michigan. In July, the slashing started and it spread like prairie fire. We have been running full-time since the past month, and Mr. Steely says we will have good business for a year." [11]

BY-PRODUCT PLANT

"One department that kept running full-time, when the others did not, was the face powder department. The nu-char has a steady demand, too. The turpentine plant was down for two months. There are two-thousand gallons of it on hand now. The fatty-acid plant is the dirtiest and stickiest place to work. From the digest liquor, they get the rosin which has dissolved from out the pine wood. Other by-products are made from the liquor, too. It was in the fatty-acid tank that the two fellows were gassed. The mill takes every precaution for safety. The state compensation laws make the employers see to that. When lives did not cost anything, it was different. In the past four years there has been every sort of improvement in the fatty-acid plant for the protection of the men employed." [12]

[Loc.: VSL/AB, box 181, 3 pp.]

Howard Reynolds *by Mary S. Venable, 8 January 1940*

It was indeed different "when lives did not cost anything." Howard Reynolds was one of the two persons referred to when G. G. Brinkley spoke of the men "gassed" in "the fatty-acid tank" at the Westvaco mill. Although Brinkley pointed to improvements made for the protection of workers in that part of the plant "in the past four years," those efforts were of no avail to Howard Reynolds in September 1933. Moreover, prior to the state workmen's compensation law of September 1938,

Roanoke, Virginia. June 1943. Paper mill. Photo by John Vachon. [LC-USW3-34477-D]

there were few, if any, means available for him even to seek redress for injuries. When Mary Venable spoke with Reynolds and his family on New Year's Day in 1940, his one lingering hope was to not die before he got the Social Security benefit that was finally promised, but after more than a year had still not been received.[13]

A few hours after "The Largest Mill In The World of its Kind" sounded a blast usher-ing in nineteen-forty, fellow citizens on the streets of Milltown exchanged wishes for family happiness and prosperity. And for the progress of the community they predicted a new high in mill production, [and] thereby [a new high for the] general welfare of the major popula-tion, employed by the company. The crisp, snowy air carried a contagious spirit of hopeful-ness in spite of the bitter wind, which drove socialites and business men to their firesides at an early hour in the afternoon to begin to continue New Year toasts from the evening before.
Down in the outskirts of the town, icicles two feet in length hung from the eaves of a

planked-up space, approximately twenty-five feet by fourteen. There was a roof with leaky spots showing. The broad barn-like door was of planks, the cracks stuffed with newspaper. Brown paper was pasted on the inside of the sidewall cracks. The lower sash of pasteboard filled one window; half of another window had a faded cloth hung over it, but it had glass panes. No footprints in the snow led to the door from the wagon-trail road, which ended beyond at the brick plant. Any passer-by, whom it might concern, would judge, "Nobody lives there. No one *would* live there." But it so happened that a very light gray "elephant's breath" of smoke issued from a small metal pipe coming out of the roof in the far corner of the summer garage, shack, or what-is-it? on New Year's Day of nineteen-forty.

As though to keep the little, old cookstove warm from the draft which came through the back door, four people stood close up to it: Howard Reynolds, his wife Jennie, William Grant Reynolds, and a half-grown daughter, Janet. From clotheslines strung near the ceiling hung paper bags puffed to full size (repositories of goods or chattels), which exclude the light from the west window. About ten feet of the interior is partitioned from the front room. There is no door to this opening. The walls are black. The ceiling is of pasteboard box sides, some curled as though from leaks in the roof.

A double bed is in the corner taking up most of the room-space. A table, size forty inches by about thirty, is a chair's distance from the front of the stove. No other table is in sight, either for work or for diners. The oilcloth, which covers it, is as nearly clean as anything in the room. On the table at 1:30 p.m., the soiled dishes remain piled in a pan on the far corner. Two chairs are grimy with grease and coal dust. The ancient make of stove is piled full of glowing coals, or is the glow an optical delusion? As another child pushes in and flattens her body against the son and daughter's, who fill the margin between the wall and the stove, the man of the house punches the fire and William Grant pours on more fine coal. Sitting appears to be an unknown posture, or at least, awaiting summer weather.

In the front room are two double beds. One covered with a dark gray blanket and the other with a ragged hand-sewn patchwork quilt. Inventorying the furniture does not take long: a small trunk, a large box probably used as a trunk, a dresser, clothing hung on a wire across the corner, no floor covering, no chair, a pair of thin ragged curtains over the southern window. No flue or chimney permits a fire in this room. It is as cold as outside. . . .[14]

"I have been out of work for six years, since the first day of September, nineteen and thirty-three," begins Mr. Reynolds . . . "It is a long story and I'll tell it just as it happened. I am fifty-three years old, born in Bedford City, Bedford County. We lived in the town but my father got some farming to do. My mother was an invalid. When I started to school I was ten years old. I went only a few days, when she took worse and I stayed [home] to nurse her and never went to school any more. I can't read, nor write, nor figger, and I've been done out of a lot of money in settling [accounts] by folks that know better. But I can't say nothin'. If it's a merchant, I pay what he says and then I stop buying from him; and if it's a man cheating me on my time, I stop workin' for him.

"When I was small," Mr. Reynolds leans forward confidentially whispering, "just as tall as a hoe-handle," then in higher pitch, "I went to help on the farm. My father had bought three-hundred and thirty acres near Haden's Switch, that is near Gala in Botetourt County. Not far away, the Longdale Iron Company was mining. After I farmed a year or two, I started to work in the mine, carrying water first. Then I saw how the work ran and when I was big enough — they didn't keep boys from working then — I got a job in the iron mines. My older brothers got married and left home, and my father lost his farm or sold it for the payments due on it. He sold it to Emery Circle. I moved up to the Iron Gate mines and boarded there. My wife's family, [the] McNaeils, had moved there a year or two before. When she was seventeen, January, twenty-fourth, nineteen and six . . ." "No, I lacked a month of being seventeen," Mrs. Reynolds interrupts. "That's so," William Grant says and laughs. "Well, then," admits the story-teller, "sixteen years and eleven months! we were married. Her parents went with me to get the license. We went to housekeeping.

"I got one and a half dollars a day for ten hours work. It was big wages for them times and we got along fine. Then I went to run the Big Hill pump, tend the boiler and keep the pump goin'. It was for less money, one dollar and fifteen cents for ten hours, but it was not so hard as mining. I liked machinery. I stayed for nine years till the mines closed, and then I moved to Iron Gate to work in the tannery. Our rent was five dollars a month. I got eight dollars and ten cents a week. A leather-hanger is what they called me there. The World War come on and I did what they called leather-splitting. The government took most of our production for gun-carriages, harnesses, and war things for soldiers. Our three children were born at Iron Gate: Fred Howard, Marion Lee, and William Grant."

"We lost a set of twins," the mother mentions. "They had cholera infantum. There's two kinds of it, the slow and the quick infantum. One of the twins had the quick kind. He died in a day. The other had the slow kind, he lived several days. And the baby who was born the next year died too. She was born in 1915, but she never lived but a few minutes." [15]

"Fred was five when we left Iron Gate," Mr. Reynolds resumes. "I got a job for more money with a firm in Harrisonburg, same business, tannery! Rent there was six dollars at the first place, then we moved to the A and B Row." "The company houses were named for the men who owned the plant. They were good houses for the rent," Mrs. Reynolds explains. "Mr. A and Mr. B," murmurs Mr. Reynolds. "I can't think of those men's names, as well as I know them. Some days my head don't work clear." "It don't matter what their names are," says his wife very sympathetically. "Go on."

"We lived in Harrisonburg from 1913 to 1922, and I came to Milltown because the wages at the mill here was higher. I came first and left the chillun there till I got a job and my first pay-check; then my fambly come. We have rented all over town. That is too long a story! I went to work on the lime kiln at the mill, eight hours, thirty-five cents an hour, burning lime. From there I was moved to the bleach-maker. Nothing more than a case of flu had ever happened to me in all the years I had been in public work, because I was careful first for myself, and that meant careful for the other man beside me. I had worked where accidents would have happened from carelessness, but I had never been in any accident.

"I was not at fault, either, the night I got gassed. The man who went off [the shift] before I came [to work], left the cells on the back row choked. It was the business of the foreman, Clarence Lackey, to know how everything stood about his work when the fellow left, but Clarence was out on the lime kiln. Had he told me to be careful and watch to unchoke the back row, I would have known what to do. But as it was, nobody knew the gas was collecting.

"It is hard to explain to them what don't know about cells or anything in the bleach-maker. Chromaline gas don't smell. It gives no warning. I had worked in the place eleven years and eight months, that night I had half the cells to watch. I climbed up on a ladder or steps; it is kept there for getting up to the top row. When I come to 44 cell and the brine was not runnin' on it, I started to unchoke it and the gas come from the back row, where the fellow had left

[it] choked. I sucked in a big lot of gas. I aimed to run for water, but I never did get to it.

"I was gassed alright! Somebody found me unconscious. Clarence Lackey told the mill folks that he pulled me off the ladder, where I had a heart attack. But he was out on the lime kiln and did not know I was gassed till Dr. Jeter had come in his car and taken me home. Clarence did not dare to tell that before the Commissioners, because it was easy to prove that he had never seen me. But he told the mill foremen that to save his own skin for not knowing about the condition of the cells when I took them over. I was sick for days at home and my head felt queer. My heart would miss beats and a knot was on the back of my shoulder, high up, under my collar-like. It drawed up some days and went down some days. I didn't want to eat and was sick at my stomach, but I got better, able to walk around. Dr. Jeter, the company doctor, patted me on the back and says, 'You write up an O.K. and go back to work. The mill will put you on er easy job.' But I wanted my insurance and I was too sick to work. I went to another doctor in this town. He says, 'Go to a GOOD doctor, not in this place where the mill owns all of them what are mill doctors, or are hopin' to be if the one what has it dies,' by 'it' he meant the mill practice. So I remembered my Harrisonburg doctor. He is well-known over the state and here is what he wrote. Jennie, get his letter.

"But in the meantime I had been down to the Clifton Forge hospital, which is the mill hospital or it was then. The mill wanted me to be thoroughly examined and I wanted to be, too, because I knew there was effects of gassin' workin' on me. I thought their doctors would maybe do the right thing, though I knew if the cells got a bad name, it was one of the worst places in the mill to bring on damages. Since then, two fellows have died. I don't know what Dr. Jeter called it, heart attacks, I reckon. Their hearts sure stopped! And Clarence Lackey got a dose, too, the next year. He said he went off on a long vacation the company give him. He got gassed! But not as bad as I was!

"I was wanting my insurance. When you work at the mill, each man pays in so much on his insurance each month. I figured that was mine and I needed it, so I wrote and asked for it. Here is the letter I got in answer from the office manager, Ed Crawford:

Dear Mr. Reynolds,
This is to advise you, that you were discharged from insurance by Dr. N. B. Jeter on September 28th and of course, no further insurance will be paid to you or medical attention given.

If this does not meet with your approval and you want to ask for a hearing before the Compensation Commission, it will be alright with us. You can get the blanks for application for a hearing by writing to the office of the Compensation Commission in Richmond, Virginia."[16]

By this time, Mr. Reynolds says, he had made up his mind to get a settlement through the Compensation Commission, but he still felt that his insurance was due. He wrote the President of the mill, Mr. George Miller, whose reply advised him to write for blanks for application of hearing before the Compensation Commission. The letter [gave] no explanation as to the insurance.

During this month and for a year or more previously, his mother states, a son of this family, Howard Jr., had worked in the calender room of the same mill with always one helper, and in case of a rush order to get out, two helpers. Mrs. Reynolds explains that the room given the name "calender" is where the large rolls of pulp or paper are wrapped and put on trucks to be taken to the car for shipment. The rolls are heavy and it had been the practice, heretofore, to have two men to lift the large-sized rolls. But after the decision of his father to get a hearing before the State Commission, Howard Jr.'s helper was transferred and some trifling reason given as to why he remained on other work.

Howard Jr. was the only person at work to support a family of (at that time) eight. He felt it obligatory to hold his place though he came home utterly worn out, so his mother states: "He would fall into a chair and as soon as he ate, roll over in the bed till morning. He would say, 'I don't think I can stand it much longer.' One night when the work was heavy, he asked for a helper, 'like has always been in the calender room since I've been there, till this month,' says he. The boss told him, 'If you can't keep the work up, then get out!' He got his dinner-bucket and left. He knew that the roller was under him and he might as well quit.

"Now what do you think the mill people told about his leaving?" continues Mrs. Reynolds. "They tell that he said, 'I won't work for a company that treats my father like you have,' and left, quit. They don't tell how it happened, that they piled the work on him to run him off. There was the way the mill would have give my husband a light job like Dr. Jeter told him. That's the kind of dirty work they would have put over him, after he had give 'um an OK. He knew they would find a way to run him off, and what they did to Howard Jr. was the kind of light job that would have settled his father's claim once he went back to work for them. A body don't know till they are on public works what can be done and sound like nothing at all when a fellow tells it, but those who are working there know that those things are hard to take.

"Folks will tell you that Howard Jr. was a fool to quit when we needed bread and had to go on the county. And when it come to the county agent on welfare, Charles Campbell from the mill bleacher-make-room, told the Welfare not to allow us anything because the mill was paying [us] eighty-cents a day, when the mill was not giving us what HE had paid in for insurance. Of course, the Welfare would believe a mill department-head before they would Howard (Sr.), so it took a long time for us to get the five dollars a month that the three children are allowed now. We heard that Charles Campbell went to the Welfare and told, for the truth, that the mill give us money. What business of his was it? If the mill runs the County Welfare and fires everybody in the family of those who take their claim before the State Compensation Commission, that's about the same as the mill tryin' to run the county."

Mrs. Reynolds' exasperation has no tinge of neuroticism. "If they don't, they try to," mentions Howard, who seems exhausted with excitement but brings forward some papers, from which he selects the reports of examination from the Harrisonburg physicians.[17]

"The State Compensation Commission heard us more than once," Mr. Reynolds relates, as he breathes irregularly and grows excited. "Nichols didn't do nothin'. He was a man from Richmond. Persley come one time. The last man what heard it, I can't remember his name, he done all that has been done. The hearing was at the county courthouse in June 1934. My witnesses from the mill, some of 'um hated to come, but they did: Skelding from Low Moor; Noel ——— from Covington, (I can't remember his last name), we all call him Noel over at the mill. Rev. Robinson was another of my witnesses, and Lloyd Parker who ran a store at the bridge. He had seen me in Dr. Jeter's car as they took me home after being gassed. And agin' me was the four doctors of the mill: Dr. Jeter, Dr. Emmett, his X-ray man, and one of his helpers what had examined me at the Clifton Forge Hospital, which was then the mill hospital.

"Every time the hearing was called, the mill had important business for Clarence Lackey out of town. He was never there. It was his *not* inspecting the cells before I went on that was the cause of the accident. But there was a Mr. Leek, a Department Superintendent, a big man at the mill, who went on the witness stand and was telling all about how it happened and my heart attack. And the Commission Judge asked him: 'Mr. Leek, where was you at the time?' 'I was in New York,' says Mr. Leek. 'Get off the stand, Mr. Leek,' says the Judge. 'You don't know nothin' 'bout it.'

"My witnesses, Lloyd Parker and Rev. Robinson, did not get to the stand. The four doctors told what all was NOT wrong with me and how I was able to work. They said things, words that I didn't know. And the Judge at last asked 'um, 'what was in that cell room THAT night of September first,' that had not been there the years I had worked there and not been put in bad condition. They said, 'twa'n't nothin'.' The Judge told 'um, 'Nothin' but the gas over at the mill would have put Reynolds in this condition, if he has worked for years in exactly the same place and never before been like this.'

"The Clifton Forge Hospital doctors didn't have any X-ray pictures with them but of my teeth. They asked the Judge if he wanted to see them. 'Put 'um back in your pocket,' says the Judge, 'I don't want to see no picture of Reynold's TEETH.' The Judge knew of Canady and Wright, good doctors! He handed Jeter one of the reports on me they made in Harrison-burg. It looked like Dr. Jeter didn't know enough to read 'um. I don't think he knows much medicine!" "Maybe there was some things Jeter didn't want to read on them reports," offers Mrs. Reynolds.[18]

"The Judge put me on the stand and told me to tell what they done at the mill hospital at Clifton Forge when they examined me. Well, I don't know nothin' 'bout taken X-ray pic-tures. I didn't even know when they took 'um. I'm an ig'nunt fellow, but I told the Judge this, 'When the Harrisonburg doctors examined me, they didn't give me a shot to deaden me first.'" Mr. Reynolds becomes very excited recalling the episodes. To all appearances there is neurosis from some cause. One wonders if it might be from lack of food, six years is a long time for slight rations!

"Dr. Jeter, he fit so hard agin me." The respiration of Mr. Reynolds is labored and when one tries his pulse, it is weak and irregular. Mrs. Reynolds tells him to be calm. She men-tions that a doctor in town, who does not wish his name to be known in connection with Mr. Reynolds, has told her that she may expect Mr. Reynolds to have a heart attack now since he is so depleted. But he will not be sh-ssshed: "When the man, Arrington, who was gassed at the rayon plant brought the Philadelphia doctor here to his trial, it was a noted doctor on gas *poison*." (The best Howard can make of the doctor's name sounds like *Trumper*.) "I went to him and he told me to come to him for an examination. But I have no money to go to him. I think he was pretty sure from the things he said, the questions he asked, and my answers, but of course, there would have to be a goin' over before a doctor would put his name to any report that could be used at a Commission hearing. I can understand that, and if I had the money I certainly would go to that expert for examination.

"The last thing the Commission people wrote was telling me that my papers and all were sent to the Roanoke office. And a year ago, I got a letter from that office saying that three or four points were being cleared up that would be good for me. They sent me a book, *Brief Explanation of the Social Security Act, Circular #1, Information Source, July 1937*. That was a year ago. I hope I won't die before I get it."[19]

[Loc.: VSL/AB, box 181, 16 pp., 5,230 wds.]

Roy C. Fix *by Mary S. Venable, 16 August 1940*

Some experiences in the lives of Roy C. Fix and his wife, the former Myrtle Fridley, were common also to those of a number of other couples (such as Noah and Lizzie Gibson in chapter 2). For instance, they each left their rural homes or farms for nearby cities, where they all worked in textile mills and met their future spouses. Prior to her marriage, Myrtle Fix worked in the Covington silk mill. And in 1926, shortly after Industrial Rayon Corporation's mill in South Covington was built—as he recalled—Roy Fix went to work in its aging room, where the viscose was made.[20]

By 1929 the Covington mill was employing upwards of a thousand workers. Despite the depression, the United States in 1933 was producing "about one-third of the world's supply of rayon." Almost one-third of that amount was manufactured by the five rayon mills, including the Covington plant, in the state of Virginia.[21]

On 30 March 1937, several hundred members of the Synthetic Yarn Federation branch of the United Textile Workers began a sit-down strike in the rayon plant. They left the mill peaceably in response to a court order after ten days, but they continued to picket outside the plant. However, when the mill tried to reopen with nonunion men in July 1937, a riot broke out and a car was overturned. Several union members who were put in prison for their part in the rioting were later pardoned by the governor.

That strike had been called over "seniority rights." Reportedly, management was bringing unskilled workers in from other locations and starting them at pay rates that were higher than entry level. At the same time, it was charged that the company was engaging in a practice of breaking down the higher earnings of experienced workers by laying them off and then rehiring them after some interval at beginning wage rates. As one man put it, "The mill made such a point of experience, when they first put up the place. . . . But funny enough if you got laid off, no matter how long you'd been there, when you'd start back it was nineteen cents [an hour] again!"[22]

As Roy Fix was being interviewed in late 1940, there were rumors of yet another possible strike over essentially the same grievance: the mill was not honoring "its agreement as to seniority rights among the employees."

Roy Fix came to Alleghany from Rockbridge County about 1922 to help his brother who was a tenant farmer. Both had grown up on a farm which their father rented near Lexington, Virginia. Roy says, "It was not a big farm and the house we lived in was not much of a house. There were two girls and two boys in our family. After my father's death, we gave the farm up and I came here, where—my brother wrote—I could get work. My Dad had us up by daylight and when school time came, we had done all there was to be done on a farm excepting the crop gathering. He hired extra help for the corn cutting, but seeding wheat we could manage without extra help. Dad sent us to school, though my brother and I stopped in the seventh grade. That was as far as that school taught and in those days there were no buses.

"I stayed with Mother till I came to work for old man Hart, where my brother Bob was working. Before the year was up the old man died and his widow run the farm for a year or two, and then sold it to the Rayon Mill Housing company. Mother had come to this county after her girls married and moved away. She bought a lot and built a four-room, frame cottage on it. This is the lot we are standing on, but the house she built burned. My brother and sisters agreed that she would deed it to me and she [would] live with me. I started to repair the burned house and found out it would cost more than to put up a good house and make

Botetourt County, Virginia. Eagle Rock Limestone Works. Photo by W. Lincoln Highton. VSL/PC. [43460]

it as large as I wanted for my family and mother. I added a bathroom too! I got a loan from the U.S. Housing Company. It was expensive but now I pay no more, in fact less, than rent would be. And in fifteen years, I will own something instead of having nothing to show for the monthly costs. That Housing Loan is a wonderful thing to poor people. You have to own something, though, to start with.

"I'm a sort of carpenter. I did a lot of work on my house myself. My mother lived with us till she died. Then I paid the cost of putting her away. The others did not say I had to do it all, but I knew they thought I ought to, when she had made her lot over to me." Mrs. Roy Fix interrupts, "That is not a thing to talk over, when it happens. Nobody would have words over who was to bury their Mother."

The house is a five-room and bath, frame cottage on a sloping half-acre facing the secondary road through Mallow, Virginia—a settlement of about fifty homes. The lot runs back about one hundred and fifty feet. The cellar has not been excavated. When this is done, the dirt that comes from it will be used to build the road to the garage. . . . At present the model 1926, sits in the rain, close beside the window.[23]

Mr. Fix makes seventy cents an hour. He began working for the Industrial Rayon Corporation of South Covington five months after it started up, to be exact, "November eighteenth, nineteen and twenty-six. I went to work there and have never missed a day till," he smiles sheepishly, "the strike." Mrs. Fix does not smile, "We had a hard time during the strike with our house payments coming due, besides getting along. I hope they never have another," she says with decision.

"I started in at thirty-two cents an hour," resumes the man. "I work in what is called the Ageing Room. It is there the viscose is made. The crumbs come in large drums, that is, paper or fiber crumbled up fine. It is pure white, till we put a chemical on it that turns it as yellow as a pumpkin. It has to stand in that a certain number of hours to age, that is where the room gets its name. We wash the cs out, and it turns white again after standing awhile. The drums are two sizes; some hold four batches. In the next room they add something that turns it into [a mixture that], looks like, molasses. It goes through pipes to the lower floor and there it is kept moving from one drum to another. I reckon there are as many as a hundred drums in that room. The mixture flows from one to the other. It must not be allowed to settle. When that process has been going on the right length of time, it is brought up a pipe by vacuum into the room above, then driven through filters. They are thin cloth over the end of the pipes that take out the dregs and black specks. Then it has aged and is ready to flow to the spinning machines, where it contacts acid in the troughs and makes a fiber. The nozzles in the pipes are as fine as needles and every year they get finer and finer.

"I started in the ageing room at thirty-two cents an hour, have gone up to seventy cents an hour, and I *like* the work. I would rather have my job of operator than be foreman. It would pay very little more and would add responsibility. We keep starting batches, so that each day a batch is ready to go to the jets. This ageing process is what makes the rayon business expensive to stop or to start up again. Once started, the stuff has to be thrown out if not used on the right day."

Inquiring as to rumors of a coming strike in a plant, Mr. Fix replies that the mill has not fulfilled its agreement as to seniority rights among the employees. He is a member of the union. "The company union was disbanded at the request of the mill authorities," he tells us. "And it *left* those fellows, that had stuck to it!"

Mr. Fix is a tall, rather thin man, with a head unusually small and narrow. He does not carry his shoulders erectly, but walks with quick, nervous manner. His wife came from an isolated section of this county, where she had gone through all the grades her country school afforded. Then she came to work at the silk mill in town. There she made from one dollar a day, during apprenticeship, up to "thirty-seven and forty, a half (month). I stopped when they gave me a worn-out loom. Jess Kimberlin's wife had been working on it. They told me, when I complained of mine that they would give me hers, it was better. But they knew all the time, that it was a wore-out-loom and I couldn't keep up on it. So I left. That was a long time ago, before my oldest girl was born. She is fourteen now, and will go to Covington High School this coming year. I have four girls. I reckon whatever a body has is what they think is the nicest. I like boys, but I'm glad my children are girls."

The home of this couple is well furnished for comfort. The living room has an upholstered New England couch, we presume for guests. The inevitable overstuffed divan and chairs are far from new. A large library table holds a convenient reading lamp, but there are no magazines in sight and only two books. One is large (we think it is a Bible), and another is of like size and as little worn. The rug is of linoleum in subdued colors. The chairs are comfortable. In the bedroom of the girls, there is a dressing table draped in turquoise blue. The metal bedstead is blue, also the rug. Bed linens are clean and their schoolbooks are on a shelf under the table. The bathroom is spotless and has a linen cabinet. Mrs. Fix's kitchen is bright. It fronts the east and they use it for dining room as well. The white and green scheme is well carried out in stove, cabinet, table, rug, chairs and shelves. Steps lead from the back porch to the ground. Beyond is a very good garden. Mrs. Fix canned more than a hundred quarts of tomatoes last year, but this wet season will ruin her vegetables, she fears. The blackberry crop has been abundant, however, "sort of evens things up," she thinks.

The idea of recreation is taboo. Mr. Fix drives his eldest daughter to take her lesson in music. She plays the guitar and hopes to be in the high school orchestra. She is overweight but engages in no sports. All three girls are becomingly dressed in prints and broadcloths. The baby is less than a year old and is large and fine-looking.

When [the baby] was born Mrs. Fix suffered from varicose veins. The dark knotted areas look dangerous and interfere with her walking. Scattered from her ankles to her thigh, the doctor told her it was impossible to wear rubber stockinette bandages "over and above the knees. He gave me a tonic and I manage to get along. But ironing is hard on me. These places hurt dreadfully," she says pointing to a clump of dark knots, below a swollen vein crossing her shin.

The guiding purpose of this couple is ambition for their children. When they came to live in this small village, their church connections were in the town from which they had moved. The Sunday School friends of the girls in their old church home were pleasant, and so the family went to the town three miles distant on Sundays. Mrs. Fix says she found out that "the folks around here held it against you if you live here and go to Sunday School somewhere else. And, it is sensible! If you come to live in a place and expect to make it your home, it is good enough to be your church home. That is, if the denomination suits you. This Sunday School is a union church and so they do not teach anything but the Bible. So we stopped going to town and send the children here. We found it was a good way to get friendly with the neighbors. They seem to think a lot more of us, since we began going here."[24]

Community progress is also a concern of Mrs. Fix. She tells us of the homeowners appointing a representative to appear before the county supervisors to ask for a sewerage line to the river. There is a water system, of private-ownership, which meets the needs of most of the houses, but the disposal of water from bathrooms is not in safe septic tanks. Some have open sewers for wash water. "It's dangerous," she says, "the washsuds trickling slowly over weeds and decaying vegetation." Mrs. Fix has been alarmed by the report of a case of infantile paralysis last week in the neighborhood. "It is a little girl about the size of my second girl," she concludes tenderly. The outside toilets of this village have been inspected by the county Health Agent, but some are built on low ground which floods with summer rains. It is for this reason that Mrs. Fix is alive to progress and doing all she can to promote sentiment for putting in sewerage lines.

To her credit, be it said, that Mrs. Fix has come a long way from her early environments on Big Ridge. For her children, she has jumped two generations of the usual slow progressiveness, which is usual for slow minds. And whilst in appearance, she is not wasting any funds on herself, from somewhere (aside from reading) she is progress-conscious.[25]

[Loc.: VSL/AB, box 181, 5 pp., 1,485 wds.]

Kate Beale *by Mary S. Venable, rec. 12 May 1939*

In the preceding life history, Roy Fix, who worked in the Industrial Rayon plant in Covington, described how rayon fiber was produced by moving the aged viscose mixture into the spinning machines and bringing it into contact with acid. No matter how careful one was around the nozzles of spinning machines and troughs of acid, inevitably workers suffered acid burns, such as Junior Beale had on his feet. Those raw wounds could be crippling, even if treated. Yet workers often avoided going to the company nurse for fear of being laid off because of their injuries. Instead, workers resorted to other means, such as raw beef poultices when acid got in the eyes or a "homeopathic doctor who had some medicine-like water that took out the acid-burning immediately." Admittedly, "that doctor had a good practice" in the "Rayon Village."[26]

The family circumstances and description in the life history of Kate Beale bear a striking similarity to another text with Mrs. Jim (Jennie) Mays, even to the detail of both women washing their fresh-picked dryland cress "greens" while they spoke with VWP worker Mary Venable. However, the interviews differ in one significant detail: Jennie Mays's son, Junior, was apparently one of the persons arrested and jailed for taking part in the riot during the rayon plant strike in July 1937. Kate Beale makes no mention of her son, Junior, having participated in that strike.

It is quite likely that Venable used a pseudonym—in one or both texts—to protect persons who had been involved in events that were still much too close and controversial. Further, it is suspected that both names—Kate Beale *and* Jennie Mays—probably refer to the same person. There is sufficient corroborative information in a series of other life histories not included here to suggest that is the case, although neither the actual identity nor the reliability of this subject can be verified at this moment.

Kate Beale is the wife of Mr. James Madison Beale, "Jim" for short. Two-score summers have faded her light hair, and the like number of winters have drawn her skin into wrinkles at the corners of her eyes till they radiate like wheel-spokes from the hub. She says that smiling "will put the wrinkles on to a body," with that she adds another with a broad smile. "I'm behind with my mornin' work," she monotones.

"Sonny and I went out to pick dry land creases and if I'm goin' to have them for dinner, I've got to be gettin' them cleaned and in the pot. If you don't mind the back porch clutter, you can come out there. Takes a long time to wash the greens and pick 'um. We can talk, have this chair—the back's broke in the other.

"I'm plain as an old shoe! We lived on mountain farms till we moved into this mill town. All my chillun was born on the places that we rented on the shares. We have five chillun: Sadie, she's twenty now; and Junior come next, he's nineteen. Bertha is sixteen. She's the only one that took to her books and if I live an' nothin' happens, I'm goin' to put her through high school, before she goes to work at the mill. Charlie is fourteen, and Sonny is twelve. Mebbe YOU don't know that boys the ages of those last two can eat as much as full grown men and then some.

"Sadie is the one who got her Dad to leave the farm and come to mill work. She wanted to go to work at the mill an' we wouldn't hear to her comin' and bein' tu'nned (turned) loose with none of us to look after her. Jim said he'd seen too many girls made fools with a few checks from town work, and then come back home to the farm to leave a kid for Dad and Mom to keer for the rest of its life. When Sadie seen he *wa'n't* goin' to budge from that, she

Covington, Virginia. January 1939. City limits. Photo by Arthur Rothstein. [LC-USF34-26767-D]

Covington, Virginia. View of mill and workers' homes. Photo by W. Lincoln Highton. VSL/PC. [44143]

began talkin' him into movin' us all here. And that's how we happened to turn from farmin' to mill workin'."

"Which is the best for you and the children?" "I have never made up my mind. Farmin' is good for some things and bad for others. The same that is good on the farm, you do without at the mill, but you get more cash to buy clothes and things. It ain't so hard on the woman of the family here," explains Kate. She goes on to compare the broad fields and diversified occupations for children on the farm. "Work is the same as play to them, if you don't make 'um go at it too hard." The contracted lot in the mill village must be endured because of neighbor's children, "They're allus gettin' in fusses, and the boys have to stay in after dark because so many rowdies have been breakin' windows and tearin' down the lattices. We don't want our boys blamed for destroyin' property. They don't do it, that is, I reckon they don't, but a body never knows what younguns'll do when they get out."

She continues to list the food shortage in town, compared to plentiful gardens in the country, saying, that there she could can for the winter season enough to "keep goin' till late spring. We have a garden, here. The mill gives every man a garden space. They draw for the spot, and if you get a piece of poor ground it's jes too bad! Or if you get one a half mile away and somebody steals most of the vege'bles, what can you do about it?" reasons Katie. It seems that the garden has been of some help since coming to the mill, but not comparable with the farm gardens which Jim used to plant and the children tend[ed] under Katie's watchful eye.

They have two pigs in a pen on the border of the village. The cost of "store feed" for the hogs has been calculated to meet the pork production, "jus" about even for what it would cost. Katie smiles again as she admits, "But we wouldn't buy it at the meat counter. It would sound too high. Scattered out along the five months' pay checks, the feed bill does not seem too extravagant. Jim likes the hogs. He takes the slop and goes to look at the hogs twice a day and talks to the other fellows feedin' their pigs along the same row," says his wife. Thus we learn that Jim finds recreation, as well as pork, for his investment in "store feed."

The Beale's cow, that came to enjoy town bright lights, gave up the ghost shortly after getting into her neighbor's feed storage closet though "Jim worked with her all that night." Katie is proud of Jim's father. He was a veterinarian, "and a lot of people called him Doctor. He wanted Jim to take up veterinary practice but Jim couldn't operate on dumb brutes, like his Pa." Jim left school about the fifth grade and Katie left after finishing the seventh. She thinks the schools in the village far superior to country schools which she attended. "I tell Junior and Sadie that the time is coming when you can't get work unless you've been through high school. Folks think if you have no brains to go to school, then you'll have none to work with. Sadie finished her second year high school, and I mean that the two youngest shall finish." Katie's determination is almost fierce.

"The kids call this the beanery," meaning the home. "They say I have October beans Mondays and Tuesdays, pintos on Wednesdays and Thursdays and brown ones on Fridays and Saturdays, with baked beans on Sundays. They don't miss it very far because, since we ate all the canned stuff we brought from the farm, I have to get something to fill them and beans is about the best. That's why I went after these creases, today," she shakes the water in a shower as she carefully examines each piece and places it in another pan of water. "It takes three washin's for greens. I never eat greens away from home. Maybe I'd trust my mother's washing greens to suit me, but nobody else." Katie thinks corn bread goes with greens and bacon.

After putting the cress in a kettle with a generous "slab" of bacon she says "We'll go in the front room till time to make the cornbread."

A congoleum rug almost covers the floor. A New England couch is covered with an "Indian" blanket, won at bingo during the county fair. From the same source came a composition doll with Bettie Boop eyes and Hawaiian costume, surmounted by a rose catharm cap of gauze and tinsel. She stands guard beside a lot of Kodak pictures on the radio. There arc a number of chairs in the room, which Katie mentions were here when the church guild met last night. "We had a big number out. I told some of the women I was goin' to bake a cake and they brought some ginger ale. It is queer how a bite to eat will bring folks to a meetin' when you know they're *not* hungry." Katie explains that the couch was an innovation [for] Sadie's social contacts. There had been a bed in this room, but Sadie thought it looked better to take the bed out, when she got to having beaux.

To counteract the influences of movies and road-house dances for the girls and the "car-craze" of her boys, Katie is finding substitution most difficult. She invents "all sorts of things to do at home, like taffy-pullin's," but Sadie has gotten beyond childish entertainments. She also wants a bedroom to herself, but as there are only three bedrooms this is impossible, for the younger daughter must room with Sadie. The boys have a room together. It is clean and comfortable, but nothing of beauty is wasted. Katie's room has a pile of mending on one chair, which, she says, is "never finished till some more comes in, torn." Here is a hand-woven basket, which her grandfather made for her when she was a little girl. It holds the socks awaiting darning. The mirror of Katie's dressing table has Kodak pictures of her children around its edge, as though she preferred looking at them to examining her image in the mirror. She feels there is little about her present appearance to warrant such a waste of time, but assures one, "I was not bad to look at when I was a girl." The evidence lingers today.

The bathroom is scrubbed and has an odor of antiseptics. In the corner are clothes of one of the boys cast carelessly there. Katie lifts them, with mutterings of displeasure, but there is no dust under them proving true her statement that "Junior left them off when he came in from work last evening." Toothbrushes hang in a row. Two have cellnese [*sic*] wrappers enclosing them. Katie spreads out a washrag on the windowsill to sun, "Charlie never washes his ring off the tub nor spreads out his washrag. I tell him, I ain't goin' to let him go to see his uncle in Newport News, till he learns bathroom manners. But here it is! He figures I'll never get the ticket for him to go, and I guess he is right. He wants to be a mechanic and if I could get him down to Newport News, there would be a chance for him to learn. There's no machinery trainin' for boys around here unless they have the pull of some relative in a garage, who can take 'em on for helper. In the summer he asks for helper's place with no pay, but the garage men think a boy will steal to make up for wages. They have no time to find out if the boy is honest, just say NO."

Junior and Charles have taken two cars to pieces and patched the worn parts of one with replacements from the other till they got one to run. They traded it for another sick car, continued till they dissolved partnership each with "something that would go, if you would call them *cars*. Jim aims to buy a car one of these days, but with this last cut-on-hours he'll not be buying one this year."

Jim was "too clumsy," Katie "reckons" to tend the spinning machines. He has been on the labor force at the mill. Sometimes he is helper for the repair gang or material man, for "trucking the stuff," when they are building something new. He is well satisfied with his surroundings since the new superintendent came. Jim says that things changed with his coming. One thing is that a "body can get at him to talk things over and ask for what they want. He's not always too busy to see an employee. And since the Wagner Act, the nineteen-cent-per-hour wage has moved up to twenty-five cents. This new 'super' does not cut a fellow back after laying him off, just to get him hired again at the lowest rate."

Jim is of average height, five feet, ten inches, weighs about one-hundred and sixty pounds. His shoulders are broad and he walks with swinging stride. He is slightly stooped, but he carries his head erect. His blonde head is kept in tonsorial perfection for he is the barber for himself and sons. He refused to lend his clippers after the neighbor, whose sons had "wire-terrier-hair took the edge off my clippers." His features are Scotch, in rugged mounds of high bones, with valleys in each cheek. His eyes are of the trouble-sighting-type of discerning Scots. From his bearing, one guesses him to be a "follower," with no initiative or desire for leadership.

The majority opinion, Jim considers, "must be right, if they *all* think so," yet he reasons for himself between elections, that is, with Katie at the rudder. In local politics, his outlook is personal and seldom based on the principle involved if some civic point is to be decided in the election at hand. Partiality to the candidate, or the reverse, is Jim's deciding factor. "Forest Hanna always knows me when I go to town and he's an all-round fellow. I voted for him for county supervisor last election. If I had thought about his bein' for a change in the highway routin', I would have voted for the other man, but Forest asked me to vote for him and so I did.

"The children do a lot of reading but I don't get time for much. I read the paper, sometimes." So Jim passes his time till the fishing season opens and at dawn on the first day he can be found about twenty miles from his home, rod in hand, the particulars of each hole in the "crick" tabulated in his memory. And as he tells it, "with a worm on my hook, I was waitin' for daylight. The Game Warden wrote in the paper a notice not to drop your line in the water till sun-up, and you can never tell when them deputies is around. I waited for the first slant-o-sun, but *not* the second one!" Deer hunting is also a sport which Jim loves. He is sorry that he let his Buddie take the head of the deer he killed last fall. "But you see it takes ten dollars to have the head mounted. Jim Stull does 'em up fine for his price, but I didn't see the ten dollars then. Now I wish I had kept it. Jim would have waited and give me time to pay him. I'd like to see it on my wall. It had five points on its horns. Some that the others killed had more than five. But he was the one that come my way and I brought him down."

Jim thinks the family "ought to get along with Junior, Sadie, and me workin' if we don't get layed off too long at a time. This rent eats you up when you get a layoff." Jim makes sixty-five cents an hour, but Sadie makes as much as ninety dollars a month. Junior is now at thirty-five cents per hour with the hope of a raise in the near future. Next to a layoff, Jim thinks sickness and medical attention "get you behind." The family of Beales's have had no sickness since coming off the farm, excepting Junior's acid-burn on his feet. The mill nurse cured the raw place on his instep with ointment, but it took time and it was very painful to walk during the process.

"If we keep our health, what we make ought to cover our *need*cessities. If Sadie would stop spending what she does on foolishness, I could get a car for the family. But she pays board and gets a chair now and then, or a porch swing, gives her mother a dress onct a year, and where the rest goes nobody can find out," Jim complains, as the cause of resentment comes into the room. "Here's Sadie, now. This is her Swing Day and she's swung all her money away up town, more'n likely."

Sadie turns on the radio, then draws close to talk above its din. Her permanent "pipe curls" on crown and behind each ear gives her [a] very youthful appearance, and she later tells one she plucks her own brows. The slant produces an inquisitive expression to her large, blue eyes. With good texture of skin and splendid regular teeth, she came near being beautiful. A nose, just like her father's, could not be improved by a beautician, and there she missed her claim to beauty. She has been on the night shift ever since she went to work. To circumvent being on that schedule, she has gotten leave-of-absence till some other girl on the daylight shift would leave "for good," but on returning to work her old schedule is again given. She does not mind it in the winter, but in the summer the heat makes sleep in the afternoon quite impossible. She wears the slackers and shirt regulation uniform at work, also low-heel shoes. After punching the clock and showing her hands to the inspector, she stands by the machine, if reeling, waiting to tie broken ends, keep the yarn steadily coming, and waiting to place the tags at the proper place. The tags have her number on them, also the dernier that is being run, as well as the brand.

At first when she went to work, she tired with standing. There is a break in the eight hours for lunch and then she could sit. There is a clean restroom where they may eat lunches, but some of the girls go to the cafeteria for coca-colas or coffee and sandwiches. Sadie prefers her mother's pie, cake and sausage-between-biscuits.

When she works in the finishing room, she stretches the skeins, looks for loose broken ends, and with lightning speed ties the two ends, "This way." She illustrates taking two ends of the string around her package of merchandise [and] with quick movement—[such that] one's eye cannot follow the motion—the knot appears. "I learned to tie it, right off," she boasts. "Some of the girls have to practice knot-tying to get it at right speed, but after the instructor showed me once, I got it."

Sadie would not return to the farm. Her social contacts are of paramount importance. Aristocracy of mill job has weight in the selection of her sweethearts. "The first fellow that I went with was just a forty-cent-an-hour man. I had just come in from the country, but the fellow I go with now is a room-foreman. He wears the *best* looking clothes. I like a man to dress up. Don't you! He makes a-plenty to dress on and when he takes me out, of course, I have to wear good clothes. Dad don't know about all these things like a woman would. Mother understands!

"There are barn-dances and movies, anywhere along the road from here to fifty miles each way. The Bloody Bucket is the name of one. It is next to the skating rink. Terrible sounding name, isn't it? We go weekends or swing days over to ——— (nearby city). A bunch usually goes the same place and we have dinners and go to the *big* shows. Four of us went to see the Washington cherry blossoms. Three cars full saw the Winchester Apple Blossom Festival. In the fall, we go to the county fairs and see the horse-racing. I've been in one or two car wrecks. It always happens because we have stayed too long and have to make time to get somebody back to work, so he won't lose his job."

Jim Beale and his daughter, Sadie, do not attend Sunday School, but the rest of the family have kept up their connections with religion since coming to town. Jim says he is tired and that he has "work clothes but no Sunday suit." But Sadie gives the reason for non-attendance that she always has some sort of trip planned for weekends. She says she has as much regard for religion as when she came from the country, but "I can't sit still during a sermon. When you get keyed up with hurrying to keep time with machines, it sort of keeps running inside after you come off from work," she thinks.

When asked if she thinks her physical self will always be able to keep going at the mechanical rate of speed, she replies, "O! I know machinery wears out and breaks down sooner or later, but it's a long time till I get OLD." At the suggestion of self-enforced relaxation on swing days or weekends, she claims, it is a task to "break myself in again" to the whir and rapid action required of the worker when back at work cooperating with machine tempo. With an endless chain of activities over the "time off," no extra effort is needed to get back to work. When one drives, dances and swims Saturdays and Sundays "so as not to slow down," Monday's work comes easy.

The mention of athletics disgusts her. Nothing of the kind is included in her program of speeding. Rather contradictorily she says, "If a body stands eight hours with one break for lunch, wouldn't they want to get off their feet the rest of the twenty-four?" "What do you call dancing?" asks Katie. "It is all I can do to get my clothes washed—my rayon things that don't go in Mom's wash—and get my permanent set, my nails done and look for the specials in bargains. You have to be there early to get the bargains, so there is no time left for ball games or tennis."

Jim thinks it would do her good to help Katie with the washing, or beat the rug out on the line, or iron the kid's clothes. Sadie's alibi for the first suggestion is that she would be laid off if a rough cuticle appeared to catch in the yarn. "The inspector is tight about our hands. She laid a girl off for two weeks for a hangnail not long ago."

Katie is of the opinion, "Ironing don't make hangnails." But Sadie has disappeared up the stairs, she returns with a good-looking foulard. "When did you get that? Only last payday you got a new dress," Katie expostulates. "Put the hem up one inch," orders Sadie, "while you're sitting still."

[Loc.: VSL/AB, box 181, 8 pp., 2,378 wds.]

Nancy Carter *by Everett Anderson, 14 February 1939*

Although Nancy Carter felt "like a machine" and hated the deafening sound of the tobacco factory's whistle, she admitted that packing cigarettes on the production line of a Richmond factory was a "good-paying job." Her job and industrial routine were both direct results of the entrepreneurial efforts of James B. ("Buck") Duke of Durham, North Carolina, in the late nineteenth and early twentieth century. With his American Tobacco Company and control of rights to the "newly developed Bonsack cigarette machine," Duke developed global markets for machine-made cigarettes and revolutionized the industry along corporate lines.[27]

In 1940, the WPA's Virginia *Guide* acknowledged that "in the production of cigarettes Virginia [was] second only to North Carolina, having produced about 53,000,000,000 in the year ending July 1937—more than one-fourth of the National output." It noted, too, that this part of the industry employed nearly five thousand workers, most of them concentrated in factories in Richmond.[28]

"I must be at my table at five minutes to seven, so I get up early. The night before, I washed and starched my white uniform no matter what time I got in. It's dry by morning, if I hang it by the stove or the room is warm, and I iron it before breakfast. Most of the girls are married, or soon will be, and have kids they must prepare cereal and lunch for. Then some of us live a good way from the plant. I'm five or six miles from it and it takes me three-quarters of an hour to get there; I ride two street cars. So I'm up by five-thirty.

"But when I'm deafened for the first time that day at five to seven, I'm at a table with from five to eleven young women, waiting for the first cartons of cigarettes to come down by carrier belts from the floor above. Without makeup we look like ghosts. Some work is usually left finished upstairs the day before just so we won't have to wait in the morning.

"The table is of wood and about eight feet long and three feet wide. Our elbows bump together, we're so close. There is a narrow shelf in the center of the table. As the cartons of ten packs of cigarettes come down from the floor above on a carrier belt that levels out for about six feet before it comes to the edge of the table, a girl pushes the cartons up the center of the table between the posts that support the shelf. I and the other girls at the table pick the cartons from beneath the shelf, put them on a carton flat, and then quickly join the ends of this second carton and slip the flap of its top into its edge. The carton within a carton is then put atop the shelf above the middle of the table. So on, until a girl has twenty-five completed, when she signals a boy who comes to carry them to the labelling machine or table. This boy gives the girl a ticket to check to show that he took her work, and she gives him a slip to mark to show that she finished that much work.

"The stack of flat cartons before a girl cannot be very high, because she has to reach over it and beneath the shelf to get the cartons to wrap. That reaching motion, by the way, can get one quite tired. At rush periods, like before Christmas, four carrier belts take the work to four tables. Sometimes maybe only one table is working, and all four belts swing into action carrying the cartons to one table. Then things hum, and jokes, and giggling, and wisecracking don't add to the noise of the machinery above and about us. But it's better to have a lot to do rather than too little. Because when there are gaps of from five to ten minutes, even of half an hour, in the flow of the work, then one has to find something to fill up the time or else the foreman will give you a black look, besides finding some work for you.

"Sometimes I work on the labelling machine. Two persons operate it together. A boy catcher receives the labelled cartons from the end of the machines, while I, at the other end, see that the cartons go in evenly and sidewise. When the roll of cellophane has run out and has to be replaced or when two or three labels, despite the thorough ruffling given them, cling together until one is stuck to the carton and the other then falls into the mechanism and prevents its working, then either the boy or I—whichever is not remedying the situation— puts the brake on the machine. A loose label in the machine can be a nuisance, besides bringing you a good balling [bawling] out from the foreman.

"For some reason, when I ask about any of the plant's operations the answer is always, 'I don't know.' The whistle flattens out one's brains several times within the first two hours. There ought to be a law. It blows at five to seven, seven, seven-thirty, five to eight, eight, and eight-thirty. Then it blasts us out at noon, and back a half hour later, and out again at three-thirty.

"Before going out for lunch the girls put on make-up. Then there's a rush for a seat in the restaurant across the street. If you bring your lunch, you eat at one of the tables in the plant and perhaps buy a coke or a bottle of milk. Or maybe you're one of the girls who sit with the boyfriend—who also works there—in his car, and eat. That's one reason for make-up.

"The front part of the restaurant is taken up by the white workers. The Negroes pass by us and go behind a partition that sets off the back of the place; we hear them, but we don't see them.[29]

"We eat like we work when there's a rush. What talking there is, is about what's wrong with the baby or something it did that was cute, about the date last night, the dance the company is giving Friday night, the foreman's latest favorite among the girls, and a couple of jokes. And then we're whistled back to work.

"Maybe around two o'clock the woman foreman tells you that you're going to work an hour or two overtime today to get through. If the boyfriend is going to meet you, there's no way of letting him know; he'll either wait or he won't. It may be that you will be told to work Saturday. Or again, perhaps you will be told not to come to work the next two days, there isn't much doing. This information, like all that connected with the factory, is given you at the last minute, and of course, it isn't a good idea to protest.

"It is a well-paid job. When I first went there, I signed a contract which promised me a full week's work and wages every week at forty cents an hour. At the end of two months, I was being told when to come or not to come to work. All the workers, whether old hands or not, are treated the same way. The cigarette business is seasonal, too, you know; for instance, after the Christmas rush, work practically stops for a month or so. After about four months, I was raised to fifty cents an hour, which meant that when I worked a full week of forty hours, I got $20 instead of $16. Overtime was paid time and a half, or seventy-five cents an hour. If I had joined the union, I would have been among the first to be put back to work after a layoff, that was the main advantage union membership offered.

"But whenever the day ends, at three-thirty, four-thirty, I, like the others, change to street clothes and meet the boyfriend, shop in town, or go by the market on the way home to clean-up, read the paper, or maybe see an early show, and try to get to bed as early as possible—not forgetting to wash and starch the white uniform.

"If I don't work Saturdays, I straighten up the room I pay $3 a week for, launder clothes, shop and market, and so on. Sunday, I iron, and eat, and try to sleep a little longer. I feel like a machine, but it's a good-paying job."

[Loc.: VSL/AB, box 191, 4 pp.]

Epilogue
VIRGINIA ON THE EVE OF WORLD WAR II

In May 1939, more than two and a half years before the Japanese attack on Pearl Harbor, a Richmond truck driver observed: "Everything seems to be so uncertain now. Papers are full of war talk. 'Twas just the other day—Friday, I believe—that we saw three airplanes flying across here. We don't want any war."[1] Today, three planes flying overhead on the same day would not command our attention; but his comment tells us that such an occurrence then was rare enough to be worthy of note. Moreover, his remarks reflect a public state of apprehension in Virginia, even at that date, about the approach of war.

As time passed and the conflict in Europe intensified with the news becoming ever more ominous and disturbing, the Virginia Writers' Project life histories contained lengthier and more specific statements concerning war, especially with regard to the ongoing U.S. role as noncombatant observer. For its treatment of the Allies following World War I, England received particular censure from a number of individuals, including a twenty-three-year-old native of Rocky Mount, Virginia, who said: "If England had acknowledged that we won the war for her in 1918 we would have been over there long ago to assist her in winning this one. But a nation—like a person who goes back on his friends—cannot expect them to give them the same opportunity twice, and Americans will hesitate a long time before sending their boys across the water again on a thankless and bloody mission."[2] Past experience thus provided both a scapegoat and a sufficient justification for further detachment and xenophobia.

Nevertheless, the "war scare" did provoke a groundswell of nationalistic fervor and an increasing demand for patriotic display of all kinds. Some Virginians, like persons elsewhere in the country, reported an aversion to the prospect of war based on their memories of earlier such hostilities. Others rejected war altogether on the basis of deeply felt religious convictions; but all religious beliefs were not recognized as equally valid. This was especially true for so-called fringe religious sects such as the Jehovah's Witnesses, whose rise as a mass movement in the interim between world wars was seen as threatening the "most sacred influences and institutions of this country."[3]

Norfolk, Virginia. March 1941. A group of Public school children reciting the Oath of Allegiance.
Photo by John Vachon. [LC-USF34-62482-D]

Thus in June and July 1940, when several members of the sect in Alleghany County re-fused, as a matter of faith, to salute the American flag, their act was perceived as disloyalty and a threat to the national interest. One of the religious dissenters reported that in the West-vaco plant where he worked, he heard "a lot of talk about Communists, though *they* don't call me one. What *could* be more opposed to Christianity than anti-Christ communism, unless it is Nazi Fascism destroying liberty and life. Those widespread destroyers of today had a small beginning twenty years ago. They looked harmless. Not so much different from a group here, today, telling a fellow what he shall or shall not do, when the Constitution guarantees him free speech and action." Still there were near riots in the Industrial Rayon and Westvaco plants in Covington, and fellow workers threatened to throw the "Witnesses" in the Jackson River for their rejection of important symbols and rituals of national identity.[4]

Images of schoolchildren pledging allegiance to the flag in early 1941 were part of a planned campaign to prepare the American public for inevitable U.S. involvement in the war. It was not then a matter of "whether" to enter the fray but of "when" it would happen. And it could not be denied that, in fact, defense readiness and preparation for war had already been under way for some time. An attitude of aloofness from the battle was gradually replaced by one of martial zeal, such as that stated by a shipyard worker who told vwp worker Rone Sidney in March 1941, "Nothing would suit me better than dropping a boom on Hitler's head."[5]

In the fall of 1940, Eudora Ramsay Richardson notified her workers that the Virginia Writers' Project no longer needed the life histories that it had been asking them to send. Some such materials continued to arrive in the Richmond office up through May 1941, but the vwp life history program was virtually ended prior to the country's entry into World War II. The photographs and supporting textual records of the Office of War Information provide some documentation, however, for the post–May 1941 period of war preparation in the Old Dominion.

There were many different individual circumstances "pushing" and "pulling" people into urban centers and industrial settings during the depression and early in the developing war effort. One writer concerned with the impact of such internal migrations on the public welfare in Virginia asserted: " 'The hope of a nation at war is centered in the mobility of its working population.' Since industry began to expand under the stimulus of war production, even as early as 1940, mass migration of the civilian population in the United States has become not only a 'hope' but a major problem of the Nation."[6] So it was, too, in Virginia. And in fact, if the United States had not entered the war after such long and intensive buildup to that end, then there would surely have been many more serious social problems to follow as a consequence of the massive population dislocations it had already caused.

People from all parts of Virginia, as well as from other states, flocked into the Hampton Roads area, including Newport News, Norfolk, and Portsmouth, to fill jobs created by defense contracts awarded to its primary industry—shipbuilding. The largest privately owned shipyard in the United States was that established by Collis P. Huntington in Newport News, and the country's second-oldest navy yard, established in 1800, was located in Portsmouth.

Between June 1940 and October 1941, the area had received more than nine hundred million dollars' worth of defense contracts, and by September 1942 "civilian employees at the Navy Yard were increasing at the rate of 1,000 per month." One of this number, a young shipyard employee, in March 1941 declared his own interests in that expansion bluntly, "Afraid of war, who, me? Let those Germans raise all the cane they want, because as long as they do Uncle Sam will build ships and that means money for me."[7]

By May 1942 the country was at war, and any fears defense workers may have had about their vulnerability as wartime targets were being allayed by photo essays such as that by Pat Terry of owi. Terry's series of photographs documented a shipyard worker at his job, at home with his family, doing various chores, at his station as a volunteer air raid warden, and playing in a local orchestra—all emphasizing normalcy and the routine aspects of life going on despite the backdrop of conflict.

(Opposite) Newport News, Virginia. Newport News shipbuilding and drydock company. October 1941. Workmen knocking out shores preparatory to launching a C-3. This process raises the ship slightly, then sends it down the greased ways. The stocks shown in this picture float down to the water with the ship. Photo by Alfred Palmer. [LC-USE6-00704-D]

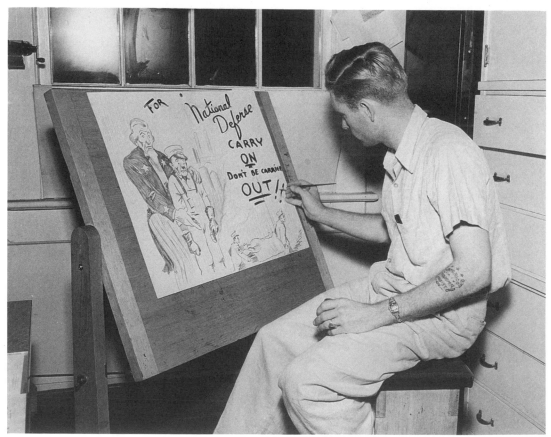

Newport News, Virginia. May 1942. Negro shipyard worker. Photo by Pat Terry. [LC-USW3-01892-C]

(Opposite, top left) Newport News, Virginia. Newport News shipbuilding and drydock company. October 1941.
[Caption missing—general view of a ship about 30 percent complete.] Photo by Alfred Palmer. [LC-USE6-00694-D]

(Opposite, top right) Portsmouth, Virginia. Norfolk navy yard. October 1941. Rhythm in defense! Music, both popular and
classical, news, sports events and other programs are broadcast all day long to the thousands of workers at the Yard. Officials
have found that these broadcasts are beneficial to the morale of the men, and cut down the fatigue brought on by difficult or
monotonous tasks. Photo by Alfred Palmer. [LC-USE6-01729-D]

(Opposite, bottom) Portsmouth, Virginia. Norfolk navy yard. October 1941. Shirley Hogge is listed on the rolls as a chipper
and caulker, but actually his job is to draw cartoons and safety posters. Most of his posters are on the all-important subject of
safety on the job. He is believed to be the only cartoonist employed in a government navy yard. Photo by Alfred Palmer.
[LC-USE6-01746-D]

Newport News, Virginia. May 1942. Negro shipyard worker at his rural home. Photo by Pat Terry. [LC-USW3-01917-E]

Newport News, Virginia. May 1942. Negro shipyard worker and one of his sons going to milk.
Photo by Pat Terry. [LC-USW3-01910-E]

Large numbers of all categories of workers likewise poured into other areas of Virginia, such as Arlington, Alexandria, and Radford, as a result of the prewar boom. In Arlington County, the rapid 45 percent population increase between 1940 and 1942 caused tremendous strains on community resources. Police and social welfare agencies could not handle the greater incidence of crime or the problems caused by the disruptions in home and family life. Housing was totally inadequate; water, electric, and sewerage facilities were not much better. The use of trailers was adopted as one immediate solution to the problems of providing housing for torpedo plant and other defense workers in the area.[8]

Some of the need for housing in northern Virginia was attributable to the influx of workers to fill white-collar governmental positions in metropolitan Washington, D.C. A large number of these were female clerical workers, who commuted by bus or other means into the District of Columbia to work. Under similar circumstances during World War I, Emily Palmer Stearns worked to find and inspect homes that were appropriate for young, single women

Newport News, Virginia. May 1942. Negro shipyard worker's family. Photo by Pat Terry. [LC-USW3-01903-C]

Newport News, Virginia. May 1942. Negro shipyard worker (second from right) participates in a musical organization. Photo by Pat Terry. [LC-USW3-01901-C]

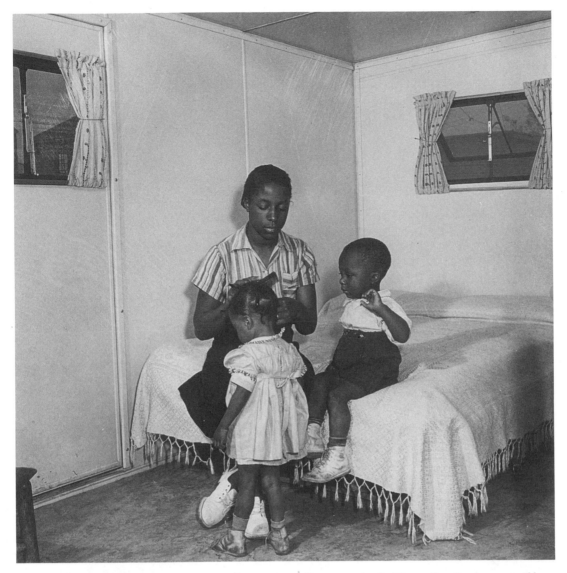

Arlington, Virginia. April 1942. Farm security administration trailer camp project for Negroes. Interior of an expansible trailer, showing one wing used as a bedroom. Photo by Marjory Collins. [LC-USF34-100006-E]

to live in and board while they worked in Washington. In World War II, the problem was resolved, in part, by constructing dormitory-style residences for these women.[9]

The housing situation was bad enough in the larger cities of northern Virginia and the Hampton Roads area, but it was critical in the town of Radford, Virginia. Radford had a population of seven thousand and was expecting twenty thousand workers to staff the newly built Hercules powder plant and its associated bag-packing plant. In December 1940, John Vachon was the first of three RA/FSA photographers to go to Radford to document conditions there. He photographed the town and its severely overcrowded conditions. John Collier followed afterward, in July 1941, to photograph the developing housing projects. And Marion Post Wolcott photographed Sunset Village, an RA/FSA project in Radford, in October 1941.

In Caroline County, Virginia, 1,122 tracts of land totaling 77,215 acres were appropriated by purchase in the fall of 1940 and spring of 1941 to create Fort A. P. Hill—a "maneuver area for intensive training of troops." Towns, stores, churches, and homes were condemned, and about four thousand people were dispossessed. In June 1941, Jack Delano was sent to

Arlington, Virginia. June 1943. Waiting for the bus at Arlington farms, a residence for women who work in the U.S. government for the duration of the war. Photo by Esther Bubley. [LC-USW3-26037-E]

(Opposite) Radford, Virginia. December 1940. Workers from Lynchburg, Virginia, who arrived in town today, sleeping in their car. They will go to work tomorrow and get a place to live when they get time. The one in the front seat is a steamfitter. Photo by John Vachon. [LC-USF34-61984-D]

Radford, Virginia. October 1941. Sunset Village, FSA *housing project. Homes for defense workers.*
Photo by Marion Post Wolcott. [LC-USF34-90238-D]

Radford, Virginia. 1988. Sunset Village. Rephoto of above view by Charles L. Perdue Jr.

Radford, Virginia. October 1941. Sunset Village, FSA *housing project. Fred B. Williams from Savannah, Georgia, a safety engineer at the powder plant, leaving his home at 803 9th Street. Photo by Marion Post Wolcott.* [LC-USF34-90186-D]

Radford, Virginia. 1988. Sunset Village. Rephoto of above view by Charles L. Perdue Jr.

Caroline County, Virginia. June 1941. A negro farmer carting some of his farm equipment out of the area that is being taken over by the Army. Photo by Jack Delano. [LC-USF34-44867-D]

photograph the dislocation and resettlement of some of those people into new prefabricated homes built by the RA/FSA. Although some soldiers were already there by June, the Second Corps and the Twenty-ninth Infantry, which arrived in December 1941, constituted the first major influx of troops to Fort A. P. Hill. Following training there, most of these troops were shortly sent into the North African campaign.[10]

By the time the Roanoke Scrap Program and the Virginia Defense Programs were photographed in October and November 1942, respectively (for the Office of Emergency Management and Office of War Information), there was no longer any need for subtlety or for disguising the propagandistic message. The nation had been at war for almost a year, and its children were being charged to put their "playthings aside for a more important game" and to mobilize themselves into the "newest home front fighters, the Junior Army." Even when the photograph itself appeared innocuous, such as was the case with two little boys looking at a piece of paper, the caption "Two barefoot Junior Commandos . . ." made the intent explicit.

The Virginia Defense series of photographs was clearly intended to show both the resolve and capabilities of the state's military resources, to inspire greater public support for the war effort, and to reassure Virginians that they were protected "should enemy visitors embark on [their] shore." These photographs were, to a large degree, deliberately posed and manipulated to shape attitudes in the most direct manner possible.

In June 1942, the Virginia Writers' Project office in Richmond closed. Director Eudora Ramsay Richardson stayed on, however, until February 1943 to oversee final production of

Caroline County, Virginia. June 1941. Children of William Corneal, a farmer who must move out of the area which is being taken over by the Army for maneuver grounds. Photo by Jack Delano. [LC-USF33-21001-M2]

the VWP's last publication, *Roanoke: Story of County and City*. The VWP hope to publish "a book devoted to the lives of typical Virginians" was not realized. Richardson subsequently went to work as a writer for the Quartermaster Technical Training Service at Camp Lee. There she wrote speeches for the commandant of the fort to deliver on the Fourth of July and at Memorial Day services, and she published, with Sherman Allen, a history of the Quartermaster Supply in Europe. She retired in 1950 with a meritorious service commendation.[11]

At the Office of War Information, Roy Stryker stayed on longer, leaving in September 1943 to work for Standard Oil of New Jersey. There he directed a team of photographers—in some cases the same RA/FSA photographers he had supervised earlier—whose task it was to document the pervasiveness and importance of oil in everyday life and create a more favorable public attitude toward oil producers, specifically Standard Oil of New Jersey. The OWI continued to function and to produce photographs for wartime propaganda use, but the heyday of the so-called RA/FSA documentary photography ended with Stryker's departure.[12]

The world war provided what the WPA and other New Deal programs had set out to provide—jobs for millions of workers. More than that, these jobs were not make-work but were important to the war effort and the nation's future and therefore full of cultural meaning as significant work. That was a point that many of the WPA programs failed to understand or were unable to address because of their inherent nature; it was especially true for the cultural programs.

For some individuals it was, and is still, a source of embarrassment that they were ever obliged to work on New Deal projects. On the other hand, many of the cultural program directors and supervisory staff were idealists who felt that they were "remaking the world"

Roanoke, Virginia. October 1942. Two barefoot Junior Commandos wriggle their toes with delight as they study their instructions for collecting scrap for Uncle Sam's great army. Directions for the scrap collection were given the children at the huge star-spangled rally that launched the campaign. Photo by Valentino Sarra. [LC-USW3-06423-D]

and taking part in an important social movement—one that would endure and guarantee progress toward greater social equality and justice. Jerre Mangione reports a momentous and instructive exchange between the then librarian of Congress, Archibald MacLeish, and Florence Kerr, assistant WPA commissioner. At a conference of "cultural leaders" held at the Library of Congress shortly before the attack on Pearl Harbor in 1941, an aggravated Mac-Leish charged: "What you people did in WPA was completely hypocritical. . . . You kept telling yourself you were actually giving people a job, but you were really more interested in your program." To this Florence Kerr responded, "You must admit . . . it was one of the higher forms of hypocrisy."[13]

For the workers on the ground, the WPA/VWP provided a means to the end of feeding

Roanoke, Virginia. October 1942. Nobody played hookey the day teacher Doris Jordan at Jamison Elementary School explained how every pupil can help win the war. These youngsters, along with some 30 million other young Americans, are being mobilized into the nation's newest home front fighters, the Junior Army, to collect scrap for ammunition. Photo by Howard Liberman. [LC-USW3-06436-D]

(Above left) Roanoke, Virginia. October 1942. She's put her playthings aside for a more important game. This youngster is one of America's thousands of school age boys and girls who are self-appointed scrap collectors for the duration. Photo by Valentino Sarra. [LC-USW3-06452-D]

(Above right) Roanoke, Virginia. October 1942. The charge of the scrap brigade in Roanoke, Virginia, includes such methods of collection as this pony cart. The patriotic and energetic youngsters of the town are making an all-out effort to corner every available piece of scrap in the city, so that their soldier and sailor brothers will have the shells and guns and tanks with which to beat the Axis. Photo by Valentino Sarra. [LC-USW3-06457-D]

(Top) Fort Belvoir, Virginia. November 1942. Member of an all-Negro tank crew in training. The hard, steady routine of war exercises at this post is changing men with little or no previous experience into competent tank crew members, infantrymen and specialists in the manifold tasks of the Engineer Corps. Photo by Alfred Palmer. [LC-USW3-08733-D]

(Bottom left) Fort Story, Virginia. March 1942. Men and 16 inch gun prepare to resist Axis aggression. Photo by Alfred Palmer. [LC-USE6-03619-D]

(Bottom right) Fort Story, Virginia. March 1942. A sergeant of the CAC stands beside the muzzle of a 16 inch howitzer at Fort Story. Photo by Alfred Palmer. [LC-USE6-03669-D]

(Opposite) Fort Story, Virginia. March 1942. Ninety-six pounds of steel and high explosive make a very special burden for one of Fort Story's soldiers. Should enemy visitors embark on the Virginia shore, headache capsules like this would greet him. Photo by Alfred Palmer. [LC-USE6-03615-D]

Langley Field, Virginia. May 1942. Silhouetted against the dawn a soldier of a bombardment squadron keeps faithful watch over a giant YB-17 bomber. Photo by Alfred Palmer. [LC-USW3-04896-D]

themselves and their families, whether or not they shared in its ideology. From another perspective, that "higher [form] of hypocrisy" produced a lasting and invaluable, even if partial, portrait of Virginia lives at a critical juncture of rapid social change and transformation—already long in progress in some areas—from a rural-based agricultural society to a modern industrial state.

With the war mobilization and an abundance of jobs, there was less and less reason for the WPA's existence, and scarce resources were more urgently needed elsewhere. The WPA ended with a whimper; the war ended with a bang that is still resounding. But the aftermath of those events—on their own terms and by their own measure—left the world a significantly changed place in time.

RFC   *Reconstruction Finance Corporation* (January 1932–June 1957), authorized initially to extend aid to agriculture, commerce, and industry by direct loans to banks, other credit agencies, and railroads. Its powers were expanded by subsequent legislation such as the *Emergency Relief and Construction Act* (21 July 1932). A small portion of RFC money supported handicrafts, amateur dramatics, music, and folk dancing in Los Angeles County, California.

CCC   *Civilian Conservation Corps* (June 1937–June 1943), created to succeed the *Emergency Conservation Work* program established by executive order of 31 March 1933.

FERA   *Federal Emergency Relief Act* (May 1933–July 1935), passed by the new administration of Franklin Delano Roosevelt in May 1933 and administered by Harry Hopkins; provided $500 million for outright grants to the states with administration left to individual localities. This act funded public works of art and music projects. It was succeeded by the WPA, but some FERA activities continued into 1936.

PWA   *Public Works Administration* (June 1933–July 1943). Originally the *Federal Emergency Administration of Public Works,* the PWA was established by the *National Industrial Recovery Act,* with Harold L. Ickes as administrator. Its purpose was to initiate large public construction projects through grants and loans. The PWA was transferred to the Federal Works Agency under the President's Reorganization Plan on 1 July 1939. The PWA funded public works of art under the *Public Works of Art Project* (PWAP).

CWA   *Civil Works Administration* (November 1933–July 1934), established under the authority of the *National Industrial Recovery Act* and administered by Harry Hopkins. This program, with an initial fund of $400 million, was federally financed and administered. More than four million people were employed by the CWA during the winter of 1933–34. Its programs included documentation of historic buildings, music projects, folklore collecting, handicraft instruction, and art projects.

WPA   *Works Progress Administration* (May 1935–June 1939); *Work Projects Administration* (July 1939–June 1943), administered by Harry Hopkins. The WPA's main purpose was to remove 3.5 million employables from the relief rolls. The WPA succeeded the FERA and absorbed most of its administrative personnel.

WPA   *Division of Professional and Service Projects:*
Federal No. 1
FMP *Federal Music Project* (July 1935–June 1942), Nikolai Sokoloff, director.
     WPA/VMP *Virginia Music Project* (December 1935–June 1942), Wilfrid Pyle, director.
FAP *Federal Art Project* (July 1935–June 1942), Holger Cahill, director.
     WPA/VAP *Virginia Art Project* (February 1936–July 1942), Adele Clark, director.
FAP/IAD *Index of American Design* (January 1936–June 1942), Adolph C. Glassgold, director.
FTP *Federal Theatre Project* (July 1935–June 1939), Hallie Flanagan, director.
     WPA/VTP *Virginia Theatre Project* (January 1936–April 1936), T. Beverly Campbell, director. Project aborted following accusation of misuse of federal funds.
FWP *Federal Writers' Project* (July 1935–June 1942), Henry G. Alsberg, director. Became the Writers' Program after the 1939 reorganization; John D. Newsome, director beginning spring of 1939.
     WPA/VWP *Virginia Writers' Project* (October 1935–June 1942), Hamilton J. Eckenrode, part-time director October 1935–March 1937; Eudora Ramsay Richardson, director March 1937–June 1942.
HRS *Historic Records Survey* (November 1935–June 1942), Luther H. Evans, director. The HRS began under the Federal Writers' Project but became a separate unit under Federal One in October 1936.
     WPA/HIP *Historic Inventory Project* (October 1935–December 1938). Began under W. A. Moon Jr. as acting state supervisor; followed by M. F. Pleasants as state supervisor. Thirty microfilm reels of information on houses, mills, Indian sites, relics, and so on compiled by two hundred workers in eighty-five Virginia counties. Includes numerous photographs.
     WPA/VHP *Virginia Handicraft Project* (March 1940–July 1942), taught the weaving of linen, wool,

and cotton from homegrown raw materials; taught woodworking skills; operated at least one craft outlet store north of Fredericksburg, Virginia.

WPA/DR *Division of Recreation* (June 1936–1943), Loula Clyde Woody, director.

NYA *National Youth Administration* (June 1935–December 1944), was nominally within the WPA but was essentially an autonomous organization. The NYA provided educational, cultural, and work programs for youths aged sixteen to twenty-four. Under the President's Reorganization Plan the NYA became part of the Federal Security Agency on 1 July 1939, and on the same date, the WPA (renamed *Work Projects Administration*) became part of the Federal Works Agency with primary control and sponsorship transferred to the state level.

HABS   *Historic American Buildings Survey* (July 1935–present), work actually began under funding from the CWA in 1933. The survey is operated by the National Park Service.

HAMMS   *Historic American Merchant Marine Survey* (July 1935–), Eric J. Steinlein, director. This was a project sponsored by the Smithsonian Institution; it measured, photographed, and generally documented traditional watercraft.

RA   *Resettlement Administration* (April 1935–September 1937), created to aid economically distressed rural people through programs of land use, rural and suburban resettlement, and rehabilitation. On 1 September 1937 the RA became the *Farm Security Administration* (FSA), and the FSA was succeeded by the *Farmers Home Administration* (FHA) in August 1946. The Historical Section in the Information Division of RA/FSA employed photographers to record depression conditions and to document various RA/FSA projects.

OWI   *Office of War Information.* In October 1942 the Historical Section of the FSA (see RA) was transferred to the OWI.

OEM   *Office for Emergency Management.* In May 1943 the OWI's photography units were consolidated and combined with those of the OEM, creating the Division of Photography, OWI, with Roy Stryker continuing as division chief.

The following supplemental material is presented in the same order as the life history subjects appear in the chapters of this book. The birthplace of all persons (and their parents where given) is Virginia unless otherwise noted—for example, b: W.Va./W.Va./W.Va. for self/father/mother. Further, all persons are white unless they are indicated as B or MU (for black or mulatto) in accordance with the racial identity reported in the census.

Although not consistently reported, the 1850, 1860, and 1870 censuses did include categories for the value of real estate and personal property owned by household heads; for example, James Adams had real/personal property = $2,000/$1,200 in 1860. In 1900 and 1910, the censuses indicate instead if the household head owned a farm or home free of or with mortgage (OFF/OMF or OFH/OMH) or rented either a farm or home (RF/RH). In a few cases, primarily in the Virginia Piedmont areas of Rappahannock and Culpeper Counties, only an "H" appeared in this category—quite likely to indicate that the house was neither technically "rented" nor "owned" by the person enumerated but was provided for that person's use under terms of the "findings" or perquisite wage/labor system that was operative in the area.

The relationship of the head to other persons in a household is given regularly beginning with the 1880 census. The 1900 and 1910 censuses indicate if a person was single (S), married (M), or widowed (Wd); the number of years married—for example, M7 for 7 years or (in 1910 only) M2/7 if it was a second marriage of the same length; and the number of children a woman had borne and the number of those that were still living—for example, 10/8 below indicates that Mary E. Arritt reported having had 10 children, but only 8 of those were surviving in 1900. The 1910 census also reported if a man was a Confederate (CA) or Union (UA) veteran of the Civil War.

Age is generally the most variable, and therefore least reliable, information available from census records. The 1900 census is the possible exception. It reports the month and year of birth for each individual, in addition to his or her age—for example, Daniel F. Aritt, 39, was born in December 1860, or 12/60. Maybe the birthdate acted as a control for the usual misstatements of age, but for whatever reason the 1900 census age data seem to hold up better alongside other sources of such information. There is some variation in the spelling of names in the records; they are given below without change. Names in boldface indicate those people whose life histories are included in this book.

It is quickly apparent that there is a greater volume of accessible documentary evidence pertaining to older people in the life histories than there is for either younger persons (born after 1910) or African Americans. Some of the latter do begin to appear as infants or as migrants in the 1920 federal census made available after March 1992. A few people have not been located in any public records, and some possible reasons for that absence are offered in the notes to their individual life histories. Those persons are not, then, included in this appendix.

CHAPTER 1

Benjamin Christopher Thacker

8 December 1849: Samuel Thacker to Harriet Yancey. Father: Jeremiah Yancey. Marriage Book 1-158, Campbell Co. Courthouse.

1850 Campbell Co. Census, no district/township given, 72-72:

Jeremiah Yancey	62	Farmer	RE = $——
Sarah H.	64		
Samuel Thacker	28	——	
Harriett "	24		
Edmond Welch	28	Carpenter	
Jane "	26		
Andrew "	2		
James "	1/12		

1860 Bedford Co. Census, South Dist., 1281-1281:

S. [Samuel] Thacker	39	Farmer	$1,500/$300
H. [Harriett]	35		

D. J.		6	[m]		
M. M.		4	[f]		
Wm. H.		1	[m]		
Infant [**Benjamin**]		2/12	[m]		b: June

1870 Bedford Co. Census, Otter Dist., 348-337:

Samuel Thacker	50	Farmer $555/$200
David	16	
Melissa	13	
Wm. H.	11	
Benj. C.	10	
Saml. R.	5	
Harriet L.	2	

2 January 1878: Thomas A. Wood, 22, farmer, born in Campbell Co. to Sarah M. Wood, 23, born in Bedford Co. Parents: Archibald and T. C. Wood; John T. and Mary E. Wood. Married by W. S. Bishop. Marriage Book 2-77, Bedford Co. Courthouse.

1880 Bedford Co. Census, Otter Dist., 39-39:

Thomas Wood	Head	23	M	Works on Farm
Sarah	Wife	26	M	
Pearl	Dau	1	S	

40-40:

Sam'l Thacker	Head	59	Wd	Farming
Mary	Dau	23	S	
Benj. C.	Son	20	S	Works on Farm
Samuel	Son	15	S	Works on Farm
Hariet	Dau	12	S	

1900 Bedford Co. Census, Otter Dist., 326-325:

Benjamin C. Thacker	Head	39	S	Farmer	OMF	06/60
Harriett "	Sis	31	S	Housekeeper		11/68
Bettie Adams	Brdr	50	S			02/50

1910 Bedford Co. Census, Otter Dist., 247-248:

Benjamin C. Thacker	Head	49	M9		Farmer	OFF
Leona P.	Wife	31	M9	5/5		
Joel D.	Son	8	S			
Malcolm T.	Son	7	S			
Harry C.	Son	5	S			
Samuel G.	Son	3	S			
Hettie L.	Dau	1	7/12			

248-249:

*Waivily Adams	Brdr	41	S		Farm Laborer

In HH of:

Charles L. Wills	Head	35	M8	Farmer	OFF

+ wife; 4 children; fa, Thomas Wills, 80 Wd, CA; Pearl Sims, Srvt

*Brother of California Adams StClair; see following.

1920 Bedford Co. Census, Otter Dist., E.D. 6, 222-222:

B. C. Thacker	Head	59	M	Farmer	OMF
Leonia P.	Wife	40	M		
Joel	Son	18	S		
Malcolm	Son	17	S		
Harry C.	Son	14	S		

Guy	Son	12	s
Hattie	Dau	11	s
Isabell	Dau	8	s
Louise	Dau	6	s
Earle	Son	4	
Frances	Dau	4	

Hill's Roanoke, Virginia, City Directory, 1931 (Richmond: Hill Directory Co.):

B. Chris Thacker (Pearl), carpenter

　h. 359 Day Avenue, S.W., Roanoke

California Elizabeth Adams StClair

25 November 1833: Joseph D. StClair to Lucinda W. McGhee, James McGhee, Surety. Married by James Leftwich. Marriage Record in Burlap Book, Bedford Co. Courthouse.

1 July 1840: Will for John StClair, dec. of Bedford Co. Leaves $100 each to son, Joseph D., and daughter, Rhoda W. Mentions other children: Nancy, Adline, Susan, Sally, Henry T., and Catherine. Appoints son, Joseph D., and widow, Catharine, to be administrators and guardians of last four children above, who are infants. Rec. 22 May 1843. Will Book 11-303, Bedford Co. Courthouse.

14 December 1846: James Adams to Elizabeth Roberts. Father: John Roberts. Marriage Book 1-1, Campbell Co. Courthouse.

1850 Campbell Co. Census, no district/township given, 361-361:

James Adams	30	Blacksmith
Elizabeth	23	
Texanna	1	

1860 Bedford Co. Census, South Dist., 1268-1268:

Jas. Adams	46	Blacksmith	$2,000/$1,200
E.	40		
T.	9		
C. [**California**]	7		
W.	5		
Infant [Dau]	1/12		
A. T. Adams	17	Blacksmith	

28 July 1862: Will of William A. Adams, dec. of Bedford presented in Court. Gives house and land on Arise [?] Creek to sons Samuel, Wilson, Abraham, and Cornelius; all the rest of estate to sons James, Richard, and Nathan and daughters Martha Huse and Elizabeth Fisher. Tilghman A. Cobbs Jr. to be executor. Dated: 11 February 1857. Witnesses: Joshua C. Adams, Abram Austin, and W. [Waddy] Burton. Will Book T-19-91, Campbell Co. Courthouse.

11 October 1862: Appraisal of estate of William A. Adams, dec. Included: set of Cooper's Tools; Carpenter's Tools; 3 Firkins; 1 Loom; 1 Hackle; 1 Cut Reel; 1 Flax Wheel; 1 Cotton Wheel; 1 Candle stick and Moulds; 1 Shot Gun; 1 Waggon; 1 Bay Mare, and more. Value = $225.65. Appraised by J. C. Adams, Geo. W. Goode, and Abner Hewitt. Will Book T-19-141, Campbell Co. Courthouse.

[*Note:* In the 1870 Bedford Co. Census, Abram Adams, a farmer, his family, and brother Cornelius, a carpenter, are living in HH# 278-273; Joshua C. Adams, a retired merchant, and his family are in HH# 305-297; and Wilson Adams, a farmer and miller, along with his family are in HH# 343-333.]

1870 Bedford Co. Census, Otter Dist., 275-270:

James Adams	57	Blacksmith	$800/$340
Elizabeth	50		
Texanna	20		
California	19		
Waverly D.	14		
Ossa	10		

Staunton Dist., 305-300:

Joseph D. StClair	62	Farmer
Lucinda	57	
James H.	20	

25 November 1875: James H. StClair, 25, mechanic, to **Callie E. Adams**, 24, both born in Bedford Co. Parents: Jos. D. and Lucinda W. StClair; James and Elizabeth Adams. Married by C. L. Anthony, minister. Marriage Book 2-53, Bedford Co. Courthouse.

1880 Bedford Co. Census, Otter Dist., 55-55:

James Adams	Head	66	M	Farmer
Lizzie	Wife	60	M	
Wavelly	Son	24	S	Farm Work
Ollie [?] W.	Dau	18	S	Teacher

Staunton Dist., 3-3:

Joseph StClair	Head	73	M	Farmer
L. W.	Wife	66	M	

4-4:

Jas. H. StClair	Head	30	M	Farmer
C. E. [**California**]	Wife	29	M	
L. E.	Son	3	S	
Jno. W.	Son	2	S	
Jas. D.	Son	1	S	
S. E. Adams	Cous	18	S	[f]

1900 Bedford Co. Census, Staunton Dist., 29-31:

James StClair	Head	50	M25	Farmer	OFF	06/50
Callie	Wife	50	M25			11/50
Louiston	Son	23	S	Clerk/Grocery		08/76
John	Son	22	S	Farm Laborer		11/77
James W.	Son	20	S	Farm Laborer		06/79
Frank P.	Son	19	S	Farm Laborer		09/80
Kate	Dau	18	S			03/82
Benjamin	Son	16	S	Farm Laborer		11/83
Lillian	Dau	15	S			03/85
Lizzie	Dau	13	S			04/87
Emmett	Son	9	S			11/90
William O.	Son	6	S			11/93

1920 Roanoke City Census, E.D. 22, 716 Highland & 10th Ave., 209-253:

John W. StClair	Head	42	M	Car Repair/RR Shop	OMH
Mollie L.	Wife	42	M		
Nedia L.	Dau	5	S		
William H. Lee	Fa-i-law	69	Wd	Carpenter	

E.D. 128, 517 Dennison Ave., 66-69:

Orval D. Amburn	Head	35	M	Hostler/RR	OF	
Elizabeth W.	Wife	30	M			
James O.	Son	5	S			
Edward G.	Son	4 2/12				
Muriel C.	Dau	1 1/12				
Callie E. StClair	Mo-i-law	69	Wd	None		

Hill's Roanoke, Virginia, City Directory, 1931 (Richmond: Hill Directory Co.):
John W. StClair (Mollie), carpenter
    h. 716 Highland Ave., S.E., Roanoke

George (Strausburg) Strawsburg

1850 Augusta Co. Census, 2nd Dist., 837-837:

Elias Strawsburg	44	Blacksmith	RE = $800
Elizabeth	38		
Ephraim Y.	17	Blacksmith	
Robert M.	16	Blacksmith	
James M.	14		
David L.	12		
William H.	3		
Elizabeth A.	10		
Susanah Hill	21		

28 June 1852: Michael Yessler, John G. Hausman, and Jacob Shuey put up bond of $1,800 for Yessler to be administrator of the estate of Elias Strausburg, dec. Recorded the same day. Will Book 32-108.

1 July 1853: "Michael Yesler, Guardian of Ephraim Y. Strasburg, In acct with his Ward" pays Ephraim $57.10. Will Book 34-179. Other guardian accounts involving both Yesler and the widow Elizabeth Strausburg appear in the following: Will Book 32-178, 515; Will Book 34-162, 178; and Will Book 37-120-121.

19 July 1852: Estate of Elias Strausburg appraised by Daniel Fisher, John B. Fairbairn, George F. Hoover. Total value = $1,446.85. Recorded October term, 1852. Will Book 32-213-214.

October Term, 1852: Estate sale of Elias Strausburg, dec. Among other persons indicated, Ephraim Y. Strausburg bought: "one saddle @ $14.00"; "1 skillet @ .07"; "3 States [?] @ .16 1/4"; "shaving box & razor & etc @ .12 1/2"; "1 sugar box @ .06 1/4"; "1 blacking box @ .03"; "1 shot gun @ 5.50"; "2 window curtains @ .15"; "1 Mason Hammer and Trowel, .31"; "1 Plough pattern @ 1.00"; one 2 horse Waggon @ 74.50"; and "1 Sett Gears for 2 horses @ 15.25." Bill of sale of property of Elias Strausburg, dec., for total of $270.49 was presented in court term as given above. Will Book 32-211-13.

17 September 1860: Marriage contract between widow Elizabeth Strausburg and Jacob Shaver. Agree to allow her separate and sole use of land and personal property she holds prior to marriage. At her death, if he survives her, Jacob Shaver shall deliver said property to her children or their descendants. Deed Book 79-560-61. All the above from Augusta Co. Courthouse Records.

1860 Augusta Co. Census, 1st Dist., Staunton, 1789-1734:

Ephraim Y. Strausburg	27	Blacksmith	$——/$75
Elizabeth	26		
George L.	3		
James Watson	5/12		

1870 Augusta Co. Census, 1st Dist., Staunton, 757-545 [?]:

William Carter	[?]	Farmer	$5,000/$3,000
Martha B.	69	Keeps House	
Anthony Lefew [?]	22	Laborer	
James J. Paxton	22	Laborer	
Ellen Henderson	19	At School	
George Strawsburgh	10	Domestic	
Elizabeth Hollen [?]	50	Housekeeper	

1900 Augusta Co. Census, Riverheads Dist., 264-274:

James W. Strausburg	Head	40	Wd	Farmer	OFF	04/60
Albert R.	Son	9	S			04/91
Eva C.	Dau	6	S			06/93
Bessie M.	Dau	4	S			08/95

1900 Rockbridge Co. Census, Kerr's Creek Dist., 50-50:

George L. Strasburg	Head	42	M18	Laborer	OFF	07/57
Martha F.	Wife	53	M18	3/3		10/46
Mary E.	Dau	17	S			04/85

1910 Rockbridge Co. Census, Kerr's Creek Dist., 155-164:

George L. Strasburg	Head	54	M26		Carpenter	OFF
Martha F.	Wife	60	M26	3/2		
Margarette Hinckle	Srvt	75	Wd			

Daniel F. Arritt

1860 Alleghany Co. Census, Covington, 704-708:

John L. Aritt	30	Farmer	$900/$400
Phebe	27		
Virginia A.	8		
Moses W.	5		
Elizabeth A. Bush	20	Domestic	
Jacob D. Ferry	22	Farmer	$20/$70

1870 Alleghany Co. Census, Boiling Springs Dist., 144-144:

Moses G. Wright	47	Farmer	$1,000/$500
Pheba	38	Keeps House	
Andrew L.	5	At Home	
Henry	3		
William	1		
Virginia Aritt	18	At Home	
Moses W. Aritt	15	At Home	
Daniel F. Aritt	10		
John L. Aritt	8		
Frances Scipower	18	Domestic Servant	

12 April 1882: **Daniel F. Aritt,** 21, farmer, born Alleghany Co., to M. E. Riddlesbarger, 21, born Botetourt Co. Parents: John and [not readable] Aritt; M. C. and M. A. Riddlesbarger. Marriage Book, Alleghany Co. Courthouse.

1900 Alleghany Co. Census, Boiling Springs Dist., 54-50:

Daniel F. Aritt	Head	39	M18		Farmer	OFF	12/60
Mary E.	Wife	40	M18	10/8			10/59
Stella M.	Dau	16	S				09/83
Willie L.	Son	15	S				02/85
Henry F.	Son	12	S				06/87
Waldo P.	Son	9	S				08/90
Amber G.	Dau	9	S				08/90
Minnie P.	Dau	7	S				03/92
Roda A.	Dau	5	S				07/94
Ernest H.	Son	2	S				08/98

1910 Alleghany Co. Census, Boiling Springs Dist., 68-68:

Daniel Aritt	Head	49	M28		Farmer		OFF
Mary E.	Wife	50	M28	12/7			
Ambria	Dau	19	S				
Waldin	Son	19	S				
Minnie	Dau	17	S				
Grady [?]	Son	14	S				
Hawes [Ernest?]	Son	12	S				
Lowel	Son	7	S				
Clarence Young	Brdr	27	S		Teamster/Lumber Wagon	b: W.Va./W.Va./W.Va.	

1920 Alleghany Co. Census, Boiling Springs Dist., Potts Creek Rd., 184-184:

Daniel F. Arritt	Head	59	M	Farmer	OF
Mary E.	Wife	60	M		
Hawes [?] E.	Son	21	S	Laborer/Home Farm	
Lowell W.	Son	18	S	Laborer/Lumber Mill	

19 February 1945: List of heirs of **Daniel Arritt** include wife Emma, age 87; four daughters; and three sons, living in Alleghany County; Seattle, Washington; and Kalamazoo, Michigan. Charles E. Wolfe [who married daughter Amber Arritt] and Frank E. Miller, executors. Witnesses: R. B. Stephenson and A. C. Sizer. E. A. Robinson, Delbert Hepler, Henry Bowen, M. G. Wright, and G. N. Wright, or any three to appraise estate. Will Book 7-204-205, Alleghany Co. Courthouse.

George and Celia (McKnight) Brown

1860 Scott Co. Census, Estillville, 1853-1853:

John Brown	23	Farmer		$——/$110	
Elizabeth	20	*Spinster	b: Tenn.		

*This term was used consistently in this census district for women, married or single.

1900 Wise Co. Census, Richmond Dist., 302-476:

George Brown	Head	39	M14		Tipple Boss	RH		02/61
Celia	Wife	41	M14	1/1			b: Ky./Ky./Ky.	04/59
Joseph	St-son	20	S		Salesman		b: Ky./Ky./Ky.	10/79

1910 Wise Co. Census, Richmond Dist., Appalachia, 203-203:

George Brown	Head	48	M23		House Carpenter	OFH	
Celia	Wife	50	M23	1/1			b: Ky./Ky./Ky.

1920 Wise Co. Census, Richmond Dist., Appalachia, 104-109:

George Brown	Head	58	M	House Carpenter	OF	
Celey	Wife	60	M	None		b: Ky./Ohio/Ky.

Lycurgus Drumheller

1870 Nelson Co. Census, Rockfish Twnshp., 33-34:

John Drumheller	41	Carpenter	$400/$200
Elvira J.	40	Keeps House	
Lycurgus	27	Farm Laborer	
Masiah	15	Farm Laborer	
Mace Ellis	13	At Home	
William C.	9	At Home	
Zachariah E.	5	At Home	

1910 Nelson Co. Census, Schuyler Dist., 11:

Lycurgus Drumheller	Head	62	M37		House Carpenter	OFF
Sarah L.	Wife	55	M37	11/9		
Thos. D.	Son	18	S		Laborer/Odd Jobs	
Aubrey	Son	16	S			
Zelma	Dau	13	S			

——/13:

Lorenzo Drumheller	Head	26	M6		House Carpenter	OFF
Geneva	Wife	22	M6	3/2		
Iowa	Dau	2	S			
Iva	Dau	8/12	S			

——/236:

Siah Drumheller	Head	55	M33		House Carpenter	OFF
Belle	Wife	49	M33		———	
Lottie	Dau	12	S			
Mary	Dau	9	S			
Adeline P. Witt	Mo-i-law	74	Wd	2/1	Blind	

1920 Nelson Co. Census, Rockfish Dist., 192-192:

L. Drumheller	Head	73	M	Merchant/Grocery	OF
Sarah L.	Wife	66	M		
Aubrey C.	Son	27	S	Brakeman/R.W. [*sic*]	

193-193:

Thomas Drumheller	Head	21	M	Carpenter/R.W. [*sic*]	OF
Eva	Wife	26	M		
Margaret	Dau	6	S		
Robert	Son	4	S		

Orthodox Creed Strictler (Smith)

1850 Campbell Co. Census, Leesville Dist., 1040-1040:

William B. Smith	40	Farmer	RE = $615
Catharine F. W.	36		
Watson L.	16	Farmer	
Robert B.	14		
Mary A.	13		
Susan A.	11		
William C.	8		
John T.	6		
Orthodox C.	4		
Adolphus A.	2		

1041-1041:

Paalett Clark	80	Farmer	
Mary A.	73		
O. Creed	36	Farmer	RE = $2,250
Susan	31		
John F.	27	Overseer	
William Irvine	60		

1860 Campbell Co. Census, Hat Creek P.O., 119-127:

| O. C. Clark | 41 | Farmer | $6,915/$12,600 |
| Susan E. N. [?] | 47 | Domestic | $———/$4,500 |

120-125:

Catherine W. Smith	41	Farmer	$1,818/$7,975
Robt. B.	24	Farm Laborer	
Susan E.	19	Domestic	
Wm. E. Smith, Jr.	17	Farm Laborer	
Jas. T.	16		
O[rthodox] C[reed]	14		
Adolphus A.	12		

1910 Henry Co. Census, Martinsville Twnshp., Church St., 87-98:

Orthodox C. Smith	Head	60	M35		Tobacconist/Leaf Prizing [*sic*]	OFH	CA
Mary C.	Wife	51	M35	3/3			
Cabbel	Son	31	M11		Real Estate Agent		
Ray Cabbel	Dau	18	S				
*Essie W.	Dau-i-law	30	M11	2/2	Teacher/Public School		

Laura B[utler]	———	15	S		[Step-Gdau]
Mary C.	Gdau	10	S		
Martha	Srvt	24	M	B	Servant/Private Family

*Essie W. is Essie Wade Smith, the vwp interviewer.

1920 Henry Co. Census, Martinsville, Church St., 340-440:

O. C. Smith	Head	73	M		Retired Tobacconist	OF
Mary C.	Wife	66	M			
Cabel	Son	44	M		Deputy U.S. Marshall	
Martha Meck [?]	Srvt	43	M	B	Servant	
Margaret Smith	Srvt	14	S	B	Servant	

Nannie Isabel Webb Price

1850 Franklin Co. Census, no district/township given, 2023-2011:

Theodorick F. Webb	50	Farmer	RE = $1,500
*Nancy [Calloway]	40		
Tazewell	25		
Henry	22		
Mary C.	18		
Theodorick	15		
Benjamin F.	13		
Ursula	10		
Louisa	8		
James	6		
Ramsey	4		

*Nancy Calloway was the daughter of James Calloway and Betsy Greer; the latter was the daughter of Moses Greer Sr. (b. Md., 2 June 1744) and Nancy Bailey. Wingfield, *Pioneer Families,* 87.

1860 Franklin Co. Census, S.W. Dist., 614-610:

Theodorick F. Webb	59	Farmer/Baptist Clergy	$12,000/$29,070
Julia C.	43		
Serena	13		
James	11		
Ramsay	9		
Nancy	4		
Julia	2		
John H. Wade	19		$———/$3,200
Elizabeth M. "	14		$———/$3,000
*Zachary T. "	8		$———/$3,000

Slave census lists 37 slaves for Theodorick F. Webb.

*Zachary Taylor Wade and his wife, Catherine Greer, were the parents of vwp worker Celestia (Essie) Wade Smith. "History of Franklin County, Virginia—Unfinished Manuscript and Notes," by Essie Wade Smith, Stanley Library, Franklin County Historical Society. See the records above for Orthodox Creed Strictler (Smith).

725-721:

T[azewell]. A. Webb	36	Farmer	$———/$1,000
J. Adaline	29		
Theodorick H.	4		
Nancy I.	2		

726-722:

| Richard F. Darnell | 46 | Farmer | $12,000/$8,660 |
| Susan I. | 36 | | |

Jemima E.   19
Lucy M.   16
Sarah M.   14
Susan I.   9
Richard Q.   5
Henry M.   2

727-723:
Henry P. Webb   24   Farmer $800/$3,305
Sarah A.   23
Charles H.   1

728-724:
Theo. F. Webb   25   Farmer $——/$1,000
Mary   19
Nancy A.   1
Caroline M.   [?]

Long Branch Dist., 366-363:
Owen Price   59   Farmer $10,000/$34,300
Mildred C.   43
Thomas G.   3
Edward H.   1
James M. Price   19   Ward $2,900/$4,000
Owen H. Price   17   Ward $22,500/$16,020
Sallie Price   78
Thomas P. Jones   39

1870 Franklin Co. Census, Snow Creek Twnshp., Glade Hill, 438-479:
Tazewell Webb   47   Farmer
Jemima   40   Keeps House
Henry   15   Farm Laborer
Nancy   12
Sarah   9
William   6
Mary   4
Ursula   1/12

439-480:
Theodorick Webb   69   Minister $5,000/$1,000
Julia   53   Keeps House
Ramsey   21   Farm Laborer
Nancy   15   At School
Julia   13   At School
Gustave   9
Daniel Webb   20   B   Farm Laborer

1870 Franklin Co. Census, Blackwater Dist., 85-85:
Mildred Price   54   Keeps House $8,000/$2,000
James M.   28   Farmer
Thomas   13
Edward   11
Henry   8
Thomas Jones   49   Farmer
Sally S.   "   37
Nancy Price   16   B   Servant

1880 Franklin Co. Census, Blackwater Dist., 1-1:

Benj. B. Webb	Head	39	M	Farmer	
Sallie M.	Wife	34	M		b: Va./N.C./Va.
Ella T.	Dau	12	S		
Mary J.	Dau	10	S		
Wayland W.	Son	8	S		
Benj. M.	Son	2	S		
Jemimah Darnall	Si-i-law	36	S		b: Va./N.C./Va.

63-63:

Edward Price	Head	21	M	Farmer
Nannie	Wife	22	M	
Rosy L.	Dau	7/12	S	

102-102:

Tazewell Webb	Head	57	M	School Teacher
Adaline	Wife	50	M	
Sallie	Dau	18	S	
Willie L.	Son	16	S	
Mary T.	Dau	14	S	
Mosca T.	Dau	12	S	
Fannie B.	Dau	8	S	

Blackwater Dist., 394-395:

Millie Price	Head	63	Wd	Keeps House
James M.	Son	39	S	Farm Hand
Thomas G.	Son	22	S	Farm Hand
Henry G.	Son	18	S	Farm Hand

1900 Roanoke Co. Census, Salem Dist., 98-98:

Edward H. Price	Head	41	M20		RR Foreman	OFH	11/58
Nannie I.	Wife	42	M20	7/7			02/58
Charles E.	Son	18	S		Day Laborer		04/82
Hattie G.	Dau	15	S		Weaver in Mill		07/84
Luther T.	Son	12	S		Day Laborer		06/87
Lula B.	Dau	10	S				05/90
Mary T.	Dau	4	S				12/95
Annie D.	Dau	1	S				02/99

1910 Roanoke Co. Census, Salem Town, 361-385:

Luther T. Price	Head	22	M4		Machinist/Tannery	RH
Amy	Wife	22	M4	2/2		
Cledist [?]	Son	2				
Clifton	Son	6/12				

362-386:

Edward H. Price	Head	53	M22		Laborer/Tannery	OFH
Nannie I.	Wife	52	M22	8/8		
Lula	Dau	19	S			
Mary	Dau	14	S			
Annie	Dau	11	S			
Vernon	Son	7	S			

1920 Roanoke Co. Census, Salem Town, 218-237, 303 Chestnut St.:

Nannie I. Price	Head	62	Wd	None	OFH
Annie	Dau	21	S	Sales/Ice Cream Parlor	
Vernon	Son	17	S	Driver/Grocery Wagon	

Howard D.	Gson	16	s	In School		
Mildred	Gdau	8	s	In School		

CHAPTER 2

Mrs. J. L. (Josephine) Wright

30 July 1894: Marriage license for John L. Wright, 24, single, b: Alleghany Co., Va., to **Josephine Lipes,** 20, single, b: Craig Co., Va. Parents are John H. and Barbara Wright, and Oscar L. and Sarah E. Lipes. Marriage performed next day at home of Oscar L. Lipes in Craig Co. by minister John B. Davis. Marriage Record, Craig Co. Courthouse.

1900 Alleghany Co. Census, Boiling Springs Dist., 63-64:

John L. Wright	Head	30	M6		Farmer	RH	05/70
Josia	Wife	25	M6	3/3			10/74
Roxie M.	Dau	4	s				08/95
Lester L.	Son	2	s				08/97
Virgy H.	Dau	8/12	s				09/99

1910 Alleghany Co. Census, Boiling Springs Dist., 82-83:

John L. Wright	Head	38	M16		Lumberman	RF
Josphine	Wife	36	M16	7/7		
Rox Anna	Dau	14	s			
Lester L.	Son	12	s			
Virgie Lee	Dau	10	s			
Bessie M.	Dau	8	s			
Effey E.	Dau	6	s			
Leliah E.	Dau	3	s			
Ruth A.	Dau	11/12				

1920 Alleghany Co. Census, Boiling Springs Dist., Mill Run Rd., 220-220:

John L. Wright	Head	50	M	Farmer		R
Josephine	Wife	45	M			
Lester L.	Son	21	M	Laborer/Lumber Mill		
Virgie H.	Dau	20	s			
Bessie M.	Dau	17	s			
Effie E.	Dau	15	s			
Edna L.	Dau	13	s			
Ruth A.	Dau	10	s			
Harry F.	Son	8	s			
Fay J.	Dau	5	s			
Grady A.	Son	1 9/12				
Emmet W.	Gson	2 7/12				
Gordon L.	Gson	1 1/12				
Margie L.	Dau-i-law	19	M			

Margaret Wolfe

1860 Alleghany Co. Census, 709-713:

Abraham Wolf	64	Farmer	$600/$410	
Hetta H.	39			
King A.	19	Farming		
Caroline	11			
Phebe H.	9			
Sina	4			

1880 Alleghany Co. Census, E.D. 1, 89-94:

C. W. Wright	Head	23	Clerk in Store
Sinia W. [Wolfe]	Wife	24	Keeping House
Paris L.	Son	7/12	b. Nov.

89-95:

Hettie Wolf	Gr-mo [?]	60
George W.	Son	18

1900 Alleghany Co. Census, Boiling Spring Dist., 69-70:

George W. Wolfe	Head	39	M17		Farmer	OFF	12/60
Wilsona	Wife	32	M17	1/1			11/67
Frank	Son	16	S		Farm Laborer		10/83
Hettie H.	Mo	79	Wd	6/5			12/20

1910 Alleghany Co. Census, Boiling Spring Dist., 84-85:

Frank Wolfe	Head	26	M5		Farmer	RF
Rose E. [?]	Wife	25	M5	1/1		
Aurther [sic] C.	Son	3	S			

Note: Reference in another VWP interview strongly suggested that Frank and Rose Wolfe were Margaret's parents, though that was not yet obvious in either the 1910 or 1920 census. A telephone conversation with Margaret Lee (née Wolfe) on 8 June 1993 confirmed her parents as above and also the names of her siblings: Arthur, Clara, Dorothy, Gertrude Missouri, Lucy Marie, George F., and Daisy.]

1920 Alleghany Co. Census, Boiling Springs Dist., Potts Creek Rd., 176-176:

Frank C. Woolf	Head	27	M	Farmer	OF
Rosie M.	Wife	37	M		
Arthur C.	Son	12	S		
Clara L.	Dau	9	S		
George F.	Son	6	S		
Missouri G.	Dau	3 3/12			
Lucy M.	Dau	1 9/12			

177-177:

George W. Woolf	Head	59	M	Farmer	OF
Wilsonia	Wife	54	M		

Lizzie (Sallie Newman) Gibson

1850 Patrick Co. Census, Ararat P.O., 41-42:

Fountain Howell	40	Farmer	$1,500
Nancy	36		
Elijah P. [?]	11	At School	
Mary E.	6		
Lucinda	3		

494-520:

Joseph Newman	30	Farmer
Sarah E.	18	
James M.	2	
Hynam W. [?]	1/12	

1860 Patrick Co. Census, Ararat P.O., 370-370:

Fountain Howell	49	Farmer	$3,000/$4,900
Nancy	45		
Lucinda	12		
Rosabel H.	9		
Susan J. [Newman]	6		

| Samuel F. | | 2 | | |

371-371:

Elijah Howell		20	Farmer	$500/$175
Martha		19		
William P.		1		

1870 Patrick Co. Census, Dan River Twnshp., 466-487:

Fountain Howell		59	Farmer	$1,300/$200
Nancy		55	Keeping House	
Samuel H.		13	Laborer	

467-487:

| James M. Newman | | 22 | Farmer | $400/$160 |
| Susan J. | | 17 | Keeping House | |

468-488:

Elijah P. Howell		31	Farmer	$1,750/$280
Martha J.		30	Keeping House	
Wm. P.		12	Laborer	
Victoria		9		
Charles F.		4		

1880 Patrick Co. Census, Dan River Mag. Dist., E.D. 157, 36-41:

James Newman	——	32	M	Farmer	
Susan J.	Wife	25	M	Keeping House	
Nancy	Dau	9	S	At School	
Elijah	Son	7	S	At School	
Cybella	Dau	5	S	At School	
Wooster	Son	3	S		
Edward	Son	4/12			b. Feb

5 February 1874: James L. F. Gibson, 20, single, farmer, to Minerva McCommack, 17, single. Both born in Franklin Co. and reside in same. Parents: Abnerton and Martha Gibson; Andrew J. and —— McCommack. Married by Daniel Bowman. Marriage Record Book 1-113, Franklin Co. Courthouse.

1880 Franklin Co. Census, Maggodee Mag. Dist., E.D. 106, 69-69:

J. F. F. Gibson	——	27	M	Farmer	
Minerva	Wife	22	M	Keeping House	
Isaac	Son	6	S	At Home	
Virginia	Dau	2	S	At Home	
Daniel	Son	1	S	At Home	
John W.	Son	1/12	S	At Home	b. Apr

1900 Franklin Co. Census, Maggodee Mag. Dist., E.D. 31, 90-90:

James F. Gibson	Head	46	M24		Farmer	RF	04/54
Manerva J.	Wife	45	M24	12/10			10/54
James O.	Son	18	S		Farm Laborer		03/82
Isabel	Dau	16	S		At School		03/84
Annie M.	Dau	12	S		At School		05/88
Elijah H.	Son	9	S		At School		04/91
David L.	Son	6	S				06/93
Thomas N.	Son	3	S				07/97

Little Creek Mag. Dist., E.D. 29, 270-270:

Otey Peters	Head	45	M21		Farmer	OMF	11/54
Martha	Wife	38	M21	10/10			11/61
Lelia	Dau	20	S				03/80

Ema [?]	Son	17	S			09/82
Sallie B. [Gibson]	Dau	15	S			07/84
Nettie	Dau	14	S		At School	07/86
Jennie	Dau	11	S		At School	12/88
Harry	Son	8	S			09/91
Henry	Son	5	S			11/94
Nancy	Dau	3	S			12/96
Clarence	Son	1	S			02/99

17 June 1904: Daniel B. Gibson, 25, single, laborer, to Sallie Peters, 20, single. Both born in Franklin Co. and reside in same. Parents: J. F. and Menerva Gibson; Otey and Martha Peters. License dated 15 June 1904. Married by D. A. Naff. Marriage Book 2-35, Franklin Co. Courthouse.

1910 Botetourt Co. Census, Amsterdam Dist. (Troutville), E.D. 53, 104-104:

Daniel C. Gibson	Head	29	M11		Farmer/Rented Farm
Sallie	Wife	27	M11	7/3	
Noah L.	Son	8			
Eddie	Son	4			
Carl	Son	NR	[Not Reported]		

[*Note:* Daniel Gibson's brother, James O. Gibson, 28, farm laborer, and his family are listed just a few households away from Daniel and Sally.]

1910 Patrick Co. Census, Dan River Mag. Dist., E.D. 74, 146-146:

E. G. Newman	Head	37	M10		Farmer/Home Farm	OFF
Jettie B.	Wife	27	M10	4/4		
Howell U.	Son	7	S			
Sally Sue [?]	Dau	5	S			
J. Harry	Son	3	S			
Myrtle	Dau	1 8/12				

1920 Patrick Co. Census, Dan River Twnshp., E.D. 125, 62-65:

Elijah G. Newman	Head	47	M	Farmer	OF
Jettie R.	Wife	37	M		
Eugene H.	Son	17	S	Laborer/Home Farm	
Sallie Lieu	Dau	15	S		
Joseph H.	Son	13	S		
Myrtle R.	Dau	11	S		
Tom A.	Son	7	S		
Nellie L.	Dau	4 7/12	S		
Dorothy E.	Dau	1 7/12	S		

1920 Bedford Co. Census, Chamblissburg, 187-189:

Darniel [?] Gibson	Head	38	M	Farmer	R
Ocie	Wife	39	M		
Noel L. [*sic*]	Son	18	S		
Eddy M	Son	13	S		
Carl D.	Son	8	S		
Cecil	Son	7	S		
Bularni [?]	Dau	3 7/12			
James E. Trout	St-son	17	S		
Annie E. "	St-dau	15	S		
Susie M. "	St-dau	13	S		
Kathleen "	St-dau	11	S		

20 February 1926: Noah Lee Gibson, 24, single, farmer, b. in Franklin Co., Va., to **Sallie Lou Newman**, 21, single, b. in Patrick Co., Va. Reside at: 1209 Penmar Ave., S.E. Roanoke; 122 Penmar Ave., S.E. Roanoke. Parents: Daniel C. and Sallie Anne Gibson; Elijah G. and Jettie Ruth Newman. License dated 17 Feb 1926. Married in Roanoke by H. J. Goodwin. Marriage Register 4-25, Roanoke City Courthouse.

Sat., 9 June 1973: Obituary notice in the *Roanoke World-News:* "Noah Lee Gibson, 71, 1623 Stewart Ave., SE, died today. Funeral will be Monday at 10 a.m. at Lotz Roanoke."

25 August 1976: **Sallie N. Gibson,** widow, sells property (Lot 8, Block 8 on Map of Oakridge Land Co.) in 1600 block of Stewart Ave., SE Roanoke, to Rufus R. Wray and Glenna P. Wray for the sum of $10.00 "and other good and valuable considerations." This tract bought by N. L. and Sallie N. Gibson on 28 August 1964. Deed Book 1385-453, Roanoke City Courthouse.

Letitia Jane Lumpkins

1880 Franklin Co. Census, Dickenson's Voting Precinct, 232-238:

James Lumpkins	Head	35	B	M	Farm Laborer
Letitia	Wife	27	B	M	
John S.	Son	8	B	S	
Sallie	Dau	6	B	S	
[Not Named]	Dau	3/12	B		

1900 Franklin Co. Census, Rocky Mount Dist., E.D. 32, 349-363:

Ticia Lumpkins	Head	41	BF	Wd	9/6	Day Labor	RH	05/51
Mary J.	Dau	20	B	S		Day Laborer		05/79
Belle	Dau	19	B	S		Washer Woman		05/81
William T.	Son	13	B	S				08/86
Willie Dan	Gson	2	B	S				02/98
Sallie T.	Gdau	2	B	S				05/98

E.D. 43, 84-93:

John Lumpkins	Head	33	B	M18		Laborer/Odd Jobs	RH
Fanny F.	Wife	29	B	M18	5/5		
Charlie	Son	11	B	S			
Lou E.	Dau	8	B	S			
John S.	Son	6	B	S			
George W.	Son	3	B	S			
Sam W.	Son	8/12	B				

15 February 1911: Obie Lumpkins, 28, farmer, born in Franklin Co., to Jennie Haywood, 17, born in Pittsylvania Co. Parents: Jim and Tishey [Letitia] Lumpkins; Ben and Eliza Lumpkins. Marriage Records, Franklin Co. Courthouse.

1920 Franklin Co. Census, Rocky Mount Dist., E.D. 58, 63-64:

John Lumpkins	Head	45	B	M	Laborer/Groc. Store	R
Fannie	Wife	38	B	M		
Stephen	Son	14	B	S	Laborer/Groc. Store	
George	Son	10	B	S	Laborer/Groc. Store	
Mary J.	Dau	7	B	S		
Marie	Dau	4	B	S		
Etheline	Dau	2 3/12	B	S		
Vinie Boothe	Mo-i-l	60	B	Wd		

E.D. 59, 101-101:

Obe Lumpkins	Head	36	B	M	Laborer/Pub. Hghwy	OF
Jennie	Wife	25	B	M		
Lillie	Dau	9	B	S		

Tishie	Dau	4 2/12	B	S
Tishie	Mo	74	B	Wd

7 April 1930: Sam Lumpkins, 17, laborer, to **Letitia Lumpkins**, 18, both born in Franklin Co. Parents: John and Fannie (Boothe) Lumpkin; Obe and Jennie Dickerson [*sic*] Lumpkin. Marriage Records, Franklin Co. Courthouse.

Mrs. Susie Young Smith

1880 Norfolk Co. Census, Norfolk City, E.D. 78, 119-125:

Theodore Smith	Head	49	M	Barber	b: Prussia/Prussia/Prussia
Christiana	Wife	46	M		b: Hesse-Darmstadt/HD/HD
Theodore J.	Son	19	S	Laborer	b: Va./Prussia/HD
Charles J.	Son	8	S		b: Va./Prussia/HD

1900 Portsmouth City Census, E.D. 120, Sheet 2, #85, Fourth St.:

Robert Young	Head	42	M	b: England	10/57
Mary J.	Wife	35	M	b: England*	04/65
Robert A.	Son	14	S	b: England*	01/86
Richard	Son	12	S	b: England*	01/88
Susanna	Dau	6			01/94
James	Son	2			08/97
Thomas	Son	1			01/99

*Naturalized citizen

1910 Portsmouth City Census, E.D. 102, 1502 "A" St., 169-173:

Theodore J. Smith	Head	49	M1/25		Shipwright	OMH	b: Va./Germany/Germany
Hattie B.	Wife	42	M1/25	11/9			
Theodore A.	Son	19	S		Toolmaker		
Linwood T.	Son	14	S				
Jesse R.	Son	12	S				
Clifford V.	Son	9	S				
Rosa	Dau	7	S				
Clarence	Son	5	S				
Kenneth	Son	2	S				

E.D. 107, #18:

Robert H. Young	Head	52	M	Machinist/R.R. Shop	b: London, England
Mary J.	Wife	45	M		b: London, England
Robert N.	Son	24	S	Boiler Maker/R.R. Shop	b: N.J.
Richard	Son	22	S	Machinist/R.R. Shop	b: N.J.
Susan	Dau	16	S	Machine Worker	
James	Son	12	S		
Thomas	Son	11	S		
Mary J.	Dau	8			
Willie	Son	5			

The *Portsmouth Star,* obituary for Theodore A. Smith, Saturday, 9 June 1928: "Theodore A. Smith, 411 Owens street, died last night at a local hospital at 7:30 o'clock. . . . Mr. Smith, who was a native of Portsmouth and was employed at the Navy Yard as a machinist, is survived by his father, Theodore J. Smith; a widow, Mrs. Susan Smith; five children, the Misses Edna, Mildred, Harriett and Mary C. and Melvin Smith; four brothers, . . . and two sisters. . . . Mr. Smith held membership in St. Paul's Catholic church, and St. Paul's Council, Knights of Columbus." The funeral services were to be conducted at St. Paul's Church the following Monday.

An article in the second edition of the Sunday *Portsmouth Star,* 10 June 1928, p. 12, was titled "Death Takes Victim of Typhoid." It noted that Theodore A. Smith died "after an illness of a week." He "contracted typhoid fever and only lived a few days after. The five children in the family also have typhoid and are thought to be seriously affected with the disease."

Mrs. Nola (Geneva Fowlkes) Thompson

1900 Chesterfield Co. Census, Matoaca Dist., E.D. 7, 310-323:

Thomas Fulkse [*sic*]	Head	30	B	M10		Log sawer [?]	OFH	10/69
Minnie	Wife	30	B	M10	7/7			12/69
Arthur	Son	13	B	S		At school		05/87
Worther	Son	9	B	S				10/90
Carrie	Dau	7	B	S				05/92
Susie	Dau	6	B	S				03/94
Lilian	Dau	4	B	S				02/96
Blanch	Dau	2	B	S				04/98
Libirdia [?]	Dau	1/12	B					04/00

1910 Chesterfield Co. Census, Matoaca Dist., E.D. 10, River Rd., 47-51:

Tom Fultz	Head	43	B	M18		Laborer/Saw Mill	OFH
Minnie	Wife	44	B	M18	10/9		
Carry	Dau	18	B	S		Washwoman/Private Family	
Susie	Dau	17	B	S			
Lyllian	Dau	16	B	S			
Blanch	Dau	15	B	S			
Berta	Dau	14	B	S		Washwoman/Private Family	
Elnora	Dau	13	B	S			
Arthur	Son	12	B	S		Laborer/Saw Mill	
Rosevelt	Son	10	B	S		Laborer/Saw Mill	
Gennever	Dau	4	B	S		Laborer/Saw Mill [?]	

12 May 1930: Mack Thompson to **Mary Geneva Fowlkes.** He was born in Asheville, N.C., in 1892, the son of Mack Thompson Sr. and Frances Worthy Thompson. She was born in 1904 in Chester, Va., the daughter of Tom and Minnie Lee Fowlkes. Marriage Records, Hopewell City Courthouse.

Hill's Petersburg (Dinwiddie Co., Va.) City Directory, 1937, (Richmond: Hill Directory Co.):

> **Geneva Thompson** (c) tobwkr
> h. 12 E. Byrne

Vol. 25, 1941:

> David Moore (c)
> h. 12 E. Byrne St; rear of same address:
> Minnie Fulkes [no Geneva Thompson listed]
> Wother [Worther] Foulkes (c, Irene), lab.
> h. 532 Virginia
> 1943:
> Minnie Fulkes (c)
> h. 1459 E. Byrne

Julia Keesee (Carwile)

1860 Campbell Co. Census, West. Dist., Castle Craig, 949-1043:

Richard Keesee	40	Overseer	$——/$40
Tabitha A.	32		
Booker	18	Laborer	
Jenny	16		
Jesse	14		

Harriett	12		
Avery [Geo. A.?]	9		
Volney	6		
James	4		
Ida	2		

1870 Campbell Co. Census, Western Dist., 1476-1572:

Richard Keesee	57	Farm Work	$2,500/$150
Tibitha [*sic*]	42		
Virginia	23		
Harriet J.	20		
George A.	18	Farm Work	
Volney	15	Farm Work	
Jas. R.	13	Farm Work	
P. J.	11	[f]	
Ivenhoe	10		
C. V. [Charles V.]	4		
Abner	8/12		

Lynchburg P.O., 1114-1153:

Jacob Carwile	43	Farmer
Judy	35	Keeps House
Martha A.	14	
Richard H.	12	
James B.	10	
Walter R.	8	
John S.	6	
Fannic	4	
Sam	1	

16 January 1878: Appraisement of personal estate of Richard Keesee, dec. Included: 1 yoke of oxen; 1 ox yoke; 3 cows and 1 yearling; 1 horse; 1 mule; 1 hog & 250# pork; 2 stocks of oats; 1000# of tobacco; 5 bu. wheat; 20# muddy corn; 1 wagon & 2 old wheels; 1 set harness; 2 harvesting cradles & pitch forks; 1 cutting knife; 1 hillside plow; 1 lot of old plows; lot of hoes, chirres [shears?] &c; 1 grindstone; 2 axes & lot of iron; 1/2 bu. nails; 1 reel & spinning wheel; 1 set of mechanics tools; 1 lot of cooking utensils, buckets & tub; 4 chairs; 1 Press and contents; 1 folding table; 1 bed/straw/ & stead; 1 bed/straw/ & bedstead; 1 Rifle; 1 Clock; 1 Bureau; 1 Chest; 2 sets of Beds, Bedsteads and Furniture. Value = $431.25. Appraised by D. R. Arnold, N. M. Oliver, B. N. Anthony. Will Book 15-26.

25 December 1890: Charles V. Keesee, 23, to Willie K. Boley, 21. Married by J. S. Mason. Marriage Book 2-161. This and the will record above are both from the Campbell Co. Courthouse.

1900 Campbell Co. Census, Rustburg Dist., 80-80:

Chas. V. Keesee	Head	34	M9		Farmer	OFF	02/66
Willie K.	Wife	30	M9	8/4			11/69
Clarence E.	Son	7	S				10/92
Mary H.	Dau	6	S				01/94
Orville V.	Son	3	S				03/97
Julia E.	Dau	1	S				04/99
William Gregory	Srvt	14	S		B	Servant	03/86

1910 Campbell Co. Census, Rustburg Dist., 302-302:

Charles V. Keesee	Head	43	M20		Farmer	OFF
Willie K.	Wife	41	M20	15/10		
*Clarence E.	Son	18	S	———		
May Hilda	Dau	16	S			

Orville V.	Son	14	S		Farm Laborer	
Julie E.	Dau	11	S			
Olive Kate	Dau	9	S			
Carrie E.	Dau	7	S			
Mattie H.	Dau	5	S			
Dora	Dau	3	S			
Marcey	Dau	2	S			
Wilbur	Son	7/12				

*Clarence E. was erroneously listed in this census as a female/daughter, although his name was clearly spelled out.

15 June 1918: **July Elva Keesee**, 21, born in Campbell Co., to Watsy [*sic*] M. Carwile, 21, born in Halifax Co. Parents: Charles V. and Willie Kate Keesee; W. R. and Martha Sarah [?] Carwile. Married by Jim A. Eider. Marriage Book 3-98, Campbell Co. Courthouse Records.

1920 Campbell Co. Census, Rustburg, E.D. 80, 95-95:

Walter R. Carwile	Head	57	M	Farmer		OM
Martha A.	Wife	47	M			
Walter D.	Son	25	S	Merchant/Gen. Store		
Thomas L.	Son	21	S	Farmer		
Claude W.	Son	18	S	Laborer/Home Farm		
Marvin G.	Son	15	S	Laborer/Home Farm		
Richard E.	Son	14	S			
Ray D.	Son	11	S			
Roy W.	Son	11	S			
Hector E.	Son	9	S			
Dorothy P.	Dau	7	S			

96-96:

Watsy Carwile	Head	23	M	Farmer		
Julia E.	Wife	20	M			

140-140:

Charles V. Keesee	Head	54	M	Farmer		OF
Willie K.	Wife	56	M			
Clarence E.	Son	27	M	Farmer/Home Farm		
Olive K.	Dau	19	S	Teacher/Pub. School		
Carrie E.	Dau	17	S			
Ellen W.	Dau-i-law	22	M			
Mattie H.	Dau	14	S			
Dora A.	Dau	13	S			
Margery C.	Dau	11	S			
Wilbur C.	Son	10	S			
Milton E.	Son	7	S			

E.D. 81, 82-87:

James E. Carwile	Head	58	M	Farmer	OF	
Kate E.	Wife	54	M			
*Paul E.	Son	13	S			
Mary J.	Dau	10	S			
Elbert F.	Son	7	S			
Albert H.	Son	7	S			

*Paul E. Carwile married Mattie H. Keesee, Julia's sister.

14 August 1939: List of Heirs of C. V. Keesee. Three daughters, Olive K. Keesee, **Julia (Mrs. W. M.) Carwile**, and Mattie (Mrs. Paul) Carwile, were living in Lynchburg. His other four surviving daughters and three sons remained in Rustburg, Va. Will Book 27-198.

October 1939: Account of distribution of estate of C. V. Keesee, dec. Total estate value = $1,924.12. Will Book 27-469-71. Appraisal of personal property of C. V. Keesee, dec., included: mostly farm tools, 2 mules, one 2 horse wagon, 1 grain cradle, 2 hay forks, saddle, 2 cows, 1 set carpenter tools, 1 bedroom set, and more. Value = $354.50. Will Book 27-533. Will records from Campbell Co. Courthouse.

Emily Palmer Stearns

1860 Henrico Co. Census, Richmond, Va., 370-355:

Franklin Stearns	45	Financc/Distiller	$155,000/$200,000	b: Vt.
Caroline V.	39			
Zeuus [*sic*] B.	14			
Franklin, Jr.	11			
Erastus W.	8			
Alcine L.	6			
Jane G. O'Willie	53			

1870 Culpeper Co. Census, Jeffersonton Dist., 312-322:

Franklin Stearns [Jr.]	21	M		Farmer	$100,000/$9,000
Emily S.	17	M — June/70			b: N.Y.

1880 Culpeper Co. Census, Stevensburg Dist., 140-148:

Franklin Stearns	Head	31	M	Farmer	b: Va./Vt./Va.
E. S.	Wife	27	M		b: N.Y./N.Y./N.Y.
Franklin [III]	Son	9	S		b: Va./Va./N.Y.
J. L.	Dau	7	S		b: " " "
S. S.	Dau	5	S		b: " " "
E. S. [Emily S. P.]	Dau	3	S		b: " " "
A. R.	Dau	1	S		b: " " "
C. P.	Son	2/12			b: " " "
George Palmer	Br-i-law	32	S	————	b: N.Y./N.Y./N.Y.
N. M. Hansbrough	Brdr	30	S	[f] School Teacher	

CHAPTER 3

John Lee Wright

(See also Josephine Wright in previous chapter.)

1870 Alleghany Co. Census, Boiling Springs Dist., Covington, 96-96:

John H. Wright	30	Farm Laborer
Barbary	22	Keeps House
Mary	2	
John	1	
Catherine Switzer	20	Domestic Servant

John Ernest Bess Sr.

1860 Alleghany Co. Census, Covington, 703-707:

Hamilton Bess	53	Farmer	
Jesse V.	33	Farmer	$———/$100
William H.	28	Farmer	$500/$150
Charles L.	26	Farmer	$———/$50

John L.		23	Teacher in Common Schools	$250/$75
Rebecca		17		
Cara A.		16	Farming	

1900 Alleghany Co. Census, Boiling Spring Dist., 7-7:

John L. Bess	Head	61	M30		Farmer		OFF	03/38
Mary F.	Wife	53	M30	7/5				02/47
Wilbur C.	Son	25	S		At School			11/74
Walter E.	Son	21	S		Farm Laborer			09/78
John E.	Son	20	S		Farm Laborer			05/80
*Blanch	Dau	16	S					01/84
Lonnie E.	Son	13	S		Farm Laborer			09/86

*Blanch is Leila Blanche Bess, the VWP worker.

1910 Alleghany Co. Census, Boiling Spring Dist., 83-84:

John L. Bess	Head	69	M40		Farmer		OFF	CA
Mary F.	Wife	60	M40	7/4				
Earnest	Son	26	S		Farm Laborer			
Blanche	Dau	24	S					
Lonnie	Son	23	S		Civil Engineer			

1920 Alleghany Co. Census, Boiling Spring Dist., Mill Run Rd., 219-219:

John E. Bess	Head	39	M	Farmer	OM	
Nannie E.	Wife	33	M			
Mary F.	Mo	72	Wd			b: Va./Va./W.Va.
Leila B.	Sis	35	S			

23 December 1955: **John Ernest Bess** of Covington died 21 December 1955. Heirs: Nannie Reid Bess, 68, widow; John Ernest Bess Jr., 35, son; Nelda Bess Kessinger, 34, daughter. Will Book 9-63, Alleghany Co. Courthouse Records.

Arthur Garrett

1900 Nelson Co. Census, Lovingston Dist., E.D. 83, 146-146:

Arthur Garret	Head	26	M2		Farmer	RF	09/73
Emma W.	Wife	26	M2	2/2			06/73
Agnes R.	Dau	1					11/98
James E. [Jimmie]	Son	7/12					10/99

Hill's Richmond City Directory, 1938 (Richmond: Hill Directory Co.):

Hester L. Crocker, clerk, Standard Drug Co.

   r. 111 E. Franklin

1941–1943:

Arth. W. Garrett (Emma W.), watchman

   h. 320 Cowardin Ave.

Hester G. Crocker (wid Albert L.), emp. Nell Mar.

   Corp. [1942]; canvasser [1943]

   h. 320 Cowardin Ave.

1944:

No entry after 1943 for either Arthur or Emma Garrett.

Hester L. Crocker, agent, Life & Casualty Inv. Co. of Tenn.

   no h. given

Mr. and Mrs. Charles Crawley

1870 Dinwiddie Co. Census, Petersburg City, 4th Ward, 497-592:

Sarah Crowley	40	B	Keeping House
Charles	13	B	At Home
Sarah	12	B	At School

1880 Dinwiddie Co. Census, Petersburg City, 4th Ward, 207 Plum St., 201-275:

William Goode	Head	40	M	B	Laborer
Sarah	Wife	40	M	B	Cook
Charles Crawley	St-son	24	S	B	Out of Work/Sick Bilious Liver

7 July 1880: **Charles Crawley,** 23, single, factory hand, to Martha Tylor, 21, single, both born in Petersburg. Parents: Armistead Crawley and Sarah [?]; Henry Tylor and Marsha [?]. Marriage Records, Petersburg City Courthouse.

1900 Dinwiddie Co. Census, Petersburg, 4th Ward, 207 Plum St., 232-254:

James Givings	Head	60	B	M		Laborer	H	12/39
Sarah	Wife	50	B	M	10/1	Cook		01/49
Anna	Dau	15	B	S		Cook		

1910 Dinwiddie Co. Census, Petersburg City Dist., 207 Plum St., 147-159:

Sarah Givens	Head	60	B	Wd	Home Laundress	OFH
Charles Crawley	Son	45	B	S	Plasterer/Mechanic	

1920 Dinwiddie Co. Census, Petersburg, 4th Ward, 515 Plum St., 162-177:

Sarah Givens	Head	75	B	Wd	Wash Woman	R
Charles Crawley	Son	60	B	M	Laborer	
Mattie	Dau i law	40	B	M		

1919 Land Books indicate Sarah Gibbons [*sic*] as owning three lots in Petersburg: two on N. Plumb [*sic*] Street and one on E. Donoughs [Doans?] Alley.

23 March 1922: Will of Sarah Gibbons. Gives and bequeaths to "my children my real estate which consist of three lots. My son **Charlie Crawley,** one. And at his death to his widow, as long as she remains his widow, Mattie Crawley. And one to my grand daughter, Edith Russel Washington, and one to my great-grandson Byron Douglas Washington. And my persona [*sic*] property, and money to my daughter Sarah Washington." Wit: Annie D. Fields; Henry Jones; Fannie Foster. List of Heirs:

Sarah Washington	Daughter	53	Petersburg, Va.
Charles Crawley	Son	56	Petersburg, Va.

Presented in court and recorded 7 April 1923. Will Book 12-237, Petersburg City Courthouse.

Petersburg (Dinwiddie Co.) City Directory (Richmond: Hill Directory Co.) for 1941, 1943, and 1946, all list:

Charles Crawley (c; Mattie), h. 515 Plum Street

Marvin Broyhill

1900 Wilkes Co., N.C., Census, Reddies River Twnshp., 71-71:

Thomas J. Broyhill	Head	52	M18		Lumber Dealer	OFF	06/52	*N.C./N.C./N.C.
Sallie M.	Wife	35	M18	14/10			10/64	
Rural [*sic*] V.	Son	15	S		Farm Laborer		03/85	
Marvin T.	Son	11	S		Farm Laborer		07/88	
Dessie M.	Dau	9	S				09/90	
Thomas G.	Son	9	S				09/90	
Phelix [*sic*] H.	Son	3	S				02/97	
Annie L.	Dau	3	S				02/97	

*In both the 1900 and 1910 censuses, the birthplaces for all members of the household were the same as for Thomas J. Broyhill: N.C./N.C./N.C.

1910 Wilkes Co., N.C., Census, Reddies River Twnshp., 310-310:

Thomas J. Broyhill	Head	58	M28	Farmer	OFF
Sallie M.	Wife	42	M——	11/7	
F. Gipson	Son	19	S		
Dessie M. E.	Dau	19	S		
Annie L.	Dau	13	S		
Phelix	Son	13	S		
Lincoln [Pete]	Son	8	S		

1920 Prince George Co. Census, City of Hopewell, Petersburg Rd., 6-6:

Gibson Broyhill	Head	29	M	Mechanic/DuPont Co.	OF	b: N.C./N.C./N.C.
Daisy	Wife	29	M			b: " " "
Ruby	Dau	5	S			b: " " "
Paul	Son	2 6/12				b: Va./N.C./N.C.
Gabrielle	Dau	4/12				b: " " "

33 2nd Ave., 119-119:

Marvin T. Broyhill	Head	32	M	Clerk/DuPont Co.	R	b: N.C./N.C./N.C.
Nellie M.	Wife	32	M			b: " " "
Marvin T. Jr.	Son	1 7/12				b: Va./N.C./N.C.
Joel T.	Son	2/12				b: " " "

1st Ave., 129-129:

Ruiel V. Broyhill	Head	34	M	Machinist/Own Shop	OF	b: N.C./N.C./N.C.
Fannie C.	Wife	35	M			b: " " "
Sallie S.	Dau	11	S			b: " " "
Thomas J.	Son	9	S			b: " " "
Ruel Ray	Son	7	S			b: " " "

Charles Tucker

1860 Alleghany Co. Census, Covington, 716-720:

James A. Tucker	39	Farmer	$250/$250
Mary E.	29		
Alfred	11	At School	
Josephine	9	At School	
Elvira A.	7	At School	
John M.	5	At School	
Elizabeth F.	3		
Sarah A.M.	1		

1870 Alleghany Co. Census, Boiling Springs Dist., 145-145:

James A. Tucker	56	Farm Laborer
Elizabeth	42	Keeps House
Alfred	21	Farm Laborer
Josephine	19	At Home
Elvira	17	At Home
John M.	15	At Home
Elizabeth F.	13	At Home
Sarah M.	11	
James R.	9	
Delia J.	7	
Joseph U. Sg.[?]	5	
Otis F.	3	

1900 Alleghany Co. Census, Boiling Spring Dist., 72-74:

Levi Wolfe	Head	56	M31		————	OFF	04/44
Mariah P.	Wife	56	M31	9/7			02/44
Virginia A.	Dau	21	S				03/79
Jane M.	Dau	16	S				03/84

74-75:

Josephine Tucker	Head	54	S	4/3	————	RF	03/46
Charles	Son	20	S		————		05/80
John D.	Son	12	S		————		09/87

4 November 1902: Charles F. Tucker, 23, farmer, to Jane M. Wolfe, 17, both born in Alleghany Co. Parents: ————— and Josie Tucker; L. V. and A. M. Wolfe. Marriage Book, Alleghany Co. Courthouse Records.

1910 Alleghany Co. Census, Boiling Spring Dist., 157-161:

Charles Tucker	Head	33	M8		Farmer	RH
Jane M.	Wife	21	M8	5/5		
Robert L.	Son	7	S			
Ruby E.	Dau	5	S			
Mattie S.	Dau	3	S			
Roxie M.	Dau	2	S			
John H.	Son	7/12				

158-162:

Levi Wolfe	Head	65	M2/7	Farmer	OFF
Johisphine [*sic*]	Wife	50	M1/7		

1920 Alleghany Co. Census, Boiling Springs Dist., E.D. 2, Turnpike, 147-147:

Charles S. Tucker	Head	47	Wd	Farmer	R
Robert E.	Son	16	S	Laborer/Home Farm	
Ruby E.	Dau	14	S		
Roxie M.	Dau	11	S		
John H.	Son	8	S		
Harvey M.	Son	5	S		
Joseph L.	Son	1 6/12			

Isaiah Wallace

1900 Rappahannock Co. Census, Stonewall Dist., 157-157:

Charles Wallis	Head	50	M26		B	Blacksmith	OH	11/49
Annie E.	Wife	45	M26	13/11	B			05/55
Henry C.	Son	25	S		B	Farm Laborer		04/75
Isaac	Son	23	S		B	Farm Laborer		09/76
Martha	Dau	21	S		B			09/78
Sidonia	Dau	17	S		B			07/82
Annie Bell	Dau	15	S		B			04/85
Malinda	Dau	12	S		B			04/88
Rebecca	Dau	10	S		B			02/90
Silas	Son	7	S		B			12/92
Clarence	Son	5	S		B			11/94
Alberta	Dau	3	S		B			02/97
James L.	Son	11/12			B			07/99

1910 Rappahannock Co. Census, Hawthorne Dist., 155-155:

Charles H. Wallace	Head	61	M36		MU	————	OFF
Annie	Wife	54	M36	13/11	MU		
Annie B.	Dau	21	S		MU		

Silas J.	Son	17	S		MU		
Clarence	Son	15	S		MU		
Alberta	Dau	13	S		MU		
James S.	Son	10	S		MU		
Raymond	Son	6	S		MU		

169-169:

Isaiah Wallace	Head	33	M9		MU	Farm Laborer	H
Malinda	Wife	43	M9 0/0		B	Laundress	

Tom Hand

1860 Rappahannock Co. Census, Hawthorne Dist., 134-122:

Thomas Hand, Sen.	53	Farmer	$——/$13,098	
Ada [?]	65			
Mary	35			
Fannie	30			
William	28	Farm Hand	$4,000/———	
Olivia	25			
Eastham	22			
Robert	21			

1900 Rappahannock Co. Census, Hawthorne Dist., 29-29:

Robert Hand	Head	60	S		Farmer	OFF	11/39
Mary E.	Sis	80	S				06/20
Fannie C.	Sis	76	S				09/25
Livia E.	Sis	70	S				11/30
John Matthews	Srvt	18	S	B	Farm Laborer		05/81

Stonewall Dist., Woodville, 132-132:

William Hand	Head	73	M25		Farmer	OFF	10/26
Mary O. [?]	Wife	48	M25 6/6				07/67
Thomas	Son	24	S		Farm Laborer		05/76
Annie M.	Dau	21	S				03/79
Eddie G.	Son	18	S				02/82
John W.	Son	15	S				02/85
Lizzie M.	Dau	11	S				02/89
Jimmie	Son	11	S				02/89

1910 Rappahannock Co. Census, Hawthorne Dist., 151-155:

Robert Hand	Head	71	S	Farmer	OFF	
Olivia	Sis	80	S			

Stonewall Dist., Woodville, 149-149:

William Hand	Head	83	M35	Own Income	OFF	CA
Mary V.	Wife	59	M35 6/6			
George E.	Son	28	S	———		
Elizabeth	Dau	21	S			
James	Son	21	S	———		

1920 Culpeper Co. Census, Catalpa Dist., West St., ——— 386:

Thomas Hand	Head	43	M	Farmer	OF
Willie S.	Wife	41	M		
Bessie O.	Dau	9	S		
Thomas C.	Son	3	S		
Eustice Johnson	Brdr	26	S	Mail Carrier	

CHAPTER 4

Aunt Mattie Perndon

1870 Culpeper Co. Census, Jeffersonton Dist., 125-130:

Joseph Ficklin	22	B	Farm Laborer	$——/$175	
Martha	20	B			
Fannie Stewart	55	B			
Robert "	9	B			

1900 Culpeper Co. Census, Catalpa Dist., 270-272:

Henderson Purnton	Head	——	B	M23	Farm Laborer	RH	00/59
Mattie	Wife	54	B	M23	0/0		00/46

1920 Culpeper Co. Census, Catalpa Dist., Culpeper/Rixeyville Rd., 71-73:

Susan Stewart	Head	61	MU	Wd	Wash Woman	OF
Roland	Son	30	MU	M	Farm Laborer	
James Tibbs	Gson	16	MU	S	Farm Laborer	
Arthur Stewart	Son	42	MU	S	Farm Laborer	

74-76:

Mattie Purinton	Head	65	B	Wd		OF
Arthur Steward [?]	Neph	30	B	S	Laborer	

Willis J. Madden

1880 Culpeper Co. Census, Stevensburg Dist., 177-192:

Mariah Fields	Head	43	B	Wd	Farming & Keeping House
Thos. O. Madden	Son	20	B	S	Works on Farm
W[illis]. J. Madden	Son	17	B	S	Works on Farm
Richard Brooks	Srvt	13	B	S	Works on Farm

1900 Culpeper Co. Census, Catalpa Dist., 289-292:

Willis J. Madden	Head	37	B	MI	Teacher	OH	08/62
Netta D.	Wife	19	B	MI	1/1		12/80
Maria F.	Dau	10/12	B				07/99

1910 Culpeper Co. Census, Catalpa Dist., 264-264:

Willis J. Madden	Head	47	MU	M2/7		Teacher	OFF
Ida A.	Wife	32	MU	MI/7	4/4		
Willis L.	Son	6	MU	S			
Maria F.	Dau	10	MU	S			
Abner G.	Son	4	MU	S			
Lilburn B.	Son	2	MU	S			
Irma T.	Dau	2/12	MU				

269-275:

T[homas]. O. Madden	Head	50	MU	M20		Teacher	OFF
L. R.	Wife	43	MU	M20	12/10		
Odenla	Dau	19	MU	S			
Ruth C.	Dau	18	MU	S			
Sallie M.	Dau	17	MU	S			
Oliver W.	Son	14	MU	S			
Edward E.	Son	11	MU	S			
Malissa	Dau	13	MU	S			
Hannible	Son	9	MU	S			
T. O. [Jr.]	Son	7	MU	S			

Nathaniel	Son	4	MU	S		
Landonia	Dau	11/12	MU			

1920 Culpeper Co. Census, Catalpa Dist., Culpeper/Sperryville Rd., 11-12:

Willis J. Madden	Head	57	MU	M	Preacher	OF
Ida A.	Wife	42	MU	M		
Willis L.	Son	16	MU	S	Chauffer [sic]	
Abram G.	Son	14	MU	S	Laborer/Farm	
Lilburn	Son	12	MU	S		
Erma T.	Dau	9	MU	S		
Samuel	Son	8	MU	S		
Sumner G.	Son	6	MU	S		
Ida	Dau	4	MU	S		
Thaddeus	Son	3	MU	S		
Mabel	Dau	15/12	MU			

Lillie R. Vaughn

1900 Pittsylvania Co. Census, Danville City, E.D. 103, 142 Rison St., 46-50:

Waldin Yancey	Head	36	B	M9		Teamster	RH	b: N.C./N.C./N.C.	04/64
Henrita	Wife	33	B	M9	5/3			b: N.C./N.C./N.C.	05/67
Willie A.	Dau	7	B	S				b: Va./N.C./N.C.	07/92
Ada B.	Dau	5	B	S				b: Va./N.C./N.C.	10/94
Addie L.	Dau	4	B	S				b: Va./N.C./N.C.	12/95

1920 Pittsylvania Co. Census, Danville City, E.D. 38, 142 Rison St., 1-1:

Weldon Yancey	Head	48	B	M	Plasterer/Tile Firm	RH
Henrietta	Wife	48	B	M	Servant/Day	
Ada B.	Dau	24	B	S	Servant/Private Family	
Adale	Dau	22	B	S	Servant/Private Family	
John Albert	Son	20	B	S	Laborer/Tile Firm	
Lois	Dau	16	B	S		
Henry	Son	12	B	S	Butler/Private Family	
*Jollie	Son	11	B	S		
*Knowledge	Dau	11	B	S		
Minnie J.	Dau	9	B	S		

*Twins

Hill's Danville (Pittsylvania County) Directory, 1935, (Richmond: Hill Directory Co.):

Weldon Yancey, c. (Henrietta), plasterer
   h. Branch Corner Winslow (Almagro)

Cleveland Buchanan

1910 Botetourt Co. Census, Amsterdam Dist., E.D. 52, 299-306:

Grover C. Buchanan	Grnr	22	MU	S		Gardener		
Living in HH of:								
Hunter G. Breckenridge	Head	36		M5		Farmer	OFF	
Grace V.	Wife	30		M5	2/2			b: Pa./Pa./Pa.
Dorothy A.	Dau	3		S				b: Va./Va./Pa.
Gracie O.	Dau	2		S				b: Va./Va./Pa.
Susan Hayes	Cook	26	B	M		Cook		
Robert "	Son	4	B	S				
Annie "	Dau	6	B	S				

Louise	"	Dau	1 6/12	B		
Dick	"	Son	6/12	B		
William K. Hayes		Srvt	15	B	S	Farm Laborer

1930–33: During this period Cleveland Buchanan and wife Dorothy buy six town lots in Covington; in one case Cleveland is acting as trustee for Covington Lodge No. 60, Knights of Pythias. Deed Books 66-475; 68-239; 70-67, 432, 481; & 71-108.

1 July 1935: Cleveland and Dorothy Buchanan take a deed of trust on above real estate. Recorded in 1938. Deed Book 81-429-430, Alleghany Co. Courthouse Records.

Mollie Williams

1900 Pittsylvania Co. Census, Danville City, E.D. 104, 220 Ross St., 84-92:

Mary Jennings	Head	33	B	M	Cook	RH		08/66

84-93:

Mollie Williams	Head	25	B	S	Cook	RH		05/75
Roxy Stamper	Brdr	18	B	S	Tobacco Stemmer			12/87
Henry Word	Son	3/12	B					03/00

84-94:

Sally Evans	Head	35	B	S	Cook	H	b: N.C./N.C./N.C.	05/65
Ward Scales	Neph	16	B	S	Tobacco Stemmer			04/84
Laura Roane	Mo	63	B	S 1/1	Nurse		b: N.C./N.C./N.C.	05/35

1920 Pittsylvania Co. Census, Danville City, E.D. 39, 220 Ross St., 182-186:

George Richmond	Head	[?]	B	M	Driver/Food Store	R
Maria W.	Wife	[?]	B	M	Cook/Private Family	
Sallie M.	Dau	14	B	S		
Conrad Malone [?]	St-son	——	B	S		
Nettie Matthews	Ldgr	[?]	B	S	Hand/Tobacco Factory	

Rev. J. H. Coleman

1910 Wise Co. Census, Gladesville Dist., 854-896:

John Coleman	Head	43	MU	M7		Pastor/Church House	RH
Willie	Wife	27	MU	M7	1/1		
Isabella	Dau	7	MU	S			

Bernice Reid

1900 Greensville Co. Census, Zion Mag. Dist., E.D. 32, 406-406:

Rosa Chatman		50	B	Wd	3/3		05/50
Turner Chatman	Head	40	B	M1		Farm Laborer RH	06/59
Mary	Wife	21	B	M1	1/1		05/79
Driad [?]	Son	16	B	S		Farm Laborer	03/84
Mollie	Dau	12	B	S			11/87
Fillie	Son	3	B	S			10/96

1910 Greensville Co. Census, Zion Mag. Dist., E.D. 37, 52 53:

Turner Chatman	Head	41	B	M2/10		Butler/Private Family
Mary	Wife	27	B	M1/10	8/5	Wash Woman/ "
Lelia	Dau	14	B	S		
Prince	Son	9	B	S		
Julie	Dau	6	B	S		
Anna	Dau	3	B	S		
St.Lena	Dau	1	B	S		

1920 Greensville Co. Census, E.D. 34, 280-281:

Turner Chatman	Head	50	B	M	Farm Laborer	R
Mary	Wife	45	B	M		
Julia	Dau	15	B	S		
Anna	Dau	11	B	S		
Lena	Dau	10	B	S		
Odel Reid	Gson	4	B	S		

20 April 1936: Odell Reid, 21, res. 435 Doans Alley, to **Bernice Inez Dyson,** 18, res. 1104 Willcox St., both born in Petersburg. Parents: Walter Reid and Lelia Chapman [*sic*]; Eddie Dyson and Mamie Dandridge. Elder Christian performed marriage service. Penciled note at bottom of record: "Father of the female appeared too." Marriage Record Book.

18 September 1941: List of Heirs of **Bernice Inez Reed:**

Odell Reed	Husband	25	644 Pegram St., Petersburg
Arthur McDaniel Reed	Son	4	As above
Rose Dicie Reed	Dau	3	As above

Husband, Odell Reed, Adm. Will Book 16-432.

[However, *Hill's Petersburg City Directory, vol. 25, 1941,* lists: Odell Reid (c; **Burnice I.**) student; h. 517 S. Dunlop.]

26 Jan 1944: Odell Reed inducted into the navy at Richmond, Va. Address: 517 S. Dunlop St., Petersburg, Va. Born: Petersburg, 2 October 1915. Negro. Male. 5'6". 143 lbs. Brown eyes. Black hair. Dk. brown complexion. Occupation: Brick Mason. Marital status: M. Citizen: Yes. No further service information or indication of discharge given. Induction & Discharge Bk. 5-41.

13 September 1947: Odell Reid, 31, widow, b. Petersburg, res. 644 Pegram St., to Eula Mae Williams, 33, single, b. Spring Hope, N.C., res. 437 E. Halifax St. His occupation: lens grinder for Titmus Optical Co. Parents: Walter Reid and Lelia Chapman; Cato Williams and Ora Cooper. Marriage performed by Linwood L. Christian. Marriage Record Book. All of the above records, except as noted, are from Petersburg City Courthouse.

Ben James

Hill's Richmond City Directory, 1938 (Richmond: Hill Directory Co.):
Benj James, lab, 2309 E. Franklin

Hill's Richmond City Directory, 1942 (Richmond: Hill Directory Co.):
Benj. James, lab, 609 N. 9th Street

Hill's Richmond City Directory, 1943 (Richmond: Hill Directory Co.):
Benj James, lab
Frank Contey of Va,
609 N. 9th Street

Hill's Richmond City Directory, 1944 (Richmond: Hill Directory Co.):
Benj James
609 N. 9th Street, U.S.A.

CHAPTER 5

Sam Harrison (Buzzell Peebles)

1870 Northampton Co., N.C., Census, Seaboard Township, p. 670, 104-104:

Britton Jerdan	22	B	Farm Laborer	b: N.C.	
Francis	18	B	Keeps House	b: N.C.	
Anny [?-unclear]	1	B			

1880 Northampton Co., N.C., Census, Seaboard Township, E.D. 183, 254-271:

Fannie Jordan	———	26	B	M	Keeps House	b: N.C./N.C./N.C.
Mittie	Dau	11	B	S	At Home	b: " " "

Peter	Son	4	B	S		b:	"	"	"
Jernigan [?]	Son	1	B	S		b:	"	"	"

1880 Southampton Co. Census, Town of Franklin, E.D. 103, pp. 30–31:

Robbert Peoples	Head	49	B	Public Work	b: N.C./N.C./N.C.				
Caroline	Wife	49	B	Public Work	b:	"	"	"	
Hardy	Son	23	B	Public Work	b:	"	"	"	
Robbert	Son	16	B	Work on Steamboat	b:	"	"	"	
Estella	Dau	14	B		b:	"	"	"	
Waverly	Son	10	B		b:	"	"	"	
Louisa	Dau	9	B		b:	"	"	"	

24 January 1885: Robert Peebles, 23, to Mit Jordan, 19, both born in N.C. but residing in Southampton Co., Va. His occupation listed as farming; parents not given. Her parents indicated as Brit and Fanny Jordan. Married by H. C. Smith. Marriage Book, Southampton Co. Courthouse.

1910 Southampton Co. Census, Boykins Dist., Beale & Grizzard Rd., pp. 93–94:

Mittie Peebles	Head	35	B	Wd	8/16	Farm Labor/Works Out	b: N.C./N.C./N.C.		
Robert J.	Son	28	B	S		Farm Laborer	b: Va./Va./N.C.		
Napoleon	Son	24	B	S		Farm Laborer	b: " " "		
Estelle	Dau	16	B	S		Farm Laborer	b: " " "		
Courtney	Dau	14	B	S		Farm Laborer	b: " " "		
Fad	Son	11	B	S			b: " " "		
Barzel	Son	10	B	S			b: " " "		
Henretta	Dau	5	B	S			b: " " "		
Beatrice Laurene	Dau	4	B	S			b: " " "		
Golden	Son	1 10/12	B	S			b: " " "		

1920 Southampton Co. Census, Boykins Dist., E.D. 207, E. side of Griffin Rd. to Branchville, 409-465:

Codny [?] Peeples	Head	38	B	M	Farmer	R	
Willie	Wife	22	MU	M			
May Z.	Dau	4 2/12	MU	S			
Marvin	Son	3 2/12	MU	S			
Ethel	Dau	2/12	MU	S			
Henretta	Sis	15	B	S			
Beatress L.	Sis	13	B	S			
Borzel	Bro	19	B	S			

E.D. 266, County Rd., 21-21:

Napoleon Peebles	Head	36	B	M	Farmer	R	
Ella	Wife	30	B	M			
Pearl	Dau	12	B	S			
Joseph W.	Son	8	B	S			
Peter	Son	4 2/12	B	S			
Clorene	Dau	1 3/12	B	S			
James Parham	Srvt	23	B	S	Farm Laborer		

18 December 1920: **Barzelle Peebles,** 21, resides in Branchville, to Virgie Worrell, 21, resides in Newsoms; both born in Southampton Co. Parents: Robert and Mit Peebles; and Ed and Phoebe Worrell. Married by Rev. W. A. Butts. Marriage Record, Southampton Co. Courthouse.

Herman Hooker

1910 Alleghany Co. Census, Clifton Mag. Dist., 159-159:

Henry Hooker	Brdr	21	S	Farm Laborer	
George Hooker	Brdr	18	S	Farm Laborer	

In HH of:

Austin A. Robinson	Head	34	M8		Farmer	OMF
Hortense	Wife	27	M8	3/3		

    + 3 children & sister Maud Robinson, 31 S

2 December 1914: George Washington Hooker, 23, single, farming, to Miss Lillie Margaret Landrum, 17, single, both born in Alleghany Co. Parents: Charles and Dollie Hooker; A. R. and Julia Landrum. Marriage Book, Alleghany County Courthouse.

1920 Alleghany Co. Census, Covington Mag. Dist., E.D. 5, Covington and Healing Springs Rd., 18-18:

George W. Hooker	Head	24	M	Farmer		R
Lillian G.	Wife	22	M			
Henry H. [**Herman?**]	Son	4 3/12				
Lillian P.	Dau	2 2/12				
Charles R.	Fa	62	Wd	None		

21-21:

Samuel B. Surber	Head	44	M	Farmer	OF
Lou B.	Wife	45	M		
Robert O.	Son	19	S	Farmer/Home Farm	

    + John Sutphin, 71, Hired Man & Geary Fisher, 39, Srvt/Cook

43-43:

Archer Landrum	Head	57	M	Farmer	R
Julia A.	Wife	45	M		
Clyde	Son	25	S	Farm Laborer/Home Farm	
Guile [?]	Son	22	S	Farm Laborer/Home Farm	
Nattie P.	Dau	19	S		
Hugh	Son	21	S		
John	Son	17	S		
Andrew	Son	15	S		
Charlie	Son	13	S		
Cora	Dau	11	S		
Fred	Son	9	S		
Sallie	Dau	7	S		
Thomas	Son	5	S		

John E. Bess

See chapter 3 (John Ernest Bess Sr.) for John E. Bess records.

CHAPTER 6

John H. Flemming Jr.

1910 Norfolk Co. Census, Portsmouth City, E.D. 102, 144 Armstrong St., 193-202:

James H. Flemming	Head	66	M2/17	Oyster Planter		OFH
Lyda V. S.	Wife	34	M1/17	0/0	b: Md./Md./Md.	

E.D. 104, 726 Webster Avenue, 1-1:

John H. Fleming	Head	30	M6		Oyster Packer	OMH
Emmaline	Wife	28	M6	2/2	b: Md./Ire./Va.	
Margaret	Dau	3	S		b: Va./Va./Md.	
Edward	Son	1 6/12			b: " " "	
Mamie Williams	Srvt	10	S	MU	Nurse/Private Family	

Hill's Norfolk and Portsmouth (Norfolk Co.) City Directory, 1941, (Richmond: Hill Directory Co.), vol. 91:

Portsmouth:

Fleming, J. H. Co. (**John H. Jr.**, Edw. J. Fleming) crab pkrs ft. [factory] Armstrong

John H. Fleming, Jr. (Emelyn C.; J. H. Fleming Co.)

    h. 1740 Spratley

Elsie Wright

1870 Norfolk Co. Census, Tanner's Creek Twnshp., 385-479:

J. S. Lambert	22		Farmer	
James Lambert	70		At Home	
Ann	59		Keeps House	b: N.C.
Wm. F.	24		Oysterman	
Virginia	22		At Home	
Joseph	7/12	b. Oct.		
Charles	15		At Home	

387-481:

Henry J. Lambert	39		Farmer	$1,925/$200
Lucinda	32		Keeps House	b: N.Y.
Georgiana	11		At School	
Gussie	2	[f]		

388-482:

Hillory Lambert	36		Oysterman	$——/$200
Margaret	32		Keeps House	
Wm. J.	16		At School	
Laura J.	14		At Home	
Henritta	10			
Walter	3			
James E.	1			

1880 Norfolk Co. Census, E.D. 69, 126 Tenchurch St., 92-156:

Hillory Lambert	Head	48	M	Oysterman [Rheumatism]
Margaret	Wife	44	M	
John	Son	20	S	Oysterman [Dispepsia]
Laura	Dau	19	S	
Henrietta	Dau	18	S	
Walter	Son	14	S	At School
James E.	Son	11	S	At School
[?]	Son	7	S	At School
Eva	Dau	3	S	

1910 Norfolk Co. Census, Tanners Creek Twnshp., 145-148:

James E. Lambert	Head	34	M 11		Proprietor/Fishing Pound	R
Mary L.	Wife	32	M 11	6/6		
Edward Y.	Son	10	S			
Elsie M.	Dau	8	S			
Amanda M.	Dau	7	S			
James R.	Son	5	S			
Ruth M.	Dau	3	S			
Mary A.	Dau	1 6/12				

Hill's Norfolk-Portsmouth Virginia Directory, 1920–1921 (Norfolk: Hill Directory Co.), 1921:

Norfolk:

James E. Lambert, fish, 640 Maysville Avenue,

    h. 1501 Church Street

Ellie E. Lambert [Wright], clerk J. E. Lambert,
  h. 1623 Lovett Avenue

Hill's Norfolk and Portsmouth (Norfolk Co.) City Directory, 1941, (Richmond: Hill Directory Co.), vol. 91:

Norfolk:
Jos. T. Wright (**Elsie M.**) fisherman
  h. 1339 E. Ocean View

Charlie Johnson

1910 Norfolk Co. Census, Portsmouth City, 751 Caledonia Street, 352-391:

Charlie Johnson	Head	25	B	M6		Laborer/Lumber Mill	RH	b: Va./N.C./N.C.
Emma [Mary?]	Wife	21	B	M6	3/3		b: N.C./N.C./N.C.
Lolie	Dau	5	B	S			b: " " "
Jensie	Dau	4	B	S			b: " " "
Archie	Son	2	B	S			b: Va./N.C./N.C.

1920 Norfolk Co. Census, Portsmouth City, E.D. 179, 584-600:

Charlie Johnson	Head	34	B	M1	Laborer/U.S. Navy Yard	b: N.C./N.C./N.C.
Emma	Wife	33	B	M1		b: " " "
Lallie	Dau	14	B	S		b: " " "
Janie	Dau	12	B	S		b: " " "
Archie S.	Son	11	B	S		b: Va./N.C./N.C.
Ella	Dau	6	B	S		b: " " "
Sophie	Dau	2 3/12	B			b: " " "

CHAPTER 7

Mr. John S. Powell

1920 Henrico Co. Census, Richmond City, E.D. 147, 766-Ninth St., 415-642:

John S. Powell	Head	54	MU	M	Barber/Own Shop	OF
M. Ellen	Wife	52	MU	M		
Harvey Lewis	Brdr	23	B	M	Porter/Confectionary Shop	
Inez "	Brdr	19	B	M	Elev. Oper./Dry Goods Store	
Lucille Woodson	Brdr	2 6/12	B			

Articles on John Powell in *Richmond News Leader,* Tuesday, 23 May 1933, p. 14: "Familiar Names Appear on Gilded 'Mugs' in John Powell's Glistening Collection." Also in *Richmond Times Dispatch,* Sunday magazine section, 18 November 1934, pp. 9 and 11: "Lathering Richmond for Fifty Years."

Hill's Richmond City Directory, 1934 (Richmond: Hill Directory Co.):
  John S. Powell (c) (M. Ellen) Powell's Barber Shop
    h. 766 N. 9th Street
    shop 6 S. 14th Street

Hill's Richmond City Directory, 1940 (Richmond: Hill Directory Co.):
  John S. Powell—Jim's Barber Shop
    h. 766 N. 9th Street

23 January 1950: Will of **John S. Powell** of Richmond. Bequeathed houses and lots at 609 and 754 N. 9th Street; stock in East End Memorial Cemetery Association; and watch and jewelry to his brother Frank S. Powell. Left house and lot at 766 N. 9th Street; personal effects and household goods in that house; and stock in Southern Aid Insurance Company and Consolidated Bank and Trust Company to his foster daughter, with rights of survivorship to her daughter. And gave $100.00 to the First African Baptist Church at 14th and Broad St., Richmond. Brother Frank S. Powell to be executor; witnessed by Walter R. Myers and W. M. Granderson. Will was probated 14 March 1958. Will Book 68-471. John Marshall Courthouse, Richmond.

Mr. And Mrs. Thomas McCaleb

1910 Alleghany Co. Census, Covington Dist., Covington Town, E.D. 7, 218 Oak Street, 532-555:

Margaret L. McCaleb	Head	65	Wd	1/1		RH
Blanche L.	Gdau	18	S			
Thomas	Gson	17	S		Salesman/Hardware	
Dorotha M.	Adpt Dau	16	S			

1920 Alleghany Co. Census, Covington Dist., Covington Town, E.D. 8, 109 S. Marion St., 32-34:

Thomas Leon McCaleb	Head	26	M	Clerk/Grocery	R
Esta	Wife	22	M		
Thos. Leon Jr.	Son	2	S		
V. C. Tyree	Mo-i-l	54	Wd		

Mrs. Roxy Prescott Dodson

23 December 1890: Will of **Roxie Prescott** of North Danville. Gives to son Edward A. Prescott furniture and lot on Franklin Street, at corner of lot 101, along Spring Street, and all real property. Also names son Charles Prescott and two daughters, Mattie Sherwood and Jennie Aarn. Son Edward to be executor, or F. Baumhardt if Edward not of age at her death. Witnesses were E. C. White and J. S. Willis. Will recorded 6 January 1891; Edward Prescott was under 21. Will Book B-91, Danville City Courthouse.

1900 Pittsylvania Co. Census, Danville City, E.D. 102, 822 Beaufort St., 216-217:

Edward A. Prescott	Head	27	M4		Salesman (Grocery)	12/72
Ida G.	Wife	23	M4	2/2		11/76
Zonie R.	Son [*sic*]	3	S	[f]		01/97
Roxiana	Dau	1	S			02/99

1910 Pittsylvania Co. Census, Danville, 44-54:

Edward E. Prescott	Head	38	M15		City Police Officer	OMH
Ida G.	Wife	34	M15	6/6		
Dona R.	Dau	13	S			
Roxia A.	Dau	11	S			
Carumar [?]	Son [?]	8	S			
Charley R.	Son	6	S			
Ida M.	Dau	4	S			
Edward R.	Son	2	S			

1920 Pittsylvania Co. Census, Danville City, E.D. 34, 855 Pine St., 99-136:

Edward Prescott	Head	48	M	Fruit Stand/Street	OM
Ida	Wife	43	M		
Cumer	Dau	18	S	Saleslady/Fruit Store	
Charlie	Son	16	S		
Ida	Dau	14	S		
Edward	Son	12	S		
Roxie Walsh	Dau	20	D		
Francis "	Gr-Son	5/12			

George G. Hodges

1910 Clifton Forge City, Alleghany Co. Census, E.D. 125, 101 Main St., 269-269:

[Not given] Hodges	Head	25	M7		Photographer/Gallery	RH
Cora	Wife	22	M7	3/3		
Winifred	Son	4	S			
Ruby	Dau	2	S			
Tiny	Dau	1/12				

19 July 1930: Estate of Letcher B. Hodges:

Winifred Hodges	24	Son
Ruby M.	22	Dau
Juanite I.	20	Dau
L. B. Jr.	17	Son
William E.	14	Son
George G.	12	Son
Jack	10	Son
James	8	Son
Joseph D.	7 mos	Son

Executor: [widow] Cora E. Hodges. Will Book 5-602.

10 June 1941: **George Gooden Hodges,** 23, paper maker, born in Covington, to Hilda Frances Lockridge, 21, born in Bath Co. Parents: L. B. Hodges and C. E. Gooden; C. H. Lockridge and Reathie Obedience Lovings. Marriage Book, Alleghany Co. Courthouse.

William D. Deal

1870 Fayette Co., West Virginia Census, Mountain Cove Tshp., 298-298:

Thaddeus Deal	25	Farmer	$2,400/$150
Henrietta	20	At Home	
John R.	1		b: W.Va.

1920 Fayette Co., West Virginia Census, Sewell Mountain M.D., E.D. 34, 61-61:

Walter D. Deal	Head	44	M	Coal Miner	R	b: W.Va./Va./W.Va.
Sadie	Wife	29	M	Keeps House		b: W.Va./W.Va./Ohio
Orville	Adpt	7				b: W.Va./Unk/Unk
Thad H.	Fa	75	M [?]			

1942: W. D. Deal buys part of Lot 96 in the town of Covington. Deed Book 90-430.

5 August 1952: List of heirs of **Walter Daniel Deal** [William D. Deal] gives the names of twenty-three legatees: one brother, two sisters, and various nieces and nephews—some of whom were living in the vicinity of Fayette County, W.Va. Will Book 7-85-86, Alleghany Co. Courthouse Records.

CHAPTER 8

F. W. Lilly

1880 Rockbridge Co. Census, South River Dist., 306-316:

Miller Lilly	Head	51	M	Laborer
Lee Anna	Wife	39	M	
Nannie	Dau	17	S	
Sedalia	St-dau	6	S	
Howard	Son	1	S	

Walker's Creek Dist., 4-4:

M. B. Cash	Head	35	M	Blacksmith
Sarelda	Wife	30	M	
Blanch	Dau	10	S	
William	Son	7	S	
Eva	Dau	5	S	
Infant	Dau	1/12		

1900 Rockbridge Co. Census, Walker's Creek Dist., 382-390:

Matthew Cash	Head	56	Wd		Blacksmith	OFH	11/43
Lee Lilley	Keep House	50	Wd	9/6	Housekeeper		09/49

| Howard N. Lilley | —— | 20 | S | Day Laborer | 07/79 |
| Carrie Lee " | —— | 17 | S | | 10/82 |

1910 Rockbridge Co. Census, Walker's Creek Dist., 84-87:

Matthiew B. Cash	Head	60	M2/2		Blacksmith	OFH
Lucy J.	Wife	39	M2/2	1/1		
Mathew B.	Son	1	S			

171-179:

Howard N. [F. W.] Lilly	Head	29	M9		Blacksmith/Repair Shop	RH
Belle M.	Wife	27	M9	2/2		
Earnest M.	Son	7	S			
Sadie B.	Dau	5	S			

1920 Bath Co. Census, E.D. 51, Sheet 5, #26:

Howard N. [F. W.] Lilly	Head	40	M	Blacksmith/Lumber Co.	R
Bell M.	Wife	38	M		
Ernest M.	Son	17	S	Laborer/Ban[d] Mill	
Sadie B.	Dau	16	S		
Otha T. Coiner	Cous	18	S	Laborer/Ban[d] Mill	
Survells Hinckle	Srvt	17	S	Housekeeper/Priv. Fam.	

25 May 1931: Homestead Exemption for H. N. Lilly for $68.85 in pay due from Columbia Gas Co. Deed Book 68-199, Alleghany Co. Courthouse.

Joe Hippert

1900 Alleghany Co. Census, Clifton Forge Mag. Dist., E.D. 3, 164-179:

| Edward Hibbert | Head | 25 | M0 | | Clerk | 11/74 | b: Mich./Eng./Ohio |
| Mary | Wife | 21 | M0 | 0/0 | | | |

Boarding in HH of: Robert Monteith

1910 Alleghany Co. Census, Clifton Dist., 412-431:

Joseph A. Hibbert	Head	34	M9		Ship Clerk/Iron Co.	RH	b: Mich./Eng./Eng.
Carrie C.	Wife	34	M9	2/2			b: N.Y./N.Y./N.Y.
John F.	Son	6	S				b: Va./Mich./N.Y.
Mabel A.	Dau	4	S				b: " " "
Mary Jackson	Srvt	35	Wd	B	Servant/Priv. Family		

413-433:

Edward Hibbert	Head	35	M10		Cashier/Iron Co.	RH	b: Mich./Eng./Eng.
Mary L.	Wife	30	M10	1/1			
Mary E.	Dau	8	S				b: Va./Mich./Va.

1920 Alleghany Co. Census, Clifton Mag. Dist., Low Moor, 288-307:

J. A. Hibbert	Head	46	M	Manager/Iron Co.	R	b: Mich./Eng./Eng.
Caroline	Wife	46	M			b: N.Y./N.J./N.Y.
John	Son	18	S	Machinist/Iron Co.		b: Va./Mich./N.Y.
Mabel	Dau	15	S			b: " " "

Oscar William Gross

1900 Botetourt Co. Census, Amsterdam Dist., E.D. 46, 92-94:

Joseph W. Gross	Head	24	M1		Iron Ore Miner	RH	06/75
Malissa	Wife	25	M1	1/0			02/75
George McDonald	Brdr	35	M		Iron Ore Miner		01/65

1910 Craig Co. Census, New Castle Dist., 200-200:

Joseph M. Gross	Head	36	M13		Car Carpenter/RR		RH
Malissie	Wife	36	M13	6/4 [?]			
Carl	Son	12	S				
Erly M.	Son	10	S				
Mary L.	Dau	7	S				
Henry Y.	Son	4	S				
Oscar W.	Son	3	S				
Infant	Son	1/12					
Lottie Craft	Srvt	22	S		Housekeeper/Works Out		
Viola P. "	———	2	S				

John B. Davidson

1880 Lee Co. Census, Jonesville Dist., 98-100:

Milton B. Fleenor	Head	19	M	Farmer
Sarah	Wife	24		
Carry M.	Dau	1		

1910 Wise Co. Census, Richmond Dist., Appalachia, 522-522:

John B. Davison	Head	33	M2/15		Store Salesman	RH
Carrie	Wife	31	M1/15	6/4		
Earnest	Son	12	S			
Verna	Dau	9	S			
Homer	Son	7	S			
Clide	Son	3	S			
Fielding Morton	Brdr	21	S		Store Salesman	b: Tenn./Tenn./Tenn.

1920 Wise Co. Census, Richmond Dist., Roda Coal Plant, #96, 840-854:

John B. Davidson	Head	42	M	Foreman/Coal Mine
Carry	Wife	41	M	
Earnest R.	Son	22	S	Fireman/R.R.
Homer	Son	17	S	
Clyde	Son	12	S	
Wilma	Dau	8	S	

CHAPTER 9

G. G. Brinkley

11 October 1917: Will of Claude C. Brinkley of Covington names wife Florence M., two sisters of Alderson, W.Va., a brother in Alderson, and a brother, George Brinkley of New York City. Will Book 5-577-579, Alleghany Co. Courthouse.

Howard Reynolds

1900 Botetourt Co. Census, Fincastle Dist. [Includes part of incorporated town of Iron Gate], 112-118:

R. Q. Reynolds	Head	53	M27		Farmer	OFF	03/47
Catherine V.	Wife	52	M27	8/7			08/47
Howard	Son	22	S		Day Laborer		04/78
Eubank B.	Son	17	S		Day Laborer		07/82
Nancie B.	Dau	16	S				02/83
Maggie P.	Dau	12	S				01/87
Catherine	Dau	10	S				10/89

M. G. Armentrout	Brdr	65	M		Pedlar/Silverware	02/35
John McNeiles	Brdr	52	S		Pedlar/Notions	10/47
	Immigrated in 1860*			b: Ire./Ire./Ire.		

*Naturalized citizen

24 January 1906: **Howard Reynolds,** 26, sawmill man, born in Bedford Co., to Janet Lee McNeal, 17, born in Augusta Co. Parents: Richard and Charlotte Reynolds; A. J. and Joanna McNeal. Marriage Record Book, Alleghany Co. Courthouse.

1910 Alleghany Co. Census, Clifton Dist., Iron Gate Town, 66-79:

Howard Reynolds	Head	31	M4		Oils Leather/Tannery	RH
Jennie L.	Wife	21	M4	1/1		
H. Frederick	Son	1 8/12				
Joseph J. McNeal	Br-i-law	23	MO		RR Section Hand	
Fannie "	Si-i-law	14	MO	0/0		

69-82:

Andrew J. McNeale	Head	47	M25		Flesher/Tannery	RH
Joanna	Wife	45	M25	9/8		
Henry A.	Son	17	S		Laborer/Tannery	
Ollie R.	Dau	14	S			
Margery M.	Dau	11	S			
Nellie F.	Dau	9	S			
Mary Eliz.	Dau	7	S			
James W.	Son	24	M3 [?]		Hide Splitter/Tannery	

Roy C. Fix

14 March 1857: Will of John Fix, leaves farm and personal property to sisters, Margaret Fix and Polly Fix, and brother Christian, who is executor. Will Book 14-272. Rockbridge Co. Courthouse.

1860 Rockbridge Co. Census, 6th Dist., Collierstown, p. 218, 1936-1936:

Christian Fix	50		Farmer	$700/$375
Sarah	31			
P. H.	10	[m]		
John A.	8			
S. M.	6	[f]		
Wm. C.	3			
Clemency	8/12	[f]		

10 February 1862: Stuart Fix born to Christian and Sarah Fix. Birth Records Book 1-269, Rockbridge Co. Courthouse.

1870 Rockbridge Co. Census, Buffalo Township, 402-402:

Sarah Fix	42		Housekeeper	$2,500/$200
Philip H.	20		Laborer	
John A. [?]	19		Laborer	
Sarah M.	16		At Home	
William C.	14		At Home	
Clemency	13	F	At Home	
Stuart	9		At Home	

1880 Rockbridge Co. Census, Buffalo Township, 447-457:

Sarah Fix	Head	51	Wd	Housekeeper	
Maggie	Dau	26	S	At Home	Maimed/Cripple
William C.	Son	23	S	Works on Farm	
Stewart B.	Son	17	S	Works on Farm	

1910 Rockbridge Co. Census, Lexington Dist., 130-130:

Stewart Fix	Head	48	M18		Farmer	RH
Ella P.	Wife	38	M18	4/4		
Daniel P.	Son	16			Farm Laborer	b: Nebr.
Lula	Dau	14				b: "
William L.	Son	11				b: "
Elsworth	Son	2				b: "
Sarah	Mo	80	Wd	6/5		
Margaret	Sis	55	S			

1910 Alleghany Co. Census, Boiling Springs Dist., 242-249:

Hen. Fridley	Head	30	M6		Farmer	OFF
Ellen	Wife	27	M6	3/3		
Myrtle	Dau	5	S			
Charles	Son	2	S			
Agnes	Dau	1	S			

18 August 1919: Will of Stuart Fix, leaves all real estate and personal property to wife, Ella P. Fix; at her death to be equally divided among his children. Will Book 40-150, Rockbridge Co. Courthouse.

1920 Alleghany Co. Census, Covington Mag. Dist., E.D. 5, Covington and Mallow Rd., 235-237:

Daniel P. Fix	Head	26	M		Laborer/Flour Mill	[?]	b: Nebr./Nebr./Va.
Mattie S.	Wife	29	M				
Mamie G.	Dau	4 4/12					
Mildred L.	Dau	3					
Roy L. Fix	Bro	20	S		Laborer/Iron Mines		b: Nebr./———/Va.
Ella	Mot	47	Wd				b: U.S./U.S./U.S.
Elsworth	Bro	13	S				b: " , " "

4 July 1925: **Roy C. Fix,** 23, born in Nebraska, to Myrtle C. Fridley, 20, born in Alleghany Co. Parents: Stewart and Ella Fix; H. M. and Ella S. Fridley. Roy Fix's occupation: railroad section man. Marriage Book, Alleghany Co. Courthouse.

9 May 1989: List of heirs of Myrtle C. Fix, dec. Her will, dated 12 October 1970, left everything to her four daughters, Phyllis, Loretta, Dorothy, and Charlotte. Will Book 26-368-69, & 371, Alleghany Co. Courthouse.

SHORT BIOGRAPHIES OF SELECTED VWP INTERVIEWERS

The biographies for these seven workers are based on information they themselves provided for the files at the time of their VWP work; on examination by these editors of censuses, courthouse records, and unpublished manuscripts; on telephone conversations, interviews, or other contacts with family members, friends, or persons who knew the worker; and in some cases, on secondary sources, such as county histories. Some of these sources are acknowledged in the text, but more extensive individual citation would have been intrusive and unnecessary.

Leila Blanche Bess (ca. 1886–1959) was born in Alleghany County, Va., and never married. Her father, John L. Bess, was a member of the "Rocky Point Grays" and was wounded at Lewisburg in the Civil War. He had been a farmer/merchant, until his home and store were both destroyed by fire, considerably reducing the family's moderate circumstances. They were Methodists and claimed descent from Rev. Joseph Pinnell, a local Methodist minister who died at Potts Creek in 1849. Leila Bess apparently did some of her life histories by riding with her brother to homes along his rural mail route. See the life histories with John Ernest Bess Sr. (chapters 3 and 5) for more information on her.

30 April 1959: Leila Blanche Bess died intestate. Her heirs were listed as:

Wilbur C. Bess	Brother	83	St. Petersburg, Fla.
L. E. Bess	Brother	73	Keokee, Fla.

John E. Bess, Jr.	Nephew	39	Ft. Riley, Kans.
Nelda B. Kessinger	Niece	37	Covington, Va.

Signed 28 May 1959 by J. E. Bess, Jr. and Nelda B. Kessinger Will Book 9-363, Alleghany Co. Courthouse.

Gertrude Blair (1871–1945) was born in Blue Ridge Springs, Botetourt County, Va. Her father, Lycurgus Blair, was from Amherst County; her mother, Paulina H. Price, who died when Gertrude was in her twenties, was from Bedford County, Va. Blair never married; she lived at home and kept house for her father and brothers, who were building contractors and a real estate broker in Roanoke, Va. She mentions having attended Sunday school class in Philadelphia with John Wanamaker, but she was a charter member of Trinity Church (Methodist) in Roanoke. Her early life seems to have been comfortable: she was taught by private governesses and then studied Renaissance and ancient art in this country and in Italy. She listed as a special skill her "ability to ride horses that a man wouldn't mount."

Walsh's Roanoke, Virginia, City Directory for 1900 (Charleston, S.C.: W. H. Walsh Directory Co.):

Miss Gertrude Blair

h: 420 5th S.W., at same residence: Lycurgus Blair [Gertrude's father], retired; Lycurgus Blair, Jr., bookkeeper with Hurr, Andrews & Moyler Co; and William J. Blair, real estate at 104 Jefferson St.

1910:

Gertrude Blair is listed with her brother Lycurgus, a broker, at 21 Highland (10th) Ave., S.E. She continues to be indicated at the Highland Ave. address in 1915, 1919–20, and 1924.

9 September 1945: Gertrude Blair died on this date. List of heirs names seven stepnephews. Wills: Laws and Chancery, 7-223, Roanoke Co. Courthouse.

Susie R. C. Byrd (1899–1960) was born in Keswick, Albemarle County, Va., where she lived for several years with her parents and grandmothers before being adopted in 1903 by her maternal aunt in Petersburg, Va. She graduated from the Peabody school in 1911 and entered Virginia Normal and Industrial Institute, where she majored in Home Economics—graduating in 1913. Byrd served as principal and taught at Dewitt Training School for two years, after which she was a substitute—then regular—teacher for black schools in the Petersburg public school system until she married in 1921. She took courses at Hampton Institute and worked at various times toward a degree in social work at Virginia State College. In 1933–34 she worked in an FERA nursery school; in 1935–36 on a WPA adult night school class, which renamed itself the Susie R. C. Byrd Literary Club; and in January 1937, she began work for the VWP Negro Studies project. Byrd was a member of the Zion Baptist Church, Petersburg. See Susie R. C. Byrd autobiography, VSL/AB, box 191.

Records in Petersburg Hustings Court indicate that Susie R. C. *Bolling,* age 43, married Willie James Monroe in 1943. She used her maiden name, however, on all her VWP work. Her will indicated that she was unmarried and left no issue, but it listed three Byrd nephews as heirs.

John W. Garrett (1900–1990) was born in Nelson County, Va. He was the son of Arthur and Emma (Carter) Garrett (see the life history with Arthur Garrett and also the incident with Jimmie Garrett, John's brother, cited in the introductory material to chapter 4). John Garrett's first wife, Susie, died in 1935, leaving him a widower with three daughters. On 1 June 1936 he married Annie Lou Broyhill, one of Marvin T. Broyhill's sisters (see Broyhill's life history in this work also). Later he spent seventeen years working for Hercules Powder Company in Hopewell, Va. In an undated letter to Marvin T. Broyhill III, Annie Lou Garrett wrote that she and John had two sons and that "John [was] an ordained minister in the Pentecostal Holiness Church and ha[d] worked in this church as a pastor for thirty five years."

Hill's Hopewell and City Point Directory, 1929 (Richmond: Hill Directory Co.):

J. Garrett (Susie), both w. at Tubize

no h. address copied

18 June 1936: **John William Garrett,** widow, born 1901 in Nelson Co., Va., to Annie Lou Broyhill, single, born 1897 in Wilkes Co., N.C. He resided at 207 N. 3rd Avenue; her residence was 915 Buren Street. Parents: Arthur

Watson Garrett and W. Carter Garrett; Thomas Jefferson Broyhill and Sally Gilreath. Marriage Record Book, Hopewell City Courthouse.

28 February 1990: Obituary for **John W. Garrett**, *Richmond News-Leader*, p. 26: "The Rev. John W. Garrett, a retired pastor of Schuyler Pentecostal Church in Schuyler in Nelson County, died yesterday at home. He was 89.

"A native of Nelson County, Mr. Garrett had been a minister for about 50 years. He was a pastor in churches in Elizabeth City, N.C., and Deep Creek. He retired from the ministry about 1970." He was also "a retired laboratory maintenance worker for Hercules Inc. in Hopewell." Survivors include two daughters, two sons, ten grandchildren, eight stepgrandchildren, and eighteen great-grandchildren. Funeral was held in the Hopewell Pentecostal Holiness Church, and burial was in Appomattox Cemetery, Hopewell.

Margaret Jeffries (1899–1979) was born in Culpeper County, Va., the daughter of William Lewis and Maggie E. Jeffries. William Jeffries was a lawyer and judge in the county (he was fifty-seven in the 1910 census but died that same year). Her mother, born in 1860, was the daughter of Major William Anderson of Anderson, S.C., who was killed in the Civil War, and his wife, Lucretia McFall. Margaret Jeffries never married; she remained at home with her widowed mother. She wrote poetry and, like her mother, had a talent for art. She was a member of the Woman's Missionary Union of the Baptist General Association of Richmond. Jeffries exhibited a continuing interest in writing after her VWP experience, and in 1948–49 she took a writing course by correspondence from the Newspaper Institute of America.

1910 Culpeper Co. Census, Catalpa Dist., 371-371:

William L. Jeffries	Head	57	M27		Lawyer	OMF
Maggie E.	Wife	50	M27	11/7		
Mary E.	Dau	26			Teacher	
Mildred M.	Dau	19				
William L., Jr.	Son	18			Farm Laborer	
Thomas A.	Son	16				
Dudley M.	Son	12				
Margaret	Dau	11				
Blank [?] B.	Dau	9				

Essie W. Smith (1872–1963) was born Celestia Wade in Rocky Mount, Franklin County, Va., the daughter of Zachary Taylor Wade and his wife, Catherine Greer. Essie's grandfather Henry Hobson Wade was an Episcopal minister, educated at Princeton. Essie Wade married first Benjamin Waldo Butler of South Carolina and then Cabell Smith of Martinsville, Va.; she had a daughter by each marriage. In the 1910 Henry County, Va., census, Cabell Smith was a real estate agent; Essie Smith was a public school teacher; and her father-in-law, Orthodox Creed Smith, was a "leaf prizing" tobacconist (see Orthodox Creed Strictler life history and also Appendix B). When she died, Essie Smith was "honorary president of the United Daughters of the Confederacy."

1850 Franklin Co. Census, Ntl., 173-173:

John Wade	68	Farmer	RE = $12,000
Elizabeth	55		
Elizabeth	24		
Benjamin	21		
John	26		
Lucy A.	16		
Julia F.	14		
Josephin [?]	14		
Richard Hopson	18		
Willis Jenkins	21	Laborer	

1807-1798:

*Henry Wade	35	Farmer	RE = $2,000
Julia	32		

Andrew P.	12
John H.	10
Elizabeth M.	5
Zachary T.	2
Charles P.	18

1860 Franklin Co. Census, Glade Hill P.O., 42-42:

John Wade	77	Farmer	$30,000/$27,000
Elizabeth	65		
Peter P. Davis	40	Merchant	$3,000/$10,000
John P.	"	8	

*By 1860 Henry Hobson Wade's widow, Julia Patterson Wade, was remarried to widower Theodorick F. Webb, the grandfather of Nannie Isabel Webb Price (see chapter 1). Zachary Taylor Wade, who was shown in his father's household in 1850 and in the household of Theodorick Webb in 1860, was Celestia (Essie) Wade Butler Smith's father. John and Elizabeth (Hobson) Wade were Smith's great-grandparents, and Theodorick Webb was, by marriage, her stepgrandfather.

1 August 1961: Handwritten will of Essie W. Smith (Mrs. Cabell Smith): Leaves estate to sister, Josephine Epperson; two daughters of her brother, T. G. Wade; three granddaughters; and niece, Winnifred Davis. Russell L. Davis, executor. Presented in court 26 January 1963. Will Books 42-338, 340-41; and 43-148, Franklin Co. Courthouse.

Thursday, 24 January 1963: Obituary for **Essie Wade Smith,** *Roanoke World News.* "Mrs. Essie Wade Smith, 89, honorary president of the United Daughters of the Confederacy, died Wednesday at Hopewell. Surviving are two sisters, Mrs. A. L. Edmundson, Rocky Mount; Mrs. Josephine Epperson, Hopewell; three grandchildren, seven great-grandchildren. Funeral will be at 9 a.m. at Hopewell. Graveside service will be at 3:00 p.m. Friday at High Street Cemetery here. The family asks that flowers be omitted."

Mary S. Venable (1878–1962) was born in Alleghany County, Va., the daughter of General William Skeen and his second wife, Georgia. William Skeen was born in 1818 in Rockbridge County, Va.; he was a land lawyer both in Pocahontas County (in 1850) and in Alleghany County (see Morton, *History of Alleghany County,* 138). Mary Skeen married Edward W. Venable on 28 October 1903, but on the same date in 1922 they were divorced. Like Leila Blanche Bess, Venable was also a Methodist, but she appears to have been more liberal and associated with the progressive/reform activities of the Women's Home Mission Movement.

1850 Pocahontas Co. Census, 47th Dist., [298] 133-126:

William Skeen	32	Atty.-at-Law	$1,500
Catharine	30	At Home	
Charles	4	At School	
Robert	1		

22 November 1869: William Skeen, 52, wid., b. in Rockbridge County, lawyer, parents Robert and Polly Skeen, to G. A. Payne, 27, single, b. in Alleghany County, parents G. H. and S. A. Payne. Married by J. M. [page torn]. Marriage Book, Alleghany Co. Courthouse.

1870 Alleghany Co. Census, Covington Twnshp., 141-141:

William Skeen	Head	52	M	Lawyer	$45,000/$27,000
Robert A.	Son	20	S	Powder Agent	
Isaac H.	Son	14	S	At School	
Joseph C.	Son	10	S	At School	

1880 Alleghany Co. Census, S.D. 5, E.D. 325, Page 6, 56-56:

William Skeen	Head	60	M		Lawyer
Georga A.	Wife	37	M	KH	
Virginia	Dau	6			
Jessie	Dau	3			

Mary	Dau	2			
Joseph C.	Son	20	S		Works on Farm
William Wallice	Srvt	20	S	B	Servant

Tuesday, 2 July 1962: Obituary for **Mrs. Mary Skeen Venable,** *Roanoke World News.* "Mrs. Mary Skeen Venable, 84, formerly of Covington, died Sunday in Los Angeles, California. She was the author of a number of books of poetry."

Photographs Taken by Year*

Year	Number of Photos Taken	Number Surviving	Number Killed
1935	312	160	154
1936	59	53	2
1937	147	53	63
1938	29	14	9
1939	50	39	10
1940	276	273	1
1941	1,081	975	71
1942	626	551	52
1943	703	513	175
1944	10	10	0
Total	3,293	2,641	537

Photographs Taken by Individual Photographers

Photographer	Photographs Taken	Number Killed	Prints Not Found
Bonn, Philip	209	76	0
Bubley, Esther	184	45	5
Carter, Paul	35	0	0
Collier, John	236	23	17
Collins, Marjorie	50	15	9
Delano, Jack	420	61	6
Dixon, Royden	20	0	0
Driscoll, Norman	3	0	3
Ealand, Maria	10	0	0
Evans, Walker	2	0	0
Hollem, Howard	71	27	0
Hotchkiss, Reginald	1	0	0
Lange, Dorothea	14	2	4
Lee, Russell	20	8	4
Liberman, Howard	44	0	0
Locke, Edwin	1	0	0
McMillan, Martha	19	0	0
Palmer, Alfred	332	0	0
Parks, Gordon	26	6	0
Rosener, Ann	10	0	6
Rothstein, Arthur	448	185	31
Sarra, Valentine	41	0	0
Shahn[?], Ben	156	0	0
Terry, Pat	27	0	0
Vachon, John	590	79	16
Wolcott, Marion Post	301	10	21
Unknown	23	0	7
Total	3,293	537	129

*Because the Prints and Photographs Division has no overall indexes to its prints and negatives, these figures are subject to some amount of error. In the first list above, there is a cumulative difference of 115 photographs unaccounted for between the number indicated by various sources as having been taken and the sum of the photos known to survive or to have been killed during the entire period. But the second list indicates 14 more — or 129 — prints not accounted for or found. Presumably, negatives exist for some or all of the photographs not found in the files, and prints of them could be ordered. Furthermore, negatives exist for many of the "killed" photographs, and these could be ordered as well. However, many (though by no means all) of these prints would display evidence of the holes punched in their negatives by Roy Stryker.

NOTES

ABBREVIATIONS OF DEPOSITORIES

HU/AH   Dr. Arthur Howe Papers, Federal Works Agency (WPA), Archives, Hampton University, Hampton, Virginia

HU/REL   Roscoe E. Lewis Papers, Archives, Hampton University, Hampton, Virginia

LC/M   Manuscripts Division, Library of Congress, Washington, D.C.

LCP&P   Prints and Photographs Division, Library of Congress, Washington, D.C.

NA/B   Work Projects Administration, Record Group 69, Bourne Guide, State Series, National Archive, Washington, D.C.

NA/D   Work Projects Administration, Record Group 69, Davidson Guide, National Archive, Washington, D.C.

NG/IAD   Index of American Design Collection, National Gallery of Art, Washington, D.C.

RPL   Virginiana Room, Roanoke Public Library, Roanoke, Virginia

UL/RS   Roy Stryker Papers, 1912–72, Horvath Guide, University of Louisville Photographic Archives, University of Louisville, Louisville, Kentucky

UNC/SHC   Southern History Collection, Manuscripts Department, Wilson Library, University of North Carolina at Chapel Hill

UVA/ERR   Eudora Ramsay Richardson Papers (Accession No. 9766), Manuscripts Division, Special Collections Department, Alderman Library, University of Virginia, Charlottesville

UVA/FC   WPA Virginia Writers' Project Folklore Collection (Accession No. 1547), Manuscripts Division, Special Collections Department, Alderman Library, University of Virginia, Charlottesville

UVA/KBP   Kevin Barry Perdue Archive of Traditional Culture, Department of Anthropology, University of Virginia, Charlottesville

UVA/MJ   Margaret Jeffries Papers (Accession Nos. 10366-a and 10366-b), Manuscripts Division, Special Collections Department, Alderman Library, University of Virginia, Charlottesville

VCU/AC   Adele Clark Papers, Special Collections and Archives, James Branch Cabell Library / Tompkins-McCaw Library, Virginia Commonwealth University, Richmond

VSL/AB   WPA-FWP Papers, Archives Branch, Virginia State Library, Richmond

VSL/HIP   Historic Inventory Project, Film 509, Library Division, in the Reference Department and Picture Collection, Virginia State Library, Richmond

VSL/PC   Picture Collection, Library Division, Virginia State Library, Richmond

INTRODUCTION

1. The title quote is from "The Mother of a Family," life history with Mrs. Jo (Joseph) Morris by Anne Worrell, 5 pp., 1,450 wds., 3 April 1939, VSL/AB, box 182. The Morris text is not included in this book, but excerpts from it are cited in the introductory text of chapter 2.

2. Heinemann in *Depression and New Deal,* 92, and again in "Alphabet Soup," erroneously attributes both *Virginia: A Guide* and *Negro in Virginia* to Hamilton J. Eckenrode as VWP director, rather than to Richardson. For a presentation of the extant Virginia ex-slave interviews, see Perdue, Barden, and Phillips, *Weevils in the Wheat.* For a discussion and background of *The Negro in Virginia* and the Negro Studies program at Hampton Institute, see the foreword by Charles L. Perdue Jr. to the 1994 reprint. Regrettably, this edition of *The Negro in Virginia* excluded the original foreword by Eudora Ramsay Richardson and all its photographs, including those by African American photographer Robert McNeill, who was specifically assigned to that project. On the life history project, see copy of letter from Richardson to Venable on "Social-Ethnic Studies interviews," 2 November 1938, HU/REL.

3. John S. Widdicombe to Margaret Jeffries, 17 October 1939 and 22 November 1939, UVA/MJ. As state offices closed, many sent their project materials to the Washington office, to be housed finally among the WPA holdings of the Manuscripts Division in the Library of Congress. But Virginia is little represented in that depository. Ac-

cording to our best estimate, *none* of the VWP life history or social-ethnic and youth studies texts and only about 10 percent of the state's folklore/folksong collection and ex-slave narratives were sent to Washington. At the behest of Arthur Kyle Davis Jr., professor of English at the University of Virginia and president/archivist of the Virginia Folklore Society, the VWP folklore/folksong collections and associated administrative materials were deposited in the Manuscripts Department of the University of Virginia's Alderman Library in Charlottesville. Documents and accompanying photographs produced under the state's WPA Historical Inventory Project were placed in the Virginia State Library in Richmond. Some ex-slave interviews and other texts produced by the VWP's Negro Studies Program survive only in the archives at Hampton University. But the bulk of the life histories, social-ethnic and youth studies, and ex-slave interviews, along with materials from the Historic Records Survey and other separate WPA projects, were deposited in the Archives Branch of the state library in Richmond, where they currently fill some 547 Hollinger boxes. In the course of our examination of this collection in August 1984, we compiled an unpublished 124-page listing titled "Work Projects Administration Records—A Partial Inventory," a copy of which was provided to the VSL/AB staff. In May 1993, it remained in use as a provisional guide to the collection.

The term *endangered* as applied here reflects our concern and that of many others about conditions affecting the Virginia State Archives and its large holdings of poorly housed WPA/VWP and other New Deal records. This concern was forcefully voiced in a letter received by the editors from the Virginia Genealogical Society (VGS) on 5 January 1994, which enclosed a report entitled "The Virginia State Archives: A Treasure in Trouble" urging the public to lobby on behalf of archive funding and adequate housing. The VGS cites the archive's current overseer as saying that "Virginians will find their documentary heritage in irreversible jeopardy by 2007, the Commonwealth's 400th Anniversary" (personal files). From our own observations, the designation of these collections as "endangered" is justified.

4. The discussion here of history and culture is adapted from historian Lawrence Levine's *Black Culture,* 5. But folklorist Barre Toelken similarly defines "folklore" as process in *Dynamics of Folklore,* 32–38. For other folklorists who have synthesized the approaches of folklore and history in their work, see Glassie, *Passing the Time;* Joyner, *Down by the Riverside;* and Montell, *Saga of Coe Ridge.*

5. There is an enormous literature on the life history as method, as a form of biography, and as it has been used by history and the social sciences generally. Among these works, the *Use of Personal Documents* by Gottschalk, Kluckhohn, and Angell (1945) is a benchmark survey of life history use and method; its anthropology component by Kluckhohn is definitive to that date. In *Lives* (1981), Langness and Frank update Kluckhohn's coverage and include a "general review" of more than five hundred works, which they note could not at that time constitute a "comprehensive bibliography" given the growth of "important work in the life-history field" (157). Runyan, *Life Histories and Psychobiography,* gives a good overview of the use of life histories, particularly from the perspectives of psychology and psychobiography, and he also includes an extensive bibliography.

From the turn of the century until recently, anthropologists have used the term *autobiography* to refer primarily to the life histories of so-called primitive peoples, as translated and written down by the ethnographer from the (mostly) unwritten languages of the native. However, Linde, a sociolinguist, currently views autobiography (apart from its nearest relative, the oral life story form) to be generally accepted as both a written, first-person account or exemplum from one's life and a literary genre with its own peculiar history, demands, and market: see *Life Stories,* 38–42.

For a few recent publications that have made use of FWP life history materials, see: Banks, *First-Person America;* Brown, *Up before Daylight;* Cohen, *America, the Dream;* Newby, *Plain Folk;* Terrill and Hirsch, *Such as Us;* and Weigle, *New Mexicans in Cameo and Camera; Two Guadalupes;* and *Women of New Mexico.*

6. The Works Progress Administration was renamed the Work Projects Administration after the agency's general reorganization in July 1939. For further information on that development, see McDonald, *Federal Relief Administration,* 104–6, 129–32, 309. See also Mangione, *Dream and the Deal;* Penkower, *Federal Writers' Project;* and McKinzie, "Writers on Relief." For a bibliography of resources on the WPA, see Bloxom, *Pickaxe and Pencil.* This last work has a generally useful appendix of WPA administrators and their positions at federal or state levels; however, none of Virginia's administrators or directors are included in it.

7. "RA/FSA" will be used to refer generally to the images produced under Roy Stryker's authority in all the various agencies with which the Historical Section was associated, including the Office of Emergency Management and, later, the Office of War Information. In *Anthropology as Cultural Critique,* 125–30, Marcus and Fischer com-

ment on the 1930s documentary mode in America and the use of the "photographic medium to capture 'human experience'" with the implicit goal of effecting cultural change. See also William Stott, *Documentary Expression.*

8. Garnett's state-sponsored survey began in August 1939 under the reorganized and renamed Work Projects Administration of Virginia. See Norfleet to Jeffries, 28 September 1939, UVA/MJ. The Anna Watts interview (in chapter 4) is one of the urban black youth studies conducted out of Hampton Institute. So, too, are the interviews with rural white youths George Hodges (in chapter 7) and Margaret Wolfe (in chapter 2) by Mary Venable and Leila Blanche Bess of Alleghany County.

9. Eckenrode, who was appointed as the first VWP director on a part-time basis on 28 October 1935, was forced by FWP director Henry Alsberg to resign from the position as of 27 February 1937. Richardson served as the first and only full-time VWP director from 9 March 1937 until after the program officially ended in 1942. Regarding Eckenrode's dismissal, see NA/D, entry 1, Virginia, box 1 of 2, and Eckenrode to William A. Smith, 27 February 1937, NA/D, entry 1, box 1 of 2. On hiring Richardson, see Alsberg to Woodward, 8 March 1937, and Browning to Alsberg, 19 March 1937, NA/D, entry 1, boxes 1 and 2. See also Garner, "Richmond's Own Eudora," and Richardson to Landin, 31 August 1943, UVA/ERR, box 1. Regarding Richardson's suffrage activities, see newspaper clippings, 24 September 1917 and 3 October 1917, and undated broadside with picture of Richardson, UVA/ERR, box 1. Comments on Richardson's personality are in a memorandum from Reed Harris to Lawrence Morris, 18 March 1937, NA/B, entry 12, 651.317.

10. Sternsher, *Rexford Tugwell,* 303. See also Fleischhauer and Brannan, *Documenting America,* 3–6. Although there were never more than six official RA/FSA photographers working at any given time, Fleischhauer and Brannan attribute the aggregated photographs in the FSA file to approximately forty-four individuals—only sixteen of whom they name. It is difficult to determine from this exactly who the persons are who fit within what they call "the Stryker opus" (337). See also Baldwin, *Poverty and Politics,* 91–92; Stoeckle and White, *Plain Pictures,* 31; and Hurley, *Portrait of a Decade,* 36.

11. By some estimates, there are some 140,000 negatives, 77,000 black-and-white prints with captions, and 1,600 Kodachrome slides in the RA/FSA collection deposited in the Prints and Photographs Division, Library of Congress. Personal communication, Beverly Brannan, LCP&P. Based on his own "recent systematic survey," Nicholas Natanson (an archivist in the Still Picture Branch, National Archives) states there are 182,000 RA/FSA negatives and "some 110,000 black-and-white prints," but he agrees with Brannan on the number of 1,600 color transparencies. See Natanson, *Black Image,* 269–70. In fact, no one knows the exact number of RA/FSA photographs that were taken, since photographers did not always send in all of their negatives and then only about half of the extant negatives have been printed. These are the prints housed in the Library of Congress (along with an unknown quantity of photographs by other government or private photographers that were copied and deposited among the RA/FSA collection) that Brannan estimated above.

12. Letter of authorization for Rothstein's trip, 22 October 1935, lot 12024, FSA-OWI Written Records, 1935–46, reel no. 5, LCP&P. Stryker "killed," that is, he deliberately mutilated, destroyed, or simply did not use, some number of the RA/FSA negatives submitted. Slightly more than 2,600 Virginia RA/FSA photographs were actually located in the files at LCP&P, but an unknown number of the 537 Virginia photographs that were supposedly killed exist in negative files and may, in fact, be printed—as the example of the Shenandoah project photo with Stryker's trademark (the hole punched in the negative) indicates. Only five RA/FSA photographs, in addition to those by Rothstein, were taken in Virginia in 1935; another 285 RA/FSA photographs were made statewide between 1936 and 1939. But most of the total Virginia RA/FSA photographs were taken between January 1940 and October 1943.

13. McDonald, *Federal Relief Administration,* 657–58, 688. On tourism, see Weigle, "Southwest Lures"; Sears, *Sacred Places;* and MacCannell, *The Tourist.* In terms of MacCannell's process of "sight sacralization," the guidebooks were participants in "*naming,*" that is, of authenticating or marking the site off "as worthy of special attention by signage or decree," as cited by Kirshenblatt-Gimblett and Bruner in "Tourism," 302. See discussion in MacCannell, 43–48.

14. See VWP, *Virginia: A Guide,* vii. Alsberg to Richardson, 31 October 1938, and Harris to Morris, 18 March 1937, NA/D, entry 1, WPA Administrative Correspondence, Utah-Virginia, 1935–39.

15. Heaton to Jeffries, 6 May 1939, UVA/MJ. It has generally been assumed by those researching the Federal Writers' Project that most, if not all, fieldworkers had copies of program manuals and applied them in their work. For a recent example of this assumption, see Barden, *Virginia Folk Legends.* He gives a critical reading of Botkin's manual in terms of its coverage of the category "legend" and then writes that "what folklore training

[VWP fieldworkers] got was on the job, from the written guidelines of the Washington and Richmond offices" (6). A thirteen-page version of Botkin's nineteen-page folklore manual (much modified by VWP's folklore consultant Miriam Sizer) and Couch's "Instructions to Workers" were eventually sent to some VWP workers. But even these were received too late to be of much value to the project's overall efforts. Further, there is no evidence that the people who worked *only* on life history programs ever received the folklore manual, even in modified form. See also below, n. 26.

16. There was some overlap of workers between the VWP folklore-collecting and life history interview programs, but by and large, the workers who were most productive on the life history projects did not correspond to those who were the most prolific folklore collectors. For works presenting VWP-collected folklore materials, see Perdue, *Outwitting the Devil;* Perdue, *Pigsfoot Jelly;* and Barden, *Virginia Folk Legends.* See Douglas Southall Freeman, "The Spirit of Virginia," in VWP, *Virginia: A Guide,* 5. Couch to Richardson, January 1939, NA/D, entry 1, WPA Administrative Correspondence, Utah-Virginia, 1935–39.

17. McDonald, *Federal Relief Administration,* 679. For Couch's statement regarding such a series, see "Instructions to Writers" in FWP, *These Are Our Lives,* app., 419–20; see also the preface by Couch, ix and 417. For his concerns about the image of the South presented in various media, see Terrill and Hirsch, *Such as Us,* xviii–xxi, and Brown, *Up before Daylight,* 7.

18. Hirsch, "Culture on Relief," 23–26, 30, 56–65, 69. Brown, *Up before Daylight,* 4–7, 10–23, esp. 14. In its final form, *These Are Our Lives* included twenty life histories from North Carolina, fourteen from Tennessee, and one from Georgia (xi). The fact that Couch included no Virginia life histories in that work was not missed by Richardson; still, she encouraged her workers to obtain "material for future volumes that [were] to be published." Anne Heaton, VWP supervisor of field assignments, to Margaret Jeffries, 6 May 1939, UVA/MJ. Although none of the planned sequels to *These Are Our Lives* appeared at the time, Terrill and Hirsch's *Such as Us,* published in 1978, was composed of texts from the FWP southeastern region's collection deposited in UNC/SHC. Several VWP texts, which were also deposited among those materials, have subsequently been published. See Newby, *Plain Folk,* and Robinson, *Living Hard,* which contains a version of the life history of Sam Harrison (Buzzell Peebles) in chapter 5, under yet another pseudonymous name.

19. FWP, *These Are Our Lives,* x, xii–xiii.

20. Comaroff and Comaroff, *Ethnography and the Historical Imagination,* 17. In the "Theory, Ethnography, Historiography" section of this work, esp. 7–31, the Comaroffs give a valuable and insightful overview of recent debates in anthropology and history regarding the representation of "others." They warn that "social science persists in treating biography as a neutral, transparent window into history [and] in so doing, it serves to perpetuate [what Bourdieu calls] the 'biographical illusion,'" that is, to locate the creations of both history and biography "in rational individualism, and to pay little heed to the social and cultural forms that silently shape and constrain human action" (26). For some other discussions of representation, life writing, and related issues, see Krupat, *For Those Who Come After;* Lavie, Narayan, and Rosaldo, *Creativity/Anthropology;* Myerhoff, *Remembered Lives,* esp. introduction by Marc Kaminsky, 1–97; and Van Maanen, *Representation in Ethnography,* esp. 1–35.

21. Penkower, *Federal Writers' Project,* 152, 153 n. 43. The reviewer cited was Lewis Gannett writing in the *New York Herald Tribune* on 20 May 1939. Brown, *Up before Daylight,* 14. Thompson, *Voice of the Past,* 255–59.

22. Banks relied heavily on a self-proclaimed intuition for recognizing the authenticity of the texts she selected from the "more than 150,000 pages" of FWP life histories deposited in the "Folk Song Archive" (Archive of Folk Song) and later transferred to the Manuscripts Division of the Library of Congress. The Archive of Folk Song (now renamed the Archive of Folk Culture) has been incorporated into the American Folklife Center at the Library of Congress. Through the work of Carl Fleischhauer and others on the Library of Congress's current American Memory Project, some, if not all, of the 150,000 pages of FWP texts examined by Banks are now available on the electronic World Wide Web. See Banks, *First-Person America,* xiv.

Leonard Rapport has rightly questioned intuitive "ring of truth" tests, such as that used by Banks, and discussed the general tendency of persons to ignore, insofar as these FWP life histories are concerned, otherwise accepted rules of evidence and historiographic practice. See Rapport, "How Valid Are the Federal Writers' Project Life Stories," 8.

23. There is, however, a growing body of serious research devoted to the comprehensive coverage of FWP programs in specific states. Besides our own work in Virginia and that of Barden, *Virginia Folk Legends,* these include, in New Mexico, Weigle, *New Mexicans in Cameo and Camera, Two Guadalupes,* and *Women of New Mexico,* and

Weigle and White, *Lore of New Mexico;* in Alabama, Brown, *Up before Daylight;* and in New Jersey, Cohen, *America, the Dream.* These investigators, to varying extents, have either given such biographical data as are known about project workers and staff or attempted to locate and interview those surviving to provide further background both on them and on the programs.

24. We contend that the extent to which Virginia fieldworkers on various cultural projects injected themselves, family members, friends, and neighbors into their work has not been generally recognized. As one case in point, Lucille B. Jayne of Capahosic, Virginia, submitted an extensive autobiography to the VWP personnel files and also a very lengthy, anonymous, written portrait of herself and her family to the life history program. See a long excerpt from the latter in the introductory text of chapter 6. Further, when her relief certification ended, Jayne wrote a desperate letter full of personal details to Eleanor Roosevelt pleading for the first lady's help to get her VWP job back. NA/B, 651.3179—Miscellaneous Correspondence, 1939–42, folder 2: "H-J."

25. For the source of biographical information on workers in this and the following paragraphs, see Appendix B.

26. Couch's instructions to writers specifically admonished against the "expression of judgment" in interviews; so, too, did Botkin's interview guidelines—in the six-page section of the folklore manual that was edited out by Miriam Sizer. But because even those modified manuals were not necessarily sent out to all VWP workers, there is much more discretionary expression of the individual writers' personality and opinions and a far greater variability in the VWP life histories than might otherwise exist. As has been noted previously in the text, this is both a strength and a weakness in the VWP materials. However, these particular programmatic circumstances make it all the more imperative to consider each VWP interviewer and his or her body of work separately, on its own merits, within its own specific context, and according to its own idiosyncracies. Sidney Mintz, "The Anthropological Interview and the Life History," in Dunaway and Baum, *Oral History,* 312. This article is a somewhat shortened and revised version of one first printed in *Oral History Review* in 1979.

27. Barbara Myerhoff and Jay Ruby, "A Crack in the Mirror: Reflexive Perspectives in Anthropology," in Ruby, *Crack in the Mirror,* 4. See also Riv-Ellen Prell in Barbre et al., *Interpreting Women's Lives,* 254, and Myerhoff, *Remembered Lives,* 307–40.

28. Regarding this use of the obsolete questionnaire forms, see communications from John S. Widdicombe, VWP supervisor of field assignments, to Jeffries, UVA/MJ.

29. Van Maanen, *Tales of the Field,* 137. See also S. A. Tyler, "Post-modern Ethnography," in Clifford and Marcus, *Writing Culture.* Jerrold Hirsch refers to the FWP life histories as "conversational narratives," using a term he attributes to oral historian Ronald Grele. But Hirsch's use of the term projects an idealized structure onto the life history interview situation and does not address the underlying issues pointed out by Van Maanen and others. Hirsch, letter to Charles L. Perdue Jr., 8 October 1979; see also Terrill and Hirsch, "Replies," 87. Others have confused the situation further by their particular use or definition of these narratives of experience or life history texts. For example, some writers use "personal narrative" (which has specific meaning among folklorists as a recounting of first-person experience) to encompass several other kinds of "life writing," including biographies, diaries, and journals, as well as life histories. See Barbre et al., *Interpreting Women's Lives,* 4.

30. Robert K. Merton attributes the statement "If men define situations as real, they are real in their consequences" to W. I. Thomas, "the dean of American sociologists," and refers to it as "the Thomas theorem." But Merton further allows that Bishop Bossuet, J. Mandeville, Karl Marx, Sigmund Freud, and William Graham Sumner had each expressed essentially the same idea in their own times; see Merton, *Social Theory and Social Structure,* 421. John Dollard in *Criteria for the Life History,* 33–34, stressed that life history material had to be "organized and conceptualized" in some way because it "does not speak for itself." He was not dismissing the value of narrated subjective experience. Rather, his remark introduced a caveat on the deliberate, as well as unconscious, processes of selection that affect a person's communication of his or her life history. He pointed out that it was too easy to "accept the result [the interview text] as a valid life history" without further research or analysis into the meanings of a particular self-representation at a particular moment in time. It is a point well taken: one that sixty years ago foreshadowed the current concerns in various disciplines with questions of representation. Dollard's near contemporary, Roy Stryker similarly stated that "the photograph cannot ordinarily stand by itself" and stressed the need for contextual information to assess the cultural value of the RA/FSA canon of documentary photographs; see Ware, *Cultural Approach to History,* 324–30, esp. 326. See also Arnold Krupat in the foreword to Radin's *Crashing Thunder,* ix.

31. FWP, *These Are Our Lives*, xiii, x.

32. Linde, *Life Stories*, 20–31, esp. 21. Titon also distinguishes between "life story" and "life history" but his concept of life story is more narrowly performance oriented and not as potentially useful as Linde's broader linguistics approach; see Titon, "The Life Story."

33. Cruikshank, *Life Lived like a Story*, 2.

34. Runyan, *Life Histories and Psychobiography*, 3. Ayers, *Promise of the New South*, viii.

35. A text written to accompany an RA/FSA photographic project in the Shenandoah Valley has also been included to exhibit yet another type of New Deal writing for comparative purpose. A few items from the state's Historic Inventory Project, Historic American Building Survey, and the Art Project's Index of American Design and some examples of VWP folklore are included for illustrative purpose as well.

36. See the preface for coverage of some individual cases in which the editors' experiences were particularly relevant. See Appendix B for discussion of specific problems in the documentary records and their implications for some of the subjects not found.

37. See interview with Robert McNeill in 1989, cited in part in Natanson, *Black Image*, 265–67. In addition, there are 365 OEM photographs made in Virginia before April 1942 in the FSA picture file at LCP&P. Of these, 110 were made by John Vachon and Royden Dixon, who were FSA photographers. The rest, some of which are also included in this work, were made by Alfred Palmer, who was not FSA trained. See Palmer's comments also quoted in *Black Image*, 257–58.

PART ONE

1. For a good coverage of the Hoover administration's response to the depression, see Biles, *New Deal for the American People*. Figures based on unemployment rolls tend to underenumeration and therefore do not adequately reflect the actual amount of unemployment that existed. It is likely that as much as a third of the population was, in fact, out of work. But the lack of accurate records for the period accounts for the varying figures offered by different writers.

2. See Himmelberg, *Great Depression*, v; see also Biles, *New Deal for the American People*, 11–12. For further background on a selection of federal relief agencies and programs, see Appendix A.

3. The "Roosevelt Song" was collected by Emory Hamilton, a fieldworker for the VWP folklore program, as it was sung by Mrs. Pearl Potter of Coeburn, Virginia, on 12 July 1939. Hamilton noted on the manuscript, "This sounds like a 1939 version of Casey Jones." UVA/FC. Roosevelt's "flagman" was Vice President John Nance Garner. President Hoover's passion for trout fishing was well known. This indulgence was deliberately used by Virginia officials to entice Hoover into purchasing a fishing camp on the Rapidan River in Madison County and, indirectly, to bring him into the movement to establish the Shenandoah National Park in that area.

4. These ideas were made explicit in Roosevelt's "Fireside Chat" of 14 April 1938. "Franklin D. Roosevelt: Plans For Recovery," quoted in Himmelberg, *Great Depression*, 22.

5. For a discussion of the development of early radio, see Daniel, *Pickin' on Peachtree*, 110–11; Fowler and Crawford, *Border Radio*, 1–6; and Malone, *Country Music USA*, 34–35.

6. Fowler and Crawford, *Border Radio*, and Daniel, *Pickin' on Peachtree*.

7. McElvaine, *Down and Out*, 37. The interview, recorded in September 1981, was taped as part of the editors' ongoing research on the history of families displaced by the creation of the Shenandoah National Park. A work on that topic tentatively titled " 'To Build A Wall around These Mountains' " is in progress. The interview tapes are available at UVA/KBP. This subject probably referred to either "Hoover's Blues" or "The Bonus Blues" written by country musician Buddy Starcher about the Bonus Army in Washington, D.C., in 1932. She thought it had been a Carter Family record, but they did not record either of the above. See Lornell, *Virginia's Blues*, 35–58, and Tribe, *Mountaineer Jamboree*, 80–81.

8. McElvaine, *Down and Out*, 6–7.

9. Gee and Corson, *Statistical Study of Virginia*, 186–88.

10. Campbell, Bair, and Harvey, *Educational Activities*, 48–49. "Questions to Be Asked by Federal Writers' Project Workers Who Are Gathering Life Histories," UVA/MJ. See Mrs. J. L. (Josephine) Wright life history in chapter 2. Life history of Sarah Colleen Powell by Bessie Scales, 1,789 wds., no date given, VSL/AB, box 178.

11. Sarah Colleen Powell told VWP interviewer Scales, "Don't you dare though, put my name in any survey of any kind," and Scales promised not to use her real identity. But the *Hill's Directory* for Danville in the years 1935 and 1937 lists Sarah Colleen Powell as office secretary for the *Register* newspaper (just as was reported in the life history), revealing that Scales did not, in fact, disguise the name in this case.

12. Some ex-slaves were interviewed elsewhere in the state by white VWP workers under the general heading of life history programs. A few of these were included in Perdue, Barden, and Phillips, *Weevils in the Wheat,* for comparison with the extant interviews from the Negro Studies ex-slave interviewing project at Hampton. None of the texts published in that prior work are reprinted here. The text for Aunt Mattie Perndon (in chapter 4) is one of those life history interviews with a former slave that was not previously published.

13. On "life review," or reminiscence, as used in the literature, see Mullen, *Listening to Old Voices,* 16–19. See also Myerhoff, *Remembered Lives,* esp. 101–26, 231–55.

14. See Margaret Wolfe life history in chapter 2. Life history with Mr. Beale [surname omitted by editor] by Mary S. Venable, 2,340 wds., 6pp., 9 January 1939, VSL/AB, box 181. The life history referred to is not included in this work.

15. Monies from the Literary Fund "were apportioned to the counties on the basis of their *white* population and were managed by school commissioners appointed annually by the county court." The definition of a poor or indigent child was usually that of an "unmarried person from seven to twenty-one years of age" and whose parents "by reason of a lack of property, labor or skill [were] not able to defray the expenses" of their education. Virginia legislation in 1846 allowed county citizens to tax themselves in order to set up and support free public schools for all county children, but few areas implemented that option prior to the later mandate requiring it. See Daniel, *Bedford County,* 179. See also Perdue, "Movie Star Woman," 44–52.

16. Social-ethnic study with Charlie Smith by Mary S. Venable, 16 October 1939, VSL/AB, box 181.

17. Overall, the composition of school populations statewide averaged 51 percent females to 49 percent males. U.S. Bureau of the Census, *Fifteenth Census: Population,* vol. 3, table 6, p. 1145.

18. Ibid., tables 7 and 13. The eight counties exceeding 30 percent were Charlotte, Cumberland, Dinwiddie, Greenville, Richmond, Sussex, Patrick, and Lee.

19. Negro economic conditions interview with Ralph and Elizabeth Fitzgerald by Susie R. C. Byrd, 10 pp., legal-size, handwritten ms., rec. 17 December 1938, HU/REL, box 4. F. J. Spencer, "Epidemics and Eubiotics," in Hughes and Leidheiser, *Virginia's Human Resources,* 110–15.

20. This epidemic is referred to as the "Spanish Lady" in Reynolds and Shachtman, *Gilded Leaf,* 100. See David Brown, "Moving like Prairie Fire, Flu from Kansas Took Estimated 30 Million Lives," *Washington Post,* A, 15, Sunday, 15 March 1992. Interview with Lillie R. Vaughn by Bessie A. Scales, 7 pp., legal-size, handwritten ms., 1,843 wds., 19 August 1940, VSL/AB, box 178. From evidence in the interview, Lillie Vaughn was born about 1919.

21. Richard W. Garnett Jr., "Mental Health in Virginia," in Hughes and Leidheiser, *Virginia's Human Resources,* 134–38. Greenhow cited by Barbara L. Bellows in "'My Children, Gentlemen, Are My Own,'" in Fraser, Saunders, and Wakelyn, *Web of Southern Social Relations,* 54.

22. Life history with Icy May Paitzel by Leila Blanche Bess, 6 pp., 1,697 wds., 20 March 1940, VSL/AB, box 184. For discussion of traditional beliefs about prenatal influences or "marking" in various cultures, see Hand, *Magical Medicine,* 59–61. See also Randolph, *Ozark Magic and Folklore,* 196–99, and *Frank C. Brown Collection,* 6:18–23. Items 102 and 103 in Brown refer specifically to the effects of seeing animals die and of children being marked "with some resemblance or feature of the animal seen" (20).

CHAPTER ONE

1. See *Webster's 3rd International Dictionary* for definitions of *infare* and *callithump.* The latter term has origins in eighteenth-century Dorsetshire and Devonshire, England, where it meant "a disturber or disturbance of elections." A few cases of the use of these expressions are given in this work; but there are other life histories, not included here, that also use the terms. Moore cites T. P. Abernethy's *Historical Sketch of the University of Virginia* (1948) as the source of his account of this "calathump" in *Albemarle: Jefferson's County,* 138–41.

2. Robert P. Swierenga, "Agriculture and Rural Life: The New Rural History," in Gardner and Adams, *Ordinary People,* 107. For descriptions of these and other social gatherings, see Paul G. Brewster, "Beliefs and

Customs," in *Frank C. Brown Collection,* 1:243–47; Botkin, *Folk-Say,* 79–85; and Wingfield, *Franklin County,* 49–51. For a description of a slave corn shucking on a plantation in Mecklenburg County, Virginia, about 1838, see Livermore, *Story of My Life.*

3. Burke, *Popular Culture in Early Modern Europe.* In many cases the educated classes shunned their native languages, leaving them to be spoken only by perceived inferiors, such as craftsmen and peasants. Thus Gaelic was abandoned for British English in the Scottish Highlands; Finnish for Swedish in Finland; and Norwegian for Danish in Norway. Burke's book is useful generally, but for his discussion of the withdrawal of the upper classes, see 270–81.

4. See Shapiro, *Appalachia on our Mind,* 6. Cogan, *All-American Girl,* cites information from *Bibliotheca Americana,* 16.

5. Swierenga presents a cogent overview of several different perspectives on rural history and change, including Jensen's behavioral model, Nugent's concept of systemic change and periodization, and Shover's view of the radical transformations of rural life wrought by the technological revolution and agribusiness following World War II. All of these models project different times for the beginnings of American "modern cosmopolitan" culture, and all have merit. But to some extent, all assume a concurrent or uniform process of change that seldom, if ever, exists. The appropriate conditions required for certain kinds of change to take place do not occur everywhere at the same time. Thus even now, hegemony of the modern or postmodern is not seamless and complete: there are still farmers in this country who plow horses and agricultural communities that are not "merely a microcosm of urban mass culture." See Swierenga, "Agriculture and Rural Life," 91–113, esp. 107. See also Samuel S. Hill, "Region and Religion," in Lich, *Regional Studies,* 75–76.

6. Swierenga, "Agriculture and Rural Life."

7. Social-ethnic study with William West by Mary S. Venable, 8 pp., 2,400 wds., rec. 25 April 1939, VSL/AB, box 181.

8. Life history with James Berkley by John W. Garrett, 7 pp., legal-size, handwritten ms., 1,353 wds., rec. 25 June 1940, VSL/AB, box 187. See also Fite, *Cotton Fields No More,* 3.

9. John S. Green Account Book, 1824–1839, Manuscripts Division, Special Collections Department, Alderman Library, University of Virginia, Charlottesville; VWP interview with Fleety Dodson by Margaret Jeffries, undated, UVA/MJ. The specific terms of the findings system varied but normally included a house, garden plot, windfall fruit, a cow to milk, meat, cornmeal, flour, and in later times, some amount of cash.

10. Life history with Charles Smith by Mary S. Venable, 6 pp., rec. 15 August 1939, VSL/AB, box 181. See also preceding discussion of "rituals of local bonding" and its accompanying note (2).

11. Although some interviews by Gertrude Blair in the first few months of 1939 were labeled as social-ethnic studies, the Benjamin Thacker text was submitted as part of the VWP folklore-collecting project. See Informant Information Form for Benjamin Thacker, UVA/FC, box 10. Although the Thackers had lived in Roanoke for twenty years (since about 1919), they were not living at the same location during that entire period. The city directory for 1931 gave their address as 359 Day Avenue SW, Roanoke.

12. See Livermore, *Story of My Life.* See similar description of a corn shucking as given by former slave Uncle John Spencer in Perdue, Barden, and Phillips, *Weevils in the Wheat,* 278. See also Abrahams, *Singing the Master,* esp. 203–305.

13. For analogues of these beliefs collected in North Carolina, see "Popular Beliefs and Superstitions," in *Frank C. Brown Collection,* vol. 7: #7994, #8066, and #8072—"Beans should be planted when the sign is in the Twins." No specific reference was made in this source to corn or potatoes being planted under Gemini, however. #8464 includes a source stating, "Lay a fence rail in the light of the moon, or it will sink in the ground and create a wobbly fence." Randolph, *Ozark Magic and Folklore* reports just the opposite, that neither fence rails nor posts should be put up during the waxing or light period of the moon (41–42). Likewise, the cluster of beliefs in *Brown* regarding cutting wood (#8441, #8444–47) emphasize the reverse of that reported by Benjamin Thacker, namely, #8447—"Pine wood must be cut during light nights or it will be soggy." There is similar mixed belief regarding the best time for butchering one's hogs, but #7697 and #7699 agree with #7707 that "pork produces more grease if hogs are killed when the moon is full." And *Frank C. Brown Collection,* vol. 6, includes #4695, "If you keep black cats at home, you'll never marry" (also #4696 and #4697), and #3802, "If a long-tailed animal should cross your path, you will have good fortune."

14. Puckett discusses the contents of "conjure-balls," which often include needles or pins, along with other

items such as salt, roots, herbs, hair, silver coins, snakes, and insects; see *Folk Beliefs,* 230–31 esp., and 435 for reference to cows dying if one kills a daddy longlegs, or "harvestman," spider. See also *Frank C. Brown Collection,* vol. 7, #5543, for discussion of conjure balls, and also #5545 for the use of needles in conjuration. Both *Brown,* #7611, and Randolph, *Ozark Magic and Folklore,* 48, report the use of daddy longlegs to locate lost cows. One asked the spider to tell the cow's whereabouts and then followed the direction in which the spider crawled or pointed with its leg. See also the use of spider legs in conjure as related by Rev. J. H. Coleman in chapter 4 of this section. Benjamin Thacker's account of Dr. Ding's use of a needle in a ball to find the lost cow brings together several related elements of belief from both African American and Anglo-American traditions.

15. The placing of some object, the "trick" or "charm," in the path to a person's house to cause that individual harm is common in conjuration. But as Benjamin Thacker relates, the belief in such practice could be used effectively by whites to cause Negroes to avoid certain areas. J. A. Tillinghast noted in a similar vein, "Any house . . . known to have a charm . . . in charge of it, is seldom molested by thieves," cited in Puckett, *Folk Beliefs,* 278, and 222, generally on placing the charm. *Frank C. Brown Collection,* vol. 7, #7256, specifies that "if a mockingbird sings all night long, . . . it is a true sign of a great sorrow or trouble that is coming to the family." In the same volume, items #6744–57 suggest that the belief associating dead snakes and rain is quite widespread. See in particular #6751—"If you hang a dead snake in a tree, it will rain."

16. A number of fieldworkers found the tobacco-chewing habits of their subjects repugnant. It is clear from their comments that chewing tobacco was associated with being common or "low class" and was not viewed as acceptable social behavior. But the use of tobacco (and other plants of the genus *Nicotiana*) has long figured in Western folk medicine, where "chewing seems to be the orthodox method of use." It was thought to cure toothache, draw poison from a snakebite, stop bleeding, and help digestion and growth. For the last, chewing tobacco was often recommended for "puny, delicate children who [did] not grow as they should." Walter R. Smith, "Animals and Plants in Oklahoma Folk Cures," in Botkin, *Folk-Say,* 74. See also *Frank C. Brown Collection,* vol. 6, #944 (for boils), #1165 (for colic), #1266 (for cuts), and #2232–2235, #2250–2256 (for insect stings).

17. See Appendix B.

18. Mrs. Adams's prohibition may have derived from a belief similar to the following: "If you keep a hat on your bed, you will have a disappointment." This item was collected by VWP worker Sue K. Gordon from Mildred Jackson of Fredericksburg, Virginia, on 21 October 1939; see UVA/FC, box 2, item #357.

19. It is not altogether clear from Callie Adams StClair's account with which side the family sympathized or if her father actually fought in the Civil War. However, neither the Adamses nor Samuel Thacker, who lived near various Adams family members, owned slaves.

20. The interviewer appears to accept this story of the turkeys in red flannel clothes as factual, but it has all the earmarks of a tall tale. In fact, the motif of making clothes for mistakenly plucked fowl of some description often turns up in the form of a jest. In one example of this, a similarly plucked rooster is observed holding down a hen while attempting to unbutton the fly of his homemade suit. See Burrison, *Storytellers,* 189–90, and Legman, *No Laughing Matter,* 2:596–97. A variant of StClair's story, reported by a Rappahannock County, Virginia, native and raconteur, consists of the initial part of the tale only, without the motif of making clothes for the plucked fowl. In it, turkeys belonging to a woman who lived in a hollow above Sperryville had eaten their fill of a neighboring moonshiner's mash. Thinking they were dead, she had picked the birds and left them in a pile, only to find "her flock of cold, naked, and embarrassed-looking turkeys" at "their accustomed feeding place" the next morning. See Johnson and Johnson, *Rappahannock County,* 254–55.

21. Bedford County was an important site in the early southwestward migration of Quakers from Pennsylvania and other northern states, as well as from other areas within the state of Virginia. Among the latter group, almost 80 percent of those who moved during the 1780s transferred their certificates to the South River and Goose Creek meetings in Bedford County. See Gragg, *Migration in Early America,* 30–31. As Niebuhr states, Methodism later reaped harvests "in the regions first tilled by Quaker missionaries"; see *Social Sources of Denominationalism,* 166–67, 190–97. See also Daniel, *Bedford County,* 142–78, esp. 156–61 and 170, for a discussion of religion in the county in the period 1840–60.

22. At the bottom of the page of text, Blair noted, "Of course, the congregation didn't know anything about the yellow jackets but they soon found out." Jones, *Preacher Joke Book,* 67, relates a variant of this tale from Kentucky with the punchline "I've got love in my heart but hell in my britches!"

23. Garrett contributed a total of 119 items to the WPA-VWP Folklore Collection. The earliest date given on

any of those items was 26 May 1939. But among the folklore texts submitted by Garrett that were dated, the majority were collected in the latter part of 1940 and in 1941. In the life history that follows, the subject's name was given as "Strawsburg" on the title page, but it was used interchangeably with "Strausburg" on the page headings throughout the text.

24. This tall tale may be classified generally as Motif X1761, Absurd disregard of the nature of holes, and is related to Motif X1611.1.15.1*(cb), Wind blows wells inside out; see Baughman, *Type and Motif-Index*, 561, 588.

25. For record sources cited here and in the subsequent paragraph, see Appendix B.

26. There are several discrepancies here between the text and other information that is available. Strausburg states that he and his wife had only one child, a daughter Betty (Mary E. in the census). But both the 1900 and 1910 censuses agree that Martha Strausburg had borne three children, only two of whom were living in 1910. Although this could be an error, the consistency between the two censuses suggests not in this case. Given the age difference between George and Martha, however, it is possible that she had two children by a prior marriage not mentioned in the interview. In addition, their daughter Betty was not living at home with the couple in 1910. By then Betty was about twenty-seven years old, and it would seem likely she was already married, though according to George's account she did not marry until after her mother's death.

27. Driver, "Social Differentiation and Cohesion," 386–87. Rawson, *Candleday Art*, 101, 103–7, esp. 104. The texts with Daniel "Arrit" cited in Rawson's work are in many ways similar to those in the earlier Historic Inventory report by Leila Blanche Bess. Still there is enough additional material in Rawson to suggest that she also interviewed him herself. It is clear from sketches and references to various Alleghany County sites in several of her books that she did have some contact with and knowledge of the area. And *Candleday* is dedicated to "Elva Rachal" of Low Moor, the main seat of the iron industry in the county. This does not preclude the possibility, however, that there was also some mutual contact or relationship between Rawson and Bess.

28. The Fulton Pottery information is presented here in the same format (without cover sheet) in which the original was typed in the Works Progress Administration of Virginia offices in Richmond. With regard to other treatments of Fulton Pottery, it is worth noting that Morton, in his *History of Alleghany County,* 70, gives a bare mention, without name, of pottery works in the Potts Creek area. For more information on George N. Fulton and his pottery site in Botetourt County, see Russ, *The Fincastle Pottery,* 6–10.

29. A narrative about selling ware to a competitor in Blacksburg constitutes the rest of this section of the Historical Inventory report. It was later duplicated in the life history with Arritt and is included therein following, rather than in this format.

30. Virginia Historical Inventory Project, film 509, VSL/HIP. There are thirty microfilm reels of inventory material organized by county; in addition, there is a separate file of the photographs that accompanied some of the inventories in VSL/PC.

31. The remainder of this sentence, composed of Bess's personal and enigmatic musings on the significance of Arritt's chin, has been omitted.

32. Rawson presents a variant of this story and alleges that the competitor was Thomas Waddle of Sugar Run; see *Candleday Art,* 106.

33. A paragraph in which Bess engages in moralizing speculation about Arritt's status as a Christian is omitted here.

34. Robert Weise, "Big Stone Gap and the New South, 1880–1900," in Ayers and Willis, *Edge of the South,* 188. See also the life history of John B. Davidson in chapter 8 for another account of the developing coal fields and towns.

35. Eller, *Miners, Millhands, and Mountaineers,* 76, cited by Weise, "Big Stone Gap," 173.

36. "Narrative of John F. D. Smyth, 1769–1775," cited in Morrison, *Travels in Virginia,* 18.

37. Weise, "Big Stone Gap," 186. U.S. Bureau of the Census, *Fifteenth Census: Population,* vol. 3, pt. 2, "Virginia," table 11, p. 1160. See also life history of John B. Davidson in chapter 8.

38. Speers Ferry is just south of Clinchport in Scott County, Virginia. The C. C. and O. refers to the Carolina, Clinchfield, and Ohio Railroad, formerly the South and Western Railway. See Eller, *Miners, Millhands, and Mountaineers,* 150–52.

39. Duplicated line deleted here.

40. The VWP worker states that the Browns had no children, but the census (see Appendix B) indicates that

Celia had borne a son, who was twenty years old, living at home, and working as a salesman in 1900. He is listed as George Brown's stepson.

41. Lycurgus Drumheller's ledger, or account book, is the property of his great-granddaughter Janet Drumheller. We owe her a special debt of gratitude for allowing us to use it as a source for the additional biographical information included here.

42. In some of his accounts with M. W. Woodson, Lycurgus Drumheller mentions receiving pay in the form of meal or flour from a mill referred to as the "Faber Mill." However, "the only mill referred to as Woodson's Mill was up the Rockfish River near Rockfish Depot," according to Drumheller's grandson. He adds that it had been washed away in a flood by at least 1920 or earlier, though the logs from its dam may have remained there on the riverbank until as recently as 1969. Janet Drumheller, letter to editors, 25 June 1992. There appears to be another mill that has more recently been identified by some as a Woodson's Mill; it is still standing and operating elsewhere in Nelson County.

43. It is interesting to compare his expenditures with those of John Gregory of Franklin County, who in 1940 estimated that his family spent fifty dollars per year for coffee, sugar, gas for the car, and other necessities; see chapter 5.

44. Form B, Personal History of Informant, filled in by Gertrude Blair, uva/fc, "Games" folder. See also Appendix B.

45. Felldin, *Index to the 1820 Census of Virginia*, indicates two William Drumhellers residing in Albemarle County, Virginia. It also reports two Jacobs, a George and George Sr., and an Adam Drumheller in the same county; these are the only Drumhellers listed for Virginia in that period. The single entry from John Drumheller's store account remaining in the old ledger points to a possible inconsistency in the text: it would appear that either John Drumheller *could* read and write or that some other family member kept his accounts for him.

46. White reports in *American Negro Folk-Songs*, 178, that this verse was common in pre–Civil War minstrel songbooks as far back at least as 1846. The town named is usually Lynchburg, but occasionally it is Richmond or Vicksburg.

47. The suggestion to "let the person interviewed ramble on" is attributed here by Blair to the "manual on Folklore." But it seems to refer to the statement "You should put at ease the person with whom you are talking and let him ramble on," which is taken from the two-page form letter of instructions for the Social-Ethnic Studies project sent by state director Eudora Ramsay Richardson to vwp fieldworkers on various dates in November 1938. Several copies of these instructions survive in manuscript materials at the University of Virginia and Hampton University.

The reference, as cited or as given by Richardson, does not appear in the FWP's *Supplementary Instructions to the American Guide Manual, Manual for Folklore Studies*, revised in August 1938 by Benjamin Botkin, national folklore consultant and, later, FWP national folklore editor. Blair's parenthetical comment offers some additional evidence for the argument that the "official" FWP folklore manual by Botkin was *not* generally distributed to vwp workers.

48. Blair reports that Drumheller went to Ohio after he had been employed at the soapstone quarry at Schuyler, Virginia, but her chronology is confused. Given his report that the verse from "Jenny" was written about 1871 and that he returned from Ohio to marry his childhood sweetheart (in 1873), along with the fact that he was in the Nelson County census in 1870 (see Appendix B), Drumheller must have gone to Ohio in the period between 1870 and 1873—about three years. As to the Virginia Soap Stone Company, Drumheller's ledger indicates that he worked framing company houses for owner J. W. Foster in November and December 1897; that he spent one day putting in windows for the same in November 1898; and that he did day work for the company from 17 July through 2 November 1899.

49. The portion of Drumheller's interview beginning with this line and continuing through the description of how to play "London Bridge" was included in vwp, *Roanoke: Story of County and City*, 126–27.

50. See Botkin, *American Play-Party Song*, 225, 226. Botkin states that this song is "based on a Jacobite song," and he gives two versions plus bibliography.

51. Newell, in *Games and Songs of American Children*, 155–58, 215–21, states that this game, known under a variety of names including "Hawk and Chickens," is centuries old, widespread over most of Europe from Russia to Italy, and common also in America.

52. "London Bridge" is an ancient game thought to have its origin in rituals of human sacrifice in which vic-

tims were chosen whose bodies were to be buried beneath the foundations of bridges and other structures. See Gomme, *Traditional Games,* 1:333–50.

53. A leather-backed commonplace book stuck between the pages of the old ledger contained the following note about his Odd Fellow membership: "On Saturday night August 11/96 L. Drumheller joined Rockfish Lodge #198 Transferred from Schuyler lodge #233."

54. In several pages from a manuscript deposited among her papers, Essie Smith discussed the relationship between these individuals and other families in the general area. See "History of Franklin County, Virginia — Unfinished Manuscript and Notes," by Essie Wade Smith, reproduced by the Franklin County Bicentennial Commission, 1977, in the Franklin County Historical Society's Gertrude C. Mann Archives, Stanley Library, Rocky Mount, Virginia. See also Early, *Campbell Chronicles,* 26–31, 373–74.

55. The 1910 census (see Appendix B) indicated that Mary C. Smith had borne only three children, who were not all identified though all were living then. Since miscarriages or children that had died were often not reported, the figure for the total number of children borne is quite likely wrong. But Smith's comment that he had no grandchildren (unless he really was referring only to *males* to carry on his name) is strange given that Cabell and Essie Wade Smith did have a daughter, Mary C., living with them in Smith's household in 1910. The will and list of heirs for Essie Smith in 1963 in Franklin County name several nieces and granddaughters, at least one of whom was certainly a descendant of the Smith family line.

56. This interview is titled "A Calvinist of the Old School."

57. Early, *Campbell Chronicles,* 25, 31–33, 358–65.

58. This and subsequent information on these families is from the U.S. census records of 1830 through 1910 for Franklin and Roanoke Counties and is supplemented by Wingfield, *Pioneer Families of Franklin County* and *Marriage Bonds of Franklin County.* See Appendix B.

59. See biography of Henry Mauze Darnall in Jack and Jacobs, *History of Roanoke County,* 183. See also Appendix B.

60. See Jack and Jacobs, *History of Roanoke County,* and also Appendix B.

61. See Samuel P. Hays, "Politics and Social History," in Gardner and Adams, *Ordinary People,* 170–71.

62. When she was interviewed in 1939, Mrs. Price lived on Chestnut Street in Salem, Virginia. The interview with her was copied from a typescript of "The Folk of Roanoke," by Gertrude Blair of Roanoke, Virginia, 1940, compiled under the direction of the Virginia Writers' Project, Eudora Ramsey Richardson, state supervisor, WPA.

Thirty-four of the forty interviews in "The Folk of Roanoke" are attributed to the FWP's Social-Ethnic Studies program and are included in the VSL/AB holdings. Of the six other interviews in the typescript, a duplicate of the Nannie Isabel Webb Price text is in the UVA/FC, #1547, item #1544. The five interviews remaining seem to be extant only in the RPL typescript and in copies made therefrom for working files in UVA/KBP.

CHAPTER TWO

1. Matthews, *Good and Mad Women,* 17.

2. It should be pointed out that this latter characteristic was also typical of some male project workers, as witness John W. Garrett, who interviewed his father, a brother, a sister, and a future son-in-law, as well as at least nine other persons related to him by marriage.

3. This quote (emphasis added) is from the first youth study with Virginia ———— by Mary S. Venable, 8 pp., 2,996 wds., 19 July 1940; a second study with the same individual is 5 pp., 25 July 1940; VSL/AB, box 182 for both. The surname in this case has been omitted by the editors. In the life histories written by Venable, her judgments about spouse abuse were always severe. In several of those instances she referred to men as "tyrants," and she was clearly not at all hesitant to refer such a case to the Klan for action. Accounts of Klan behavior, similar to that which she reported, have been collected as well in some of the areas that became part of the Shenandoah National Park in the 1930s. In those reports, the abusive husband was given a warning (such as was described here), and if the advice was not heeded, it was followed up with a severe beating or "thumping" of the offender's body.

4. The Ku Klux Klan's operation with regard to black men and women was usually of a different order, see Dilcie Gum in chapter 4 for contrast. An ex-slave interview from South Carolina offers a humorous case of inversion, in terms of both race and gender, of the Klan's activities. In that instance, a group of black women

(including the victimized wife) masked their identity by wearing the robed and gloved garb of Klansmen, mimicked their behavior, and gave the abusive husband "a most terrible whaling, beat him very badly with rocks and sticks." See Fry, *Night Riders*, 165.

5. Youth study with Virginia ———, cited in n. 3 above. Matthews, *Good and Mad Women*, 15–16. See Barbara Welter, "The Cult of True Womanhood: 1820–1860," reprinted in idem, *Dimity Convictions*, 21, for her discussion of the "four cardinal virtues" of "true womanhood": "piety, purity, submissiveness and domesticity"; see also Cogan, *All-American Girl*, especially the introduction, 3–26, and Beverly J. Stoeltje, "'A Helpmate for Man Indeed': The Image of the Frontier Woman," in Farrer, *Women and Folklore*, 30–38. The supposedly conflicting ideals posed by Welter and Cogan of "true" or "real" womanhood, based on their respective readings and content analysis of nineteenth-century periodical literature, more likely reflect the range of values assumed to be held by different middle-class American women between 1840 and 1880. It is far more problematic, however, to determine the extent to which the literature itself mirrored reality or shaped it, and for whom.

6. "The Mother of a Family," life history with Mrs. Jo (Joseph) Morris by Anne Worrell, 5 pp., 1,450 wds., 3 April 1939, VSL/AB, box 182. In the context of this work it is doubtful that Worrell intended any pun or that she seriously contemplated the implications of using "Lot's wife" to connote length of time or antiquity in conjunction with "salt of the earth."

7. Social-ethnic study with Mrs. Forest E. ——— by Mary S. Venable, 4 pp., 1,477 wds., rec. 30 June 1939, VSL/AB, box 181. Surname omitted by editors. See also Kate Beale in chapter 9 and Mrs. J. L. (Josephine) Wright in this chapter for comments on cross-generational changes. Project worker Mary S. Venable makes a number of references linking speed with lifestyle changes, but she is not alone in making such observations.

8. See the texts for Margaret Wolfe and Lizzie (Sallie Newman) Gibson in this chapter.

9. Life history with Mrs. Thomas ——— by Russell Carpenter, 4 pp., 1 June 1939, VSL/AB, box 191. Social-ethnic study with Maggie Jane ——— by Gertrude Blair, 4 pp., 1,288 wds., rec. 10 April 1939, VSL/AB, box 186. Surnames omitted by editors.

10. See urban black youth study with Anna Watts (a pseudonym used by the editors) in chapter 4. For similar statements from a white, rural farm woman, see Mrs. J. L. (Josephine) Wright in this chapter. See also Faye Ginsburg, "Dissonance and Harmony: The Symbolic Function of Abortion in Activists' Life Stories," in Barbre et al., *Interpreting Women's Lives*, 59–84.

11. Hagood, *Mothers of the South*, 56. Hagood's work was first published in 1939, but her findings of lower divorce rates among rural farm families relative to nonfarm or urban families are still valid. See Linda Bescher-Donnelly and Leslie Whitener Smith, "The Changing Roles and Status of Rural Women," in Coward and Smith, *Family in Rural Society*, 168. Life history of Paulina Persinger-Crowder by Leila Blanche Bess, 7 pp., 7 March 1940, VSL/AB, box 184, and life history of Mrs. Jo (Joseph) Morris by Anne Worrell, cited in n. 6 above.

12. This is from a social-ethnic study by Leila Blanche Bess titled "Julia Tinsley Breaks up Housekeeping," 4 pp., 1,672 wds., rec. 19 December 1938, VSL/AB, box 183.

13. See U.S. Bureau of the Census, *Fifteenth Census: Population*, vol. 3, tables 10 and 20, and vol. 5, chap. 2, table 13. In 1930 there were ninety-five black and ninety-seven white women employed in planer mills or sawmills in Virginia. It is significant, however, that a total of only 314 black and white women were reported in that category (which also included box factories) in the entire United States. In an unpublished paper, "Folk Narratives of Spotsylvania County," Black and Mackay collected stories about a white woman (in her sixties in 1972) who worked in a sawmill and was subjected to community speculation as to whether she was truly a female, a male, or a hermaphrodite. It was told that several men plotted to take her hunting in the woods for the purpose of determining her gender. When she discovered their intent, she beat them up and left them all, there in the woods, still ignorant. Local talk about her included reference to the fact that "she" had several "pretty" sisters, which made her appearance and behavior even greater cause for gossip and invidious comparison. Although the social distinction of women as being "other than men" is universal, gender alone does not determine femininity or ideals concerning appropriate gender behavior. For discussion of some of these issues, see introductions to Matthews, *Good and Mad Women* and Barbre et al., *Interpreting Women's Lives*. See also Joyce, *A Woman's Place*, 3–5, 211–36, and the special issue of the *Journal of American Folklore* 88, no. 347 (January–March 1975), since reissued as Farrar, *Women and Folklore*, especially the introduction by Farrer, vii–xxi.

14. Negro economic conditions interview with Mrs. Allie Jones by Susie R. C. Byrd, 3 pp., legal-size, handwritten ms., rec. 27 February 1939, HU/REL, box 5. Such evaluations underscore Jacqueline Jones's critique that

black females "endured a degree and type of workplace exploitation for which the mere fact of having a job could not compensate." Jones, *Labor of Love,* 199.

15. Agnew Hall at Virginia Polytechnic Institute is named for Ella Agnew, who was also the country's first home demonstration agent. See Heinemann, *Depression and New Deal,* 74–75. The Virginia division of the FERA—VERA—preceded, overlapped with, and had the same director as the state WPA. However, VWP interview subjects referred to Lee Park as a WPA-, rather than a VERA-, sponsored project. Several African American women spoke in their VWP interviews of the inequitable and discriminatory work conditions they and others experienced working on the Lee Park project. See, for instance, Mrs. Allie Jones interview, cited in n. 14, and Mrs. Catherine Johnson in chapter 4. For a case study of federal New Deal jobs programs in Baltimore, Maryland, and a discussion of gender roles and job discrimination (particularly with regard to African American women) in those programs, see Argersinger, *Toward A New Deal,* 72–79.

16. See social-ethnic study with Julia Keesee (Carwile) in this chapter.

17. See life history with Kate Beale by Mary S. Venable in chapter 9. The song by Nancy Dixon is recorded on the album *Babies in the Mill,* Testament Records, T3301.

18. See text for Nannie Isabel Webb Price in the preceding chapter; see also Appendix B. In a telephone conversation with Charles L. Perdue Jr. on 8 June 1993, Margaret Wolfe Lee gave additional information about her life and confirmed the names of family members and of others interviewed by Leila Blanche Bess. She also remembered Bess but did not recall being interviewed by her for the Writers' Project.

19. The Covington Silk Mill, which was built in 1921 by the Schwarzenbach-Huber Company, had been sold to Burlington Mills by the time of Wolfe's VWP interview. However, Roy Fix's wife, Myrtle (in chapter 9), worked in the same silk mill under its earlier ownership.

20. The Potts Creek mail carrier with whom Margaret Wolfe rode was John E. Bess; see his life history in the following chapter and also in chapter 5.

21. This is a reference to land in Alleghany County taken by the U.S. Forest Service for the George Washington National Forest.

22. Based only on the life history, it at first seemed that "Howe" might be Lizzie Gibson's maiden name. Further research showed that the name Howe was not commonly found in Patrick County, but the surname "Howell" *did* occur there with some frequency. The fact that Noah L. Gibson was heard and recorded as "Noel" in the 1920 Bedford County census (see Appendix B) suggested the additional possibility that a similar confusion—intended or otherwise—might have occurred between the surnames Howe and Howell. As it turned out, Howell was *not* Lizzie (actually Sally) Gibson's surname; but it *was* that of her paternal grandmother, Susan J. Howell Newman.

23. See Appendix B. The former Gibson home is located in a busy working-class neighborhood composed of houses that appear to date from the World War II era.

24. "Fairy stone" or "fairy crosses" are names given to naturally occurring intergrown crystals—sometimes twinned in the shape of an *X* or of a Greek (or Roman) cross—of the mineral staurolite, which is found in abundance "in the Piedmont counties not far from the Blue Ridge, particularly in Grayson and Patrick counties." Humbert et al., *Virginia: Economic and Civic,* 114.

25. Sally Newman Gibson was *not* the "baby of the family"; in fact, she was the eldest daughter of Elijah and Jettie Newman. With regard to her parents' education, the 1880 census shows Elijah Newman attending school, and the 1910 and 1920 censuses (see Appendix B) agree that both Elijah Newman and his wife, Jettie R., could read and write (although the latter information was not included in the appendix because of space limitations).

26. Since Sallie Newman was the oldest daughter in her family, the "oldest" of her younger sisters would have been Myrtle R., who would have been no more than thirty years old, not fifty, at the time of the VWP interview.

27. Noah's father, Daniel C. Gibson, and stepmother, the widow Ocie Anna Trout, did buy a farm on Goose Creek, north of Montvale near Thaxton in July 1930. But that property was left, at the deaths of Ocie in 1954 and Daniel in 1959, to the stepchildren. The "oldest boy" referred to in the text is likely the eldest stepson in this case, since Noah is the oldest son otherwise. For the above, see Deed Book 159-219, 221, and Will Books 62-127 and 65-361, Bedford County Courthouse.

28. A rewrite of this life history by Richmond editor Gordon Thornton is dated 26 May 1939 and titled "Dutch Colonial"; see VSL/AB, box 180, 7 pp., 2,366 wds. Another revised version as above, but 7 pp., 2,550 wds. long, is in VSL/AB, box 191. Both of these rewrites vary significantly from the text included here. For instance, all references to Patrick County (and the fact that Sallie Gibson was born there), which allowed an informed guess about

the name "Howell" and suggested further areas for investigation and verification, were omitted from the rewritten versions. Most of the variation in these texts, however, resulted not from omission but from the addition of material, such as the discussion of preparing foods such as "White Creasy Beans" or of the use of a "stick plow" by Grandfather "Howe." The rewrites are the more insidious, however, in that they also include alleged bits of dialogue or interaction, such as a supposed conversation between "Lizzie" and her mother as the latter was dying (it is hinted, of tuberculosis); a description of the breakup of the family as a result of her father not caring "a mite" for anything following his wife's death; and the comment that he supposedly told the boys who were going off to work in the coal mines "not to worry none how to git back [home] if they left." All of the above-described additions appear to have been introduced and completely fabricated by the editor.

29. Miss Crane is identified in the textual material accompanying Collier's photographs. The other information is from Deed Books 106, 107, and 114, Prince William County Courthouse. See also the discussion in "Portraits of Peasantry or Pastures of Plenty?" in chapter 5.

30. From the records, it is clear that Jenny Lumpkins died sometime after the 1920 census; see Appendix B.

31. See reference to "Aunt Viney" in Perdue, *Pigsfoot Jelly,* 63. See also Appendix B.

32. This prologue to the interview is apparently based on a conversation with the doctor's wife (the woman witness to the "near tragedy"), on Smith's own knowledge, or on local gossip about the event. It sets a dramatic scene in a clearly different time frame and place from the interview with Letitia, a fact recognized by the separation indicated in the text.

33. There are some important, and unreconciled, differences here between statements in the text and supplemental information from other records; see Appendix B. The marriage record in 1930 for Sam Lumpkins to Letitia gives her age as eighteen and his as seventeen. The census indicates she was four years old in 1920 and thus would have been fourteen when they married, consistent with the age given in the text. However, if Sam was eight months old in 1900 as the census shows, he was considerably older when they married—over thirty, rather than nineteen (as given in the text) or seventeen (as stated above). In addition, the census does not indicate that Letitia had a brother, "older" or otherwise, in 1920. It is possible that her mother, Jenny, died giving birth to a son sometime after that date, but that is mere speculation at this point. One must wonder, moreover, at the seeming inconsistency between the Obe Lumpkins presented in the census in 1920 as owning a farm and working as a laborer on the public highway, and the man crippled by scrofula, who "never was no hand for steady work," portrayed in the text. At the very least, it calls for a cautionary note.

34. The children's names as given in the obituary were Edna (Elsie in the text), Mildred, Harriett, Mary C., and Melvin. It also gave their address as 411 Owens Street and that of the elder Smith as 1502 A Street, Portsmouth. The elder Smith's father, Theodore, a barber in Portsmouth in 1880, was born in Prussia in about 1831; his wife Christiana was born in Hesse-Darmstadt, Germany in 1834. For census and newspaper records, see Appendix B.

35. At the end of the interview text, VWP worker Sarah Moore inserted a parenthetical aside, "Mrs. Smith enjoys talking and speaks awfully loud," which suggests the possibility that Mrs. Smith may also have been somewhat deaf. However, this statement was intrusive and has been removed by the editors to this note for the sake of readability and to strengthen the text's ending.

36. See VWP, *Negro in Virginia,* 143, and Perdue, Barden, and Phillips, *Weevils in the Wheat,* 92–96. See also Appendix B.

37. See U.S. Bureau of the Census, *Fifteenth Census: Population,* vol. 3, pt. 2, table 20, p. 1186, and vol. 5, table 17, p. 110. There were 3,109 African American women in the labor force in Petersburg City at the time of the 1930 census.

38. There are a number of possible explanations for Geneva Thompson's absence in the directory without necessarily denying her physical presence. She could have married again and David Moore was her husband—or a son-in-law. In either case, she might have been living in Moore's household or in that of her mother at the back of the house. A much more speculative suggestion is that Moore was a kinsman of Minnie Fowlkes, who in the ex-slave interview was referred to at one point as "Miss Moore." Perdue, Barden, and Phillips, *Weevils in the Wheat,* 96. But the fact that in 1943 Minnie Fowlkes was again living at the location at 459 [1459] E. Byrne, where she was when Byrd interviewed her in 1937, suggests a more disturbing possibility: that she had moved into the back of the house at 12 E. Byrne to care for an ailing Geneva and possibly returned to her own home after her daughter had died. No death records for Geneva Thompson, in that period or otherwise, were found in the Petersburg courthouse, but that does not preclude the last explanation.

39. See Appendix B. It can be seen from the children listed in the censuses that Geneva (Nola) was close to, if not, the youngest child of Thomas and Minnie Fowlkes. In addition, none of the names of her siblings given in the text match those in the census records. It is not characteristic of Susie R. C. Byrd to change the names of the people she interviewed, so it is assumed these alterations were made by editors at Hampton or in Richmond. Geneva's statement that her mother lost four children in infancy is in general agreement with the testimony of Minnie Folkes in 1937 that she had eleven children but four were dead. See Perdue, Barden, and Phillips, *Weevils in the Wheat,* 96. However, even allowing for age errors in the census, it is likely that there were two sons named Arthur in the family, with the younger one named for the eldest son, who died as a young adult.

40. Thomas Fowlkes worked as a laborer in a sawmill prior to his death. Afterward, his widow, Minnie, may simply have taken his place on the job. Note that several of his small children, including four-year-old Geneva, also worked as laborers in the sawmill in 1910. See Appendix B.

41. See Appendix B for census and other vital records cited in this and subsequent paragraphs of this headnote.

42. See *Folklore and Folklife in Virginia* 4 (1988): 15, for a photograph of Charles V. Keesee's brother, Abner Keesee, from whom Virginia Folklore Society members collected ballads in 1932.

43. There is a some apparent confusion regarding the Franklin graves mentioned by Julia. One grave was probably that of Major Thomas Franklin, *not* Henry. Jane Campbell, of the other marked grave, was a granddaughter of Major Thomas and Letitia Franklin. It was their son, Henry, who was still alive in 1850 and was the father of Joanna, the "infidel," referred to in the following paragraph. See Will Books 9-30 and 13-118, Campbell County Courthouse; see also U.S. Census Manuscripts, Virginia, Campbell County, 1850, household nos. 1162, 1164, and 1165, p. 207.

44. In 1900 George W. Wheeler, his wife, Margaret, and their six children were listed in the second household (#82-82) following the Charles V. Keesee family in the census for the Rustburg District, Campbell County.

45. In the 1910 census for Rustburg District, Campbell County, John L. Dickey, seventy-one, and his wife, Elvira L. (Akers) Dickey, sixty-six, were listed in household #12-12. The Dickeys had been married for twenty-two years and indicated they had never had any children. Charles V. Keesee's older brother, George A., and his family lived fairly close to the Dickeys in household #37-37, whereas Charles and his family were located in household #302-302. The differences in the numerical listings for family households give a rough indication of the relative location or (depending on population density) an approximate distance between specific family groupings. The above arrangement of families would certainly seem to be consistent with and supportive of the circumstances described in the text.

46. Between 28 February and 4 March 1938, the *Los Angeles Times* reported an estimated 144 persons dead or missing and $65 million in damages as the result of a massive Pacific coast storm system that brought heavy snows in the mountains, gale-force winds on the coast, and 4.40 inches of rain in three days to the city and surrounding counties. New Deal flood-control projects were being planned for the Los Angeles area, but unfortunately they had not yet begun to be implemented. And in environs highly susceptible to flash flooding, the stalled storm and ongoing rain caused a disaster of major proportions for its time. Coverage of the flood and its aftermath commanded much of the reportage in the *Times* for March 1938 — until attention was diverted by Hitler's occupation of Austria. See also the comment in the preface to this work.

47. The history of the "studio" that was then so well known that it was not considered worthwhile to recount is, at this time, more difficult to recover. In a telephone conversation on 23 July 1993, Robert Stovall, the son of Virginia artist Queena Stovall, recalled that the business was started (possibly in the early 1920s) by two sisters and that it was located in a private residence — a beautiful old home on Church Street near the armory — now restored and occupied by government offices. He offered that "it was a tough go for those ladies" and "sometimes [they] couldn't make the payroll," which he knew for a fact because at least one or two of his sisters had worked for them. Stovall's sister, Mrs. Judy Fairfax, later added that the business was begun by a Mrs. Thornhill and her spinster sister, Miss Mamie Rohr, whom she remembered as "the smart one" and the bigger of the two women. She also agreed that it was always Miss Rohr who came around and announced that the women would have to wait for their pay because the company had not been paid for their orders, even though they made very fine bags (which did use eyelet materials from Madeira, Spain) and sold to Bloomingdale's and other "big accounts." Mrs. Fairfax did not know when the company began or how long it continued in operation; however, she did remember Julia Keesee Carwile. Julia, she said, was "older than herself" and worked upstairs "in the plant itself,"

whereas she worked downstairs and part-time in the summers only, packing bags in boxes and sending them out to fill orders. However, she recalled Julia Carwile as "a real sweet person."

48. The last sentence in the paragraph seems to hint that "piece work" was done, outside the plant and outside regular working hours, under conditions aimed at getting around NRA restrictions. Mrs. Fairfax (see n. 47, also) reported that she made about six dollars a week. But she also hinted that there was a difference in status between the women who worked in the plant upstairs, doing the sewing and manufacturing of the bags, and those who worked in the offices downstairs, doing essentially clerical work. Whether it was the spatial or social distance between them, there was apparently not much interaction between some of the groups of women workers. Mrs. Fairfax noted also that Julia Carwile stood out and was not like most of the women who worked "upstairs."

49. The Virginia Art Goods Studios, here referred to by the abbreviated name "Virginia Arts," is not in any way related to the present-day Lynchburg business, Virginia Arts, with which the formerly mentioned Mr. Robert Stovall is associated.

50. This interview is identified as a social-ethnic study.

51. Slaughter, *St. Mark's Parish,* 122. See also Appendix B.

52. Fleury, "Emily Summers Palmer Stearns," 13, UVA/KBP.

CHAPTER THREE

1. Matthews, *Good and Mad Women,* 18. In 1977 Lawrence Levine cataloged the need for a more encompassing social history in *Black Culture,* x. By 1983 Peter Stearns observed that the new social history, focused on "ordinary people, rather than the elite," had brought "a rapid advance in historical knowledge of the working class, of blacks and ethnic groups, of women." Note that he does not mention men apart from those presumably included under the categories of "working class," "blacks," or ethnics. See Peter N. Stearns, "The New Social History: An Overview," in Gardner and Adams, *Ordinary People,* 4–5. In the same volume, Elizabeth H. Pleck, in "Women's History: Gender as a Category of Historical Analysis," extended the critique to *include* the new social history, stating that "the great promise of a democratized history was never achieved when it came to women. . . . *Social history too often turned out to be the history of the common man in a man-made world*" (53; emphasis added). See also Pleck and Pleck, *American Man,* esp. 1–5. But Robert J. Samuelson in an editorial titled "I Love the Census" noted that the Census Bureau estimated that "the population was undercounted by 1.4 percent" in 1980 "and that blacks and Hispanics were undercounted by 5 to 6 percent." In general, the undercount was composed largely of men in these racial/ethnic or lower socioeconomic categories. *Washington Post,* 4 April 1990.

2. Barbre et al., *Interpreting Women's Lives,* 4–5. It should be noted here that this group uses the term *personal narratives* to include "biography, autobiography, life history . . . diaries, journals, and letters."

3. U.S. Bureau of the Census, *Fifteenth Census: Population,* vol. 5, tables 10–11, pp. 102–3, and tables 15–16, pp. 216–27. In contrast to men's labor force participation, little more than 15 percent of the total number of females above ten years old were gainfully employed. At the peak of their labor force participation between the ages of eighteen through twenty-nine, the percentage of women working at each age level ranged from 28 to 35 percent. This number declined steadily until only about 10 percent of all women aged seventy to seventy-four and 7 percent over seventy-five were still employed.

Pointing out that work was man's most significant gender-related experience in 1930 is not intended to deny the importance of family life to males. We do intend it to suggest, however, that men's personal narratives about work correspond to those by women about their roles as wives and homemakers; that each focuses on that part of their gender experience that occupies—or is normatively expected to occupy—the larger portion of their lives; and that such narratives are thus equally marked as gender specific. The last becomes most apparent when the boundaries of occupational roles are crossed, such as in the case of the female sawmill worker (see chapter 2 and n. 13 there) or the male WPA worker who thought that social surveys and life history interviewing were woman's work (as discussed in the introductory material to Part II and n. 18 there).

For other discussions of men's personal narratives and the complex relationships between work and identity that are expressed therein, see Lloyd and Mullen, *Lake Erie Fishermen,* esp. 161–73; McCarl, *District of Columbia Fire Fighters' Project;* and Santino, *Miles of Smiles.*

4. See the life history with John Lee Wright in this chapter. He is the husband of Josephine Wright, whose life history is included in chapter 2.

5. See Labov and Waletzky, "Narrative Analysis: Oral Versions of Personal Experience," in Helm, *Essays on the Verbal and Visual Arts,* 12–44. Although this personal narrative was written down by the interviewer, it follows the form of the oral narratives elicited by Labov and Waletzky when they asked subjects, "Were you ever in a situation where you were in serious danger of being killed?"

6. See Joseph H. Pleck, "Men's Power with Women, Other Men, and Society: A Men's Movement Analysis," in Pleck and Pleck, *American Man,* 417–33, esp. 423–24.

7. Life history with Elbert Lee Byer by Leila Blanche Bess, 13 pp., 3,827 wds., rec. 22 April 1940, VSL/AB, box 184. See also Lloyd and Mullen, *Lake Erie Fishermen,* 173.

8. See Elbert Lee Byer interview cited in n. 7.

9. Life history with A. L. Parrish by Maude R. Chandler, 9 pp., legal-size, handwritten ms., 1,446 wds., rec. 12 August 1940, VSL/AB, box 189. Emphasis in quote added by editors.

10. Thompson, *Voice of the Past,* 259–60. "Henry Cowles Comes Back to the Soil," life history with Henry Cowles (Crowder) by Leila Blanche Bess, 6 pp., 1,895 wds., rec. 21 March 1939, VSL/AB, box 185. Henry Cowles was a pseudonym used by Bess for the son of Thomas and Paulina Persinger Crowder. For a comment on divorce from Bess's life history with Paulina Crowder, see the introductory text in the preceding chapter. "Extract wood" is a reference to various types of wood, such as hemlock, chestnut, and chestnut oak, that were sources of tannic acid for use in tanneries prior to the development of synthetic chemical tanning agents.

11. Henry Cowles (Crowder) interview cited in n. 10.

12. Thompson, *Voice of the Past.*

13. Social-ethnic study with Edward ("Ned") H—— by Mary S. Venable, 19 pp., 5,670 wds., rec. 27 March 1939, VSL/AB, box 181. Emphasis added by the editors. Although Venable gave only an initial for the surname of this fifty-six-year-old subject, research has tentatively identified him as Edward Harnsberger, who was living in Jenkins, Kentucky, when his father, Robert M., died in 1919. Based on that evidence, then "Ned's" grandfather was George Harnsberger, who was forty-nine and lived in Fishersville in 1870. See Deed Book 198-69 and Muster Roll Book, Augusta County Courthouse; see also U.S. Census Manuscripts, Virginia, Augusta County, p. 478.

14. See Edward ("Ned") H—— (Harnsberger) interview cited in n. 13. See also another photograph by FSA photographer Marion Post-Wolcott of hog butchering (fig. 3-9). Although a lone woman is cutting up the meat by herself and away from other activities, this photograph still demonstrates the obvious—that hog butchering is not exclusively men's work, despite Harnsberger's perception and memory of it as such. In general, domestic hog butchering involves a division of labor between both males and females and assigns different parts of the process—in part but not altogether—on the basis of gender attributes, such as physical strength.

15. Matthews, *Good and Mad Women,* 17.

16. Social-ethnic study titled "A Visit to Rocky Point Farm" [John Lee Wright] by Leila Blanche Bess, 8 pp., 1,877 wds., rec. 20 February 1939, VSL/AB, box 185.

17. "Holy Roller" is a derogatory term—usually used in reference to Pentecostal/Holiness church members—that arose from descriptions of religious fervor exhibited in frenzied body movement and shouting.

18. See chapter 1 of this section for Daniel F. Arritt life history. See also Morton, *History of Alleghany County,* 161. For additional information from the life history of John E. Bess ("A Land Owner Speaks His Mind on Share Croppers"), see chapter 5. See also Appendix B.

19. See Appendix B. See also social-ethnic study with Nelda Reid Bess (daughter of John E. Bess) by Leila Blanche Bess, 6 pp., 1,451 wds., rec. 9 October 1939, VSL/AB, box 185.

20. The tenant referred to here is not the man who is the subject of John Bess's tirade against sharecroppers in chapter 5. This tenant and "right good fellow" (identified by yet another VWP life history) was Joseph Knight Tucker, the son of Charles Tucker. Charles Tucker's life history follows later in this chapter.

21. John E. Bess was the interviewer's brother; see Appendix B.

22. The date of this accident is not known; however, Susie Garrett died in 1935 leaving the widower John W. Garrett with three small children—all girls. Annie Broyhill Garrett to Marvin T. Broyhill III, undated, personal files. Copy sent to editors courtesy of Marvin T. Broyhill III on 28 May 1990, in response to queries about Marvin Broyhill Sr., whose life history follows in this chapter. For several years before the Broyhill communication, we had considered that VWP worker John William Garrett might be the son John mentioned in Arthur Garrett's text.

It was already clear from internal clues in the texts that Arthur and Jimmie Garrett were father and son. Further family connections between the Garretts and others with surnames such as Crocker, Crews, Bryant, Word, Noble, and Broyhill progressively became apparent through subsequent research, comparative analysis, and correspondence. See Appendix B for additional biographical data on John William Garrett and other records for Arthur Watson Garrett.

23. Life history with Hester Crocker by John W. Garrett, 8 pp., legal-size, handwritten ms., 1,658 wds., rec. 19 February 1940, VSL/AB, box 188. Hester met Albert L. Crocker of Rocky Mount, Edgecombe County, North Carolina, when she worked as a classifier and he was a spinner in the silk mill in Hopewell. Crocker had lost his job at the silk mill and had decided to move the family to his father's farm after the second baby was born. He left Hester with her parents and had gone in advance to make arrangements in Rocky Mount. While there, a dispute between his father and a cousin escalated into a shooting incident, in which the latter wounded the father and killed Allie Crocker, just a week after his daughter was born.

24. Life history with Hester Crocker, cited in n. 23. See also information from Richmond city directories in Appendix B.

25. There is a discrepancy between Garrett's report of Hester and her family living with him and Emma and that reported by John Garrett in the Hester Crocker interview. Although the Crockers lived (and boarded for five dollars a week) with the elder Garretts for the first year of their marriage, they afterward lived and both worked in Richmond for some period of time before their first child was born. And Allie brought Hester "back to [her] mothers to stay" when he left for North Carolina about two weeks before the second daughter was born. But it does not appear that all four members of the Crocker family ever lived all together at one time with the Garretts.

26. In the Richmond city directories for 1941 to 1943, Arthur Garrett is listed as a watchman. It is possible that he was still employed by the WPA, but that is not known for certain because no employer was named.

27. According to the 1860 slave census for Lunenburg County, Robt. H. Allen owned twenty-seven slaves. See Perdue, Barden, and Phillips, *Weevils in the Wheat*, 78–80, for an ex-slave interview with the same Charles Crawley by Susie R. C. Byrd. It was done about two years before this life history text and was ultimately deposited in the Virginia State Library. The language in that earlier interview contrasts sharply with this account from Crawley, as well as with other interviews by Byrd, which were deposited instead at Hampton University (see Ben James, Bernice Reid, and Mrs. Catherine Johnson in the next chapter). It can only be inferred that the former text was reworked and put in heavy dialect by editors in the Richmond VWP office. As far as can be determined, content was not so consciously altered.

28. In this text, we use "Givens" consistently, even though the surname appears in a single instance each as "Givings" and as "Gibbons" in census records or other documents. See Appendix B. This case also points up the problems of the age category in census records. For instance, Sarah "Crawley's" age is given as forty in both 1870 and 1880, and it is reported as fifty in 1900. Thus in an actual span of thirty years, she had aged only ten years! Given the age variability, as well as the different male heads of household and surnames, the only reliable way of recognizing this as the same family unit through time was the consistent house address. The change from 207 to 515 Plum Street that shows up in the 1920 census (and also the VWP interview) may reflect a renumbering of houses in the area owing to growth, or these numbers may simply be the separate addresses of two of the three lots owned in 1919 by Sarah "Gibbons" according to Petersburg Land Books.

29. Such living and working arrangements are not uncommon and are found among socially marginalized peoples, in particular, through time and in many places around the world, including native white Appalachian migrants earlier in this century and ethnic immigrants to this country from the early Irish on to more recent influxes of Hispanic, Caribbean, and Asian peoples; present-day West Indians and Turks in England and Germany; and various tribal peoples moved from their homelands into urban ghettos and tin or diamond mining areas in Africa in the nineteenth century onward.

30. The house form he describes is basically the traditional Virginia "I" house, or "two over two" room house, with a detached kitchen, often referred to as a "summer kitchen."

31. Letter from Marvin T. Broyhill III cited in n. 21 above, 2. Life history of Thomas Broyhill by John W. Garrett, 4 pp., no date given, VSL/AB, box 187.

32. Calos, Easterling, and Rayburn, *Old City Point and Hopewell*, 46–48.

33. There is some confusion and disagreement as to when various Broyhill family members went to Hopewell. In his *Broyhill Family History*, Marvin T. Broyhill III reports that Ruel Broyhill bought a lot at a land auction

in Hopewell in April. The date of that auction was 13 April *1914,* according to Calos, Easterling, and Rayburn, *Old City Point and Hopewell,* 46. That would place Ruel Broyhill in Hopewell more than a year before any of the other family members arrived. One of the family stories reported in the *Broyhill Family History* above is that after Ruel sold the said lot for an immediate profit, he wrote Marvin about the opportunities in Hopewell and asked him to come see for himself. Marvin did so and stayed on. This exchange supposedly took place, and Marvin arrived sometime before their parents did in July 1915. By that account, Marvin was in Hopewell and he and Ruel were in business together at the time of the Hopewell fire in December 1915. But in a 1970s interview with M. T. Broyhill III, Nellie Broyhill told him she met his grandfather Marvin when he was a telegraph operator in Wilkesboro in 1916 and that he had left for Hopewell that fall. Despite such apparent discrepancies, however, the main point remains the same: in the period between 1914 to 1917 most of Marvin T. Broyhill's immediate family, including himself, migrated from western North Carolina to Hopewell, Virginia. For a picture of housing built by the Broyhills in the town's B area, see Calos et al., ibid., p. 77.

34. Calos, Easterling, and Rayburn, *Old City Point and Hopewell,* 46. See also Appendix B. His brother Ruel remained in Hopewell, but Felix and Pete also moved to Arlington and worked with Marvin on various projects there or in Front Royal.

35. See obituary for M. T. Broyhill Sr., *Washington Post,* Thursday, 24 November 1966. In addition to the life history with Marvin Broyhill, there are at least nine vwp life histories with Broyhill family members and affines, including Thomas Jefferson Broyhill; Gipson (Gibson) and several of his children; Felix's wife, Mary; and others. The vwp interviewer John W. Garrett was married to Marvin T. Broyhill's sister, Annie Lou, who was the probable source for material in several of the life histories, including that of her father, Thomas J. Broyhill, since he died early in 1936 — prior to the apparent date of the interview.

36. It is useful to compare this very difficult paragraph (to read and edit without substantial rewriting, which has been resisted) with a piece from an undated letter written by Annie Lou Broyhill to Marvin T. Broyhill III: "In the late 18 hundreds [my father Thomas Jefferson Broyhill], bought a tract of land about 300 acres for its timber as he was a manufacturer of lumber and builder. . . . The land recession (Cleveland Recession) hit the country and large part of the land was cleared as the people could not get work. He [Thomas Broyhill] gave them jobs clearing the land so that they could get food. He settled down, built a house and continued to live there until about 1915." There are similarities, beyond mere content, between this statement from the letter, the paragraph in the Marvin Broyhill text, and a passage on the same topic in the vwp text for Thomas Jefferson Broyhill.

37. Marvin Talmadge Broyhill Sr. and Nellie Magdalene Brewer were married in Huntington, West Virginia, on 8 April 1917; see Broyhill, *Broyhill Family History,* pt. 2, "The Descendants of James Broyhill I, 1975."

38. The 1920 census (see Appendix B) indicates that Marvin and Nellie Broyhill had only two children at that time: nineteen-month-old Marvin Jr. and two-month-old Joel. Based on that information and the statement that they had three sons when he opened his real estate office again, that date would had to have been about 1921 at the earliest. According to the vwp's *Guide to Prince George and Hopewell,* 21–23, the Tubize Artificial Silk Company of America began producing rayon at the Hopewell site in 1921.

39. The records of Fork Union Military Academy indicate that Joel Thomas Broyhill (born 4 November 1919; mother: Nellie Broyhill) attended Fork Union during the academic year 1938–39 and graduated in 1939. *Who's Who in American Politics,* 1st ed., vol. 29 (New York: Bowker, 1967–68), also lists Representative Joel T. Broyhill of Arlington, Virginia, born in Hopewell, Virginia, on 4 November 1919; attended George Washington University; and served in the army in World War II. His business was given as real estate and builder.

40. See article on recent historical work on the influenza virus in the *Washington Post,* Sunday, 15 March 1992, A15.

41. Life history with Joseph Knight Tucker by Leila Blanche Bess, 12 pp., 5 February 1940, vsl/ab, box 184.

42. About a page of text was deleted here because of the writer's unwarranted and slanderous judgments based on gossip and class prejudices.

43. Another half page deleted for the same reason as given in the previous note.

44. The final paragraph is omitted here for the same reason cited in n. 42.

45. John Jackson, personal communication with editors, 1 January 1992.

46. See also the interview with Isaiah's mother, Annie Wallace, in Perdue, Barden, and Phillips, *Weevils in the Wheat,* 292–96. In her interview she told a slightly different story about the knitted "socks and gloves." She said that she "used to take the socks and clothes that *Miss Polly made* and *sell* 'em to the soldiers" (emphasis added).

Jeffries emphasizes that Isaiah's sister is "not just normal" several times in this text and also in that with Annie Wallace just cited. This probably tells more about Jeffries's concerns than about the Wallaces' candor.

47. In an interesting extension and use of statements about mixed Indian and African American ancestry, such as are found in this text and also in the ex-slave interviews with Annie Wallace and others in Perdue, Barden, and Phillips, *Weevils in the Wheat,* Peter Wallenstein has examined the implications of Virginia laws that granted the status of the mother to her offspring (if she was free, her children were free; if she was a slave, her children were slaves) and that repealed other laws allowing the enslavement of "native American Indians." Descendants of mothers having some amount of Indian ancestry could, and did, sue under those conditions for their freedom from slavery. See Wallenstein, "Indian Foremothers," esp. 20.

48. The Rosenwald Fund was established by Sears magnate Julius Rosenwald to help build schools for African Americans. John Hope Franklin notes that "between 1913 and 1932 the Fund aided in the construction of more than 5,000 Negro school buildings in 15 Southern states," among them those in Rappahannock and Culpeper Counties, Virginia. See Franklin, *From Slavery to Freedom,* 547–48.

49. A copy of the Madden interview is also located in UVA/MJ, box 1.

50. See Hite, *Rappahannock Story Book,* 75, 200–202. See also Appendix B.

51. For a discussion of the "Tom Hand's Mule" story and variants of it still in oral tradition in the vicinity, see the Preface.

52. This form of fox hunting, known as "hilltopping," is widely practiced and is not, of itself, illegal. A valid state hunting license is currently required for any sport involving the chase, on horseback or with dogs, of a wild animal whether or not it is killed; but even today there is no limited season placed on fox hunting in Culpeper County. In the Piedmont counties of Virginia, the distinctive styles of both the elite, formal fox hunt with horse and hound and the informal hilltopping with pickup truck and foxhounds have long coexisted. See Lyne, "What Are They Saying?," esp. 42–56, for a discussion of hilltopping, its history, and its jargon.

53. The description of Jeffries's visit with Tom Hand's family in his home, but without him present, raises a question as to whether she actually did interview him at some other time. In addition, her admission that some statements in the text came from her own recollections of Hand from times past does not reassure with regard to the interview question. A copy of "Tom Hand" is also in UVA/MJ, box 1. There is, in addition, a four-page version of this interview titled "Sandy Small's Mule," which was rewritten and edited by Richmond VWP editor Thomas Leonard, located in VSL/AB, box 191.

CHAPTER FOUR

1. Sobel, *World They Made,* 233. A nephew of Rev. Willis J. Madden, T. O. Madden Jr., communicated much the same message to these editors in conversations with him in the fall of 1978.

2. This letter written by George Lightfoot to Captain Thomas Humphreys in 1823 was found among papers in a trunk belonging to the Madden family and cited by T. O. Madden Jr. in *Madden's Tavern,* n.p.

3. See interview with Dilcie Gum in this chapter. Life history with Perkins Worley by John W. Garrett, 7 pp., legal-size, handwritten ms., 1,694 wds., rec. 18 March 1940, VSL/AB, box 188.

4. Interview with "C. H." by M. D. Gore, 2 pp., 484 wds.; rec. 12 January [?] 1939, VSL/AB, box 190. This interviewer commonly used only initials to identify her subjects.

5. Life history with Jimmie Garrett by John W. Garrett, 7 pp., 1,446 wds., rec. 1 April 1940, VSL/AB, box 187. This account was written in the third person, that is using "Jim" instead of "I" and "his gun" instead of "my gun," but was edited as indicated in brackets to eliminate the confusion of voice that existed otherwise. However, this life history was clearly the product of John Garrett's own personal knowledge of his brother's experience, not the direct result of a first-person interview. See the life history with Arthur Garrett in the preceding chapter.

6. Life history with Wallace Samson by Bessie A. Scales, 7 pp., 1,687 wds., handwritten ms., 26 August 1940, VSL/AB, box 178. See also Roger Wilkins, "On Being Uppity," in the "Uncommon Ground" department of *Mother Jones* 15, no. 4 (June 1990): 6.

7. The interview with Bernice Reid follows in this chapter.

8. See Perdue, Barden, and Phillips, *Weevils in the Wheat,* particularly Appendix 8, "Susie R. C. Byrd Notes on Interviewing Ex-Slaves," 383–88; see also Appendix 10, "Recordings of Virginia Ex-Slave Narrative Material in

the Archive of Folk Song, Library of Congress," 390, for a listing of the Petersburg ex-slaves recorded on aluminum disks.

9. See the photographic essay on Aberdeen Gardens in this chapter. See also Conkin, *Tomorrow a New World,* 200–201.

10. Bernard M. Fagelson, state adviser on NYA resident projects, in "Final Report—National Youth Administration for the State of Virginia," 24.

11. Projects such as Chopawamsic did more, however, than just provide jobs to some African Americans. An area in Chopawamsic (Prince William Forest Park) named Camp Pleasant was set aside specifically for the use of black children. In 1941, "one thousand under-privileged children from the District of Columbia spent the summer at the Camp, learning various craft, recreational, and other skills." See the frontispiece photograph with caption "A Little Negro Girl Helping to Serve the Food. Camp Pleasant, Virginia. August 1941," in Perdue, *Pigsfoot Jelly.* See also Parker, *The Hinterland,* which gives an overview of the history of Prince William Forest Park.

12. Margaret Baskerville, who lived at 216 Maple Lane (formerly "Guineham's Alley"), Petersburg, Virginia, was interviewed by Susie R. C. Byrd, 2 pp., handwritten ms., rec. 20 March 1939, HU/REL, box 5. Although there are several other separate texts identified with this woman, all of them were received in the VWP office on the same day. One handwritten, nine-page manuscript follows the format of other interviews that Byrd labeled "Home Conditions among Negroes" and concentrates on a description of Mrs. Baskerville's living arrangements and neighborhood. On another page Mrs. Baskerville describes the source of the name for Black Swan Twist tobacco.

13. Youth study with Harrison Blair by Mary S. Venable, 5 pp., 1,654 wds., 24 June 1940, VSL/AB, box 182.

14. Interview with James Cooke Jr. by Rone Sidney, 1 p., legal-size, handwritten ms., rec. 17 April 1941, 300 wds., VSL/AB, box 186. The Newport News Shipbuilding and Dry Dock Company, founded by Collis P. Huntington in 1886, was the largest privately owned shipyard in the world and could, therefore, exclude blacks, if desired, from its apprentice program established in 1919. See VWP, *Virginia: A Guide,* 261–62. After 1939, five NYA "Defense" Resident Programs for males were developed, but the only one that served African Americans was at Virginia State College. That program gave 110 young black men work experience in the "construction of a brick vocational shop building, electricity, sheet metal, and automobile mechanics." The other four units served only white youths and had the capacity to train 975 young men in radio, welding, carpentry and general woodworking, plumbing, machine shop operation, blacksmithing, and various specialized aviation trades. See "Final Report—National Youth Administration for the State of Virginia," 22–24. See also Reiman, *New Deal and American Youth,* 174–78.

15. See Cleveland Buchanan life history in this chapter.

16. See Appendix B. Since Mattie Stewart was next to the youngest of twelve children in her family and her father was sold away when she was little, the nine-year old Robert Stewart in the household is probably not her brother. He is more likely Fannie Stewart's grandson, and another of Mattie's nephews. Virginia Writers' Project worker Jeffries hints that Mattie Ficklin was widowed, but a Joseph Ficklin of about the right age and with another wife continues to appear in the Jeffersonton area up through at least 1910.

17. Margaret Jeffries had interviewed Rev. Willis J. Madden on 11 January 1940, several months prior to her conversation with Perndon. He likewise spoke candidly about his white and free black ancestry; Madden's interview text follows.

18. For a folklore class with Charles L. Perdue Jr. in 1978, Clara Steele (Eden), a University of Virginia student from Culpeper County, interviewed the Reverend Mr. Willis's nephew, Thomas Obed Madden Jr. She subsequently wrote an article about Madden and his family manuscript collection for the *Culpeper News,* 7 December 1978, reprinted 28 December 1978. See Steele, #1978-56, UVA/KBP. T. O. Madden Jr., with researcher Ruth Fitzgerald, later compiled the pamphlet *Madden's Tavern.* Neither of the family accounts connecting the Maddens to Washington or Jefferson were reported in that work. The factual links to the father and brother of the future president, James Madison Jr., was discovered by Ann Brush Miller through references in papers and records relating to James Madison Sr. Given the other purported ties to presidents, it is no doubt significant that the Madison connection is not mentioned in the Maddens' oral traditions about their origins. T. O. Madden Jr. reported, in a personal conversation with the editors in 1978, that the Irish indentured servant ancestor (that is, Mary Madden) was impregnated by a black coachman belonging to George Washington. But a variant of this story, attributing the liaison as between the coachman and Sarah Madden (daughter of Mary) and suggesting him

as father of the early Willis Madden, is reported and rejected with good cause (since Sarah was already living at Madison Mills at the time) in the following work: Madden, with Miller, *We Were Always Free,* 15–25, 41.

19. For a much more comprehensive and accurate account of the Madden family's history, see, Madden, with Miller, *We Were Always Free.*

20. Birth date of 22 August 1862 is from Willis Madden's family Bible (published by Jesper Harding, #57 S. Third St., Philadelphia, 1850; sold by Harrold & Murray, 177 Broad St., Richmond, Virginia). On the flyleaf is written, "Willis Madden, 1st July. 1854." Information given by Ann Brush Miller.

21. The retired missionary of note was Mr. John Stone, whose son of the same name was an early collector of ballads and folksongs and president of the Virginia Folklore Society for a number of years. In 1880, the John Stone family lived four dwellings away from Mariah Fields and her sons in the Stevensburg District of Culpeper County.

22. The words and music for the hymn "Look and Live" were written by W. A. Ogden and first copyrighted by the E. O. Excell Company in 1887. Ogden also wrote such other songs as "Seeking the Lost," "He Is Able to Deliver Thee," and "Bring Them In." Although Madden thought it had "been forgotten" and could not "find the music anywhere," the hymn was published by the Ruebush-Kieffer Company of Dayton, Virginia, in *Gospel Message in Song* (undated but at least after 1915, based on song copyright dates given), #142. See also Grace I. Showalter, ed., *The Music Books of Ruebush and Kieffer, 1866–1942: A Bibliography* (Richmond: Virginia State Library, 1975). "Look and Live" was also printed in a compilation "used exclusively in the Gipsy Smith Campaigns," *Wonderful Jesus and Other Songs* (Chicago: Biglow-Main-Excell Company, 1927), #133, and it has since been reprinted in *All Time Favorite Hymns* (Shreveport, La.: Jimmie Davis Music Co., 1965), #190, with a note that the copyright to E. O. Excell had been renewed in 1915. The song seems to have remained in print fairly consistently over time in this type of paperback, popular gospel/hymn song book and was not exactly "forgotten."

23. His behavior here is not without basis or precedent. See n. 2 (in this chapter) for earlier discussion urging caution against offending white people.

24. In the VSL/AB location cited, this interview with Madden has an attached "Survey of Rural White Youth" form and is in a folder titled "Youth Survey, Jeffries (Year 1940)." A copy of the interview is also in UVA/MJ, 10366-a, box 1.

25. See Appendix B.

26. Ada Lee Yancey (shown as Addie L. and Adale in the census) was listed on the Personal History or "Form A—Circumstances of Interview" for both Stevens and Johnson in response to question four: "Who put you in touch with Informant?" These interview forms were completed only for the folklore program—not for the life history project—and then relatively few of them seem to have survived. Where they do survive, they are invaluable. For instance, it is a matter of considerable curiosity that the informant information given for Johnson bears some similarity to that of Dilcie Gum and that some of the traditional figures of speech collected from Stevens seem to be incorporated in either the Dilcie Gum or Mollie Williams texts, which are themselves likely conflated. See discussion of Dilcie Gum's life history and also Mollie Williams's folklore text and personal history form following in this chapter.

27. See "Final Report—National Youth Administration for the State of Virginia," 31, 123, 127–28, 144.

28. The source cites *Democracy Paid For,* 1919, Negro Film. Depicts Negro soldiers in France, by Cleveland Buchanan and ———— Franklin. Directed by James Rodney Smith. Made in France. First showing 10 September 1919, Manhattan Casino, New York City. Lieutenant W. U. Bowman, publicity man. "It depicts our boys in France as they worked during the closing days of the War." Reel 7 of the George P. Johnson Collection, University of California at Los Angeles, Film Library. Our thanks to Michelle Branigan for locating this reference in the Indiana University Film Archives.

29. At the time of the VWP interview, Cleveland Buchanan and his family lived at 522 Alleghany Avenue, Covington, Virginia. Venable added a note here: "The County Supervisors raised the price allowance to undertakers from $25 to $45 and the white undertaker got more of the business. The body of one pauper (negro) was sold to a Richmond Medical University." She also commented that Buchanan "made no mention of figures in profits, though given an opportunity."

30. Charlotte Courthouse was the site of Patrick Henry's "last appearance in public life" and the first in that of John Randolph of Roanoke, when they "matched oratory" during the 1799 political campaign. This match is supposedly the source for the name given to Randolph Henry High School. See FWP, *Virginia: A Guide,* 518.

Specific information about the Bruce donation and other details in subsequent paragraphs about the history, renovation, and integration of the two schools, Randolph Henry High and Central High, are personal communications by phone to the editors from Mr. Larry Dunn, assistant superintendent of Charlotte County schools, 6 October 1995.

31. A Bonn photograph captioned "Central high school buildings" was, in fact, another view in the series on the white Randolph Henry High School. Since there was no contemporary photo of Central High by Bonn, a photograph of the vacant "Central Middle School" taken by editor Charles L. Perdue Jr. on 18 June 1995 is included in the following collection instead. Exterior views of the shop buildings at Randolph Henry and at Central Middle School, taken on the same day, are also included here.

32. See life history of Letitia Jane Lumpkins in chapter 2. For additional commentary on the reputations of black female cooks and their importance to Virginia foodways as reported by the workers of the vwp, see Charles L. Perdue Jr., *Pigsfoot Jelly*. In one specific example from that work, another vwp worker from Danville refers to "one of them old-time nigger cooks . . . known far and near as, 'Tishie Lewis, the Cake Baker from Milton, North Carolina'" (32). Such commentary, intended to be complimentary, assured and spread the reputations of Lewis and other women like her. But use of the vernacular, and generally derogatory, term *nigger* was, and is, still a recognizable marker signaling the social distance and inequality existing between black and white persons—even while acknowledging the skills of those such as Tishie Lewis. For one African American's view of the changing use and implications of various color terms, see Madden, with Miller, *We Were Always Free,* xxv.

33. This copy of the cookbook is in the Special Collections Division, Rare Books Department of Alderman Library, University of Virginia, Charlottesville. There are only two entries in the book attributed to black cooks: one for "Grated Potato Yeast" to "'Aunt' Mary, Lexington, Va. (Mrs. John R. Anderson's cook)," and for "Before the War Corn Batter Cakes" from "Aunt Creasy." Black women could make their reputations as cooks in the community's oral tradition and history; however, it was not uncommon for the white ladies they worked for to deny them their "good name" and take credit for their productions in print. In the 1900 Pittsylvania County census, Augusta Yates, forty-seven and single, born in Virginia, was living in the household of her brother-in-law, Judge A. M. Aiken, fifty-one, a lawyer, born in North Carolina and married for eighteen years; his wife, Mary E. Aiken, fifty, also born in North Carolina; and their only child, Archie M. Aiken, twelve. See U.S. Census Manuscripts, Virginia, Pittsylvania County, 1900, Household #586-603, Tunstall District, Stokesland Precinct.

34. In the 1920 Pittsylvania County census, Dilsa Ingram, an eighty-year-old widow living alone without any occupation and born in North Carolina, was the head of household #612-642, Almagro Village, in Tunstall District. In 1910, Dis Ingraham, age given as sixty-five, widowed after forty-five years of marriage and having two living children, was with her daughter, Alice Ingraham, and her seven children, aged two to sixteen years of age, in household #981-992, as above. However, Dilcy Ingram, seventy, born May 1830, a laundress, is listed in the 1900 census with her husband, Amos Ingram, seventy, born September 1829 in North Carolina, a day laborer, in household #663-681, E.D. 88, Tunstall District, Stokesland Precinct—not far from Augusta Yates. See U.S. Census Manuscripts, Virginia, Pittsylvania County, 1900, Tunstall District, Stokesland Precinct; 1910, Household #981-992; 1920, Household #612-642.

35. There are quite a number of Mary Williamses in the Danville City and Pittsylvania County censuses, and Molly is the diminutive form of Mary. However, Molly Williams is very likely the woman of that same name who, in 1900, shared a house on Ross Street in Danville with two other single African American women cooks, their various relatives, and several boarders. By 1920 a Maria (Molly?) W. (Williams?) at the same address is married to a George Richmond and has a daughter. Since she is not at that time in Almagro (neither are the Yanceys), she cannot be positively identified as the person in the folklore text, but the circumstantial evidence is suggestive. See Appendix B. See also n. 26 above, which suggests some connections between this text and that for Lessie Johnson and Bettie Stevens, both of whom Scales interviewed under the folklore program.

36. See Fry, *Night Riders,* esp. 110–69, for discussion of the Ku Klux Klan and other agents used for social control of blacks.

37. See use of the expression "cemetery dead" in the following Mollie Williams interview as well.

38. Bessie Scales turned in a number of "*Negro Folklore Expressions,*" which she states she collected between 17 and 21 February 1941 (after the date of this life history) from yet another source, Bettie Stevens of Almagro. Included among these sayings is the statement "When ah wurks, ah wurks hard, an when ah sets, ah looses. An when ah wurry's, ah jest goes ter sleep." This expression is quoted in Dilcie Gum as "When I sets, I sets loose."

But as given in that form from Gum, it also loses a dimension of meaning referring to work and wages that becomes apparent in the version "when ah sets, ah looses," attributed to Stevens. See UVA/FC, box 2, item #462.

39. See also the discussion of covering clocks and mirrors after a death in the family in the Mollie Williams interview following.

40. The expression "Talkin o' de ole booger man will sho' scare up his imps" is attributed elsewhere by Scales to Bettie Stevens, Almagro. See n. 36 above for more discussion of this source. UVA/FC, box 2, item 462.

41. For the use of black cat bones to become a witch as reported by white ballad singer Texas Gladden of Salem, and also as reported by a "colored woman" from Roanoke, Virginia, see *Folklore and Folklife in Virginia* 2 (1980–81): 71–72, 86. See also the discussion of the black cat bone in Puckett, *Folk Beliefs,* 256–59, and *Frank C. Brown Collection,* vol. 7, #5590, and esp. #5591.

42. Along with paths and crossroads, doorsteps are among the most important and frequently mentioned sites for the working of conjuration or witchcraft. For some discussion of the use of these boundaries and of spiders in conjuring, see nn. 13 and 14 in chap. 1. For more on the practice of conjuring among Virginia slaves, see Perdue, Barden, and Phillips, *Weevils in the Wheat;* for a recent general discussion of conjuring, see Levine, *Black Culture,* 55–80.

43. See *Frank C. Brown Collection,* vol. 7, #5671: "If a knife is placed under the pillow, witches can do no harm to the one in bed"; see also #5672. For a variation of the practice, see tale by Mardia Queseberry in *Folklore and Folklife in Virginia* 2 (1980–81): 77. The Rev. J. H. Coleman text is given here just as it was reported by VWP worker James Taylor Adams, who apparently omitted some material before sending it to Richmond. For a heavily edited and extended version of this same Coleman text, see "Firm Believers in Witchcraft," in Davis, *Silver Bullet,* 202–3.

44. See Baldwin, *Poverty and Politics,* 68–76; Dr. Arthur Howe Papers, box 22, folder: Newport News Housing Project (Aberdeen Homestead), (1934), HU/AH.

45. Report indicating variation in houses planned, dated 22 January 1935; *Newport News Daily Press* report of 27 February 1935; and news release of 13 March 1935, all located in Dr. Arthur Howe Papers, box 22, folder: Aberdeen Homesteads (1935), HU/AH.

46. See Conkin, *Tomorrow a New World,* 113, and *First Annual Report: Resettlement Administration,* 48.

47. Conkin, *Tomorrow a New World,* 167, 201, 202.

48. Howe Papers, box 22, folder: Aberdeen Homesteads (1936), HU/AH.

49. Howe Papers, box 22, folders for 1937 and 1938, HU/AH.

50. Conkin, *Tomorrow a New World,* 334.

51. See Appendix B for census and other records.

52. The dwelling at that address was occupied in 1920 by Henry Bolling, thirty-five, and his wife, Annie Bolling, twenty-eight; he was a driver, and she worked in the peanut factory. This information further underscores the point that this particular area was a working-class neighborhood with a considerable degree of transient occupancy as indicated by the city directories over time. See Appendix B.

53. No cause of death or obituary for Bernice Reid was found, even though courthouse records and papers were checked for such. The only evidence found for her death was the list of heirs recorded in the Petersburg City Courthouse. See Appendix B for records relating both to this paragraph and the one following.

54. See life history of John S. Powell in chapter 7 and also Appendix B. Although it cannot be proved that the Benj. James in the Richmond directories is the same person as that in the VWP life history, this speculation is based on a diligent search of available records in courthouses, archives, and libraries. At least the surname James is well represented in the public records of Caroline and Henrico Counties and of Richmond of the time; it is not so, however, in the courthouse and other records for Petersburg. In fact, the only evidence so far that clearly establishes Ben James's presence in Petersburg is that of the VWP life history itself, which further suggests that he was probably not from Petersburg and did not remain there for long. Because of his age, the census records for 1930 and 1940 would be most helpful in this case, but these will not be available for general use until well into the twenty-first century. Ben James may also represent a good case in point of a member in what has been called in recent times an underclass. Such individuals—because of race or ethnicity, poverty, homelessness, unemployment, or a combination thereof—are regularly undercounted or missed altogether in the censuses and other public records that routinely document some aspects of most people's lives.

55. No marriage record for any Catherine to a male Johnson (in a period extending a decade or more before the age of her eldest child to the time of the VWP interview) was found in the Petersburg courthouse. Despite her

designation in the interview as "Mrs.," there is still the possibility (which cannot be entirely ruled out) that she was not married and that Johnson was actually *her* surname.

56. There was a Frederick Johnson, driver, with a wife, Kate, living at 345 Federal Street, as well as a Katie Johnson, student, at 404 Federal Street, in the 1929 Petersburg city directory. In the 1920 census for Dinwiddie County, E.D. 85, #299-319, no age was given for Frederick, but his wife, Kate, fifty-six, was a laundress, and they had no children listed at home. She is likely the Kate Johnson listed as a laundress for Bock Woo Laundry in the 1931 city directory. In any case, she was too old to be the Catherine Johnson of the VWP interview, though Katie Johnson, the student, who was perhaps a daughter of Frederick and Kate, might be a remote possibility, that is, *if* Catherine was unmarried or if Johnson was her maiden name as well as her married name. There is also a Kathryn Johnson at 218 N. Old Church in the 1941 city directory, who may or may not be the Catherine in question. But no courthouse or other records have as yet been found to specify with certainty who these persons are in relation to the Catherine Johnson of the life history.

57. This interview represents an investigator's report for the black urban youth study; part of it is from a personal interview with Anna, and part of it results from an interview with Anna's in-laws. The interviewer gave addresses for Anna Watts as 208 S. Second Street and for her in-laws, 222 S. Second Street, Richmond, Virginia, but these have not been verified by city directories, which suggests that Gow may have changed either the subjects' names or addresses in this text. Since that cannot be confirmed, however, the editors used the pseudonym Anna Watts in this case because of the subject matter. Only the principal names have been changed, however; all other information is as it was given in the interview.

58. "Cot," or "caught," is a descriptive term often used by midwives rather than "delivered" in reference to the birth of a baby.

PART TWO

1. Clarence E. Cason, "Middle Class and Bourbon," in Couch, *Culture in the South,* 490–91.

2. Ibid. See also Heinemann, *Depression and New Deal,* esp. 69–87.

3. U.S. Bureau of the Census, *Fifteenth Census: Population,* vol. 3, pt. 2, pp. 1140–1205. See esp. tables 1 and 2. All figures based on census records have been rounded off to the nearest percentage.

4. Ibid.; see also tables 10, 13, 14, and 16 and vol. 5, tables 10 and 11, pp. 102–3. Using figures from these tables, the U.S. white labor force (based on the number of all gainfully occupied "persons *10 years old* and over") was 79 percent male and 21 percent female; the black labor force was 67 percent male and 33 percent female. Thus, Alleghany County did, in fact, come close to the national average. The comparable figures for Virginia were 83 percent male and 17 percent female white workers versus 70 percent male and 30 percent female black workers. Although the census includes a category of "unpaid family workers" under the heading of Agriculture, many argue that large numbers of women who should have been included in the labor force under this category were greatly underenumerated though there was some attempt to correct for this in the 1930 census. See Oppenheimer, *Female Labor Force,* 3–6.

5. U.S. Bureau of the Census, *Fifteenth Census: Population,* vol. 3, table 20, pp. 1182–97. See also interviews with Joe Hippert in chapter 8 and Howard Reynolds, Roy C. Fix, and Kate Beale in chapter 9, who comment on some of the Alleghany County industries specifically mentioned here. Still others note the effects of strikes, slowdowns in production, or factory closings in places such as the DuPont de Nemours Powder Company and Tubize Silk Company in Hopewell, tobacco factories in Richmond, and the Dan River Mills textile plant in Danville.

6. U.S. Bureau of the Census, *Fifteenth Census: Population,* vol. 3, tables 13, 14, and 20. See also Gee and Stauffer, *Rural and Urban Living Standards,* 14. Culpeper County was one of three Virginia localities selected for this 1929 social science research monograph, which reported that "in progressive agricultural development, Culpeper [took] rank among the leading counties of Virginia."

7. U.S. Bureau of the Census, *Fifteenth Census: Population,* vol. 3, p. 1 and table 22, p. 1205. Urban areas were defined as "cities and other incorporated places having 2,500 inhabitants or more, the remainder being classified as rural." "Culpeper town" was indicated as having 2,379 residents, so it was included in the rural category. Jeffries, "Culpeper, a Typical Town of Northern Virginia," UVA/MJ.

8. Jeffries, "Culpeper, a Typical Town of Northern Virginia," UVA/MJ.

9. Skyline Drive and Shenandoah National Park were dedicated by President Franklin D. Roosevelt on 3 July 1936. See vwp, *Virginia: A Guide,* 392–93, 414–15. Youth study with Elma Good by Margaret Jeffries, 7 pp., 2,400 wds., no interview date, vsl/ab, box 188.

10. U.S. Bureau of the Census, *Fifteenth Census: Population,* vol. 3, tables 14 and 15. In the three counties—Floyd, Shenandoah, and Grayson—that had more females, however, the difference was negligible for the most part. The point remains the same: the sex ratio favored males in rural Virginia populations, whereas the reverse was true in the state's largest cities. Although they were included in table 15, Bristol and Bluefield were excluded here because their actual in-state populations were under 10,000. The fourteen cities referred to include Danville, Hopewell, Lynchburg, Norfolk, Petersburg, Portsmouth, Newport News, Hampton, Roanoke, Staunton, and Richmond; all but Hampton are represented in vwp life history texts in this volume.

11. Ibid., table 20. vwp, *Guide to Prince George,* 19. Personal communication from Marvin T. Broyhill III. See also Calos, Easterling, and Rayburn, *Old City Point and Hopewell,* and Brian Kelly, "Life among the Smoking Stacks," *Washington Star,* 20 September 1976.

12. U.S. Bureau of the Census, *Fifteenth Census: Population,* vol. 3, table 20. See also vol. 5, p. 20. The public service category included members of all branches of the military; police, marshals, and sheriffs; firemen; other city, county, state, or federal officials and inspectors; and other public service pursuits not otherwise classified.

13. Ibid., vol. 3, table 20.

14. Ibid., table 10, p. 1149. See also vol. 5, chap. 2, table 13, pp. 60–61. The percentages given in the text are from vol. 3, but there is some discrepancy between these figures and the summary numbers and percentages given in vol. 5, table 13, which lists all geographic divisions and the states within them.

15. Ibid., vol. 3, tables 10 and 20. The percentage of women in domestic service in Portsmouth is based on 2,238 white women and 2,166 black women in those jobs. The percentages of women in the labor force in the cities of Norfolk, Portsmouth, and Richmond, however, are striking and are well above the averages for both the United States and the state of Virginia (see n. 4 above). In Portsmouth 26 percent of white and 37 percent of black workers were female; for Norfolk, the respective figures were 28 percent and 41 percent; in Richmond, they were 34 percent and 43 percent.

16. Ibid.

17. Ibid., table 20. See also Tilley, *R. J. Reynolds Tobacco,* and Reynolds and Shachtman, *Gilded Leaf.*

18. Social-ethnic study with Mrs. Kennedy Sr. (a pseudonym), titled "A Widow and Her Household," by Edith C. Skinner, 4 pp., 1,003 wds., rec. 10 December 1938, vsl/ab, box 178. Such comments regarding the wpa have been made directly to us in conversations with former fieldworkers and others. In addition, personnel files for the Virginia Writers' Project contain a number of complaints and job actions that cite low morale and lack of productivity, particularly among some male workers.

19. U.S. Bureau of the Census, *Fifteenth Census: Population,* vol. 3, table 10. When the categories for white and black females are separated, they show that 2.4 percent of white women and not quite 0.2 percent of black women were in public service. Susie R. C. Byrd of Albemarle County, who took courses at both Hampton Institute and Virginia State College and taught school in the Petersburg school system, also worked for the Virginia Writers' Project. But she worked on the de facto segregated unit operating out of Hampton Institute. The women referred to here are Eudora Ramsay Richardson, Mary S. Venable, Margaret Jeffries, Pearl Morrissett, Lucille Jayne, and Essie Wade Smith, respectively.

CHAPTER FIVE

1. See life history with Sam Harrison following in this chapter.

2. See discussion of the development of coal and timber holdings in Eller, *Miners, Millhands, and Mountaineers.* For a contemporary extension of this issue, see Appalachian Land Ownership Task Force, *Who Owns Appalachia?: Landownership and Its Impact* (Lexington: University of Kentucky Press, 1983).

3. Garnett, "Rural Marginal Population," 22. It is interesting to note that, with the exception of the recommended use of the eugenics program, the Area Redevelopment Acts under Eisenhower's administration in the 1950s and 1960s proposed much the same solutions for rural farm poverty levels as did Garnett in 1934. See Rohrer and Douglas, *Agrarian Transition in America,* 79–104, esp. 100–103.

4. Garnett, "Rural Marginal Population."

5. LCP&P, Lot 12024, FSA-OWI Textual Records, 1935–46, reel no. 5.

6. Gee and Corson, *Statistical Study of Virginia,* 60, 61, 64, 117, 155.

7. Daniel, *Breaking the Land,* 163.

8. Gee and Corson, *Statistical Study of Virginia,* 183–85.

9. Youth study with Reginald Shires by Leila Blanche Bess, 13 pp., 3,630 wds., 29 May 1940, VSL/AB, box 185. Interview with Emma Lou Lee by Essie W. Smith, 7 pp., 20 December 1939, VSL/AB, box 179 (there is another version of this interview: 7 pp., 1,800 wds., 27 June 1939, VSL/AB, box 180). The expression—to be paid in "chips and whetstones"—seems to bear some relationship to the notion, traced to the sixteenth century, of giving a whetstone, "i.e., a wit-sharpener," to whomever could tell the biggest lie. Thus, the expression might suggest that one should "sharpen one's wit" in bargaining for wages or, conversely, imply lying, broken promises, and not being true to one's contract on the part of others. See Farmer and Henley, *Slang and its Analogues,* 328.

10. Life history with Minnie T. Kilbourne, 6 pp., 1,642 wds., rec. 19 December 1938, VSL/AB, box 190; and with Earl Spurrier, 4 pp., 1,087 wds., rec. 19 December 1938, VSL/AB, box 190. Both interviews by Anne Davidson Meiman (mistakenly identified in VWP files as Anne M. Davidson). Additional information on both persons and on VWP worker Anne Meiman from personal interview by the editors with Mrs. Kenneth Davidson, Bristol, Virginia, 10 August 1988.

11. Daniel, *Breaking the Land,* 253.

12. Wingfield, *Franklin County,* 59, notes that his father often said tobacco "required thirteen months of the year to grow and market." Humbert et al., *Virginia: Economic and Civic,* 4–5.

13. "Tobacco Song," collected by VWP worker Bessie A. Scales from Belle Jackson, Rison Alley, Danville, Virginia, 20–24 January 1941, UVA/FC, box 2, #466. A slightly different version of the same verse was collected as part of the life history of Margaret Ozena (Bane) Reed by VWP worker Gertrude Blair in Roanoke on 6 July 1940. Reed had written it on her school tablet and recited it for her class. Her old teacher, Mr. Cab Holland, who "chewed and smoked tobacco incessantly" was not amused by her recitation: "Tobacco is an evil weed and from the Devil did proceed, It spoils your breath and soils your clothes, And makes a chimney of your nose." VSL/AB, box 186.

14. See Appendix B for census records and data for Buzzell Peebles. The surname appears variously in the records as Peeples and Peoples, and the given name, which sometimes is indicated as Borzell or Barzell, may in fact be derived from Burwell. See also VWP, *Negro in Virginia,* 323.

15. The surnames Harrison (sometimes confused with Hairston), Davidson, and Jackson, used in different VWP versions of the interview, *all* appear in censuses for the city of Danville, as well as those for Pittsylvania and Nansemond Counties. However, examination of the records for those areas between 1900 and 1920 has revealed no family or individual that fits the profile given in versions of the Sam Harrison texts. Without further data to support a case for any of those other names, the circumstantial evidence favors the contention that the subject of this interview is Buzzell Peebles.

16. The version of the Sam Harrison text sent to Chapel Hill was about half the length of the one included in this work. See FWP Papers, #3709, box 8, UNC/SHC, and Robinson, *Living Hard,* 111–15. See also "A Black Mr. Peanut," 4 pp., by Thomas C. Leonard, VSL/AB, box 191.

17. For another detailed account of tobacco culture, from planting, harvesting, and curing it to hauling it to market and also including a description of tobacco auctions, see Wingfield, *Franklin County,* 49–59. He writes also that in setting out tobacco shoots "a strong man could make 1000 hills per day" (52).

18. For further discussion of tobacco grades, see ibid., 57.

19. The text reports that Herman Hooker was born in January 1922 and was the sixth child—fifth son—out of ten in his family. But George and Lillian Hooker had only two children in 1920, and it is highly unlikely that they had four more by 1922. Therefore the birth order as indicated by Venable is probably incorrect, even if Herman was born in 1922 as reported. Another, more likely possibility is that Herman is actually the son Henry H., aged four, already listed in the 1920 census. See Appendix B.

20. Donald Holley, "The Sharecropper," in Peterson, *Farmers, Bureaucrats, and Middlemen,* 121.

21. Garnett, "Rural Marginal Population," 5. See also Heinemann, *Depression and New Deal,* 113, 121–22. Heinemann cites the same figures on the makeup of this marginal population as those given in the Garnett article, but he credits them to a much later Virginia Polytechnic Institute bulletin by Garnett and Allen D. Edwards.

22. Venable identifies this "Youth Study" as being with "Herman Hooker, Falling Spring, Va.," but she fre-

quently refers in the text to "Hiram" and has written "Herman" over that typed name in at least one place. The usage of "Herman" in brackets in the text indicates places where "Hiram" was used and replaced. In actual fact, the voice most often heard in this text is that of "Herman's" father—presumably George Washington Hooker.

23. It was likely the Hookers' former landlord, S. B. Surber, who was responsible for Sills's participation in the AAA wheat reduction program. Heinemann quotes the extension agent on the benefits in Alleghany County of price increases in 1934 as a result of the AAA-supported programs. Surber said, "I believe my farmers are really beginning to appreciate this effort our government is making to put farming on a level with other industries." Heinemann, *Depression and New Deal,* 107.

24. There are at least three separate VWP texts with John E. Bess. The first, titled "A Land Owner Speaks on Share Croppers," by Leila Blanche Bess (5 pp., 1,663 wds., rec. 14 March 1939, VSL/AB, box 185), did not identify him as the subject. A second text—the one reported here—is identified as being with John E. Bess and has the same title as the first, but it is indicated as having been written in the period March to July and on 2 August 1939 (thus overlapping with, extending, and also duplicating much of the first text above). This manuscript, received in the VWP office on 7 August 1939, is sixteen pages long, or 5,534 words, and it encompasses the earlier five-page text, which underwent some slight modifications in the process. The first version was impersonal in its writing: the pronouns *he* or *they* were used throughout; the sharecropper was never named; and the hunting and cat drowning incidents were not mentioned as they are in this more subjective and lengthier version. A little more than two pages were omitted at the end of this longer text because they duplicate material contained in yet a third John E. Bess life history, dated 15 August 1940, which is given in its entirety in chapter 3.

25. A paragraph between this and the one following detailed the concerns and speculations of the mother and aunts about what *might* have happened if John had been left out on the farm to hunt. Because their conversation and personal thoughts are outside the general thrust of the narrative about the sharecropper from John Ernest Bess's perspective, they are intrusive and have been omitted here.

26. A brief paragraph, indicated by ellipsis between the bracketed text and the final sentence in this paragraph, has been left out. The next paragraph follows directly after the quoted last sentence just as it does in the original text. In the material omitted, however, Bess makes personal judgments and stereotypical statements about Sampson's character and ethnicity that are intrusive and not appropriate here.

27. Johnson, *Mountaineers to Main Streets,* 77. It is useful to compare Delano's statement about migrants' wages with the testimony of others in the life histories, such as Charles Tucker in chapter 3 and Ben James in chapter 4.

28. See life history of Elva Lee Beheler by Essie W. Smith, 10–11 April 1940, 5 pp., VSL/AB, box 178. Both John Gregory and James Beheler were prosperous farmers; owned about the same amount of land; and lived in houses described almost exactly the same. Each of them had wives who were former schoolteachers and who had only one sibling—a brother serving as a missionary in the Far East. Likewise they each had four children— an older daughter, two sons, and a younger daughter—of about the same age, and both of them took their children to school in the car when the weather was good; when it was bad, the children rode horseback or walked because the car could not get out over the bad roads. John Gregory's daughter was finishing high school in 1939; in 1940, Elva Lee Beheler had finished high school about a "year ago" and was working "in a sandwich shop on the highway between Rocky Mount and Gogginsville."

29. In arguing the Wickersham claim as an exaggeration, Smith did not deny its validity altogether. And she herself was not loath to project similar views on others elsewhere in her life history writings.

30. It appears that they not only heard about Jesse James but they may also have sung about him. In May 1939, about one month before John Gregory's interview was sent to Richmond, VWP folklore project worker Raymond Sloan sent in a text for the ballad "Jesse Jeames" (in manuscript, dated 26 September 1898), which he collected from Mrs. Onie Meadors Slone. According to descriptions in the life history, she likely lived within ten miles of John Gregory.

31. "Final Report, National Youth Administration," 15. Because of her age and the lack of other significant information about Marietta Holley's family, it has not been possible to establish her identity beyond what is given in the life history. There are many Holley/Holly families in Franklin County, but that is not necessarily a reliable indicator of anything of a factual nature relative to Marietta Holley, given Smith's tendencies to change surnames and other details in interviews.

32. The rest of this page and a few subsequent lines of text contain unsubstantiated allegations by Smith about various members of the Holley family and are excluded here.

1. For quote in the title of this chapter, see life history with Joe New by Sarah Moore (revised by Ann Heaton), 9 pp., 14 February 1939, VSL/AB, box 191. Humbert et al., *Virginia: Economic and Civic,* 158–61. See also *Washington Post,* Sunday, 8 August 1993, A1, A19.

2. Susan Brait writes that the Susquehanna River "drains thirteen million acres of land over a course of four hundred and forty-four miles" and that "more than half of the Bay's fresh water comes from it" at a rate of "nineteen million gallons of water" a minute. See Brait, *Chesapeake Gold,* 121–22.

3. Johnson, *Working the Water,* 11. Humbert et al., *Virginia: Economic and Civic,* 160–62. See also Wennersten, *Oyster Wars,* 13–17, and Frye, *Men All Singing,* 49–52.

4. Excerpts from "Life History of Two Sisters," by Lucille B. Jayne, 20 pp., 2,625 wds., 7 February 1939, VSL/AB, box 191. See also VSL/AB, box 190.

5. Brewington, *Chesapeake Bay,* 172.

6. Ibid. For a detailed history of the oyster wars, see Wennersten, *Oyster Wars.* See also Johnson, *Working the Water.* Both of the latter works focus primarily on the fishing industry in Maryland but provide useful background information on fishing in the bay area generally.

7. Humbert et al., *Virginia: Economic and Civic,* 165–66.

8. Ibid.

9. Ibid. See also Gregory Power, "More about Oysters Than You Wanted to Know," *Maryland Law Review* 30, no. 3 (1970): 199–225, cited by G. Terry Sharrer, "The Patuxent Fisheries," in Johnson, *Working the Water,* 17–18.

10. Frye, *Men All Singing,* 181–88. See the essay and notes on work songs of the menhaden fishermen by Glenn Hinson for *Virginia Traditions: Virginia Work Songs,* BRI 007, a record series of the Blue Ridge Institute, Ferrum College, Ferrum, Virginia. For more on the work and lore of the Gulf Coast fishermen, see Mullen, *I Heard the Old Fisherman Say.*

11. Humbert et al., *Virginia: Economic and Civic,* 158–62.

12. Quoted in Wennersten, *Oyster Wars,* v.

13. Sharrer states that "commercial crabbing had a stronger and earlier start in Virginia than in Maryland," because of the lower Chesapeake Bay's saltier water and higher crab population. He also notes that the first commercial crab cannery was not established in Oxford, Maryland, until 1900. See "Patuxent Fisheries," 14.

14. Humbert et al., *Virginia: Economic and Civic,* 167, and Sharrer, "Patuxent Fisheries," 16.

15. Flemming mentioned that five cents a pound was the wage he paid for picking crabmeat, and according to Sharrer, that was the standard rate paid in 1940 as well. However, that rate was only "two cents per pound more" than the wages paid for that job in 1890, even though the retail price for crabmeat had tripled between 1920 and 1940. See Sharrer, "Patuxent Fisheries," 16.

16. Flemming's remarks here are prejudicial, but, based on other life histories and evidence, the attitudes expressed by him are not atypical of many white Virginians of the period. His negative statements about an anonymous group of generalized oyster workers did not, however, exclude the possibility—noted by the interviewer earlier—of a "lack of caste feeling" between himself and the workers in his plant. Such contradictions between the treatment of depersonalized "others" and of individuals who are known and recognized to be separate, real persons (despite having the same ethnic or racial identity as those stigmatized others) are characteristic of paternalistic behavior.

17. VWP, *Virginia: A Guide,* 240. See also Appendix B.

18. See VWP, *Virginia: A Guide,* 465. The 183-million-pound finfish catch in Virginia in 1930 was almost three times that of the shellfish catch, yet the total market value of the finfish was slightly less than that of the shellfish. Humbert et al., *Virginia: Economic and Civic,* 164–68, 218–19. For an aesthetic approach to the value of different kinds of fish, see Forrest, *Lord I'm Coming Home,* 70–72, esp. the comment on 72 contrasting "old [inedible] bass" to "really good fish" such as "spot or bluefish."

19. Julia Keesee's husband, Watson, worked for the Pender Company in grocery stores in Altavista, Lynchburg, Bedford, and Chatham (see chapter 2). These locations are in south central, not eastern, Virginia. Thus the range of these chain stores was apparently broader than the interviewer reported.

20. This verse from African American folksong tradition was reported by White as sung by various kinds of gang laborers, including deckhands on the Tennessee River, in *American Negro Folk-Songs,* 280, 306–7. See also

Scarborough, *On the Trail,* 236. The verse cited is as it is sung by John Jackson, a native of Rappahannock County, Virginia, on *Blues and Country Dance Tunes from Virginia,* Arhoolie Record F1025.

21. Census records are presented for a Charlie Johnson, who was living in Portsmouth and was about the right age to be the person interviewed here. But other details, such as his wife's name and the presence of several older surviving children, are inconsistent with the life history as given. Moreover, there was a Charlie Johnson who was about the same age, had a wife Mary and no children, and, in addition, had a married couple rooming in his household. But he was born in South Carolina rather than North Carolina and lived in Newport News, not Portsmouth. In this particular case, there is not as much confidence that the records presented do, in fact, pertain to the actual person in the vwp interview. See U.S. Census Manuscripts, Virginia, Warwick County, 1920, E.D. 102, #236-237 and Appendix B.

22. See vwp, *Virginia: A Guide,* 483.

23. Louisa Chase represents a good case in point of the problems of tracing women's lives. It has not been possible to find Louisa Chase, who was orphaned at a young age and then moved out of state, in the usual record sources. Because her maiden name is not known, census records for the earlier period of her life are eliminated from possible search, and later censuses that date from after her marriage are not yet available. And though several men named John Chase were found in Baltimore records, none of these can clearly be identified as the person in this interview.

24. The latter circumstance (like that of abortion in the case of Anna Watts) transcends the time and person of Louisa Chase. The issues concerning adoption in Chase's case have their parallels still in highly publicized cases, which are presently challenging existing laws.

25. There are at least nine George Harrises in the 1910 census for Norfolk and Portsmouth cities and Norfolk County. Out of these, there are two possibilities, neither of which can be proved to be the George of the vwp interview. These two men in the census were both in their thirties and married, and each had a son; one also had a daughter. But neither of them were fishermen at that time. One was a machinist in Portsmouth; the other was a confectionery salesman in Norfolk city. No reference was found in the soundex (phonetic index) to the censuses for an Amos Harris at all. Given their living circumstances, they might likely have been missed by the census in 1920 altogether.

26. Johnson describes an attempt to unionize the oyster shuckers at the J. C. Lore Oyster House in St. Mary's County, Maryland, in 1936. It failed because the Lore family closed the oyster house down and moved its operation to another location. When talk of unionization dwindled the next year, the family reopened the shucking room at its former location without any further problem. See Johnson, *Working the Water,* 42 and n. 19.

CHAPTER SEVEN

1. Bernard Fagelson in "Final Report—National Youth Administration for the State of Virginia," 22. In 1913, there were 9,022 cars and trucks in the state. By 1927, Virginia had 336,384 such vehicles, with one car per 7.56 persons in the state. *University of Virginia News Letter* 4, no. 17 (1 June 1928): 1.

2. Cited by Dr. Walter S. Newman in "Final Report—National Youth Administration," 10.

3. See also Reiman, *New Deal and American Youth,* 152-54, 178-81, and his discussions of Lyndon Johnson's participation in and views on the nya with regard to Great Society programs such as the Job Corps and Upward Bound, 194-95.

4. Ayers, *Promise of the New South,* 64-66.

5. Biography of Henry Mauze Darnall in Jack and Jacobs, *History of Roanoke County,* 183. Darnall had about the same "education, money, social connections, self-confidence, and morality" provided by his parents as did other kinsmen and peers among the Webb and Price families, yet some of them were working as laborers in a Roanoke tannery in 1910 and 1920. See Nannie Isabel Webb Price in chapter 1 and Appendix B. See also Ayers, *Promise of the New South.*

6. Humbert et al., *Virginia: Economic and Civic,* 297–308.

7. For discussion of possibilities for comparing and analyzing the seeming disparate experiences of individuals, see Clyde Kluckhohn and Henry Murray cited in Runyan, *Life Histories and Psychobiography,* 6–9; and Sidney Mintz, "The Anthropological Interview and the Life History," in Dunaway and Baum, *Oral History,* 18–26. For

occupational histories and personal stories and another approach, see also Lloyd and Mullen, *Lake Erie Fishermen,* 161–73.

8. Marvin Broyhill was referred to thusly by his grandson, Marvin T. Broyhill III, in a letter, previously cited in chapter 3, n. 30, 7. The reference to John Powell was made in the *Richmond Times-Dispatch,* "Lathering Richmond for Fifty Years," 18 November 1934, Sunday Magazine Section, sec. 5, pp. 9, 11.

9. Wood, *Black Majority,* 104. The date of his birth is based on a report in the *Richmond Times-Dispatch* article (cited in n. 8), and it holds up well with his age given in the 1920 Henrico County census. See Appendix B. However, if he was indeed sixty-eight when Susie Byrd interviewed him, then the date of this interview would have been in 1934.

10. "Lathering Richmond," *Richmond Times-Dispatch,* 18 November 1934, 9. The *Greater Richmond Directory, 1905* (Richmond: Hill Directory Co., 1905), vol. 41, listed John Powell working as a barber at 1408 E. Main Street in Richmond and living at 732 N. Ninth Street. See also Ben James in chapter 4 and Appendix B.

11. See Tyler-McGraw and Kimball, *Bondage and Freedom,* 27–30 and nn. 30 and 31. According to their sources, Lomax Smith's support of the southern cause was largely rhetorical, but from Powell's knowledge and recall Smith actually served as a soldier in the Confederate army. Tyler-McGraw and Kimball also claim that Russell in *Free Negro in Virginia* misread William Meekin as "Mundin." But it is not a misreading; rather, it seems to be their confusion, not Russell's. The 1920 Henrico County census lists William Mundin, eighty, barber/own shop; wife Leonead, seventy-eight; daughter Maude, forty-two, single, registered private nurse; and son Reginald, thirty-five, single, medical doctor, all living at 717 Sixth Street. At 715 Sixth Street is a Herbert Mundin, forty, tailor/own shop, and wife Minnie, thirty-eight. And John Scott, fifty-three, barber/works in barber shop (possibly that of his brother Cornelius at 816 Sixth Street), and his wife Willanna, thirty-two, trained nurse/private family, lived at 711 Sixth Street.

12. See reference to John Scott in n. 11 above.

13. This article was previously cited in n. 9 above. However, there was also an earlier article in the *Richmond News-Leader,* "Familiar Names Appear on Gilded 'Mugs' in John Powell's Glistening Collection," Tuesday, 23 May 1933, n.p.

14. Tilley, *R. J. Reynolds Tobacco,* 237.

15. Virginia Writers' Project worker Anderson reported Cipriani as living at 203 Thirty-fifth Street, Richmond, in 1939, but that address does not appear in any of the city directories checked for a range of years around that time. There is, however, a Jos. Cipriani (Ciprai in some), cabinetmaker, antique shop, with a wife Mary F., h. 14 E. Main Street, listed in *Hill's Directory* for 1934 and 1936. By 1938, Mrs. Mary Ciperani, seamstress, is listed alone at r. 1435 (1427) W. Main. This Mary Ciperani is likely the widow of Joseph and also, in all probability, the Nana Cipriani of the interview. But there are other complications: Salvatore Cipriana, born 1895, who emigrated from Italy in 1912, is in Newport News in 1920 but appears in Richmond city directories beginning in 1924. In 1933 he is listed as living at *14 W. Main* (Joseph and Mary are at *14 E.* Main), and he is a clerk in an antique shop. He married a woman from Fredericksburg named Mary Magdalene Bosher, they continued living in Richmond, and she (or a Mary, at least) worked for Phillip Morris as a machine operator. Grandchildren of this couple still living in Richmond claim no knowledge of or kinship with the earlier Joseph and Mary Cipriani; personal communication with R. Cipriani, June 1994.

16. See Jones and Park, "From Feedbags to Fashion," for mention of such tobacco bag usage.

17. We have deleted a paragraph here of Anderson's musings about federal relief programs ruining the morale of the people.

18. About four and one-half pages follow in which Anderson reports bits of overheard conversations between the young woman in charge of the station and various unidentified people who came in conducting their business; that part of the account is left out here. The listing that follows, "Five Cent Bags of Smoking Tobacco," was included with the interview on an attached, separate page.

19. A typed note at the top of the interview indicates that Thomas McCaleb began work in the grocery store with "Mr. Jos. Payne." In the 1910 census for Alleghany County, Joseph W. Payne, forty-seven, with a wife and two daughters, was listed as the proprietor of a livery stable. Not far away, however, George A. Payne, also forty-seven, with a wife and one daughter, was proprietor of a grocery store and was so also in 1920.

20. See Gipsy Smith, comp., *Wonderful Jesus and Other Songs* (Chicago: Biglow-Main-Excell Co.), 1927,

UVA/KBP. The title song, "Wonderful Jesus," was the campaign song for the evangelist's tours. This collection also contains the song "Look and Live" referred to by Rev. Willis Madden in chapter 4.

21. See Heinemann, *Depression and New Deal*, 6–7.

22. The cleaning business run by Roxie's parents, Edward and Ida Prescott, appeared in the Danville city directory in 1931; by 1939 the directory listed it as being managed by Roxie's brother, Charles A. Prescott. The establishment is still listed in the telephone book, but now it is "Crane Cleaners, Formerly Prescott's Cleaners."

23. Scales is referring here to Francis J. Gorman, a vice president of the United Textile Workers of America, who led the organizing drive for the strike in Danville. See Smith, *Mill on the Dan*, 299–324, for a detailed account of the strike and its effects; see also 390–91 and n. 78 for comment on Gorman and a later attempt to organize in 1931.

24. This information is from correspondence dated 29 July 1991 and telephone conversation between Mrs. Hilda Frances Hodges and Nancy J. Martin-Perdue, 21 March 1991.

25. This information was cited by Venable as being from the Miscellaneous Lien Book, Deed Books, and Will Book #5 in Alleghany County Courthouse records.

26. See Appendix B.

27. Ibid. In the 1870 census for Mt. Cove District, Fayette County, West Virginia, Thaddeus Deal, twenty-five, farmer, born in Virginia, is listed in household 298, along with his wife, Henrietta, twenty, also born in Virginia, and son John R., one, born in West Virginia. See Geraldine Workman and Dreama Blevins, comp., *1870 Census, Fayette County, West Virginia* (Page, W.Va.: Loup Creek Press, n.d.).

CHAPTER EIGHT

1. Wust, *Virginia Germans*, 20–21, and Humbert et al., *Virginia: Economic and Civic*, 10–14.

2. See U.S. Census Manuscripts, Virginia, census for Alleghany County, 1860, #947-942 and #955-951. See also Humbert et al., *Virginia: Economic and Civic*, 31.

3. VWP, *Roanoke: Story of County and City*, 202.

4. Noe, *Southwest Virginia's Railroad*, 63.

5. Eller, *Miners, Millhands, and Mountaineers*, 149, 150. For the story of coal in the southern mountains generally, see 128–242 and also Shifflett, *Coal Towns*.

6. See Shifflett, *Coal Towns*, 162–75, 198–212, and 220 n. 50 on Lee County, which is where John Davidson was from. Although his argument for a particular type of working culture specific to the experiences and conditions of mining is persuasive, Shifflett is essentially describing a subset of working-class culture.

7. In regard to the killing of "Henry Walker," Lilly almost certainly referred to the murder of Henry Miller by Doctor Z. J. Walker, following Miller's examination by a justice of the court on 8 November 1889. In the disturbance that followed, Walker and his wife were killed by Miller's sons, and one of them was seriously wounded. See Morton, *History of Rockbridge County*, 156–57.

8. This is a reference to the former Low Moor Iron Company furnace, Low Moor, Alleghany County. See the following interview with Joseph Hippert.

9. According to Venable's notes, Lilly's blacksmith shop was located between Court and Bridge Streets, in the alley parallel with the Jackson River, Covington, Virginia.

10. Athey, *Kaymoor*, 5–7. See also Driver, "Social Differentiation and Cohesion," 396–403, and Appendix B.

11. Athey, *Kaymoor*, 7–8, and Driver, "Social Differentiation and Cohesion." See also life history with F. W. (Howard N.) Lilly in this chapter.

12. The Oriskany mine in Botetourt County was named for the Devonian sandstone formation, known variously as the Oriskany or Ridgely formation. This formation occurs "in various places from Tennessee to Maryland, but it is mainly in Alleghany, Botetourt, Craig, and Augusta counties, particularly in the region about Clifton Forge, that the iron ores have their best development." Humbert et al., *Virginia: Civic and Economic*, 121.

13. The reference in the life history text to the "Paymaster" may, in fact, refer to Edward Hibbert, who was listed in the census as the "Cashier" for the Iron Company.

14. The Virginia Iron, Coal, and Coke Company (referred to as George Carter's "I.C.C." in the text) had a

share in the Low Moor Iron Company and in the management of its mines and furnaces. For coverage of Carter, the Blairs (a syndicate of New York bankers), and others involved in developing the "I.C.C." and other related coal companies in the area, see Eller, *Miners, Millhands, and Mountaineers,* 12, 59–60, 75–76, 150–51.

15. The president and manager of Low Moor, Ellison R. (C.) Means, with his wife, Ruby; two children; his mother-in-law, Sallie C. Rings of Kentucky; brother-in-law, Bolivar B. Rings; and an Irish servant, also lived in the furnace village. According to the 1910 census, Means and his family occupied dwelling no. 410; his assistant treasurer, Samuel G. Cargill, and his family were next door in no. 411; and Joseph and Edward Hibbert occupied nos. 412 and 413, respectively. See also Athey, *Kaymoor,* 12, 15.

Although these were supposedly Hippert's words, Venable made similar comments elsewhere on the paternalism of the iron foundry owners. Writing about the "capitalist-owner of the Lucy-Selina Furnace," she commented: "He lived in the midst of his feudal kingdom. . . . He shared 'hard times' with his employees and reduced his living expenses till the market went up. He was the padre to three generations of most of the families on his payroll." Life history with Nona Craft, 28 May 1940, VSL/AB.

16. Even though they had lived in the county for thirty years, Hippert and his family *were* outsiders in the Potts Creek community by reasons both of birth and of class. His assessment that his not being a native of the area affected the treatment he received with regard to jobs was likely well founded. Driver found strong evidence of efforts to maintain social distance and boundaries between distinct "insider/outsider components" still existing in this same settlement in 1978. See Driver, "Social Differentiation and Cohesion," 478.

17. Driver cites local orchardist and Chamber of Commerce member Benjamin Moomaw for the 1931 closing date. Ibid., 403. But an earlier date is suggested by Venable's life history with Jimmie Hunt, 17 June 1940, VSL/AB, box 181. Hunt, who lived in Canada before World War I, returned there and met Sanger after the armistice. It was apparently Sanger's influence that brought Hunt to Covington to serve a four-year apprenticeship as a mechanic under Alfather at the Covington Machine Shop. The shop closed within a year after Hunt arrived there, and he finished his apprentice's term at the Westvaco mill.

18. The six and one-third pages presented here are edited down from the eleven-and-one-half-page original report.

19. The phrase "in the horse and covered-wagon days" was omitted, because its placement here made it describe the birthplace of Milton Joseph Gross, rather than the old ford.

20. In a footnote, Venable observes that Olin Payne is the county clerk and that he "owns the house Oscar lives in."

21. See the life history of George and Celia Brown in chapter 1.

22. The headnote provided here with "The Explosion at Derby" was written by James Taylor Adams to accompany the text, which was included in the VWP folklore/folksong materials, UVA/FC. See Rosenberg, *Folksongs of Virginia,* 33. Writers' Project worker James Taylor Adams included essentially the same ballad text in his publication *Death in the Dark.* In that work, Adams gave the following additional information: "This ballad was sent me on May 20, 1940, by Miss Anna Belle Kilgore, teacher in the Coeburn (Virginia) High School. She obtained it from Miss Pauline Carico of the Sandy Ridge section of Wise County. A notation in pencil on the ballad says: 'Composed by Leslie Ketron. 4th and 5th stanzas by Ruth Crowder and Maude Hall' " (117).

CHAPTER NINE

1. MacDonald, *Southern Mill Hills,* 6–8.

2. John W. Speake, 2 May 1926, quoted in ibid., 17.

3. Broadus Mitchell, quoted in MacDonald, *Southern Mill Hills,* 21.

4. Hall et al., *Like a Family,* 74. Allen Tullos's *Habits of Industry* is useful here as well.

5. Hall et al., *Like a Family,* 183–236.

6. Alan Lomax, "Bluegrass Background: Folk Music with Overdrive," *Esquire* (October 1959): 108.

7. Humbert et al., *Virginia: Economic and Civic,* 43. For a fairly detailed description of the viscose process, see the entry "The American Viscose Corporation Plant" in the Roanoke tour section of VWP, *Virginia: A Guide,* 304. For comparison, see Roy Fix's account in this chapter.

8. Life history with Henry Cowles (Crowder) by Leila Blanche Bess, 6 pp., 1,895 wds., rec. 21 March 1939, VSL/AB, box 185.

9. See Zieger, "Union Comes to Covington," 52–56.

10. Ibid., 65. Zieger names various officers of Local 152 through time, but does not mention Brinkley. In his will in 1917, Claude C. Brinkley mentioned a brother, George, who was in New York at the time and was likely G. G. Brinkley. It also appears that Brinkley was not president of the union for long.

11. Zieger notes that the secretary of Local 152, S. N. Montgomery, "found company officials unusually forthcoming and cordial [in October 1938], although he suspected that this was largely due to the fact that they were seeking union acceptance of a 10 percent wage reduction." Ibid., 68. The company was also beginning to be subjected to pressures from the more "militant unionism" of the CIO.

12. Despite improvements in working conditions and increased safety precautions, work in a pulp and paper mill can never be considered to be without hazard. As recently as 5 May 1988 the *Washington Post* reported "17 Workers Injured in Va. Chemical Spill." About 300,000 gallons of toxic sodium sulfide gas used "in preparing wood to make pulp" was released when a 400,000-gallon storage tank ruptured at the Covington Westvaco paper mill. The workers were injured when they inhaled the gas, and an unknown amount of the gas leaked into the Jackson River.

13. See Heinemann, *Depression and New Deal,* 162.

14. In the almost three pages that follow, Venable informs us that for the quarters described, the Reynolds pay four dollars a month rent to a landlord who winters in Richmond. She also notes that the county welfare office found the housing for them and provides the family with fifteen dollars a month, which buys their "groceries and coal." Most of this part of the interview is composed, however, of Venable's description of and judgments concerning each family member and is deleted here.

15. The "Family Register" attached to the interview indicated that the twins were born and died at Iron Gate in 1914, and it noted that their "caskets cost $10 each and were paid for at $1 per month. Burial expenses were not extra."

16. The letter is typed by Venable in facsimile in the text of the interview. She indicates that it is on West Virginia Pulp and Paper Company letterhead stationery, dated 18 October 1933, addressed to Mr. H. D. Reynolds of 206 Oak Street, Covington, and signed by E. A. Crawford for Westvaco.

17. These two documents, both dated October 1933, from Drs. Jos. L. Wright and A. C. Byers of Harrisonburg, Virginia, were typed in facsimile by Venable as part of the interview. Reynold's medical examination results are omitted here for reasons of privacy; only the physician's conclusions will be given. Wright reported: "Probable diagnosis neurosis from accident, September 1st, 1933 by inhalation of Chromaline gas." Byers likewise concluded: "Neurosis, breaking down of nervous system by inhalation of Chromaline gas."

18. The reference here to Canady and Wright does not agree with the medical reports referred to above, which were by Wright and "Byers." This is a discrepancy; it may or may not be an error.

19. We have deleted the last page and a half of text, which contained mostly unwarranted conjecture by Venable.

20. See Driver, "Social Differentiation and Cohesion," 406. She reports that the rayon plant was established in 1928. Zieger gives the date as 1929; see "Union Comes to Covington," 53.

21. Humbert et al., *Virginia: Economic and Civic,* 43–44.

22. See Heinemann, *Depression and New Deal,* 166–67. See also Fry, "Rayon, Riot, and Repression," 3–18. The speaker cited is supposedly John Harvey, cited in the life history with Mrs. Jim (Jennie) Mays by Mary S. Venable, 4 pp., 1,489 wds., 15 July 1940, VSL/AB, box 182.

23. A long paragraph is omitted in which Venable details the argument between Mr. and Mrs. Fix about where their garage is going to be built.

24. In a note on the interview, Venable commented that the church the Fix family attended was "a Presbyterian Church but a 'Union' congregation." In its institutional character the church presumably was Presbyterian, but its congregation seems to have fit Niebuhr's description of the church of the Disciples as being "somewhat more interested in the social principle of union than in the individual principle of the salvation of souls" (180). See Niebuhr, *Social Sources of Denominationalism,* 179–80, 197–99, 218–20, for discussion of Union movements, especially with regard to Scotch Presbyterians.

25. Venable ends this interview with the following paragraph quoted just as shown here:
"Scheinfeld claimed 'if we shake the bottle and equalize the environment, the levels of mentality in which classes of people now appear to be stratified would disappear. . . . with the constant intermingling that has taken

place among peoples of all levels . . . we have no basis for assuming that parents in the unskilled, laboring group carry, or will transmit to their offspring, genes for intelligence inferior to those of parents in the professional class.' From *You and Heredity,* pp. 217–19." See also Amram Scheinfeld, *Your Heredity and Environment,* in which he also notes "the enormous jumps that have been made in various groups from grossly inferior levels to ever higher stages of respectability," cited in Ainsworth, *Eclectic Essays,* 35. These quotations help to explain the several previous sentences by Venable as well as some of the ideas and sources influencing her thinking at the time.

26. "Jennie Mays in Rayon Village" by Mary S. Venable, 10 pp., rec. 6 March 1939, VSL/AB, box 181.

27. Smith, *Smoke Signals,* 15–18. See also Tullos, *Habits of Industry,* 162, and Tilley, *R. J. Reynolds Tobacco,* 96.

28. See VWP, *Virginia: A Guide,* 108–9.

29. A Nancy Carter, tobacco worker, was indicated in Hill's Richmond Directory in the years 1941, 1942, and 1943, *but* she is listed as "colored." Given the preceding statement, the Nancy Carter of this interview was white, that is, unless VWP interviewer Anderson deliberately changed her race and the text to disguise her identity.

EPILOGUE

1. Life history with Robert Sheckel by Russell Carpenter, 4 pp., 20 May 1939, VSL/AB, box 191.

2. Interview with James Cassell Ford by Essie W. Smith, 6 pp., 1,200 wds., 6 June 1940, VSL/AB, box 183.

3. See "Veterans Ask Proper Respect for the Flag," *Covington Virginian,* 12 June 1940. This notice from the local chapter of the Veterans of Foreign Wars warned local people "to avoid and shun" members of this sect "even as one would avoid and shun a rattlesnake or the small-pox." They also called on "all public-spirited, loyal Americans" to burn its "pernicious" literature and on "all loyal, patriotic employers of labor to get out of their employ and to refuse to hire others all such who will not salute the American flag."

4. Life history with Jimmie Hunt by Mary S. Venable, 11 pp., 3,251 wds., 17 June 1940, VSL/AB, box 181; life history with Mrs. Jim (Jennie) Mays by Mary S. Venable, 4 pp., 1,489 wds., 15 July 1940, VSL/AB, box 182.

5. Life history with Daniel Holmes by Rone Sidney, 2 pp., handwritten ms., rec. 3 March 1941, VSL/AB, box 186.

6. Shields, "Wartime Migration," 1.

7. Ibid., 3. Life history with Lenard Lipscomb by Rone Sidney, 2 pp., 350 wds., rec. 3 March 1941, VSL/AB, box 186.

8. Shields, "Wartime Migration," 3.

9. See Stearns's life history in chapter 2.

10. The land for Fort A. P. Hill was acquired at an average of about thirty-three dollars per acre. Information on use of Fort A. P. Hill as a maneuver area and a training ground for troops going to fight in the North African campaign is from a typescript (pp. 7–10) accompanying a letter dated 4 February 1981 from L. E. Rice Jr., chief, Real Estate Division, Naval Facilities Engineering Command, Corps of Engineers, Department of the Army, to Charles L. Perdue Jr.

11. UVA/ERR, box 1.

12. For the Standard Oil story, see Plattner, *Roy Stryker,* and Lemann, *Out of the Forties.* As a matter of historical curiosity and coincidence, the editors have in their possession Roy Stryker's personally inscribed, December 1943 edition of Pratt's *Oil in the Earth.* Wallace E. Pratt was at that time the vice president of Standard Oil of New Jersey; apparently his work was given to Stryker to supply background information for his new venture. This book was given to Charles L. Perdue Jr. by Stryker's daughter, Phyliss Stryker Wilson, when both were employed by the United States Geological Survey.

13. Mangione, *Dream and the Deal,* 347.

BIBLIOGRAPHY

Abrahams, Roger D. *Singing the Master: The Emergence of African-American Culture in the Plantation South.* New York: Penguin Books, 1992.

Adams, James Taylor. *Death in the Dark: A Collection of Factual Ballads of American Mine Disasters.* Big Laurel, Va.: Adams-Mullins Press, 1941; facsimile reprint, Folcroft Library Editions, 1976.

Ainsworth, Catherine Harris. *Eclectic Essays.* Dubuque, Iowa: Kendall/Hunt Publishing Co., 1974.

Anderson, James C. *Roy Stryker: The Humane Propagandist.* Louisville: University of Louisville, Photographic Archives, 1977.

Argersinger, Jo Ann E. *Toward a New Deal in Baltimore: People and Government in the Great Depression.* Chapel Hill: University of North Carolina Press, 1988.

Athey, Lou. *Kaymoor: A New River Community.* [Philadelphia]: Eastern National Park and Monument Association, 1986.

Ayers, Edward L. *The Promise of the New South: Life after Reconstruction.* New York: Oxford University Press, 1992.

Ayers, Edward L., and John C. Willis, eds. *The Edge of the South: Life in Nineteenth-Century Virginia.* Charlottesville: University Press of Virginia, 1991.

Bach, Marcus. *Strange Sects and Curious Cults.* New York: Dodd, Mead & Co., 1961.

Baldwin, Sidney. *Poverty and Politics: The Rise and Decline of the Farm Security Administration.* Chapel Hill: University of North Carolina Press, 1968.

Banks, Ann, ed. *First-Person America.* New York: Vintage Books, 1981.

Banks, Ann, and Robert Carter. *Survey of Federal Writers' Project Manuscript Holdings in State Depositories.* Washington, D.C.: American Historical Association, 1985.

Barbre, Joy Webster, et al. (Personal Narratives Group). *Interpreting Women's Lives: Feminist Theory and Personal Narratives.* Bloomington: Indiana University Press, 1989.

Barden, Thomas E., ed. *Virginia Folk Legends.* Charlottesville: University Press of Virginia, 1991.

Baughman, Ernest W. *Type and Motif-Index of the Folktales of England and North America.* The Hague: Mouton & Co., 1966.

Bauman, Richard, ed. *Folklore, Cultural Performances, and Popular Entertainments: A Communications-Centered Handbook.* New York: Oxford University Press, 1992.

Biles, Roger. *New Deal For The American People.* DeKalb: Northern Illinois University Press, 1991.

Black, Sandra K., and Kathleen M. MacKay. "Folk Narratives of Spotsylvania County." Paper no. 1972-89. Kevin Barry Perdue Archives of Traditional Culture, University of Virginia, 1972.

Bloxom, Marguerite D., comp. *Pickaxe and Pencil: References for the Study of the WPA.* Washington, D.C.: Library of Congress, 1982.

Botkin, B[enjamin] A. *The American Play-Party Song.* 1937. Reprint, New York: Frederick Ungar, 1963.

———. "We Called It 'Living Lore.'" *New York Folklore Quarterly* 14, no. 3 (Fall 1958).

———. "WPA and Folklore Research: 'Bread and Song.'" *Southern Folklore Quarterly* 3 (March 1939): 7–14.

———, ed. *Folk-Say: A Regional Miscellany.* Norman: Oklahoma Folk-Lore Society, 1929.

———, ed. *Lay My Burden Down: A Folk History of Slavery.* Chicago: University of Chicago Press, 1945.

Bourne, Francis T. *Preliminary Checklist of the Central Correspondence Files of the Work Projects Administration and Its Predecessors, 1933–1944.* Washington, D.C.: National Archives, 1946.

Brait, Susan. *Chesapeake Gold: Man and Oyster on the Bay.* Lexington: University Press of Kentucky, 1990.

Brewington, M. U. *Chesapeake Bay: A Pictorial Maritime History.* New York: Bonanza Books, 1956.

Brown, James Seay, Jr., ed. *Up before Daylight: Life Histories from the Alabama Writers' Project, 1938–1939.* University: University of Alabama Press, 1982.

Broyhill, Marvin Talmadge, III. *The Broyhill Family History.* Petersburg, Va.: privately printed, 1975.

Burgess, Robert G., ed. *Field Research: A Sourcebook and Field Manual.* London: George Allen and Unwin, 1982.

Burke, Peter. *Popular Culture in Early Modern Europe.* New York: Harper & Row, 1978.

Burrison, John A., ed. *Storytellers: Folktales and Legends from the South.* Athens: University of Georgia Press, 1989.

Calos, Mary Mitchell, Charlotte Easterling, and Ella Sue Rayburn. *Old City Point and Hopewell: The First 370 Years.* Norfolk/Virginia Beach, Va.: Donning Co., n.d.

Campbell, Doak S., Frederick H. Bair, and Oswald L. Harvey. *Educational Activities of the Works Progress Administration.* Washington, D.C.: U.S. Government Printing Office, 1939.

Clifford, James, and George E. Marcus, eds. *Writing Culture: The Poetics and Politics of Ethnography.* Berkeley and Los Angeles: University of California Press, 1986.

Cogan, Frances B. *All-American Girl: The Ideal of Real Womanhood in Mid-Nineteenth-Century America.* Athens: University of Georgia Press, 1989.

Cohen, David Steven, ed. *America, the Dream of My Life: Selections from the Federal Writers' Project New Jersey Ethnic Survey.* New Brunswick, N.J.: Rutgers University Press, 1990.

Collier, John, Jr., and Malcolm Collier. *Visual Anthropology: Photography as a Research Method.* Rev. and exp. edition. Albuquerque: University of New Mexico Press, 1986.

Comaroff, John, and Jean Comaroff. *Ethnography and the Historical Imagination.* Boulder, Colo.: Westview Press, 1992.

Conkin, Paul K. *The New Deal.* New York: T. Y. Crowell & Co., 1967.

———. *Tomorrow a New World: The New Deal Community Program.* New York: Da Capo Press, 1976.

Couch, W. T., ed. *Culture in the South.* Chapel Hill: University of North Carolina Press, 1934.

Coward, Raymond T., and William M. Smith. *The Family in Rural Society.* Boulder, Colo.: Westview Press, 1981.

Cruikshank, Julie, with Angela Sidney, Kitty Smith, and Annie Ned. *Life Lived Like A Story: Life Stories of Three Yukon Native Elders.* Lincoln: University of Nebraska Press, 1990.

Curtis, James C. *Mind's Eye, Mind's Truth: FSA Photography Reconsidered.* Philadelphia: Temple University Press, 1989.

Daniel, Pete. *Breaking the Land: The Transformation of Cotton, Tobacco, and Rice Cultures since 1880.* Urbana: University of Illinois Press, 1985.

Daniel, Pete, Merry A. Foresta, Maren Stange, and Sally Stein. *Official Images: New Deal Photography.* Washington, D.C.: Smithsonian Institution Press, 1987.

Daniel, W. Harrison. *Bedford County, Virginia, 1840–1860: The History of an Upper Piedmont County in the Late Antebellum Era.* Bedford, Va.: Print Shop, 1985.

Daniel, Wayne W. *Pickin' on Peachtree: A History of Country Music in Atlanta, Georgia.* Urbana: University of Illinois Press, 1990.

Davidson, Katherine H. *Preliminary Inventory of the Records of the Federal Writers' Project, Work Projects Administration, 1935–1944.* Washington, D.C.: National Archives Publication No. 54-2, 1953.

Davis, Hubert J., ed. *The Silver Bullet and Other American Witch Stories.* Middle Village, N.Y.: Jonathan David, 1975.

Dixon, Penelope. *Photographers of the Farm Security Administration: An Annotated Bibliography, 1930–1980.* New York: Garland Publishing, 1983.

Dollard, John. *Caste and Class in a Southern Town.* 1937. 3d ed. Reprint, Garden City, N.Y.: Doubleday Anchor Books, 1957.

———. *Criteria for the Life History.* New Haven: Yale University Press, 1935.

Driver, Rebecca Virginia. "Social Differentiation and Cohesion in an Appalachian Community." Ph.D. diss., University of Virginia, 1978.

Dunaway, David K., and Willa K. Baum, eds. *Oral History: An Interdisciplinary Anthology.* Nashville: American Association for State and Local History, 1984.

Dundes, Alan. "Defining Identity through Folklore." In *Identity: Personal and Socio-Cultural, a Symposium,* edited by Anita Jacobson-Widding, 235–61, Studies in Cultural Anthropology 5. Uppsala: Academiae Upsaliensis, distributed by Almqvist & Wiksell, 1983.

Early, R. H. *Campbell Chronicles and Family Sketches: Embracing the History of Campbell County, Virginia, 1782–1926.* Lynchburg, Va.: J. P. Bell Co., 1927.

Eller, Ronald D. *Miners, Millhands, and Mountaineers: Industrialization of the Appalachian South, 1880–1930.* Knoxville: University of Tennessee Press, 1982.

Farmer, J. S., and W. E. Henley. *Slang and Its Analogues.* 1890–1904. New York: Arno Press, 1970.

Farrer, Claire R., ed. *Women and Folklore: Images and Genres.* Prospects Heights, Ill.: Waveland Press, 1975.

Federal Writers' Project. *These Are Our Lives.* Written by members of the Federal Writers' Project, Works Progress Administration. Chapel Hill: University of North Carolina Press, 1939.

Felldin, Jeanne Robey, comp. *Index to the 1820 Census of Virginia.* Baltimore: Genealogical Publishing Co., 1976.

"Final Report, National Youth Administration for the State of Virginia." 31 December 1943. Copy in Alderman Library, University of Virginia, Charlottesville.

First Annual Report: Resettlement Administration. Washington, D.C.: U.S. Government Printing Office, 1936.

Fisher, Andrea. *Let Us Now Praise Famous Women: Women Photographers for the US Government, 1935 to 1944.* London: Pandora, 1987.

Fite, Gilbert C. *Cotton Fields No More: Southern Agriculture, 1865–1980.* Lexington: University Press of Kentucky, 1984.

Fleischhauer, Carl, and Beverly W. Brannan, eds. *Documenting America, 1935–1943.* Berkeley and Los Angeles: University of California Press, 1988.

Fleury, Alice. "Emily Summers Palmer Stearns and the Farley House." Paper No. 1, 1989-79. Kevin Barry Perdue Archives of Traditional Culture, University of Virginia, 1989.

Folklore and Folklife in Virginia (journal of the Virginia Folklore Society) 2 (1980–81).

Forrest, John. *Lord I'm Coming Home: Everyday Aesthetics in Tidewater North Carolina.* Ithaca, N.Y.: Cornell University Press, 1988.

Foster, Stephen William. *The Past Is Another Country: Representation, Historical Consciousness, and Resistance in the Blue Ridge.* Berkeley and Los Angeles: University of California Press, 1988.

Fowler, Gene, and Bill Crawford. *Border Radio.* Austin: Texas Monthly Press, 1987.

The Frank C. Brown Collection of North Carolina Folklore. Edited by Newman Ivey White. Durham, N.C.: Duke University Press, 1952–64.

Franklin, John Hope. *From Slavery to Freedom: A History of Negro Americans.* 3d ed. New York: Vintage Books, 1967.

Fraser, Steve, and Gary Gerstle, eds. *The Rise and Fall of the New Deal Order, 1930–1980.* Princeton: Princeton University Press, 1989.

Fraser, Walter J., Jr., R. Frank Saunders Jr., and Jon L. Wakelyn. *The Web of Southern Social Relations: Women, Family, and Education.* Athens: University of Georgia Press, 1985.

Fry, Gladys-Marie. *Night Riders in Black Folk History.* Knoxville: University of Tennessee Press, 1975.

Fry, Joseph A. "Rayon, Riot, and Repression: The Covington Sit-Down Strike of 1937," *Virginia Magazine of History and Biography* 84, no. 1 (January 1976): 3–18.

Frye, John. *The Men All Singing.* Norfolk/Virginia Beach, Va.: Donning Co., 1978.

Gardner, James B., and George Rollie Adams, eds. *Ordinary People and Everyday Life: Perspectives on the New Social History.* Nashville, Tenn.: American Association for State and Local History, 1983.

Garner, Anita M. "Richmond's Own Eudora." *Richmond Quarterly* 7, no. 3 (Winter 1984): 15–19.

Garnett, W. E. "Our Rural Marginal Population," *Commonwealth: The Magazine of Virginia Business* 1, no. 6 (October 1934): 5–6, 22.

———. *Virginia's Marginal Population: A Study in Rural Poverty.* Blacksburg: Virginia Polytechnic Institute, 1941.

Gee, Wilson, and John J. Corson. *A Statistical Study of Virginia.* University, Va.: Institute for Research in the Social Sciences, 1927.

Gee, Wilson, and William Henry Stauffer. *Rural and Urban Living Standards in Virginia.* Institute for Research in the Social Sciences, monograph no. 6. Charlottesville, Va.: Michie Co., 1929.

Glassberg, David. *American Historical Pageantry: The Uses of Tradition in the Early Twentieth Century.* Chapel Hill: University of North Carolina Press, 1990.

Glassie, Henry. *Passing the Time in Ballymenone: Culture and History of an Ulster Community.* Philadelphia: University of Pennsylvania Press, 1982.

Gomme, Alice Bertha. *The Traditional Games of England, Scotland, and Ireland.* Vol. 1. 1894. Reprint, New York: Dover, 1964.

Gottschalk, Louis, Clyde Kluckhohn, and Robert Angell. *The Use of Personal Documents in History, Anthropology, and Sociology.* New York: Social Science Research Council, 1945.

Gragg, Larry Dale. *Migration in Early America: The Virginia Quaker Experience.* Ann Arbor: University of Michigan Research Press, [ca. 1980].

Hagood, Margaret Jarman. *Mothers of the South: Portraiture of the White Tenant Farm Woman.* 1939. Reprint, New York: W. W. Norton & Co, 1977.

Hall, Jacquelyn Dowd, James Leloudis, Robert Korstad, Mary Murphy, Lu Ann Jones, and Christopher B. Daly.

Like a Family: The Making of a Southern Cotton Mill World. Chapel Hill: University of North Carolina Press, 1987.

Hammer, Andrea. But Now When I Look Back: Remembering St. Mary's County through Farm Security Administration Photographs. Westminster, Md.: Opera House Printing, 1988.

Hand, Wayland D. Magical Medicine: The Folkloric Component of Medicine in the Folk Belief, Custom, and Ritual of the Peoples of Europe and America. Berkeley and Los Angeles: University of California Press, 1980.

Heinemann, Ronald L. "Alphabet Soup: The New Deal Comes to the Relief of Virginia." Virginia Cavalcade 33, no. 1 (Summer 1983).

———. Depression and New Deal in Virginia: The Enduring Dominion. Charlottesville: University Press of Virginia, 1983.

Helm, June, ed. Essays on the Verbal and Visual Arts: Proceedings of the 1966 Annual Spring Meeting of the American Ethnological Society. Seattle: University of Washington Press, 1967.

Hendrickson, Paul. "Double Exposure." Washington Post Magazine, 31 January 1988.

Himmelberg, Robert F., ed. The Great Depression and American Capitalism. Boston: D. C. Heath and Co., 1968.

Hirsch, Jerrold Maury. "Culture on Relief: The Federal Writers' Project in North Carolina, 1935–1942." M.A. thesis, University of North Carolina, 1973.

———. "Folklore in the Making: B. A. Botkin." Journal of American Folklore 100 (January–March 1987):3–38.

———. "Portrait of America: The Federal Writers' Project in an Intellectual and Cultural Context." Ph.D. diss., University of North Carolina, 1984.

Hite, Mary Elizabeth. My Rappahannock Story Book. Richmond, Va.: Dietz Press, 1950.

Hughes, Roscoe D., and Henry Leidheiser Jr. Exploring Virginia's Human Resources. Charlottesville: University Press of Virginia, 1965.

Humbert, R. Lee, Willard H. Humbert, Melville L. Jeffries, and Clarence W. Newman, eds. Virginia: Economic and Civic. Richmond, Va.: Whittet & Shepperson, 1933.

Hurley, F. Jack. Portrait of a Decade: Roy Stryker and the Development of Documentary Photography in the Thirties. Baton Rouge: Louisiana State University Press, 1972.

Jack, George S., and E. B. Jacobs. History of Roanoke County, History of Roanoke City, and History of the Norfolk & Western Railway Company. Roanoke, Va.: Stone Printing and Manufacturing Co., 1912.

Johnson, Brooks. Mountaineers to Main Streets: The Old Dominion As Seen through the Farm Security Administration Photographs. Norfolk, Va.: Chrysler Museum, 1985.

Johnson, Elisabeth B., and C. E. Johnson Jr. Rappahannock County, Virginia: A History, Fact, Fiction, Foolishness and the Fairfax Story. Orange, Va.: Green Publishers, 1981.

Johnson, Paula J., ed. Working the Water: The Commercial Fisheries of Maryland's Patuxent River. Charlottesville: University Press of Virginia, 1988.

Jones, Jacqueline. Labor of Love, Labor of Sorrow: Black Women, Work, and the Family, from Slavery to the Present. New York: Vintage Books, 1985.

Jones, Loyal. The Preacher Joke Book: Religious Anecdotes from the Oral Tradition. Little Rock, Ark.: August House, 1989.

Jones, Lu Ann, and Nancy Grey Osterud. "Breaking New Ground: Oral History and Agricultural History." Journal of American History 76, no. 2 (September 1989): 551–64.

Jones, Lu Ann, and Sunae Park. "From Feedbags to Fashion." Paper, Division of Agriculture and Natural Resources and Division of Textiles, Smithsonian Institution, Washington, D.C.

Joyce, Rosemary O. A Woman's Place: The Life History of a Rural Ohio Grandmother. Columbus: Ohio State University Press, 1983.

Joyner, Charles. Down by the Riverside: A South Carolina Slave Community. Urbana: University of Illinois Press, 1984.

Key to the Pantry: Choice Tried Recipes Collected by the Ladies of the Church of the Epiphany, Danville, Virginia. Danville, Va.: Boatwright Bros., 1898.

Kirshenblatt-Gimblett, Barbara, and Edward M. Bruner. "Tourism." In Folklore, Cultural Performances, and Popular Entertainments: A Communications-Centered Handbook, edited by Richard Bauman. New York: Oxford University Press, 1992.

Krupat, Arnold. For Those Who Come After: A Study of Native American Autobiography. Berkeley and Los Angeles: University of California Press, 1985.

Kyvig, David E., and Mary-Ann Blasio. *New Day/New Deal: A Bibliography of the Great American Depression, 1929–1941*. New York: Greenwood Press, 1988.

Langness, L. L., and Gelya Frank. *Lives: An Anthropological Approach to Biography*. Novato, Calif.: Chandler & Sharp, 1981.

Lavie, Smadar, Kirin Narayan, and Renato Rosaldo, eds. *Creativity/Anthropology*. Ithaca, N.Y.: Cornell University Press, 1993.

Legman, G. *No Laughing Matter: An Analysis of Sexual Humor*. Vols. 1, 2 (2d ser.). New York: Breaking Point, 1968, 1975.

Lemann, Nicholas. *Out of the Forties*. Austin: Texas Monthly Press, 1981.

Leuchtenburg, William E. *Franklin D. Roosevelt and the New Deal, 1932–1940*. New York: Harper Torchbooks, 1963.

Levine, Lawrence W. *Black Culture and Black Consciousness: Afro-American Folk Thought from Slavery to Freedom*. New York: Oxford University Press, 1977.

Lich, Glen E., ed. *Regional Studies: The Interplay of Land and People*. College Station: Texas A&M University Press, 1992.

Linde, Charlotte. *Life Stories: The Creation of Coherence*. New York: Oxford University Press, 1993.

Livermore, Mary A. *The Story of My Life; or, the Sunshine and Shadow of Seventy Years*. Hartford, Conn.: A. D. Worthington, 1897.

Lloyd, Timothy C., and Patrick B. Mullen. *Lake Erie Fishermen: Work, Identity, and Tradition*. Urbana: University of Illinois Press, 1990.

Lornell, Kip. *Virginia's Blues, Country, and Gospel Records, 1902–1943: An Annotated Discography*. Lexington: University Press of Kentucky, 1989.

Lowenthal, David. *The Past Is a Foreign Country*. New York: Cambridge University Press, 1985.

Lyne, David C. "What Are They Saying? A Study of the Jargon of Hilltopping." M.A. thesis, Western Kentucky University, 1976.

MacCannell, Dean. *The Tourist: A New Theory of the Leisure Class*. 1976. Reprint, New York: Schocken Books, 1989.

MacDonald, Lois. *Southern Mill Hills: A Study of Social and Economic Forces in Certain Textile Mill Villages*. New York: Alex L. Hillman, 1928.

MacLeish, Archibald. *Land of the Free*. New York: Harcourt, Brace, 1938.

Madden, T. O., Jr. *Madden's Tavern: A History*. Elkwood, Va.: privately printed, 1981.

Madden, T. O., Jr., with Ann Brush Miller. *We Were Always Free: The Maddens of Culpeper County, Virginia: A 200-Year Family History*. New York: W. W. Norton and Co., 1992.

Malone, Bill C. *Country Music USA: A Fifty-Year History*. Austin: University of Texas Press, 1975.

Mangione, Jerre. *The Dream and the Deal: The Federal Writers' Project, 1935–1943*. New York: Equinox Books, 1972.

Marcus, George E., and Michael M. J. Fischer. *Anthropology as Cultural Critique*. Chicago: University of Chicago Press, 1986.

Matthews, Jill Julius. *Good and Mad Women: The Historical Construction of Femininity in Twentieth-Century Australia*. Sydney: George Allen & Unwin, 1984.

McCarl, Robert. *The District of Columbia Fire Fighters' Project: A Case Study in Occupational Folklife*. Washington, D.C.: Smithsonian Institution Press, 1985.

McDonald, William F. *Federal Relief Administration and the Arts: The Origins and Administrative History of the Arts Projects of the WPA*. Columbus: Ohio State University Press, 1969.

McElvaine, Robert S. *Down and Out in the Great Depression: Letters from the "Forgotten Man."* Chapel Hill: University of North Carolina Press, 1983.

McKinzie, Kathleen O'Connor. "Writers on Relief: 1935–1942." Ph.D. diss., Indiana University, 1970.

Melville, Annette. *Farm Security Administration, Historical Section: A Guide to Textual Records in the Library of Congress*. Washington, D.C.: Library of Congress, 1985.

Merton, Robert K. *Social Theory and Social Structure*. 1949. Revised and enlarged ed., Glencoe, Ill.: Free Press, 1962.

Montell, William Lynwood. *The Saga of Coe Ridge: A Study in Oral History*. Knoxville: University of Tennessee Press, 1970.

Moore, John Hammond. *Albemarle: Jefferson's County, 1726–1976*. Charlottesville: University Press of Virginia, 1976.

Morrison, A. J., ed. *Travels in Virginia in Revolutionary Times*. Lynchburg, Va.: J. P. Bell Co., 1922.

Morton, Oren F. *A Centennial History of Alleghany County, Virginia*. Dayton, Va.: J. K. Ruebush Co., 1923.

———. *A History of Rockbridge County, Virginia*. Staunton, Va.: McClure Co., 1920.

Mullen, Patrick B. *I Heard the Old Fishermen Say: Folklore of the Texas Gulf Coast*. Austin: University of Texas Press, 1978.

———. *Listening to Old Voices: Folklore, Life Stories, and the Elderly*. Urbana: University of Illinois Press, 1992.

Myerhoff, Barbara. *Remembered Lives: The Work of Ritual, Storytelling, and Growing Older*. Edited by Marc Kaminsky. Ann Arbor: University of Michigan Press, 1992.

Natanson, Nicholas. *The Black Image in the New Deal: The Politics of FSA Photography*. Knoxville: University of Tennessee Press, 1992.

Newby, I. A. *Plain Folk in the New South: Social Change and Cultural Persistence, 1880–1915*. Baton Rouge: Louisiana State University Press, 1989.

Newell, William Wells. *Games and Songs of American Children*. 1903. Reprint, New York: Dover, 1963.

Niebuhr, H. Richard. *The Social Sources of Denominationalism*. 1929. Reprint, New York: World Publishing Co., 1957.

Noe, Kenneth W. *Southwest Virginia's Railroad: Modernization and the Sectional Crisis*. Urbana: University of Illinois Press, 1994.

O'Neal, Hank. *A Vision Shared: A Classic Portrait of America and Its People, 1935–1943*. New York: St. Martin's Press, 1976.

Oppenheimer, Valerie Kincade. *The Female Labor Force in the United States*. University of California Monograph Series, no. 5, Berkeley and Los Angeles: University of California Press, 1970.

Parker, Patricia L. *The Hinterland: An Overview of the Prehistory and History of Prince William Forest Park, Virginia*. Occasional Report #1, Regional Archeology Program, National Capital Region. Washington, D.C.: National Park Service, United States Department of the Interior, September 1986.

Penkower, Monty Noam. *The Federal Writers' Project: A Study of Government Patronage of the Arts*. Urbana: University of Illinois Press, 1977.

Perdue, Charles L., Jr. "Movie Star Woman in the Land of the Black Angries: Ethnography and Folklore of a Negro Community in Rural Virginia." Ph.D. diss., University of Pennsylvania, 1971.

———. *Outwitting the Devil: Jack Tales from Wise County, Virginia*. Santa Fe, N.Mex.: Ancient City Press, 1987.

———. *Pigsfoot Jelly and Persimmon Beer: Foodways from the Virginia Writers' Project*. Santa Fe, N.Mex.: Ancient City Press, 1992.

Perdue, Charles L., Jr., Thomas E. Barden, and Robert K. Phillips. *Weevils in the Wheat: Interviews with Virginia Ex-Slaves*. 1976. Reprint, Charlottesville: University Press of Virginia, 1992.

Peterson, Sally. "Tin Plate Town: Coping with New Concepts on the Writers' Project in Pennsylvania." *New York Folklore*, special issue: "Folklore: The State of the Field," 9, nos. 3–4 (Winter 1983).

Peterson, Trudy Huskamp, ed. *Farmers, Bureaucrats, and Middlemen: Historical Perspectives on American Agriculture*. Washington, D.C.: Howard University Press, 1980.

Plattner, Steven W. *Roy Stryker: U.S.A., 1943–1950: The Standard Oil (New Jersey) Photography Project*. Austin: University of Texas Press, 1983.

Pleck, Elizabeth H., and Joseph H. Pleck. *The American Man*. Englewood Cliffs, N.J.: Prentice-Hall, 1980.

Puckett, Newbell Niles. *Folk Beliefs of the Southern Negro*. 1926. Reprint, Montclair, N.J.: Patterson Smith Publishing, 1968.

Radin, Paul, ed. *Crashing Thunder: The Autobiography of an American Indian*. With a foreword by Arnold Krupat. Lincoln: University of Nebraska Press, 1983.

Randolph, Vance. *Ozark Superstitions*. 1947. Reprinted as *Ozark Magic and Folklore*, New York: Dover, 1964.

Rapport, Leonard. "How Valid Are the Federal Writers' Project Life Stories: An Iconoclast among the True Believers." *Oral History Review* (1979): 6–17.

———. "On Interviewing." *International Journal of Oral History* 2 (February 1981): 46–52.

Rawson, Marion Nicholl. *Candleday Art*. New York: E. P. Dutton, 1938.

Reiman, Richard A. *The New Deal and American Youth: Ideas and Ideals in a Depression Decade*. Athens: University of Georgia Press, 1992.

Reynolds, Patrick, and Tom Shachtman. *The Gilded Leaf: Triumph, Tragedy, and Tobacco: Three Generations of the R. J. Reynolds Family and Fortune.* Boston: Little, Brown and Co., 1989.

Richter, Gerald J. "The Folklore Program of the Federal Writers' Project, 1935–1939." Term paper, University of Pennsylvania, 2 May 1974.

Robinson, John L. *Living Hard: Southern Americans in the Great Depression.* Washington, D.C.: University Press of America, 1981.

Rohrer, Wayne C., and Louis H. Douglas. *The Agrarian Transition in America: Dualism and Change.* Indianapolis: Bobbs-Merrill, 1969.

Rosenberg, Bruce A. *The Folksongs of Virginia: A Checklist of the WPA Holdings, Alderman Library, University of Virginia.* Charlottesville: University Press of Virginia, 1969.

Ruby, Jay, ed. *A Crack in the Mirror: Reflexive Perspectives in Anthropology.* Philadelphia: University of Pennsylvania Press, 1982.

Runyan, William McKinley. *Life Histories and Psychobiography: Explorations in Theory and Method.* New York: Oxford University Press, 1982.

Russ, Kurt C. *The Fincastle Pottery (44Bo304): Salvage Excavations at a Nineteenth-Century Earthenware Kiln Located in Botetourt County, Virginia.* Technical Report Series 3. Richmond: Virginia Department of Historic Resources, 1990.

Russell, John H. *The Free Negro in Virginia, 1619–1865.* 1913. Reprint, New York: Dover, 1969.

Saloutos, Theodore. *The American Farmer and the New Deal.* Ames: Iowa State University Press, 1982.

Santino, Jack. *Miles of Smiles, Years of Struggle: Stories of Black Pullman Porters.* Urbana: University of Illinois Press, 1989.

Scarborough, Dorothy. *On the Trail of Negro Folk-Songs.* 1925. Reprint. Hatboro, Pa.: Folklore Associates, 1963.

Scheinfeld, Amram. *Your Heredity and Environment.* Philadelphia: J. B. Lippincott Co., 1965. First published as *You and Heredity,* with Morton David Schweitzer. New York: Frederick A. Stokes Co., 1939.

Sears, John F. *Sacred Places: American Tourist Attractions in the Nineteenth Century.* New York: Oxford University Press, 1989.

Shapiro, Henry D. *Appalachia on Our Mind: The Southern Mountains and Mountaineers in the American Consciousness, 1870–1920.* Chapel Hill: University of North Carolina Press, 1978.

Shields, Carrington. "Wartime Migration: A Problem for the Commonwealth." *Virginia Public Welfare* 20, no. 11 (November 1942): 1, 3, 4.

Shifflett, Crandall A. *Coal Towns: Life, Work, and Culture in Company Towns of Southern Appalachia, 1880–1960.* Knoxville: University of Tennessee Press, 1991.

Siegel, Frederick F. *The Roots of Southern Distinctiveness: Tobacco and Society in Danville, Virginia, 1780–1865.* Chapel Hill: University of North Carolina Press, 1987.

Sitkoff, Harvard, ed. *Fifty Years Later: The New Deal Evaluated.* Philadelphia: Temple University Press, 1985.

Slaughter, Rev. Philip. *A History of St. Mark's Parish, Culpeper County, Virginia, with Notes of Old Churches and Old Families.* 1877. Reprint, Bowie, Md.: Heritage Books, 1990.

Smith, Jane Webb. *Smoke Signals: Cigarettes, Advertising, and the American Way of Life.* Richmond, Va.: Valentine Museum, 1990.

Smith, Robert Sidney. *Mill on the Dan: A History of Dan River Mills, 1882–1950.* Durham, N.C.: Duke University Press, 1960.

Sobel, Mechal. *The World They Made Together: Black and White Values in Eighteenth-Century Virginia.* Princeton: Princeton University Press, 1987.

Sontag, Susan. *On Photography.* New York: Farrar, Straus & Giroux, 1977.

Steiner, Jesse F. "Research Memorandum on Recreation in the Depression." Social Sciences Research Council, bulletin 32. New York, 1937.

Sternsher, Bernard. *Rexford Tugwell and the New Deal.* New Brunswick, N.J.: Rutgers University Press, 1964.

Stoeckle, John D., M.D., and George Abbott White. *Plain Pictures of Plain Doctoring: Vernacular Expression in New Deal Medicine and Photography.* Cambridge: MIT Press, 1985.

Stott, William. *Documentary Expression and Thirties America.* 1973. Reprint, Chicago: University of Chicago Press, 1986.

Stryker, Roy. Papers, 1912–72. University of Louisville Photographic Archives, Louisville, Ky.

Stryker, Roy Emerson, and Nancy Wood. *In This Proud Land: America, 1935–1943, As Seen in the FSA Photographs.* New York: Galahad Books, 1973.

Terrill, Tom E., and Jerrold Hirsch. "Replies to Leonard Rapport's 'How Valid Are the Federal Writers' Project Life Stories: An Iconoclast among the True Believers.' " *Oral History Review* (1980): 81–92.

———, eds. *Such as Us: Southern Voices of the Thirties.* Chapel Hill: University of North Carolina Press, 1978.

Thompson, Paul. *The Voice of the Past: Oral History.* Oxford: Oxford University Press, 1978.

Tilley, Nannie M. *The R. J. Reynolds Tobacco Company.* Chapel Hill: University of North Carolina Press, 1985.

Titon, Jeff Todd. "The Life Story." *Journal of American Folklore* 93 (July–September 1980): 276–92.

Toelken, Barre. *The Dynamics of Folklore.* Boston: Houghton Mifflin Co., 1979.

Tribe, Ivan M. *Mountaineer Jamboree: Country Music in West Virginia.* Lexington: University Press of Kentucky, 1984.

Tugwell, Rexford Guy, Thomas Munro, and Roy E. Stryker. *American Economic Life and the Means of Its Improvement.* New York: Harcourt, Brace, 1925.

Tullos, Allen. *Habits of Industry: White Culture and the Transformation of the Carolina Piedmont.* Chapel Hill: University of North Carolina Press, 1989.

Tyler-McGraw, Marie, and Gregg D. Kimball. *In Bondage and Freedom: Antebellum Black Life in Richmond, Virginia.* Richmond, Va.: Valentine Museum, 1988.

U.S. Bureau of the Census. Census Manuscripts, Population Schedules, Virginia, 1850–1920.

———.*Fifteenth Census of the United States,* 1930. Washington, D.C.: U.S. Government Printing Office, 1931–33.

Vance, Rupert Bayless. *Human Factors in Cotton Culture.* Chapel Hill: University of North Carolina Press, 1929.

Van Maanen, John. *Tales of the Field: On Writing Ethnography.* Chicago: University of Chicago Press, 1988.

———, ed. *Representation in Ethnography.* Thousand Oaks, Calif.: Sage Publications, 1995.

Virginia Writers' Project. *A Guide to Prince George and Hopewell.* Compiled by workers of the Writers' Program of the Work Projects Administration in the state of Virginia. N.p., 1939.

———. *The Negro in Virginia.* Compiled by workers of the Writers' Program of the Work Projects Administration in the state of Virginia. New York: Hastings House, 1940. Reprint, New York: Arno Press, 1969, and Winston-Salem, N.C.: John F. Blair, Publisher, 1994, with new foreword by Charles L. Perdue Jr.

———. *Roanoke: Story of County and City.* Work Projects Administration, Virginia Writers' Project. Roanoke, Va.: Stone Printing, 1942.

———. *Virginia: A Guide to the Old Dominion.* Compiled by workers of the Writers' Program of the Work Projects Administration in the state of Virginia. New York: Oxford University Press, 1940. Reprint, Richmond: Virginia State Library and Archives, 1992.

Wallenstein, Peter. "Indian Foremothers: Race, Sex, Slavery, and Freedom in Early National Virginia." Paper, 19 July 1992. In possession of author.

Ware, Caroline F., ed. *The Cultural Approach to History.* New York: Columbia University Press, 1940.

Watkins, Charles Alan. "The Blurred Image: Documentary Photography and the Depression South." Ph.D. diss., University of Delaware, 1982.

Weigle, Marta. "Southwest Lures: Innocents Detoured, Incensed Determined." *Journal of the Southwest* 32 (1990): 499–540.

———, ed. *New Mexicans in Cameo and Camera: New Deal Documentation of Twentieth-Century Lives.* Albuquerque: University of New Mexico Press, 1985.

———. *Two Guadalupes: Hispanic Legends and Magic Tales from Northern New Mexico.* Santa Fe, N.Mex.: Ancient City Press, 1987.

———. *Women of New Mexico: Depression Era Images.* Santa Fe, N.Mex.: Ancient City Press, 1993.

Weigle, Marta, and Peter White. *The Lore of New Mexico.* Albuquerque: University of New Mexico Press, 1988.

Welter, Barbara. *Dimity Convictions: The American Woman in the Nineteenth Century.* Athens: Ohio University Press, 1976.

Wennersten, John R. *The Oyster Wars of Chesapeake Bay.* Centreville, Md.: Tidewater Publishers, 1981.

White, Newman I. *American Negro Folk-Songs.* 1928. Reprint, Hatboro, Pa.: Folklore Associates, 1965.

Wilson, Bryan. *Religious Sects: A Sociological Study.* New York: McGraw-Hill, 1970.

Wingfield, Marshall. *Franklin County, Virginia: A History.* Berryville, Va.: Chesapeake Book Co., 1964.

———. *Marriage Bonds of Franklin County, Virginia, 1786–1858*. Baltimore, Md.: Genealogical Publishing Co., 1973.

———. *Pioneer Families of Franklin County, Virginia*. Berryville, Va.: Chesapeake Book Co., 1964.

Wood, Peter H. *Black Majority: Negroes in Colonial South Carolina from 1670 through the Stono Rebellion*. New York: W. W. Norton & Co., 1974.

Wust, Klaus. *The Virginia Germans*. Charlottesville: University Press of Virginia, 1969.

Yetman, Norman R. *Life under the 'Peculiar Institution': Selections from the Slave Narrative Collection*. New York: Holt, Rinehart & Winston, 1970.

Zieger, Robert H. "The Union Comes to Covington: Virginia Paperworkers Organize, 1933–1952." *Proceedings of the American Philosophical Society* 126, no. 1 (1982): 51–89.

INDEX

Page numbers in italics refer to illustrations.

Carter, William, 36

Carter, William Champe, 97, 99

Carter Coal Company, 310

Cash, Matthew, 303, 304

Catawba Sanatorium (Roanoke Co.), 68

Catawba Stock Farm (Botetourt Co.), 173, 176

Catt, Carrie Chapman, 3

Central High School (Charlotte Court House), 21, 178, *179–83*

Chamberlayne, The, 286

Chappell, Buddy, 278

Charlotte Court House, 159, 178

Charlottesville (Albemarle Co.), 20

Chase, Louisa and John, 268, 458 (n. 23)

Chatham (Pittsylvania Co.), 95, 220

Chatman family, 196, 409

Chelf, Dr. (Culpeper Co.), 149

Cheriton (Northampton Co.), 235

Chesapeake Bay, 251–57, 268

Childbearing, 77, 78; attitudes toward, 63, 64, 70, 71, 84, 85, 161, 201–3; and abortion, 63, 202, 203; midwives, 71, 202; premature birth, 322, 323, 324

Children and adolescents: labor of, 22, 28, 29, 36, 37, 42, 45, 78, 85, 138, 144, 145, 171, 225, 227, 266; given to others, 22, 36, 269; training or punishment of, 33, 36, 43, 44, 52, 140, 148, 170, 171, 225, 331; placed in foster homes or in care of kin, 36, 44, 45, 83, 84, 90, 140, 145, 268, 269, 290; as runaways, 36, 145; aspirations for, 43, 67, 76, 79, 89, 97, 120, 167, 171, 223, 225, 229, 240, 243, 257, 260, 286, 292, 293, 350, 351; views of, 63, 64, 84, 120, 131, 152, 161, 166, 171, 266, 305; behavior of, as source of worry, 71, 120, 140; wages of, 86, 90, 118, 125, 139, 304, 336, 337; illegitimate, 138, 163; and relations with grandparents, 142, 152, 153, 196, 323; unhappy with living situations, 244, 245; concern for neglected, 299, 305. *See also* Domestic economy; Education; Family; Household composition

Chrysler Museum, 13

Churches: Antioch Church (Culpeper), 162, 164, 165; Christian Holiness Church (Danville), 186; Christ's Church (Brandy, Culpeper Co.), 103; Dillwyn Baptist Church (Buckingham Co.), 154; First African Baptist Church (Richmond), 414; First Baptist Church (Covington), 176; High Street Baptist Church (Danville), 172; Hopewell Pentecostal Holiness Church, 422; Saint Paul's Catholic Church (Portsmouth), 85, 397; Saint Paul's Evangelical Reformed Church (Weyer's Cave, Rockingham Co.), *24*; Schuyler Pentecostal Church (Nelson Co.),

422; Shiloh Baptist Church (Rappahannock Co.), 148; Trinity Methodist Church (Roanoke), 421; Zion Baptist Church (Petersburg), 421

Cipriani, Nana, 281

Circle, Emery, 343

Civilian Conservation Corps, 140; camp near Lynchburg, 327; cook in Dolly Ann camp, 327

Civil servants: judge, 8, 149; magistrate, 44, 45; commissioner of revenue, 56; commonwealth attorney, 232, 233; clerk of the court, 322, 328; mounted policeman, 334

Civil War, 19, *27*, 39, 45, 49, 50, 143; socioeconomic and cultural change as result of, 25, 36, 56, 78, 251, 309; Union sympathizers, 28, 29; casualty of, 28, 31, 36, 41, 49, 53, 54, 122; particular sites, soldiers, or regiments, 33, 34, 45, 53, 54, 122, 143, 150, 161, 308; civilians' experience of, 33, 34, 309; provisions to troops in, 34; attitudes toward Yankees, 34, 56, 143; surrender in, 50, 251; prison experience in, 54; specific hospitals, 56, 143, 161; Confederate service, 122, 150, 241, 278; resident traitor's role in, 309. *See also* Slaves/slavery

Civil Works Administration, xi, 4

Clark, Paulett, 52

Clark, R. M., 278

Clarke, Aaron, 308

Class and status, 7–10, 20, 106, 295; altered by socioeconomic change, 8, 55, 56, 65, 134, 135, 210; conditioned by race, 8, 64, 65, 83, 134, 143, 156, 174, 266; attached to reputation and morality, 8, 65, 83, 84, 150, 171, 184, 185, 226, 277, 279, 327; manifest in differences of social power, 10, 36, 63, 65, 84, 96, 138, 143, 198–200, 210, 304, 322, 324; justified by pseudo-scientific notions, 20, 75, 76, 210, 211; spectrum of, 20, 97–105, 198–99; effects of social or geographic mobility on, 25, 27, 28, 46, 55, 56, 66, 78, 134, 135, 150; reflected in social relations and behavior, 33, 37, 83–85, 96, 98–100, 138, 149, 150, 152, 164–69, 170–72, 174–77, 305; intelligence unrelated to, 461–62 (n. 25). *See also* Blacks and whites; Discrimination; Gender; Language

Cleveland (Grover) Administration, 135, 145

Clifton Forge (Alleghany Co.), 206, 302, 310

Clifton Forge hospital, 344–46

Clinchport, 46, 436 (n. 38)

Clinch River, 46

Clothing, 53, 54, 75, 117, 121, 131, 144, 257, 266, 271, 330; disapproval of modern dress, 30, 59, 305; festive dress, 34, 35; of schoolteachers, 57; for work, 74, 103, 227; given to families, 88, 138, 225; dressmaking and sewing, 167, 172, 244; need for, 167,

305, 326; milliner, 262; for babies, 323, 324; and importance of "dressing up," 356

Coal mining, *331*; growth of mines and camps, 45–47; wage for, 46, 47, 330; miners, 46, 47, 330, 334; and expansion of railroads, 46, 303; in other states, 77, 298; hazards of, 77, 298, 331, 332; cokeyard worker, 189; effects of replacing employees with young, inexperienced workers, 298; use of physical exams to get rid of workers, 298; and depression in the industry, 303; and opening of Wise County fields, 303; and Derby mine disaster, 303, 332, 333, 334, 335; work culture in, 303, 333, 334; men instructed in safety of, 330; diagram of Derby mine, 332; list of Derby victims, 333; and bond between miners, 334; improved safety conditions in, 334

Coeburn (Wise Co.), 334, 432 (n. 3)

Coleman, J. H., 189; family of, 409

Colonial Heights project (WPA, Petersburg), 156, 196

Columbia Gas Company, 417

Columbia University, 3, 4

Comaroff, John and Jean, 6

Concord (Campbell Co.), 94

Conjure and witchcraft, 30, 31, 188, 434–35 (nn. 14, 15); death associated with, 188; bundle or bottle, 188, 189; prevention of, 188, 189; "two-head man," 188, 189; and education, 189; strength of belief in, 189; and use of black cat bone, 189. *See also* Folklore/folklife

Consolidated Bank and Trust Company, 414

Cooke, James, 159

Cooper, William M., 190

Corneal, William: children of, *375*

Corn-shuckings, 23, 28, 33, 43; apple brandy at, 30; singing at, 30

Couch, William Terry, 2, 5, 6, 10, 11, 220

Courtship and marriage: marriage, 1, 41, 45, 48, 52, 67, 128, 134, 140, 145, 161, 176, 270, 285, 292, 330, 343; weddings, 23, 34, 35, 58, 59, 95; and in-laws, 28, 32, 37, 64, 68, 202, 203, 330; proposal, 30; contract, 36; husband's view of, 37, 43, 50, 51, 54, 120, 137, 141, 142, 166, 202, 203; wife's view of, 47, 63, 64, 68, 86, 142, 185, 196, 201, 202; courtship, 50, 51, 62, 66, 68, 78, 90, 94, 95, 260; elopement, 54, 90, 117; disapproval of, 54, 120; changes in affection for mate, 63, 166, 201; attitudes toward, 66, 67, 68, 74, 78, 84, 172, 222; changes in patterns of, 70, 71; with kin relations, 75, 76, 83, 84; extra-marital relationships, 84, 140, 201; records, 89, 95, 132, 196, 220, 226; desire for daughters to avoid wedding farmers, 225; marriage to older widower, 269. *See also* Death; Divorce and separa-

tion; Domestic economy; Family; Household composition; Widowhood

Covington (Alleghany Co.), 20, 39, 66, 124, 126, 173, 206, 274, 276, 284, 304, 325, 327, 339, *352*, 361

Covington High School, 349

Covington Post Office, 60

Covington Silk Mill, 68, 75, 347, 349, 440 (n. 19)

Cowles (Crowder), Henry, 337, 338, 444 (n. 10)

Coxe, Tench, 302

Craddock and Terry Shoe Company, 96

Crafts: blacksmiths, 31, 36, 138, 143, 277; potter and helper, 39, 41; salt-glazing technique described, 39, 40, 42, 43; women's handicraft sweatshop, 96, 97; and paternalism in workplace, 96; shoemaker, 277, 297. *See also* Fulton Pottery; Virginia Art Goods Studio

Craigsville (Augusta Co.), 339

Crane, Mary McKim, Jr., *80–82*

Crawford, Ed, 344

Crawley, Mr. and Mrs. Charles, 132, 445 (n. 27); family of, 132, 403, 445 (n. 28)

Creach, Henry, 46

Creasy, Bettie, 30

Crops, 210; corn, 26, 27, 30, 48, 49, 56, 74, 118, 125, 129, 139, 226, 227, 234, 242; tobacco, 26, 90, 93, 95, 221, 222, 242; snap beans, 30; wheat, 30, 126, *139*, 226, 227, 230, 234, 242; potatoes, 30, 129, 130; peeling pulp wood as a cash crop to buy or support, 72, 117, 121, 231; flax, 77; sweet potatoes, 129, 224; cabbage, 130; peanuts, 221, 223, 224; alfalfa, 225; grass or hay, 230, 234, 242; oats, 234, 242; apples, 242; planting peas to improve soil, 242; rye, 242; tomatoes, 242; watermelons and cantaloupes, 242

Cross Roads (near New London, Campbell Co.), 31

Crowder, T. O., 40

Culpeper (Culpeper Co.), 8, 19–21, 50, 145, 150, 161, 167, 206, 212

Culpeper Training School, 166

Customary occasions: shivarees, 23; "infairs," 23, 28, 29; house or barn raisings, 23, 28, 43, 112; for sociability or cooperative work, 23, 33, 41; "callithumps," 23, 59; apple butter boilings, 28, 33; log rollings, 28, 33, 43, 112, 116; apple and peach peelings, 30, 32, 33; parties, 30, 32, 33; school pageants or plays, 159. *See also* Animals, butchering of; Domestic economy: quilts and quilting

Dances/dancing, 23, 59, 72, 128, 130, 137, 268, 295; negative views of modern, 30, 32, 51; square, 30, 51, 58, 128; "Johnny Picking Up Rocks," 51; "Virginia Breakdown," 51; "Virginia Reel," *58*, 128;

man's role as "good provider," 43, 67, 106, 120, 122, 142, 240, 257; woman's role as "helpmate," 60, 62, 64, 68, 69, 71, 72, 93, 120, 137, 142, 231, 232, 240, 269, 324; ideals of femininity or masculinity, 62, 65, 66, 106, 109, 119, 129, 292, 295, 439 (n. 5); husband jailed for nonsupport of family, 201, 203; and beauty, 285

General Electric Company, 312, 313

Geographic mobility: to get jobs, 3, 32, 37, 46, 47, 55, 66, 68, 77, 78, 90, 91, 95, 101, 110, 111, 124, 129, 131, 132, 134, 220; out-of-state, 46, 50, 77, 91, 95, 110, 122, 125, 126, 132, 134, 145, 146, 162, 165, 166, 220, 269; role of family-based networks in, 47, 55, 90, 91, 111, 112, 126, 134, 136, 137, 145, 149; from other countries, 85; from other states, 85, 89, 111, 134, 135, 201, 220, 252, 269; in wartime, 95, 175, 186; to preach, 165; to pursue education, 165; to teach, 165–67; as factor in choice of place to live, 173; as job requirement, 173; to other countries, 175; to serve apprenticeship in Richmond, 293; to buy land, 329; to enter defense work in World War II, 363. *See also* Dislocation

Gibson, Lizzie (Sally Newman), 62, 76; family of, 76–78, 393–96, 440 (n. 27)

Ginseng, 47, 118

Givens, James, 132, 159, 160, 403, 445 (n. 28)

Goode, William, 132, 403, 445 (n. 28)

Gorman, Francis J., 291, 459 (n. 23)

Goshen (Rockbridge Co.), 37, 38

Government and military occupations: fire tower workers, 74, 75; inspector for government worker housing, 101, 453 (n. 19); wireless telegrapher, 135–36; chief steward, U.S. Merchant Marines, 176

Grange, *61*

Graves, John, 278

Green, John S., 27

Greenhow, George, 22

Gregory, John, 239, 455 (n. 28)

Greno Mine (Wise Co.), 334

Grimsley, George, 27

Grist mills and millers, 26, 31, 48, 50, 55, 56, 150, *300*, 305

Grocery stores: A&P Tea Company, 92, 95; Bibees Grocery (Lynchburg), 92, 95; Grimes Market (Covington), 308; Kroger Grocery Company (Covington), 286; M and M Grocery (Covington), 284; Pender Grocery Company (Altavista, Bedford, Chatham, Lynchburg and Norfolk), 92, 95, 262, 456 (n. 19)

Gross, Oscar William, 322; family of, 323, 417, 418

Grubb Mines (Bedford Co.), 324

Gum, Dilcie, 10, 154, 184, 187

Gypsies, 124

Haden's Switch (Botetourt Co.), 342

Hairston, Mary L., 55

Hall, Sidney, 191

Hammerstein, Oscar, 175

Hampton Institute, 3, 8, 19, 156, 158, 166, 428 (n. 3)

Hand, Tom, 11, 150; family of, 150, 406

Hand's Mill (Rappahannock Co.), xii, 150

Hanna, Forest, 355

Hardy, Charles, 90

Harnsberger, Edward, 444 (nn. 13, 14)

Harris, Ben, 278

Harris, George and Amos, 251, 256, 270

Harris, Reed, 3

Harrison, Sam, 10, 210, 220; family of, 220, 410, 411, 430 (n. 18)

Harrisonburg (Rockingham Co.), 66, 343–46

Harvard University, 156

Hat Creek (Campbell Co.), 55

Hawkins, Charlie, 146

Hazel River (Rappahannock Co.), 150

Health and sickness, 3, 21, 72, 91, 95, 111, 132, 160, 242, 261, 267, 270, 287; physical disabilities, 31, 32, 37, 38, 83, 143, 146, 266, 267; effects of industrial work on, 68, 74, 75, 111, 330, 334, 344, 345, 351, 355; cost of medical treatment, 72, 91, 223, 287, 324; treatment at clinic, 92; sanitary instruction, 174; benefits from public health nurses, 223, 224; and concern about poor sanitation, 350. *See also* Public institutions: asylums; Public institutions: hospitals or sanitariums

—Specific infirmities: appendicitis, 67, 72; blindness, 35, 36, 38, 136, 160, 267; blood poisoning, 37, 72; Bright's disease, 122, 126; cholera infantum, 343; "creeping paralysis," 63; deafness, 35, 54; diptheria, 21, 78, 138–40; dropsy, 174; dysentery, 54; flu ("Spanish Lady"), 21, 138, 140, 306; hay fever, 95; heart disease, 120, 174; infantile paralysis, 350; insanity or retardation, 63, 120, 143, 162, 166; kidney disease, 87, 88, 92; malaria, 21; measles, 47; pneumonia, 78, 174, 223; rheumatism, 73, 74, 188, 224; scarlet fever, 54; scrofula, 83; smallpox, 21; stroke, 84, 149; tuberculosis (TB), 21, 22, 68, 170, 174; typhoid fever, 21, 85, 87, 151

Hepler, W. D., 39, 40

Hercules Powder Company (Pulaski Co.), 8, 369

High Hat Restaurant (Culpeper), 207

Hillsman, Thomas, 32

Hines, James J., 176

value of Jordan ironmasters's property in 1860, 302; competition from other regions and rapid reduction of manufacture, 302, 310; use of auctioned furnace anvil in blacksmith shop, 306, 309; close of Low Moor, 309; sale of Low Moor furnace inventory, 309; description of Low Moor village, 310; monthly payroll of, 310; railroads and, 310, 311; traffic manager for, 311; paternalism in, 311, 460 (n. 15); and wages for, 325; and rivet-sticker in shop, 325, 326, 327; hazards of, 326, 327

Iron Gate (Alleghany Co.), 343
Iron Gate mines (Alleghany Co.), 343
Iron Mountain (Alleghany Co.), 109, 118
Irvine, John, 52

Jackson, Andrew Jackson, 308
Jackson River (Alleghany), 310, 326, 361
Jesse James (film), 242
James, Mr. and Mrs. Ben, 20, 198, 410, 451 (n. 54)
James River, 55, 129, 251, 262
Jamison Elementary School, 377
Jayne, George, 252–54
Jayne, Lucille, 252–54, 431 (n. 24)
Jefferson, Thomas, 148, 164, 293
Jeffersonton (Culpeper Co.), 147, 159
Jeffriestown (Culpeper), 166
Jeter, N. B. (Westvaco Doctor), 344, 345
Jim Crow: in churches, 154, 155, 186; white violence justified by black defiance of laws, 155, 156
Johnson, Albert, 149
Johnson, Catherine, 199
Johnson, Charlie, 266; family of, 414, 457 (n. 21)
Johnson, Lessie, 170
Johnson, Mr. (landlord), 223–25
Johnson, Powerton, 278
Johnson Creek School (Alleghany Co.), 20
Jones, Royal and Eva, 187
Jones, T. Richie, 198
Jonesville (Lee Co.), 330
Jordan, Doris, 377
Jordan, Edwin, 302
Jordan, Isa F., 302
Jordan, John, 309
Jordan Furnace, 302
Jordan Mines (Alleghany Co.), 39, 40

Karnes Creek (Alleghany Co.), 310
Kaymoor mines (West Virginia), 309–11
Keesee (Carwile), Julia, 66, 92; family of, 92, 93, 214, 398–401, 442 (n. 46)
Kelly, Jack, Jr., 48

Kelly, John, 45
Kemper, James, 143, 149
Keokee (Lee Co.), 110
Kerr, Florence, 376
Keswick (Albemarle Co.), 421
Key to the Pantry, The, 184, 185
Keysville (Charlotte Co.), 178, *179*
Kilbourne, Joe, 45, 46
Kilbourne, Minnie T., 212, 214
Kimberlin, Jess, 349
King, John, 91,
King and Queen Co., 269
Ku Klux Klan, 60, 62, 186, 438 (nn. 3, 4)

Lackey, Clarence, 343–45
Lafayette River (formerly Tanners Creek, Norfolk Co.), 260
Lambert family, 260, 413, 414
Lambert Fisheries, 260, 261
Lambert's Point (Norfolk), 261
Landrum, Lillie Margaret, 226, 411, 412
Langley Field (Hampton), *380*
Language, 151; as possibly offensive to listener, 75, 271; and speech impediment, 151; dialect as indicator of class or racial difference, 185–88, 220; artificially constructed by editors, 220
Lee, Emma Lou, 212
Lee, Robert E., 251, 262
Lee Park (Petersburg), 65, 200
Leesburg (Loudoun Co.), 50, 260
Leisure activities: camp parties, 62; road trips, 62, 137, 286, 356; listening to radio, 72, 79, 168, 356; movies, 79, 84, 172, 186, 228, 242, 291, 328; reading, 126, 127, 131, 148, 149, 168, 172, 295, 299, 328, 355, 359; card games, 137; negative view of programs on, 168; reading aloud to nonreading adult, 171; swimming, 295; amusing children, 299; taffypullings, 354
Leonard, Thomas C., 220
Leviss, Susanna and Ursula, 58
Lewis, Benjamin, 256
Lexington (Rockbridge Co.), 304, 347
Liberty. *See* Bedford
Library of Congress, 376
Life history, 1–3, 5–11, 19, 41, 71, 77; southern life history project, 2, 5, 6, 430 (n. 18); as oral history, 2, 6, 7, 12; contextualization of, 2, 6, 12, 431 (n. 30); discussions of, 2, 428 (n. 5); and editing or alterations of texts, 6, 10, 184, 220, 351, 440–41 (n. 28), 447 (n. 5), 449 (n. 26); in connection with literary figures on FWP, 7; authenticity as issue for, 7,

Murder. *See* Unlawful acts

Music, 72, 137; at callithumps, 23; at corn-shuckings, 30; need for lessons in schools, 171; accompanist or choral work in churches and clubs, 176, 286; private lessons, 286, 350. *See also* Dances/dancing
—Instruments: banjo, 30, 59, 128; fiddle, 30, 51, 59, 72
—Musicians: Faulkner, Ned, 51; Thacker, Jim, 30
—Songs: "The Explosion at Derby," 334, 335; "Going Down to Town" (Lynchburg), 50; "Jesse Jeames," 243; "Look and Live," 168, 169; "Roosevelt Song," 17, 18; "Shuck away, shuck away," 30; textile mill song, 66; "Tobacco Song," 454 (n. 13); tobacco verse, 215

Naming practices, 31, 32, 53, 54, 76, 83, 143, 144, 288

Narratives, personal: selling stoneware, 43; story about "senging," 47; taking brandy to school, 57; fear of "old colored man," 93; brother drowned in floods, 95; near disaster in Iron Mountain snowstorm, 109, 118–20; hunter almost shoots neighbors, 142; hunting dogs fight with something in deep hole, 142; church members eat all the tripe, 144; attitudes toward southerners and slavery used to coerce vote, 148; smoking of tobacco, 221; owner's son arranges foreclosure on Peebles farm, 224, 225; move from New York to Chesapeake Bay on inland waterways, 253, 254; young coal miner ignores foreman's warning, 331, 332; underground during the Derby mine disaster, 332, 333

National Labor Relations Act (Wagner-Connery Act, 1935), 337, 340, 355

National Labor Relations Board, 340, 355

National Park Service, 66, 158

National Recovery Administration, 96, 340

National Woman's Suffrage Association, 3

National Youth Administration, 3, 244, 245; civilian defense project at Aberdeen Gardens, 156; work of black project on white Home Economics cottage in Charlotte County, 170; job at recreation center, 171; playground and library at colored school, 171–73; school cafeteria, 172; Roosevelt's view of purpose, 273; residential projects a model for modern vocational training, 273, 274; other projects for blacks, 448 (n. 14)

Natural disasters, xxi, 95, 109, 118–20, 442 (n. 46); floods in 1933, 224

Negro in Virginia, The, (Virginia Writers' Project), 1, 9, 89, 220

New, Harry S., 176

New Deal, 1, 12, 22; child labor laws, 86; attitudes toward governmental programs or regulations, 96, 227; and effect on apprenticeship in trades, 279; and price-fixing and sanitation laws, 284, 287, 288; and wage-hour and minimum wage laws, 313; idealism of some workers, 376. *See also* Relief and welfare

New Dealers, 3

New London (Campbell Co.), 28, 56

Newman, Walter S., 244

Newport News, 85, 129, 155, 156, 190, *191*, 207, 261, *307*, 354, 363

Newsome, Mr. (Mr. Johnson), 210

Newsoms (Southampton Co.), 220

Newspapers, 33. *See* Periodical literature

Norfolk, 87, 207–9, 256, 258, 262, 268, 269, 363

Norman (Culpeper Co.), 147

Norton (Wise Co.), 189, 210

Nugent, Walter, 25

Ocean View (Norfolk City), 261, 266

Office for Emergency Management, 374, 432 (n. 37)

Office of War Information, 363, 374, 375

Old age, 19, 23, 160–63; attitudes toward, 38, 69, 70, 121, 142; work and living in, 69, 70, 120, 121, 131, 141, 142, 167, 168

Old Age pension. *See* Relief and welfare

Oliver and Robinson, 278

O'Neals Photography Studio (Portsmouth), 292

Onley (Accomac Co.), 235

Oral history. *See* Life history: as oral history

Oriskany (Botetourt Co.), 310, 459 (n. 12)

Osaka (Wise Co.), 329

Otter River (Lunenburg or Bedford Co.), 56

Paint Bank (Alleghany Co.), 124

Palmer, Emily Somers, 98, 401

Parker, Lloyd, 345, 346

Parker, W. C., 296

Parker's Hosiery Mill (Portsmouth), 85, 88

Parks, resorts, and tourism, 210; and effects of on localities, 207; seasonal effects of on business, 298
—Specific parks and resorts: Chopawamsic, *141*, *157*, 158, 448 (n. 11); Shenandoah National Park and Skyline Drive, *4*, *26*, *33*, 77, 207, 432 (nn. 3, 7); Sweet Springs (Monroe Co., West Virginia), 118, 228; White Sulphur Springs, 159, 173, 298

Paul, Alice, 100

Payne, Elizabeth, 201

Payne, Olin J., 311, 322, 328

Peabody School (Petersburg), 421

Peebles, Buzzell. *See* Harrison, Sam

and for collective bargaining, 288, 289; apprentice in finishing room, 289; attitudes toward five-day week, 289; harder work in dark rooms, 289; weaver, 289; leaders never rehired by mill, 290; the southern cotton mill movement as moral venture, 336; employment of children in mills, 336–37; changing conditions following World War I, 337; hazardous nature of synthetic textile production, 337; introduction of rayon processes, 337; mill as "family," 337; reflected in music, 337; effects of speed-up of machinery on lives of workers, 337, 357; apprentice in ageing room, 348; description of viscose making process, 348; silk mill pressures worker to quit, 349; wages as operator, 349; wages as weaver, 349; spinner's description of working with yarn, 356. *See also* Strikes; Unions/unionization

Thacker, Benjamin Christopher, 23, 28; family of, 28, 31, 32, 381–83

Thaxton (Bedford Co.), 78

These Are Our Lives (Federal Writers' Project), 2, 6, 7, 10, 11, 430 (n. 18)

Thompson, Mrs. Nola (Geneva Fowlkes), 65; family of, 89, 398, 441 (n. 38), 442 (n. 39)

Thompson, Paul, 7

Thornhill, Mrs. (co-owner of Virginia Art Goods Studio), 96

Thurmond (West Virginia), 126

Timber industry: lumber, 46, 47, 111, 126, 134, 135, 136; sawmills, 47, 55, 56, 65, 89, 134, 136, 439 (n. 13); wages at, 90; railroad ties, 109, 118, 139; shakes/shingles, *141*. *See also* names of specific companies/industries

Timmons family, 201

Tobacco industry: use and attitudes toward, 31, 59, 84, 133, 221, 233, 271, 306, 308, 435 (n. 16); tobacco markets and roads, 32, 50; tobacco buyer, 54; superintendent of factory, 55; cigar factories, 68, 170, 185; attitudes toward work, 89, 91, 221, 358, 359; paid with tobacco prunings, 90; growing tobacco, 90, 95, 208, 215; wages at, 91, 92, 359; close of factory and layoffs, 91, 156; work quarrels and sectional difference, 159; and importance of as major cash crop, *215–19*, 222; description and grades of, 221, 222; curing of, 233; stringing bags for smoking tobacco, 281–83; description of storefront tobacco bag station, 283, 284; and costs of materials in nickel bag of tobacco, 284; Bonsack cigarette machine, 357; cigarette production in state, 357; cigarette factory work described, 358, 359. *See also* Health and sickness: tuberculosis; Music: "Tobacco Song"; Music: tobacco verse

—Specific tobacco companies: American, 357; Beech, 199; British American, 89, 91; Brown and Williamson, 196; R. J. Reynolds, 209, 281

Tom's Creek (Wise Co.), 329, 330

Transportation, 84; horse, 109, 139; truck drivers, 109, 152, 185, 261; stage driver, 118; streetcar conductor, 129, 155; and livery stable, 145, 330; oil wagon driver, 151; by sloop, 253, 254; by passenger steamship, 262; by boat, 263–65; failed bus company, 323; by train, 330. *See also* Automobiles; Railroads

Traylor, Mark, 29

Tubal-cain, 306

Tubize Artificial Silk Company (Hopewell), 7, 131, 137, 446 (n. 38)

Tucker, Charles, 21, 106, 138; family of, 138, 404, 405

Tugwell, Rexford Guy, 4

Turner, Julia, 57

Tuskegee Institute, 173

Unemployment. *See* Work and unemployment

Union Depot (Washington, D.C.), 151

Unions/unionization: attitudes toward, 96, 196, 272, 290, 298, 313; open shop and collective bargaining, 96, 196, 289, 312, 313; and results of disputes, 111; association of foreigners or "outsiders" with, 159, 313; of "reds," 272; efforts at, 288–90, 457 (n. 26), 461 (n. 11); leaders and organizers of, 289, 291; and safety in coal mines, 298; company-sponsored, 349. *See also* Accidents; Strikes; names of specific unions

United Daughters of the Confederacy, 8, 423

U.S. Bureau of Fisheries, 255

U.S. Congress, 100

U.S. Merchant Marines, 174, 176

U.S. Navy, 208

U.S. Signal Corps, 135

United Textile Workers of America, 459 (n. 23)

University of North Carolina, 220

University of North Carolina Press, 6

University of Richmond, 257

University of Virginia, 23, 167, 184

Unlawful acts, 163; murder, 23, 128, 131, 155, 162, 163, 241, 242, 304, 445 (n. 23), 459 (n. 7); theft, 31, 285; theft of cattle, 75; knife attacks, 83, 197, 201; arrest or imprisonment for, 84, 140, 152, 201, 242; attempted robbery, 94; illegal whiskey business, 140, 239; assault for defiance of Jim Crow laws, 156; hanged for crime, 162; nonsupport of family, 201, 203